SOTHIS PRESS

Sothis Press aims to completely reimagine the public domain book with an emphasis on universal access to captivatingly designed print editions. We believe that technology will enable every single book ever published to be perpetually accessible in beautiful print form. Sothis is beauty in ubiquity.

www.sothis.press
1 Waterhouse Square, London, ECIN 2ST

International Law

A Treatise; War and Neutrality

L. Oppenheim

SOTHIS PRESS

ISBN 978-1-0365-0784-8

This edition is published by
Sothis Press © 2023. The company
is registered in England and Wales.
The Company Number is 14900389.

INTERNATIONAL LAW

A TREATISE

By L. OPPENHEIM, M.A., LL.D.

FORMERLY WHEWELL PROFESSOR OF INTERNATIONAL LAW IN THE UNIVERSITY OF CAMBRIDGE, MEMBER OF THE INSTITUTE OF INTERNATIONAL LAW, HONORARY MEMBER OF THE ROYAL ACADEMY OF JURISPRUDENCE AT MADRID, CORRESPONDING MEMBER OF THE AMERICAN INSTITUTE OF INTERNATIONAL LAW

Vol. II.—WAR AND NEUTRALITY

THIRD EDITION

EDITED BY

RONALD F. ROXBURGH

OF THE MIDDLE TEMPLE, BARRISTER-AT-LAW, FORMERLY WHEWELL SCHOLAR IN THE UNIVERSITY OF CAMBRIDGE, FORMERLY SCHOLAR OF TRINITY COLLEGE, CAMBRIDGE

LONGMANS, GREEN AND CO.

39 PATERNOSTER ROW, LONDON

FOURTH AVENUE & 30TH STREET, NEW YORK

BOMBAY, CALCUTTA, AND MADRAS

1921

PREFACE

TO THE THIRD EDITION

OPPENHEIM'S work upon the revision of this volume was unfinished when he died; but most of the material had already been collected, and many passages rewritten. He intended, as he once told me, to introduce the events of the war when they illustrated, extended, or challenged general principles hitherto accepted. But for the history of the war he would have relied on his friend Garner's *International Law and the World War,* which he had already read in manuscript. By kindly lending me the proofs of that book (since published), Professor Garner has enabled me to make frequent references to it according to the author's plan.

The war has involved changes in this volume; yet they are surely fewer than might have been expected. So Oppenheim felt; and some notes intended for this preface show with what force he would have argued against the prevalent impression that the war has made an end of the laws of war. Confronted with the many brutal violations of these laws which marred the struggle, he would have argued that in almost every case the offender felt constrained either to deny the charge or to plead justification. This seemed to him to be in itself an admission of the power of the law in normal times. But the times were abnormal, and the laws of war and neutrality were admittedly in partial suspense. This he would have attributed in part to the unusual impotence of the neutral States and in part to new conditions—aircraft, submarines, mines, and the network of Continental railways—for which the old rules were not wholly adapted. Neutrals naturally demanded from belligerents that they should obey the old rules notwithstanding the changes. But the claim of the belligerents that the rules should undergo corresponding change was quite as natural. Again, since neutrals did not see to it that the fundamental rules were not broken by either belligerent, there were bound to be reprisals. Reprisals may injure neutrals as well as States at war, and they provoke counter-reprisals and more reprisals in an unending chain. This Oppenheim held to be a principal cause of the partial anarchy of the war, which he likened to revolution within the State. When order is re-established, the law revives. Even then, no doubt, many criminals escape unpunished. But no one would argue on that account that there was no law.

In the edition of 1912, Oppenheim urged that the Declaration of London should be ratified. But when the war came, he saw that the declaration, even if it had been ratified, could not have survived when Germany had pulled down in Belgium the pillars upon which International Law stood.

Considerations such as these are reflected in Oppenheim's revisions in the chapter on the means of securing legitimate warfare. Other important changes and additions which he himself made are to be found in § 53 in the discussion upon the legality of war, in § 57*a* dealing with the threatened disappearance of the distinction between members of armed forces and civilians, in §§ 294, 299 which concern neutral duties and the recognition of neutrality by belligerents, in § 319 discussing the legality of measures of reprisal affecting neutrals, in § 348*a* examining the status of shipwrecked combatants coming into neutral territory, in the sections dealing with the right of angary, in many of the sections relating to contraband, in § 413*a* concerning the seizure of enemy reservists at sea, in § 428*a* relating to the call at an enemy port of a vessel with a neutral destination, and in § 434 discussing the law administered by Prize Courts.

The establishment of the League of Nations called for modifications and additions in the chapters dealing with the settlement of disputes without resort to war; but Oppenheim had not yet made them when his last illness came upon him, and this task fell upon the present writer. New material has also been introduced in §§ 88-92 on enemy character, in § 100*a* on *persona standi in judicio*, in § 101 on trading with the enemy, and in § 102 on enemy private property and debts. Reference, for which Oppenheim is not alone responsible, has also been made to the treatment of enemy merchantmen found by the belligerents in their harbours at the outbreak of the World War, to the treatment of prisoners, and to other important controversies which sprang up during the contest. The author's notes on air warfare have been brought together and expanded in a new chapter. The fate of the Declaration of London and recent changes in the conception of neutrality are recorded in § 292. Two new sections have been added to § 390 relating to the long-distance blockade. On the other hand, the chapter on International Prize Courts has been curtailed, as the Hague project of 1907 has lost the position which it held in 1912.

Mr. C. E. A. Bedwell, Mr. H. A. C. Sturgess, and Messrs. T. and A. Constable, Ltd., have again kindly made their respective contributions in revising the Index and Table of Cases and attending to the typography of the book.

RONALD F. ROXBURGH.

4 NEW SQUARE, LINCOLN'S INN.

[Events are recorded in this volume down to the end of February 1921.]

ABBREVIATIONS

OF TITLES OF BOOKS, ETC., QUOTED IN THE TEXT

The books referred to in the bibliography and notes are, as a rule, quoted with their full titles and the date of their publication. But certain books, periodicals, and conventions which are very often referred to throughout this work are quoted in an abbreviated form, as follows :—

A.J.	=	The American Journal of International Law.
Alvarez, *Grande Guerre*	=	Alvarez, La Grande Guerre Européenne et la Neutralité du Chili (1915).
Annuaire	=	Annuaire de l'Institut de Droit international.
Ariga	=	Ariga, La Guerre Russo-Japonaise (1908).
Barboux	=	Barboux, Jurisprudence du Conseil des Prises pendant la Guerre de 1870-71 (1871).
Barclay, *Problems*	=	Barclay, Problems of International Practice and Diplomacy (1907).
Bernsten	=	Bernsten, Das Seekriegsrecht (1911).
Bluntschli	=	Bluntschli, Das moderne Völkerrecht der civilisirten Staaten als Rechtsbuch dargestellt, 3rd ed. (1878).
Boeck	=	Boeck, De la Propriété privée ennemie sous Pavillon ennemi (1882).
Boidin	=	Boidin, Les Lois de la Guerre et les deux Conférences de la Haye (1908).
Bonfils	=	Bonfils, Manuel de Droit international public, 7th ed. by Fauchille (1914).
Borchard	=	Borchard, The Diplomatic Protection of Citizens Abroad (1915).
Bordwell	=	Bordwell, The Law of War between Belligerents (1908).
Bulmerincq	=	Bulmerincq, Das Völkerrecht (1887).
Calvo	=	Calvo, Le Droit international théorique et pratique, 5th ed , 6 vols. (1896).

Convention I.	=	Hague Convention for the Pacific Settlement of International Disputes.
Convention II.	=	Hague Convention respecting the Limitation of the Employment of Force for the Recovery of Contract Debts.
Convention III.	=	Hague Convention relative to the Opening of Hostilities.
Convention IV.	=	Hague Convention concerning the Laws and Customs of War on Land.
Convention V.	=	Hague Convention respecting the Rights and Duties of Neutral Powers and Persons in War on Land.
Convention VI.	=	Hague Convention relative to the Status of Enemy Merchant-ships at the Outbreak of Hostilities.
Convention VII.	=	Hague Convention relative to the Conversion of Merchant-ships into War-ships.
Convention VIII.	=	Hague Convention relative to the Laying of Automatic Submarine Contact Mines.
Convention IX.	=	Hague Convention respecting Bombardment by Naval Forces in Time of War.
Convention X.	=	Hague Convention for the Adaptation of the Principles of the Geneva Convention to Maritime Warfare.
Convention XI.	=	Hague Convention relative to certain Restrictions on the Exercise of the Right of Capture in Maritime War.
Convention XII.	=	Hague Convention relative to the Establishment of an International Prize Court.
Convention XIII.	=	Hague Convention respecting the Rights and Duties of Neutral Powers in Naval War.
Despagnet	=	Despagnet, Cours de Droit international public, 4th ed. by de Boeck (1910).
Deuxième Conférence, Actes	=	Deuxième Conférence internationale de la Paix, Actes et Documents. 3 vols. (1908-1909).
Dupuis	=	Dupuis, Le Droit de la Guerre maritime d'après les Doctrines anglaises contemporaines (1899).
Dupuis, *Guerre*	=	Dupuis, Le Droit de la Guerre maritime d'après les Conférences de la Haye et de Londres (1911).

Field	=	Field, Outlines of an International Code, 2 vols. (1872-1873).
Fiore	=	Fiore, Nouveau Droit international public, deuxième édition, traduite de l'Italien et annotée par Antoine, 3 vols. (1885).
Fiore, *Code*	=	Fiore, International Law Codified. Translation from the 5th Italian edition by Borchard (1918).
Gareis	=	Gareis, Institutionen des Völkerrechts, 2nd ed. (1901).
Garner	=	Garner, International Law and the World War (1920).
Gessner	=	Gessner, Le droit des Neutres sur Mer (1865).
Grotius	=	Grotius, De Jure Belli ac Pacis (1625).
Hague Regulations	=	Hague Regulations respecting the Laws and Customs of War on Land, adopted by the Hague Peace Conference of 1907.
Hall	=	Hall, A Treatise on International Law, 7th ed. (1917) by A. Pearce Higgins.
Halleck	=	Halleck, International Law, 4th English ed. by Sir Sherston Baker, 2 vols. (1908).
Hartmann	=	Hartmann, Institutionen des praktischen Völkerrechts in Friedenszeiten (1874).
Hautefeuille	=	Hautefeuille, Des Droits et des Devoirs des Nations neutres en Temps de Guerre Maritime, 2nd ed. 3 vols. (1858).
Heffter	=	Heffter, Das europäische Völkerrecht der Gegenwart, 8th ed. by Geffcken (1888).
Heilborn, *Rechte*	=	Heilborn, Rechte und Pflichten der neutralen Staaten in Bezug auf die während des Krieges auf ihr Gebiet übertretenden Angehörigen einer Armee und das dorthin gebrachte Kriegsmaterial der kriegführenden Parteien (1888).
Heilborn, *System*	=	Heilborn, Das System des Völkerrechts entwickelt aus den völkerrechtlichen Begriffen (1896).
Hershey	=	Hershey, The Essentials of International Public Law (1912).
Higgins	=	Higgins, The Hague Peace Conferences (1909).
Holland, *Prize Law*	=	Holland, A Manual of Naval Prize Law (1888).

Holland, *Studies*	=	Holland, Studies in International Law (1898).
Holland, *Jurisprudence*	=	Holland, The Elements of Jurisprudence, 11th ed. (1910).
Holland, *War*	=	Holland, The Laws of War on Land (1908).
Holtzendorff	=	Holtzendorff, Handbuch des Völkerrechts, 4 vols. (1885-1889).
Hurst	=	Hurst and Bray, Russian and Japanese Prize Cases, vol. i. (1912), vol. ii. (1913).
Kleen	=	Kleen, Lois et Usages de la Neutralité, 2 vols. (1900).
Klüber	=	Klüber, Europäisches Völkerrecht, 2nd ed. by Morstadt (1851).
Kriegsbrauch	=	Kriegsbrauch im Landkriege (1902). (Heft 31 der kriegsgeschichtlichen Einzelschriften, herausgegeben vom Grossen Generalstabe, kriegsgeschichtliche Abtheilung I.).
Land Warfare	=	Edmonds and Oppenheim, Land Warfare. An Exposition of the Laws and Usages of War on Land for the Guidance of Officers of His Majesty's Army (1912).
Lawrence	=	Lawrence, The Principles of International Law, 4th ed. (1910).
Lawrence, *Essays*	=	Lawrence, Essays on some Disputed Questions of Modern International Law (1884).
Lawrence, *War*	=	Lawrence, War and Neutrality in the Far East, 2nd ed. (1904).
Lémonon	=	Lémonon, La Seconde Conférence de la Paix (1908).
Liszt	=	Liszt, Das Völkerrecht, 6th ed. (1910).
Longuet	=	Longuet, Le Droit actuel de la Guerre terrestre (1901).
Lorimer	=	Lorimer, The Institutes of International Law, 2 vols. (1883-1884).
Maine	=	Maine, International Law, 2nd ed. (1894)
Manning	=	Manning, Commentaries on the Law of Nations, new ed. by Sheldon Amos (1875).
Martens	=	Martens, Völkerrecht, German translation of the Russian original, 2 vols. (1883).

Martens, G. F.	=	G. F. Martens, Précis du Droit des Gens moderne de l'Europe, nouvelle éd. par Vergé, 2 vols. (1858).
Martens, R. Martens, N.R. Martens, N.S. Martens, N.R.G. Martens, N.R.G. 2nd Ser. Martens, N.R.G. 3rd Ser.	}	These are the abbreviated quotations of the different parts of Martens, Recueil de Traités (see p. 118 of vol. i.), which are in common use.
Martens, *Causes célèbres*	=	Martens, Causes célèbres du Droit des Gens, 2nd ed., 5 vols. (1858-1861).
Mérignhac	=	Mérignhac, Traité de Droit public international, vol. i. (1905), vol. ii. (1907), vol. iii[a]. (1912).
Meurer	=	Meurer, Die Haager Friedenskonferenz, 2 vols. (1905-1907).
Moore	=	Moore, A Digest of International Law, 8 vols., Washington (1906).
Moore, *Arbitrations*	=	Moore, History and Digest of the Arbitrations to which the United States have been a Party, 6 vols. (1898).
Nippold	=	Nippold, Die zweite Haager Friedenskonferenz, 2 vols. (1908-1911).
Nys	=	Nys, Le Droit international, 3 vols., 2nd ed. (1912).
Ortolan	=	Ortolan, Règles internationales et Diplomatie de la Mer, 2 vols., 3rd ed. (1856).
Perels	=	Perels, Das internationale öffentliche Seerecht der Gegenwart, 2nd ed. (1903).
Phillimore	=	Phillimore, Commentaries upon International Law, 4 vols., 3rd ed. (1879-1888).
Piedelièvre	=	Piedelièvre, Précis de Droit international public, 2 vols. (1883-1895).
Pillet	=	Pillet, Les Lois actuelles de la Guerre (1901).
Pistoye et Duverdy	=	Pistoye et Duverdy, Traité des Prises maritimes, 2 vols. (1854-1859).
Pradier-Fodéré	=	Pradier-Fodéré, Traité de Droit international public, 8 vols. (1885-1906).
Pufendorf	=	Pufendorf, De Jure Naturae et Gentium (1672).

Reddie, *Researches*	=	Reddie, Researches, Historical and Critical, in Maritime International Law, 2 vols. (1844).
R.G.	=	Revue générale de Droit international public.
R.I.	=	Revue de Droit international et de Législation comparée.
Rivier	=	Rivier, Principes du Droit des Gens, 2 vols. (1896).
Satow, *Diplomatic Practice*	=	Satow, A Guide to Diplomatic Practice, 2 vols. (1917).
Schramm	=	Schramm, Das Prisenrecht in seiner neuesten Gestalt (1913).
Scott, *Conferences*	=	Scott, The Hague Peace Conferences of 1899 and 1907, vol. i. (1909).
Spaight	=	Spaight, War Rights on Land (1911).
Takahashi	=	Takahashi, International Law applied to the Russo-Japanese War (1908).
Taylor	=	Taylor, A Treatise on International Public Law (1901).
Testa	=	Testa, Le Droit public international maritime, traduction du Portugais par Boutiron (1886).
Twiss	=	Twiss, The Law of Nations, 2 vols., 2nd ed. (1884, 1875).
Ullmann	=	Ullmann, Völkerrecht, 2nd ed. (1908).
U.S. Naval War Code	=	The Laws and Usages of War at Sea, published on June 27, 1900, by the Navy Department, Washington, for the use of the U.S. Navy and for the information of all concerned.
Vattel	=	Vattel, Le Droit des Gens, 4 books in 2 vols., nouvelle éd. (Neuchâtel, 1773).
Walker	=	Walker, A Manual of Public International Law (1895).
Walker, *History*	=	Walker, A History of the Law of Nations, vol. i. (1899).
Walker, *Science*	=	Walker, The Science of International Law (1893).
Wehberg	=	Wehberg, Das Seekriegsrecht (1915) in Stier-Somlo, Handbuch des Völkerrechts.

Wehberg, *Kommentar*	=	Wehberg, Kommentar zu dem Haager Abkommen betreffend die friedliche Erledigung internationaler Streitigkeiten (1911).
Westlake	=	Westlake, International Law, 2 vols., 2nd ed. (1910-1913).
Westlake, *Chapters*	=	Westlake, Chapters on the Principles of International Law (1894).
Westlake, *Papers*	=	The Collected Papers of John Westlake on Public International Law, ed. by L. Oppenheim (1914).
Wharton	=	Wharton, A Digest of the International Law of the United States, 3 vols. (1886).
Wheaton	=	Wheaton, Elements of International Law, 8th American ed. by Dana (1866).
Zorn	=	Zorn, Das Kriegsrecht zu Lande in seiner neuesten Gestaltung (1906).
Z.I.	=	Zeitschrift für internationales Recht.
Z.V.	=	Zeitschrift für Völkerrecht.

TABLE OF CASES

CONTENTS

OF

THE SECOND VOLUME

PART I

SETTLEMENT OF STATE DIFFERENCES

CHAPTER I

AMICABLE SETTLEMENT OF STATE DIFFERENCES

I. *State Differences and their Amicable Settlement in General*

II. *Negotiation*

III. *Good Offices and Mediation*

IV. *Arbitration*

V. *Arbitration according to the Hague Convention*

VI. *The League of Nations and State Differences*

CHAPTER II

COMPULSIVE SETTLEMENT OF STATE DIFFERENCES

I. *On Compulsive Means of Settlement of State Differences in General*

II. *Retorsion*

III. *Reprisals*

IV. *Pacific Blockade*

V. *Intervention*

VI. *Economic Boycott*

PART II

WAR

CHAPTER I

ON WAR IN GENERAL

I. *Characteristics of War*

II. *Causes, Kinds, and Ends of War*

II. *Effects of the Outbreak of War*

CHAPTER III

WARFARE ON LAND

I. *On Land Warfare in General*

II. *Violence against Enemy Persons*

III. *Treatment of Wounded, and Dead Bodies*

IV. *Captivity*

V. *Appropriation and Utilisation of Public Enemy Property*

VI. *Appropriation and Utilisation of Private Enemy Property*

VII. *Requisitions and Contributions*

VIII. *Destruction of Enemy Property*

IX. *Assault, Siege, and Bombardment*

X. *Espionage and War Treason*

XI. *Ruses*

XII. *Occupation of Enemy Territory*

CHAPTER IV

WARFARE ON SEA

I. *On Sea Warfare in General*

II. *Attack and Seizure of Enemy Vessels*

CHAPTER IVA

AIR WARFARE

CHAPTER V

NON-HOSTILE RELATIONS OF BELLIGERENTS

I. *On non-Hostile Relations in general between Belligerents*

II. *Passports, Safe-conducts, Safeguards*

III. *Flags of Truce*

IV. *Cartels*

V. *Capitulations and Simple Surrender*

VI. *Armistices*

CHAPTER VI

MEANS OF SECURING LEGITIMATE WARFARE

I. *On Means in general of securing Legitimate Warfare*

II. *Complaints, Good Offices and Mediation, Intervention*

III. *Reprisals*

IV. *Punishment of War Crimes*

V. *Taking of Hostages*

VI. *Compensation*

CHAPTER VII

END OF WAR, AND POSTLIMINIUM

PART III

NEUTRALITY

CHAPTER I

ON NEUTRALITY IN GENERAL

I. *Development of the Institution of Neutrality*

II. *Characteristics of Neutrality*

III. *Different Kinds of Neutrality*

IV. *Commencement and End of Neutrality*

CHAPTER II

RELATIONS BETWEEN BELLIGERENTS AND NEUTRALS

I. *Rights and Duties deriving from Neutrality*

II. *Neutrals and Military Operations*

III. *Neutrals and Military Preparations*

IV. *Neutral Asylum to Land Forces, War Material and Airmen*

V. *Neutral Asylum to Naval Forces and Shipwrecked War Material*

CHAPTER III

BLOCKADE

I. *Conception of Blockade*

CHAPTER IV

CONTRABAND

I. *Conception of Contraband*

II. *Carriage of Contraband*

III. *Consequences of Carriage of Contraband*

CHAPTER V

UNNEUTRAL SERVICE

I. *The Different Kinds of Unneutral Service*

II. *Consequences of Unneutral Service*

CHAPTER VI

VISITATION, CAPTURE, AND TRIAL OF NEUTRAL VESSELS

I. *Visitation*

II. *Capture*

III. *Trial of Captured Neutral Vessels*

CHAPTER VII

THE PROPOSED INTERNATIONAL PRIZE COURT

I. *Proposals for International Prize Courts*

II. *The Hague Project for an International Prize Court*

PART I

SETTLEMENT OF STATE DIFFERENCES

CHAPTER I

AMICABLE SETTLEMENT OF STATE DIFFERENCES

I

STATE DIFFERENCES AND THEIR AMICABLE SETTLEMENT IN GENERAL

Twiss, ii. §§ 1-3 — Hershey, No. 304 — Ullmann, §§ 148-150 — Bulmerincq in *Holtzendorff*, iv. pp. 5-12—Heffter, §§ 105-107—Rivier, ii. § 57—Bonfils, No. 930—Despagnet, No. 469—Pradier-Fodéré, vi. Nos. 2580-2583—Calvo, iii. §§ 1670-1671—Martens, ii. §§ 101-102—Fiore, ii. Nos. 1192-1198, and *Code*, No. 1251—Wagner, *Zur Lehre von den Streiterledigungsmitteln des Völkerrechts* (1900).

Legal and Political International Differences.

§ 1. International differences can arise from a variety of grounds. Between the extremes of a simple and comparatively unimportant act of discourtesy committed by one State against another, and so gross an insult as must necessarily lead to war, there are many other grounds, varying in nature and importance. State differences are correctly divided into legal and political. Legal differences arise from acts for which States have to bear responsibility, be it acts of their own or of their parliaments, their judicial and administrative officials, their armed forces, or individuals living on their territory.[1] Political differences are the result of a conflict of political interests. But although this distinction is certainly theoretically correct and of practical importance, frequently in practice a sharp line cannot be drawn. For in many cases States either

[1] See above, vol. i. § 149.

hide their political interests behind a claim for an alleged injury, or make a positive, but comparatively insignificant, injury a pretext for the carrying out of political ends. Nations which have been for years facing each other armed to the teeth, waiting for a convenient moment to engage in hostilities, are only too ready to obliterate the boundary line between legal and political differences. Between such nations a condition of continuous friction prevails which makes it difficult, if not impossible, in every case which arises, to distinguish the legal from the political character of the difference.

International Law not exclusively concerned with Legal Differences.

§ 2. It is often maintained that the Law of Nations is concerned with legal differences only, political differences being a matter, not of law, but of politics. Now it is certainly true that only legal[1] differences can be settled by a juristic decision of the underlying juristic question, whatever may be the way in which such a decision is arrived at. But although political differences cannot be the objects of juristic decision, they can be settled short of war by amicable or compulsive means. And legal differences, although within the scope of juristic decision, can be of such kinds as to prevent the parties from submitting them to juristic decision, without being of such a nature that they cannot be settled peaceably at all.[2] Moreover, as has just been pointed out, although the distinction between legal and political differences is correct in theory and of practical importance, nevertheless, in practice, a sharp line frequently cannot be drawn. Therefore the Law of Nations is not exclusively concerned with legal differences, for in fact most amicable means of settling legal differences are likewise means of settling political

[1] On the 'justiciability' of international differences, see Reeves and Scott in the *Proceedings of the American Society of International Law*, ix. (1916), pp. 78-95.

[2] See Balch in *R.G.*, xxi. (1914), pp. 137-182.

differences, and so are two of the compulsive means of settling differences—namely, pacific blockade and intervention.

Amicable in contradistinction to Compulsive Settlement of Differences.

§ 3. Political and legal differences can be settled either by amicable or by compulsive means. Before the establishment of the League of Nations there were four kinds of amicable means—namely, negotiation between the parties, good offices of third parties, mediation, and arbitration.[1] And there were also four kinds of compulsive means—namely, retorsion, reprisals (including embargo), blockade, and intervention of third States. No State was allowed to make use of compulsive means before negotiation had been tried, but there was no necessity for the good offices or mediation of third States, and eventually arbitration,[2] to be tried beforehand also. Frequently, however, States made use of the so-called Compromise Clause [3] in their treaties, which stipulated that any differences arising between them with regard to matters regulated by the treaties concerned, or their interpretation, should be settled through the amicable means of arbitration to the exclusion of all compulsive means. And in a few cases States had even concluded treaties stipulating that all differences, without exception, that might arise between them should be amicably settled by arbitration.[4] These exceptions, however, only confirmed the rule that no international legal duty as yet existed for States to settle, or even try to settle, their differences

[1] Some writers (see Hall, § 118, and Heilborn, *System*, p. 404) refuse to treat negotiation, good offices, and mediation as means of settling differences, because they cannot find that these means are of any legal value, it being within the choice of the parties whether or not they agree to make use of them. They forget, however, the enormous political value of these means, which alone well justifies their treatment; moreover, there are some positive legal rules in existence concerning these means—see below, §§ 5-10.

[2] Except in the case of contract debts claimed from the Government of one country by the Government of another country as being due to its nationals. See Convention II.; above, vol. i. § 135; and below, § 19.

[3] See above, vol. i. § 553.

[4] See below, § 17.

amicably through arbitration, before they made use of compulsive means.

But after the World War, the Powers, anxious 'to achieve international peace and security by the acceptance of obligations not to resort to war,' adopted in the Covenant of the League of Nations three new means of settling international disputes. They were: inquiry and report by the Council of the League, inquiry and report by the Assembly, and a judgment of the proposed International Court of Justice. Moreover, the members of the League have undertaken that they will not go to war without attempting to reach a settlement in the manner laid down by the Covenant, and will act in concert against any member which disregards its undertaking.[1]

II

NEGOTIATION

Twiss, ii. § 4—Lawrence, § 220—Moore, vii. § 1064—Taylor, §§ 359-360—Heffter, § 107—Bulmerincq in *Holtzendorff*, iv. pp. 13-17—Ullmann, § 151—Bonfils, Nos. 931-932—Despagnet, Nos. 470 and 477—Pradier-Fodéré, vi. Nos. 2584-2587—Rivier, ii. § 57—Calvo, iii. §§ 1672-1680—Martens, ii. § 103—Nys, ii. pp. 539-542.

In what Negotiation consists.

§ 4. The simplest means of settling State differences, and that to which States always resort before they make use of other means, is negotiation. Indeed the Covenant of the League of Nations indirectly recognises it as the first step towards the settlement of all international disputes. It consists in such acts of intercourse between the parties as are initiated and directed for the purpose of effecting an understanding, and thereby amicably settling the difference that has arisen between them.[2] Negotiation as a rule begins by a

[1] The United States of America is not a member of the League.

[2] See above, vol. i. §§ 477-482, where the international transaction of negotiation in general is discussed.

State complaining of a certain act, or lodging a certain claim with another State. The next step is a statement from the latter making out its case, which is handed to the former. It may be that the parties at once come to an understanding through this simple exchange of statements. If not, other acts may follow according to the requirements of the special case. Thus, for instance, other statements may be exchanged, or a conference of diplomatic envoys, or even of the heads of the States at variance, may be arranged, for the purpose of discussing the differences and preparing the basis for an understanding.

§ 5. Failure to reach a settlement by diplomacy is often due to the difficulty of arriving at the real facts. So the contracting Powers of the Hague Convention for the Pacific Settlement of International Disputes deemed it expedient and desirable that, if ordinary diplomatic negotiation had failed to settle such differences as did not involve either honour or vital interests, the parties should, so far as circumstances allowed, institute an International Commission of Inquiry [1] to elucidate the facts underlying the difference by an impartial and conscientious investigation. The Convention of 1899 had only six articles (9-14) on the subject. The Second Conference of 1907, profiting by the experience gained by the Commission of Inquiry in the *Dogger Bank* [2] case, the first occasion on which a Commission

International Commissions of Inquiry.

[1] See Herr, *Die Untersuchungskommissionen der Haager Friedenskonferenzen* (1911); Meurer, i. pp. 129-166; Higgins, pp. 167-170; Lémonon, pp. 77-91; Wehberg, *Kommentar*, pp. 21-46; Nippold, i. pp. 23-35; Scott, *Conferences*, pp. 265-273; Politis in *R.G.*, xix. (1912), pp. 149-188; Lammasch, *Die Lehre von der Schiedsgerichtsbarkeit* (1914), pp. 224-239.

[2] On October 21, 1904, during the Russo-Japanese War, the Russian Baltic fleet, which was on its way to the Far East, fired into the Hull fishing fleet off the Dogger Bank, in the North Sea, whereby two fishermen were killed, and considerable damage was done to several trawlers. Great Britain demanded from Russia, not only an apology and ample damages, but also severe punishment of the officer responsible for the outrage. As Russia maintained that the firing was caused by the approach of some Japanese torpedo-boats, and that she could therefore not punish the officer in command, the parties

of Inquiry was set up, remodelled the institution. A commission was to investigate the circumstances of the case, and issue a report 'limited to a statement of facts' and having in no way 'the character of an award'; the parties were to be free as to the effect to be given to it. The more important of the twenty-eight articles (9-36) dealing with Commissions of Inquiry in Hague Convention I. were the following:—

(1) A commission was to be constituted by a special treaty between the parties. It was to determine the facts to be examined, the manner and period within which the commission was to be formed, and the extent of the powers of the commissioners (Article 10). If the treaty did not stipulate the manner in which the commission was to be formed, it was to be formed in the same manner as an arbitration tribunal under Articles 45 and 57 (Article 12). The parties might appoint assessors, agents, and counsel (Articles 10, 14).

(2) The International Bureau of the Permanent Court of Arbitration was to act as registry for the commissions which sat at the Hague; but if they sat elsewhere, a Secretary-General was to be appointed whose office was to serve as registry (Articles 15-16).

(3) The parties might agree upon rules of procedure; otherwise the rules comprised in Articles 19-32 were to be

agreed upon the establishment of an International Commission of Inquiry. This commission was charged, not only to ascertain the facts of the incident, but also to pronounce an opinion concerning the responsibility for the incident, and the degree of blame attaching to the responsible persons. The commission consisted of five naval officers of high rank —one British, one Russian, one American, one French, and one Austrian—and sat at Paris in February 1905. The report of the commission stated that no torpedo-boats had been present, that the opening of fire on the part of the Baltic fleet was not justifiable, that Admiral Rojdestvensky, the commander of the Baltic fleet, was responsible for the incident, but that these facts were 'not of a nature to cast any discredit upon the military qualities or the humanity of Admiral Rojdestvensky or of the *personnel* of his squadron.' In consequence of the last part of this report Great Britain could not insist upon punishment of the responsible Russian admiral, but Russia paid a sum of £65,000 to indemnify the victims of the incident and the families of the two dead fishermen. See Martens, *N.R.G.*, 2nd Ser. xxxiii. pp. 641-716; Mandelstam in *R.G.*, xii. (1905), pp. 161 and 351; Lammasch, *Die Lehre von der Schiedsgerichtsbarkeit* (1914), pp. 236-239.

applicable (Article 17), and details of procedure not covered by the treaty or by Articles 19-32 were to be determined by the commission (Article 18).

(4) The report of the commission was to be signed by all its members; if a member refused to sign, the fact was to be mentioned, but the validity of the report was not to be thereby affected (Article 33). The report of the commission was to be read in open court, the agents and counsel of the parties being present or duly summoned to attend; a copy was to be furnished to each party (Article 34).

These stipulations are still in force as between the parties to Hague Convention I., although it may be that the new machinery devised by the League of Nations or provided in more recent treaties may have robbed them of much of their value. The author did not live to express an opinion.

Different from these International Commissions, but inspired by the idea underlying them, were the Permanent Commissions of Inquiry constituted for differences between the United States of America and a great number of foreign States,[1] by the series of so-called Bryan Arbitration Treaties signed at Washington in the autumn of 1914. These treaties were not all identical, but had the following features in common:—

The High Contracting Parties agreed to refer all disputes which diplomatic methods had failed to adjust to a Permanent International Commission for investigation and report, and they agreed not to begin hostilities before the report was submitted. The Permanent Commissions were to be composed of five members; each of the parties choosing one of its own subjects and one citizen of some third country,

[1] See above, vol. i. § 50, and *A.J.*, vii. (1913), p. 823, viii. (1914), p. 565, and ix. (1915), pp. 195 and 494. The treaty with Great Britain was signed on September 15, 1914 (Treaty Ser. (1914), No. 16, Cd. 7714), and ratified on November 10, 1914.

and the fifth member, also a subject of a third State, being chosen by common agreement between the two parties. The commission might, by unanimous agreement, offer its services in a dispute even before the parties were compelled by failure of diplomatic negotiation to resort to it. Its report had to be completed within one year, unless the parties limited or extended the time by mutual agreement. The parties, having received the report, were to be at liberty to take such action as they might think fit.

All these treaties were concluded for a period of five years; they were, however, to continue in force at the end of that time until twelve months after one of the parties had given notice of withdrawal. Accordingly, many of them are still in operation.[1]

Effect of Negotiation.

§ 6. The effect of negotiation may be to make it apparent that the parties cannot come to an amicable understanding at all. But frequently the effect is that one of the parties acknowledges the claim of the other party. Again, sometimes negotiation results in a party, although it does not acknowledge its opponent's alleged rights, waiving its own rights for the sake of peace, and for the purpose of making friends with its opponent. And, lastly, the effect of negotiation may be a compromise. Frequently the parties, after having come to an understanding, conclude a treaty in which they embody the terms. The practice of everyday life shows clearly the great importance of negotiation as a means of settling international differences. The modern development of international traffic and transport, the fact that individuals are constantly travelling on foreign territories, the keen interest taken by all powerful States in colonial enterprise, and many other factors, make the daily rise of differences between States un-

[1] A somewhat different International Commission was agreed upon by Argentina, Brazil, and Chili by the Treaty of Buenos Ayres of May 25, 1915. See the text of the treaty in Alvarez, *Grande Guerre*, p. 68, and *R.G.*, xxii. (1915), p. 475.

avoidable. Yet the greater number of such differences are settled through negotiation of some kind or other.

III

GOOD OFFICES AND MEDIATION

Maine, pp. 207-228—Phillimore, iii. §§ 3-5—Twiss, ii. § 7—Lawrence, § 220—Moore, vii. §§ 1065-1068—Hershey, Nos. 306-308—Taylor, §§ 359-360—Wheaton, § 73—Bluntschli, §§ 483-487—Heffter, §§ 107-108—Bulmerincq in *Holtzendorff*, iv. pp. 17-30—Ullmann, §§ 152-153—Bonfils, Nos. 932[1]-943[1]—Despagnet, Nos. 471-476—Pradier-Fodéré, vi. Nos. 2588-2593—Mérignhac, i. pp. 429-447—Rivier, ii. § 58—Nys, ii. pp. 543-546—Calvo, iii. §§ 1682-1705—Fiore, ii. Nos. 1199-1201, and *Code*, Nos. 1253-1298—Martens, ii. § 103—Holls, *The Peace Conference at the Hague* (1900), pp. 176-203—Zamfiresco, *De la Médiation* (1911)—Lammasch, *Die Lehre von der Schiedsgerichtsbarkeit* (1914), pp. 11-23—Politis in *R.G.*, xvii. (1910), pp. 136-163.

§ 7. When parties are not inclined to settle their differences by negotiation, or when they have negotiated without effecting an understanding, a third State [1] may be able to procure a settlement through its good offices or its mediation. Such assistance may have been asked for by one or both the parties at variance, or it may have been spontaneously offered. Collective mediation is also possible, several States acting at the same time as mediators. It is further possible for a mediatorial conference or congress to meet for the purpose of discussing the terms of an understanding between the conflicting parties. And it must be especially mentioned that good offices and mediation are not confined to the time before the parties at issue have appealed to arms; they can also be offered and sought during hostilities, for the purpose of bringing the war to an end. It is during war that good offices and mediation are of particular value, neither of the belligerents as a rule being inclined to open peace negotiations on his own account.

Occasions for Good Offices and Mediation.

[1] Or the League of Nations, see below, §§ 25*b*–25*g*.

Right and Duty of offering, requesting, and rendering Good Offices and Mediation.

§ 8. As a rule, a third State has no duty to offer its good offices or mediation, or to respond to a request from conflicting States for this service, nor is it, as a rule, the duty of conflicting parties themselves to ask or to accept a third State's good offices and mediation. But by special treaty such a duty may be stipulated. Thus, for instance, by Article 8 of the Peace Treaty of Paris of March 30, 1856, between Austria, France, Great Britain, Prussia, Russia, Sardinia, and Turkey, it was stipulated that, in case a difference which threatened peace should arise between Turkey and one or more of the signatory Powers, the parties should be obliged, before resorting to arms, to ask for the mediation of the other signatory Powers. Moreover, the Hague Convention for the Pacific Settlement of International Disputes laid down some stipulations respecting the right and duty of offering or accepting good offices and mediation, which will be found below in § 10.

Good Offices in contradistinction to Mediation.

§ 9. Diplomatic practice frequently does not distinguish between good offices and mediation. But although good offices can easily develop into mediation, they must not be confounded with it. The difference between them is that, whereas good offices consist in various kinds of action tending to call negotiations between the conflicting States into existence, mediation consists in direct conduct of negotiations between the parties at issue on the basis of proposals made by the mediator. Good offices seek to induce conflicting parties, who are disinclined to negotiate, to do so, or those who have negotiated without effecting an understanding, to renew the attempt. Good offices may also consist in advice, in submitting a proposal of one of the parties to the other, and the like, but States tendering them never take part in the negotiations themselves. On the other hand, a mediator is a middleman who does take part in the negotiations. He makes certain propositions on the basis of which the States at variance may come to an understanding. He even conducts the negotiations himself, always anxious to reconcile the opposing claims and to appease the feeling of resentment between the parties. All the efforts of the mediator may often, of course, be useless, the parties being unable or unwilling to consent to an agreement. But if an understanding is arrived at, the position of the mediator as a party to the negotiation, although not a party to the difference, frequently becomes clearly apparent either by the drafting of a special act of mediation which is signed by the States at variance and the mediator, or by the fact that in the convention between the conflicting States, which embodies their understanding, the mediator is mentioned.

Good Offices and Mediation according to the Hague Arbitration Convention.

§ 10. The Hague Convention for the Pacific Settlement of International Disputes[1] undertook in Articles 2-8 the task of making the signatory Powers have recourse more frequently than theretofore to good offices and mediation, and recommended a new and particular form of mediation in the following rules :—

(1) The contracting Powers agreed before they appealed to arms, to have recourse, as far as circumstances allowed, to good offices or mediation (Article 2). And independently of this recourse, they considered it expedient and desirable that contracting Powers who were strangers to the dispute should, on their own initiative, offer their good offices or mediation (Article 3). A real legal duty to offer good offices or mediation was not thereby created ; only the expediency and desirability of such an offer was recognised. In regard to the legal duty of conflicting States to ask for good offices or mediation, it is obvious that, although literally such a duty was agreed upon, the condition 'as far as circumstances allow' made it more or less illusory,

[1] See Meurer, i. pp. 104-129 ; Higgins, p. 167 ; Barclay, *Problems*, pp. 191-197 ; Lémonon, pp. 69-73 ; Wehberg, *Kommentar*, pp. 10-21 ; Nippold, i. pp. 21-22 ; Scott, *Conferences*, pp. 256-265.

as it was in the discretion of the parties to judge for themselves whether or not the circumstances of the special case allowed them to have recourse to good offices and mediation.

(2) The contracting Powers agreed that (Article 3) a right to offer good offices or mediation existed for those of them who were strangers to a dispute, and that this right existed also after the conflicting parties had appealed to arms. Consequently, every contracting Power, when at variance with another, be it before or after the outbreak of hostilities, was in duty bound to receive an offer of good offices or mediation, although it need not accept it. And it was specially stipulated that the exercise of the right to offer good offices or mediation might never be regarded by the conflicting States as an unfriendly act (Article 3). It was further stipulated that the contracting Powers considered it their duty in a serious conflict to remind the parties of the Permanent Court of Arbitration, and that the advice to have recourse to this court might only be considered as an exercise of good offices (Article 48, paragraphs 1 and 2). And, finally, in case of dispute between two Powers, one of them might always address to the International Bureau of the Permanent Court of Arbitration a note containing a declaration that it would be ready to submit the dispute to arbitration, whereupon the Bureau was at once to inform the other Power of this declaration (Article 48, paragraphs 3 and 4).

(3) Mediation was defined (Article 4) as reconciliation of the opposing claims and appeasement of the feelings of resentment between the conflicting States, and it was specially emphasised that good offices and mediation have exclusively the character of advice.

(4) The acceptance of mediation—and, of course, of good offices, which was not mentioned—was not (Article 7) to have the effect of interrupting, delaying, or hindering mobilisation or other preparatory measures for war, or of interrupting military operations when war had broken out before the acceptance of mediation, unless there should be an agreement to the contrary.

(5) The functions of the mediator were to be at an end

(Article 5) when once it was stated, either by one of the conflicting parties or by the mediator himself, that the means of reconciliation proposed by him were not accepted.

(6) A new and particular form of mediation was recommended by Article 8. Before appealing to arms, each conflicting State was to choose a State as umpire, to whom it entrusted the mission of entering into direct communication with the umpire chosen by the other side for the purpose of preventing the rupture of pacific relations. The period of the mandate extended, unless otherwise stipulated, to thirty days, and during such period the conflicting States were to cease from all direct communication on the matter in dispute ; it was to be regarded as referred exclusively to the mediating umpires, who were to use their best efforts to settle it. Should such mediation not succeed in bringing the conflicting States to an understanding, and a definite rupture of pacific relations take place, the chosen umpires were jointly charged to take advantage of any opportunity to restore peace.

Value of Good Offices and Mediation.

§ 11. The value of good offices and mediation for the amicable settlement of international conflicts, be it before or after the parties have appealed to arms, cannot be over-estimated; and the Hague Convention, which is still in force between the parties to it, greatly enhanced the value of such assistance by giving third States a legal right to tender it. Hostilities have been frequently prevented through the authority and the skill of mediators, and furiously raging wars have been brought to an end through good offices and mediation of third States.[1] The Dogger Bank incident of 1904 may be quoted as a case in which probable war was averted, for it was through the mediation of France that Great Britain and Russia agreed upon the establishment of an International Commission of Inquiry.[2] And the good offices of the President of the United

[1] See the important cases of mediation discussed by Calvo, iii. §§ 1684-1700, and Bonfils, Nos. 936-942.

[2] See above, § 5, n. 2.

States of America were the means of bringing a war to an end by inducing Russia and Japan, in August 1905, to open the negotiations which led to the conclusion of the Peace of Portsmouth on September 5, 1905. Nowadays the importance of these means of settlement of international differences is even greater than in the past.[1] The outbreak of war is under the circumstances and conditions of our times no longer a matter of indifference to all except the belligerent States, and no State which goes to war knows exactly how far such war may affect its very existence. Since the World War, this truth has found expression in the Covenant of the League of Nations, which has devised new means for settling international disputes. But still, if good offices and mediation are interposed at the right moment, they will in many cases not fail to effect a settlement of a conflict which could not be so well settled by other methods.

IV

ARBITRATION

Grotius, ii. c. 23, § 8—Vattel, ii. § 329—Hall, § 119—Westlake, i. pp. 350-368—Lawrence, § 221—Maine, pp. 210-218—Phillimore, iii. §§ 3-5—Twiss, ii. §§ 5-6—Taylor, §§ 357-358—Wharton, iii. § 316—Hershey, Nos. 309-313—Moore, vii. §§ 1069-1088—Bluntschli, §§ 488-498—Heffter, § 109—Bulmerincq in *Holtzendorff*, iv. pp. 30-58—Ullmann, §§ 154-156—Bonfils, Nos. 944-969—Despagnet, Nos. 722-741—Pradier-Fodéré, vi. Nos. 2602-2630—Mérignhac, i. pp. 448-485—Rivier, ii. § 59—Calvo, iii. §§ 1706-1806—Fiore, ii. Nos. 1202-1215, and *Code*, Nos. 1299-1385—Nys, ii. pp. 547-576—Martens, ii. § 104—Rouard de Card, *L'Arbitrage international* (1877)—Mérignhac, *Traité théorique et pratique de l'Arbitrage* (1895)—Moore, *History and Digest of the Arbitrations to which the United States has been a Party*, 6 vols. (1898)—Darby, *International Tribunals*, 4th ed. (1904)—Dumas, *Les Sanctions de l'Arbitrage international* (1905), and in *A.J.*, v. (1911), pp. 934-957—Nippold, *Die Fortbildung des Verfahrens in völkerrechtlichen Streitigkeiten* (1907)—Reinsch in *A.J.*, v. (1911), pp. 604-614—Scott, *Conferences*, pp. 188-253—Lapradelle et Politis, *Recueil des Arbitrages internationaux*, i. (1798-

[1] The editor believes that the author would have still held this view. Moreover, the League of Nations may itself use its good offices or mediation as a means of settling a dispute. See below, §§ 25*b*–25*g*.

1855), (1905)—Fried, *Handbuch der Friedensbewegung*, 2nd ed. (1911), i. pp. 137-184—Morris, *International Arbitration and Procedure* (1911) —Lammasch, *Die Rechtskraft internationaler Schiedssprüche* (1913), and *Die Lehre von der Schiedsgerichtsbarkeit* (1914)—Balch, *International Courts of Arbitration* (6th ed., with an introduction and additional notes by Thomas Willing Balch, 1915)—Barclay, *New Methods of Adjusting International Disputes and the Future* (1917)—Dungern in *Z. V.*, vii. (1913), pp. 257-271—Jong van Beek en Donk in the *Jahrbuch des Volkerrechts*, i. (1913), pp. 375-403—Balch, *Arbitration as a Term of International Law* (reprint from the *Columbia Law Review*) (1915)—Penfield and Ralston in the *Proceedings of the American Society of International Law*, ix. (1916), pp. 40-62.

§ 12. Arbitration is the name for the determination of differences between States through the verdict of one or more umpires chosen by the parties. As there is no central political authority above the sovereign States, and no such international court as could exercise jurisdiction over them, State differences, unlike differences between private individuals, cannot as a rule be obligatorily settled in courts of justice. The only way in which a settlement of State differences through a verdict may be arrived at is by the conflicting States voluntarily consenting to submit themselves to a verdict of one or more umpires chosen by themselves for that purpose.[1] Conception of Arbitration.

§ 13. It is, therefore, necessary for such conflicting States as intend to have the conflict determined by arbitration to conclude a treaty by which they agree to this course. Such a treaty of arbitration imposes an obligation on both parties to submit in good faith to the decision of the arbitrators. Frequently a treaty of arbitration will be concluded after the outbreak of a difference; but it also frequently happens that States concluding a treaty stipulate by the so-called Compromise Clause,[2] that any difference arising between them respecting matters regulated by the treaty shall Treaty of Arbitration.

[1] When, however, the proposed International Court of Justice has been set up, States will have a further means of obtaining a judicial decision. See below, § 25*f*.

[2] See above, § 3.

be determined by arbitration. Two or more States can also conclude a so-called general treaty of arbitration, or treaty of permanent arbitration, stipulating that all or certain kinds of differences arising in future between them shall be settled by this method. Thus Article 7 of the Commercial Treaty between Holland and Portugal [1] of July 5, 1894, constituted such a general treaty of arbitration, as it stipulated arbitration, not only for differences respecting matters of commerce, but for all kinds of future differences which did not concern their independence or autonomy. Until the Hague Peace Conference of 1899, however, general treaties of arbitration were not numerous. Public opinion everywhere was aroused in their favour through the success of this conference, with the result that from 1900 to the present day many general arbitration treaties have been concluded.[2]

Who is to arbitrate?

§ 14. States which conclude an arbitration treaty have to agree upon the arbitrators. If they choose a third State, they have to conclude a treaty (*receptum arbitri*), by which they appoint that State as arbitrator, and it accepts the appointment. The appointed State chooses on its own behalf those umpires who actually serve as arbitrators. It can happen that the conflicting States choose a head of a third State as arbitrator. But he never himself investigates the matter; he chooses one or more individuals, who make a report and propose a verdict, which he pronounces. And, further, the conflicting States may agree to entrust the arbitration to any other individual, or to a body of individuals, a so-called arbitration committee or commission. Thus the arbitration of 1899 in regard to the Venezuelan Boundary Dispute between Great Britain, Venezuela, and the United States was conducted by a commission, sitting at Paris, consisting of American

[1] See Martens, *N.R.G.*, 2nd Ser. xxii. p. 591.
[2] See below, § 17.

and English members and the Russian Professor von Martens as president. And the Alaska Boundary Dispute between Great Britain and the United States was settled in 1903, through the award of a commission, sitting at London, consisting of American and Canadian members, with Lord Alverstone, Lord Chief Justice of England, as president.

§ 15. The treaty of arbitration should stipulate the principles according to which the arbitrators have to give their verdict. These principles may be the general rules of International Law, or they may be the rules of any Municipal Law chosen by the conflicting States, or rules of natural equity, or rules specially stipulated in the treaty of arbitration for the special case.[1] Sometimes the treaty of arbitration stipulates that the arbitrators shall compromise the conflicting claims of the parties without resorting to special rules of law. In default of any express provision, it must be presumed that the verdict is to be given according to principles of International Law,[2] or if there are none applicable, according to rules of equity. The treaty generally stipulates also rules of procedure to be followed by the arbitrators. If it does not, the arbitrators themselves have to work them out and communicate them to the parties.

On what Principles Arbitrators proceed and decide.

§ 16. An arbitral verdict[3] is final if the arbitration treaty does not stipulate the contrary, and is binding upon the parties. The members of the League of Nations have agreed by Article 13 of the Covenant to carry it out in good faith, and not to go to war with a

Binding Force of Arbitral Verdict.

[1] See Lammasch, *Die Rechtskraft internationaler Schiedssprüche* (1913), pp. 36-67, and *Die Lehre von der Schiedsgerichtsbarkeit* (1914), pp. 175-186. See also below, § 335, concerning the 'Three Rules of Washington.'

[2] That as a rule arbitrators are bound to give their award according to law, and not according to other principles, is very ably set out in Balch, *Arbitration as a Term of International Law* (reprint from the *Columbia Law Review*) (1915).

[3] Its effect is discussed in all its details in Lammasch, *Die Rechtskraft*, etc., pp. 91-128.

member complying therewith. As, however, no central authority exists above the States to execute the verdict against a State refusing to submit, in case of such a refusal the other party has the right to enforce the arbitral decision by compulsion. Moreover, under Articles 13 and 16 of the Covenant of the League of Nations, in the event of failure to carry out an award, the Council is to propose what steps should be taken to give effect to it, and the delinquent member is liable to the penalties for breach of covenant stipulated in Article 16.[1] Yet it is obvious that an arbitral verdict is only binding provided [2] that the arbitrators have in every way fulfilled their duty as umpires, and have been able to find their verdict in perfect independence. Should they have been bribed, or not followed their instructions, should their verdict have been given under the influence of coercion of any kind, or should one of the parties have intentionally and maliciously led the arbitrators into an essential material error, the arbitral verdict would have no binding force whatever. Thus the award given in 1831 by the King of Holland in the North-Eastern Boundary Dispute between Great Britain and the United States of America was not considered binding by the parties, because the arbitrator had transgressed his powers.[3] For the same reason, Bolivia refused to submit to the award given in 1909 by the President of Argentina in her boundary dispute with Peru.[4] And in October 1910, the Permanent Court of Arbitration at the Hague, deciding the case of the United States of America against the United

[1] See above, vol. i. § 167*k*.

[2] The question of an appeal against an arbitral award is discussed in a masterly way by Lammasch, *Die Rechtskraft internationaler Schiedssprüche* (1913), pp. 129-209, and *Die Lehre von der Schiedsgerichtsbarkeit* (1914), pp. 212-224. See also Donker Curtius and Nys in *R.I.*, 2nd Ser. xii. (1910), pp. 5 and 595; Casusus and M'Kenney in the *Proceedings of the American Society of International Law*, vi. (1912), pp. 59 and 63.

[3] See Moore, vii. § 1082, and Moore, *Arbitrations*, i. pp. 85-161.

[4] See Fiore in *R.G.*, xvii. (1910), pp. 225-256, and Martens, *N.R.G.*, 3rd Ser. iii. p. 53.

States of Venezuela concerning the claims of the Orinoco Steamship Company, annulled,[1] with regard to certain points, a previous arbitration award given by Mr. Barge.

What Differences can be decided by Arbitration.

§ 17. It is often maintained that every possible difference between States could not be determined by arbitration, and, consequently, efforts are made to distinguish those groups of State differences which are determinable by arbitration from others. Now, although all States may never consent to have all possible differences decided by arbitration, theoretically there is no reason to distinguish between differences on the ground that some can, and others cannot, be decided through arbitration. For there can be no doubt that, the consent of the parties once given, every possible difference might be settled through arbitration, either by the verdict being based on rules of International Law, or rules of natural equity, or by opposing claims being compromised.

But, differing from the theoretical question as to what differences are, and are not, determinable by arbitration, is the question what kind of State differences *ought* always to be settled in this manner. The latter question was answered by Article 16 of the Hague Convention of 1899, and by Article 38 of the Hague Convention of 1907 for the Pacific Settlement of International Disputes, the contracting Powers therein recognising arbitration as the most efficacious, and at the same time the most equitable, means of determining differences of a judicial character in general, and in especial differences regarding the interpretation or application of international treaties. In 1903, Great Britain and France, following the suggestion of this Article 16, concluded a treaty in which they agreed to settle by arbitration all such differences of a legal nature as did not affect their vital interests, their

[1] See Martens, *N.R.G.*, 3rd Ser. iv. p. 79.

independence, their honour, or the interests of third States, and many other States followed the lead. Great Britain, in the following years, entered into such [1] arbitration treaties with Spain, Italy, Germany, Sweden, Norway, Portugal, Switzerland, Austria-Hungary, Holland, Denmark, the United States of America, Colombia, and Brazil. These agreements were concluded for five years only, but many of them have been renewed.

Yet there is a flaw in all these treaties, because the decision as to whether a difference is of a legal nature or not, is left to the discretion of the parties. Cases have happened in which one party has claimed to have a difference settled by arbitration on account of its legal nature, whereas the other party has denied its legal nature, and, therefore, refused to go to arbitration. For this reason the arbitration treaties signed on August 3, 1911, between the United States of America and Great Britain and between the United States of America and France would have been epoch-making, had they been ratified, since Article 3 provided that, in cases where the parties disagreed as to whether or not a difference was subject to arbitration under the treaty concerned, the question should be submitted to a Joint High Commission of Inquiry; and that, if all, or all but one, of the members of that commission decided the question in the affirmative, the case should be settled by arbitration. This article was, however, struck out by the American Senate, and so these treaties were not ratified.[2]

It should be mentioned that, whereas most arbitra-

[1] It is to be noted that the arbitration treaty between Great Britain and Uruguay of April 18, 1918 (Treaty Ser. (1919), No. 3, Cmd. 150) is of a different variety, since it stipulates arbitration for all disputes of every kind.

[2] See Dennis in *A.J.*, vi. (1912), pp. 614-628; *Proceedings of the American Society of International Law*, vi. (1912), pp. 87-114; Vlietinck in *R.I.*, 2nd Ser. xv. (1913), pp. 307-332 and 417-444. As regards the so-called Bryan Arbitration Treaties, which are not all arbitration treaties, but treaties making provision for the appointment of International Commissions of Inquiry, see above, § 5.

tion treaties limit arbitration in one or more ways, exempting cases which concern the independence, the honour, or the vital interests of the parties, Argentina [1] and Chili in 1902, Denmark and Holland in 1904, Denmark and Italy in 1905, Denmark and Portugal in 1907, Argentina and Italy in 1907, the Central American Republics of Costa Rica, Guatemala, Honduras, Nicaragua, and San Salvador in 1907, Italy and Holland in 1909, and Great Britain and Uruguay in 1918, entered into general arbitration treaties according to which such cases have not been excluded from settlement by arbitration.[2]

Arbitration under the Covenant of the League of Nations.

§ 17*a*. The validity of existing treaties of arbitration has not been affected [3] by the Covenant of the League of Nations. Indeed, that Covenant, while giving added importance to arbitration as a means of settling international disputes, has made use of existing machinery. For by Articles 12 and 13 the members agreed that if there should arise between them a dispute likely to lead to a rupture, they would submit it either to arbitration or to inquiry by the Council. If they referred it to arbitration, as they undertook to do if it was one recognised by them as suitable for arbitration and incapable of satisfactory settlement by diplomacy, they agreed not to resort to war until three months after the award, which was to be made within reasonable time. Legal differences and those regarding the interpretation of treaties had already been selected by Hague Convention I. as suitable for arbitration; and

[1] Earlier than this, on July 23, 1898—see Martens, *N.R.G.*, 2nd Ser. xxix. p. 137—Argentina and Italy, and on November 6, 1899 — see Martens, *N.R.G.*, 2nd Ser. xxxii. p. 404 — Argentina and Paraguay had concluded treaties according to which all differences without exception were to be settled by arbitration, provided they did not affect the constitution of either country. See also above, § 3, concerning the Compromise Clause.

[2] A list of all the arbitration treaties which had been entered into by the several States between the First Hague Peace Conference of 1899 and 1911 is to be found in Fried, *op. cit.*, p. 185.

[3] See Article 21.

they are again recommended by the Covenant for similar treatment. 'Disputes as to the interpretation of a treaty, as to any question of international law, as to the existence of any fact which if established would constitute a breach of any international obligation, or as to the extent and nature of the reparation to be made for any such breach, are declared to be among those which are generally suitable for submission to arbitration.' The Covenant does not establish a new arbitration tribunal for such disputes, but refers them to 'the court agreed on by the parties to the dispute or stipulated in any convention existing between them.'[1]

Value of Arbitration.

§ 18. Thus arbitration every day becomes more and more important. History proves that in antiquity and during the Middle Ages it was occasionally[2] made use of as a peaceable means of settling international differences. But, although an International Law made its appearance in modern times, during the sixteenth, seventeenth, and eighteenth centuries very few cases of arbitration occurred. It was not until the end of the eighteenth century that it was frequently made use of. There were 177 cases from 1794 to the end of 1900.[3] This number shows that the inclination of States to agree to arbitration had increased, and more recent developments show that arbitration has a great future. States and the public opinion of the whole world have become more and more convinced that there are a good many international differences which may well be determined by arbitration without any danger

[1] As to the manner in which the award may be enforced, and the circumstances under which a member of the League has agreed not to resort to war, see above, § 16, and vol. i. § 167*k*.

[2] See examples in Calvo, iii. §§ 1707-1712, and in Nys, *Les Origines du Droit international* (1894), pp. 52-61.

[3] See La Fontaine, *Histoire sommaire et chronologique des Arbitrages internationaux* in *R.I.*, 2nd Ser. iv. pp. 349, 558, 623. See also Scott, *Conferences*, pp. 188-253.

whatever to the national existence, independence, dignity, and prosperity of the States concerned. Already before the World War, a net of so-called peace societies had spread over the whole world, and their members unceasingly worked for the promotion of arbitration. The parliaments of several countries had repeatedly given their vote in its favour ; and the Hague Peace Conference of 1899 created a Permanent Court of Arbitration, a step by which a new epoch in the development of International Law was inaugurated. It was certain that arbitration would gradually increase its range, although the time was not then, and is not now, in sight when all international differences will find their settlement by arbitration.

The institution of the Permanent Court of Arbitration at the Hague stood before the World War between a cross-fire of impatient pacifists and cynical pessimists. Because a number of wars had been fought since the establishment of the Permanent Court, impatient pacifists were in despair and considered the institution of the Court of Arbitration a failure, whereas cynical pessimists triumphantly pointed to the fact that the millennium seemed to be as far distant as ever. But the calm observer of the facts who possessed insight into the process of historical development, had no cause to despair, for, compared with some generations before, arbitration was an established force which daily gained more power and influence. So it was to be expected that the close of the World War would witness a strong movement of opinion in favour of arbitration, and this expectation was justified. The Covenant of the League of Nations sets arbitration in the forefront of its plans for averting war, and existing arbitration treaties gain a new importance. It is therefore desirable to discuss in some detail arbitration according to Hague Convention I.

V

ARBITRATION ACCORDING TO THE HAGUE CONVENTION

Hershey, Nos. 314-320 — Ullmann, §§ 155-156 — Bonfils, Nos. 953[1]-955[1]— Nys, ii. pp. 568-572—Despagnet, Nos. 742-746 *bis*—Mérignhac, i. pp. 486-540—Holls, *The Peace Conference at the Hague* (1900)—Martens, *La Conférence de la Paix à la Haye* (1900)—Mérignhac, *La Conférence internationale de la Paix* (1900)—Fried, *Die zweite Haager Konferenz* (1908) — Meurer, i. pp. 299-372 — Scott, *Conferences*, pp. 286-385— Higgins, pp. 164-179—Lémonon, pp. 188-219—Nippold, i. pp. 36-231— Wehberg, *Kommentar*, pp. 46-164 — Lammasch, *Die Lehre von der Schiedsgerichtsbarkeit* (1914)—Strupp, *Die internationale Schiedsgerichtsbarkeit* (1914).

Arbitral Justice in general.

§ 19. Of the ninety-seven articles of the Hague Convention for the Pacific Settlement of International Disputes, no fewer than fifty-four—namely, Articles 37-90—deal with arbitration in four chapters, headed 'On Arbitral Justice,' 'On the Permanent Court of Arbitration,' 'On Arbitral Procedure,' and 'On Arbitration by Summary Procedure.' The first chapter, Articles 37-40, contains rules on arbitral justice in general, which, however, with one exception, are not of a legal but of a merely doctrinal character. Thus the definition in Article 37, 'international arbitration has for its object the determination of controversies between States by judges of their own choice and upon the basis of respect for law,' is as doctrinal as the assertion of Article 38 : 'In questions of a judicial character, and especially in questions regarding the interpretation or application of international treaties or conventions, arbitration is recognised by the contracting Powers as the most efficacious and at the same time the most equitable method of deciding controversies which have not been settled by diplomatic methods. Consequently it would be desirable that, in disputes regarding the above-mentioned questions, the contracting Powers should, if the case arise, have recourse to arbitration, in so far as circumstances permit.' And the provision of Article 39, that an agreement of arbitration may be made respecting disputes already in existence, or arising in the future, and may relate to every kind of controversy, or solely to controversies of a particular character, is as doctrinal as the reservation of Article 40, which runs: 'Independently of general or special treaties imposing expressly the obligation to have recourse to arbitration on the part of any of the contracting Powers, these Powers reserve to themselves the right to conclude new general or special agreements with a view to extending obligatory arbitration to all cases which they consider possible to submit to it.' The only rule of legal character is that of Article 37 (second paragraph), enacting the already existing customary rule of International Law, that 'the agreement of arbitration implies the obligation to submit in good faith to the arbitral sentence.'

On the signatory Powers no obligation to submit any difference to arbitration was imposed. Even differences of a judicial character, and especially those regarding the interpretation or application of treaties (for the settlement of which the signatory Powers, in Article 38, acknowledged arbitration to be the most efficacious and at the same time the most equitable method), had not necessarily to be submitted to arbitration. Yet the principle of compulsory arbitration for a limited number of international differences was by no means negatived by the Hague Peace Conferences, especially not by the Second Conference.

The principle found indirect recognition in the Convention respecting the Limitation of the Employment of Force for the Recovery of Contract Debts.[1] In Article 1 of this convention, which stipulates that

[1] See above, vol. i. § 135, where the so-called Drago Doctrine is likewise discussed.

recourse to the employment of force for the recovery of contract debts claimed from the Government of one country by the Government of another country as being due to its nationals is not allowed unless the debtor State refuses arbitration, compulsory arbitration has been victorious.

Moreover, although it was not possible to agree upon the inclusion in Convention I. of any stipulation embodying compulsory arbitration for a number of differences, the principle itself was fully recognised, and the Final Act of the Second Peace Conference included, therefore, a declaration that the conference 'is unanimous (1) in admitting the principle of compulsory arbitration; (2) in declaring that certain disputes, in particular those relating to the interpretation and application of international agreements, may be submitted to compulsory arbitration without any restriction.'

There were, therefore, reasonable grounds for the hope and expectation that one of the future Peace Conferences would find a way out of the difficulty, and come to an agreement upon compulsory arbitration for a limited number of international differences.[1]

Arbitration Treaty and Appointment of Arbitrators.

§ 20. According to Article 52, the conflicting States which resort to arbitration sign a special Act, the *compromis*, which clearly defines: the subject of the dispute; the time allowed for appointing the arbitrators; the form, order, and time in which the communications referred to in Article 63 must be made; the sum which each party must deposit in advance to defray expenses; the manner of appointing arbitrators (if there be occasion); any special powers which may eventually belong to the tribunal, where it shall meet, the languages to be used, and any special conditions upon which the

[1] See Scott, *Conferences*, pp. 319-385, where the proceedings of both the First and Second Peace Conferences concerning compulsory arbitration are sketched in a masterly and very lucid style.

parties may agree. Should, however, the conflicting States prefer it, the Permanent Court at the Hague is competent to draw up and settle the *compromis*, and the court is likewise in some other cases competent to settle the *compromis* (Articles 53-54). The parties may agree to have recourse to the Permanent Court of Arbitration which was instituted by the convention;[1] but they may also assign the arbitration to one or several arbitrators chosen by them, either from the members of the Permanent Court of Arbitration, or otherwise (Article 55). If they choose a head of a State as arbitrator, the whole of the arbitral procedure is to be determined by him (Article 56). If they choose several arbitrators, an umpire is to preside, but in case they have not chosen an umpire, the arbitrators are to elect one of their own number as president (Article 57). If the *compromis* is settled by a commission, as contemplated by Article 54, in default of an agreement to the contrary, the commission itself shall form the arbitration tribunal (Article 58). In case of death, resignation, or disability of one of the arbitrators from any cause, his place is to be filled in accordance with the method of his appointment (Article 59). The place of session of the arbitrators is to be determined by the parties; and failing this, is to be the Hague. It may not be changed by the arbitrators without the consent of the parties; and may only be on the territory of a third State with the latter's consent (Article 60). The International Bureau of the Court at the Hague is authorised to put its offices and its staff at the disposal of parties which have preferred to bring their dispute before arbitrators other than the Permanent Court of Arbitration (Article 47).

§ 21. The parties may agree upon such rules of arbitral procedure as they like. If they fail to stipulate

[1] Details have been given above, vol. i. §§ 472-476.

Procedure of, and before, the Arbitral Tribunal.

special rules of procedure, the following rules are valid, whether the parties have brought their case before the Permanent Court of Arbitration or have chosen other arbitrators (Article 51):—

(1) The parties may appoint counsel or advocates for the defence of their rights before the tribunal. They may also appoint delegates or special agents to attend the tribunal as intermediaries between them and the tribunal. The members of the Permanent Court, however, may not act as agents, counsel, or advocates except on behalf of the Power which has appointed them members of the court (Article 62).

(2) The tribunal selects the languages for its own use and for use before it, unless the *compromis* has specified them (Article 61).

(3) As a rule there are two distinct stages: written pleadings and oral discussion. The written pleadings consist of cases, counter-cases, and, if necessary, replies, communicated by the respective agents to the members of the tribunal and to the opposite party; all papers and documents relied on must be annexed. The pleadings are to be communicated either directly, or through the International Bureau, in the order and within the time fixed by the *compromis* (Article 63). A duly certified copy of every document produced by one party must be communicated to the other party (Article 64). Unless special circumstances arise, the tribunal does not meet until the pleadings are closed (Article 65).

(4) Upon the written pleadings follows the oral discussion in court; it consists of the oral development of the pleas of the parties (Article 63). The discussions are under the direction of the president of the tribunal, and are public only if it be so decided by the tribunal with the consent of the parties. Minutes of the discussion are to be drawn up by secretaries appointed by the president, and only these official minutes, which

are signed by the president and one of the secretaries, are authentic (Article 66). During the discussion in court the agents and counsel of the parties are authorised to present to the tribunal orally all the arguments they may think expedient in support of their case. They are likewise authorised to raise objections, and to make incidental motions, but the decisions of the tribunal on these objections and motions are final, and cannot form the subject of any further discussion (Articles 70, 71). Every member of the tribunal may put questions to the agents and counsel of the parties, and demand explanations from them on doubtful points; but such questions or other remarks made by members of the tribunal may not be regarded as expressions of opinion (Article 72). The tribunal may always require from the agents of the parties all necessary explanations and the production of all papers, and in case of refusal the tribunal takes note of it in the minutes (Articles 69).

Whenever a doubt arises as to the competence of the tribunal, the tribunal itself is authorised to decide the question, by interpretation of the *compromis* and other relevant papers and documents, and by the application of the principles of law (Article 73).

During the discussion in court—Article 67 says, 'after the close of the pleadings'—the tribunal may refuse to admit fresh papers and documents which one party may desire to submit to the tribunal without the consent of the other party (Article 67), but must admit fresh papers and documents when both parties agree to their submission. On the other hand, the tribunal is always competent to take into consideration fresh papers and documents to which its attention is drawn by the agents or counsel of the parties, and in such cases the tribunal may require production of the papers and documents, but it is at the same time obliged to make them known to the other party (Article 68).

The parties must supply the tribunal, within the widest limits they may think practicable, with all the information required for deciding the dispute (Article 75). For the service of all notices by the tribunal, or the collection of evidence, in the territory of a third contracting Power, the tribunal applies direct to its Government, which must assist with the means at its disposal according to Municipal Law, unless the request seems to impair its own sovereign rights or its safety. Instead, however, of making a direct application to a third Power, the tribunal may always invoke the aid of the Power on whose territory it sits (Article 76). As soon as the agents and counsel of the parties have submitted all explanations and evidence in support of their case, the president declares the discussion closed (Article 77).

Arbitral Award.

§ 22. The arbitral award is given after deliberation behind closed doors, and the proceedings remain secret; the members of the tribunal vote, and the majority of the votes makes the decision of the tribunal (Article 78). The decision, accompanied by a statement of the considerations upon which it is based, is to be drawn up in writing, to recite the names of the arbitrators, and to be signed by the president and the registrar, or the secretary acting as the registrar (Article 79). The award is read out at a public meeting of the tribunal, the agents and counsel of the parties having been duly summoned to attend (Article 80).

Binding Force of Awards.

§ 23. The award, when duly pronounced and notified to the agents of the parties, decides the dispute finally and without appeal (Article 81). Any dispute arising between the parties as to its interpretation or execution must, in default of an agreement to the contrary, be submitted to the tribunal which pronounced it (Article 82). The parties may, however, beforehand stipulate in the *compromis* the possibility of an appeal.

In such case, unless the *compromis* stipulates otherwise, the demand for a rehearing of the case must be addressed to the tribunal which pronounced the award. It may only be made on the ground of the discovery of some new fact such as may exercise a decisive influence on the award, and which at the time when the discussion was closed was unknown to the tribunal as well as to the appealing party. Proceedings for a rehearing may only be opened after a decision of the tribunal, expressly stating the existence of a new fact of the character described, and declaring the demand admissible on this ground. The treaty of arbitration must stipulate the period of time within which the demand for a rehearing must be made (Article 83).

Award binding upon Parties only.

§ 24. The award [1] is binding only upon the parties to the proceedings. But when there is a question of interpreting a convention to which States other than the States at variance are parties, the conflicting States have to inform all the contracting Powers in good time. Each has a right to intervene in the case before the tribunal, and, if one or more avail themselves of this right, the interpretation contained in the award is binding upon them also (Article 84).

Costs of Arbitration.

§ 25. Each party pays its own expenses, and an equal share of those of the tribunal [2] (Article 85).

Arbitration by Summary Procedure.

§ 25*a*. With a view to simplifying arbitration in disputes of minor importance, Convention I. adopted the following rules for a summary procedure exclusively in writing :—

Each of the conflicting parties appoints an arbitrator, who need not necessarily be members of the Permanent Court of Arbitration. The two arbitrators thus appointed choose a third as umpire, who need not be a member of the Permanent Court either. But if they cannot agree

[1] The awards hitherto given are enumerated above, vol. i. § 476.

[2] See details in Wehberg, *Kommentar*, pp. 155-158.

upon an umpire, each of them proposes two candidates taken from the general list of the Permanent Court of Arbitration (exclusive of such members as are either appointed by the conflicting States or are their nationals), and it is to be determined by lot which of the candidates shall be the umpire. This umpire presides over the tribunal, which gives its decisions by a majority of votes (Article 87). In the absence of agreement, the tribunal settles the time within which the two parties must submit their cases (Article 88). Each party is represented by an agent who serves as intermediary between it and the tribunal (Article 89). The proceedings are conducted exclusively in writing. Each party, however, is entitled to ask that witnesses and experts should be called, and the tribunal has the right to demand oral explanations from the agents as well as from the experts and witnesses whose appearance in court it may consider useful (Article 90). Articles 52 to 85 of Convention I. apply so far as they are not inconsistent with the rules laid down in Articles 87 to 90 (Article 86).

VI

THE LEAGUE OF NATIONS AND STATE DIFFERENCES

The League of Nations as a Factor in State Differences.

§ 25*b*. Negotiation between the parties, good offices or mediation of third States, and arbitral awards,—these were the only amicable means available for the settlement of State differences before the World War. There was no organised body to detect the early growth of disputes and by timely action to avert armed conflict. No aid was tendered to the parties at issue unless they themselves sought it, or unless one or more States had sufficient interest, initiative, and prestige to offer their services. But since the war the Family of Nations has acquired an organisation in the League of Nations, and among its principal functions is the prevention of war.[1] Accordingly, the Covenant charges the League itself with

[1] See above, vol. i. § 167*i*.

special duties, and lays new obligations upon the individual members, which are designed to secure the peaceful settlement of differences.

The Duties of the League itself.

§ 25*c*. By Article 11, as has already been seen,[1] any war or threat of war, whether immediately affecting any of the members of the League or not, is declared to be a matter of concern to the whole League. Each member has the 'friendly right' to bring to the attention of the Assembly or the Council any circumstance affecting international relations which threatens to disturb international peace, or the good understanding between nations upon which peace depends. Upon the request of a member the Secretary-General must in such an emergency forthwith summon a meeting of the Council. The League is to take any action that may be deemed wise and effectual to safeguard the peace of nations. Upon the means to be employed there is no other limitation than this; accordingly, they may consist of good offices or mediation, or of one of the methods of compulsion described in the next chapter. Moreover, under Article 10,[2] if there be any threat or danger of external aggression against the territorial integrity or existing political independence of a member, the Council is to advise other members upon the means for fulfilling their obligation to preserve them. Here again the means are not specified; they may be amicable, compulsive, or even war.

The Duty of Members involved in a Dispute: Inquiry by the Council.

§ 25*d*. The members of the League have by Article 12 agreed [3] to refer any dispute between them likely to lead to a rupture either to arbitration or to inquiry by the Council, and not to resort to war until three months after the award or the report. Reference to arbitration has already been discussed.[4] A dispute not submitted to arbitration must be laid before the Council.

A dispute is brought before the Council by notifica-

[1] See above, vol. i. § 167*k*.
[2] See above, vol. i. § 167*m*.
[3] See above, vol. i. § 167*k*.
[4] See above, § 17*a*.

tion to the Secretary-General. Upon one of the parties at variance giving such notice, the Secretary-General has to make all necessary arrangements for full investigation and consideration. Each party must communicate to him as promptly as possible statements of their case, with all relevant facts and papers.[1] Either party, by request made within fourteen days after the submission of the dispute, may require it to be referred to the Assembly; and the Council may so refer it, even if no such request is made.[2] Otherwise the investigation and report are to be the work of the Council, upon which all parties to the dispute are entitled to be represented[3] for the occasion. The Council is first to endeavour to effect a settlement of the dispute; if successful, it is to publish a statement giving such facts and explanations regarding the dispute, and the terms upon which it has been settled, as it may deem appropriate. If a settlement is not reached in this way, it may be that one party will claim that the dispute arises out of a matter which by International Law is solely within the domestic jurisdiction of that party.[4] If the Council finds this contention to be well founded, it will so report, and make no recommendation. But if the dispute be within the jurisdiction of the League, the Council must make and publish a report within six months after its submission. This report is to contain a statement of the facts of the dispute, and to make such recommendations as are deemed just and proper. If the report be unanimous, or concurred in by all members of the Council other than representatives of the parties to the dispute, the members of the League agree that they will not go to war with any party to the dispute which complies with the recommendations of the report. But if the report is merely a majority

[1] Article 15. The Council, if it appears desirable, may direct their immediate publication.

[2] As to the procedure in this case, see below, § 25*e*.

[3] Article 4.

[4] See above, vol. i. § 167*i*.

report, the members of the League reserve to themselves, subject to their obligation not to resort to war until three months after the report, the right to take such action as they consider necessary for the maintenance of right and justice. Any report by the Council must secure at least a majority; but each member represented on it may publish on its own account a statement of facts and of its conclusions upon them.[1]

§ 25*e*. But, as has been stated, a dispute may be transferred from the Council to the Assembly. In that case the same procedure is to be followed, 'the Assembly' being substituted in all references to 'the Council.' But with regard to the report there is a difference. A report of the Assembly, in order to bind the members of the League not to make war against a party carrying out its recommendations, must be concurred in by the representatives of those members of the League represented on the Council and by the representatives of a majority of the other members, exclusive in each case of the representatives of the parties to the dispute. Inquiry by the Assembly.

§ 25*f*. The Covenant of the League also contemplates the settlement of differences between States by recourse to an International Court.[2] The need for such a court, and the progress then made towards its establishment, have been referred to in the first volume.[3] After that volume went to press, the committee of jurists unanimously adopted a draft project[4] for the institution of the court. The draft was amended by the Council of the League and approved in its amended form by the Assembly at its meeting at Geneva on December 13, 1920.[5] The Proposed International Court of Justice.

The Covenant does not compel the submission of any class of disputes to this court; but only provides that it should hear and determine any international

[1] Article 15.
[2] Article 14.
[3] § 476*b*.
[4] *League of Nations Official Journal*, Special Supplement (No. 2), September 1920.
[5] *League of Nations Official Journal*, Special Supplement, January 1921, p. 23.

dispute which the parties voluntarily bring before it. The proposal made by the committee of jurists that the court should nevertheless have compulsory jurisdiction in certain classes of State differences was not accepted by the League. Many of the treaties which constitute the resettlement after the World War have, however, as has been previously stated, expressly stipulated that certain differences which may arise under them should be brought before this court for decision.

Disputes in which non-Members are involved.

§ 25*g*. Disputes may arise between a State which is, and a State which is not, a member of the League, or between two States neither of which is a member. In that event, the State or States which are not members of the League are to be invited to accept the obligations of membership for the purposes of the dispute upon such conditions as the Council may deem just, and the Council is immediately to institute an inquiry into the circumstances of the dispute, and recommend such action as may seem best and most effectual under the circumstances.

If for the purpose of a dispute between a member and a non-member the non-member refuses to accept the obligations of membership, and resorts to war against the member, it is to be subjected to the same measures as a member-State which breaks its covenants.[1] If neither party to a dispute is a member of the League, and both refuse to accept the obligations of membership for the purposes of the dispute, the Council may—not must—take such measures and make such recommendations as will prevent hostilities and result in the settlement of the dispute. No special provision seems to have been made for the case in which one party consents and the other refuses to accept the obligations of membership.[2]

[1] See below, § 26.

[2] The defects of the provisions of the Covenant of the League for dealing with international differences have been discussed above, vol. i. § 167*a*.

CHAPTER II

COMPULSIVE SETTLEMENT OF STATE DIFFERENCES

I

ON COMPULSIVE MEANS OF SETTLEMENT OF STATE DIFFERENCES IN GENERAL

Hershey, Nos. 321-328—Lawrence, § 136—Westlake, ii. p. 6—Phillimore, iii. § 7—Pradier-Fodéré, vi. No. 2632—Despagnet, No. 483—Mérignhac, iii[a]. p. 44—Fiore, ii. No. 1225, and *Code*, Nos. 1886-1390—Taylor, § 431—Nys, ii. pp. 581-593—Schoenborn, *Die Besetzung von Vera Cruz* (1914), pp. 7-35.

Conception and Kinds of Compulsive Means of Settlement.

§ 26. Under the Covenant of the League of Nations, as was explained in the last chapter, member-States have undertaken not to resort to war without having first submitted a dispute either to arbitration or to inquiry, and in no case to begin hostilities against a State which complies with an arbitral award or with the recommendations of a report of the Council or the Assembly which has secured the requisite majority. But a member may break his covenants; in that case, measures of compulsion are to be taken against it by the other members of the League. These measures are laid down in Article 16, and have already been fully stated.[1] Or again, it may be necessary for the League itself to apply compulsion to a State or States for the purpose of safeguarding the peace of the world. More-

[1] See above, vol. i. § 167*k*. They are briefly, (1) the severance of all trade or financial relations between the guilty State and other members, (2) the prohibition of all intercourse between its subjects and theirs, (3) the prevention of all intercourse between its subjects and the subjects of States which are not members of the League, and if need be, (4) armed force.

over, there are still many cases in which individual States are permitted by the Covenant to take measures of compulsion against each other; and if its machinery should disappoint the hopes of its founders, the occasion for such measures will arise more often. It is the purpose of this chapter to discuss them. All the means of constraint here mentioned, except the so-called 'economic boycott,' were in use before the organisation of the League of Nations, and in a book which was written before the World War are naturally discussed without reference to the League. But it will be apparent that some of them are as appropriate for use by the League itself as for use by the individual States.

Compulsive means of settlement of differences are measures containing a certain amount of compulsion taken by a State for the purpose of making another State consent to such settlement of a difference as is required by the former. There are four different kinds of such means in use—namely, retorsion, reprisals (including embargo), pacific blockade, and intervention. But it must be mentioned that, whereas every amicable means of settling differences might find application in every kind of difference, not every compulsive means is applicable in every difference. For the application of retorsion is confined to political, and that of reprisals to legal, differences.

Compulsive Means in contradistinction to War.

§ 27. War is very often enumerated among the compulsive means of settling international differences. This is in a sense correct, for a State might make war for no other purpose than that of compelling another State to settle a difference in the way required before war was declared. Nevertheless, the characteristics of compulsive means of settling international differences make it necessary to draw a sharp line between them and war. It is, in the first place, characteristic of compulsive means that, although they frequently consist of harmful measures, they are not considered as acts of war, either by the conflicting States or by other States, and consequently all relations of peace, such as diplomatic and commercial intercourse, the execution of treaties, and the like, remain undisturbed. Compulsive means are in theory and practice considered peaceable, although not amicable, means of settling international differences. It is, further, characteristic of compulsive means that they are even at their worst confined to the application of certain harmful measures only, whereas belligerents in war may apply any amount and any kind of force, with the exception only of those methods forbidden by International Law. And, thirdly, it is characteristic of compulsive means that a State which has succeeded in compelling another to declare that it is ready to settle the difference in the manner desired must cease to apply them; whereas, war once broken out, a belligerent is not obliged to lay down arms if and when the other belligerent is ready to comply with the request made before the war. As war is the *ultima ratio* between States, the victorious belligerent is not legally prevented from imposing upon the defeated foe any conditions he likes.

Compulsive Means in contradistinction to an Ultimatum and Demonstrations.

§ 28. Since these are the characteristics of compulsive means for the settlement of international differences, it is necessary to distinguish between such means and an *ultimatum*. The latter is the technical term for a written communication by one State to another which ends amicable negotiations respecting a difference, and formulates, for the last time and categorically, the demands to be fulfilled if other measures are to be averted. An *ultimatum* is, theoretically at least, not compulsion, although it may have the same effect, and although compulsive means, or even war, may be threatened in the event of a refusal to comply with the demands made.[1] Similarly, withdrawal of diplomatic agents, military and naval demonstrations, and the like, which some publicists [2] enumerate among the compulsive means of settlement of international differences, although they may indirectly achieve the settlement of differences, are not in themselves measures of compulsion.

II

RETORSION

Vattel, ii. § 341—Hall, § 120—Westlake, ii. p. 6—Phillimore, iii, § 7—Twiss ii. § 10—Taylor, § 435—Wharton, iii. § 318—Moore, vii. § 1090—Wheaton, § 290—Bluntschli, § 505—Heffter, § 110—Bulmerincq in *Holtzendorff*, iv. pp. 59-71—Ullmann, § 159—Bonfils, Nos. 972-974—Despagnet, Nos. 484-486—Mérignhac, iii[a]. p. 46—Pradier-Fodéré, vi. Nos. 2634-2636—Rivier, ii. § 60—Nys, ii. p. 582—Calvo, iii. § 1807—Fiore, ii. Nos. 1226-1227, and *Code*, Nos. 1391-1395—Martens, ii. § 105—Rapisardi-Mirabelli in *R.I.*, 2nd Ser. xvi. (1914), pp. 223-244.

Conception and Character of Retorsion.

§ 29. Retorsion is the technical term for retaliation for discourteous, or unkind, or unfair and inequitable, acts by acts of the same, or a similar, kind. Retorsion has nothing to do with international delinquencies, as it is not a means of compulsion in the case of legal differences, but only in the case of certain political differences. The act which calls for retaliation is not an illegal act; on the contrary, it is an act that is within the competence of the doer.[3] But a State can commit many legislative, administrative, or judicial acts which, although they are not internationally illegal, involve discourtesy or unfriendliness to another State, or are

[1] See Pradier-Fodéré, vi. No. 2649, and below, § 95.

[2] See Taylor, §§ 431, 433, 441; Moore, vii. §§ 1089, 1091, 1099; Pradier-Fodéré, vi. No. 2633.

[3] For this reason—see Heilborn, *System*, p. 352, and Wagner, *Zur Lehre von den Streiterledigungsmitteln des Völkerrechts* (1900), pp. 53-60—it is correctly maintained that retorsion, in contradistinction to reprisals, is not of legal, but only of political importance. Nevertheless, a system of the Law of Nations must not omit retorsion altogether, because it is in practice an important means of settling political differences.

unfair and inequitable. If the State against which such acts are directed considers itself wronged thereby, a political difference is created which might be settled by retorsion.

§ 30. The question when retorsion is, and when it is not, justified is not one of law, and is difficult to answer. The difficulty arises from the fact that the conceptions of discourtesy, unfriendliness, and unfairness cannot be defined very precisely. It depends, therefore, largely upon the circumstances and conditions of each case whether a State will, or will not, consider itself justified in making use of retorsion. In practice, States have frequently employed retorsion in cases of unfair treatment of their citizens abroad through rigorous passport regulations, the exclusion of foreigners from certain professions, the levy of exorbitant protectionist or fiscal duties; or in cases when the courts of another State have refused the usual assistance to its courts, or another State has refused to admit foreign ships to its harbours, etc.

Retorsion, when justified.

§ 31. The essence of retorsion consists in retaliation for a noxious act by a noxious act. But a State, in making use of retorsion, is by no means confined to acts of the same kind as those complained of, acts of a similar kind being equally admissible, provided they are not internationally illegal. And, further, as retorsion is made use of only to compel a State to alter its discourteous, unfriendly, or unfair behaviour, all acts of retorsion ought at once to cease when it does so.

Retorsion, how exercised.

§ 32. The value of retorsion as a means of settling certain international differences consists in its compulsory force, which has great power in regulating the intercourse of States. It is a commonplace of human nature, and by experience constantly confirmed, that evil-doers are checked by retaliation, and that those who are inclined to commit a wrong against others are

Value of Retorsion.

often prevented by the fear of it. Through the high tide of chauvinism, protectionism, and unfriendly feelings against foreign nations, States are often tempted to legislative, administrative, and judicial acts against other States which, although not internationally illegal, nevertheless endanger friendly relations and intercourse within the Family of Nations. The certainty of retaliation may be the only force which can make States resist the temptation.

III

REPRISALS

Grotius, iii. c. 2—Vattel, ii. §§ 342-354—Bynkershoek, *Quaestiones Juris publici*, i. c. 24—Hall, § 120—Lawrence, §§ 136-137—Westlake, ii. pp. 6-11, and *Papers*, pp. 590-606—Twiss, ii. §§ 11-22—Moore, vii. §§ 1095, 1096, 1098—Taylor, §§ 436-437—Wharton, iii. §§ 318, 320—Wheaton, §§ 291-293—Bluntschli, §§ 500-504—Heffter, §§ 111-112—Bulmerincq in *Holtzendorff*, iv. pp. 72-116—Ullmann, § 160—Bonfils, Nos. 975-985—Despagnet, Nos. 487-495—Pradier-Fodéré, vi. Nos. 2637-2647—Mérignhac, iii[a]. pp. 48-60—Rivier, ii. § 60—Nys, ii. pp. 582-589—Calvo, iii. §§ 1808-1831—Fiore, ii. Nos. 1228-1230, and *Code*, Nos. 1396-1404—Martens, ii. § 105—Lafargue, *Les Représailles en Temps de Paix* (1899)—Ducrocq, *Représailles en Temps de Paix* (1901), pp. 5-57, 175-232.

Conception of Reprisals in contradistinction to Retorsion.

§ 33. Reprisals are such injurious and otherwise internationally illegal acts of one State against another as are exceptionally permitted for the purpose of compelling the latter to consent to a satisfactory settlement of a difference created by its own international delinquency. Whereas retorsion consists in retaliation for discourteous, unfriendly, unfair, and inequitable acts by acts of the same or a similar kind, and has nothing to do with international delinquencies, reprisals are acts, otherwise illegal, performed by a State for the purpose of obtaining justice for an international delinquency by taking the law into its own hands. It is, of course, possible for a State to retaliate for an illegal act committed against itself by an act of a similar kind. Such retaliation would be retorsion in the ordinary sense of the term; but not in the technical meaning of the term, as used by those writers on International Law who correctly distinguish between retorsion and reprisals.

Reprisals admissible for all International Delinquencies.

§ 34. Reprisals are admissible, not only, as some writers[1] maintain, in case of denial or delay of justice, or other ill-treatment of foreign citizens prohibited by International Law, but in all other cases of an international delinquency for which the injured State cannot get reparation through negotiation,[2] or other amicable means, be it non-compliance with treaty obligations, violation of the dignity of a foreign State, violation of foreign territorial supremacy, or any other internationally illegal act.

Thus, to give an example, Great Britain, in the case of the Sicilian Sulphur Monopoly, performed acts of reprisal against the Two Sicilies in 1840 for a violation of a treaty. By the treaty of commerce of 1816 between the Two Sicilies and Great Britain certain commercial advantages had been secured to Great Britain; and when, in 1838, the Neapolitan Government granted a sulphur monopoly to a company of French and other foreign merchants, Great Britain protested against this as a violation of her treaty rights, and demanded the revocation of the monopoly. The Neapolitan Government had declined to comply, and Great Britain in 1840 laid an *embargo* on Sicilian ships in the harbour of Malta, and ordered her fleet in the Mediterranean to seize Sicilian ships, by way of reprisal. A number of vessels were captured, but were restored after the Sicilies had, through the mediation[3] of France, agreed to withdraw the grant of the sulphur monopoly.

[1] See, for instance, Twiss, ii. § 19.

[2] As regards reprisals for the non-payment of contract debts, see below, § 41.

[3] See Satow, *Diplomatic Practice*, ii. § 636.

Again, when in 1908 de Castro, the President of Venezuela, dismissed M. de Reuss, the Dutch minister resident at Caracas, Holland considered this step to be a violation of her dignity, and sent cruisers into Venezuelan waters to take reprisals. These cruisers captured the Venezuelan coast-guard ship *Alexis* outside Puerto Cabello, and another Venezuelan public vessel; but both were restored in 1909, when de Castro was deposed, and the new President negotiated a settlement with Holland.

Reprisals admissible for International Delinquencies only.

§ 35. Reprisals are admissible in the case of international delinquencies only and exclusively. As internationally injurious acts on the part of administrative and judicial officials, armed forces, and private individuals are not *ipso facto* international delinquencies, no reprisals for them are admissible if their State discharges the obligations of its vicarious responsibility.[1] However, should it refuse to do so, its vicarious responsibility would turn into original responsibility, and thereby an international delinquency would be created, for which reprisals are indeed admissible.

The reprisals ordered by Great Britain in the case of Don Pacifico are an illustrative example of unjustified reprisals, because no international delinquency had been committed. In 1847 a riotous mob, aided by Greek soldiers and gendarmes, broke into, and plundered, the house of Don Pacifico, a native of Gibraltar, and an English subject living at Athens. Great Britain claimed damages from Greece, although Don Pacifico had not sought redress in the Greek courts. Greece refused to comply with the British claim, maintaining correctly that Don Pacifico ought to institute an action for damages against the rioters before the Greek courts. Great Britain continued to press her claim, and finally in 1850 blockaded the Greek coast and ordered, by

[1] See above, vol. i. §§ 149, 150.

way of reprisal, the capture of Greek vessels. The conflict was eventually settled by Greece paying £150 to Don Pacifico. It is generally recognised that England had no right to act as she did in this case. She could have claimed damages directly from the Greek Government only after the Greek courts had denied satisfaction to Don Pacifico.[1]

Reprisals, by whom performed.

§ 36. Acts of reprisal may nowadays be performed only by State organs such as armed forces, or men-of-war, or administrative officials, in compliance with a special order of their State. But in former times private individuals used to perform them. Such private acts of reprisal seem to have been in vogue in antiquity, for there existed a law in Athens, according to which the relatives of an Athenian, murdered in a foreign State which refused punishment or extradition of the murderer, had the right to seize, and bring before the Athenian courts, three citizens of that State (so-called ἀνδρολῃψία). During the Middle Ages, and even in modern times to the end of the eighteenth century, States used to grant so-called 'letters of marque' to subjects who had been injured abroad, either by a foreign State itself or by its citizens, and could not get redress. They authorised the bearer to commit acts of self-help against the State concerned, its citizens and their property, for the purpose of obtaining satisfaction for the wrong sustained. In later times, however, States themselves also performed acts of reprisal. In consequence, their performance by private individuals fell more and more into disuse, and finally disappeared totally with the end of the eighteenth century. The distinction between general and special reprisals, which used formerly to be drawn, is based on the fact that in former times a State could either authorise a single private individual to perform

[1] See above, vol. i. § 167. The case is reported with all its details in Martens, *Causes célèbres*, v. pp. 395-531.

an act of reprisal (*special* reprisals), or command its armed forces to perform all kinds of such acts (*general* reprisals). The term 'general reprisals' is by Great Britain nowadays used for the authorisation of the British fleet to seize in time of war all enemy ships and goods.[1]

Objects of Reprisals.

§ 37. An act of reprisal may be performed against anything and everything that belongs to, or is due to, the delinquent State or its citizens. Ships sailing under its flag may be seized, treaties concluded with it may be suspended, a part of its territory may be militarily occupied, goods belonging to it, or to its citizens, may be seized, and the like. Thus in 1895 Great Britain ordered a fleet to land forces at Corinto, and to occupy the custom-house and other Government buildings, as an act of reprisal against Nicaragua; again, in 1901 France ordered a fleet to seize the island of Mitylene, as an act of reprisal against Turkey; and in 1908 Holland ordered a squadron to seize two public Venezuelan vessels as an act of reprisal against Venezuela.[2] The persons of officials, and even of private citizens, of the delinquent State are possible objects of reprisals. Thus, when in 1740 the Empress Anne of Russia arrested without just cause Baron de Stackelberg, a natural-born Russian subject, who had, however, become naturalised in Prussia by entering Prussian service, Frederick II. of Prussia seized two Russian subjects by way of reprisal, and detained them until Stackelberg

[1] Phillimore (iii. § 10) cites the following Order in Council of March 29, 1854: 'Her Majesty having determined to afford active assistance to her ally, His Highness the Sultan of the Ottoman Empire, for the protection of his dominions against the encroachments and unprovoked aggression of His Imperial Majesty the Emperor of All the Russias, Her Majesty is therefore pleased, by and with the advice of Her Privy Council, to order, and it is hereby ordered, that general reprisals be granted against the ships, vessels, and goods of the Emperor of All the Russias, and of his subjects, or others inhabiting within any of his countries, territories, or dominions, so that Her Majesty's fleets may lawfully seize all ships, vessels, and goods,' etc.

[2] See above, § 34.

was liberated. But it must be emphasised that the only act of reprisal admissible against foreign officials or citizens is arrest; they must not be treated like criminals, but like hostages, and under no circumstance may they be executed, or subjected to punishment.

The rule that anything and everything belonging to the delinquent State may be made the object of reprisals has, however, exceptions; for instance, individuals enjoying the privilege of exterritoriality while abroad, such as heads of States and diplomatic envoys, may not [1] be made the object of reprisals, although this has occasionally been done in practice.[2] In regard to another exception—namely, public debts—unanimity does not exist, either in theory or in practice. When Frederick II. of Prussia in 1752, by way of negative reprisals for an alleged injustice of British Prize Courts against Prussian subjects, sequestrated the payments of the Silesian loan due to English creditors, Great Britain, in addition to denying that there was a just cause for reprisals at all, maintained that public debts may not be made the object of reprisals. English jurists and others, as, for instance, Vattel, agree, but German writers dissent.[3]

Positive and Negative Reprisals.

§ 38. Reprisals can be positive or negative. Positive reprisals are such acts as would under ordinary circumstances involve an international delinquency. Negative reprisals consist in a refusal to perform such acts as are under ordinary circumstances obligatory; such as the fulfilment of a treaty obligation or the payment of a debt.

[1] Grotius, ii. c. 18, § 7.

[2] See the case reported in Martens, *Causes célèbres*, i. p. 35.

[3] See Vattel, ii. § 344; Phillimore, iii. § 22, in contradistinction to Heffter, § 111, n. 5. The case is treated in all its details in Satow, *The Silesian Loan and Frederick the Great* (1915). See also Martens, *Causes célèbres*, ii. pp. 97-168, and Trendelenburg, *Friedrichs des Grossen Verdienst um das Völkerrecht im Seekrieg* (Monthly Report of the Prussian Academy of Sciences, January 1866). The dispute was settled in 1756—see below, § 437—through Great Britain paying an indemnity of £20,000.

Reprisals must be proportionate.

§ 39. Reprisals, be they positive or negative, must be in proportion to the wrong done, and to the amount of compulsion necessary to get reparation. For instance, a State would not be justified in arresting, by way of reprisal, thousands of foreign subjects living on its territory because their home State had denied justice to one of its subjects living abroad. But it would be justified in ordering its own courts to deny justice to all subjects of that foreign State, or in ordering its fleet to seize several vessels sailing under the flag of that State, or in suspending a commercial treaty with it.

Embargo.

§ 40. A kind of reprisal, which is called *embargo*, must be specially mentioned. This term of Spanish origin means detention, but in International Law it has the technical meaning of detention of ships in port. Now, as by way of reprisal all acts, otherwise illegal, may be performed, there is no doubt that ships of the delinquent State may be prevented from leaving the ports of the injured State for the purpose of compelling the delinquent State to make reparation for the wrong done.[1]

But the important point is to distinguish *embargo* by way of reprisal from detention of ships for other reasons. According to a rule of International Law, believed to be obsolete until the World War,[2] conflicting States could, when war was breaking out or impending, lay an *embargo* on, and appropriate each other's merchantmen. Another kind of *embargo* is the so-called *arrêt de prince*[3]—that is, a detention of foreign ships to prevent the spread of news of political importance. And there is, thirdly, *embargo* arising out of the so-called *jus*

[1] Thus in 1840—see above, § 34—Great Britain laid an embargo on Sicilian ships.

[2] See, however, below, § 102*a*, where the attitude of belligerents at the outbreak of the World War is discussed.

[3] See Steck, *Versuch über Handels- und Schiffahrts-Verträge* (1782), p. 355; Caumont, *Dictionnaire universel de Droit maritime* (1867), pp. 247-265; Calvo, iii. § 1277; Pradier-Fodéré, v. p. 719; Holtzendorff, iv. pp. 98-104.

angariæ—that is, the right of a belligerent State to seize, and make use of, neutral property in case of necessity, under the obligation to compensate the neutral owner.[1]

These kinds of international *embargo* must not be confounded with the so-called *civil embargo* of English Municipal Law[2]—namely, an order of the sovereign to English ships not to leave English ports.

Reprisals to be preceded by Negotiations and to be stopped when Reparation is made.

§ 41. Like all other compulsive means of settling international differences, reprisals are admissible only after negotiations have been conducted in vain for the purpose of obtaining reparation from the delinquent State. In former times, when States used to authorise private individuals to perform special reprisals, treaties of commerce and peace frequently stipulated for a certain period of time, for instance three or four months, to elapse after an application for redress before the grant of letters of marque by the injured State.[3] Although with the disappearance of special reprisals this is now antiquated, a reasonable time for the performance of reparation must even nowadays be given. On the other hand, reprisals must at once cease when the delinquent State makes the necessary reparation. Individuals arrested must be set free, goods and ships seized must be handed back, occupied territory must be evacuated, suspended treaties must again be put into force, and the like.

It must be specially mentioned that in the case of recovery of contract debts claimed from the Government of one country by the Government of another country as being due to its nationals, reprisals by means of armed forces can, according to Article 1 of Convention II., only be resorted to in case the debtor State refuses arbitration.

[1] See below, §§ 364-365.
[2] See Phillimore, iii. § 26.
[3] See Phillimore, iii. § 14.

Reprisals during Peace in contradistinction to Reprisals during War.

§ 42. Reprisals in time of peace must not be confounded with reprisals between belligerents. Whereas the former are resorted to for the purpose of settling a conflict without going to war, the latter[1] are retaliations to force an enemy guilty of a certain act of illegitimate warfare to comply with the laws of war.

Value of Reprisals.

§ 43. The value of reprisals as a means of settling international differences is analogous to the value of retorsion. States have recourse to reprisals for such international delinquencies as they think not important enough for a declaration of war, but too important to be entirely overlooked. That reprisals are rather a rough means for the settlement of differences, and that the institution of reprisals can give, and has in the past given, occasion for abuse in case of a difference between a powerful and a weak State, cannot be denied. On the other hand, as there is no court and no central authority above the sovereign States which could compel a delinquent State to make reparation, the institution of reprisals can scarcely be abolished. The influence in the future of the means for settling disputes which have been evolved since 1899 remains to be seen. If all the States would adopt one or other of these methods in all cases of an alleged international delinquency which affected neither their national honour nor their vital interests and independence, and if the machinery set up by the Covenant of the League of Nations should be effective, acts of reprisal would almost disappear.

[1] See below, § 247.

IV

PACIFIC BLOCKADE

Hall, § 121—Lawrence, § 138—Westlake, ii. pp. 11-18, and *Papers*, pp. 572-589—Taylor, § 444—Moore, vii. § 1097—Bluntschli, §§ 506-507—Heffter, § 112—Bulmerincq in *Holtzendorff*, iv. pp. 116-127—Ullmann, § 162—Bonfils, Nos. 986-994—Despagnet, Nos. 496-498—Mérignhac, iii^a. pp. 60-64—Pradier-Fodéré, v. Nos. 2483-2489, vi. No. 2648—Rivier, ii. § 60—Nys, ii. pp. 590-593—Calvo, iii. §§ 1832-1859—Fiore, ii. No. 1231, and *Code*, Nos. 1409-1419—Martens, ii. 105—Holland, *Studies*, pp. 130-150—Deane, *The Law of Blockade* (1870), pp. 45-48—Fauchille, *Du Blocus maritime* (1882), pp. 37-67—Falcke, *Die Hauptperioden der sogenannten Friedensblockader* (1891), and in *Z. I.*, xix. (1909), pp. 63-175—Barès, *Le Blocus pacifique* (1898)—Ducrocq, *Représailles en Temps de Paix* (1901), pp. 59-174—Hogan, *Pacific Blockade* (1908)—Söderquist, *Le Blocus maritime* (1908)—Staudacher, *Die Friedensblockade* (1909)—Drossos, ΤΟ ΠΡΟΒΛΗΜΑ ΤΩΝ ΕΙΡΗΝΙΚΩΝ ΑΠΟΚΛΕΙΣΜΩΝ (The Problem of Pacific Blockades, 1912).

Development of Practice of Pacific Blockade.

§ 44. Before the nineteenth century blockade was only known as a measure between belligerents in time of war. It was not until the second quarter of the nineteenth century that a so-called pacific blockade—that is, a blockade during time of peace—was first resorted to as a compulsive means of settling an international difference. All cases of pacific blockade are cases either of intervention or of reprisals.[1] The first case, one of intervention, happened in 1827, when, during the Greek insurrection, Great Britain, France, and Russia intervened in the interest of the independence of Greece, and blockaded those parts of the Greek coast which were occupied by Turkish troops. Although this blockade led to the battle of Navarino, in which

[1] A blockade instituted by a State against portions of its own territory in revolt is not a blockade for the purpose of settling international differences. It has, therefore, in itself nothing to do with the Law of Nations, but is a matter of internal police. I cannot, therefore, agree with Holland, who, in his *Studies in International Law*, p. 138, treats it as a pacific blockade *sensu generali*. Of course, necessity of self-preservation only can justify a State that has blockaded one of its own ports in preventing the egress and ingress of *foreign* vessels. And the question might arise whether compensation ought not to be paid for losses sustained by foreign vessels so detained.

the Turkish fleet was destroyed, the Powers maintained, nevertheless, that they were not at war with Turkey. In 1831 France blockaded the Tagus as an act of reprisal for the purpose of exacting redress from Portugal for injuries sustained by French subjects. Great Britain and France, exercising intervention for the purpose of making Holland consent to the independence of revolting Belgium, blockaded the coast of Holland in 1833. In 1838 France blockaded the ports of Mexico as an act of reprisal, but Mexico replied with a declaration of war. Likewise as an act of reprisal, and in the same year, France blockaded the ports of Argentina; and in 1845, conjointly with Great Britain, France blockaded the ports of Argentina a second time. In 1850, in the course of her differences with Greece relative to Don Pacifico,[1] Great Britain blockaded the Greek ports, but against Greek vessels only. Another case of intervention was the pacific blockade instituted in 1860 by Sardinia, in aid of an insurrection against the then Sicilian ports of Messina and Gaeta, but the following year saw the conversion of the pacific blockade into a war blockade. In 1862 Great Britain, by way of reprisal for the plundering of a wrecked British merchantman, blockaded the Brazilian port of Rio de Janeiro. The blockade of the island of Formosa by France during her differences with China in 1884, and that of the port of Menam by France during her differences with Siam in 1893, are likewise cases of reprisals. On the other hand, cases of intervention are the blockade of the Greek coast in 1886 by Great Britain, Austria-Hungary, Germany, Italy, and Russia, for the purpose of preventing Greece from making war against Turkey; and further, the blockade of the island of Crete in 1897 by the united Powers. In 1902, Great Britain, Germany, and Italy blockaded, by way of reprisal, the coast of

[1] See above, § 35.

Venezuela,[1] and in April 1913, Great Britain, Austria-Hungary, Germany, France (with a mandate from Russia), and Italy blockaded Antivari (Montenegro).

In December 1916, during the World War, the Allied Powers blockaded the coasts of Greece, not then a belligerent, by way of reprisals for attacks by Greek forces on Allied troops in Athens. Foreign neutral ships in blockaded ports were allowed four days to depart.[2]

Admissibility of Pacific Blockade.

§ 45. No unanimity exists among international lawyers as to whether pacific blockades are admissible according to the principles of the Law of Nations. There is no doubt that the theory of the Law of Nations forbids the seizure and sequestration of vessels other than those of the blockaded State for attempting to break a pacific blockade. For even those writers who maintain the admissibility of pacific blockade assert this. What is controverted is whether according to International Law the coast of a State may be blockaded at all in time of peace. From the first recorded instance to the last, several writers[3] of authority have denied that it can. On the other hand, many writers say that it may, differing among themselves only as to whether vessels sailing under the flag of third States could be prevented from entering or leaving ports under pacific blockade. The Institute of International Law carefully studied the question in 1887, discussed it at its meeting in Heidelberg, and finally voted a declaration[4] in favour of the admissibility of pacific blockades. Thus the most influential body of theorists approved what had been established before by practice. There ought to be no doubt that the

[1] This blockade, although represented as a war blockade so that the ingress of foreign vessels might be prevented, was nevertheless essentially a pacific blockade. See Holland in the *Law Quarterly Review*, xix. (1903), p. 133; *Parl. Papers*, Venezuela, No. 1 (1903), Cd. 1399.

[2] See *The Times*, December 9, 1916, and *A.J.*, xii. (1918), p. 806.

[3] The leader of these writers is Hautefeuille, *Des Droits et des Devoirs des Nations neutres* (2nd ed. 1858), vol. ii. pp. 272-288.

[4] See *Annuaire*, ix. (1887), pp. 275-301.

numerous cases of pacific blockade which occurred during the nineteenth century and since have, through tacit consent of the members of the Family of Nations, established the admissibility of pacific blockades for the settlement of political as well as of legal international differences.

Pacific Blockade and Vessels of third States.

§ 46. It has already been stated that all writers agree that the blockading State has no right to seize and sequestrate such ships of third States as try to break a pacific blockade. Apart from this, no unanimity exists as to the position of ships of third States in a case of pacific blockade. Some German writers[1] maintain that they have to respect the blockade, and that the blockading State has a right to stop those which try to break it. The vast majority of writers, however, deny such a right. There is, in fact, no rule of International Law which could establish such a right, as pacific (in contradistinction to belligerent) blockade is a mere matter between the conflicting parties. The declaration of the Institute of International Law in favour of pacific blockade contains, therefore, the condition: 'Les navires de pavillon étranger peuvent entrer librement malgré le blocus.'

Practice has varied. Before 1850 ships of third States were expected to respect a pacific blockade, and such as tried to break it were seized, and restored at the termination of the blockade without compensation. During the blockade of Greece in 1850 and 1886, Greek ports were only closed for Greek ships, and others were allowed to pass through. And the same was the case during the blockade of Crete in 1897. On the other hand, when France instituted a blockade of Formosa in 1884 and tried to enforce it against ships of third States, Great Britain declared that a pacific blockade could not be so enforced; whereupon France had to drop her intended establishment of a pacific blockade,

[1] See Heffter, § 112; Perels, § 30.

and consider herself at war with China. And when in 1902 Great Britain, Germany, and Italy instituted a blockade against Venezuela, they declared it a war blockade [1] because they intended to enforce it against vessels of third States.

Pacific Blockade and Vessels of the Blockaded State.

§ 47. Theory and practice seem nowadays to agree that the ships of a State under pacific blockade which try to break the blockade may be seized and sequestrated. But they may not be condemned and confiscated, but must be restored at its termination. Thus, although the Powers which had instituted a blockade against Venezuela in 1902 declared it a war blockade, all Venezuelan public and private ships seized were restored after the blockade was raised.

Manner of Pacific Blockade.

§ 48. Pacific blockade is a measure of such enormous consequences that (quite apart from the obligations of members of the League of Nations under the Covenant) it can be justified only after the failure of negotiation to settle the questions in dispute. And further, as blockade, being a violation of the territorial supremacy of the blockaded State, is *prima facie* of a hostile character, it is necessary for such State as intends in time of peace to blockade another State to notify its intention to the latter, and to fix the day and hour for the establishment of the blockade. And, thirdly, although the Declaration of Paris of 1856 enacting that a blockade to be binding must be effective concerns blockades in time of war only, there can be no doubt that pacific blockades ought likewise to be effective. The declaration of the Institute of International Law in favour of pacific blockade contains, therefore, the condition : ' Le blocus pacifique doit être déclaré et notifié officiellement, et maintenu par une force suffisante.' [2]

[1] That this blockade was essentially a pacific blockade I have already stated above, § 44.

[2] The following is the full text of this declaration, referred to above, § 45 :—

L'établissement d'un blocus en dehors de l'état de guerre ne doit

Value of Pacific Blockade.

§ 49. As the establishment of a pacific blockade has in various instances not prevented the outbreak of hostilities, its value as a means of non-hostile settlement of international differences is doubted by many writers. But others agree, and I think they are right, that the institution is of great value, be it as an act of reprisal or of intervention. Every measure which is suitable and calculated to prevent the outbreak of war must be welcomed, and experience shows that pacific blockade is, although not universally successful, a measure of this kind. That it can give, and has in the past given, occasion for abuse in case of a difference between a strong and a weak Power is no argument against it, as the same is valid with regard to reprisals and intervention in general, and even to war. And although it is naturally a measure which will scarcely be made use of in case of a difference between two powerful naval States, it might nevertheless find application with success against a powerful naval State if exercised by the united navies of several Powers.

V

INTERVENTION

See the literature quoted above in vol. i. at the commencement of § 134.

Intervention in contradistinction to Participation in a Difference.

§ 50. Intervention as a means of settling international differences is only a special kind of intervention in general, which has already been discussed.[1] It consists in the dictatorial interference of a third State in a

être considéré comme permis par le droit des gens que sous les conditions suivantes :

'1. Les navires de pavillon étranger peuvent entrer librement malgré le blocus.

'2. Le blocus pacifique doit être déclaré et notifié officiellement, et maintenu par une force suffisante.

'3 Les navires de la puissance bloquée qui ne respectent pas un pareil blocus peuvent être séquestrés. Le blocus ayant cessé, ils doivent être restitués avec leurs cargaisons à leurs propriétaires, mais sans dédommagement à aucun titre.'

[1] See above, vol. i. §§ 134-138.

difference between two States, for the purpose of settling the difference in the way demanded by the intervening State. This dictatorial interference takes place for the purpose of exercising compulsion upon one or both of the parties in conflict, and must be distinguished from such an attitude of a State as makes it a party to the conflict. If two States are in conflict, and a third State joins one of them out of friendship or from any other motive, that third State does not exercise intervention as a means of settling international differences, but becomes a party to the conflict. If, for instance, an alliance exists between one of two States in conflict and a third, and if eventually, as war has broken out in consequence of the conflict, that third State comes to the help of its ally, no intervention in the technical sense of the term takes place. A State intervening in a dispute between two other States does not become a party to their dispute, but is the author of a new imbroglio, because it dictatorially requests those other States to settle their difference in a way to which both, or at any rate one of them, objects. An intervention, for instance, takes place when, although two States in conflict have made up their minds to fight it out in war, a third State dictatorially requests them to settle their dispute through arbitration.

Intervention in the form of dictatorial interference must, further, be distinguished from efforts of a State directed to induce the States in conflict to settle their difference amicably, such as proffering its good offices or mediation, or giving friendly advice. Some jurists [1] speak incorrectly of good offices and the like as 'amicable' in contradistinction to 'hostile' intervention.

Mode of Intervention.

§ 51. Intervention in a difference between two States takes the form of a communication to one or both of the conflicting States with a dictatorial request for the

[1] Thus, for instance, Rivier, ii. § 58. See also above, vol. i. § 134.

settlement of the conflict in a certain way; for instance by arbitration, or by the acceptance of certain terms. One State may intervene alone or several States may intervene collectively. If the parties comply with the request, the intervention is terminated. If, however, one or both parties fail to comply, the intervention will be abandoned, or action more stringent than a mere request, such as pacific blockade, military occupation, and the like, will be taken. Even war can be declared for the purpose of an intervention. Of special importance are the collective interventions exercised by several great Powers in the interest of the balance of power, and of humanity.[1]

Time of Intervention.

§ 52. An intervention in a difference between two States can take place at any time from the moment a conflict arises till the moment it is settled, and even immediately after the settlement. In many cases interventions have taken place before the outbreak of war between two States for the purpose of preventing war; in other cases third States have intervened during a war which had broken out in consequence of a conflict. Interventions have, further, taken place immediately after the peaceable settlement of a difference, or after the termination of war by a treaty of peace or by conquest, on the grounds that the conditions of the settlement, or the treaty of peace, were against the interests of the intervening State, or because the latter would not consent to the annexation of the conquered State by the victor.[2]

[1] See above, vol. i. §§ 136, 137.

[2] With regard to the question of the right of intervention, the admissibility of intervention in default of a right, and to all other details concerning intervention, the reader must be referred to vol. i. §§ 135-138.

VI

ECONOMIC BOYCOTT

The so-called Economic Boycott.

§ 52*a*. Such were the measures of compulsion available for the settlement of disputes before the World War. But the experiences of that struggle revealed the potentialities of a new form of pressure, the so-called economic boycott or blockade. To be cut off from the resources of neighbouring States and driven into isolation was found to be a terrible plight for a highly developed modern State; and this discovery gave prominence to the idea that by prohibiting all trade and financial relations and all personal association with the subjects of a recalcitrant State, other States would be able to compel compliance with their demands. It is too early as yet to estimate the value of the new method, which naturally has a place in the constitution of a League of Nations inspired by the lessons of the war, and is the first punishment to be imposed by Article 16 on a member which breaks its covenants. In each particular instance its effectiveness must depend, not only upon the number of States combining to use it, but also upon the extent to which the offending State normally relies upon those States, the strength of its own internal resources, and its power to retaliate upon those who seek to constrain it.

PART II

WAR

CHAPTER I

ON WAR IN GENERAL

I

CHARACTERISTICS OF WAR[1]

Grotius, i. c. 1, § 2—Vattel, iii. §§ 1-4, 69-72—Hall, §§ 15-18—Westlake, ii. pp. 1-5—Lawrence, § 135—Lorimer, ii. pp. 18-29—Manning, pp. 131-133—Phillimore, iii. § 49—Twiss, ii. §§ 22-29—Taylor, §§ 449-451—Hershey, Nos. 326-336—Wheaton, § 295—Bluntschli, §§ 510-514—Heffter, §§ 113-114—Lueder in *Holtzendorff*, iv. pp. 175-198—Heilborn in *Stier-Somlo*, i. pp. 22-25—Klüber, §§ 235-237—G. F. Martens, ii. § 263—Ullmann, § 165—Bonfils, Nos. 1000-1001—Despagnet, Nos. 499-505—Pradier-Fodéré, vi. Nos. 2650-2660—Mérignhac, iii[a]. pp. 9-19—Rivier, ii. § 61—Nys, iii. pp. 1-28—Calvo, iv. §§ 1860-1864—Fiore, iii. Nos. 1232-1268—Martens, ii. § 106—Westlake, *Chapters*, pp. 258-264—Heilborn, *System*, pp. 321-332—Rettich, *Zur Theorie und Geschichte des Rechts zum Kriege* (1888), pp. 3-141—Wiesse, *Le Droit international appliqué aux Guerres civiles* (1898)—Rougier, *Les Guerres civiles et le Droit des Gens* (1903)—Higgins, *War and the Private Citizen* (1912), pp. 3-70—Grosch, *Der Zwang im Völkerrecht* (1912), *passim*, especially p. 63—Lammasch, *Das Völkerrecht nach dem Kriege* (1917), pp. 174-187—Jerusalem, *Kriegsrecht und Kodification* (1918).

War no Illegality.

§ 53. As within the boundaries of the modern State an armed contention between two or more citizens is illegal, public opinion has become convinced that armed contests between citizens are inconsistent with Municipal Law. Influenced by this fact, impatient pacifists, as well as those innumerable individuals who cannot grasp the idea of a law between sovereign States, frequently consider war and law inconsistent.

[1] Many statements in §§ 53-66 of this chapter have been the object of such violent criticism and attack that I consider it advisable to point out that my assertions concerning the characteristics of war, as well as the causes, kinds, and ends of war, are intended to give a realistic analysis of the facts of life. I do not teach what war ought to be, but what it actually is according to the practice of the States.

They quote the fact that wars are frequently waged by States as a proof against the very existence of an International Law. It is not difficult to show the absurdity of this opinion. As States are sovereign, and as consequently no central authority exists above them, able to enforce compliance with its demands, war cannot, under the existing conditions and circumstances of the Family of Nations, always be avoided. International Law recognises this fact, but at the same time provides regulations with which belligerents have customarily, or by special conventions, agreed to comply. Although with the outbreak of war peaceable relations between the belligerents cease, there remain certain mutual legal obligations and duties. Thus war is not inconsistent with, but a condition regulated by, International Law. It does not object to States which are in conflict waging war upon each other, provided they have—in compliance with the Covenant of the League of Nations—previously submitted the dispute to an inquiry by the Council of the League. Whenever they choose to go to war, they have agreed to comply with the rules laid down by International Law regarding the conduct of war, and the relations between belligerent and neutral States.

It is maintained[1] that this conception of war as lacking illegality includes an absolute right of every State to make war, whenever, and for whatever reason, it chooses; but this view is based on a misunderstanding. The assertion that war is no illegality is only directed against those who maintain that war and law are inconsistent, an opinion which overlooks the facts mentioned above. That International Law, if it could forbid war altogether, or permit it only under certain circumstances, would be a more perfect law than it is at present, there is no doubt. Yet eternal peace is an

[1] See Hill, *World Organisation* (1911), pp. 178-186.

impossibility in the conditions and circumstances under which mankind at present lives, although it is certainly an ideal of civilisation which will slowly and gradually be realised. The same factors make it at present impossible[1] to prevent the outbreak of war for any other purpose than 'the recognition of a right denied, or to redress a wrong inflicted.'

§ 54. War is the contention between two or more States through their armed forces, for the purpose of overpowering each other, and imposing such conditions of peace as the victor pleases. War is a fact recognised, and with regard to many points regulated, but not established, by International Law. Those writers[2] who define war as the legal remedy of self-help to obtain satisfaction for a wrong sustained from another State, forget that wars have often been waged by both parties for political reasons only; they confound a possible, but not at all necessary, cause of war with the conception of war. A State may be driven into war because it cannot otherwise get reparation for an international delinquency, and may then maintain that it exercises by war nothing else than legally recognised self-help. But when States are driven into, or deliberately wage, war for political reasons, no legally recognised act of self-help is performed by the war; and the same laws of war are valid, whether wars are waged on account of legal differences or political differences. Conception of War.

§ 55. In any case, it is universally recognised that war is a *contention*, i.e. *a violent struggle through the application of armed force.* For a war to be in existence, two or more States must actually have their armed forces fighting against each other, although its commencement may date back to a declaration of war, War a Contention.

[1] As will be shown below, §§ 62, 63.

[2] See, for instance, Vattel, iii. § 1; Phillimore, iii. § 49; Twiss, ii. § 26; Bluntschli, § 510; Bulmerincq, § 92.

or some other unilateral initiative act. Unilateral acts of force performed by one State against another without a previous declaration of war may be a cause of the outbreak of war, but are not war in themselves, as long as they are not answered by similar hostile acts by the other side, or at least by a declaration of the other side that it considers them to be acts of war. Thus it comes about that acts of force performed by one State against another by way of reprisal, or during a pacific blockade in the case of an intervention, are not necessarily acts initiating war. And even acts of force illegally performed by one State against another—for instance, occupation of a part of its territory—are not acts of war so long as they are not met with acts of force from the other side, or at least with a declaration that it considers them to be acts of war. Thus, when Louis XIV. of France, after the Peace of Nymeguen, instituted the so-called Chambers of Reunion, and in 1680 and 1681 seized the territory of the then Free Town of Strasburg, and other parts of the German Empire, without meeting with armed resistance, these acts of force, although doubtless illegal, were not acts of war.

Though war is a contention, a violent struggle through the application of armed force, other measures may be incidentally applied in connection therewith. This appears from the institution of blockade, the prohibition of the carriage of contraband, or trading with the enemy, or from the capture of sea-borne enemy property. The object of all these measures is the weakening, or destruction, of the economic power of resistance of the enemy; but it could not be achieved without application of armed force.

War a Contention between States.

§ 56. To be war, the contention must be *between States*. In the Middle Ages wars between private individuals, so-called private wars, were known, and wars between corporations, as the Hansa for instance, and States. But such wars have totally disappeared in modern times. A contention may, of course, arise between the armed forces of a State and a body of armed individuals, but this[1] is not war. Thus the contention between the raiders under Dr. Jameson and the former South African Republic in January 1896 was not war. Nor is a contention with insurgents or with pirates a war. And a so-called civil war[2] need not be war from the beginning, and may not become war at all, in the technical sense of the term in International Law. On the other hand, to an armed contention between a suzerain and its vassal[3] State the character of war ought not to be denied, for both parties are States, although the action of the vassal may, from the standpoint of Constitutional Law, be rebellion. And likewise an armed contention between a full sovereign State and a State under the suzerainty of another State, as, for instance, that between Serbia and Bulgaria[4] in 1885, is war. Again, an armed contention between one or more member-States of a Federal State and the Federal State itself ought to be considered as war in International Law, although, according to the constitution of Federal States, war between the member-States, as well as between any member-State and the Federal State itself, is illegal, and recourse to arms by a member-State may therefore, from the standpoint of the constitution, correctly be called rebellion. Thus the War of Secession within the United States between the Northern and the Southern member-States in 1861-1865 was real war.

§ 57. War nowadays is a contention of States *through their armed forces*.[5] Those private subjects of the belli-

[1] Some publicists maintain, however, that a contention between a State and the armed forces of a party fighting for public rights must be considered as war. See, for instance, Bluntschli, §512, and Fiore, iii. §1265.

[2] See below, § 59.

[3] See below, § 75.

[4] Bulgaria was at that time still a vassal State under Turkish suzerainty.

[5] See, however, below, § 57*a*.

War a Contention between States through Armed Forces.

gerents who do not directly or indirectly belong to the armed forces do not take part in it: they do not attack and defend; and no attack ought therefore to be made upon them. This is the result of an evolution of practices totally different from those in vogue in former times. During antiquity, and the greater part of the Middle Ages, war was a contention between the whole populations of the belligerent States. In time of war every subject of one belligerent, whether an armed and fighting individual or not, whether man or woman, adult or infant, could be killed or enslaved by the other belligerent at will. But gradually a milder and more discriminating practice grew up, and nowadays the life and liberty of such private subjects of belligerents as do not directly or indirectly belong to their armed forces, and, with certain exceptions, their private property, ought to be safe.

This is generally admitted. But opinions disagree as to the general position of such private subjects in time of war. The majority of the European Continental writers for three generations before the World War propagated the doctrine that no relation of enmity existed between belligerents and such private subjects, or between the private subjects of the respective belligerents. This doctrine went back to Rousseau.[1] In 1801, at the opening of the French Prize Court, the famous lawyer and statesman Portalis adopted Rousseau's [2] doctrine by declaring that war is a relation between States, and not between individuals, and that consequently the subjects of the belligerents are only enemies as soldiers, not as citizens. Although this new doctrine did not [3] spread at once, from the second half of the nineteenth century it was proclaimed on

[1] *Contrat Social*, i. c. 4.

[2] See Lassudrie-Duchêne, *Jean Jacques Rousseau et le Droit des Gens* (1906).

[3] As Hall (§ 18) shows.

the European Continent by the majority of writers. British and American-English writers, however, never adopted it, but always maintained that the relation of enmity between the belligerents extends also to their private citizens.

I think, if the facts of war are taken into consideration without prejudice, there ought to be no doubt that the British and American view is correct.[1] It is impossible to sever the citizens from their State, and the outbreak of war between two States cannot but make their citizens enemies. But the point is unworthy of dispute, because it is only one of terms without any material consequences.[2] For, apart from terminology, the parties agree in substance upon the rules of the Law of Nations regarding such private subjects as do not directly or indirectly belong to the armed forces.[3] Nobody doubts that they ought to be safe as regards their life and liberty, provided they behave peacefully and loyally; and that, with certain exceptions, their private property should not be touched. On the other hand, nobody doubts that, according to a generally recognised custom of modern warfare, the belligerent who has occupied a part or the whole of his opponent's territory, and treats such private individuals leniently according to the rules of International Law, may punish them for any hostile act, since they do not enjoy the privileges of members of armed forces. Although International Law by no means forbids, and, as a law between States, is not competent to forbid, private individuals from taking up arms against an enemy, it does give a right to the enemy to treat hostilities committed by them[4] as acts of illegitimate warfare. A

[1] See Boidin, pp. 32-44.

[2] But many Continental writers constantly make use of Rousseau's *dictum* in order to defend untenable positions. See Oppenheim, *Die Zukunft des Völkerrechts* (1911), pp. 59-61.

[3] See Breton, *Les Non-belligérants: leurs Devoirs, leurs Droits, et la Question des Otages* (1904).

[4] See below, § 254.

belligerent is under a duty to respect the life and liberty of private enemy individuals, which he can carry out only on condition that they abstain from hostilities against him. Through military occupation in war they fall under the military authority [1] of the occupant, and he may therefore demand that they comply with his orders regarding the safety of his forces. The position of private enemy individuals is made known to them through the proclamations which the commander-in-chief of an army occupying the territory usually publishes.

Owing to their position it is inevitable that he should consider and mark as criminals such of them as commit hostile acts, although they may act from patriotic motives, and may be highly praised for their acts by their compatriots. The high-sounding and well-meant words of Baron Lambermont, one of the Belgian delegates at the Conference of Brussels of 1874—'Il y a des choses qui se font à la guerre, qui se feront toujours, et que l'on doit bien accepter. Mais il s'agit ici de les convertir en lois, en prescriptions positives et internationales. Si les citoyens doivent être conduits au supplice pour avoir tenté de défendre leur pays au péril de leur vie, il ne faut pas qu'ils trouvent inscrits sur le poteau au pied duquel ils seront fusillés l'article d'un traité signé par leur propre gouvernement qui d'avance les condamnait à mort'—have no *raison d'être* in face of the fact that, according to a generally recognised customary rule of International Law, hostile acts on the part of private individuals are not acts of legitimate warfare, and the offenders may be treated and punished as war criminals. Even those writers [2] who object to

[1] The first edition of this work was wrong in stating that through military occupation private enemy individuals fall under the *territorial supremacy* of the occupant. Since military occupation by no means vests sovereignty in the occupant, but only actual authority, this authority may not be called *territorial supremacy*.

[2] See, for instance, Hall, § 18, p. 71, and Westlake, *Papers*, p. 268.

the term 'criminals' do not deny that such hostile acts by private individuals, in contradistinction to hostile acts by members of the armed forces, may be severely punished. The controversy whether or not such acts may be styled 'crimes' is again only one of terminology; materially the rule is not at all controverted.[1]

Recent Developments affecting the Distinction between Armed Forces and Civilians.

§ 57*a*. The time-honoured distinction between members of the armed forces and civilians is threatened by four developments which appeared during the World War.

(1) Wars are nowadays fought by whole nations in arms. Not only has conscription carried the day, the whole male population of military age being enrolled in the fighting forces; all other men and all fit women are asked, or even compelled, to assist the fighting forces as workers in munition factories, and to undertake all kinds of other work, so as to release fit men of military age for the armies. During the World War, thousands of women were enrolled and sent to the front as cooks, drivers, store-keepers, etc., for the army, to take the place of soldiers previously so employed. Russia even admitted women into the ranks as soldiers.

(2) The development of aerial warfare. The fact that it has been considered legitimate for air vessels to bombard, outside the theatre of war, munition factories, bridges, railway stations, and other objects of value for military communication and preparation, must necessarily blur, or even efface, the distinction between members of the armed forces and civilians. Air vessels cannot aim with any precision at their direct objects; and, if they undertake bombardment by night, such aim would seem to be entirely impossible.

(3) Democracy has for the most part conquered the world, so that wars are no longer dynastic but national.

[1] See below, § 251, and Articles 20-26 of the *Instructions for the Government of Armies of the United States in the Field*, published in 1863 during the War of Secession.

Governments are supposed to be representative, nations are supposed to be responsible for their Governments, and wars have therefore become wars between all the individuals of the warring nations.

(4) The enormous development of international means of communication for commerce and industry. To put economic pressure upon the enemy has always been legitimate; but, whereas in previous wars it only played a secondary part, during the World War it became of primary importance. The consequence is that, although war still is in the main a contention between States by their armed forces, the civilian population nowadays is exposed to extreme suffering in health and property.

War a Contention between States for the purpose of overpowering each other.

§ 58. The last, and not the least important, characteristic of war is its purpose. It is a contention between States for the purpose of overpowering each other. This purpose of war is not to be confounded with the ends[1] of war, for, whatever the ends of war may be, they can only be realised by one belligerent overpowering the other. Such a defeat as compels the vanquished to comply with any demand the victor may choose to make is the purpose of war. Therefore war calls into existence the display of the greatest possible power and force on the part of the belligerents, rouses the passion of the nations in conflict to the highest possible degree, and endangers the welfare, the honour, and eventually the very existence of both belligerents. Nobody can predict with certainty the result of a war, however insignificant one side may seem to be. Every war is a risk and a venture. Every State which goes to war knows beforehand what is at stake; and it would never go to war were it not for its firm, though very often illusory, conviction of its superiority in strength over its opponent. Victory is

[1] See below, § 66.

necessary in order to overpower the enemy; and it is this necessity which justifies all the indescribable horrors of war, the enormous sacrifice of human life and health, and the unavoidable destruction of property and devastation of territory. Apart from restrictions imposed by the Law of Nations upon belligerents, all kinds and all degrees of force may be, and eventually must be, used in war, in order that its purpose may be achieved, in spite of their cruelty [1] and the utter misery they entail. As war is a struggle for existence between States, no amount of individual suffering and misery can be regarded; the national existence and independence of the struggling State is a higher consideration than any individual well-being.

§ 59. These characteristics of war must help to decide whether so-called civil wars are war in the technical meaning of the term. It has already been stated [2] that an armed contention between a Federal State and its member-States, or between a suzerain and its vassal, ought to be considered as war because both parties are real States, although the Federal State and the suzerain may correctly designate it as rebellion. Such armed contentions may be called civil wars in a wider sense of the term. In the proper sense of the term a civil war exists when two opposing parties within a State have recourse to arms for the purpose of obtaining power in the State, or when a large portion of the population of a State rises in arms against the legitimate Government. As war is an armed contention between *States*, such a civil war need not be war from the beginning, nor become war at all, in the technical sense of the term. But it may become war through the recognition of each of the contending parties, or of the insurgents,

Civil War.

[1] To avoid misunderstanding, attention should be drawn to the preamble of Hague Convention (IV.) concerning the Laws and Customs of War on Land.

[2] See above, § 56.

as a belligerent Power.[1] Through this recognition a body of individuals receives an international position, in so far as it is for some parts, and in some points, treated as though it were a subject[2] of International Law. Such recognition may be granted by the State within the boundaries of which the civil war broke out, and then other States will in most cases, although they need not, likewise recognise a state of war as existing and bear the duties of neutrality. But it may happen that other States recognise insurgents as a belligerent Power before the State on whose territory the insurrection broke out so recognises them. In such a case the insurrection is war in the eyes of these other States, but not in the eyes of the legitimate Government.[3] Be that as it may, although a civil war becomes war in the technical sense of the term by recognition, this recognition has a lasting effect only when the insurgents succeed in getting their independence established through the defeat of the legitimate Government and a consequent treaty of peace which recognises their independence. Moreover, nothing prevents the State concerned, after the defeat of the insurgents and reconquest of the territory which they had occupied, from treating them as rebels according to the Criminal Law of the land, for the character of a belligerent Power received through recognition is lost *ipso facto* by their defeat and the reoccupation of the territory by the legitimate Government.

Guerilla War.

§ 60. The characteristics of war also determine whether so-called guerilla war is real war in the technical sense of the term.

Guerilla war must not be confounded with guerilla tactics during a war. During war commanders send small bodies of soldiers wearing uniform to the rear of the enemy for the purpose of destroying bridges

[1] See below, §§ 76, 298.
[2] See above, vol. i. § 63.
[3] See below, § 298.

and railways, cutting off communications and supplies, attacking convoys, intercepting despatches, and the like. This is in every way legal, and these parties, when captured, enjoy the treatment due to enemy soldiers. Or again, private individuals take up arms, and devote themselves mainly to similar tactics. According to the former rules of International Law such individuals, when captured, under no condition enjoyed the treatment due to enemy soldiers, but could be treated as criminals and punished with death. However, according to Article 1 of the Regulations concerning War on Land adopted by the Hague Conferences of 1899 and 1907, such guerilla fighters enjoy the treatment of soldiers provided that they (1) do not act individually, but form a body commanded by a person responsible for his subordinates, (2) have a fixed distinctive emblem recognisable at a distance, (3) carry arms openly, and (4) conduct their operations in accordance with the laws of war.[1]

On the other hand, one speaks of guerilla war or petty war when, after the defeat and the capture of the main part of the enemy forces, the occupation of the enemy territory, and the downfall of the enemy Government, the routed remnants of the defeated army carry on the contention by mere guerilla tactics. Although hopeless of success in the end, such petty war can go on for a long time, thus preventing the establishment of a state of peace, in spite of the fact that regular war is over and the task of the army of occupation is no longer regular warfare. Now the question whether such guerilla war is real war in the strict sense of the term in International Law must, I think, be answered in the negative, for two reasons. First, there are no longer the forces of two States in the field, because the defeated belligerent State has ceased to exist through the military occupation of its territory, the downfall of its estab-

[1] See also Article 2 of the Hague Regulations.

lished Government, the capture of the main part and the routing of the remnant of its forces. And, secondly, there is no longer in progress a contention between armed forces. For although the guerilla bands are still fighting when attacked, or when attacking small bodies of enemy soldiers, they try to avoid a pitched battle, and content themselves with constantly harassing the victorious army, destroying bridges and railways, cutting off communications and supplies, attacking convoys, and the like, always in the hope that some event may occur which will induce the victorious army to withdraw. If, then, guerilla war is not real war, it is obvious that in strict law the victor need no longer treat the guerilla bands as a belligerent Power, and their captured members as soldiers. It is, however, advisable that he should do so, as long as they are under responsible commanders and observe the laws and usages of war. For I can see no advantage or reason why, although in strict law it could be done, those bands should be treated as criminals. Such treatment would only call for acts of revenge on their part, without in the least accelerating the pacification of the country. And it is, after all, to be taken into consideration that those bands act, not out of criminal, but patriotic motives. With patience and firmness, the victor will succeed in pacifying them without recourse to methods of harshness.

II

CAUSES, KINDS, AND ENDS OF WAR

Grotius, i. c. 3; ii. c. 1, c. 22 and c. 23; iii. c. 3—Pufendorf, viii. c. 6, § 9—Vattel, iii. §§ 2, 5, 24-50, 183-187—Lorimer, ii. pp. 29-49—Phillimore, iii. §§ 33-48—Twiss, ii. §§ 26-30—Halleck, i. pp. 488-520—Taylor, §§ 452-454—Wheaton, §§ 295-296—Hershey, Nos. 329-336—Bluntschli, §§ 515-520—Heffter, § 113—Lueder in *Holtzendorff*, iv. pp. 221-236—Klüber, §§ 41, 235, 237—G. F. Martens, §§ 265-266—Ullmann, § 166—Bonfils,

Nos. 1002-1005—Despagnet, No. 506—Pradier-Fodéré, vi. Nos. 2661-2670—Rivier, ii. p. 219—Nys, iii. pp. 13-23—Calvo, iv. §§ 1866-1896—Fichte, *Ueber den Begriff des wahrhaften Krieges* (1815)—Rettich, *Zur Theorie und Geschichte des Rechts zum Kriege* (1888), pp. 141-291—Peyronnard, *Des Causes de la Guerre* (1901).

Rules of Warfare independent of Causes of War.

§ 61. Whatever may be the cause of a war that has broken out, and whether or no the cause be a so-called just cause, the same rules of International Law are valid as to what must not be done, may be done, and must be done by the belligerents themselves in making war against each other, and as between the belligerents and neutral States. This is so, even if the declaration of war is *ipso facto* a violation of International Law, as when a belligerent declares war upon a neutral State for refusing passage to its troops. To say [1] that, because such a declaration of war is *ipso facto* a violation of neutrality and International Law, it is 'inoperative in law and without any juridical significance' is erroneous. The rules of International Law apply to war *from whatever cause it originates.* This being the case, the question as to the causes of war is of minor importance for the Law of Nations, although not for international ethics. The matter need not be discussed at all in a treatise on International Law, were it not that many writers maintain that there are rules of International Law which determine and define just causes of war. It must be emphasised that this is by no means the case. All such rules laid down by writers on International Law as recognise certain causes as just and others as unjust are rules of writers, but not rules of International Law based on international custom or international treaties.

Causes of War.

§ 62. The causes of war are innumerable. They are involved in the fact that the development of mankind is indissolubly connected with the national develop-

[1] See Visscher in the *Grotius Society*, ii. p. 101, and in *Belgium's Case* (1916), p. 148.

ment of States. The millions of individuals who as a body are called mankind do not face one another individually and severally, but in groups as races, nations, and States. With the welfare of the races, nations, and States to which they belong the welfare of individuals is more or less identified; and it is the development of races, nations, and States that carries with it the causes of war. A constant increase of population must in the end force upon a State the necessity of acquiring more territory, and if it cannot be acquired by peaceable means, acquisition by conquest alone remains. At certain periods of history, the principle of nationality, and the desire for national unity, gain such a power over the hearts and minds of the individuals belonging to the same race or nation, but living within the boundaries of several different States, that wars break out for the cause of national unity and independence. And jealous rivalry between two or more States, the awakening of national ambition, the craving for rich colonies, the desire of a land-locked State for a sea-coast, the endeavour of a hitherto minor State to become a world-Power, the ambition of dynasties or of great politicians to extend and enlarge their influence beyond the boundaries of their own States, and innumerable other factors, have been at work, ever since history was first recorded, in creating causes of war, and likewise play their part in our own times. Although one must hope that the time will come when war will entirely disappear, there is no possibility of seeing this hope realised in the near future. The first necessities for the disappearance of war are that the surface of the earth should be shared between States of the same standard of civilisation, and that the moral ideas of the governing classes in all the States of the world should undergo such alteration and progressive development as would create the conviction that decisions of International Courts of Justice, and awards of arbitrators, are alone adequate means for the settlement of international disputes and international political aims. So long as these first necessities are not realised, war will, as heretofore, remain the *ultima ratio* of international politics, although the causes of war can be diminished by effective machinery for settling international differences without recourse to hostilities.[1]

Just Causes of War.

§ 63. However this may be, it often depends largely upon the standpoint from which they are viewed whether or no causes of war are to be called just causes. A war may be just or unjust from the standpoint of both belligerents, or just from the standpoint of one, and utterly unjust from the standpoint of the other. The assertion that whereas all wars waged for political causes are unjust, all wars waged for international delinquencies are just, if there be no other way of getting reparation and satisfaction, is certainly incorrect, because too sweeping. The evils of war are so great that, even when caused by an international delinquency,[2] it cannot be justified if the delinquency be comparatively unimportant and trifling. On the other hand, under certain circumstances and conditions, many political causes of war may correctly be called just causes. Only such individuals as lack insight into history and human nature can, for instance, defend the opinion that a war is unjust which has been caused by the desire for national unity, or by the desire to maintain the balance of power, which under the present conditions and circumstances is the basis of all International Law. Necessity for a war implies its justification, whatever may be the cause. In the past many wars have undoubtedly been waged which were unjust,

[1] Such as the Covenant of the League of Nations has endeavoured to set up. See above, §§ 25*b*-25*g*. The author had intended to reconsider this, and the following, section, in view of the establishment of the League.

[2] See above, vol. i. §§ 151-156.

from whatever standpoint they may be viewed. Yet the number of wars diminishes gradually every year, and the majority of the European wars since the downfall of Napoleon I. were wars that were, from the standpoint of, at any rate, one of the belligerents, necessary, and therefore just wars.

Causes in contradistinction to Pretexts for War.

§ 64. Causes of war must not be confounded with pretexts for war. A State which makes war against another will never confess that there is no just cause for war, and it will therefore, when it has made up its mind to make war for political reasons, always look out for a so-called just cause. Thus frequently the apparent reason of a war is only a pretext, behind which the real cause is concealed. If two States are convinced that war between them is inevitable, and if, consequently, they face each other armed to the teeth, they will find at the suitable time many a so-called just cause plausible and calculated to serve as a pretext for the outbreak of a war which was planned and resolved upon long ago. History teaches that the skill of politics and diplomacy have nowhere been more needed than when a State was convinced that it must go to war for one reason or another. Public opinion at home and abroad was often not ripe to appreciate the reason and not prepared for the scheme of the leading politicians, whose task it was to realise their plans with the aid of pretexts which appeared as the cause of war, whereas the real cause did not become apparent for some time.[1]

Different Kinds of War.

§ 65. Writers on International Law who lay great stress upon the causes of war in general, and upon the distinction between just causes and others, also lay great stress upon the distinction between different kinds of war. But as the rules of the Law of Nations

[1] The author hoped that the progress of democracy and constitutional government, and the establishment of the League of Nations, would prevent wars being embarked upon under pretexts.

are the same[1] for the different kinds of war that may be distinguished, this distinction is in most cases of no importance. Apart from that, there is no unanimity respecting the kinds of war, and it is apparent that, just as the causes of war are innumerable, so innumerable kinds of war can be distinguished. Thus one speaks of offensive and defensive, or religious, political, dynastic, national, civil wars; of wars of unity, independence, conquest, intervention, revenge, and of many other kinds. As the very name which each different kind of war bears always explains its character, no further details are necessary respecting kinds of war.

§ 66. The cause, or causes, of a war determine at its inception the ends of that war. The ends of war must not be confounded with the purpose of war.[2] Whereas the purpose is always the same—namely, the overpowering and utter defeat of the opponent—the ends may be different in each case. Ends of war are those objects for the realisation of which a war is made.[3] In the beginning of the war its ends are determined by its cause or causes, as already said. But they may undergo alteration, or at least modification, with its progress and development. No moral or legal duty exists for a belligerent to stop the war when his opponent is ready to concede the object for which war was made. If war has once broken out, the very national existence of the belligerents is more or less at stake. The risk the belligerents run, the exertion they make, the blood and wealth they sacrifice, the reputation they gain or lose through the changing fortune and chances of war—all these and many other factors work, or may work, together to influence the ends of a war, so that eventually there is scarcely any longer a relation between

Ends of War.

[1] See above, § 61.

[2] Ends of war must likewise not be confounded with aims of land and sea warfare; see below, §§ 103, 137.

[3] See Bluntschli, § 536; Lueder in *Holtzendorff*, iv. p. 364; Rivier, ii. p. 219.

them and the causes of the war. If war really were, as some writers maintain,[1] the legal remedy of self-help to obtain satisfaction for a wrong sustained from another State, no such alteration of the ends of war could take place without at once setting in the wrong a belligerent which changed the ends for which the war was initiated. But history shows that nothing of the kind is really the case; and the existing rules of International Law by no means forbid such alteration or modification of the ends of a war, which is the result of an alteration or modification of circumstances created during the progress of war, through the factors previously mentioned. It could not be otherwise, and there is no moral, legal, or political reason why it should be. And the natural jealousy between the members of the Family of Nations, their conflicting interests in many points, and the necessity of a balance of power, are factors of sufficient strength to check the political dangers which such alteration of the ends of a war may eventually involve.

III

THE LAWS OF WAR

Hall, § 17—Westlake, ii. pp. 56-63, and *Papers*, pp. 237-241—Maine, pp. 123-159—Phillimore, iii. § 50—Taylor, § 470—Hershey, No. 336—Walker, *History*, i. §§ 106-108—Heffter, § 119—Lueder in *Holtzendorff*, iv. pp. 253-332—Ullmann, §§ 167, 170—Bonfils, Nos. 1006-1013—Despagnet, Nos. 508-510—Pradier-Fodéré, viii. Nos. 3212-3213—Mérignhac, iii^a. pp. 19-44—Rivier, ii. pp. 238-242—Nys, iii. pp. 91-96—Calvo, iv. §§ 1897-1898—Fiore, iii. Nos. 1244-1260—Martens, ii. § 107—Longuet, p. 12—Bordwell, pp. 100-193—Spaight, pp. 1-19—Garner, i. §§ 1-24—*Kriegsbrauch*, p. 2—*Land Warfare*, §§ 1-7—Holland, *Studies*, pp. 40-96—Lammasch, *Das Volkerrecht nach dem Kriege* (1917), pp. 3-25—Jerusalem, *Kriegsrecht und Kodification* (1918).

§ 67. Laws of war are the rules of the Law of Nations respecting warfare. The roots of the present laws of

[1] See above, § 54.

war are to be traced back to practices of belligerents which arose, and grew gradually, during the latter part of the Middle Ages. The unsparing cruelty of the war practices during the greater part of the Middle Ages began gradually to be modified through the influence of Christianity and chivalry; and although these practices were cruel enough during the fifteenth, sixteenth, and seventeenth centuries, they were mild compared with those of still earlier times. Decided progress was made during the eighteenth century, and again after the close of the Napoleonic wars, especially in the years from 1850 to the outbreak of the World War. The laws of war evolved in this way: isolated milder practices by and by became usages, so-called *usus in bello*, manner of warfare, *Kriegs-Manier*, and these usages through custom and treaties turned into legal rules. And this evolution is constantly going on, for, besides the recognised laws of war, there are usages in existence, which have a tendency to become gradually legal rules of warfare. The whole growth of the laws and usages of war is determined by three principles. There is, first, the principle that a belligerent should be justified in applying any amount and any kind of force which is necessary for the realisation of the purpose of war—namely, the overpowering of the opponent. There is, secondly, the principle of humanity at work, which says that all such kinds and degrees of violence as are not necessary for the overpowering of the opponent should not be permitted to a belligerent. And, thirdly and lastly, there is at work the principle of chivalry, which arose in the Middle Ages, and introduced a certain amount of fairness in offence and defence, and a certain mutual respect. And, in contradistinction to the savage cruelty of former times, belligerents in the era preceding the World War reached the conviction that the realisation of the purpose of war was in no way

Origin of the Laws of War.

hampered by indulgence shown to the wounded, to prisoners, and to private individuals who do not take part in the fighting. Thus the influence of the principle of humanity has been enormous upon the practice of warfare, and its methods, although by the nature of war to a certain degree cruel and unsparing, became less cruel and more humane. But the evolution of the laws and usages of war could not have taken place at all, but for the institution of standing armies, which dates from the fifteenth century. The humanising of the practices of war would have been impossible without the discipline of standing armies; and without them the important distinction between members of armed forces[1] and private individuals could not have arisen.

But there is no doubt—the World War has made it obvious—that this distinction, and also the moderating influences of chivalry and humanity, again threaten to disappear. Conscription, with its consequences that wars are fought by whole nations in arms, and war passions infect all belligerent subjects, threatens to overthrow the barriers against excesses which the professional soldiery of the eighteenth and nineteenth centuries, and the Hague Peace Conferences of 1899 and 1907, attempted to erect.

The most important Developments of the Laws of War.

§ 68. The most important developments of the laws of war took place through the following general treaties concluded between the majority of States after 1850:—

(1) The Declaration of Paris of April 16, 1856, respecting warfare on sea. It abolished privateering, recognised the principles that the neutral flag covers enemy goods, and that neutral goods under an enemy flag cannot be seized, and enacted the rule that a blockade in order to be binding, must be effective. The declara-

[1] See above, § 57.

tion was signed by seven States, but almost all other maritime Powers acceded in course of time.[1]

(2) The Geneva Convention of August 22, 1864, for the amelioration of the condition of wounded soldiers in armies in the field, which was originally signed by only nine States, but to which in course of time almost all the civilised States acceded. A treaty containing a number of additional articles to the convention was signed at Geneva on October 20, 1868, but was never ratified. A new Geneva Convention was signed on July 6, 1906, by thirty-five States, and several others acceded. Its principles were adapted to maritime warfare by conventions [2] of the First and Second Hague Peace Conferences.

(3) The Declaration of St. Petersburg of December 11, 1868, respecting the prohibition of the use in war of projectiles under 400 grammes (14 ounces) which are either explosive, or charged with inflammable substances. It was signed by seventeen States.

(4) The convention enacting regulations respecting the Laws of War on Land agreed upon at the First Peace Conference of 1899.

The history of this convention may be traced back to the *Instructions for the Government of Armies of the United States in the Field* which the United States published on April 24, 1863, during the War of Secession. These instructions, which were drafted by Professor Francis Lieber,[3] of the Columbia College of New York, represented the first endeavour to codify the laws of war, and they are even nowadays of great value and importance. In 1874 an international conference, invited by the Emperor Alexander II. of Russia, met at Brussels to discuss a draft code of the Laws of War

[1] See above, vol. i. § 47, and Garner, i. § 11.

[2] See below, § 204.

[3] See Root in *A.J.*, vii. (1913), pp. 453-469.

on Land prepared by Russia. The body of the articles agreed upon at this conference, and known as the 'Brussels Declarations,' have, however, never become law, as ratification was never given by the Powers. But they were made the basis of deliberations on the part of the Institute of International Law, which at its meeting at Oxford in 1880 adopted a Manual[1] of the Laws of War consisting of a body of eighty-six rules under the title, *Les Lois de la Guerre sur Terre*, and a copy of this draft code was sent to all the Governments of Europe and America. It was, however, not until the Hague Peace Conference of 1899 that the Powers re-assembled to discuss again the codification of the laws of war. At this conference the Brussels Declarations were taken as the basis of the deliberations; but although the bulk of its articles were taken over, several important modifications were introduced in the convention, which was finally agreed upon and ratified, only a few Powers abstaining from ratification.

The Second Peace Conference of 1907 revised this convention, and its place is now taken by Convention IV. of the Second Peace Conference. Convention IV.,[2] as the preamble expressly states, does not aim at giving

[1] See *Annuaire*, v. pp. 157-174.

[2] For brevity Convention IV. will be referred to in the following pages as the *Hague Regulations*. These Regulations, although they are intended to be binding upon the belligerents, are only the basis upon which the signatory Powers have to frame instructions for their forces. Article 1 declares: 'The High Contracting Parties shall issue instructions to their armed land forces, which shall be in conformity with the Regulations respecting the Laws and Customs of War on Land annexed to the present Convention.' The British War Office, therefore, published in 1912 a guide, *Land Warfare: an Exposition of the Laws and Usages of War on Land for the Guidance of Officers of His Majesty's Army*, written by order of the Secretary of State for War by Colonel Edmonds and Professor Oppenheim. In it the Hague Regulations are systematically set out, and their full text is published in an Appendix. This guide was in 1914 embodied in a new edition of the official *Manual of Military Law*. The British War Office had already in 1903 published a manual, drafted with great precision and clearness by Professor Holland, for the information of the British forces, comprising 'The Laws and Customs of War on Land, as defined by the Hague Convention of 1899.' See also Holland, *The Laws of War on Land (Written and Unwritten)* (1908). Germany had in 1902 issued for the guidance of officers *Kriegsbrauch im Landkriege*. Be-

a complete code of the laws of war on land, and cases beyond its scope still remain the subject of customary rules and usages. Further, it does not create universal International Law, as Article 2 of the convention expressly stipulates that the Regulations shall be binding upon the contracting Powers only in case of war between two or more of them, and shall cease to be binding in case a non-contracting Power takes part in the war. But, in spite of this express stipulation, there can be no doubt that in time the Regulations will become universal International Law, since all the Powers represented at the Second Peace Conference signed the convention except three, although some States made certain reservations.[1]

(5) The declaration concerning expanding (dumdum) bullets.[2]

(6) The declaration concerning projectiles and explosives launched from balloons.[3]

(7) The declaration concerning projectiles diffusing asphyxiating or deleterious gases.[4]

(8) The convention for the adaptation to sea warfare of the principles of the Geneva Convention, produced by the First and revised by the Second Peace Conference.[5]

(9) The Hague Convention of 1907 concerning the opening of hostilities.[6]

(10) The Hague Convention of 1907 concerning the

fore the outbreak of the World War many other States had issued manuals: *e.g.* the French *Les Lois de la Guerre Continentale* (4th ed. 1913), and the United States *Rules of Land Warfare* (1914). See details in Garner, i. §§ 3-6.

[1] This was the author's opinion before the World War. But when it came, this convention had not been ratified by all the belligerents, and its binding force was controversial. Garner, i. §§ 16-18, collects the material, and concludes that the corresponding convention of 1899, which had been so ratified, was binding, but that the convention of 1907 was not binding, except in so far as it was declaratory of existing customary rules. In any case, it is now generally felt that the convention of 1907 requires revision; but Oppenheim did not live to discuss these questions.

[2] See below, § 112.

[3] See below, § 114.

[4] See below, § 113.

[5] See below, § 204.

[6] See below, § 94.

status of enemy merchantmen at the outbreak of hostilities.[1]

(11) The Hague Convention of 1907 concerning the conversion of merchantmen into men-of-war.[2]

(12) The Hague Convention of 1907 concerning the laying of automatic submarine contact mines.[3]

(13) The Hague Convention of 1907 concerning bombardment by naval forces in time of war.[4]

(14) The Hague Convention of 1907 concerning certain restrictions on the exercise of the right of capture in maritime war.[5]

(15) The two Hague Conventions of 1907 [6] concerning the rights and duties of neutral Powers and persons in land warfare and in sea warfare.[7]

Binding Force of the Laws of War.

§ 69. As soon as usages of warfare have by custom or treaty evolved into laws of war, they are binding upon belligerents under all circumstances and conditions, except in the case of reprisals [8] as retaliation against a belligerent for illegitimate acts of warfare by the members of his armed forces or his other subjects. In accordance with the German proverb, *Kriegsraeson geht vor Kriegsmanier* (*necessity in war overrules the manner of warfare*), many German authors [9] before the

[1] See below, § 102*a*.

[2] See below, § 84.

[3] See below, § 182*a*.

[4] See below, § 213.

[5] See below, §§ 85, 186, 187, 191.

[6] See below, § 292.

[7] A declaration concerning the Laws of Naval War was signed at the Conference of London on February 26, 1909, by Great Britain, Germany, the United States of America, Austria-Hungary, Spain, France, Italy, Japan, Holland, and Russia. It was to have enacted rules concerning blockade, contraband, unneutral service, destruction of neutral prizes, transfer of vessels to a neutral flag, enemy character, convoy, and resistance to search, but failed to secure ratification. See below, § 292.

[8] See below, § 248.

[9] See, for instance, Lueder in *Holtzendorff*, iv. pp. 254-257; Ullmann, § 170; Meurer, ii. pp. 7-15. Liszt, who in former editions agreed with these writers, deserts their ranks in the sixth edition (§ 24, iv. 3), and correctly takes the other side. See also Nys, iii. p. 202; Holland, *War*, § 2, where the older literature is quoted; Cybichowski, *Studien zum internationalen Recht* (1912), pp. 21-71, who treats the subject accurately and in more detail; Huber in *Z.V.*, vii. (1913), pp. 351-374, whose distinction between military and other kinds of necessity is very helpful; Visscher in *R.G.*, xxiv. (1917), pp. 74-108, who discusses the influence of necessity on the laws of war very thoroughly; Lammasch, *op. cit.*, pp. 20-23; Schoen, *Die*

World War were already maintaining that the laws of war lose their binding force in case of extreme necessity. Such a case was said to arise when violation of the laws of war alone offers, either a means of escape from extreme danger, or the realisation of the purpose of war—namely, the overpowering of the opponent. This alleged exception to the binding force of the laws of war was, however, not at all generally accepted by German writers; for instance, Bluntschli did not mention it. English, American, French, and Italian writers did not, so far as I am aware, acknowledge it. The protest of Westlake[1] against it was the more justified, as a great danger would have been involved in its admission.

The proverb dates very far back in the history of warfare. It originated and found recognition in those times when warfare was not regulated by laws of war, *i.e.* generally binding customs and international treaties, but only by usages (*Manier*, i.e. *Brauch*), and it says that necessity in war overrules usages of warfare. In our days, however, warfare is no longer regulated by usages only, but to a greater extent by laws—firm rules recognised, either by international treaties, or by general custom.[2] These conventional and customary rules cannot be overruled by necessity, unless they are framed in such a way as not to apply to a case of necessity in self-preservation. Thus, for instance, the rules that poisoned arms and poison are forbidden, and that it is not allowed treacherously to kill or wound individuals belonging to the hostile army, do not lose their binding force even if their breach would effect an escape from extreme danger or the realisation of the purpose of war. Article 22 of the Hague Regulations stipulates

völkerrechtliche Haftung der Staaten aus unerlaubten Handlungen (1917), pp. 112-118; Nys, *L'Occupation de Guerre* (1919), pp. 92-110. See also the Swiss-Belgian Rivier, ii. p. 242.

[1] See Westlake, ii. pp. 115-117, and *Papers*, p. 243.

[2] Concerning the distinction between usage and custom, see above, vol. i. § 17.

distinctly that the right of belligerents to adopt means of injuring the enemy is not unlimited, and this rule does not lose its binding force in a case of necessity. What may be ignored in case of military necessity are not the laws of war, but only the usages of war. *Kriegsraeson geht vor Kriegsmanier*, but not *vor Kriegsrecht!*[1]

IV

THE REGION OF WAR

Taylor, §§ 471, 498—Heffter, § 118—Lueder in *Holtzendorff*, iv. pp. 362-364—Kluber, § 242—Liszt, § 40, i.—Ullmann, § 174—Pradier-Fodéré, vi. No. 2733, and viii. Nos. 3104-3106—Rivier, ii. pp. 216-219—Boeck, Nos. 214-230—Longuet, §§ 18-25—Perels, § 33—Rettich, *Zur Theorie und Geschichte des Rechts zum Kriege* (1888), pp. 174-213—Boeckner, *Der Kriegsschauplatz* (1911)—Schramm, § 6—Wehberg, § 3, p. 55.

Region of War in contradistinction to Theatre of War.

§ 70. Region of war is that part of the surface of the earth in which the belligerents may prepare and execute hostilities against each other. In this meaning, 'region of war' ought to be distinguished from 'theatre of war.' The latter is that part of territory, or the open sea, on which hostilities actually take place.[2]

[1] For here the general rule that necessity in the interest of self-preservation is an excuse for an illegal act cannot find application, because in the preamble of Hague Convention IV. it is expressly stated that the rules of warfare were framed with regard to military necessities. 'According to the views of the High Contracting Parties, these provisions, the wording of which has been inspired by the desire to diminish the evils of war *as far as military requirements permit*, are intended to serve as a general rule of conduct for belligerents in their mutual relations and in their relations with the inhabitants.'

[2] The distinction between 'region' and 'theatre' of war, although of considerable importance, does not appear to have formerly been made by any other publicist. It becomes quite apparent from Article 39 of the Hague Regulations and Article 11 of Hague Convention v., where the 'theatre of war' means that part of territory on which hostilities actually take place. See also Schramm, § 6, p. 58, and Wehberg, p. 59. In *The Dominion Coal Co.* v. *Maskinonge Steamship Co.*, ((1916) 33 T.L.R. 132, 340; (1917) 34 T.L.R. 212), the question was of importance whether a vessel had been ordered by the charterers to trade 'in the war region.' It is, however, obvious that the parties did not thereby mean the 'region of war' in the sense used above, but the 'theatre of war.' The distinction is particularly evident in relation to the open

Legally no part of the earth which is not region of war may be made the theatre of war; but not every section of the whole region of war is necessarily theatre of war. Thus, in the war between Great Britain and the two South African Republics, the whole of the territory of the British Empire and the open sea, as well as the territory of the Republics, was the region of war, but the theatre of war was in South Africa only. On the other hand, in the World War the theatre of war was almost coextensive with the region of war.

§ 71. The region of war depends upon the belligerents. For this reason, every war has its particular region, so far, at any rate, as the territorial region is concerned. For besides the open sea,[1] and all such territories as are as yet not occupied by any State (which are always within the region of war), the particular region of every war is the whole of the territories and territorial waters of the belligerents. But any part of the globe which is permanently neutralised[2] is always outside the region of war. Particular Region of every War.

Since dominions and colonies are a part of the territory of the empire or mother country, they fall within the region of a war between the latter and another State, whatever their position may be within it. Thus

sea. For instance, the right of visit and capture may be exercised throughout this region of war, mines may only be laid on the theatre of war, that is, where actual fighting takes place. Therefore the region of war remains unaltered, but the theatre of war may shift about.

[1] Can States, through a unilateral declaration, extend the width of their neutral maritime belt beyond three miles, and thereby curtail the region of war? By a decree of October 18, 1912, France claimed a maritime belt six miles wide for all purposes of neutrality. After the outbreak of the World War, Italy, when still neutral, by a decree of August 6, 1914, likewise claimed a neutral maritime belt six miles wide. However, the decision of the German Prize Court in *The Elida*, *Z. V.*, ix. (1915), p. 109, and the arrangement between the British and the Norwegian Governments that, for the decision of *The Loekken*, (1918) 34 T.L.R. 594, the three-mile limit should be postulated, would seem to show that belligerents are not prepared to recognise the claim of any State to a neutral maritime belt more than three miles wide.

Newspapers reported at the beginning of the World War that Great Britain had refused the claim of Argentina and Uruguay to a neutral belt wider than three miles; but the author was unable to obtain confirmation of this. On the other hand, Great Britain, as a matter of policy, ordered her cruisers to respect the six miles claimed by Italy.

[2] See below, § 72.

in the World War the whole of Australia, Canada, India, and so on, were included with the British Islands in the region of war. And, further, as States under the suzerainty of another State are internationally in several respects considered to be a portion of its territory,[1] they fall within the region of a war between it and another Power. Again, such parts of the territory of a State as are under the *condominium*, or under the administration, of another State,[2] fall within the region of a war between one of the *condomini*, or the administrating State, and another Power. Thus, in the World War, Cyprus at once fell within the region of war; and also the Soudan, which is under the *condominium* of England and Egypt. On the other hand, Cyprus would not have fallen[3] within the region of a war between Turkey and any other Power than Great Britain.

Although as a rule the territories of both belligerents, together with the open sea, fall within the region of war, and neutral territories do not, exceptions may occur:—

(1) A belligerent can deliberately renounce its right to treat certain territories, or parts of the open sea, as being within the region of war, provided that such areas fulfil the duties incumbent upon neutrals. Thus, during the Turco-Italian War, in 1911 and 1912, Italy treated Crete and Egypt as though they were not parts of the region of war.[4]

(2) Cases are possible in which a part, or the whole, of the territory of a neutral State falls within the region of war. These cases arise in wars in which such neutral territories are the very objects of the war, as were Korea (then an independent State) and the Chinese province

[1] See above, vol. i. §§ 91, 169.

[2] See above, vol. i. § 171.

[3] Cyprus has since been annexed by Great Britain. See above, vol. i. §§ 50*a*.

[4] There is no doubt that this attitude of Italy is explained by the fact that Egypt, although then legally under Turkish suzerainty, was actually under British occupation, and that Crete was forcibly kept by the Powers under Turkish suzerainty.

of Manchuria [1] in the Russo-Japanese War. Or when a neutral State, either deliberately, or because it has not at its disposal sufficiently strong naval forces, does not prevent a belligerent from committing hostilities in its territorial waters, and making them a basis for military operations and preparations. These territorial waters become in consequence a part of the region of war,[2] and the other belligerent may also commit hostilities there. Or again, if a belligerent army which has crossed the frontier of a neutral State is not at once disarmed and interned, and is, therefore, able at any moment to recross the frontier and attack the other belligerent.[3] Necessity of self-defence can then compel the latter also to cross the neutral frontier, and pursue and attack the enemy on a portion of neutral territory, which would for this reason become part of the region of war.

But if in such an exceptional case neutral territory becomes the region and theatre of war, and is militarily occupied by a belligerent, the occupant does not possess such a wide range of rights with regard to the occupied country and its inhabitants as he possesses in occupied *enemy* territory. He can indeed resort to all measures which are necessary for the safety of his forces; but he cannot exact contributions or appropriate cash, funds, and realisable securities which are the property of the neutral State.[4]

[1] See below, § 320.

[2] See the judgment in the French case of *The Tinos* (1917), printed in *R.G.*, xxv. (1918), *Jurisprudence en Matière de Prises maritimes*, p. 3. The *Tinos* and twelve other German merchantmen were captured during the World War, in September 1916, in the roadsteads of several Greek ports by the Allies. Since Greece was at that time still neutral, the German owners of the vessels claimed restitution on account of these vessels having been captured in neutral waters; but the French Prize Court condemned them because a succession of hostile acts committed by the enemy had turned Greek territorial waters into a part of the theatre of war. Greece did not claim the vessels, since she had meanwhile joined the Allies.

[3] See below, § 339.

[4] See the very lucid discussion of the matter in Boeckner, *Der Kriegsschauplatz* (1911), pp. 145-208. Quite different, of course, is a case where a belligerent deliberately attacks a neutral State in order to force a passage through it, as Germany attacked Belgium in the World War.

Exclusion from Region of War through Neutralisation.

§ 72. Moreover, certain areas may be excluded from the region of war through neutralisation. This may be permanent, through a general treaty of the Powers, or temporary, through a special treaty between the belligerents. At present no part of the open sea is neutralised, as the neutralisation of the Black Sea was abolished [1] in 1871. The following are some important instances [2] of parts of territories [3] which are, or were at one time, permanently neutralised :—

(1) The provinces of Chablais and Faucigny were permanently neutralised until the resettlement after the World War.[4]

(2) The Ionian Islands were permanently neutralised [5] when they merged in the kingdom of Greece. But this neutralisation was restricted [6] to the islands of Corfu and Paxo only by Article 2 of the Treaty of London of March 24, 1864.

(3) The mouth and some parts of the River Danube were closed to vessels of war by Article 52 of the Treaty of Berlin of 1878.[7] The Rivers Congo and Niger, and all their territories, were neutralised by Articles 25 and 33 of the Berlin Congo Act of 1885; but this Act was abrogated at the conclusion of the World War.[8]

(4) The Suez Canal is permanently neutralised [9] since 1888.

The Panama [10] Canal is permanently neutralised

[1] See above, vol. i. §§ 181, 265.

[2] The matter is thoroughly treated in Rettich, *Zur Theorie und Geschichte des Rechtes zum Kriege* (1888), pp. 174-213. See also Schramm, pp. 83-87.

[3] See Krauel, *Neutralität, Neutralisation und Befriedung im Völkerrecht* (1915), pp. 48-90, where all the existing cases are discussed under the term of 'Befriedung' (Pacification). That he includes Luxemburg is very odd.

[4] See above, vol. i. § 207. Trésal, *L'Annexion de la Savoie en France* (1913), asserts that, through the annexation of Chablais and Faucigny by France in 1860, the neutralisation established by the Vienna Congress had even then fallen to the ground.

[5] Through Article 2 of the Treaty of London of November 14, 1863.

[6] See Martens, *N.R.G.*, xviii. pp. 55, 63. Nevertheless, the Allies occupied Corfu during the World War as a rest camp for the Serbian army. See Garner, ii. § 464.

[7] As to the provisions made with regard to the Danube after the World War, see above, vol. i. § 459.

[8] See above, vol. i. § 564.

[9] See above, vol. i. § 183.

[10] See above, vol. i. § 184.

through Article 3 of the Hay-Pauncefote Treaty of November 18, 1901. But this treaty is not a general treaty of the Powers, but only one between Great Britain and the United States.

By the Treaty of Peace between the Allied Powers and Turkey at the end of the World War, a zone comprising the Bosphorus and Dardanelles is placed under an International Commission of Control, and no belligerent right may be exercised in it, or hostilities be committed there, except under the authority of the League of Nations.

These three cases are cases of 'internationalisation' rather than neutralisation.

(5) The Straits of Magellan [1] are permanently neutralised through Article 5 of the Boundary Treaty of Buenos Ayres of July 23, 1881, between Argentina and Chili.

A piece of territory along the frontier between Sweden and Norway is neutralised by the Convention of Stockholm of October 26, 1905, between Sweden and Norway, which includes rules concerning a neutral zone,[2] but stipulates [3] that the neutralisation shall not be valid in a war against a common enemy.

The neutralisation provided for in these two cases is the concern of the contracting parties alone, and has no consequences for third States.

(6) The territory of the former Congo Free State was neutralised in compliance with Article 10 of the General Act of the Berlin Congo Conference. In 1908 it merged by cession into Belgium; [4] but this did not affect the neutralisation of the territory, so long as the Berlin Act was in force.[5] However, the case was unique, because Belgium was herself a neutralised State.

[1] See Martens, *N.R.G.*, 2nd Ser. xii. p. 491, and above, vol. i. § 195. *The Bangor*, (1916) 2 B. and C. P. C. 206.

[2] See Martens, *N.R.G.*, 2nd Ser. xxxiv. p. 703.

[3] See Article 1.

[4] See above, vol. i. § 101.

[5] See above, vol. i. § 564.

As regards temporary neutralisation, parts of the territories of belligerents or the open sea may become neutralised through a treaty of the belligerents for a particular war. Thus, when in 1870 war broke out between France and Germany, the commanders of the French man-of-war[1] *Dupleix* and the German man-of-war *Hertha*—both stationed in the Japanese and Chinese waters—through their embassies in Yokohama, proposed to their respective Governments the neutralisation of these waters for that war. Germany consented, but France refused. Again, at the commencement of the Turco-Italian War in 1911, Turkey proposed the neutralisation of the Red Sea, but Italy refused to agree to it.[2]

Asserted Exclusion of the Baltic Sea from the Region of War.

§ 73. That at present no part of the open sea is neutralised is universally recognised, and this applies to the Baltic Sea, which is admittedly part of the open sea. Some writers,[3] however, maintained before the World War that the littoral States of the Baltic had a right to forbid all hostilities within it in a war between States other than themselves, and could thereby neutralise it without the consent, and even against the will, of the belligerents. This opinion was based on the fact that, during the eighteenth century, these littoral States claimed that right in several conventions; but it appeared untenable, because it was opposed to the universally recognised principle of the freedom of

[1] See Perels, § 33, p. 160, n. 2.

[2] Different from cases of this kind is the special protection during war arranged in special conventions for certain establishments. Although the terms 'neutrality' and 'neutralisation' are often used, they are not strictly applicable. Thus, Article 3 of the Treaty of Tangier of May 31, 1865, provided for the 'neutrality' of the lighthouse at Cape Spartel. See Martens, *N.R.G.*, xx. p. 350; but see also Martens, *N.R.G.*, 2nd Ser. iii. p. 560, and ix. p. 227. Again, according to Article 21 of the Danube Navigation Act signed at Galatz on November 2, 1865, the works and establishments of all kinds created by the European Danube Commission were to enjoy the benefits of 'neutrality.' See Martens, *N.R.G.*, xviii. p. 144.

[3] See Perels, pp. 160-163, who discusses the question at some length and answers it in the affirmative.

the open sea. As no State has territorial supremacy over parts of the open sea, I could not see how such a claim could be justified ; [1] and, in fact, during the World War, hostilities did take place in the Baltic.

V

THE BELLIGERENTS

Vattel, iii. § 4—Phillimore, iii. §§ 92-93—Taylor, §§ 458-460—Wheaton, § 294—Bluntschli, §§ 511-514—Heffter, §§ 114-117—Lueder in *Holtzendorff*, iv. pp. 237-248—Klüber, § 236—G. F. Martens, ii. § 264—Gareis, § 83—Liszt, § 39, ii.—Ullmann, §§ 168-169—Pradier-Fodéré, vi. Nos. 2656-2660—Rivier, ii. pp. 207-216—Nys, iii. pp. 23-26—Mérignhac, iii°. pp. 136-139—Martens, ii. § 108—Heilborn, *System*, pp. 333-335.

Qualification to become a Belligerent (*facultas bellandi*).

§ 74. As the Law of Nations recognises the status of war, and its effects as regards rights and duties between the belligerents on the one hand, and, on the other, between the belligerents and neutral States, the question arises what kind of States are legally qualified to make war, and thereby to become belligerents. Publicists who discuss this question at all speak for the most part of a *right* of States to make war, a *jus belli*. But if this so-called right is examined, it turns out to be no right at all, as there is no corresponding duty in those against whom the right is said to exist.[2] A State which makes war against another exercises one of its natural functions, and the only question is whether it is, or is not, legally qualified to exercise this function. Now, according to the Law of Nations, full sovereign States alone possess the legal qualification to become belligerents ; half and part sovereign States are not legally qualified to become belligerents. Since neutralised States, as Switzerland, are full sovereign States, they are legally qualified to become belligerents, although

[1] See Rivier, ii. p. 218 ; Bonfils, § 504 ; Nys, i. pp. 448-450.

[2] See Heilborn, *System*, p. 333.

their neutralisation binds them not to make use of their qualification, except for defence. If they become belligerents because they are attacked, they do not lose their character as neutralised States; but if they become belligerents for offensive purposes, they *ipso facto* lose this character.

Possibility in contradistinction to Qualification to become a Belligerent.

§ 75. Such States as do not possess the legal qualification to become belligerents are by law prohibited from offensive or defensive warfare. But the possession of armed forces makes it possible for them in fact to enter into war, and to become belligerents. History records instances enough of such States having actually made war. Thus in 1876 Serbia and Montenegro, although at that time vassal States under Turkish suzerainty, declared war against Turkey, and on February 28, 1877, peace was concluded between Turkey and Serbia.[1] And when in April 1877 war broke out between Russia and Turkey, the then Turkish vassal State Roumania joined Russia, and Serbia declared war anew against Turkey in December 1877. Further, in November 1885 a war was waged between Serbia, which had become a full sovereign State, and Bulgaria, which was at the time still a vassal State under Turkish suzerainty. The war lasted actually only a fortnight, but the formal treaty of peace was not signed until March 3, 1886, at Bucharest; [2] and although Turkey was a party to it, Bulgaria appeared as a party thereto independently, and on its own behalf.

Whenever a State lacking the legal qualification to make war nevertheless actually makes war, it is a belligerent, the contention is real war, and all the rules of International Law respecting warfare apply to it.[3] Therefore, an armed contention between suzerain and

[1] See Martens, *N.R.G.*, 2nd Ser. iii. pp. 171-173.

[2] See Martens, *N.R.G.*, 2nd Ser. xiv. p. 284.

[3] This is quite apparent through the fact that Bulgaria by accession became a party to the Geneva Convention at a time when she was still a vassal State under Turkish suzerainty.

vassal, between a full sovereign State and a vassal State under the suzerainty of another State, and, lastly, between a Federal State and one or more of its members, is war[1] in the technical sense of the term according to the Law of Nations.

Insurgents as a Belligerent Power.

§ 76. The distinction between legal qualification and actual power to make war explains the fact that insurgents may become a belligerent Power. It is a customary rule of the Law of Nations that any State may recognise insurgents as a belligerent Power, provided (1) they are in possession of a certain part of the territory of the legitimate Government; (2) they have set up a Government of their own; and (3) they conduct their armed contention with the legitimate Government according to the laws and usages of war.[2] Such insurgents in fact, although not in law, form a State-like community, and they are in fact making war, although their contention is by International Law not considered as war in the technical sense of the term, as long as they have not received recognition as a belligerent Power.

The Case of the Czecho-Slovaks.

§ 76*a*. Different from recognition of insurgents is recognition as a belligerent Power granted by belligerents to separate armies comprising subjects of the enemy who are fighting to free their nation from subjection to him. Thus in 1918, during the World War, Great Britain, France, Italy, and the United States of America, recognised the Czecho-Slovaks as co-belligerents.[3] By a proclamation dated August 13, 1918, Great Britain recognised them 'as an allied

[1] See above, § 56, and Baty, *International Law in South Africa* (1900), pp. 66-68.

[2] See above, § 59. See also Rougier, *Les Guerres civiles*, etc. (1903), pp. 372-413, and Westlake, i. pp. 50-57. The Institute of International Law, at its meeting at Neuchâtel in 1900, adopted a body of nine articles concerning the rights and duties of foreign States in case of an insurrection; Articles 4-9 deal with the recognition of the belligerency of insurgents. See *Annuaire*, xviii. p. 227.

[3] See Garner, i. § 26.

nation,' their armies as 'an allied and belligerent army waging regular warfare against Austria-Hungary and Germany,' and their National Council 'as the supreme organ of national interests and as the present trustee of the future Czecho-Slovak Government to exercise supreme authority over this allied and belligerent army.' The Government of the United States, by proclamation dated September 3, 1918, recognised a 'state of belligerency' between the organised armies of the Czecho-Slovaks and the German and Austro-Hungarian empires, and the National Council as 'a *de facto* belligerent Government clothed with proper authority to direct the military and political affairs of the Czecho-Slovaks.'

There is no doubt that the enemy is in law not compelled to grant them similar recognition; he is justified in law in considering the members of such armies as traitors. But humanity ought to induce him to treat them, when captured, as prisoners of war, and not as criminals.

Principal and Accessory Belligerent Parties.

§ 77. War occurs usually between two States, one on each side. But in some wars there are on one or on both sides several parties, and then principal and accessory belligerents are sometimes to be distinguished.

Principal belligerents are those parties to a war who wage it on the basis of a treaty of alliance, whether concluded before or during the war. Accessory belligerents are such States as provide help and succour only in a limited way to a principal belligerent; for instance, by paying subsidies, sending a certain number of troops or men-of-war, granting a coaling station to the men-of-war of a principal party, allowing his troops a passage through their territory, and the like. Such accessory party becomes a belligerent through rendering help.

The matter need hardly be mentioned at all, were it

not that publicists formerly discussed whether or not a neutral State which fulfilled in time of war a treaty concluded in time of peace, by the terms of which it had to grant a coaling station, the passage of troops through its territory, and the like, to one of the belligerents, violated its neutrality. This question is identical with the question [1] whether a qualified neutrality, in contradistinction to a perfect neutrality, is admissible. Since the answer to this question is in the negative, such State as fulfils a treaty obligation of this kind in time of war may be considered by the other side to be an accessory belligerent. All doubt in the matter ought to have been removed, since Article 2 [2] of Hague Convention v. categorically enacted that 'belligerents are forbidden to move across the territory of a neutral Power troops or convoys either of munitions of war or of supplies.'

VI

THE ARMED FORCES OF THE BELLIGERENTS

Vattel, iii. §§ 223-231—Hall, §§ 177-181—Lawrence, §§ 148-150—Westlake, ii. pp. 64-67—Manning, pp. 206-209—Phillimore, iii. § 94—Twiss, ii. § 45—Halleck, i. pp. 555-562—Hershey, Nos. 352-354, 403—Taylor, §§ 471-476—Moore, vii. § 1109—Wheaton, §§ 356-358—Bluntschli, §§ 569-572—Heffter, §§ 124-124^a—Lueder in *Holtzendorff*, iv. pp. 371-387—Kluber, § 267—G. F. Martens, ii. § 271—Gareis, § 83—Ullmann, § 175—Liszt, § 40, ii.—Bonfils, Nos. 1088-1098—Despagnet, Nos. 520-523—Mérignhac, iii^a. pp. 139-155—Pradier-Fodéré, vi. Nos. 2721-2732, and viii. Nos. 3091-3103—Nys, iii. pp. 85-134—Rivier, ii. pp. 242-259—Calvo, iv. §§ 2044-2065—Fiore, iii. Nos. 1303-1316, and *Code*, Nos. 1460-1480—Martens, ii. § 112—Longuet, §§ 26-36—Pillet, pp. 35-59—*Kriegsbrauch*, pp. 4-8—Perels, § 34—Boeck, Nos. 209-213—Dupuis, Nos. 74-91—Lawrence, *War*, pp. 195-218—Zorn, pp. 36-73—Bordwell, pp. 228-236—*Land Warfare*, § 17-38—Meurer, ii. §§ 11-20—Spaight, pp. 45-72—Ariga, pp. 74-91—Takahashi, pp. 89-93—Schramm, §§ 12, 16—Wehberg, § 4—Garner, i. §§ 245, 250-264.

§ 78. The chief part of the armed forces of the belligerents are their regular armies and navies. What

[1] See below, § 305.

[2] See also Article 3 of Convention v.

Regular Armies and Navies.

kinds of forces constitute a regular army and a regular navy is not for International Law to determine, but a matter of Municipal Law exclusively. Whether or not so-called militia and volunteer corps belong to armies rests entirely with the Municipal Law of the belligerents; and there are several States whose armies consist of militia and volunteer corps exclusively, no standing army being provided for. The Hague Regulations expressly stipulate[1] that in countries where militia or volunteer corps constitute the army, or form part of it, they are included under the denomination 'army.' It is likewise irrelevant to consider the composition of a regular army, whether it is based on conscription or not, whether foreigners as well as subjects are enrolled, and the like.

Non-Combatant Members of Armed Forces.

§ 79. In the main, armed forces consist of combatants; but no army in the field consists of combatants exclusively. There are always several kinds of other individuals, such as couriers, doctors, farriers, veterinary surgeons, chaplains, nurses, official and voluntary ambulance men, contractors, canteen-caterers, newspaper correspondents,[2] civil servants, diplomatists, and foreign military attachés[3] in the suite of the commander-in-chief.

Writers on the Law of Nations do not agree as regards the position of these non-combatants; they are not mere private individuals, yet are certainly not combatants, although they may—as, for instance, couriers, doctors, farriers, and veterinary surgeons—have the character of soldiers. They may correctly be said to belong *indirectly* to the armed forces. Article 3 of the Hague Regulations expressly stipulates that the armed forces of the belligerents may consist of combatants and non-combatants, and that both, in case of capture,

[1] Article 1.

[2] See Rey in *R.G.*, xvii. (1910), pp. 73-102, and Higgins, *War and the Private Citizen* (1912), pp. 91-112.

[3] See Rey in *R.G.*, xvii. (1910), pp. 63-73.

must be treated as prisoners of war, provided[1] they produce a certificate of identification from the military authorities of the army which they accompany. However, when one speaks of armed forces generally, combatants only are under consideration.

The question whether women may be considered as non-combatant members of armed forces came into prominence during the World War, when thousands were enrolled, and sent to the front to serve as army cooks, drivers, store-keepers, and the like. I think the question must be answered in the affirmative.

Irregular Forces.

§ 80. Very often the armed forces of belligerents consist throughout the war of their regular armies only; but it happens frequently that irregular forces take part. Of such irregular forces two different kinds are to be distinguished—first, such as are authorised by the belligerents; and, secondly, such as are acting on their own initiative, and on their own account, without special authorisation. Formerly it was a recognised rule of International Law that only the members of authorised irregular forces enjoyed the privileges due to the members of the armed forces of belligerents; members of unauthorised irregular forces were considered to be war criminals, and could be shot when captured. During the Franco-German War in 1870, the Germans acted throughout according to this rule with regard to the so-called 'franctireurs,' requesting the production of a special authorisation from the French Government from every irregular combatant whom they captured, failing which he was shot. But according to Article 1 of the Hague Regulations this rule is now obsolete; and its place is taken by the rule that irregulars enjoy the privileges due to members of the armed forces of the belligerents, although they do not act under authorisation, provided (1) that they

[1] See below, § 127.

are commanded by a person responsible for his subordinates, (2) that they have a fixed distinctive emblem recognisable at a distance,[1] (3) that they carry arms openly,[2] and (4) that they conduct their operations in accordance with the laws and customs of war. It must, however, be emphasised that this rule applies only to irregulars fighting in bodies, however small. Such individuals as take up arms or commit hostile acts singly and severally are still liable to be treated as war criminals, and shot.[3]

Levies *en masse.*

§ 81. It sometimes happens during war that, on the approach of the enemy, a belligerent calls the whole population of the country to arms, and thus makes them a part, although a more or less irregular part, of his armed forces. Provided they receive some organisation, and comply with the laws and usages of war, the combatants who take part in such a levy *en masse* organised by the State enjoy the privileges due to members of armed forces.

Or again, sometimes a levy *en masse* takes place spontaneously, without organisation by a belligerent, and the question arises whether, or not, those who take part in such levies *en masse* belong to the armed forces of the belligerents, and therefore enjoy the privileges due to members of such forces. Article 2 of the Hague Regulations stipulates that the population of a territory not yet occupied who, on the enemy's approach, spontaneously take up arms to resist the invading enemy,

[1] The distance at which the emblem should be visible is undetermined. See *Land Warfare*, § 23, where it is pointed out that it is reasonable to expect that the silhouette of an irregular combatant standing against the skyline should be at once distinguishable from that of a peaceable inhabitant by the naked eye of ordinary individuals, at a distance at which the form of an individual can be determined. See Ariga, p. 87, concerning 120 irregulars who were treated as criminals and shot by the Japanese after the occupation of Vladimirowka on the island of Sakhaline.

[2] See *Land Warfare*, § 26; individuals whose sole arm is a pistol, hand-grenade, a dagger concealed about the person, or a sword-stick, are not such as carry their arms openly.

[3] See below, § 254.

without having time to organise themselves under responsible commanders and to procure fixed distinctive emblems recognisable at a distance, shall nevertheless enjoy the privileges due to armed forces, provided that they carry arms openly, and act otherwise in conformity with the laws and usages of war. Totally different, however, is a levy *en masse* of the population of a territory already invaded by the enemy, for the purpose of freeing the country from the invader. Article 2 of the Hague Regulations does not cover this case, in which, therefore, the old customary rule of International Law is valid, that those taking part in such a levy *en masse*, if captured, are liable to be shot.[1]

It is of particular importance not to confound invasion with occupation in this matter. Article 2 distinctly speaks of the *approach* of the enemy, and thereby sanctions only such a levy *en masse* as takes place in territory not yet *invaded* by the enemy. Once the territory is invaded, although the invasion has not yet ripened into occupation,[2] a levy *en masse* is no longer legitimate. But, of course, the term *territory*, as used by Article 2, is not intended to mean [3] the whole extent of the State of a belligerent, but only such parts of it as are not yet invaded. For this reason, if a town is already invaded, but not a neighbouring town, the inhabitants of the latter may, on the approach of the enemy, legitimately rise *en masse*. And it matters not whether the individuals, in doing so, are acting in immediate combination with a regular army or separately from it.[4]

§ 82. As International Law grew up amongst the States of Christendom, and the Family of Nations includes only civilised, although not necessarily Christian, **Barbarous Forces.**

[1] See below, § 254.

[2] Concerning the difference between invasion and occupation, see below, § 167.

[3] See *Land Warfare*, §§ 31-32.

[4] See *Land Warfare*, § 34.

States, all writers on International Law agree that, in wars between themselves, the members of the Family of Nations should not make use of barbarous forces—*i.e.* troops consisting of individuals belonging to savage tribes and barbarous races. But it can hardly be maintained that a rule of this kind has customarily grown up in practice, nor has it been stipulated by treaties, and the Hague Regulations overlook this point. It is therefore difficult to say whether such fighters, if employed in a war between members of the Family of Nations, would enjoy the privileges due to members of armed forces generally. I see no reason why they should not, provided they would or could comply with the laws and usages of war prevalent according to International Law. But the very fact that they are barbarians makes it probable that they could or would not do so; it would then be unreasonable to grant them the privileges generally due to members of armed forces, and it would be necessary to treat them according to discretion.[1] But the employment of barbarous forces must not be confounded with the enrolling of coloured individuals into the regular army and the employment of regiments consisting of disciplined coloured soldiers. There is no reason whatever why, for instance, the members of a regiment formed by the United States of America out of negroes bred and educated in America, or members of Indian regiments under English commanders, should not, in wars between members of the Family of Nations, enjoy the privileges due to the members of armed forces according to International Law. In fact, the United States employed two coloured cavalry regiments in Cuba during her war with Spain, and, during the World War, some

[1] As regards the limited use made of armed natives as scouts, and the like, on the part of the British commanders during the South-African War, see *The Times History of the War in South Africa*, v. pp. 249-251. The Boers refused quarter to any who fell into their hands.

Indian regiments were employed by Great Britain in France.

Privateers. § 83. Formerly privateers were a generally recognised part of the armed forces of the belligerents, private vessels being commissioned by the belligerents through letters of marque to carry on hostilities at sea, and particularly to capture enemy merchantmen.[1] From the fifteenth century, when privateering began to grow up, down to the eighteenth century, belligerents used to grant letters of marque to private ships owned by neutral subjects as well as by their own. But during the eighteenth century it became the practice to grant them to ships belonging to their own subjects only.[2] However, privateering was abolished by the Declaration of Paris in 1856 as between the signatory Powers and others who joined it later. Although privateering would still be legal as between other Powers, it will in future scarcely be made use of. In all the wars that have occurred since 1856 between such Powers, no letters of marque have been granted.[3]

Converted Merchantmen. § 84. A case which happened in 1870, soon after the outbreak of the Franco-German War, raised the question whether converted [4] merchantmen could be considered

[1] See Martens, *Essai concernant les Armateurs, les Prises, et surtout les Reprises* (1795); La Mache, *La Guerre de la Course* (1901); Willms, *Die Umwandlung von Kauffahrteischiffen in Kriegsschiffe* (1912); Wehberg, § 4.

[2] Many publicists maintain that nowadays a privateer commissioned by another State than that of which he is a subject is liable to be treated as a pirate when captured. With this, however, I cannot agree; see above, vol. i. § 273, Hall, § 81, and below, § 330.

[3] See below, § 177. It is confidently to be hoped that the great progress made by the abolition of privateering through the Declaration of Paris will never be undone. But it is of importance to note the fact that up to the present day endeavours have been made on the part of free-lances to win public opinion for a retrograde step. See, for instance, Munro-Butler Johnstone, *Handbook of Maritime Rights; and the Declaration of Paris Considered* (1876), and Gibson Bowles, *The Declaration of Paris of 1856* (1900); see also Perels, pp. 177-179. As the Declaration of Paris is a law-making treaty which does not bestow a right upon the several signatory Powers to give notice of withdrawal, a signatory Power is not at liberty to give such notice, although Mr. Gibson Bowles (*op. cit.*, pp. 169-179) asserts that this could be done. See above, vol. i. § 12.

[4] See Guichéneuc, *La Marine auxiliaire en Droit international* (1900); Willms, *op. cit.*; Kriege, in *Z.I.*, xxvi. (1915), pp. 71-117.

part of the armed naval forces of a belligerent. As the North-German Confederation owned only a few men-of-war, the creation of a volunteer fleet was intended. So the King of Prussia, as President of the Confederation, invited the owners of private German vessels to make them part of the German navy under the following conditions: Every ship should be assessed as to her value, and 10 per cent. of it should at once be paid in cash to the owner, as a price for the charter of the ship. The owner should engage the crew himself, but they should become for the time of the war members of the German navy, and wear the German naval uniform. The ship should sail under the German war flag, and be armed and adapted for her purpose by the German naval authorities. Should she be captured or destroyed by the enemy, the assessed value should be paid to her owners in full; but should she be restored after the war undamaged, the owner should retain the 10 per cent. received as charter price. All such vessels should only try to capture or destroy French men-of-war, and, if successful, the owner should receive between £1500 and £7500 as a premium. The French Government considered this scheme a disguised evasion of the Declaration of Paris which abolished privateering, and requested the intervention of Great Britain. The British Government brought the case before the law-officers of the Crown, who declared the German scheme to be substantially different from the revival of privateering, and consequently the British Government refused to object to it. The scheme, however, was never put into practice.[1]

Now, in spite of the opinion of the British law-officers, writers on International Law differ as to the legality of the above scheme; but, on the other hand, they are unanimous that not every scheme for a voluntary fleet

[1] See Perels, § 34; Hall, § 181; Boeck, No. 211; Dupuis, Nos. 81-84.

is to be rejected. Russia,[1] in fact, from 1877 possessed a voluntary fleet. France [2] had before the World War made arrangements with certain steamship companies according to which their mail-boats had to be constructed on plans approved by the Government, commanded by officers of the French navy, and incorporated in the French navy at the outbreak of war. Great Britain from 1887 onwards entered into agreements with several powerful British steamship companies for the purpose of securing their vessels at the outbreak of hostilities; and the United States of America in 1892 made similar arrangements with the American Line.[3]

Matters were brought to a climax in 1904, during the Russo-Japanese War, through the cases of *Peterburg* and *Smolensk*.[4] On July 4 and 6 of that year, these vessels, which belonged to the Russian volunteer fleet in the Black Sea, were allowed to pass the Bosphorus and the Dardanelles, which were closed [5] to men-of-war of all nations, because they were flying the Russian commercial flag. They likewise passed the Suez Canal under the commercial flag; but, after leaving Suez, they converted themselves into men-of-war by hoisting the Russian war flag, and began to exercise over neutral merchantmen all the rights of supervision which belligerents can claim for their cruisers in time of war. On July 13 *Peterburg* captured the British P. and O. steamer *Malacca* for alleged carriage of contraband, and put a prize-crew on board for the purpose of navigating her to Libau. But the British Government protested; the *Malacca* was released at Algiers on her way to Libau on July 27, and Russia

[1] See Dupuis, No. 85.

[2] See Dupuis, No. 86.

[3] See Lawrence, § 201, and Dupuis, Nos. 87-88. On the whole question see Pradier-Fodéré, viii. Nos. 3102-3103.

[4] See the details of the career of these vessels in Lawrence, *War*, pp. 205 *seq.*

[5] See above, vol. i. § 197.

agreed that *Peterburg* and *Smolensk* should no longer act as cruisers, and that all neutral vessels captured by them should be released.

This case was the cause of the question of the conversion of merchantmen into men-of-war being taken up by the Second Hague Conference in 1907, and dealt with in Convention VII.[1] This convention, which was signed by all the States represented at the conference except the United States of America, China, San Domingo, Nicaragua, and Uruguay, comprised twelve articles; its more important stipulations were the following: No converted vessel can have the status of a warship unless she is placed under the direct authority, immediate control, and responsibility of the Power whose flag she flies (Article 1). Such a vessel must, therefore, bear the external marks which distinguish the warships of her nationality (Article 2); the commander must be in the service of the State, must be duly commissioned, and his name must figure on the list of the officers of the military fleet (Article 3); and the crew must be subject to the rules of military discipline (Article 4). A converted vessel must observe the laws and usages of war (Article 5), and her conversion must as soon as possible be announced by the belligerent concerned in the list of the ships of his military fleet (Article 6).[2]

During the World War converted merchantmen were freely employed.

The opinion, which largely prevailed before the World War, that by permitting the conversion of merchantmen into men-of-war privateering had been revived, is absolutely unfounded, for the rules of Convention VII.

[1] See Wilson in *A.J.*, ii. (1908), pp. 271-275; Lémonon, pp. 607-622; Higgins, pp. 312-321; Dupuis, *Guerre*, Nos. 48-58; Nippold, ii. pp. 73-84; Scott, *Conferences*, pp. 568-576; Higgins, *War and the Private Citizen* (1912), pp. 115-165.

[2] It must be specially observed that a merchantman which has been armed only for the purpose of defence is not thereby converted into a man-of-war. See *A.J.*, ix. (1915), p. 188.

in no way abrogated the rule of the Declaration of Paris that privateering is and remains abolished. But the convention was unsatisfactory because it did not settle the questions where conversion may be performed, and whether it was permissible to reconvert into a merchantman, before the termination of the war, a vessel which during the war had been converted into a warship. The Powers could not come to an agreement on these two points, one party claiming that conversion could only be performed within a harbour of the converting Power, or an enemy harbour occupied by it, the other party defending the claim to convert on the high seas as well; and the preamble of Convention VII. stated expressly that the place where a conversion might be performed remained an open question. It was still open when the World War broke out, and Great Britain, which belonged to the party denying a right to convert on the high seas, at once made it known that if German vessels, after leaving American ports, were converted into men-of-war on the high seas, it would hold the United States Government responsible for resulting damage.[1] Those Powers which claim that conversion[2] must not take place on the high seas may still refuse to acknowledge the public character of any vessel which has been converted on the high seas, and may still uphold their view that a converted vessel may not alternately claim the character and the privileges of a belligerent man-of-war and a merchantman.

The Crews of Merchantmen.

§ 85. In a sense, the crews of merchantmen owned by subjects of a belligerent belong to its armed forces. For those vessels are liable to be seized by enemy men-of-war, and, if attacked for that purpose, they may

[1] See Garner, i. § 245, and *A.J.*, ix. (1915), Special Supplement, pp. 222-223.

[2] Concerning the question whether an enemy merchantman, captured on the high seas, may at once be converted into a warship, see below, § 185.

defend[1] themselves, may return the attack, and eventually seize the attacking men-of-war. The crews of merchantmen become in such cases combatants, and enjoy all the privileges of the members of armed forces. But unless attacked, they must not commit hostilities, and if they do so, they are liable to be treated as criminals, just as are private individuals who commit hostilities in land warfare. Some writers[2] assert that, although merchantmen of the belligerents are not competent to exercise the right of visit, search, and capture towards neutral vessels, they may attack enemy vessels—merchantmen as well as public vessels—not merely for the purpose of defence, but even without having been previously attacked, and that, consequently, the crews must in such case enjoy the privileges due to members of the armed forces. But this opinion is absolutely without foundation nowadays;[3] even in former times it was not generally recognised.[4]

In regard to the fate of the crews of captured merchantmen, a distinction is to be made according as to whether, or no, a vessel has defended herself against a legitimate attack. In the first case, members of the crew become prisoners of war, for by legitimately taking part in the fighting they have become members of the armed forces of the enemy.[5] In the second case, Articles 5 to 7 of

[1] *The Catharina Elizabeth*, (1804) 5 C. Rob. 232. See Wheaton, § 528; Twiss, ii. § 97; Phillimore, iii. § 340; Hall, § 182; Halleck, ii. p. 269; American Naval War Code, Article 10; Bordwell, p. 236; Fiore, *Code*, No. 1698. This rule had not been contested until shortly before the outbreak of the World War; but see now below, § 181 n.; Oppenheim and Triepel in *Z. V.*, viii. (1914), pp. 154-169, 378-406; Higgins, *Armed Merchantships* (1914) and *Defensively Armed Merchantships*, etc. (1917); Wehberg, pp. 66, 256-258, 283-286; Smith, *The Destruction of Merchantships under International Law* (1917), pp. 17-21; Anderson and Stowell in the *Proceedings of the American Society of International Law*, xi. (1917), pp. 11-23; Garner, i. §§ 250-264.

[2] See Wheaton, § 357; Taylor, § 496; Walker, p. 135, and *Science*, p. 268; and *International Law Notes*, iii. p. 51, where the assertion is still made by Gregory, Scott, and others.

[3] See below, § 181, and Hall, § 183.

[4] See Vattel, iii. § 226, and G. F. Martens, ii. § 289. As regards the case of Captain Fryatt, see below, § 181.

[5] This follows indirectly from Article 8 of Convention XI.

Convention XI. of the Second Peace Conference enacted the following rules [1]:—

(1) Such members of the crew as are subjects of neutral States may not be made prisoners of war.

(2) The captain and officers who are subjects of neutral States may only be made prisoners if they refuse to give a promise in writing not to serve on an enemy ship while the war lasts.

(3) The captain, officers, and such members of the crew as are enemy subjects may only be made prisoners if they refuse to give a written promise not to engage, while hostilities last, in any service connected with the operations of war.

(4) The names of all the individuals retaining their liberty under parole must be notified by the captor to the enemy, who is forbidden knowingly to employ them in any service prohibited by the parole.

However, the provision that members of the crew who were enemy subjects might only be made prisoners if they refused to give parole was *ipso facto* modified by the practice followed during the World War, according to which all enemy civilians of military age could be prevented from returning home, and could be interned. Accordingly, all the belligerents interned the enemy crews of captured enemy merchant vessels.

§ 86. The privileges of members of armed forces cannot be claimed by members of the armed forces of a belligerent who go over to the forces of the enemy and are afterwards captured by the former. They may be, and always are, treated as criminals. And the same is valid with regard to treasonable subjects of a belligerent who, without having been members of his armed forces, fight in the armed forces of the enemy. Even if they appear under the protection of a flag of truce, deserters and traitors may be seized and punished.[2]

Deserters and Traitors.

[1] See below, § 201.
[2] See below, § 222; Hall, § 190; *Land Warfare*, § 36.

VII

ENEMY CHARACTER

Grotius, iii. c. 4, §§ 6, 7—Bynkershoek, *Quaestiones Juris publici*, i. c. 3 *in fine*—Hall, §§ 167-175—Lawrence, §§ 151-159—Westlake, ii. pp. 163-176—Phillimore, iii. §§ 82-86—Twiss, ii. §§ 152-162—Taylor, §§ 468, 517—Walker, §§ 39-43—Wharton, iii. §§ 352-353—Wheaton, §§ 324-341—Hershey, Nos. 433-436—Moore, vii. §§ 1185-1194—Geffcken in *Holtzendorff*, iv. pp. 581-588—Ullmann, § 192—Nys, iii. pp. 70-84—Pradier-Fodéré, viii. Nos. 3166-3175—Bonfils, Nos. 1343-1349[1]—Despagnet, Nos. 650-653[5]—Calvo, iv. §§ 1932-1952—Fiore, iii. Nos. 1432-1436, and *Code*, Nos. 1723-1731—Boeck, Nos. 156-190—Dupuis, Nos. 92-129, and *Guerre*, Nos. 59-73—Lémonon, pp. 426-467—Higgins, p. 593—Nippold, ii. pp. 40-54—Wehberg, pp. 178-194—Garner, i. §§ 144, 155-161, 134-135, 121-138—Scott, *Conferences*, pp. 541-555—Frankenbach, *Die Rechtsstellung von neutralen Staatsangehörigen in kriegführenden Staaten* (1910)—Hirschmann, *Das internationale Prisenrecht* (1912), § 7—Baty in the *Journal of the Society of Comparative Legislation*, New Ser. ix. part i. (1908), pp. 157-166, and Westlake, *ibid.*, part ii. (1909), pp. 265-268—Baty in the *Juridical Review*, xxi. (1909), pp. 1-11—Oppenheim in the *Law Quarterly Review*, xxv. (1909), pp. 372-384—Visscher, *ibid.*, xxxi. (1915), pp. 289-298.

On Enemy Character in general.

§ 87. Since the belligerents, for the realisation of the purpose of war, are entitled to take many kinds of measures against enemy persons and enemy property, it must be determined what persons and what property are vested with enemy character. Now it is, generally speaking, correct to say that, whereas the subjects of a belligerent and their property bear enemy character, the subjects of a neutral State and their property do not bear enemy character. This rule has, however, important exceptions. For under certain circumstances and conditions enemy persons and the property of enemy subjects may not bear, and, on the other hand, subjects of a neutral State and their property may bear, enemy character. And it is even possible for a subject of a belligerent to bear for certain purposes enemy character as between himself and his home State.

The question of enemy character is, however, to a

great extent unsettled, since on many points connected with it no universally recognised rules of International Law are in existence. Before the World War, British and American courts had worked out a body of precise and clear rules, but the practice of other countries, and especially of France, had followed different lines. The Second Hague Conference of 1907 produced three articles of minor importance on the matter (Articles 16, 17, and 18 of Convention v.), which were accepted by all the signatory Powers, except Great Britain, which, upon signing the convention, entered a reservation against them. The Declaration of London comprised a number of rules which, apart from two important points, offered a common basis for the practice of all maritime States.[1] But neither the Hague Conference nor the Naval Conference of London reached a compromise upon the old controversies as to whether nationality exclusively, or domicile also, should determine the neutral or enemy character of individuals and their goods, and whether or not neutral vessels acquire enemy character by embarking in time of war, with the permission of the enemy, upon such trade with the latter as was closed to them in time of peace (rule of 1756).

When the World War broke out, these questions were still open; moreover, Great Britain and certain other belligerents had not ratified Hague Convention v., and no Power had ratified the Declaration of London. States had opportunity to fall back upon their divergent practices, and even these underwent far-reaching changes under the stress of new circumstances.

For the consideration of enemy character in detail, it is convenient to distinguish between individuals,

[1] At the first glance it would seem that only the four articles—57 to 60—of Chapter vi. headed 'Enemy Character' dealt with the subject, but a closer examination shows that Article 46, relating to a certain kind of unneutral service, Articles 55 and 56, dealing with transfer to a neutral flag, and, lastly, Article 63, relating to forcible resistance to the right of visitation, were also concerned with enemy character.

corporations, vessels, goods, the transfer of enemy vessels, and the transfer of enemy goods on enemy vessels.

Enemy Character of Individuals.

§ 88. The general rule with regard to *individuals* is that subjects of the belligerents bear enemy character, whereas subjects of neutral States do not. In this sense Article 16 of Convention v. stipulated: 'The nationals of a State which is not taking part in the war are considered to be neutral.' These neutral individuals can, however, lose their neutral character and acquire enemy character in several cases, and subjects of the belligerents can in other cases lose their enemy character:—

(1) Since relations of peace obtain between either of the belligerents and neutral States, the subjects of the latter can, by way of trade and otherwise, render many kinds of services to either belligerent without thereby losing their neutral character. On the other hand, if they enter the armed forces of a belligerent, or do certain other things in his favour, or commit hostile acts against a belligerent, they acquire enemy character.[1] All measures that are allowed during war against enemy subjects are likewise allowed against such subjects of neutral Powers as have thus acquired enemy character. For instance, during the World War hundreds of subjects of neutral States, who were fighting in the ranks of the belligerents, were captured and retained as prisoners until the end of the struggle. But such individuals must not be more severely treated than enemy subjects, and, in especial, no punitive measures are allowed against them.[1]

Subjects of neutral States not inhabiting the territory of the enemy, or any territory militarily occupied by him, do not, however, acquire enemy character by furnishing supplies or making loans to the enemy,

[1] Article 17 of Convention v.

provided the supplies do not come from the enemy territory, or any territory occupied by him.[1]

Article 18(*b*) of Convention v. laid down a new rule [2] that subjects of neutral States who render services to the enemy in matters of police and administration, likewise do not acquire enemy character. This stipulation must, however, be read with caution. It can only mean that such individuals do not lose their neutral character to a greater degree than other subjects of neutral States resident on enemy territory; it cannot mean that they are in every way to be considered and treated like subjects of neutral States not residing on enemy territory.

The acts by which subjects of neutral States lose their neutral, and acquire enemy, character need not necessarily be committed after the outbreak of war. They can, even before the outbreak of war, identify themselves to such a degree with a foreign State that, with the outbreak of war against that State, enemy character devolves upon them *ipso facto*, unless they at once sever their connection with such State. This, for instance, is the case when a foreign subject, in time of peace, enlists in the armed forces of a State and continues to serve after the outbreak of war.

(2) From the time when International Law made its appearance down to our own, no difference has been made by a belligerent between the treatment accorded to subjects of the enemy and subjects of neutral States inhabiting the enemy country. Thus Grotius [3] teaches

[1] Article 18(*a*) of Convention v.

[2] Since Great Britain entered a reservation against Articles 16, 17, and 18 of Convention v. she is not bound by them. But Articles 16, 17, and 18(*a*)—not 18(*b*)!—enacted only such rules as were always customarily recognised, *unless Article 16 be interpreted so as to prevent a belligerent from considering subjects of neutral States inhabiting the enemy country as bearing enemy character.* Different, however, is Article 18(*b*), which created an entirely new rule, for nobody had previously doubted that the members of the police force and the administrative officials of the enemy bore enemy character whether or no they were subjects of the enemy State.

[3] iii. c. 4, §§ 6, 7.

that foreigners must share the fate of the population living on enemy territory, and Bynkershoek[1] distinctly teaches that foreigners residing in enemy country bear enemy character. English[2] and American practice assert, therefore, that foreigners, whether subjects of the belligerents or of neutral States, acquire enemy character by being domiciled (*i.e.* resident) in enemy country, because they have thereby identified themselves with the enemy population, and contribute, by paying taxes and the like, to the support of the enemy Government. For this reason, all measures which may legitimately be taken against the civil population of the enemy territory, may likewise be taken against them, unless they withdraw from the country, or are expelled therefrom. It must, however, be remembered that they acquire enemy character *in a sense* and *to a certain degree* only; their enemy character is not as intensive as that of enemy subjects resident on enemy territory. Such of them as are subjects of neutral States do not, therefore, lose the protection of their home State against arbitrary treatment inconsistent with the laws of war; and such of them as are subjects of the other belligerent are handed over to the protection of the embassy of a neutral Power. However that may be, they are not exempt from requisitions and contributions; from the restrictions which an occupant imposes upon the population in the interest of the safety of his troops and his military operations; from punishments for hostile acts committed against the occupant; or from being taken into captivity, if exceptionally necessary.

This treatment of foreigners resident on occupied enemy territory is generally recognised as legitimate

[1] *Quaestiones Juris publici*, i. c. 3 *in fine*.

[2] See *The Harmony*, (1800) 2 C. Rob. 322; *The Johanna Emilie*, otherwise *Emilia*, (1854) Spinks 12; *The Baltica*, (1857) 11 Moore P.C. 141.

by theory[1] and practice. The proposal of Germany, made at the Second Hague Conference, to agree upon rules which would have stipulated a more favourable treatment for subjects of neutral States resident on occupied enemy territory was, therefore, rejected. Not even France supported the German proposals, although, according to the French conception then prevailing,[2] foreigners residing in enemy country did not acquire enemy character, and the German proposals were only a logical consequence of it.[3]

(3) Since enemy subjects who reside in neutral countries, or are allowed to remain resident on the territory of the other belligerent, have to a great extent identified themselves with the local population and are not under the territorial supremacy of the enemy, they lost their enemy character according to the English and American practice which prevailed before the World War,[4] although according to French practice they did not, a difference which bore upon many points, especially upon the character of goods.[5]

During the World War, however, Great Britain abandoned her former practice in many respects. As regards enemy subjects resident in neutral States, the

[1] See Albrecht, *Requisitionen von neutralem Privateigenthum*, etc. (1912), pp. 13-15, and Hirsch, *Die rechtliche Stellung der Angehorigen neutraler Staaten* (1914), pp. 80-84. See also below, § 170.

[2] See Garner, i. § 144, who points out that during the World War French trading with the enemy legislation abandoned this conception.

[3] This French conception of enemy character dated from the judgment of the *Conseil des Prises* in the case of *Le Hardy contre La Voltigeante* (1802) — see 1 Pistoye et Duverdy, 321—which laid down the rule that neutral subjects residing in enemy country do not lose their neutral character, and enemy subjects residing in neutral countries do not lose their enemy character. But this conception of enemy character had developed, not with regard to the treatment of foreigners whom an occupant finds resident on occupied enemy territory, but with regard to the exercise of the right of capture of enemy vessels and goods in warfare at sea. France did not attempt to follow out its logical consequences by meting out to foreigners resident on occupied territory treatment different from that of enemy subjects resident there.

[4] See *The Postilion*, (1779) Hay and Marriot 245; *The Danous*, (1802) 4 C. Rob. 255 n.; *The Venus*, (1814) 8 Cranch 253.

[5] See below, § 90.

Trading with the Enemy (Extension of Powers) Act, 1915,[1] authorised His Majesty by proclamation to prohibit all persons in the United Kingdom from trading with any persons in foreign countries whose *enemy nationality* or *enemy association* made such prohibition expedient, and constituted such trading trading with the enemy. Statutory lists (so-called 'black lists') were issued under this Act, which proscribed a large number of persons and firms in various States then neutral.[2] But trade with enemy subjects resident in neutral States whose names were not on these lists was not illegal. When the United States entered the war, she also adopted a policy similar to the new British policy.[3] As regards enemy subjects resident in Great Britain, orders made under the Aliens Restriction Act, 1914,[4] placed them under special restrictions; the Trading with the Enemy (Amendment) Act, 1916,[5] and later acts, singled out their property for exceptionally disadvantageous treatment with a view to eliminating their commercial influence; [6] and the Aliens Restriction (Amendment) Act, 1919,[7] saddled them with disabilities not limited to the duration of the war. American legislation was not dissimilar.[8] At the end of the war the victorious Powers reserved the general right to retain and liquidate all property of enemy subjects then within their territory.[9]

Enemy Character of Corporations.

§ 88*a*. There are no rules of International Law to determine whether a corporation possesses enemy character, and the question was much debated at the outbreak of the World War. The rapid development

[1] 5 & 6 Geo. v. c. 98.

[2] As to the resulting controversy with the United States, see *Parl. Papers*, Misc., No. 11 (1916), Cd. 8225, and No. 36 (1916), Cd. 8353, and Garner, i. §§ 156-160.

[3] See the American Trading with the Enemy Act of 1917, § 2(*c*), in *A.J.*, xii. (1918), Supplement, p. 27; Garner, i. §§ 144, 161.

[4] 4 & 5 Geo. v. c. 12.

[5] 5 & 6 Geo. v. c. 105.

[6] For details see M'Nair, *Legal Effects of War* (1920), and an article in the *Journal of Comparative Legislation*, 3rd Ser. ii. (1920), pp. 269-283.

[7] 9 & 10 Geo. v. c. 92.

[8] Garner, i. §§ 72-74.

[9] See, for example, Treaty of Peace with Germany, Article 297.

of joint stock enterprise had taken little account of warlike conditions, and the principle of company law, that a corporation is an entity distinct from its members, had not yet come into serious conflict with them.

British opinion was generally agreed, on the authority of *Janson* v. *Driefontein Consolidated Mines*,[1] that a corporation incorporated in an enemy country had enemy character. But it was doubtful whether a corporation carrying on business in an enemy country, but not incorporated there, also possessed enemy character, and, further, whether a corporation neither incorporated nor carrying on business in an enemy country could under any circumstances acquire that character. The first of these questions at once arose in connection with trading with the enemy,[2] and early proclamations, after some confusion of thought, settled down to the view that enemy character attached to companies 'wherever incorporated, *carrying on business* in an enemy country.'[3] The second question was carried to the House of Lords in the *Daimler* case,[4] where it was laid down that a company assumes enemy character 'if its agents or the persons in *de facto* control of its affairs are resident in an enemy country, or, wherever resident, are adhering to the enemy or taking instructions from or acting under the control of enemies. . . . The character of individual shareholders cannot of itself affect the character of the company.'[5]

The French courts, confronted with the same difficulty, held that, in order to determine enemy character,

[1] [1902] A. C. 484, at p. 497.

[2] See below, § 101.

[3] See M'Nair, *Legal Effects of War* (1920), p. 122, and the Proclamation of September 14, 1914.

[4] *Daimler Co. Ltd.* v. *Continental Tyre and Rubber (Great Britain) Co. Ltd.*, [1916] 2 A. C. 307.

[5] At p. 345. In *The Poona*, (1915) 1 B. and C. P. C. 275, the Prize Court had reached a different conclusion. But that decision was prior to the decision of the House of Lords in the *Daimler* case. For a detailed discussion of the nationality of corporations, see M'Nair, *op. cit.*, Schuster in the *Grotius Society*, ii. pp. 57-85, and the other literature cited above, vol. i. § 293 n. See also *The Polzeath*, [1916] P. 117.

they had the right 'to go to the bottom of things and ascertain whether the company was a French company in reality or such only in appearance.'[1]

American practice, on the other hand, while also attaching enemy character to companies incorporated, or carrying on business, in an enemy country,[2] did not attribute such character to a company neither incorporated nor doing business there. Its courts 'are entirely wedded to the doctrine that the corporators of a corporation are conclusively presumed to be citizens of the same State as the corporation.'[3]

Enemy Character of Vessels.

§ 89. The general rule before the World War with regard to vessels was that their character is determined by their flag. This is still the test in the case of a vessel sailing under the enemy flag.[4] Whatever may be the nationality of her owner—whether a subject of a neutral State, or of either belligerent—she bears enemy character. But the converse, namely that an enemy-owned vessel which sails under a neutral flag no more bears enemy character than the vessel of the subject of a neutral State sailing under the flag of another neutral State, did not secure acceptance during the World War by the Prize Courts of belligerents. Even before the World War, the flag of a neutral State was the deciding factor only when the vessel was legitimately sailing under it. Should it be found that a vessel sailing under the flag of a certain neutral State had, according to the Municipal Law of such State, no right to fly the flag she

[1] *Société Conserve Lenzbourg*, cited by Garner, i. § 153. *Journal du Droit international* (Clunet), xlii. (1915), p. 1164.

[2] See § 2*a* of the American Trading with the Enemy Act, 1917.

[3] *Fritz-Schultz Co.* v. *Raimes Co.*, (1917) 164 N.Y.S. 454, cited by Garner, i. § 154. See also *Stumpf* v. *Scheiber Brewing Co.*, (1917) 242 Fed. 80, also cited by Garner.

[4] It makes no difference that the owner be the subject of a neutral non-littoral State without a maritime flag, and that the vessel is, therefore, compelled to fly the flag of a maritime State: if the flag the vessel flies be the enemy flag, she bears enemy character. Nor, if a vessel flies an enemy flag, will she escape condemnation by being mortgaged to subjects of a non-enemy State. See *The Marie Glæser*, (1914) 1 B. and C. P. C. 38; [1914] P. 218. The Prize Court disregards mortgages and liens on enemy vessels,

showed, the real character of the vessel had to be determined in order to decide whether or no she bore enemy character. Moreover, there were exceptions to the rule.

(1) As was provided by Article 46 of the unratified Declaration of London,[1] a neutral merchantman acquired enemy character by taking a direct part in the hostilities,[2] by being in the exclusive employment of the enemy Government, and by being at the time exclusively intended either for the transport of troops or for the transmission of intelligence for the enemy. The act by which a neutral vessel acquired enemy character need not necessarily have been committed *after* the outbreak of war, for she could, even *before* the outbreak of war, to such a degree identify herself with a foreign State that, with the outbreak of war against such State, enemy character devolved upon her *ipso facto*, unless she severed her connection with it. This was, for instance, the position of a foreign merchantman which in time of peace had been hired by a State for the transport of troops or of war material, and continued to carry out her contract in spite of the outbreak of war.[3]

(2) As was provided by Article 63 of the unratified declaration, a neutral merchantman acquired enemy character *ipso facto* by forcibly resisting the legitimate exercise of the right of visit and capture.[4]

[1] See below, § 410.

[2] Whether the crew of a neutral ship taking a direct part in hostilities can only be made prisoners of war, or whether they can be punished as war criminals, does not seem to be settled. Schramm, *Das Prisenrecht* (1913), p. 358, adopts the second alternative.

[3] In the case of *The Kow-shing*, which has lost its former importance, a British ship, just before the outbreak of the Chino-Japanese War, was hired by the Chinese Government to transport Chinese soldiers and ammunition to Korea. She was met in Korean waters by the Japanese fleet, stopped, visited, and ordered to follow a Japanese cruiser. Although the British captain was ready to comply, the Chinese on board would not allow it. Thereupon the Japanese opened fire and sank the vessel. As then hostilities could be commenced without a previous declaration of war, the action of the Japanese was in accordance with the rules of International Law. See Hall, § 168*; Takahashi, *Cases on International Law during the Chino-Japanese War* (1899), pp. 27-51; Holland, *Studies*, pp. 126-128.

[4] See below, § 422.

(3) According to British practice—adopted by America and Japan[1]—neutral merchantmen likewise acquired enemy character if they violated the so-called rule of 1756,[2] by engaging in time of war in a trade which the enemy prior to the war reserved exclusively for merchantmen sailing under his own flag. The unratified Declaration of London neither rejected nor accepted this rule of 1756, for Article 57 stipulated expressly that this case remained unsettled.

These exceptions were admitted before the World War, and are still valid. But, if the Declaration of London had been ratified, no exception to the rule laid down in its Article 57 (that subject to the provisions respecting transfer to another flag, the character of a vessel was to be determined by the flag she was entitled to fly) would have been recognised on the ground that a vessel, though lawfully flying a neutral flag, was owned wholly or partly by a person with enemy character.

No doubt the British practice formerly prevailing was said to recognise such an exception where a vessel sailing under a neutral flag was in part owned by an enemy subject.[3] Thus in *The Industrie*,[4] Dr. Lushington said: 'When the vessel is sailing under a neutral flag, the captors may show that all the property is not neutral, but part of it belongs to an enemy, and in that case you divide it, and condemn the part which is hostile and not the part which is neutral.' This *obiter dictum* was all the more remarkable as in an earlier case[5] it had been held that ships had *in toto* the character with which they were invested by their flag 'to the exclusion of any claims of interest that persons living in neutral

[1] See *The Montara* in Takahashi, p. 633, and Hurst, ii. p. 403. On the other hand, the Russian Supreme Prize Court rejected the rule of 1756 in *The Thea*; see Hurst, i. p. 96.

[2] See below, § 289, and Higgins, *War and the Private Citizen* (1912), pp. 169-192.

[3] See Hall, § 169, p. 524, n. 2; Holland, *Prize Law*, § 19, No. 3; Westlake, ii. p. 170.

[4] (1854) Spinks 54.

[5] See *The Vrow Elizabeth*, (1803) 5 C. Rob. 2, at p. 4.

countries may actually have in them.' For this reason the shares of a neutral in an enemy ship were condemned.[1]

However, Article 57 of the unratified Declaration of London was put into force[2] by Great Britain at the outbreak of war, and this precluded any inquiry into the character of the owners of the vessel.

France also put Article 57 into force; but the plans adopted by Germany for buying neutral vessels and sailing them under a neutral flag[3] soon convinced both Great Britain and France that it must be abandoned. Accordingly, by Order in Council dated October 20, 1915, Great Britain abrogated this article, and declared that for the future British Prize Courts would follow the former British practice.[4] France made a similar change of policy.[5] The British Prize Court considered the character of a German-owned vessel flying a British flag in the case of *The St. Tudno*,[6] and a neutral flag in the case of *The Hamborn*,[7] and it was held that 'it is a settled rule of prize law based on the principles upon which prize courts act, that they will penetrate through and beyond forms and technicalities to the facts and realities. This . . . means that . . . the owners are

[1] See also *The Primus*, (1854) Spinks 48.

[2] As to the legal operation in British Prize Law of the Order in Council of August 20, 1914 (*London Gazette*, August 21, 1914), which put the Declaration of London into force with certain modifications, see *The Proton*, (1918) 3 B. and C. P. C. 125.

[3] See the cases of the Wagner ships (*American Transatlantic Company, owners of the steamships Kankakee, Hocking and Genesee* v. *His Majesty's Procurator-General*, (1917) reported on appeal in *The Times* of July 24, 1920), and Garner, i. § 135. A German financier in the winter of 1914 and the following year purchased eleven neutral ships through neutral agents, and made an arrangement through these agents with Wagner, an American subject of German origin, under which Wagner was to float an American company to sail the vessels and secure for them American registry. Almost as soon as American registry was obtained, however, Great Britain and France (see above) abandoned Article 57 of the Declaration of London and several of the ships were captured and condemned as being German-owned, though flying the American flag.

[4] See Garner, i. § 134.

[5] See Garner, *ibid.*, who cites the French case of *The Willkommen.*

[6] (1916) 2 B. and C. P. C. 273; [1916] P. 291.

[7] (1917) 3 B. and C. P. C. 80, 379; [1918] P. 19; [1919] A.C. 993.

bound by the flag which they have chosen to adopt, but captors as against them are not so bound.'[1]

The following rules apply to all neutral vessels which have acquired enemy character:—(*a*) all enemy goods on board may be confiscated, even if, when they were first shipped, the vessels were neutral; (*b*) all goods on board will be presumed to be enemy goods, and the owners of neutral goods will have to prove their neutral character; (*c*) the rules concerning the sinking of neutral prizes do not apply, because these vessels are now enemy vessels.

Enemy Character of Goods.

§ 90. It is an old customary rule[2] that all goods found on board an enemy merchantman are presumed to be enemy goods unless the contrary is proved by neutral owners. It is, further, generally recognised that the enemy character of goods depends upon the enemy character of their owners. As, however, no universally recognised rules exist as to the enemy character of individuals, there are no universally recognised rules as to the enemy character of goods. The unratified Declaration of London did not purport to lay down any, because the Powers could not reach agreement.

(1) Since, according to British and American practice, domicile in enemy country makes an individual bear enemy character,[3] all goods belonging[4] to individuals domiciled in enemy country are enemy goods, and all

[1] 3 B. and C. P. C. 80, at p. 83. On the case of *The Presidente Mitre*, see Garner, i. § 135.

[2] See *The Roland*, (1915) 1 B. and C. P. C. 188, and the French case of *The Porto*, (1915), *R.G.*, xxiii. (1916), Jurisprudence, p. 66, and Garner, i. § 113. The rule was embodied in the unratified Declaration of London.

[3] See, for example, the definition of 'enemy' as 'persons and bodies of persons resident or carrying on business in any country with which His Majesty is for the time being at War' in the Trading with the Enemy (Amendment) Act, 1914 (5. Geo. v. c. 12), and the definition in the American Trading with the Enemy Act of 1917 cited by Garner, i. § 144.

[4] The British Prize Court does not recognise the claims of a pledgee, but has regard to the legal ownership of the goods. *The Odessa*, (1914) 1 B. and C. P. C. 163, 554; and cp. *The Ningchow*, (1915) 1 B. and C. P. C. 288; [1916] P. 221, where the pledgors had lost their right to redeem, and had thereby ceased to be owners.

goods belonging to individuals not resident in enemy country are not, as a rule, enemy goods. For this reason, goods belonging to enemy subjects residing in neutral countries [1] do not, but goods belonging to subjects of neutral States residing in enemy country [2] do bear enemy character, although they may be the goods of a foreign consul appointed and residing in enemy country.[3] Further, the goods of subjects of one belligerent domiciled on the territory of the other and allowed to remain there after the outbreak of war, acquire enemy character in the eyes of the former, but lose it (for the purposes of prize law) in the eyes of the latter.[4] Again, the produce of an estate on enemy territory belonging to an absent neutral subject bears enemy character, for 'nothing [5] can be more decided and fixed than the principle . . . that the possession of the soil does impress upon the owner the character of the country, as far as the produce of that plantation is concerned . . . whatever the local residence of the owner may be.' Further, the property of a house of trade established in an enemy country by a neutral subject resident elsewhere likewise bears enemy character, because the owner has a 'commercial domicile' in enemy country.[6] Lastly, the enemy character of property of an enemy subject domiciled in enemy

[1] *The Postilion*, (1779) Hay and Marriot, 245; *The Danous*, (1802) 4 C. Rob. 255 n. But if an enemy subject with a neutral domicile abandons it before the capture of his goods, these goods then bear enemy character; *The Flamengo*, (1915) 1 B. and C. P. C. 509. Goods belonging to an enemy firm in a neutral country where foreigners are exterritorial (such as China) bear enemy character; *The Eumaeus*, (1915) 1 B. and C. P. C. 605.

[2] *The Baltica*, (1857) 11 Moore P.C. 141.

[3] *The Indian Chief*, (1801) 3 C. Rob. 12.

[4] *The Venus*, (1814) 8 Cranch 253.

[5] From the judgment of Sir William Scott in the case of *The Phœnix*, (1803) 5 C. Rob. 41; see also *The Asturian*, (1916) 2 B. and C. P. C. 202; [1916] P. 150; *Thirty Hogsheads of Sugar* v. *Boyle* (*Bentzen* v. *Boyle*), (1815) 9 Cranch 191.

[6] *The Anglo-Mexican* and *The Lutzow*, (1917) 3 B. and C. P. C. 24, 37. The Judicial Committee of the Privy Council, in reversing the decisions of the courts below, laid down the limit of this doctrine. See also the old cases of *The Portland*, (1800) 3 C. Rob. 41; *The Jonge Klassina*, (1803) 5 C. Rob. 297; *The Freundschaft*, (1819) 4 Wheaton 105.

territory is unaffected by the fact that he has a house of trade in a neutral State.[1]

(2) On the other hand, according to French practice prior to the World War, the nationality of the owner of the goods was exclusively the deciding factor, and it did not matter where he resided. Hence only such goods on enemy merchantmen bore enemy character as belonged to subjects of the enemy, whether they were residing on enemy or neutral territory; and all such goods on enemy merchantmen as belonged to subjects of neutral States did not bear enemy character, whether those subjects resided on neutral or enemy country.[2]

During the Turco-Italian War, the Italian courts adopted the French practice. But the exigencies of the World War[3] compelled France herself to adopt a different policy.

Transfer of Enemy Vessels.

§ 91. The question of the transfer[4] of enemy vessels to subjects of neutral States, either shortly before or during war, forms part of the larger question of enemy character, for the point to be decided is whether such transfer[5] divests these vessels of their enemy character. It is obvious that, if it does, owners of enemy merchantmen can evade the danger of having their property seized and confiscated by selling their vessels to subjects of neutral States. Before the Naval Conference of London of 1908-1909, the maritime Powers had not agreed upon common rules concerning this subject. According to French[6] practice no transfer of

[1] *The Clan Grant*, (1915) 1 B. and C. P. C. 272.

[2] See the French cases of *Le Hardy contre La Voltigeante* (1802) and *La Paix* (1803) 1 Pistoye et Duverdy 321 and 486; *Le Joan* (1870); *Le Nicolaus* (1871); *Le Thalia* (1871); *Le Laura-Louise* (1871); Barboux 101, 108, 116, 119.

[3] See Coquet in *R.G.*, xxi. (1914), pp. 253-258.

[4] This subject is fully discussed by Garner, i. §§ 121-138.

[5] See Holland, *Prize Law*, § 19; Hall, § 171; Twiss, ii. §§ 162-163; Phillimore, iii. § 486; Boeck, Nos. 178-180; Bonfils, Nos. 1344-1349[1]; Dupuis, Nos. 117-129, and *Guerre*, Nos. 62-66.

[6] See Dupuis, No. 97; Garner, i. §§ 126-127.

enemy vessels to neutrals after the outbreak of war could be recognised, and a vessel thus transferred retained enemy character; but any legitimate transfer anterior to the outbreak of war did give neutral character to a vessel. According to British and American practice,[1] on the other hand, enemy vessels could be transferred to a neutral flag, before or after the outbreak of war, and lose thereby their enemy character, provided that the transfer took place *bona fide*,[2] was not effected either in a blockaded port[3] or while the vessel was *in transitu*,[4] and the vendor did not retain an interest in the vessel, or any right to recover or repurchase the vessel after the war.[5]

Clear and decisive rules concerning the transfer of enemy vessels, which distinguished between transfer to a neutral flag *before* and *after* the outbreak of hostilities, were laid down in the unratified Declaration of London.[6]

(1) According to Article 55 the transfer of an enemy vessel to a neutral flag, if effected *before* the outbreak of hostilities, was to be *valid*, unless the captor was able to prove that it was made in order to avoid capture. However, if the bill of sale was not on board, and the transfer was effected less than sixty days before the outbreak of hostilities, it was to be presumed to be void, unless the vessel could prove that it was not effected in order to avoid capture. To provide commerce with a guarantee that a transfer should not easily be treated as void on the ground that it was effected to evade capture, it was stipulated that, if the transfer was effected more than thirty days before the outbreak of hostilities, there was to be an absolute

[1] Garner, i. §§ 127-128.

[2] *The Vigilantia*, (1798) 1 C. Rob. 1; *The Baltica*, (1857) 11 Moore P.C. 141; *The Benito Estenger*, (1899) 176 U. S. 568.

[3] *The General Hamilton*, (1805) 6 C. Rob. 61.

[4] The moment a vessel transferred *in transitu* reaches a port where the new owner takes possession of her, the voyage of the vessel is considered to have terminated. *The Vrow Margaretha*, (1799) 1 C. Rob. 336; *The Jan Frederick*, (1804) 5 C. Rob. 128.

[5] *The Sechs Geschwistern*, (1801) 4 C. Rob. 100; *The Jemmy*, (1801) 4 C. Rob. 31.

[6] Garner, i. §§ 129-130.

presumption of its validity, provided that it was unconditional, complete, and in conformity with the laws of the countries concerned, and that neither the control of, nor the profits arising from, the employment of the vessel remained in the same hands as before the transfer. But even in this case a vessel was to be suspect if the transfer took place less than sixty days before the outbreak of hostilities, and her bill of sale was not on board. Hence she might be seized and brought into a port for investigation by a prize court, and could not claim damages for the capture, even if the court released her.

(2) According to Article 56, the transfer of an enemy vessel to a neutral flag *after* the outbreak of hostilities was to be *void* unless the owner could prove that the transfer was not made in order to avoid capture. Moreover, there was to be an irrebuttable presumption that the transfer was void, if it had been made in a blockaded port, or while the vessel was *in transitu*, or if a right to repurchase or recover the vessel was reserved to the vendor, or the requirements of the Municipal Law governing the right to fly the flag under which the vessel was sailing had not been fulfilled.

The Italian courts acted upon the articles of the unratified declaration during the Turco-Italian War and condemned the two sailing vessels *Vasilios* and *Aghios Gorghios*, originally Turkish, but *after* the outbreak of war sold to a Greek subject, and registered under the Greek flag.[1]

Again, at the outbreak of the World War, Great Britain, France, and Russia determined to give effect to these articles,[2] and the important case of *The Dacia* was decided in accordance with them by the French Prize Court. The *Dacia* was purchased after the out-

[1] See Garner, i. § 129 n.

[2] For a British case where an attempt had been made to transfer a German vessel to the British flag while *in transitu* just before the outbreak of war between Great Britain and Germany, see *The Tommi*, (1914) 1 B. and C. P. C. 16; [1914] P. 251. See also the Canadian case of *The Bellas*, (1914) 1 B. and C. P. C. 95, and the French case of *The Colonia*, in *R.G.*, xxii. (1915), Jurisprudence, pp. 45-47, and Garner, i. § 123.

break of war from a German company by an American citizen, while she was lying in an American port and admitted to American registry, the United States being then neutral. She was captured by a French cruiser on the way to Rotterdam and condemned. The court held that the claimant had failed to establish that the transfer was not made to avoid capture.[1]

The rules and practices so far considered in this section relate only to the transfer of *private* enemy vessels; they do not apply to the transfer by a belligerent State to a neutral of one of his men-of-war with a view to escape capture. The question whether a war-vessel could thus divest itself of enemy character arose during the World War, when two German cruisers, *Goeben* and *Breslau*, unable to escape from the Mediterranean, ran up the Dardanelles to Constantinople, and were there reported to have been sold to Turkey, then neutral. Vessels so transferred by a belligerent to a neutral *subject* had come before the British[2] and American[3] Prize Courts in older wars and had been condemned, on the ground that a belligerent war-vessel cannot put off its enemy character during a war.

Transfer of Goods on Enemy Vessels.

§ 92. The transfer of enemy goods on enemy vessels likewise forms part of the larger subject of enemy character, for the question here also is whether such a transfer divests these goods of their enemy character,[4] and there

[1] See *R.G.*, xxii. (1915), Jurisprudence, p. 83, and *A.J.*, ix. (1915), p. 1015. Compare *The Edna*, (1919) 3 B. and C. P. C. 407. See also Garner, i. §§ 124-125, 132-133, 136, 138, who discusses the points raised, and mentions the cases of *The Brindilla*, *Platuria*, and *Petrolite*, the German case of *The Pass of Balmaha*, and abortive negotiations between Chili and Great Britain for the recognition of the validity of the transfer to the Chilian flag of German vessels which the Chilian Government desired to purchase. Later in the war, when the shortage of shipping became acute, Great Britain raised no objection to the transfer of an enemy vessel to the American flag. See Garner, i. § 136 n.

[2] *The Minerva*, (1807) 6 C. Rob. 396.

[3] See *The Georgia*, (1868) 7 Wall. 32, and Garner, i. § 139, who also cites the American case of *The Etta*, (1864) 25 Fed. Cases No. 15, p. 60.

[4] See Hall, § 172; Twiss, ii. §§ 162, 163; Phillimore, iii. §§ 487, 488; Dupuis, Nos. 141-149, and *Guerre*, Nos. 68-73; Boeck, Nos. 182, 183.

was likewise no unanimous practice among the maritime States when the Naval Conference met in London in 1908-1909. British and American practice has always refused to recognise a sale *after the outbreak of war* of goods *in transitu* if the vessel was captured before the neutral buyer had actually taken possession of the goods.[1] On the other hand, French practice used to recognise such a sale *in transitu,* provided it could be proved to have been *bona fide.*[2]

The unratified Declaration of London provided by Article 60 that enemy goods on board an enemy vessel retained their enemy character until they reached their destination, notwithstanding any transfer effected after the outbreak of hostilities while the goods were *in transitu.* Such goods might therefore be confiscated, although they had been sold *in transitu* to subjects of neutral States.[3]

At the outbreak of the World War, Great Britain and some of the other belligerents gave effect to this article. It did not, however, cover a case in which goods sold by an enemy to a neutral and consigned to him were captured in transit, and before they had actually been delivered to him. According to British practice, the material question in such a case is when did the property in the goods pass. If they had been sold to the neutral

[1] *The Jan Frederick,* (1804) 5 C. Rob. 128; *The Ann Green,* (1812) 1 Gallison 274. Where, however, goods are sold by an enemy to a neutral *in transitu bona fide* before the outbreak of war, and without expectation of war, though war intervenes, the goods are not liable to confiscation. *The Southfield,* (1915) 1 B. and C. P. C. 332.

[2] See Boeck, No. 162; Dupuis, No. 142.

[3] A special rule was provided for the case of an enemy consignee of goods on board an enemy vessel becoming bankrupt while the goods were *in transitu.* In a number of countries—Great Britain is one of them, see § 44 of the Sale of Goods Act, 1893 (56 & 57 Vict. c. 71)—an unpaid vendor has, in the event of the bankruptcy of the buyer, a recognised legal right to recover such goods as have already become the property of the buyer, but have not yet reached him (right of stoppage *in transitu*). For this reason, Article 60 stipulated that if, prior to the capture, the neutral consignor exercised, on the bankruptcy of the enemy consignee, his right of stoppage *in transitu,* the goods regained their neutral character, and might not be confiscated.

bona fide and without expectation of war, then, even though war had broken out before shipment, Municipal Law is applied to determine when the property in the goods passed to the buyer, and if it passed before shipment, the goods are not confiscated.[1] Where, on the other hand, the goods are sold after the outbreak of war (or even when war is imminent), prize law is applied to the question when the property passed, and, under prize law, goods consigned by an enemy to a neutral do not become neutral property until actual delivery.[2] On the other hand, according to prize law, goods consigned by a neutral to an enemy are liable to capture in transit, although by Municipal Law the property may still remain in the neutral vendor.[3] The captor's rights cannot be defeated by 'a mere transfer of legal ownership by documents.'[4]

[1] *The Parchim*, (1915) 1 B. and C. P. C. 579, reversed on appeal, 2 B. and C. P. C. 489.

[2] *The United States*, (1916) 2 B. and C. P. C. 390, 525; *The Kronprinsessan Margareta*, (1917) 2 B. and C. P. C. 409; *The Dirigo*, (1919) 3 B. and C. P. C. 439.

[3] An interesting case is *The Palm Branch*, (1916) 2 B. and C. P. C. 281, 3 B. and C. P. C. 241, where neutral property became enemy property after capture but before hearing. Compare *The Orteric*, [1920] A. C. 724.

[4] See *The United States*, (1916) 2 B. and C. P. C. 390, at p. 393.

CHAPTER II

THE OUTBREAK OF WAR

I

COMMENCEMENT OF WAR

Grotius, iii. c. 3, §§ 5-14—Bynkershoek, *Quaestiones Juris publici*, i. c. 2—Vattel, iii. §§ 51-65—Hall, § 123—Westlake, ii. pp. 19-28—Lawrence, § 140—Manning, pp. 161-163—Phillimore, iii. §§ 51-66—Twiss, ii. §§ 31-40—Halleck, i. pp. 521-526—Taylor, §§ 455-456—Moore, vii. §§ 1106-1108—Walker, § 37—Hershey, Nos. 338-342—Wharton, iii. §§ 333-335—Wheaton, § 297—Bluntschli, §§ 521-528—Heffter, § 120—Lueder in *Holtzendorff*, iv. pp. 332-347—Gareis, § 80—Liszt, § 39, v.—Ullmann, § 171—Bonfils, Nos. 1027-1031[2]—Despagnet, Nos. 513-516—Merignhac, iii[a]. pp. 64-84—Pradier-Fodéré, vi. Nos. 2671-2693—Nys, iii. pp. 29-49—Rivier, ii. pp. 220-228—Calvo, iv. §§ 1899-1911—Fiore, iii. Nos. 1272-1276, and *Code*, Nos. 1427-1433—Martens, ii. § 109—Longuet, §§ 1-7, 15-16—Pillet, pp. 61-72—Lawrence, *War*, pp. 26-44—Barclay, *Problems*, pp. 53-58—Boidin, pp. 116-121—Bordwell, pp. 198-200—Higgins, pp. 202-205—Holland, *War*, § 16—Lémonon, pp. 395-406—Nippold, ii. pp. 6-10—Scott, *Conferences*, pp. 516-522—Spaight, pp. 20-33—Ariga, §§ 11-12—Takahashi, pp. 1-25—*Land Warfare*, §§ 8-10—Holland, *Studies*, p. 115—Sainte-Croix, *La Déclaration de Guerre et ses Effets immédiats* (1892)—Bruyas, *De la Déclaration de Guerre*, etc. (1899)—Tambaro, *L'inizio della Guerra et la 3ª Convenzione dell'Aja del 1907* (1911)—Maurel, *De la Déclaration de Guerre* (1907)—Soughimoura, *De la Déclaration de Guerre* (1912)—Brocher in *R.I.*, iv. (1872), p. 400; Féraud-Giraud in *R.I.*, xvii. (1885), p. 19; Nagaoka in *R.I.*, 2nd Ser. vi. p. 475—Rolin in *Annuaire*, xx. (1904), pp. 64-70—Ebren and Martens in *R.G.*, xi. (1904), pp. 133, 148—Dupuis in *R.G.*, xiii. (1906), pp. 725-735—Stowell in *A.J.*, ii. (1908), pp. 50-62.

Commencement of War in general.

§ 93. According to the former practice, a condition of war could arise, either through a declaration of war, or through a proclamation and manifesto by a State that it considered itself at war with another State, or through one State committing hostile acts of force against another State. History presents many instances of wars commenced in one of these three ways. Although Grotius laid down the rule that a declaration of war is necessary for its commencement,[1] the practice of the States shows that this rule was not accepted, and many wars have taken place between the time of Grotius and our own without a previous[2] declaration of war. No doubt many writers,[3] following the example of Grotius, have always asserted the existence of a rule that a declaration is necessary for the commencement of war; but it cannot be denied that, until the Second Peace Conference of 1907, such a rule was neither sanctioned by custom, nor by a general treaty of the Powers. Moreover, many writers[4] distinctly approved of the practice of the Powers.

This does not mean that in former times a State would have been justified in opening hostilities without any preceding conflict. There was, and can be, no greater violation of the Law of Nations than for a State to begin hostilities in time of peace without previous controversy, and without having endeavoured to settle the conflict by negotiation.[5] But if negotiation had been tried without success, a State did not act treacherously by resorting to hostilities without a declaration of war, especially after diplomatic intercourse had been broken off. The rule, adopted by the First and Second Hague Conferences,[6] that, *as far as circumstances allow*, before appeal to arms recourse must be had to the good offices or mediation of friendly Powers, did not essentially alter matters, for the formula *as far as circum-*

[1] iii. c. 3, § 5.

[2] See Maurice, *Hostilities without Declaration of War* (1883).

[3] See, for instance, Vattel, iii. § 51; Calvo, iv. § 1907; Bluntschli, § 521; Fiore, iii. Nos 1274-1275; Heffter, § 120.

[4] See, for instance, Bynkershoek, *Quaestiones Juris publici*, i. c. 2; Klüber, § 238; G. F. Martens, § 267; Twiss, ii. § 35; Phillimore, iii. §§ 51-55; Hall, § 123; Ullmann (first edition), § 145; Gareis, § 80.

[5] See above, § 3, where the rule is quoted that no State is allowed to make use of compulsive means of settling differences before negotiation has been tried.

[6] Article 2 of Convention I.

stances allow in practice leaves everything to the discretion of the Power bent on making war.

The outbreak of war between Russia and Japan in 1904, through Japanese torpedo boats attacking Russian men-of-war at Port Arthur before a formal declaration of war, caused a movement for the establishment of some written rules concerning the commencement of war. The Institute of International Law, at its meeting at Ghent in 1906, adopted three principles,[1] according to which war should not be commenced without either a declaration of war or an ultimatum, and, in either case, delay sufficient to provide against treacherous surprise should be allowed before the belligerent had recourse to actual hostilities. The Second Hague Conference in 1907 took up the matter and produced Convention III. relative to the commencement of hostilities.

Declaration of War.

§ 94. According to Article 1 of Convention III. hostilities must not commence without a previous and unequivocal warning, which may take the form either of a declaration of war, stating the reasons why the Power concerned has recourse to arms, or of an ultimatum with a conditional declaration of war.

A declaration of war is a communication by one State to another that the condition of peace between them has come to an end, and a condition of war has taken its place. In former times, declarations of war used to take place with greater or lesser solemnities; but during the last few centuries all these formalities have vanished, and nowadays it may take place through a simple communication.[2] The only two conditions with

[1] See *Annuaire*, xxi. (1906), p. 283.

[2] Thus, on July 28, 1914, Austria-Hungary addressed a formal declaration of war to Serbia. (*Collected Diplomatic Documents* (1915), p. 44.) On August 2, 1914, the German ambassador at Petrograd handed a declaration of war to the Russian Foreign Minister (*ibid.*, p. 234). On August 3, 1914, the German ambassador at Paris handed to the French Minister for Foreign Affairs a letter alleging hostile acts by French forces, and stating that 'in the presence of

which, according to Article 1, declarations of war must comply, are, that they must be unmistakable, and that they must state the reason for resort to arms. No delay between the declaration and the actual commencement of hostilities is stipulated, and it is, therefore, possible for a Power to open hostilities immediately after the communication of the declaration of war to the enemy. All the more is it necessary to emphasise that there could be no greater violation of the Law of Nations than to send a declaration of war without having previously tried to settle a difference by negotiation.

How then must the communication of a declaration of war be made? Since a rule is nowhere expressly formulated that the declaration must be communicated in writing, it might be asserted that communication by any means, be it by a written document, by telegraph or by telephone message, or by direct word of mouth, is admissible. I believe that such an assertion cannot be supported. The essential importance of the declaration of war, and the fact that according to Article 1 of Convention III. it must be unmistakable and must state the reason for resort to arms, would seem to require a written document, which is to be handed over to the other party by an envoy. Further, the fact that Article 2 of Convention III. expressly enacts that the notification of the outbreak of war to neutrals *may even be made by telegraph*, points the same way, for the conclusion is justified that the declaration of war stipulated as necessary by Article 1 may *not* be made by telegraph. And if a telegraph message is inadmissible, much more are telephone messages, and communications by word of mouth. Moreover, the

these acts of aggression the German Empire considers itself in a state of war with France' (*ibid.*, p. 240). On April 6, 1917, the Congress of the United States passed a joint resolution declaring that whereas Germany had 'committed repeated acts of war' against the United States, the state of war which had thus been thrust upon the United States was 'thereby formally declared' (*A.J.*, xi. (1917), Supplement, p. 151).

practice of the States throughout the last centuries has been to hand in a written declaration of war, when any declaration has been made.

War, as between the belligerents, is considered to have commenced from the date of its declaration, although actual hostilities may not have been commenced until much later. On the other hand, as between the belligerents and neutrals, a war is not considered to have commenced until its outbreak has been notified to the neutrals, or has otherwise become unmistakably known to them. For this reason, Article 2 of Convention III. enacts that the belligerents must at once after the outbreak of war notify[1] the neutrals, even if only by telegraph, and that the state of war shall not take effect with regard to neutrals until after they have received notification, unless it be established beyond doubt that they were in fact aware of a state of war.

Ultimatum.

§ 95. The second form which the unequivocal warning may take which is provided for by Article 1 of Convention III. is an ultimatum with a conditional declaration of war.

Ultimatum[2] is the technical term for a written communication by one State to another which ends amicable negotiations respecting a difference, and formulates, for the last time and categorically, the demands to be fulfilled if other measures are to be averted. An ultimatum may be simple or qualified. It is *simple*, if it does not include an indication of the measures contemplated by the Power sending it. It is *qualified*, if it does indicate the measures contemplated, whether they be retorsion, or reprisals, pacific blockade, occupation of a certain territory, or war.[3] Now Article 1 of Con-

[1] See below, § 307.

[2] See above, § 28.

[3] Thus, on August 4, 1914, the British ambassador at Berlin handed to the German Foreign Minister a written statement that, unless Germany could give an assurance by midnight that it would proceed no further with the violation of the Belgian frontier, the British Government felt bound 'to take all steps in their power to uphold the neutrality of Belgium' (*Collected Diplomatic Documents* (1915), pp. 109-112).

vention III. provides for a qualified ultimatum, for it must be so worded that the recipient can have no doubt about the commencement of war in case he does not comply with its demands. For this reason, if a State has sent a simple ultimatum to another, or a qualified ultimatum threatening a measure other than war, it is not, in case of non-compliance, justified in commencing hostilities at once without a previous declaration of war. So Italy sent a declaration of war to Turkey in 1911, although an ultimatum threatening the occupation of Tripoli had preceded it.

Convention III. does not enact a minimum length of time which an ultimatum must grant before the commencement of hostilities; this period may, therefore, be only very short, as, for instance, a number of hours. All the more is it necessary to emphasise once again that there could be no greater violation of the Law of Nations than to send an ultimatum without previously having tried to settle a difference by negotiation.

The state of war following an ultimatum must likewise be notified to neutrals, for Article 2 of Convention III. applies to this case also. Further, for the same reason as in the case of a declaration of war, an ultimatum containing a conditional declaration of war must be communicated to the other party by a written document.

Initiative hostile Acts of War.

§ 96. There is no doubt that, in consequence of Convention III., recourse to hostilities without a previous declaration of war, or a qualified ultimatum, is forbidden. But a war can nevertheless break out without these preliminaries.[1] A State might deliberately order hostilities to be commenced without a previous

[1] Thus, in June 1913, hostilities broke out on the conquered Turkish territory of Macedonia between the Bulgarian forces and the Serbian and Greek forces, which were joined by the Montenegrins. Again, Turkey entered the World War by bombarding a Russian port. Turkey had not, however, ratified Convention III.

declaration of war, or a qualified ultimatum. Further, the armed forces of two States having a grievance against one another might engage in hostilities without having been authorised thereto, and without the respective Governments ordering them to desist from further hostilities. Again, acts of force by way of reprisals, or during a pacific blockade, or an intervention, might be forcibly resisted by the other party, hostilities breaking out in this way.

It is certain that States which deliberately order the commencement of hostilities without a previous declaration of war or a qualified ultimatum, commit an international delinquency; but they are nevertheless engaged in war. Further, it is certain that States which allow themselves to be dragged into a condition of war through unauthorised hostile acts of their armed forces commit an international delinquency; but they are nevertheless engaged in war. Again, war is actually in existence if the other party forcibly resists acts of force undertaken by a State by way of reprisals, or during a pacific blockade, or an intervention. Now in all these and similar cases, all the laws of warfare must find application, for a war is still war in the eyes of International Law, even though it has been illegally commenced, or has automatically arisen from acts of force which were not intended to be acts of war.

However that may be, Article 2 of Convention III. also applies to wars which have so broken out, and the belligerents must without delay send a notification to neutral Powers, so that these may be compelled to fulfil the duties of neutrality. But, of course, neutral Powers must in this case likewise, even without notification, fulfil the duties of neutrality, if they are unmistakably aware of the outbreak of war.

II

EFFECTS OF THE OUTBREAK OF WAR

Vattel, iii. § 63—Hall, §§ 124-126—Westlake, ii. pp. 32-55—Lawrence, §§ 143-146—Manning, pp. 163-165—Phillimore, iii. §§ 67-91—Twiss, ii. §§ 41-61—Halleck, i. pp. 526-552, and ii. pp. 124-140—Taylor, §§ 461-468—Walker, §§ 44-50—Hershey, Nos. 343-350—Wharton, iii. §§ 336-337[a]—Wheaton, §§ 298-319—Moore, v. § 779, and vii. §§ 1135-1142—Heffter, §§ 121-123—Lueder in *Holtzendorff*, iv. pp. 347-362—Gareis, § 81—Liszt, § 39, v.—Ullmann, § 173—Bonfils, Nos. 1044-1065—Despagnet, Nos. 517-519—Pradier-Fodéré, vi. Nos. 2694-2720—Mérignhac, iii[a]. pp. 84-115—Nys, iii. pp. 50-70—Rivier, ii. pp. 228-237—Calvo, iv. §§ 1911-1931—Fiore, iii. Nos. 1290-1301, and *Code*, Nos. 1444-1450—Martens, ii. § 109—Longuet, §§ 8-15—Pillet, pp. 72-84—Bordwell, pp. 200-211—Spaight, pp. 25-33—Ariga, §§ 13-15—Takahashi, pp. 26-88—Lawrence, *War*, pp. 45-55—Garner, i. §§ 27-37, 39-61, 80-98, 141-143, 162-171, 173-174, 62-79, 99-117—Sainte-Croix, *La Déclaration de Guerre et ses Effets immédiats* (1892), pp. 166-207—Meyer, *De l'Interdiction du Commerce entre les Belligérants* (1902)—Jacomet, *La Guerre et les Traités* (1909)—Markovitch, *Des Effets de la Guerre sur les Contrats entre Particuliers* (1912)—Wehberg, pp. 194-200—Borchard, §§ 46, 354—M'Nair, *Legal Effects of War* (1920)—Politis in *Annuaire*, xxiii. (1910), pp. 251-281, and xxiv. (1911), pp. 200-223—Beer and Kleinfeller in *Z.I.*, xxv. (1915), pp. 321-338, and pp. 383-395.

General Effects of the Outbreak of War.

§ 97. When war breaks out, even if it be limited to two members of the Family of Nations, nevertheless the whole Family of Nations is affected, since the rights and duties of neutrality devolve upon such States as are not parties to the war. And the subjects of neutral States may feel the consequences of the outbreak of war in many ways. War is not only a calamity to the commerce and industry of the whole world, but also involves the alteration of the legal position of neutral merchantmen on the open sea, and of subjects of neutral States within the boundaries of the belligerents. For the belligerents have the right to visit, search, and, if need be, capture neutral merchantmen on the open sea, and foreigners who remain within the boundaries of the belligerents, although subjects of neutral Powers, acquire in a degree and to a certain extent enemy character.[1] However, the outbreak of war tells chiefly and directly upon the relations between the belligerents and their subjects. Yet it would not be correct to maintain that all legal relations between the parties thereto, and between their subjects, disappear with the outbreak of war. War is not a condition of anarchy, indifferent or hostile to law, but a condition recognised and ruled by International Law, although it involves a rupture of peaceful relations between the belligerents.

Rupture of Diplomatic Intercourse and Consular Activity.

§ 98. The outbreak of war at once causes the rupture of diplomatic intercourse between the belligerents, if this has not already taken place. The respective diplomatic envoys are recalled and ask for their passports, or receive them without any previous request; but they enjoy their privileges of inviolability and exterritoriality for the period of time requisite for leaving the country.[2]

The official residence [3] of a departed envoy is, according to a usage,[4] confided to the protection of another foreign envoy, and the archives, if left behind, are placed under seals.[5] Sometimes a member of the retinue of the departing envoy is left in charge, with the permission of the local Government.

With war, consular activity likewise comes to an end, and the consular archives are left in charge of an *employé* of the consulate, or of the consul of another State.[6] But the question whether the consuls themselves must be permitted to leave aroused recrimination at the beginning of the World War. Several

[1] See above, § 88.

[2] For the incidents attending the departure of the envoys of the various belligerents at the outbreak of the World War, see Garner, i. §§ 27-33.

[3] None the less, it is stated in a German official White Paper (see Garner, i. § 32) that the German Embassy at Petrograd was wrecked by a mob in August 1914. As to the confiscation of the seat of the Austrian Legation to the Holy See in Rome, see above, vol. i. § 390 n.

[4] See details in Garner, i. § 39 n.

[5] For the arrangements made at the outbreak of the World War, see Garner, i. § 39.

[6] See above, vol. i. § 436.

belligerent States prevented enemy consuls from departing,[1] and accused one another of allowing them to suffer great indignities.[2]

§ 99. The doctrine was formerly held, and is even nowadays held by a few writers,[3] that the outbreak of war *ipso facto* cancels all treaties previously concluded between the belligerents, excepting only those concluded especially for war. But the vast majority of modern writers on International Law have abandoned this standpoint,[4] and the opinion is pretty general that war by no means annuls every treaty. But unanimity as to what treaties are or are not cancelled by war does not exist. Neither does a uniform practice of the States exist, cases having occurred in which States have expressly declared [5] that they considered all treaties annulled through war. Thus the whole question remains as yet unsettled. Nevertheless a majority of writers agree on the following propositions, and the attitude of the belligerents during the World War seems to confirm their accuracy, at any rate on many points. **Cancellation of Treaties.**

(*a*) *Treaties to which belligerents alone are parties* :—

(1) The outbreak of war cancels all political treaties between the belligerents (as, for instance, treaties of alliance) which have not been concluded for the purpose of setting up a permanent condition of things.

(2) On the other hand, it is obvious that treaties specially concluded for war are not annulled (such as treaties in regard to the neutralisation of certain parts of the territories of the belligerents).

(3) Political and other treaties concluded for the

[1] Thus Germany detained British consuls, and Great Britain German consuls, until an agreement for exchange was made. *Parl. Papers*, Misc., No. 8 (1915), Cd. 7857.

[2] Details in Garner, i. §§ 34-36.

[3] See, for instance, Phillimore, iii. § 530, and Twiss, i. § 252, in contradistinction to Hall, § 125.

[4] See Jacomet, *op. cit.*, pp. 113-128.

[5] As, for instance, Spain in 1898, at the outbreak of the war with the United States of America (see Moore, v. pp. 375-380), and Turkey in 1911, at the outbreak of her war with Italy.

purpose of setting up a permanent[1] condition of things are not *ipso facto* annulled by the outbreak of war; but nothing prevents the victorious party from imposing by the treaty of peace alterations in, or even the dissolution of, such treaties.

(4) Non-political treaties not intended to set up a permanent condition of things (such as treaties of commerce, for example) are not *ipso facto* annulled; but the parties may annul them or suspend them according to discretion.

The plan adopted in the Treaties of Peace was to regard all treaties to which two belligerents were the only parties as having been annulled by the war, but to give to the victorious Power an option to revive them upon certain conditions.[2]

(*b*) *Treaties to which many States are parties*:—

(5) So-called law-making[3] treaties (such as the Declaration of Paris, for example) are not cancelled by the outbreak of war. The same is valid in regard to all treaties to which a multitude of States are parties (such as the International Postal Union, for example); but the belligerents may suspend them, as far as they themselves are concerned, in case the necessities of war compel them to do so,[4] and they in fact did so during the World War.

The Treaties of Peace provide that only the treaties

[1] Thus American and English courts—see *The Society for the Propagation of the Gospel* v. *Town of Newhaven*, (1823) 8 Wheaton 464, and *Sutton* v. *Sutton*, (1830) 1 Russ. and M. 663—have declared that Article 9 of the treaty of November 19, 1794, between Great Britain and the United States was not annulled by the outbreak of war in 1812. See Moore, v. § 779, and Westlake, ii. p. 33; see also the foreign cases discussed by Jacomet, *op. cit.*, pp. 168-179.

[2] See the Treaty of Peace with Germany, Article 289. Great Britain has accordingly revived certain pre-war treaties with Germany. See *London Gazette*, July 23, 1920. As to Austria, see *London Gazette*, November 2, 1920.

[3] See above, vol. i. §§ 18, 492, 555-568*c*.

[4] The Institute of International Law, at its meeting at Christiania in 1912, adopted some rules with regard to the effect of war on treaties. See *Annuaire*, xxv. (1912), p. 648; *A.J.*, vii. (1913), p. 153 (where the rules are translated); and Davis in the *Proceedings of the American Society of International Law*, vi. (1912), pp. 124-132.

of an 'economic or technical character' therein mentioned are to be again applied between the Central Power concerned and those of the Allied and Associated Powers party thereto,[1] and some of them only with modification. Treaties neither economic nor technical, but to which many States are parties, are not referred to in the Peace Treaties, but the Powers correctly treat them as being again in force.

Precarious Position of Belligerents' Subjects on Enemy Territory.

§ 100. The outbreak of war affects likewise such subjects of the belligerents as are at the time within the enemy's territory. In former times they could all at once be detained as prisoners of war, and many States, therefore, concluded in time of peace special treaties for the time of war expressly stipulating for a period during which their subjects should be allowed to leave each other's territory unmolested.[2] Through the influence of such treaties, which became pretty general during the eighteenth century, it became an international practice[3] that, as a rule, enemy subjects must be allowed to withdraw within a reasonable period, and no instance of the former rule occurred during the nineteenth[4] century. Although some[5] writers even nowadays maintain that, according to strict law, the old rule is still in force, it may safely[6] be said that there

[1] See above, vol. i. § 581*b*, where this proceeding is discussed.

[2] See a list of such treaties in Hall, 4th ed., § 126, p. 407, n. 1.

[3] See Garner, i. § 40.

[4] With regard to the 10,000 Englishmen who were arrested in France by Napoleon at the outbreak of war with England in 1803, and kept as prisoners of war for many years, it must be borne in mind that Napoleon did not claim a right to make such civilians prisoners of war as were at the outbreak of war on French soil. He justified his act as one of reprisals, considering that England had violated the Law of Nations by beginning hostilities with the capture of two French merchantmen in the Bay of Audierne without a formal declaration of war. See Alison, *History of Europe*, v. p. 277, and Bonfils, No. 1052.

[5] See Twiss, ii. § 50; Rivier, ii. p. 230; Liszt, § 39, v.; Holland, *Letters upon War and Neutrality* (2nd ed. 1913), p. 39.

[6] See *Land Warfare*, § 12. The author had, however, intended to consider whether this rule could still be maintained, having regard to the practical difficulty caused by the interruption of communications and the importance attaching nowadays to man-power and espionage.

is now a customary rule of International Law, according to which all such subjects of the enemy as are not real or potential members of his armed forces must be allowed a reasonable period for withdrawal. On the other hand, such enemy subjects as are active or reserve officers, or reservists, and the like, may be prevented from leaving, and be detained as prisoners of war; for the principle of self-preservation must justify belligerents in refusing to furnish each other with resources which increase their means of offence and defence.[1]

Several States, on entering the World War, allowed enemy subjects on their territory to depart within a certain time.[2] For example, Great Britain permitted Germans to leave up to August 10, 1914.[3] On the other hand, Germany and Austria-Hungary prevented all enemy subjects from departing at the outbreak of the war.[4]

However that may be, a belligerent need not allow[5] enemy subjects to remain on his territory, although this is frequently done. Thus, during the Crimean War, Russian subjects in Great Britain and France were allowed to remain there, as were likewise Russians in Japan and Japanese in most parts of Russia during the Russo-Japanese War, and Turks in Italy during the Turco-Italian War. Moreover, during the World War, almost all the belligerents allowed enemy subjects resident within their territory to remain.[6] On the other hand, France expelled all Germans during the Franco-German War in 1870; the former South African Republics expelled most British subjects when war broke out in 1899; Russia, during the Russo-Japanese War, expelled Japanese from her provinces in the Far East;

[1] See *Land Warfare*, § 13, and the author's Introduction to Roxburgh, *The Prisoners of War Information Bureau* (1915). But a number of publicists—see, for instance, Spaight, p. 88—put forward a rule that even reservists must be allowed to leave.

[2] See Garner, i. §§ 44-61.

[3] Statement issued by the Home Office on August 5, 1914.

[4] Garner, i. § 45; Satow in the *Grotius Society*, ii. p. 8.

[5] See above, vol. i. § 324.

[6] See details in Garner, i. §§ 46-61.

in May 1912, during the Turco-Italian War, Turkey decreed the expulsion of all Italians, certain classes excepted; and, during the World War, German subjects *not* of military age were expelled from Portugal and certain British colonies.

In case a belligerent allows the residence of enemy subjects on his territory, he can, of course, impose conditions, such as an oath to abstain from all hostile acts, or a promise not to leave a certain region, and the like. Restrictions were imposed upon resident enemy aliens in almost all belligerent States during the World War.[1] Moreover, an enemy subject who is allowed to stay must not join the forces of his home State, or assist them in any way, if they occupy a part of the country in which he resides. If he does so, he is liable to be punished for treason [2] after their withdrawal.

During the World War, many belligerents not only placed all enemy aliens under strict supervision, but adopted a policy of general internment. Such aliens were looked upon as a peril to the State, and were themselves in danger from mob violence when national passions waxed hot. Thus Great Britain had in the early months of the war interned only about a third of the Germans and Austrians in the United Kingdom. But when the torpedoing of the *Lusitania,* and the drowning of more than 1100 innocent men, women, and children, so incensed public opinion that riots broke out all over the British Empire, and the life of enemy subjects was in danger, most of them were either interned or repatriated.[3] France [4] and Germany [5] also resorted to general internment, but the United States did not.[6]

[1] Garner, *ibid.*

[2] See above, vol. i. § 317, where the case of *De Jager* v. *Attorney-General for Natal*, [1907] A.C. 326, is discussed.

[3] As to the various agreements for the exchange and repatriation of enemy subjects unfitted for military service by age or sex or infirmity, see Garner, i. §§ 45, 53.

[4] Garner, i. § 52.

[5] Garner, i. § 57.

[6] Garner, i. § 61.

Persona standi in judicio on Enemy Territory.

§ 100*a*. Formerly the rule prevailed everywhere that an enemy subject had no *persona standi in judicio*, and was, therefore, *ipso facto* by the outbreak of war, prevented from either taking, or defending, proceedings in the courts. This rule dated from the time when war was considered such a condition between belligerents as justified hostilities by all the subjects of one belligerent against all the subjects of the other, the killing of all enemy subjects irrespective of sex and age, and, at any rate, the confiscation of all private enemy property. War in those times used to put enemy subjects entirely *ex lege*, and it was only a logical consequence from this principle that enemy subjects could not sustain *persona standi in judicio*. Since the rule that enemy subjects are entirely *ex lege* has everywhere vanished, the rule that they might not take or defend proceedings in the courts had in many countries, such as Austria-Hungary, Germany, Holland, and Italy, likewise vanished before the World War. But in Great Britain and the United States of America [1] enemy subjects were still prevented from taking legal proceedings,[2] although there were exceptions to the general rule.

Publicists, however, were debating whether these two States had not incurred an obligation to alter their Municipal Law in consequence of Article 23(*h*) of the Hague Regulations, by which it is forbidden 'to declare extinguished, suspended, or unenforceable in a court of law the rights and rights of action of the nationals of the adverse party.' Great Britain officially repudiated such an interpretation of this article, pointing out that neither the actual words used, nor their position among regulations for the operations of armies in the field, nor the circumstances of their origin, would justify such a construction.[3]

[1] In strict law also in France.

[2] The leading case was *The Hoop*, (1799) 1 C. Rob. 196.

[3] See above, vol. i. § 554 (11). The repudiation was contained in a letter addressed to the author and

So the question stood until the eve of the World War, when the German Government made it known that 'in view of the rule of English law' it would suspend 'the enforcement of any British demands against Germans' until reciprocity was granted.[1] No arrangement was made; Great Britain followed her earlier practice;[2] and it is very doubtful whether alien enemies in many other belligerent States enjoyed greater procedural capacity than those in the United Kingdom.[3] In fact, the exceptions to the English rule were, or became, such, that the disability to sue attached practically to non-resident alien enemies alone, and not even to them in all cases.

For, in the first place, an enemy subject resident in an allied or neutral country,[4] or having a licence,[5] was not debarred from suing; and such a licence was implied, in the case of an enemy subject resident in the United Kingdom, from mere compliance with the obligatory registration order,[6] and was not lost through internment in pursuance of general policy as a civilian prisoner of war.[7] Secondly, an enemy alien, wherever resident, was permitted to appear in the Prize Court as a claimant whenever he believed himself entitled to 'any protection, privilege, or relief under any of the Hague Conventions of 1907.'[8] And there were other

at once made public by him. See details in Oppenheim, *The League of Nations* (1919), pp. 45-55. See also Politis in *R.G.*, xviii. (1911), pp. 249-259, and the literature there quoted; Kohler in *Z.V.*, v. (1911), pp. 384-393; Holland in the *Law Quarterly Review*, xxviii. (1912), pp. 94-98; Charteris in the *Juridical Review*, xxiii. (1911), pp. 307-323; Oppenheim, *Die Zukunft des Volkerrechts* (1911), pp. 30-32; Wehberg in *R.I.*, 2nd Ser. xv. (1913), pp. 197-224; Strupp in *Z.I.*, xxiii. (1913), pt. ii. pp. 118-136, and in *Z.V.*, viii. (1914), pp. 57-66; Westlake, ii. pp. 83-86.

[1] See [1915] 1 K.B. at p. 879.

[2] See *Porter* v. *Freudenberg*, [1915] 1 K.B. 857, and M'Nair, *Legal Effects of War* (1920), pp. 26-58.

[3] See a discussion of the practice of the United States of America, France, and Germany in Garner, i. §§ 91-98.

[4] This seems correct in view of *In re Mary, Duchess of Sutherland*, (1915) 31 T.L.R. 394.

[5] *The Hoop*, (1799) 1 C. Rob. 196, at p. 201.

[6] *Princess Thurn und Taxis* v. *Moffit*, [1915] 1 Ch. 58.

[7] *Schaffenius* v. *Goldberg*, [1916] 1 K.B. 284.

[8] *The Möwe*, [1915] P. 1, at p. 15.

exceptions.[1] Even where an enemy subject does fall under a disability to sue during war, his right of action is not extinguished, but will revive with the return of peace; and even if the Treaty of Peace does not so expressly provide,[2] the statute of limitations probably does not run against him during the war.[3]

Moreover, an alien enemy, whether or not he can be plaintiff, can always be made defendant,[4] and by the Legal Proceedings against Enemies Act, 1915,[5] Parliament provided a special means for serving a writ on an alien enemy outside the jurisdiction in a certain class of proceedings.

§ 101. Before the World War, following Bynkershoek,[6] most British and American writers and cases,

[1] Thus a non-resident alien enemy could be joined as a nominal plaintiff for the purpose of pleading (*Rodriguez* v. *Speyer Bros.*, [1919] A.C. 59), and probably an enemy soldier or sailor who had been captured and made a prisoner of war could sue, on the authority of the old case of *Maria* v. *Hall*, (1800) 2 B. and P. 236, on a contract for wages. It was stated in the last edition of this book, on the authority of *Shepeler* v. *Durant*, (1854) 14 C.B. 582, that if a defendant obtained an opportunity to plead, and if subsequently war broke out with the country of the plaintiff, the defendant may not plead that the plaintiff is prevented from suing; but see now *Hellfeld* v. *Rechnitzer*, (1914) *The Times*, December 11, 1914. It was also stated, on the authority of *Ex parte Boussmaker*, (1806) 13 Ves. 71, that an alien enemy could prove for a debt in bankruptcy; but this is no longer the law, unless he is relieved from his disability on other grounds; *Re Wilson*, (1915) 84 L.J.K.B. 1893. It was also said, on the authority of *Janson* v. *Driefontein Consolidated Mines Limited*, [1902] A.C. 484, that a defendant might waive the plea of an alien enemy. But it is probable that this would no longer be allowed. See the *dictum* of Bailhache J. in *Robinson and Co.* v. *Continental Insurance Co.*, [1915] 1 K.B. 155 at p. 159.

[2] By the Treaties of Peace at the end of the World War it is stipulated that 'all periods of prescription, or limitation of right of action . . . shall be treated in so far as regards relations between enemies, as having been suspended for the duration of the War. They shall begin to run again at earliest three months after the coming into force of the treaty.' See Treaty of Peace with Germany, Article 300.

[3] The point is not settled, for the *obiter dictum* in *De Wahl* v. *Braune*, (1856) 25 L.J. (N.S.) Ex. 343, is not decisive, although Anson, *Principles of the English Law of Contract* (11th ed. 1906), p. 122, and other writers accept it as decisive. For cases arising out of the World War, the above-mentioned provision of the Treaties of Peace has received statutory force. See also the American case of *Hanger* v. *Abbot*, (1867) 6 Wall. 532, and Gregory, *The Effect of War on the Operation of Statutes of Limitation* (1915).

[4] *Robinson and Co.* v. *Continental Insurance Co.*, [1915] 1 K.B. 155.

[5] 5 Geo. v. c. 36.

[6] *Quaestiones Juris publici*, i. c. 3: '*quamvis autem nulla specialis sit commerciorum prohibitio ipso tamen jure belli commercia esse vetita.*'

Intercourse, especially Trading, between Subjects of Belligerents.

and also some French[1] and German[2] writers, asserted the existence of a rule of International Law that all intercourse, and especially trading, was *ipso facto* by the outbreak of war prohibited between the subjects of the belligerents, unless it was permitted under the custom of war (as, for instance, ransom bills), or was allowed under special licences, and that all contracts concluded between the subjects of the belligerents before the outbreak of war become extinct or suspended. On the other hand, most German, French, and Italian writers denied the existence of such a rule, but asserted the existence of another, according to which belligerents were empowered to prohibit by special orders all trade between their own and enemy subjects.

These assertions were remnants of the time when the distinction[3] between International and Municipal Law was not, or was not clearly, drawn. International Law, being a law for the conduct of States only and exclusively, has nothing to do directly with the conduct of private individuals, and both assertions are, therefore, nowadays untenable. Their place must be taken by the statement that, States being sovereign, and the outbreak of war bringing the peaceful relations between belligerents to an end, it is within the competence of every State to enact by its Municipal Law such rules as it pleases concerning intercourse, and especially trading, between its own and enemy subjects.

And if we look at the Municipal Laws of the several countries, as they stood before the World War, we find

[1] For instance, Pillet, p. 74, and Mérignhac, iii[a]. p. 107.

[2] For instance, Geffcken in his note 4 to Heffter, p. 265.

[3] See above, vol. i. § 20. But in spite of everything that speaks against it, Sir S. Evans, in *The Panariellos*, (1915) 1 B. and C. P. C. 195, again pronounced that it is a rule of *International Law* that *ipso facto* by the outbreak of war all trading with the enemy is prohibited; and the French Trading with the Enemy Decree (text in *Journal du Droit international* (Clunet), xlii. (1915), p. 103) proclaims that 'une des conséquences de l'état de guerre, *depuis longtemps admise par le droit des gens,* est d'entraîner l'interdiction de tout commerce avec l'ennemi.'

that they have to be divided into two groups. To the one group belonged those States—such as Austria-Hungary, Germany, Holland, and Italy—whose Governments were empowered by their Municipal Laws to prohibit by special order all trading with enemy subjects at the outbreak of war. In these countries trade with enemy subjects was permitted to continue after the outbreak of war unless special prohibitive orders were issued. To the other group belonged those States—such as Great Britain, the United States of America, and France—whose Municipal Laws declared trade and intercourse with enemy subjects *ipso facto* by the outbreak of war prohibited, but empowered the Governments to allow by special licence all or certain kinds of such trade. In Great Britain [1] and the United States of America, it had been, since the end of the eighteenth century, an absolutely settled [2] rule of the Common Law that, certain cases excepted, all intercourse,[3] and especially trading, with alien enemies became *ipso facto* by the outbreak of war illegal, unless allowed by special licence.

When the World War came, the belligerents by statute or decree supplemented or varied their Municipal Law

[1] See *Porter* v. *Freudenberg*, [1915] 1 K.B. 857, and besides the textbooks quoted above at the commencement of § 97, Pennant, Chadwick, and Gregory in the *Law Quarterly Review*, xviii. (1902), pp. 289-296, xx. (1904), pp. 167-185, xxv. (1909), pp. 297-316; Bentwich, *The Law of Private Property in War* (1907), pp. 47-61; Phillipson, *The Effect of War on Contracts* (1909); Latifi, *Effects of War on Property* (1909), pp. 50-58; Markovitch, *Des Effets de la guerre sur les Contrats entre Particuliers* (1912); Schuster and Strupp in *Z.I.*, xxiii. (1913), pt. ii. pp. 21, 118; Scott in the *Law Quarterly Review*, xxx. (1914), pp. 77-90, and xxxi. (1915), pp. 30-49; M'Nair, *Legal Effects of War* (1920), pp. 99-106.

[2] Whereas the Admiralty Court did at all times, the Common Law Courts did not during the eighteenth century hold trading with enemy subjects to be illegal, at any rate not in so far as insurance of enemy vessels and goods against capture on the part of English cruisers was concerned; see *Henkle* v. *London Exchange Assurance Co.*, (1749) 1 Ves. 320; *Planche* v. *Fletcher*, (1779) 1 Dougl. 251; *Lavabre* v. *Wilson*, (1779) 1 Dougl. 284; *Gist* v. *Mason*, (1786) 1 T.R. 84.

[3] That a British subject who, after the outbreak of war, becomes naturalised in the enemy country commits an act of treason was decided in *R.* v. *Lynch*, [1903] 1 K.B. 444. See above, vol. i. § 306.

relating to trading with the enemy. Thus Great Britain, in September 1914, passed the Trading with the Enemy Act, 1914,[1] forbidding (except under licence) all transactions during the war which were prohibited by Common Law, statute, or proclamation, and among them were all that would improve the financial or commercial position of a person trading or residing in an enemy country: *e.g.* paying debts to him, dealing in securities in which he was interested, handling goods destined for him or coming from him,[2] or contracting with him.[3] By a decree of September 27, 1914,[4] France, after a preamble reciting that war of itself prohibited all commerce with the enemy, expressly forbade all trade with enemy subjects or persons residing in an enemy country, all contracts (tout acte ou contrat) with such persons, and the discharge for their benefit of obligations, pecuniary or otherwise, resulting from 'tout acte ou contrat passé.'[5] Germany, by an ordinance of September 30, 1914, prohibited all payments to persons resident in the British Empire, and the ban was extended later to persons resident in other enemy countries. But German law admits trading with the enemy which is not expressly forbidden, and legislation in Germany against such trading seems to have been less rigorous

[1] 4 & 5 Geo. v. c. 87. See M'Nair, *Legal Effects of War* (1920), pp 99-106.

[2] Trading with the enemy does not become legal by the fact that goods coming from the enemy country to Great Britain, or going from Great Britain to the enemy country, are sent to their destination through a neutral country (*Moss* v. *Donohoe*, (1916) 32 T.L.R. 343: *The Jonge Pieter*, (1801) 4 C. Rob. 79). But if the goods have been bought by the subject of a neutral State *bona fide* by himself and are afterwards shipped through neutral country to the enemy, it is not a case of trading with the enemy; see *The Samuel*, (1802) 4 C. Rob. 284 n.

[3] It had long been the British rule that all contracts entered into *during* a war with alien enemies without a special licence are illegal, invalid, and can never be enforced; but prior to the Trading with the Enemy Act, 1914, and the proclamation thereunder, two exceptions to it had been recognised: (1) where the contract was entered into in a case of necessity (*Antoine* v. *Morshead*, (1815) 6 Taunt. 237); (2) where it was in order to supply an invading English army or the English fleet (*The Madonna delle Gracie*, (1802) 4 C. Rob. 195).

[4] Text in *Journal du Droit international* (Clunet), xlii. (1915), p. 103.

[5] See Garner, i. §§ 162-163.

than in Great Britain or France.[1] The United States, by the Trading with the Enemy Act of October 6, 1917,[2] prohibited all trading or contracting with persons resident or doing business in an enemy country, all payments to such persons, and all business or commercial communication with them.

It has been by the application of their trading with the enemy doctrine that the courts have determined the effect of war in English law upon contracts concluded before its outbreak.[3] For all such contracts are regarded as abrogated by outbreak of war if for their further performance they require intercourse with the enemy.[4] Thus partnerships with alien enemies are dissolved; [5] a contract of affreightment must not be fulfilled; and therefore English ships must not load or unload goods in an enemy port.[6] Moreover, even if the further performance of the contract would not appear necessarily to involve intercourse with the enemy (as where the contract contains an express provision that its execution should be suspended during war), it is still liable to be treated as abrogated if its continued existence is against public policy as laid down in the decided cases.[7] On the other hand, contracts belonging to certain classes, particularly those which 'are really the concomitants of rights of property' (a contract of tenancy,[8] for instance), are not abrogated, but suspended.[9]

[1] See Garner, i §§ 164-167.

[2] *A.J.*, xii. (1918), Supplement, p. 27.

[3] As to the Municipal Law in other countries, see Garner, i. §§ 168-171, 173-174.

[4] The leading case in *Ertel Bieber and Co.* v. *Rio Tinto Co.*, [1918] A.C. 260. For details, see M'Nair, *op. cit.*, pp. 59-74, 106-162.

[5] *Hugh Stevenson and Sons* v. *A.-G. für Cartonnagen Industrie*, [1917] 1 K.B. 842, [1918] A.C. 239. The property of the enemy partner, and the fruits which it earned during the war, do not however belong to the British partner.

[6] *Esposito* v. *Bowden*, (1857) 7 E. and B. 763. See also *Arnhold Karberg and Co.* v. *Blythe, Green, Jourdain and Co.*, [1916] 1 K.B. 495, at p. 505.

[7] *Ertel Bieber and Co.* v. *Rio Tinto Co.*, [1918] A.C. at p. 269. But rights which had accrued prior to the outbreak of war are not abrogated, but suspended.

[8] *Halsey* v. *Lowenfeld*, [1916] 2 K.B. 707.

[9] *Ertel Bieber and Co.* v. *Rio Tinto Co.*, [1918] A.C., at p. 269.

The Treaties of Peace have laid down certain rules which are to be applied by all the belligerents in the World War [1] to determine the position of pre-war contracts, and these rules generally follow British practice. The governing principle is that such contracts were abrogated as from the date when trading between the parties became unlawful; [2] but this principle does not apply to leases, mortgages, and other important classes of contracts mentioned in the treaties.

Position of Belligerents' Property in the Enemy State.

§ 102. In former times belligerents could confiscate all private and public enemy property, immoveable or moveable, on each other's territory at the outbreak of war, and also enemy debts; and the treaties [3] concluded between many States for the withdrawal of their subjects at the outbreak of war provided likewise for the unrestrained withdrawal of the private property of their subjects. Through the influence of such treaties, and of Municipal Laws and decrees enacting the same, an international usage and practice grew up that belligerents should neither confiscate private enemy property on their territory nor annul enemy debts. The last case of confiscation of private property was that of 1793, at the outbreak of war between France and Great Britain. No case occurred during the nineteenth century, and although several writers maintain that, according to strict law, the old rule, in contradistinction to the usage which they do not deny, is still valid, it may safely be maintained that it is obsolete,[4]

[1] Except the United States, Japan, and Brazil.

[2] 'Except in respect of any debt or other pecuniary obligation arising out of any act done or money paid thereunder.' See Article 299 of the Treaty of Peace with Germany.

[3] See above, § 100; Moore, vii. § 1196; Scott, *Conferences*, pp. 559-563.

[4] The position in English law of private enemy property on land was scrutinised in *Re Ferdinand, Ex-Tsar of Bulgaria*, [1921] 1 Ch. 107, and the Court of Appeal held that the Crown had a right to confiscate such property until the passing of the Trading with the Enemy Acts, but that as the powers conferred by these acts for dealing with such property were inconsistent with the exercise of the Common Law right of forfeiture, that right must be held to have been abandoned. See also

and that there is now a customary rule of International Law in existence prohibiting the confiscation of private enemy property and the annulment of enemy debts on the territory of a belligerent. This rule, however, does not prevent a belligerent from seizing *public* enemy property on his territory, such as funds, ammunition, provisions, rolling stock of enemy state railways, and other valuables; from preventing the withdrawal of private enemy property which may be made use of by the enemy [1] for military operations, such as arms and munitions; from seizing and using rolling stock belonging to private enemy railway companies, and other means of transporting persons or goods and appliances for the transmission of news, although they are private enemy property, provided all these articles are restored, and indemnities are paid for them, after the conclusion of peace; [2] or from suspending the payment of enemy debts till after the conclusion of peace in order to prevent the increase of the resources of the enemy.

The rule that private property on land is not liable to confiscation guided the policy of the belligerents in the early stages of the World War. Thus the British Trading with the Enemy (Amendment) Act, 1914,[3] created a custodian of enemy property whose general duty it was to receive dividends and other sums which became payable to enemies, invest them, and hold

Hugh Stevenson and Sons v. *A.-G. fur Cartonnagen Industrie*, [1917] 1 K.B. 842, at p. 848, [1918] A.C. 239, at p. 244; and *Porter* v. *Freudenberg*, [1915] 1 K.B. 857, at p. 870.

[1] The indulgence granted to enemy merchantmen in Russian and Japanese ports at the outbreak of the war in 1904, to leave unmolested within a certain time, was conditional upon there being no contraband in the cargoes. See Lawrence, *War*, p. 52.

[2] As the seizure of all these articles is, according to Article 53 of the Hague Regulations, permissible in occupied enemy country, provided they are restored and indemnities paid after the conclusion of peace, seizure must likewise—under the same conditions—be permissible in case these articles are on the territory of a belligerent. As regards rolling stock belonging to private enemy railway companies, see Nowacki, *Die Eisenbahnen im Kriege* (1906), § 15.

[3] 5 Geo. v. c. 12.

them (subject to the payment of debts in certain cases) until the end of the war. But the desire to eliminate the financial and commercial influence of the enemy, and other motives, presently led in most States to exceptional war measures against the businesses and property of enemies, which, though not confiscation, inflicted great loss and injury. Sometimes these measures stopped short of divesting the enemy ownership of the property; but in other cases the businesses or property were liquidated, and were represented at the close of hostilities by nothing else than the proceeds of their realisation, often enough out of all proportion to their value.[1]

The readjustment of rights of private property on land was provided for by the Treaties of Peace. The general principles underlying their complicated arrangements were that the validity of all completed war measures was reciprocally confirmed, but that while uncompleted liquidations on the territories of the Central Powers were to be discontinued, and the subjects of the victorious Powers were to receive compensation for the loss or damage inflicted on their property by the emergency war measures, the property of subjects of the vanquished Powers on the territories of the Allied and Associated Powers might be retained and liquidated, and the owner was to look for compensation to his own State. The proceeds of the realisation of such property were not to be handed over to him, or to his State, but were to be credited to his State as a payment on account of the sums payable by it under the treaties.[2] Between some States, Great Britain and Germany for example, clearing offices were established for the collection and payment of pre-war debts.[3]

[1] For details, see Garner, i. §§ 62-79.

[2] See, for example, Treaty of Peace with Germany, Articles 297-298.

[3] See Treaty of Peace with Germany, Article 296.

Property found by a belligerent on one of his merchantmen does not enjoy any immunity from confiscation, since enemy private property at sea,[1] unlike private property on land, is liable to capture everywhere except on a neutral vessel or neutral territory.[2] Accordingly, during the World War, British Prize Courts in several cases condemned enemy goods on British merchantmen whether seized before or after they had been landed in British ports.[3]

Further, enemy goods discharged before the outbreak of war into a bonded warehouse in a British port, and found in bond at the outbreak of war, are still considered by British practice as sea-borne.[4]

Effect of the Outbreak of War on Merchantmen.

§ 102*a*. In former times International Law empowered States when war was impending, or at its outbreak, to lay an embargo upon all enemy merchantmen in their harbours in order to confiscate them. Further, enemy merchantmen at sea could at the outbreak of war be captured and confiscated, although they did not even know of the outbreak of war. As regards enemy merchantmen in the harbours of the belligerents,

[1] In 1905, during the Russo-Japanese War, a Russian vessel, the *Thalia* (see Takahashi, pp. 605-620; *Russian and Japanese Prize Cases*, ii. p. 116), was seized while undergoing repairs in a Japanese shipyard, and condemned as an enemy vessel, although, being on land beside a dock, she was not at sea. This was prior to Hague Convention vi., which forbade confiscation of enemy merchantmen in harbour at the outbreak of war. (See below, § 102*a*.)

[2] The assertion—see Latifi, *Effects of War on Property* (1909), p. 90—that as 'from the point of view of Municipal Law, ships are floating portions of the national jurisdiction,' enemy goods found in a belligerent's own ships 'are not subject to the law of maritime capture, but will be on the footing of the moveable property of enemy subjects found on a belligerent's territory,' is wrong, because merchantmen are not really floating portions of the flag State. See above, vol. i. § 264.

[3] *The Miramichi*, (1914) 1 B. and C. P. C. 137; *The ten bales of silk at Port Said*, (1916) 2 B. and C. P. C. 247; *The Dandolo*, (1916) 2 B. and C. P. C. 339. See below, § 177 and § 197. *The Roumanian*, (1914) 1 B. and C. P. C. 75, 536. On the meaning of the term 'port' see Baty in the *Law Quarterly Review*, xxxiv. (1918), pp. 420-427, who denies that quays and dry docks are part of a port. And it matters not whether enemy cargo itself is concerned, or the proceeds of its sale, because it had been sold in a British port on account of its perishable character. *The Glenroy*, (1918) 3 B. and C. P. C. 161.

[4] *The Eden Hall*, (1916) 2 B. and C. P. C. 84.

it became, from 1854, during the Crimean War, a usage, if not a custom, that no embargo[1] should be laid on them for the purpose of confiscating them, and that a reasonable time, so-called days of grace, should be granted them to depart unmolested; but no rule was in existence until the Second Hague Conference of 1907, which produced a Convention (VI.) 'relative to the Status of Enemy Merchant-ships at the Outbreak of Hostilities.'[2] In coming to an agreement on the subject, two facts had to be taken into consideration. There was, first, the fact that in all maritime countries numerous merchantmen were being built from special designs in order that they might quickly, at the outbreak of, or during, war, be converted into cruisers; it would therefore have been folly for a belligerent to grant any lenient treatment to such vessels. There was, secondly, the fact that a belligerent fleet could not remain effective for long without being accompanied by a train of colliers, transport vessels, and repairing vessels; it was, therefore, of the greatest importance for a belligerent to have as many merchantmen as possible at his disposal to give such assistance to the fleet. For this reason Convention VI. represented a compromise, and distinguished between vessels in the harbours of the belligerents and vessels on the sea.

(*a*) *Vessels in harbour*:—

(1) Article 1 of the convention enacts that, in case an enemy merchant ship is at the beginning of the war in the port[3] of a belligerent, or having left its last port of departure before the commencement of the war,

[1] See above, § 40.

[2] See Lémonon, pp. 647-661 Higgins, pp. 300-307; Nippold, ii. pp. 146-153; Scott, *Conferences*, pp. 556-568; Dupuis, *Guerre*, Nos. 74-81; Scott in *A.J.*, ii. (1908), pp. 260-269; Wehberg, pp. 194-200.

[3] To enjoy the benefit of this article, a vessel must be inside a *port*; it is not sufficient that she is inside a roadstead leading to a port. See *The Belgia*, (1915) 1 B. and C. P. C. 303, 2 B. and C. P. C. 32; see also *The Möwe*, (1914) 1 B. and C. P. C. 60; *The Fenix*, *Z.I.*, ix. (1915), p. 103, *A.J.*, x. (1916), p. 909.

enters a belligerent port in ignorance of its outbreak, it is *desirable* that she should be allowed freely to depart, either immediately or after a reasonable number of days of grace, and, after being furnished with a pass, to proceed direct to her port of destination, or to any other port indicated. It is obvious that, since only the desirability of free departure of such vessels is stipulated, even a belligerent which is a party to the convention is not compelled to grant free departure; nevertheless there must be grave reasons for not acting in accordance with what is considered desirable by Article 1. Secondly, such a belligerent may make a distinction in the treatment of the several enemy vessels in his harbours, and may grant free departure to one or more of them, and refuse it to others, according to discretion.

(2) The former usage that enemy merchantmen [1] in the harbours of the belligerents at the outbreak of war might not be confiscated, was made a *binding rule* upon the parties by Article 2, which enacts that such vessels as are not allowed to leave,[2] or are by *force majeure* [3] prevented from leaving during the days of grace, may not be confiscated, but may only be detained for restora-

[1] The British Prize Court was called upon to decide what kinds of vessels came within the term merchantmen (*navires de commerce*). It condemned the *Germania*, a racing yacht found at Cowes at the outbreak of war (1 B. and C. P. C. 573, and, on appeal, 2 B. and C. P. C. 365; see Zitelmann in *Z. V.*, xi. (1918), pp. 1-19), and the *Oriental*, a Hungarian yacht found in the same place (1 B. and C. P. C. at p. 575), on the ground that they were not merchantmen. The author would have preferred to include within the term private vessels of all kinds (as did the German Prize Court in another connection — see *The Primavera*, *Journal du Droit international* (Clunet), xliv. (1917), p. 1804). In *H.M. Procurator in Egypt* v. *Deutsches Kohlen Depot Gesellschaft*, (1916) 2 B. and C. P. C. 439, 3 B. and C. P. C. 264, the Privy Council held that a fleet of lighters used in port to coal vessels, and the tugs used to tow them, were not merchantmen. See also *The Atlas and Lighters*, (1916) 2 B. and C. P. C. 470.

[2] There were several cases in which vessels did not avail themselves of a pass, and were therefore condemned. See *The Pindos*, (1915) 1 B. and C. P. C. 248, 2 B. and C. P. C. 146.

[3] Lack of funds is not *force majeure*: *The Concadoro*, (1915) 1 B. and C. P. C. 390, 2 B. and C. P. C. 64.

tion, without compensation, after the conclusion of peace, or requisitioned on payment of compensation to the owners.

(3) Both these articles apply also to enemy cargo on board these vessels.[1]

(4) The convention does not apply to merchant ships which by their construction show that they are intended for conversion into war vessels.[2]

By Article 6 this convention was made applicable only if all the belligerents in a war were party to it. During the World War, several belligerents, including the United States and Italy, were not parties, and the question arose whether in strict law it was binding.[3]

However this may be, at the outbreak of the war Germany proposed to the Allied Powers that days of grace should be allowed to merchant vessels found in enemy ports to depart unmolested, and France, by decrees of August 4 and August 13, 1914, granted seven days' grace to German and Austrian vessels in French harbours, or entering them in ignorance of the outbreak of hostilities.[4] Great Britain, by Order in Council of August 4, 1914,[5] declared that if information was received by a certain hour that no less favourable treatment was being accorded by Germany to British merchantmen and cargoes, German merchantmen (with certain exceptions) in British ports, or entering them subsequently in ignorance of the declaration of war, might load and depart within ten days. But no such information was received, and all German vessels were detained.[6] On the other hand, reciprocal permission to depart within a period of grace was granted by Great Britain to Austrian merchant vessels and by

[1] Article 4.

[2] Article 5. *The Derfflinger*, (1916) 2 B. and C. P. C. 36.

[3] See Garner, i. § 104, who holds that it was not binding. The author had expressed no opinion.

[4] See Garner, i. § 105, and *R.G.*, xxii. (1915), Documents, pp. 9-10.

[5] *London Gazette*, August 7, 1914.

[6] *London Gazette*, August 11, 1914; *The Chile*, (1914) 1 B. and C. P. C. 1, at p. 7.

Austria-Hungary to British merchant vessels found in their harbours or entering them in ignorance of the outbreak of war.[1]

The first German vessel found in port to come before the British Prize Court was *The Chile*, and she was not then condemned, but ordered to be detained until further order.[2] A similar decree was made in many other cases.[3] Among them was that of *The Marie Leonhardt*, which came again before the court after the conclusion of peace as a test case.[4] After argument upon the binding force[5] of Article 2 of Hague Convention VI. the German owners abandoned their claim under that convention, and the court held that (apart from the convention upon which it had become unnecessary to express an opinion) 'ships of the enemy in our ports at . . . the outbreak of hostilities are detained in our ports to be confiscated if no reciprocal agreement is made.'[6]

(*b*) *Vessels on the sea* :—

(1) Enemy merchant ships which left their last port of departure before the outbreak of war,[7] and, while still ignorant of the outbreak of war, are met at sea[8] (*en mer*) by cruisers of the belligerents, may, according to Article 3, be captured; they may not, however, be confiscated, but may either be detained for restora-

[1] *London Gazette*, August 14, 1914; Garner, i. § 106. As to the attitude of other belligerents, see Garner, i. §§ 105, 106, 115.

[2] See 1 B. and C. P. C. at p. 12.

[3] *The Bellas*, (1914) 1 B. and C. P. C. 95; *The Gutenfels*, (1916) 2 B. and C. P. C. 36; *The Turul*, (1919) 3 B. and C. P. C. 356; *The Prinz Adalbert*, (1916) 2 B. and C. P. C. 70, reversed on appeal, 3 B. and C. P. C. 70; *The Kronprinzessin Cecilie*, see 3 B. and C. P. C. 363 at p. 365, also reversed on appeal. In these last two cases the German ship had taken refuge in a British port prior to the outbreak of war between Great Britain and Germany in order to escape capture by French cruisers.

[4] [1921] P. 1.

[5] See above, p. 163.

[6] At p. 11.

[7] See also below, § 188, concerning so-called days of grace.

[8] Article 3 is not applicable to an enemy merchantman at anchor in a port of its home State, and there captured by a cruiser of the other belligerent. See the case of the Turkish vessel *Sabah* captured by an Italian cruiser in a Turkish port, which is discussed by Coquet in *R.G.*, xxi. (1917), pp. 261-265.

tion after the war, without compensation, or be requisitioned, or even destroyed, on payment of compensation, so long as provision is made for the safety of the persons on board, and the security of the ship's papers.

It is obvious that, in case such vessels are not ignorant of the outbreak of war—having, for instance, received the news by wireless telegraphy—they may not any longer claim the privileges stipulated by Article 3. And this article stipulates expressly that, after having touched a port of their own or of a neutral country, such vessels are no longer privileged.

(2) This article applies also to enemy cargo on board such vessels.

(3) It does not apply to merchant ships which by their construction show that they are intended for conversion into war vessels.

Germany and Russia entered reservations against this article; consequently the British [1] and French [2] Prize Courts condemned German vessels, and the German [3] Prize Court condemned a Russian vessel, captured at sea while still ignorant of the outbreak of war.

[1] *The Marie Glæser*, (1914) 1 B. and C. P. C. 38, [1914] P. 218; *The Perkeo*, (1914) 1 B. and C. P. C. 136.

[2] *The Porto*, and other cases cited by Garner, i. § 113.

[3] *The Fenix*, *Z.I.*, ix. (1915), p. 103; *A.J.*, x. (1916), p. 909.

CHAPTER III

WARFARE ON LAND

I

ON LAND WARFARE IN GENERAL

Vattel, iii. §§ 136-138—Hall, §§ 184-185—Phillimore, iii. § 94—Taylor, § 469—Wheaton, § 342—Bluntschli, §§ 534-535—Heffter, § 125—Lueder in *Holtzendorff*, iv. pp. 388-389—Gareis, § 84—Bonfils, Nos. 1066-1067—Pradier-Fodéré, vi. Nos. 2734-2741—Longuet, § 41—Pillet, pp. 85-89—*Kriegsbrauch*, p. 9—*Land Warfare*, § 39—Holland, *War*, Nos. 1-15.

Aims and Means of Land Warfare.

§ 103. The purpose of war, namely, the overpowering of the enemy, is served in land warfare through two aims [1]—first, defeat of the enemy armed forces on land, and, secondly, occupation and administration of the enemy territory. The chief means by which belligerents try to realise those aims, and which are always conclusively decisive, are the different sorts of force applied against enemy persons. But besides such violence against enemy persons, there are other means which are not at all unimportant, although they play a secondary part only. Such means are: appropriation, utilisation, and destruction of enemy property; siege; bombardment; assault; espionage; utilisation of treason; ruses. All these means of warfare on land must be discussed in this chapter, as must also occupation of enemy territory.

§ 104. But—to use the words of Article 22 of the Hague Regulations—'the belligerents have not an

[1] Aims of land warfare must not be confounded with ends of war; see above, § 66.

unlimited right as to the means they adopt for injuring the enemy.' For not all possible practices of injuring the enemy in offence and defence are lawful, certain practices being prohibited under all circumstances and conditions, and other practices being allowed only under certain circumstances and conditions, or only with certain restrictions. The principles of chivalry and of humanity have been at work for many hundreds of years to create these restrictions, and their work is not yet at an end.[1] However, apart from these restrictions, all kinds and degrees of force, and many other practices, may be made use of in war.

Lawful and Unlawful Practices of Land Warfare.

§ 105. In a sense, all means of warfare are directed against one object only—namely, the enemy State, which is to be overpowered by all legitimate means. Apart from this, the means of land warfare are directed against several objects.[2] Such objects are chiefly the members of the armed forces of the enemy, but likewise, although in a lesser degree, other enemy persons; further, private and public property, fortresses, and roads. Indeed, apart from certain restrictions, everything may eventually be the object of a means of warfare, provided the means are legitimate in themselves, and are capable of promoting the realisation of the purpose of war.

Objects of the Means of Warfare.

§ 106. Land warfare must be distinguished from sea warfare chiefly for two reasons. First, their circumstances and conditions differ widely, and, therefore, their means and practices also differ. Secondly, the law-making conventions which deal with warfare rarely deal with land and sea warfare at the same time, but generally treat them separately. Thus, whereas some conventions deal exclusively with warfare on sea, the

Land Warfare in contradistinction to Sea Warfare.

[1] See, however, above, § 67.

[2] See Oppenheim, *Die Objekte des Verbrechens* (1894), pp. 64-146, where the relation of human actions with their objects is fully discussed.

Hague Regulations (Convention IV.) deal exclusively with warfare on land.

II

VIOLENCE AGAINST ENEMY PERSONS

Grotius, iii. c. 4 and c. 11—Vattel, iii. §§ 139-159—Hall, §§ 128, 129, 185—Westlake, ii. pp. 76-83—Lawrence, §§ 161, 163, 166-169—Maine, pp. 123-148—Manning, pp. 196-205—Phillimore, iii. §§ 94-95—Halleck, ii. pp. 14-18—Moore, vii. §§ 1111, 1119, 1122, 1124—Hershey, Nos. 375-380—Taylor, §§ 477-480—Walker, § 50—Wheaton, §§ 343-345—Bluntschli, §§ 557-563—Heffter, § 126—Lueder in *Holtzendorff*, iv. pp. 390-394—Gareis, § 85—Klüber, § 244—Liszt, § 40, iii.—G. F. Martens, ii. § 272—Ullmann, § 176—Bonfils, Nos. 1068-1071, 1099, 1141—Despagnet, Nos. 525-527—Mérignhac, iii[a]. pp. 240-270—Pradier-Fodéré, vi. Nos. 2742-2758—Rivier, ii. pp. 260-265—Nys, iii. pp. 144-148—Calvo, iv. §§ 2098-2105—Fiore, iii. Nos. 1317-1320, 1342-1348, and *Code*, Nos. 1481-1488—Martens, ii. § 110—Longuet, §§ 42-49—Pillet, pp. 85-95—Holland, *War*, pp. 70-76—Zorn, pp. 127-161—Bordwell, pp. 278-283—Meurer, ii. §§ 30-31—Spaight, pp. 73-156—*Kriegsbrauch*, pp. 9-11—*Land Warfare*, §§ 39-53—Garner, i. §§ 175-190—Schultze in *Z.I.*, xxvii. (1918), pp. 1-39.

On Violence in general against Enemy Persons.

§ 107. As war is a contention between States for the purpose of overpowering each other, violence consisting of different sorts of force applied against enemy persons is the chief and decisive means of warfare. These different sorts of force are used against both combatants and non-combatants, but with discrimination and differentiation. The purpose of the application of violence against combatants is their disablement so that they can no longer take part in the fighting; and this purpose may be realised through killing or wounding them, or making them prisoners. But to non-combatant members of armed forces, private enemy persons showing no hostile conduct, and officials in important positions, only minor means of force may as a rule be applied, since they do not take part in the armed contention of the belligerents.

Killing and Wounding of Combatants.

§ 108. Every combatant may be killed or wounded, whether a private soldier or an officer, or even the monarch or a member of his family. Some publicists [1] assert that it is a usage of warfare not to aim at a sovereign or a member of his family. Be that as it may, there is in strict law [2] no rule preventing the killing and wounding of such illustrious persons. But combatants may only be killed or wounded if they are able and willing to fight or to resist capture. Therefore, combatants disabled by sickness or wounds may not be killed. Further, such combatants as lay down their arms and surrender, or do not resist being made prisoners, may neither be killed nor wounded, but must be given quarter. These rules are universally recognised, and are now expressly enacted by Article 23(*c*) of the Hague Regulations, although the fury of battle frequently makes individual fighters [3] forget and neglect them.

Refusal of Quarter.

§ 109. However, the rule that quarter must be given has exceptions. Although it has of late been a customary rule of International Law, and although the Hague Regulations now expressly stipulate by Article 23(*d*) that belligerents are prohibited from declaring that no quarter will be given, quarter may nevertheless be refused to members of a force who continue to fire after having hoisted the white flag as a sign of surrender; further, by way of reprisal [4] for violations of the rules of warfare committed by the other side; and, thirdly, in case of imperative necessity, when the

[1] See Klüber, § 245; G. F. Martens, ii. § 278; Heffter, § 126.

[2] Says Vattel, iii. § 159: 'Mais ce n'est point une loi de la guerre, d'épargner en toute rencontre la personne du roi ennemi; et on n'y est obligé que quand on a la facilité de le faire prisonnier.' The example of Charles XII. of Sweden (quoted by Vattel), who was intentionally fired at by the defenders of the fortress of Thorn, besieged by him, and who said that the defenders were within their right, ought to settle the point.

[3] See Baty, *International Law in South Africa* (1900), pp. 84-85, and the many charges made by belligerents in the World War against their adversaries.

[4] See Pradier-Fodéré, vii. Nos. 2800-2801, who opposes this principle, but discusses the subject in a very detailed way; and Spaight, p. 89.

granting of quarter would so encumber a force with prisoners that its own security would thereby be vitally imperilled.[1] But it may well be doubted whether under modern conditions of civilised warfare such a case of imperative necessity can ever arise, and it must be emphasised that the mere fact that numerous prisoners cannot safely be guarded and fed [2] by the captors, or that prisoners might regain their liberty through an impending success of their own army, does not justify a refusal of quarter unless vital danger to the captors is involved. The former rules that quarter could be refused to the garrison of a fortress carried by assault, to the defenders of an unfortified place against an attack of artillery, and to a weak garrison which obstinately and uselessly persevered in defending a fortified place against overwhelming enemy forces, are now obsolete.

Lawful and Unlawful Means of Killing and Wounding Combatants.

§ 110. As already mentioned, Article 22 of the Hague Regulations stipulates expressly that the right of belligerents to adopt means of injuring the enemy is not unlimited. Some means are expressly prohibited by treaties; others are condemned by custom. But apart from those expressly prohibited by treaties or by custom, all means of killing and wounding that exist, or may be invented, are lawful. And it matters not whether the means used are directed against single individuals, as are swords and rifles, or against large bodies of individuals, as are, for instance, shrapnel, Gatlings, and mines. On the other hand, all means are unlawful that render death inevitable [3] or that needlessly aggravate the sufferings of wounded combatants. A customary rule of International Law, also expressly enacted by Article 23(*e*) of the Hague Regulations, prohibits, therefore,

[1] See Payrat, *Le Prisonnier de Guerre* (1910), pp. 191-220, and *Land Warfare*, § 80.

[2] Accordingly, the Boers frequently during the South African War set free British soldiers whom they had captured.

[3] There are indications in the author's manuscript that he had intended to reconsider this statement.

the employment of poison and of such arms, projectiles, and material[1] as cause unnecessary injury.[2] Accordingly: wells, pumps, rivers, and the like from which the enemy draws drinking water must not be poisoned;[3] poisoned weapons must not be made use of;[4] rifles must not be loaded with bits of glass, irregularly shaped iron, nails, and the like; cannons must not be loaded with chain shot, crossbar shot, red-hot balls, and the like. Another customary rule, also enacted by Article 23(*b*) of the Hague Regulations, prohibits any treacherous way of killing and wounding combatants. Accordingly: no assassin must be hired, and no assassination of combatants be committed; a price may not be put on the head of an enemy individual; proscription and outlawing are prohibited; no treacherous request for quarter must be made; no treacherous simulation of sickness or wounds is permitted.

§ 111. In 1868 a conference met at St. Petersburg for the examination of a proposition made by Russia with regard to the use of explosive projectiles in war. The representatives of seventeen Powers signed, on December 11, 1868, the so-called Declaration of St. Petersburg,[5] which stipulates that the signatory Powers, Explosive Bullets.

[1] In 1915, during the World War, the Germans used so-called 'flame projectors'—see details in Garner, i. § 189—which threw burning liquid on the combatants of the enemy. There is no doubt that this practice is unlawful, because it causes 'unnecessary injury.'

[2] As to the controversy between the United States and Germany during the World War whether shot-guns were arms of this category, see Garner, i. § 179.

[3] Is it lawful to poison the drinking water, provided a notice is posted up informing the enemy that the water has been poisoned? The German commander in South-West Africa attempted to justify such a practice during the World War; but it must be condemned. See *Parl. Papers*, Cd. 8306, pp. 74-78, and Garner, i. § 190.

[4] The diffusion of poisonous and asphyxiating gases from cylinders or otherwise than by projectiles (which is discussed below, § 113)—a practice instituted by the Germans during the World War (see details in Garner, i. §§ 180-183)—whether or not within the prohibition of the use of 'poison or poisoned weapons' contained in Article 23(*a*) of the Hague Regulations (as to which the author had expressed no opinion), was illegal because it exposed combatants to unnecessary suffering.

[5] See above, vol. i. § 562, and Martens, *N.R.G.*, xviii. p. 474.

and those who should accede later, renounce in case of war between themselves the employment, by their military and naval forces, of any projectile of a weight below 400 grammes (14 ounces) which is either explosive, or charged with fulminating or inflammable substances. This engagement is obligatory only upon the contracting Powers, and it ceases to be so in case a non-contracting Power takes part in a war between any of the contracting Powers.

Expanding (Dum-Dum) Bullets.

§ 112. As Great Britain had introduced bullets manufactured at the Indian arsenal of Dum-Dum, near Calcutta, the hard jacket of which did not quite cover the core, and which therefore easily expanded and flattened in the human body, the First Hague Conference adopted a declaration, signed on July 29, 1899, by fifteen Powers, stipulating that they should abstain, in case of war between two or more of them, from the use of bullets which expand or flatten easily in the human body, such as bullets with hard envelopes which do not entirely cover the core, or are pierced with incisions.[1]

Projectiles diffusing Asphyxiating or Deleterious Gases.

§ 113. The First Hague Conference also adopted a declaration, signed on July 29, 1899, by sixteen States, stipulating that the signatory Powers should, in a war between two or more of them, abstain from the use of projectiles the sole object of which is the diffusion of asphyxiating or deleterious gases.[2]

Violence directed from Air Vessels.

§ 114. The First Hague Conference had adopted likewise a declaration, signed on July 29, 1899, prohibiting *for a term of five years* the launching of projectiles or

[1] During the World War the belligerents charged one another with using these bullets. See details in Garner, i. § 177, who considers that (§ 178) 'the evidence at hand . . . does not indicate that any general use of [this type of bullet] was authorised by any belligerent, or that it was in fact used except perhaps in occasional instances.'

[2] During the World War, however, Germany introduced such shells, and her adversaries also used them by way of reprisals. See details in Garner, i. § 188.

explosives from balloons or other kinds of aerial vessels. The Second Hague Conference, on October 18, 1907, had renewed this declaration *up to the close of the Third Hague Conference*, but out of twenty-seven States which signed it only a few—(among them Great Britain and the United States of America)—had ratified it before the World War, and Germany, France, Italy, Japan, Russia—not to mention smaller Powers—did not even sign it. When the World War broke out, not one of the Central Powers had ratified the declaration; its provisions were not binding, and were not observed.[1]

Violence against Non-Combatant Members of Armed Forces.

§ 115. It will be remembered[2] that numerous individuals belong to armed forces without being combatants. Now, since and in so far as these non-combatant members of armed forces do not take part in the fighting, they may not directly be attacked and killed or wounded. However, they are exposed to all injuries indirectly resulting from the operations of warfare. And, with the exception of the personnel[3] engaged in the interest of the wounded, such as doctors, chaplains, persons employed in military hospitals, official ambulance men, who, according to Articles 9 and 10 of the Geneva Convention, are specially privileged, such non-combatant members of armed forces may certainly be made prisoners, since the assistance they give to the fighting forces may be of great importance.

Violence against Private Enemy Persons.

§ 116. Whereas in former[4] times private enemy persons of either sex could be killed or otherwise badly treated according to discretion, and whereas in especial the inhabitants of fortified places taken by assault used to be abandoned to the mercy of the assailants, in the eighteenth century it became a universally recognised customary rule of the Law of Nations that private

[1] See below, § 214*a*.
[2] See above, § 79.
[3] See below, § 121.
[4] See Grotius, iii. c. 4, §§ 6, 9.

enemy individuals should not be killed or attacked. In so far as they do not take part in the fighting, they may not be directly attacked and killed or wounded. They are, however, like non-combatant members of the armed forces, exposed to all injuries indirectly resulting from the operations of warfare. Thus, for instance, when a town is bombarded, and thousands of inhabitants are thereby killed, or when a train carrying private individuals as well as soldiers is wrecked by a mine, no violation of the rule prohibiting attack on private enemy persons has taken place.

As regards captivity, the rule is that private enemy persons may not be made prisoners of war.[1] But this rule has exceptions conditioned by the carrying out of certain military operations, the safety of the armed forces, and the order and tranquillity of occupied enemy territory. Thus, for instance, influential enemy citizens who try to incite their fellow-citizens to take up arms may be arrested and deported into captivity. And even the whole population of a province may be imprisoned in case a levy *en masse* is threatening.[2]

But if a levy *en masse* is not threatening, an occupant has no right to take into captivity[3] private enemy individuals of military age, although, of course, he can resort to measures of restraint to prevent them from escaping and joining the forces of the enemy, and can punish them if they attempt to do so.

Apart from captivity, restrictions of all sorts may

[1] This statement refers only to the treatment of private enemy individuals by an invader and has no reference to enemy subjects found by a belligerent on his own territory at the outbreak of war. See above, § 100.

[2] Civilians who render assistance to the enemy as drivers, or as labourers to construct fortifications or siege works, or in a similar way, if captured while they are so engaged, may not be detained as prisoners of war, whether they render these services voluntarily or are requisitioned or hired. See *Land Warfare*, § 58 n. (*a*).

[3] When in 1914, during the World War, the Germans took into captivity all men of military age in Belgium and the occupied part of France, Great Britain and France resorted to reprisals. See below, § 413, and Wehberg, p. 315.

be imposed upon, and means of force may be applied against, private enemy persons for many purposes; such as keeping order and tranquillity on occupied enemy territory; prevention of any hostile conduct, especially conspiracies; prevention of intercourse with, and assistance to, the enemy forces; securing the fulfilment of commands and requests of the military authorities, such as those for the provision of drivers, hostages, farriers; securing compliance with requisitions and contributions, and securing the execution of public works necessary for military operations, such as the building of soldiers' quarters, roads, bridges, and the like; provided the requisitioned services do not make part of the military operations.[1]

What kinds of violent means may be applied for these purposes is in the discretion of the military authorities, who will act according to expediency, and the rules of martial law established by the belligerents. But there is no doubt that, if necessary, capital punishment and imprisonment[2] are lawful means for these purposes. The limits within which violence may be applied to private individuals in modern warfare find expression in Article 46 of the Hague Regulations: 'family honour and rights, individual lives[3] and private property, as well as religious convictions and liberty, must be respected.'

[1] Can private enemy persons be compelled to build fortifications, construct trenches, and the like? The matter is not settled in practice. See below, § 170. See also Holland, *War*, No. 77; Spaight, p. 151; Ferrand, *Des Requisitions en matière de Droit international public* (1917), p. 60; Garner in *A.J.*, xi. (1917), p. 111.

[2] That, in case of general devastation, the peaceful population may be detained in so-called concentration camps, there is no doubt; see below, § 154. And there is likewise no doubt that hostages may be taken from the peaceful population; see below, §§ 170, 259.

[3] That the lives of civilians must be respected is a principle so universally recognised, that the following case has roused the indignation of the whole civilised world. It was published by the *Munchner Neueste Nachrichten* on October 7, 1914. A German lieutenant, giving an account of the occupation of St. Dié, at the end of August 1914, by the Germans, relates that a German column had entered the town and had barricaded itself into a house to await reinforcements; he then continues: 'We had

Violence against the Head of the Enemy State and against Officials in Important Positions.

§ 117. The head of the enemy State and officials in important posts, in case they do not belong to the armed forces, occupy, so far as their liability to direct attack, death, or wounds is concerned, a position similar to that of private enemy persons. But they are so important to the enemy States, and they may be so useful to the enemy and so dangerous to the invading forces, that they may certainly be made prisoners of war. If a belligerent succeeds in obtaining possession of the head of the enemy State or its cabinet ministers, he will certainly remove them into captivity. And he may do the same with diplomatic agents and other officials of importance, because, by weakening the enemy Government, he may thereby influence the enemy to agree to terms of peace.

III

TREATMENT OF WOUNDED, AND DEAD BODIES

Hall, § 130—Westlake, ii. pp. 72-76—Lawrence, § 165—Maine, pp. 156-159—Manning, p. 205—Phillimore, iii. § 95—Halleck, ii. pp. 36-39—Moore, vii. § 1134—Taylor, §§ 527-528—Hershey, Nos. 369-374—Bluntschli, §§ 586-592—Lueder in *Holtzendorff*, iv. pp. 289-318, 398-421—Liszt, § 40, v.—Ullmann, § 178, and in *R.G.*, iv. (1897), pp. 437-445—Bonfils, Nos. 1108-1118[7]—Despagnet, Nos. 551-554—Pradier-Fodéré, vi. No. 2794, vii. Nos. 2849-2881—Rivier, ii. pp. 268-273—Nys, iii. pp. 499-510—Calvo, iv. §§ 2161-2165—Fiore, iii. Nos. 1365-1372, and *Code*, Nos. 1594-1609—Martens, ii. § 114—Longuet, §§ 85-90, 92-93—Mérignhac, iii[a]. pp. 186-240—Pillet, pp. 165-192—*Kriegsbrauch*, p. 25—*Land*

---

arrested three civilians, and a good idea occurred to me. They were put on chairs, and told to go and sit in the middle of the street. Little by little one becomes terribly hard. Well, there they sat in the street. How many prayers of anguish they uttered I do not know, but their hands were clasped as though with cramp. I am sorry for them, but the method was immediately efficacious. The fire from the houses on our flanks weakens immediately, and we are able to occupy the opposite house and so are masters of the principal street.' The officer then explains how St. Dié was cleared of the enemy, and adds: 'As I learned afterwards, the reserve regiment which entered St. Dié more to the north had experiences quite like ours. The four civilians whom they compelled to sit in the street were killed by French bullets. I myself saw them lying in the middle of the street near the hospital.'

Warfare, §§ 174-220—Zorn, p. 122—Bordwell, pp. 249-277—Spaight, pp. 419-460—Higgins, pp. 35-38—Holland, *Studies*, pp. 61-65—Holland, *War*, Nos. 41-69—Garner, i. §§ 313-318—Gurlt, *Zur Geschichte der internationalen und freiwilligen Krankenpflege* (1873)—Lueder, *Die Genfer Convention* (1876)—Moynier, *La Croix rouge, son Passé et son Avenir* (1882); *La Révision de la Convention de Genève* (1898); *La Fondation de la Croix rouge* (1903)—Buzzatti, *De l'Emploi abusif . . . de la Croix rouge* (1890)—Triepel, *Die neuesten Fortschritte auf dem Gebiet des Kriegsrechts* (1894), pp. 1-41—Müller, *Entstehungsgeschichte des rothen Kreuzes und der Genfer Konvention* (1897)—Munzell, *Untersuchungen über die Genfer Konvention* (1901)—Gillot, *La Révision de la Convention de Genève, etc.* (1902)—Meurer, *Die Genfer Konvention und ihre Reform* (1906)—Schneider, *Die Genfer Konvention* (1911)—Roszkowski in *R.I.*, 2nd Ser. iv. (1902), pp. 199, 299, 442—Delpech in *R.G.*, xiii. (1906), pp. 629-724—Macpherson in *Z.V.*, v. (1911), pp. 253-277.

Origin of Geneva Convention.

§ 118. Although,[1] since the seventeenth century, several hundred special treaties have been concluded between different States regarding the tending of each other's wounded and the exemption of army surgeons from captivity, no general rule of the Law of Nations on these points was in existence until the second half of the nineteenth century, other than one prohibiting the killing, mutilation, or ill-treatment of the wounded. A change for the better was initiated by Jean Henry Dunant, a Swiss citizen from Geneva, who was an eye-witness of the battle of Solferino in 1859, where many thousands of wounded died who could, under more favourable circumstances, have been saved. When he published, in 1861 and 1863, his pamphlet, *Un Souvenir de Solférino*, the Geneva Société d'Utilité Publique, under the presidency of Gustave Moynier, created an agitation in favour of better arrangements for tending the wounded on the battlefield, and convoked an international congress at Geneva in 1863, where thirty-six representatives of nearly all the European States met and discussed the matter. In 1864 the Bundesrath, the Government of the Federal State of Switzerland, took the matter in hand officially,

[1] See Macpherson, *op. cit.*, p. 254.

and invited all European, and several American, States to send official representatives to a congress at Geneva for the purpose of discussing and concluding an international treaty regarding the wounded. This congress met in 1864, and twelve States were represented. Its result was the Convention[1] for the Amelioration of the Condition of Soldiers wounded in Armies in the Field (commonly called 'Geneva Convention'), signed on August 22, 1864. By and by States other than the original signatories joined the convention, and finally all the civilised States of the world, with the exception of Costa Rica, Monaco, and Lichtenstein, became parties. That its rules were in no wise perfect, and needed to be supplemented regarding many points, soon became apparent. A second international congress met at the invitation of Switzerland in 1868 at Geneva, where additional articles[2] to the original convention were discussed, and signed. These additional articles were, however, never ratified. The First Hague Conference in 1899 unanimously formulated the wish that Switzerland should shortly take steps for the meeting of another international congress to revise the Geneva Convention. This congress assembled in June 1906, and on July 6, 1906, a new Geneva Convention[3] was signed by the representatives of thirty-five States, including all the Great Powers. No less than twenty-six of these States ratified the convention, and at least eight others have acceded.

The new convention consisted of thirty-three articles, and provided rules for the treatment of the wounded and the dead; and rules concerning military hospitals and mobile medical units; the personnel engaged in the interest of the wounded, including army chaplains;

[1] See Martens, *N.R.G.*, xviii. p. 607, and above, vol. i. § 560.

[2] See Martens, *N.R.G.*, xviii. p. 612.

[3] See Martens, *N.R.G.*, 3rd Ser. ii. p. 620, and Treaty Ser. (1907), No. 15.

the material belonging to mobile medical units, military hospitals, and voluntary aid societies; convoys of evacuation; the distinctive emblem; the carrying out of the convention; and the prevention of abuses and infractions.

In the final protocol the conference expressed a desire that, in order to arrive at a unanimous interpretation of the convention, the parties should, so far as the cases and the circumstances permitted, submit to the International Court of Arbitration at the Hague [1] any differences which *in time of peace* might arise between them concerning its interpretation; but Great Britain and Japan refused to become parties to this.

When the World War broke out, almost all the belligerents were parties to the convention, but not quite all; and it was provided by Article 24 that it ceases to be binding in any war from the moment when a State which is not a party to it becomes a belligerent. However, all the belligerents were parties to the old convention of 1864, which remained in force between those Powers which were parties to it without being parties to the convention of 1906.[2] None the less, the provisions of both conventions were often violated during the war.[3] The main rules of the convention of 1906 are as follows [4]:—

§ 119. According to Articles 1-5, sick or wounded persons belonging, or officially attached, to armies must be respected and cared for, without distinction of nationality, by the belligerent in whose power they may be. Should, however, a belligerent be compelled The Wounded and the Sick.

[1] See above, vol. i. § 472.

[2] See above, vol. i. § 560.

[3] See details in Garner, i. §§ 313-318.

[4] The stipulations of the convention are for the most part of a technical military character, and it is impossible in a general treatise to enter into details. Readers who take a deeper interest in them must be referred to the most valuable article by Macpherson in *Z.V.*, v. (1911), pp. 253-277.

to abandon them to the enemy, he must, so far as military exigencies permit, leave behind with them a portion of his medical personnel to assist in taking care of them, together with the necessary material. The sick and wounded who have fallen into the hands of the enemy are prisoners of war, but belligerents may exchange or release them, or even hand them over to a neutral State, which has to intern them until after the conclusion of peace. After each engagement, the commander in possession of the field must have search made for the wounded, and must take measures to protect them against pillage and maltreatment. A nominal roll of all wounded and sick who have been collected must be sent as early as possible to the authorities of the country or army to which they belong, and the belligerents must keep each other mutually informed of any internments and changes as well as of admissions into hospital. Article 5 stipulates that the military authority may appeal to the charitable zeal of the inhabitants to collect and take care of the wounded and sick of the armies under his direction, granting to those who have responded to his appeal special protection and certain immunities.

Medical Units and Establishments, and Material.

§ 120. In order that the wounded and sick may receive proper treatment, mobile medical units, and fixed [1] establishments of the medical service, must be respected and protected by the belligerents; but this protection ceases if they are made use of to commit acts harmful to the enemy, such as sheltering combatants, carrying on espionage, and concealing arms and ammunition (Articles 6 and 7).[2]

[1] It was one of the saddest experiences of the World War that German airmen frequently and deliberately bombed hospitals of the Allies, and that a German publicist attempted to justify this abominable practice. See Köllreuter in *Z. V.*, x. (1918), p. 499.

[2] But Article 8 expressly enacts that the units and establishments do not forgo protection:—(*a*) because the personnel are armed, and use their arms for their own defence, or for the defence of the wounded

As regards *material*, a distinction is drawn between material of mobile medical units, of fixed medical establishments, and of voluntary aid societies.

(*a*) Mobile medical units which fall into the hands of the enemy must not be deprived of their material, including their teams, whatever may be the means of transport, and whoever may be the drivers employed (Article 14). The competent military authority is, however, permitted to make use of the material in captured medical units for the treatment of the wounded and the sick at hand, but it must be restored under the same conditions, and so far as possible at the same time, as the medical personnel.[1]

(*b*) The buildings and material of fixed medical establishments which, because the locality where they are is militarily occupied, fall into the hands of the enemy, remain, according to Article 15, 'subject to the laws of war.' That means that they remain entirely in the power of the captor. But they may not be diverted from their medical purpose so long as they are required for the wounded and sick. Should, however, urgent military necessity demand it, a commander may dispose of them, provided he makes previous arrangements for the welfare of the wounded and sick found in them.

(*c*) The material of voluntary aid societies, which are duly recognised, is, according to Article 16, considered private property, and must, therefore, be respected as such under all circumstances, although it may be requisitioned.

§ 121. The personnel engaged exclusively in the collection, transport, and treatment of the wounded Personnel.

and sick; (*b*) because in default of armed orderlies, units or establishments are guarded by pickets, or by sentinels furnished with authority in due form; (*c*) because weapons and cartridges, taken from the wounded, and not yet handed over to the proper department, are found there.

[1] See below, § 121.

and sick, and also in the administration of mobile medical units and establishments, the chaplains attached to armies, and, lastly, pickets and sentinels guarding medical units and establishments, must, according to Article 9, under all circumstances[1] be respected and protected. If they fall into the hands of the enemy, they must not be treated as prisoners of war. According to Article 12, however, they are not free to act or move without let or hindrance; for they are to continue to carry on their duties under the direction of the captor, until their assistance is no longer indispensable. They must then be sent back to their army, or to their country, at such time, and by such route, as may be compatible with military exigencies. They must be allowed to take with them such effects, instruments, arms, and horses as are their private property.[2]

The personnel of voluntary aid societies employed in the medical units and establishments is, according to Article 10, privileged to the same extent as the official personnel, provided that the society concerned is duly recognised and authorised by its Government and its personnel is subject to military law and regulations. Each State must notify to the other, before actually employing them, the names of societies which it has authorised to render assistance to the regular medical service of its armies.[3]

[1] Does this article prevent the punishment of such persons by the enemy for so-called war-crimes? Strupp in *Z.I.*, xxv. (1915), p. 357, says 'no'; but there is no reason to accept this answer as correct. See Markman in *Z.V.*, xi. (1918), pp. 76-83.

[2] So long as they are detained by the enemy he must, according to Article 13, grant them the same allowances and pay as are due to personnel holding the same rank in his own army.

[3] A recognised voluntary aid society of a *neutral* country cannot, according to Article 11, afford the assistance of its personnel and its units to a belligerent unless it has previously received the consent of its own Government and of the belligerent concerned; and a belligerent who accepts such assistance is bound, before making any use of it, to give notice to the enemy.

§ 122. Convoys for evacuating the wounded and sick must be treated in the same way as mobile medical units, but subject to the following special provisions of Article 17 :— **Convoys of Evacuation.**

A belligerent intercepting a convoy may, if military exigencies demand, break it up, provided that he takes charge of the sick and wounded who are in it. In this case, the obligation to send back the medical personnel when their assistance is no longer indispensable, extends also to the military personnel detailed for the transport or the protection of the convoy, and furnished with an authority in due form to that effect; and the obligation to restore the medical material extends to railway trains and inland boats which are specially arranged for evacuating sick and wounded, and to material belonging to the medical service and used for fitting up ordinary vehicles, trains, and boats for the transport of the wounded. Military vehicles, other than those of the medical service, may, however, be captured with their teams; and the civilian personnel and the various means of transport obtained by requisition, including railway material and boats used for convoys, are subject to the general rules of International Law.

§ 123. According to Article 18, the Swiss heraldic device of the red cross on a white ground, formed by reversing the federal colours, is adopted as the emblem and distinctive sign of the medical service of the armies, but there is no objection to the adoption of another emblem by non-Christian States which object to the cross on religious grounds. Thus Turkey has substituted a red crescent, and Persia a red sun.[1] The following are the rules concerning the use of this emblem :— **Distinctive Emblem.**

(1) It must be shown, with the permission of the

[1] See below, § 207.

competent military authority (Article 19), on the flags, the armlets (*brassards*), and on all the material belonging to the medical service.

(2) Medical units and establishments fly the red cross flag accompanied by the national flag of the belligerent to which they belong (Article 21).[1]

(3) All the personnel, according to Article 20, wear, on the left arm, an armlet (*brassard*) with a red cross on a white ground, stamped by the competent military authority.[2]

(4) The red cross on a white ground and the words 'Red Cross' or 'Geneva Cross' must not, according to Articles 23 and 27, be used, either in peace or war, except to indicate the protected medical units, establishments, personnel, and material.[3]

Treatment of the Dead.

§ 124. According to a customary rule of the Law of Nations, belligerents have the right to demand from one another that dead soldiers shall not be disgracefully treated, and, in particular, that they shall not be mutilated, but shall be, so far as possible, collected and buried [4] or cremated on the battlefield by the victor. The Geneva Convention does not stipulate any rule concerning the collection and burial or cremation of the dead; but Article 3 enacts that, after each engagement, the commander in possession of the field must take measures to ensure protection of the dead against pillage and maltreatment, and that bodies must be carefully examined, in order to see that life is really extinct, before they are buried or cremated. Each

[1] But medical units while in the hands of the enemy fly only the red cross. Neutral medical units rendering assistance in accordance with the convention, fly, along with the red cross flag, the national flag of the belligerent to whose army they are attached (Article 22).

[2] Accompanied by a certificate of identity, in the case of persons attached to the medical service who do not wear the military uniform.

[3] See below, § 124*a*.

[4] See Grotius, ii. c. 19, §§ 1, 3. Regarding a valuable suggestion by Ullmann concerning sanitary measures for the purpose of avoiding epidemics, see above, vol. i. p. 764, n. 4.

belligerent must send, as soon as possible, to the authorities of the country or army to which they belong the military identification marks or tokens found on the dead (Article 4). Pieces of equipment found upon the dead of the enemy are public enemy property, and may, therefore, be appropriated as booty[1] by the victor. On the other hand, letters, money, jewellery, and other articles of value, found upon the dead on the battlefield, or on those who die in the medical units or fixed establishments, which are apparently private property, are not booty, but must, according to Article 4 of the Geneva Convention and Article 14 of the Hague Regulations, be collected and handed over to the bureau of information[2] concerning prisoners of war, which has to transmit them to the persons interested through the authorities of their own country.

§ 124*a*. By Article 27, Governments whose representatives signed the convention, but whose legislation was not then adequate for the purpose, undertook to take, or introduce in their legislatures, the measures necessary to prevent, at all times, the employment of the emblem or the name of 'Red Cross' or 'Geneva Cross' by private individuals or by societies other than those entitled to use them. The Governments had likewise to take, or introduce in their legislatures, in the event of their military law being inadequate, measures necessary for the repression in time of war of individual acts of pillage and maltreatment of the wounded and sick, and also for the punishment of the improper use of the Red Cross flag and armlet (*brassard*) (Article 28).[3]

Prevention of Abuses.

[1] See below, § 139.

[2] See below, § 130.

[3] By reason of the uncertainties of parliamentary proceedings, Great Britain, in signing and ratifying the Geneva Convention, entered a reservation against Articles 23, 27, and 28; but by the Geneva Convention Act, 1911 (1 & 2 Geo. v. c. 20), Great Britain was enabled to carry out their stipulations. This Act imposes a penalty for the improper use of the 'Geneva Cross.'

IV

CAPTIVITY

Grotius, iii. c. 7 and c. 14—Bynkershoek, *Quaestiones Juris publici*, i. c. 3—Vattel, iii. §§ 148-154—Hall, §§ 131-134—Westlake, ii. pp. 67-72—Lawrence, § 164—Maine, pp. 160-167—Manning, pp. 210-222—Phillimore, iii. § 95—Twiss, ii. § 177—Halleck, ii. pp. 19-30—Taylor, §§ 519-524—Hershey, Nos. 355-368—Moore, vii. §§ 1127-1131—Wharton, iii. §§ 348-348*d*—Wheaton, § 344—Bluntschli, §§ 593-626—Heffter, §§ 127-129—Lueder in *Holtzendorff*, iv. pp. 423-445—Ullmann, § 177—Bonfils, Nos. 1119-1140—Despagnet, Nos. 544-550—Pradier-Fodéré, vii. Nos. 2796-2842, and viii. No. 3208—Rivier, ii. pp. 273-279—Nys, iii. pp. 511-530—Calvo, iv. §§ 2133-2157—Fiore, iii. Nos. 1355-1362, and *Code*, Nos. 1572-1593—Martens, ii. § 113—Longuet, §§ 77-83—Mérignhac, iii[a]. pp. 156-186—Pillet, pp. 145-164—*Kriegsbrauch*, pp. 11-18—Zorn, pp. 73-122—Bordwell, pp. 237-248—*Land Warfare*, §§ 54-116—Spaight, pp. 260-319—Holland, *War*, Nos. 24-40—Garner, i. §§ 331-360—Eichelmann, *Über die Kriegsgefangenschaft* (1878)—Romberg, *Des Belligérants et des Prisonniers de Guerre* (1894)—Triepel, *Die neuesten Fortschritte auf dem Gebiet des Kriegsrechts* (1894), pp. 41-55—Holls, *The Peace Conference at the Hague* (1900), pp. 145-151—Cros, *Condition et Traitement des Prisonniers de Guerre* (1900)—Beinhauer, *Die Kriegsgefangenschaft* (1908)—Payrat, *Le Prisonnier de Guerre dans la Guerre continentale* (1910)—Davis in *A.J.*, vii. (1913), pp. 521-545.

Development of International Law regarding Captivity.

§ 125. During antiquity, prisoners of war could be killed, and they were very often at once actually butchered or offered as sacrifices to the gods. If they were spared, they were as a rule made slaves, and only exceptionally liberated. But belligerents also exchanged their prisoners, or liberated them for ransom. During the first part of the Middle Ages prisoners of war could likewise be killed or made slaves. Under the influence of Christianity, however, their fate in time became mitigated. Although they were often most cruelly treated during the second part of the Middle Ages, they were not as a rule killed; and, with the disappearance of slavery in Europe, they were no longer enslaved. By the time modern International Law gradually came into existence, killing and enslaving prisoners of war had disappeared; but they were still often treated as criminals, and as objects of personal revenge. They were not considered in the power of the State by whose forces they were captured, but in the power of those forces themselves, or of the individual soldiers that had made the capture; and it was considered lawful for captors to make as much profit as possible out of their prisoners by way of ransom, if no exchange of prisoners took place. So general was this practice that a more or less definite scale of ransom became usual. Thus, Grotius[1] mentions that in his time the ransom of a private was the amount of his pay for one month. And since the pecuniary value of a prisoner as regards ransom rose in proportion with his fortune and his position in life and in the enemy army, it became usual for prisoners of rank and note not to belong to the capturing forces but to the sovereign, who had, however, to recompense the captors. During the seventeenth century, the custom of considering prisoners to be in the power of their captors died away. They were now considered to be in the power of the sovereign by whose forces they were captured. But rules of the Law of Nations regarding their proper treatment were hardly in existence. The practice of liberating prisoners in exchange, or for ransom only, continued. Special cartels were often concluded at the outbreak of, or during, a war, for the purpose of stipulating a scale of ransom according to which either belligerent could redeem his soldiers and officers from captivity. The last[2] instance of such a cartel is that between England and France in 1780, stipulating the ransom for members of the naval and military forces of both belligerents.

It was not until the eighteenth century, with its general tendencies to mitigate the cruel practices of warfare, that matters changed for the better. The

[1] iii. c. 14, § 9.

[2] See Hall, § 134.

conviction in time became general that captivity should only be the means of preventing prisoners from returning to their corps and taking up arms again, and should, as a matter of principle, be distinguished from imprisonment as a punishment for crimes. The Treaty of Friendship [1] concluded in 1785 between Prussia and the United States of America was probably the first to stipulate (Article 24) proper treatment for prisoners of war, prohibiting confinement in convict prisons and the use of irons, and insisting upon their confinement in a healthy place, where they may have exercise, and where they may be kept and fed as troops. During the nineteenth century, the principle that prisoners of war should be treated by their captor in a manner analogous to that meted out to his own troops became generally recognised, and the Hague Regulations, by Articles 4 to 20, enacted exhaustive rules regarding captivity. These rules were drawn up in time of peace before the World War, and they are still valid at the close of the World War. But the experiences of that war disappointed many hopes founded upon them.

Treatment of Prisoners of War.

§ 126. According to Articles 4-7 and 16-19 of the Hague Regulations, prisoners of war are not in the power of the individuals or corps who capture them, but of the Government of the captor. They must be humanely [2] treated. All their personal belongings remain their property, with the exception of arms, horses, and military papers, which are booty; [3] and

[1] See Martens, *R.*, pt. ii. iv. p. 37.

[2] The treatment meted out, during the World War, to British prisoners in the hands of the Germans was in many cases not only in direct violation of the Hague Regulations and not humane, but shameful. The treatment of wounded British prisoners on their way to German camps or hospitals was in numerous cases particularly cruel, all the more so as German Red Cross nurses habitually refused them food and drink. See *The Times History and Encyclopaedia of the War*, vi. (1916), pp. 241-280; M'Carthy, *The Prisoner of War in Germany* (1918); Garner, i. §§ 331-360; and the following *Parl. Papers*: Misc., No. 3 (1918), Cd. 8984; Misc., No. 19 (1918), Cd. 9106; Misc., No. 27 (1918); Misc., No. 28 (1918).

[3] See below, § 144.

in practice [1] personal belongings are understood to include military uniform, clothing, and kit required for personal use, although technically they are Government property.[2] They may only be imprisoned as an unavoidable matter of safety, and only while the circumstances which necessitate the measure continue to exist. They may, therefore, be detained in a town, fortress, camp, or any other locality, and may be bound not to go beyond a certain fixed boundary; but they may not be kept in convict prisons. The labour of prisoners of war who are not officers may be utilised by the Government according to their rank and aptitude; but their tasks must not be excessive and must have nothing to do with military operations.[3] Work done by them for the State must be paid for in accordance with tariffs in force for soldiers of the national army employed on similar tasks, or, in case there are no such tariffs in force, at rates proportional to the work executed. But prisoners of war may also be authorised to work for other branches of the public service, or for private persons, under conditions of employment to be settled by the military authorities, and they may likewise be authorised to work on their own account. All wages they receive go towards improving their position, and the balance must be paid to them at the time of their release, after deducting the cost of their maintenance.[4] But whether they earn wages or not, the Government is

[1] See *Land Warfare*, § 69.

[2] Charges were made that the Germans during the World War often deprived prisoners of their overcoats, and Garner (i. § 342) finds that the truth of the charges was substantiated in some instances by the reports of neutral inspectors.

[3] The question whether prisoners of war can be compelled to construct fortifications, and the like, is just as controverted as the question whether enemy civilians can be forced to do such work. See above, § 116 n., and below, § 170. See also Holland, *War*, No. 26; Pillet, p. 155; Spaight, p. 212.

[4] For the extent to which prisoners of war were compelled or enabled to work by the various belligerents during the World War, the nature of their tasks, and the scales of their remuneration, see Garner, i. §§ 350-353.

bound under all circumstances to maintain them, and, failing a special agreement between the belligerents, to provide quarters,[1] food,[2] and clothing[3] for them on the same footing as for its own troops. Officer prisoners must receive the same pay[4] as officers of corresponding rank in the country where they are detained, the amount to be repaid by their Government after the conclusion of peace. All prisoners of war must enjoy every latitude in the exercise of their religion, including attendance at their own church service, provided only that they comply with the regulations for order issued by the military authorities. If a prisoner wants to make a will, it must be received by the authorities or drawn up on the same conditions as for soldiers of the national army. And the same rules are valid regarding death certificates and the burial of prisoners of war, and due regard must be paid to their grade and rank. Letters, money orders, valuables, and postal parcels destined for, or despatched by, prisoners of war must enjoy free postage, and gifts and relief in kind for them must be admitted free from all customs and other duties as well as payments for carriage by Government railways[5] (Article 16).

[1] For details as to the quarters provided for officer prisoners of war during the World War, see Garner, i. § 336; and as to the quarters for other prisoners of war, see Garner, i. §§ 337-341.

[2] For details as to the food supplied to prisoners by the various belligerents during the World War, see Garner, i. §§ 343-347, who concludes, with regard to prisoners of war in Germany, that 'had it not been for the enormous quantities of food that were sent from England and France . . . it is not improbable that many prisoners would have died of starvation.'

[3] For details as to clothing supplied to prisoners by the various belligerents during the World War, see Garner, i. § 342, who concludes, with regard to prisoners in Germany, that 'The reports of the representatives of the American Embassy substantiate in a number of instances the charges made against the Germans in respect to the insufficient supply of clothing.'

[4] During the World War the British Government was prepared to carry out this stipulation of Article 17 of the Hague Regulations, but the German Government refused. See *The Times History and Encyclopaedia of the War*, vi. p. 263. See also Garner, i. § 335.

[5] For the manner in which the various belligerents in the World War carried out these provisions, see Garner, i. §§ 348-349.

Who may claim to be Prisoners of War.

§ 127. Every individual who is deprived of his liberty, not for a crime, but for military reasons, has a claim to be treated as a prisoner of war. Article 13 of the Hague Regulations expressly enacts that non-combatant[1] members of armed forces, such as newspaper correspondents, reporters, sutlers, and contractors, who are captured and detained, may claim to be treated as prisoners of war, provided that they can produce a certificate from the military authorities of the army which they were accompanying. The Hague Regulations do not contain anything regarding the treatment of *private* enemy individuals, and enemy officials, whom a belligerent thinks it necessary[2] to make prisoners of war; but it is evident that they may claim all the privileges of such prisoners. They are not convicts, but are taken into captivity for military reasons, and are therefore prisoners of war.

And the same is valid with regard to enemy civilians who at the outbreak of war are on the territory of a belligerent, and, for military reasons, are interned. They are not convicts either, but are deprived of their liberty for military reasons only, and are therefore prisoners of war.[3]

Discipline.

§ 128. Articles 8 and 9 of the Hague Regulations lay down the discipline to be observed in the case of prisoners of war:—Every prisoner who, if questioned, does not declare his true name and rank is liable to a curtailment of the advantages accorded to prisoners of his class. All prisoners are subject to the laws, regulations, and orders in force in the army of the belligerent that keeps them in captivity. Any act of insubordination on the part of prisoners may be

[1] See above, § 79.

[2] See above, §§ 116, 117.

[3] See above, § 100, and the author's Introduction to Roxburgh, *The Prisoners of War Information Bureau in London* (1915).

punished in accordance with these laws,[1] but apart from these laws, all kinds of severe measures are admissible to prevent a repetition of such acts. Escaped prisoners, who, after having rejoined their national army, are again taken prisoners, are not liable to any punishment for their flight. But if they are recaptured before they succeed in rejoining their army, or before they have quitted the territory occupied by the capturing forces, they are liable to disciplinary punishment.[2]

Release on Parole.

§ 129. Articles 10 to 12 of the Hague Regulations deal with release on parole [3] in the following manner :—No belligerent is obliged to assent to a prisoner's request to be released on parole, and no prisoner may be forced to accept such release. But if the laws of his country authorise him to do so, and if he acquiesces, any prisoner may be released on parole. In such a case he is in honour bound scrupulously to fulfil the engagement he has contracted, both as regards his own Government, and the Government that released him. And his own Government is formally bound neither to request, nor to accept, from him any service incompatible with the parole given. Any prisoner released on parole and recaptured bearing arms against the belligerent who released him, or against his allies, forfeits the privilege of being treated as a prisoner of war, and may be tried by court-martial. The Hague Regulations do not lay down the punishment for such a breach of parole; but according to a customary rule of International Law the punishment may be capital.

[1] Concerning the question whether after conclusion of peace such prisoners as are undergoing a term of imprisonment for offences against discipline may be detained, see below, § 275.

[2] For the disciplinary measures taken against prisoners by the various belligerents during the World War, see Garner, i. 354.

[3] See Knorr, *Das Ehrenwort Kriegsgefangener in seiner geschichtlichen Entwickelung* (1916).

§ 130. According to Articles 14 and 16 of the Hague Regulations every belligerent, and likewise a neutral State which receives and detains members of the armed forces of the belligerents, must institute on the commencement of war a bureau of information relative to prisoners of war. This bureau is intended to answer all inquiries about prisoners. It must be furnished by all the services concerned with all the necessary information to enable it to make out, and keep up to date, a separate return for each prisoner, and it must, therefore, be kept informed of internments and changes as well as of admissions into hospital, of deaths, releases on parole, exchanges, and escapes. It must state in its return for each prisoner the regimental number, surname and name, age, place of origin, rank, unit, wounds, date and place of capture, of internment, of the wounds received, date of death, and any observations of a special character. This separate return must, after conclusion of peace, be sent to the Government of the other belligerent. Bureau of Information.

The bureau must likewise receive and collect all objects of personal use, valuables, letters, and the like, found on battlefields,[1] or left by prisoners who have been released on parole, or exchanged, or who have escaped, or died in hospital or ambulances, and must transmit these articles to those interested. The bureau must enjoy the privilege of free postage.[2]

§ 131. A new and valuable rule, taken from the Brussels Declaration, was introduced by Article 15 of the Hague Regulations, which makes it a duty for every belligerent to grant facilities to relief societies to serve as intermediaries for charity to prisoners of war. The condition of the admission of such societies Relief Societies.

[1] See above, § 124.

[2] Such bureaux were set up at the outbreak of the World War; see Garner, i. § 332. As to the bureau established by Great Britain, see Roxburgh, *The Prisoners of War Information Bureau in London* (1915).

and their agents is that the former are regularly constituted in accordance with the law of their country. Delegates of such societies may be admitted to the places of internment for the distribution of relief, as also to the halting-places of repatriated prisoners, through a personal permit of the military authorities, provided they give an engagement in writing that they will comply with all regulations by the authorities for order and police.

Prisoners of War during the World War.

§ 131*a*. These rules of the Hague Convention had, as has been said, been laid down in time of peace; and in war the attitude of belligerents towards prisoners is liable to change.[1] All the States involved in the World War charged one another with violating the Hague Regulations by the maltreatment of prisoners of war, and at an early stage they arranged for inspection by a neutral representative of the camps on their territory.[2] The reports of the inspectors disclosed conditions at certain times in certain German camps which were very bad, and made it clear that almost everywhere in Germany prisoners were suffering great hardships through insufficient food and clothing. The reports on British and French camps were almost uniformly satisfactory. None the less, Germany disbelieved them, and resorted to reprisals for the alleged maltreatment of German prisoners, while the Allies, in their turn, feared that conditions in the camps in Germany were even worse than appeared from the reports. Whatever may be the value as evidence of some of the charges, undoubtedly the Hague Regulations were grievously violated by Germany in letter and in spirit.

During 1916, Great Britain, France, and Germany

[1] See an address by Lord Justice Younger in *The Times* of May 31, 1920.

[2] See details in Garner, i. §§ 333-334.

mutually agreed to transfer to Switzerland, for internment there, wounded prisoners and those suffering from certain diseases, and to repatriate certain classes of interned civilians. Germany and Russia later reached an agreement for the repatriation of incapacitated prisoners. In 1918, France and Germany arranged to repatriate those combatant prisoners (other than officers) who had been long in captivity and were over a given age, and a similar agreement between Great Britain and Germany was under negotiation when hostilities ended.[1]

But these measures brought relief to comparatively few, and the position of the far greater number of prisoners who did not belong to these categories was still exercising all the belligerent Governments at the close of hostilities. To secure better treatment for American prisoners, the United States had induced Germany to send delegates to Berne, and there, on November 11, 1918, an agreement was signed concerning prisoners of war, sanitary personnel, and civil prisoners.[2] Although this agreement was not ratified, because hostilities came to an end through the general armistice of the same date, it is epoch-making.

§ 132. Captivity can come to an end in different ways. Apart from release on parole, and exchange, which have already been mentioned, it comes to an end—(1) through simple release without parole; (2) through successful flight; (3) through liberation by an invasion of the army to which the prisoners belong; (4) through prisoners[3] being brought into neutral territory by captors who take refuge there; and, lastly (5), through the war coming to an end. Release of prisoners for ransom is no longer practised, except in

End of Captivity.

[1] See details in Garner, i. § 357-360.

[2] See *A.J.*, xiii. (1919), pp. 97-101, and Supplement, pp. 1-72.

[3] See below, § 337.

the case of the crew of a captured merchantman released on a ransom bill.[1] But the practice of ransoming prisoners might be revived if convenient, provided that the ransom is to be paid, not to the individual captor, but to the belligerent whose forces made the capture.

As regards the end of captivity through the war coming to an end, a distinction must be made according to the different modes of ending war. If the war ends by peace being concluded, captivity comes to an end at once [2] with the conclusion of peace, and, as Article 20 of the Hague Regulations expressly enacts, the repatriation of prisoners must be effected as speedily as possible. If, however, the war ends through conquest and annexation of the vanquished State, captivity comes to an end as soon as peace is established. It ought to end with annexation, and it will in most cases do so. But as guerilla war may well go on after conquest and annexation, and thus prevent a condition of peace from being established, although real warfare is over, it is necessary not to confound annexation with peace.[3] The point is of interest regarding such prisoners only as are subjects of neutral States. For other prisoners become, through annexation, subjects of the State that keeps them in captivity, and that State is, therefore, so far as International Law is concerned, unrestricted in taking any measure it likes with regard to them. It can repatriate them; and it will in most cases do so. But if it thinks that they might endanger its hold over the conquered territory, it might likewise prevent their repatriation for any definite or indefinite period.[4]

[1] See below, § 195.

[2] That, nevertheless, the prisoners remain under the discipline of the captor until they have been handed over to the authorities of their home State, will be shown below, § 275.

[3] See above, § 60.

[4] Thus, after the South African War, Great Britain refused to repatriate those prisoners of war who were not prepared to take the oath of allegiance.

V

APPROPRIATION AND UTILISATION OF PUBLIC ENEMY PROPERTY

Grotius, iii. c. 5—Vattel, iii. §§ 73, 160-164—Hall, §§ 136-138—Westlake, ii. pp. 113-121—Lawrence, §§ 171-175—Maine, pp. 192-206—Manning, pp. 179-183—Twiss, ii. §§ 62-71—Halleck, ii. pp. 58-68—Moore, vii. § 1148—Taylor, §§ 529-536—Wharton, iii. § 340—Wheaton, §§ 346, 352-354—Bluntschli, §§ 644-651*a*—Heffter, §§ 130-136—Lueder in *Holtzendorff*, iv. pp. 488-500—G. F. Martens, ii. §§ 279-280—Ullmann, § 183—Bonfils, Nos. 1176-1193—Despagnet, Nos. 592-604—Pradier-Fodéré, vii. Nos. 2989-3018—Rivier, ii. pp. 306-314—Nys, iii. pp. 252-266—Calvo, iv. §§ 2199-2214—Fiore, iii. Nos. 1389, 1392, 1393, 1470, and *Code*, Nos. 1562-1565—Martens, ii. § 120—Longuet, § 96—Mérignhac, iii[a]. pp. 459-494—Pillet, pp. 249-254—Garner, ii. § 398—*Kriegsbrauch*, pp. 57-60—Holland, *War*, Nos. 113-116—*Land Warfare*, §§ 426-432—Meurer, ii. §§ 65-69—Spaight, pp. 410-418—Zorn, pp. 243-270—Rouard de Card, *La Guerre continentale et la Propriété* (1877)—Bluntschli, *Das Beuterecht im Krieg, und das Seebeuterecht insbesondere* (1878)—Depambour, *Des Effets de l'Occupation en Temps de Guerre sur la Propriété et la Jouissance des Biens publics et particuliers* (1900)—Wehberg, *Das Beuterecht im Land und Seekriege* (1909; an English translation appeared in 1911 under the title *Capture in War on Land and Sea*)—Latifi, *Effects of War on Property* (1909)—Huber in *R.G.*, xx. (1913), pp. 657-697.

Appropriation of all the Enemy Property no longer admissible.

§ 133. Under a former rule of International Law, belligerents could appropriate all public and private[1] enemy property which they found on enemy territory. This rule is now obsolete. Its place is taken by several rules, since distinctions are to be made between moveable and immoveable property, between public and private property, and, further, between different kinds of public and private property. These rules must be discussed *seriatim*.

[1] It is impossible for a treatise to go into historical details, and to show the gradual disappearance of the old rule. Even during the nineteenth century—see, for instance, G. F. Martens, ii. § 280; Twiss, ii. § 64; Hall, § 139—it was asserted that in strict law all private enemy moveable property found on enemy territory was as much booty as public property, although the growth of a usage was recognised which under certain conditions exempted it from appropriation. In the face of Articles 46 and 47 of the Hague Regulations these assertions have no longer any basis, and all the text-books of the nineteenth century are now antiquated with regard to this matter.

Immoveable Public Property.

§ 134. Appropriation of public immoveables is not lawful so long as the territory on which they are has not become State property of the occupant through annexation. During mere military occupation of enemy territory, a belligerent may not sell, or otherwise alienate, public enemy land and buildings, but may only appropriate their produce. Article 55 of the Hague Regulations expressly enacts that a belligerent occupying enemy territory shall only be regarded as administrator and usufructuary of the public buildings, real property, forests, and agricultural works belonging to the hostile State and situated on the occupied territory; and that he must protect the stock and plant, and administer them according to the rules of usufruct. He may, therefore, sell the crops from public land, cut and sell timber in the public forests,[1] let public land and buildings for the time of his occupation, and the like. He is, however, only usufructuary, and is, therefore, prohibited from exercising his right in a wasteful or negligent way so as to decrease the value of the stock and plant. Thus, for instance, he must not cut down a whole forest, unless the necessities of war compel him.

Immoveable Property of Municipalities, and of Religious, Charitable, and the like Institutions.

§ 135. It must, however, be observed that only the produce of public immoveables belonging to the State itself may be appropriated, and not the produce of those belonging to municipalities, or of those which, although they belong to the hostile State, are permanently set aside for religious purposes, for the maintenance of charitable and educational institutions, or for the benefit of art and science. Article 56 of the Hague Regulations expressly enacts that such property is to be treated as private property.

§ 136. So far as the necessities of war demand, a belligerent may make use of public enemy buildings

[1] For details of the German practice during the World War, see Garner, ii. § 398.

for all kinds of purposes. Troops must be housed, horses stabled, the sick and wounded nursed. Public buildings may in the first instance, therefore, be made use of for such purposes, although they may thereby be considerably damaged. And it matters not whether the buildings belong to the enemy State or to municipalities, whether they are regularly destined for ordinary governmental and municipal purposes, or for religious, educational, scientific, and similar purposes. Thus, churches may be converted into hospitals, schools into barracks, buildings used for scientific research into stables. But it must be observed that such utilisation of public buildings as damages them is justified only if it is necessary. A belligerent who turned a picture gallery into stables without being compelled thereto would certainly commit a violation of the Law of Nations.

Utilisation of Public Buildings.

Moveable Public Property.

§ 137. Moveable public enemy property may certainly be appropriated by a belligerent, provided that it can directly or indirectly be useful for military operations. Article 53 of the Hague Regulations unmistakably enacts that a belligerent occupying hostile territory may take possession of the cash, funds, realisable securities, depots of arms, means of transport, stores, supplies, appliances (on land, or at sea, or in the air) adapted for the transmission of news or for the transport of persons or goods, and of all other moveable property of the hostile State which may be used for military operations. Thus, a belligerent is entitled to seize not only the money and funds[1] of the hostile State, munitions of war, depots of arms, stores and supplies, but also the rolling stock of public

[1] As regards the funds of *public* banks, see Schiemann, *Rechtslage der öffentlichen Banken im Kriegsfalle* (1902), pp. 39-64, and Dicker, *Unterliegt die Reichsbank im Kriegsfalle dem Beuterecht des Feindes* (1912), especially pp. 58-69; see also Huber in *R.G.*, xx. (1913), pp. 667-679. As to the funds of private banks, see below, § 143*a*.

railways[1] and other means of transport, and everything and anything that he can directly or indirectly make use of for military operations. He may, for instance, seize a quantity of cloth for the purpose of clothing his soldiers.

Moveable Property of Municipalities, and of Religious, Charitable, and the like Institutions.

§ 138. But just as the produce of certain public immoveables may not be appropriated, so certain public moveables may not be appropriated. For Article 56 of the Hague Regulations exempts the property of municipalities, of religious, charitable, educational institutions, and of institutions of science and art. Thus the moveable property of churches, hospitals, schools, universities, museums, and picture galleries, even when belonging to the hostile State, cannot lawfully be appropriated by a belligerent. As regards archives, they are no doubt institutions for science, but a belligerent may nevertheless seize such State papers deposited therein as are of importance to him in connection with the war.

Moveable Public Property during the World War.

§ 138*a*. Such are the rules regarding moveable public property found in enemy territory; but they were during the World War systematically violated by the Central Powers, which carried off public moveable property of all kinds, even though of no military value, following the example of Napoleon I., who seized works of art during his numerous wars and had them taken to the galleries of Paris. But just as the property seized by Napoleon had to be restored to its former owners in 1815, the property taken away by the Central Powers had to be restored under the Armistices and the Treaties of Peace.[2]

[1] See Nowacki, *Die Eisenbahnen im Kriege* (1906), §§ 15, 19. Some writers—see, for instance, Bonfils, No. 1185, and Wehberg, *op. cit.*, p. 22—maintain that such rolling stock may not be appropriated, but may only be made use of during war, and must be restored after the conclusion of peace. The assertion that Article 53, second paragraph, is to be interpreted in that sense, is unfounded, for restoration is there stipulated for such means of transport and the like as are *private* property.

[2] Thus Article 245 of the Treaty of Peace with Germany provides for

Booty on the Battle-field.

§ 139. The case of moveable enemy property found by an invading belligerent on enemy territory is different from that of moveable enemy property on the battlefield. According to a former rule of the Law of Nations, all enemy property, public or private, which a belligerent could get hold of on the battlefield was booty, and could be appropriated. Although some modern publicists[1] who wrote before the Hague Conference of 1899 teach the validity of this rule, it is obvious from Articles 4 and 14 of the Hague Regulations that it is now obsolete as regards *private*[2] enemy property, except military papers, arms, horses, and the like. But as regards *public* enemy property, this customary rule is still valid. Thus not only weapons, munitions, and valuable pieces of equipment which are found upon the dead, wounded, and prisoners, may be seized, but also the war-chest and State papers in possession of a captured commander, enemy horses, batteries, carts, and all other public property found on the field of battle that is of value. To whom the booty ultimately belongs is not for International but for Municipal Law[3] to determine, since International Law simply states that public enemy property on the battlefield can be appropriated by belligerents. The restriction in Article 53 of the Hague Regulations that only such moveable property may be appropriated as can be used for the operations of war, does not apply to property found on the battlefield, for Article 53 speaks of 'an army of occupation' only. Such property may be appropriated, whether it can be used for military operations or not; the mere fact that it was seized on the battlefield entitles a belligerent to appropriate it.

the restoration of the trophies, archives, historical souvenirs, or works of art carried away from France by the German authorities. See also Articles 238, 244, Annex.

[1] See, for instance, Halleck, ii. p. 73, and Heffter, § 135.

[2] See above, § 124, and below, § 144.

[3] According to British law, all booty belongs to the Crown. See Twiss, ii. §§ 64, 71.

VI

APPROPRIATION AND UTILISATION OF PRIVATE ENEMY PROPERTY

Grotius, iii. c. 5—Vattel, iii. §§ 73, 160-164—Hall, §§ 139, 141-144—Westlake, ii. pp. 103-104—Lawrence, §§ 172-175, 179—Maine, pp. 192-206—Manning, pp. 179-183—Twiss, ii. §§ 62-71—Halleck, ii. pp. 73-75—Moore, vii. §§ 1121, 1151, 1152, 1155—Taylor, §§ 529, 532, 537—Wharton, iii. § 338—Wheaton, § 355—Bluntschli, §§ 652, 656-659—Heffter, §§ 130-136—Lueder in *Holtzendorff*, iv. pp. 488-500—G. F. Martens, ii. §§ 279-280—Ullmann, § 183—Bonfils, Nos. 1194-1206—Despagnet, Nos. 579-590—Pradier-Fodéré, vii. Nos. 3032-3047—Rivier, ii. pp. 318-323—Nys, iii. pp. 252-266—Calvo, iv. §§ 2220-2229—Fiore, iii. Nos. 1391, 1392, 1472, and *Code*, Nos. 1535-1536, 1622-1623—Martens, ii. § 120—Longuet, §§ 97-98—Mérignhac, iii^a. pp. 418-427—Pillet, pp. 333-342—*Kriegsbrauch*, pp. 53-56—Zorn, pp. 270-283—Meurer, ii. § 54—Spaight, pp. 188-201—Garner, ii. §§ 395-397, 399—Holland, *War*, Nos. 106-107—*Land Warfare*, §§ 407-415—Bentwich, *The Law of Private Property in War* (1907)—Borchard, § 104—See also the monographs of Rouard de Card, Bluntschli, Depambour, Wehberg, and Latifi, quoted above at the commencement of § 133.

Immoveable Private Property.

§ 140. Immoveable private enemy property may under no circumstances or conditions be appropriated by an invading belligerent. Should he confiscate and sell private land or buildings, the buyer would acquire no right [1] whatever to the property. Article 46 of the Hague Regulations expressly enacts that 'private property may not be confiscated.' [2] But confiscation differs from the temporary use of private land and buildings for all kinds of purposes demanded by the necessities of war. What has been said above [3] with regard to utilisation of public buildings applies equally [4] to private buildings. If necessary, they may be con-

[1] See below, § 283.

[2] Although the Hague Regulations cannot literally be applied in occupied enemy colonies populated by natives and having only a few white settlers, their real estate must not be sold, as was done in German East Africa, Togoland, Samoa, and the Cameroons, during the World War.

[3] § 136.

[4] The Hague Regulations do not mention this; they simply enact in Article 46 that private property must be 'respected,' and may not be confiscated.

verted into hospitals, barracks, and stables without compensation for the proprietors, and they may also be converted into fortifications. A humane belligerent will not drive the wretched inhabitants into the street if he can help it. But under the pressure of necessity he may be obliged to do this, and he is certainly not prohibited from doing it.

Private War Material and Means of Transport.

§ 141. All kinds of private moveable property which can serve as war material, such as arms, ammunition, cloth for uniforms, leather for boots, saddles, and also all appliances (whether on land or at sea or in the air) which are adapted for the transmission of news or for the transport of persons and goods, such as railway rolling stock,[1] ships, telegraphs, telephones, carts, and horses, may be seized and made use of for military purposes by an invading belligerent; but they must be restored at the conclusion of peace, and compensation must be paid for them. This is expressly enacted by Article 53 of the Hague Regulations. It is evident that the seizure of such material must be duly acknowledged by receipt, although Article 53 does not say so; for otherwise how could compensation be paid after the conclusion of peace? As regards the question who is to pay the compensation, Holland [2] correctly maintains that 'the Treaty of Peace must settle upon whom the burden of making compensation is ultimately to fall.'

Works of Art and Science, Historical Monuments.

§ 142. On the other hand, works of art and science, and historical monuments, may not under any circumstances or conditions be appropriated or made use of for military operations. Article 56 of the Hague Regulations enacts categorically that 'all seizure' of such works and monuments is prohibited. Therefore,

[1] See Nowacki, *Die Eisenbahnen im Kriege* (1906), § 15. Different, of course, is the seizure of the railway *tracks*, and their removal to other countries, as to which see Garner, ii. § 397.

[2] War, No. 113.

although the metal of which a statue is cast may be of the greatest value for cannons, it must not be touched.

Other Private Personal Property.

§ 143. Private personal property which does not consist of war material or means of transport serviceable for military operations may not as a rule be seized.[1] Articles 46 and 47 of the Hague Regulations expressly stipulate that 'private property may not be confiscated,' and 'pillage is formally prohibited.' But it must be emphasised that these rules have, in a sense, exceptions demanded and justified by the necessities of war. Men and horses must be fed; men must protect themselves against the weather. If there is no time for ordinary requisitions [2] to provide food, forage, clothing, and fuel, or if the inhabitants of a locality have fled, so that ordinary requisitions cannot be made, a belligerent must take these articles wherever he can get them, and he is justified [3] in so doing. Moreover, quartering [4] of soldiers (who, together with their horses, must be well fed by the inhabitants of the houses where they are quartered) is likewise lawful, although it may be ruinous to the private individuals upon whom they are quartered.[4]

Moveable Private Property in the World War.

§ 143*a*. Such are the rules regarding moveable private property found in enemy territory; but they were systematically violated by the Central Powers during the World War. Live stock, particularly cattle and horses, were seized in Belgium and the occupied parts of France and carried off to Germany.[5] Factories and workshops were dismantled, and their machinery and materials carried away.[6] Cash was taken from private

[1] See above, § 133 n. Nor may the occupant liquidate the businesses of enemy subjects in occupied territory, although he can control them, and must certainly not sell their real estate (see above, § 140), even if the proceeds are to be handed over to them after the war.

[2] See below, § 147.

[3] The Hague Regulations do not mention this case.

[4] See below, § 147.

[5] See Garner, ii. § 395, who quotes Lord R. Cecil as stating on March 19, 1918, 'Belgium had 1,500,000 cattle; we know that practically half of these have gone to Germany.'

[6] See Garner, ii. § 396.

banks.[1] These are but examples of the wholesale seizure of private property practised by Germany and her allies in the countries which they occupied.[2] However, reparation has to be made under the Armistices and Treaties of Peace. Thus Germany must effect 'restitution in cash of cash taken away, seized or sequestrated, and also restitution of animals, objects of every nature, and securities taken away, seized, or sequestrated, in the cases in which it proves possible to identify them in territory belonging to Germany or her allies,'[3] and pay compensation for 'damage in respect of all property wherever situated belonging to any of the Allied or Associated States or their nationals (with the exception of naval and military works or materials) which has been carried off, seized, injured, or destroyed by the acts of Germany or her allies.'[4]

§ 144. Private enemy property on the battlefield is no longer in every case an object of booty.[5] Arms, horses, and military papers may indeed be appropriated,[6] even if they are private property, as may also private means of transport, such as carts and other vehicles which an enemy has made use of. But letters, cash, jewellery, and other articles of value found upon the dead, wounded, and prisoners must, according to Article 14 of the Hague Regulations and Article 4 of the Geneva Convention, be handed over to the Bureau of Information regarding Prisoners of War, which must

Booty on the Battle field.

[1] See Garner, ii. § 399. Cash was also apparently taken by the Russians from private banks during their occupation of Lemberg; see Cybichowski in *Z.I.*, xxvi. (1916), at p. 470.

[2] See also below, § 147. See also the account of the removal by the Russians of valuables, pictures, and other property from Lemberg during their occupation given by Cybichowski in *Z.I.*, xxvi. (1916), at pp. 445, 468.

[3] Article 238.

[4] Article 244, Annex 1.

[5] See above, § 139.

[6] See above, § 139, and Article 4 of the Hague Regulations. This article only mentions arms, horses, and military papers; but saddles, stirrups, and the like go with horses, as ammunition goes with arms, and these may for this reason likewise be appropriated; see *Land Warfare*, § 69, note (*e*).

transmit them to those interested. Through Article 14 of the Hague Regulations and Article 4 of the Geneva Convention it becomes apparent that nowadays private enemy property found on the battlefield, other than military papers, arms, horses, and the like, is no longer booty, although individual soldiers often take as much spoil as they can get. It is impossible for the commander to bring the offender to justice in every case.[1]

Private Enemy Property brought into a Belligerent's Territory.

§ 145. Such is the position of private property found by a belligerent on enemy territory; different, however, is the case of enemy private property brought into the territory of a belligerent during war. Since such property found there at the outbreak of war may not be confiscated,[2] and private property found on enemy territory is nowadays likewise, as a rule, exempt from confiscation, there can be no doubt that private enemy property brought into a belligerent's territory during time of war may not, as a rule, be confiscated.[3] On the other hand, a belligerent may prohibit the withdrawal of articles of property which can be used by the enemy for military purposes, such as arms, ammunition, provisions, and the like. And by analogy with Article 53 of the Hague Regulations, there can be no doubt that a belligerent may seize such articles and use them for military purposes, provided that he restores them at the conclusion of peace and pays compensation for them.

[1] During the Russo-Japanese War, Japan carried out to the letter the stipulation of Article 14 of the Hague Regulations. Through the intermediary of the French Embassies in Tokio and St. Petersburg, all valuables found on the Russian dead and seized by the Japanese were handed over to the Russian Government.

[2] See above, § 102.

[3] The case of enemy merchantmen seized in a belligerent's territorial waters is, of course, an exception, as is also the case of enemy goods found by a belligerent on one of his own merchantmen and seized in one of his ports. See above, § 102, and below, §§ 177 n., 197 n.

VII

REQUISITIONS AND CONTRIBUTIONS

Vattel, iii. § 165—Hall, § 140-140*—Lawrence, § 180—Westlake, ii. pp. 106-113—Maine, p. 200—Twiss, ii. § 64—Halleck, ii. pp. 68-70—Taylor, §§ 538-539—Moore, vii. § 1146—Bluntschli, §§ 653-655—Heffter, § 131—Lueder in *Holtzendorff*, iv. pp. 500-510—Ullmann, § 183—Bonfils, Nos. 1207-1226—Despagnet, Nos. 587-590—Pradier-Fodéré, vii. Nos. 3048-3064—Rivier, ii. pp. 324-327—Nys, iii. pp. 328-392—Calvo, iv. §§ 2231-2284—Fiore, iii. Nos. 1394, 1473-1476, and *Code*, Nos. 1565, 1614-1620—Martens, ii. § 120—Longuet, §§ 110-114—Mérignhac, iii[a]. pp. 427-459—Pillet, pp. 215-235—Zorn, pp. 283-315—*Kriegsbrauch*, pp. 61-63—Holland, *War*, Nos. 111-112—Bordwell, pp. 314-324—Meurer, ii. §§ 56-64—Spaight, pp. 381-408—Ariga, §§ 116-122—Garner, ii. §§ 387-394, and in *A.J.*, xi. (1917), pp. 74-112—*Land Warfare*, §§ 416-425—Thomas, *Des Réquisitions militaires* (1884)—Keller, *Requisition und Kontribution* (1898)—Pont, *Les Réquisitions militaires du Temps de Guerre* (1905)—Albrecht, *Requisitionen von neutralem Privateigentum, etc.* (1912), pp. 1-24—Gregory, *Contributions and Requisitions in War* (1915)—Borchard, § 105—Ferrand, *Des Réquisitions en matière de Droit international public* (1917)—Risley in the *Journal of the Society of Comparative Legislation*, New Ser. ii. (1900), pp. 214-223.

War must support War.

§ 146. Requisitions and contributions in war are the outcome of the eternal principle that war must support war.[1] This means that every belligerent may make his enemy pay, as far as possible, for the continuation of the war. But this principle, though it is as old as war, and will only die with war itself, has not the same effect in modern times on the actions of belligerents as it formerly had. For thousands of years, belligerents used to appropriate all private and public enemy property they could obtain, and, when modern International Law grew up, this practice found legal sanction. But after the end of the seventeenth century, this practice grew milder, under the influence of the experience that the provisioning of armies in enemy territory became more or less impossible when the inhabitants were treated according to the old principle.

[1] Concerning the controversy as to the justification of requisitions and contributions, see Albrecht, *op. cit.*, pp. 18-21.

Although belligerents retained, in strict law, the right to appropriate all private as well as all public property, it became usual to abstain from enforcing this right, and in lieu thereof to impose contributions of cash and requisitions in kind upon the inhabitants of the invaded country.[1] When this usage developed, no belligerent ever thought of paying in cash for requisitions, or giving a receipt for them. But in the nineteenth century another practice became usual; and commanders often gave a receipt for contributions and requisitions, in order to avoid abuse, and to prevent further demands for fresh contributions and requisitions by succeeding commanders without knowledge of the former impositions. And there are cases during the nineteenth century on record in which belligerents actually paid in cash for all requisitions they made. The usual practice at the end of the nineteenth century was that commanders always gave a receipt for contributions, and that they either paid in cash for requisitions, or acknowledged them by receipt, so that the inhabitants could be indemnified by their own Government after conclusion of peace. However, no restriction whatever was imposed upon commanders with regard to the amount of contributions and requisitions, or with regard to the proportion between the resources of a country and the burden imposed.

The Hague Regulations made a progressive settlement of the question by enacting rules which put it wholly on a new basis. That war must support war remains a principle under these regulations also. But they were widely influenced by the demand that the enemy State as such, and not the private enemy individuals, should be made to support the war, and that

[1] An excellent sketch of the historical development of the practice of requisitions and contributions is given by Keller, *Requisition und Kontribution* (1898), pp. 5-26.

only so far as the necessities of war demanded it, should contributions and requisitions be imposed. Although, therefore, certain public moveable property and the produce of public immoveables may be appropriated as heretofore,[1] requisitions must be paid for in cash or, if this is impossible, acknowledged by receipt.

§ 147. Requisition is the name for the demand for the supply of all kinds of articles necessary for an army, such as provisions for men and horses, clothing, or means of transport. Requisition of certain services may also be made, but they will be treated [2] together with occupation, requisitions in kind only being within the scope of this section. Now, what articles may be demanded by an army cannot once for all be laid down, as they depend upon its actual needs. According to Article 52 of the Hague Regulations, requisitions may be made from municipalities as well as from inhabitants, but so far only as they are really necessary for the army.[3] They may not be made by individual soldiers or officers, but only by the commander in the locality. All requisitions must be paid for in cash, and if this is impossible, they must be acknowledged by receipt,[4] and the payment of the amount must be made as soon as possible. The principle that requisitions must be paid for by the enemy is thereby

Requisitions in Kind, and Quartering.

[1] See above, §§ 134, 137.

[2] See below, § 170.

[3] Article 52 was entirely ignored by the Germans while they occupied Belgium and part of France during the World War, for they made requisitions, not only for the needs of the army of occupation, but for the needs of Germany in general. See details in Ferrand, *op. cit.*, pp. 434-444, and Garner, ii. §§ 393, who concludes that 'as the blockade of Germany became more effective, and her own domestic stocks of raw materials were reduced, the policy of requisition in the occupied territories was pushed to the extreme limit. By the spring of 1918 it appears to have degenerated into a system of indiscriminate pillage . . . the same policy . . . is alleged to have been carried out in Serbia, Roumania, Poland, Northern Italy, and other territories occupied by the armies of the Central Powers.'

[4] See Garner, ii. § 393, who quotes a report from Belgian sources that at Antwerp, prior to March 1915, 85,000,000 francs' worth of supplies were requisitioned by the Germans, that at the date of the report less than half that amount had been paid, and in most cases no receipts had been given.

absolutely recognised, but, of course, commanders-in-chief may levy contributions[1] in case they do not possess cash for payment of requisitions. However this may be, from the rule that requisitions must always be paid for, it again becomes apparent, and beyond all doubt, that private enemy property is, as a rule, exempt from appropriation by an invading army.

A special kind of requisition is the quartering[2] of soldiers in the houses of private inhabitants of enemy territory who are required to supply lodging and food for them, and sometimes also stabling and forage for horses. Although the Hague Regulations do not specially mention quartering, Article 52 is nevertheless to be applied to it, since quartering is nothing else than a special kind of requisition. If cash cannot be paid at once for quartering, every inhabitant concerned must get a receipt for it, stating the number of soldiers quartered, and the number of days they were catered for, and the payment of the amount must be made as soon as possible.

However, neither in the case of ordinary requisitions, nor in the case of quartering of troops, is a commander compelled to pay the prices asked by the inhabitants. On the contrary, he may fix the prices himself, although it is expected that they shall be fair.

Contributions.

§ 148. Contribution is a payment in ready money demanded either from municipalities or from inhabitants, whether enemy subjects or foreign residents. Whereas formerly no general rules concerning contributions existed, Articles 49 and 51 of the Hague Regulations enacted that contributions might not be demanded extortionately, but exclusively[3] for the needs of the

[1] See below, § 148.
[2] See above, § 143.
[3] As regards contributions as a penalty, see Article 50 of the Hague Regulations. See also Keller, *op. cit.*, pp. 60-62.

army, in order, for instance, to pay for requisitions, or for the administration of the locality in question. They might be imposed by a written order of a commander-in-chief only, in contradistinction to requisitions, which might be imposed by a mere commander in a locality. They might not be imposed indiscriminately on the inhabitants, but must so far as possible be assessed upon them in compliance with the rules laid down by their own Government regarding the assessment of taxes. And, finally, for every individual contribution a receipt had to be given. It is apparent that these rules of the Hague Regulations sought to exclude all arbitrariness and despotism on the part of an invading enemy with regard to contributions, and to secure to the individual contributors, as well as to contributing municipalities, the possibility of being indemnified afterwards by their own Government, thus shifting, so far as possible, the burden of supporting the war from private individuals and municipalities to the State proper.[1]

But the Hague Regulations relating to contributions, as well as those relating to requisitions, were violated by the Central Powers in the territories which they occupied during the World War. In Belgium and Northern France, for example, the contributions which they levied were undoubtedly excessive, for they were required neither for the needs of the army of occupation nor for the administration of the country.[2]

[1] It is strange to observe that *Kriegsbrauch*, pp. 61-63, does not mention the Hague Regulations at all.

[2] See details in Garner, ii. §§ 388-389. By the Treaty of Peace (Article 244, Annex 1), Germany is liable to pay compensation for damage 'in the form of levies . . . upon the civilian population.'

VIII

DESTRUCTION OF ENEMY PROPERTY

Grotius, iii. c. 5, §§ 1-3; c. 12—Vattel, iii. §§ 166-168—Hall, § 186—Lawrence, § 206—Manning, p. 186—Twiss, ii. §§ 65-69—Halleck, ii. pp. 63, 64, 71, 74—Taylor, §§ 481-482—Wharton, iii. § 349—Moore, vii. § 1113—Wheaton, §§ 347-351—Bluntschli, §§ 649, 651, 662, 663—Heffter, § 125—Lueder in *Holtzendorff*, iv. pp. 482-487—Klüber, § 262—G. F. Martens, ii. § 280—Ullmann, § 176—Bonfils, Nos. 1078, 1178-1180—Pradier-Fodéré, vi. Nos. 2770-2774—Rivier, ii. pp. 265-268—Nys, iii. pp. 160-164—Calvo, iv. §§ 2215-2222—Fiore, iii. Nos. 1383-1388, and *Code*, Nos. 1530-1534, 1610-1611—Martens, ii. § 110—Longuet, §§ 99, 100—Garner, i. §§ 206-213—*Kriegsbrauch*, pp. 53-56—Holland, *War*, Nos. 3 and 76(*g*)—Bordwell, p. 284—Spaight, pp. 111-140—*Land Warfare*, §§ 414, 422, 426, 427, 434.

Wanton Destruction prohibited.

§ 149. In former times invading armies frequently used to fire and destroy all enemy property they could not make use of or carry away. Afterwards, when the practice of warfare grew milder, belligerents in strict law retained the right to destroy enemy property according to discretion, although they did not, as a rule, any longer make use of such right. Nowadays, however, this right is obsolete. For in the nineteenth century it became a universally recognised rule of International Law that all useless and wanton destruction of enemy property, be it public or private, was absolutely prohibited; and this rule was expressly enacted by Article 23(*g*) of the Hague Regulations: 'to destroy . . . enemy's property, unless such destruction . . . be imperatively demanded by the necessities of war, is prohibited.'

Destruction for the Purpose of Offence and Defence.

§ 150. All destruction of, and damage to, enemy property for the purpose of offence and defence is *necessary* destruction and damage, and therefore lawful, whether it be on the battlefield during battle, or in preparation for battle or siege. To strengthen a defensive position, a house may be destroyed or damaged.

To cover the retreat of an army, a village on the battlefield may be fired. The district around a fortress held by an enemy may be razed, and, therefore, all private and public buildings, all vegetation may be destroyed, and all bridges blown up within a certain area. If a farm, a village, or even a town is not to be abandoned, but prepared for defence, it may be necessary to damage in many ways, or entirely destroy, private and public property. Further, if and where a bombardment is lawful, all destruction of property involved in it becomes likewise lawful. When a belligerent force obtains possession of an enemy factory which makes ammunition or supplies provisions for the enemy troops, if it is not certain that it can hold it against an attack, it may at least destroy the plant, if not the buildings. Or if a force occupies an enemy fortress, it may raze the fortifications. Even a force entrenching itself on a battlefield may be obliged to resort to the destruction of many kinds of property.

Be that as it may, in every case destruction must be '*imperatively* demanded by the necessities of war,' and must not merely be the outcome of a spirit of plunder or revenge such as, during the World War, prompted the dreadful and utter devastation [1] of houses, orchards, vineyards, trees in the area from which the German armies in France withdrew in the spring of 1917, and of the coal-mines, factories, and dwellings in Cambrai and elsewhere which marked the German line of retreat in the autumn of the following year.[2]

Destruction in Marching, Reconnoitring, and Conducting Transport.

§ 151. Destruction of enemy property in marching troops, conducting military transport, and in reconnoitring, is lawful if unavoidable. A reconnoitring party need not keep on the road if they can better serve

[1] See Garner, i. § 206, who quotes a German newspaper as saying: 'in front of our new positions runs, like a gigantic ribbon, an empire of death.'

[2] See Garner, i. § 211. See also below, § 154.

their purpose by riding across the tilled fields. And troops may be marched, and transport may be conducted, over crops when necessary. A humane commander will not unnecessarily allow his troops and transport to march and ride over tilled fields and crops. But if the purpose of war necessitates it, he is justified in so doing.

Destruction of Arms, Ammunition, and Provisions.

§ 152. Whatever enemy property a belligerent may appropriate he may likewise destroy. To prevent the enemy from making use of them a retreating force may destroy arms, ammunition, provisions, and the like, which they have taken from the enemy, or requisitioned and cannot carry away. But they may not destroy provisions in the possession of private enemy inhabitants in order to prevent the enemy from making use of them in the future.[1] Nor is a commander allowed to requisition such provisions in order to have them destroyed, for Article 52 of the Hague Regulations expressly enacts that requisitions are only admissible for the necessities of the army.

Destruction of Historical Monuments, Works of Art, and the like.

§ 153. All destruction of, and damage to, historical monuments, works of art and science, buildings for charitable, educational, and religious[2] purposes are specially prohibited by Article 56 of the Hague Regulations, which enacts that the perpetrators of such acts must be prosecuted (*poursuivis*), *i.e.* court-martialled. But these objects enjoy this protection only during military occupation of enemy territory. Should a battle be waged around an historical monument on open ground, should a church, a school, or a museum be defended and attacked during military operations, these

[1] Spaight, p. 138, objects to this statement. His arguments are not conclusive, because they concern the case of justified general devastation.

[2] According to Grotius (iii. c. 5, §§ 2 and 3), destruction of graves, tombstones, churches, and the like is not prohibited by the Law of Nations, although he strongly (iii. c. 12, §§ 5-7) advises that they should be spared, unless their preservation is dangerous to the interests of the invader.

otherwise protected objects may be damaged or destroyed under the same conditions as other enemy property.[1]

General Devastation.

§ 154. The question must also be considered whether, and under what conditions, general devastation of a locality, be it a town or a larger part of enemy territory, is permitted. There cannot be the slightest doubt that such devastation is, as a rule, absolutely prohibited, and only in exceptional cases permitted when, to use the words of Article 23(*g*) of the Hague Regulations, it is 'imperatively demanded by the necessities of war.' It is impossible to define once for all the circumstances which make a general devastation necessary, since everything depends upon the merits of the special case. But the fact that a general devastation can be lawful must be admitted. It is, for instance, lawful in case of a levy *en masse* on already occupied territory, when self-preservation obliges a belligerent to resort to the most severe measures. It is also lawful when, after the defeat of his main forces and occupation of his territory, an enemy disperses his remaining forces into small bands which carry on guerilla tactics and receive food and information, so that there is no hope of ending the war except by a general devastation which cuts off supplies of every kind from the guerilla bands. But it must be specially observed that general devastation is only justified by imperative necessity, and by the fact that there is no better and less severe way open to a belligerent.[2]

There was, for example, no imperative necessity to justify the general devastation by the German armies of the Somme area of France in the spring of 1917, during the World War, or of the country through which they were rolled back in the following autumn.[3]

[1] See further below, § 158.

[2] See Hall, § 186, who gives *in nuce* a good survey of the doctrine and practice of general devastation from Grotius down to the beginning of the nineteenth century. See also Spaight, pp. 125-139.

[3] See Fauchille, *L'Évacuation des Territoires occupés par l'Allemagne dans le Nord de la France* (1917);

Be that as it may, whenever a belligerent resorts to general devastation, he ought, if possible, to make some provision for the unfortunate peaceful population of the devastated tract of territory. It would be more humane to take them away into captivity rather than let them perish on the spot. The practice, resorted to during the South African War, of housing the victims of devastation in concentration camps, must be approved. The purpose of war may even oblige a belligerent to confine a population forcibly[1] in concentration camps.

IX

ASSAULT, SIEGE, AND BOMBARDMENT

Vattel, iii. §§ 169-170—Hall, § 186—Lawrence, § 204—Westlake, ii. pp. 87-89—Moore, vii. § 1112—Halleck, ii. pp. 59 n. 67, 185—Hershey, No. 382—Taylor, §§ 483-485—Bluntschli, §§ 552-554*b*—Heffter, § 125—Lueder in *Holtzendorff*, iv. pp. 448-457—G. F. Martens, ii. §§ 286-287—Ullmann, § 181—Bonfils, Nos. 1079-1087—Despagnet, Nos. 528-535—Pradier-Fodéré, vi. Nos. 2779-2786—Rivier, ii. pp. 284-288—Nys, iii. pp. 148-160—Calvo, iv. §§ 2067-2095—Fiore, iii. Nos. 1322-1330, and *Code*, Nos. 1524-1529—Longuet, §§ 58-59—Mérignhac, iii[a]. pp. 270-284—Pillet, pp. 101-112—Zorn, pp. 161-174—Holland, *War*, Nos. 80-83—Bordwell, pp. 286-288—Meurer, §§ 32-34—Spaight, pp. 157-201—Garner, i. §§ 269-272—*Kriegsbrauch*, pp. 18-22—*Land Warfare*, §§ 117-138—Rolin-Jaequemyns in *R.I.*, ii. (1870), pp. 659, 674, iii. (1871), pp. 297-307—Fauchille in *R.G.*, xxiv. (1917), pp. 56-74.

Assault, Siege, and Bombardment, when lawful.

§ 155. Assault is the rush of an armed force upon enemy forces in the battlefield, or upon entrenchments, fortifications, habitations, villages, or towns, such rushing force committing every violence against opposing persons, and destroying all impediments. Siege is the surrounding and investing of an enemy locality by an armed force, cutting off those inside from all

and in *R.G.*, xxiv. (1917), pp. 317-336, and Garner, i. §§ 206-213. See also above, § 150.

[1] See above, § 116 n. As regards devastation during the South African War, and the concentration camps instituted in consequence, see Beak, *The Aftermath of War* (1906), pp. 1-30; *The Times History of the War in South Africa*, v. pp. 252-254; Spaight, pp. 306-310.

communication, for the purpose of starving them into surrender, or for the purpose of attacking the invested locality and taking it by assault. Bombardment is the throwing by artillery of shot and shell upon persons and things. Siege can be accompanied by bombardment and assault, but this is not necessary, since a siege can be carried out by mere investment and starvation caused thereby. Assault, siege, and bombardment are severally and jointly perfectly legitimate means of warfare.[1] Neither bombardment nor assault *on* the battlefield need special discussion, as they are allowed under the same circumstances and conditions as force in general. The only question here is under what circumstances assault and bombardment are allowed *outside* the battlefield. The answer is indirectly given by Article 25 of the Hague Regulations, where it is categorically enacted that 'the attack or bombardment, by any means whatever, of towns, villages, habitations, or buildings, which are not defended, is prohibited.'[2] This provision involved a decided advance in the view taken by International Law, for it was formerly asserted by many writers[3] and military experts that, for certain reasons and purposes, undefended localities also might, in exceptional cases, be bombarded; and it is doubtful how far the practice of the World War came up to the new standard.[4] It matters not, however, whether the defended locality be fortified or not, since an unfortified place can be

[1] The assertion of some writers—see, for instance, Pillet, pp. 104-107, and Mérignhac, iii^{a}. p. 273—that bombardment is lawful only after an unsuccessful attempt by the besiegers to starve the besieged into surrender is not based upon a recognised rule of the Law of Nations.

[2] Siege is not there specially mentioned, both because no belligerent would dream of besieging an undefended locality, and because it would involve unjustifiable violence against enemy persons, and would, therefore, be unlawful.

[3] See, for instance, Lueder in *Holtzendorff*, iv. p. 451.

[4] For details of the many charges of bombarding undefended places which the belligerents made against each other, see Garner, i. §§ 269-270.

defended; but under what circumstances a place is to be regarded as defended is not always free from doubt.[1] Nothing prevents a belligerent who has taken possession of an undefended fortified place from destroying the fortifications by bombardment as well as by other means.

The words 'by any means whatever' were added by the Second Hague Conference so as to cover bombardment by aircraft. Nevertheless, it is maintained by some that, by analogy with bombardment by naval forces,[2] railway junctions, munition factories, and the like may be bombarded from the air though situated in undefended places. The question of law is controversial.[3] All belligerents resorted to such bombardments during the World War.

Assault, how carried out.

§ 156. Undefended towns, villages, habitations or buildings may not be assaulted;[4] but when assault is lawful, no special rules of International Law exist with regard to the mode of carrying it out. Therefore, only the general rules respecting offence and defence apply. It is in particular not[5] necessary to give notice of an impending assault to the authorities of the locality, or to request them to surrender before an assault is made. That an assault may, or may not, be preceded, or accompanied, by a bombardment, need hardly be mentioned, nor that, by Article 28 of the Hague Regulations, pillage of towns taken by assault is expressly prohibited.

Siege, how carried out.

§ 157. With regard to the mode of carrying out siege *without bombardment* no special rules of International Law exist, and here too only the general rules respect-

[1] See Holls, *The Peace Conference at the Hague* (1900), p. 152. According to *Land Warfare*, § 119, a locality 'may be deemed to be defended, if a military force is in occupation of, or marching through, it.'

[2] See below, § 213.

[3] See below, § 214*a*-*c*. The author had marked this question for consideration.

[4] See above, § 155.

[5] This may be inferred from Article 26 of the Hague Regulations.

ing offence and defence apply. Therefore, an armed force besieging a town may, for instance, cut off the river which supplies drinking water to the besieged, but must not poison[1] the river. Moreover, no rule of law exists which obliges a besieging force to allow all non-combatants, or even women, children, the aged, the sick and wounded, or subjects of neutral Powers, to leave the besieged locality unmolested. Although such permission[2] is sometimes granted, it is in most cases refused, because the fact that non-combatants are besieged together with the combatants, and have to endure the same hardships, may, and very often does, exercise pressure upon the authorities to surrender. Further, should the commander of a besieged place expel the non-combatants, in order to lessen the number of those who consume his store of provisions, the besieging force need not allow them to pass through its lines, but may drive them back.[3]

That diplomatic envoys of neutral Powers may not be prevented from leaving a besieged town is a consequence of their exterritoriality. However, if they voluntarily remain, may they claim uncontrolled[4] communication with their home State by correspondence and couriers? When Mr. Washburne, the American diplomatic envoy at Paris during the siege of that city in 1870 by the Germans, claimed the right of sending a messenger with despatches to London in a sealed bag through the German lines, Bismarck declared that he was ready to allow foreign diplomats in Paris to send a courier to their home States once a week, but only if their despatches were open and did not contain any remarks concerning the war. Although

[1] See above, § 110.

[2] Thus in 1870, during the Franco-German War, the German besiegers of Strasburg as well as of Belfort allowed the women, the children, and the sick to leave the besieged fortresses.

[3] See *Land Warfare*, § 129.

[4] The matter is discussed by Rolin-Jaequemyns in *R.I.*, iii. (1871), pp. 371-377.

the United States and other Powers protested, Bismarck did not alter his decision. The whole question must be treated as open.[1]

Bombardment, how carried out.

§ 158. Bombardment by land forces was not generally considered prior to the World War except in connection with assault or siege. But the experiences of that war, and in particular the new uses of aircraft and long-range guns, have raised the question[2] how far bombardment is lawful when it is solely for destructive purposes, and is not intended to be a prelude to occupation by armed forces. If, as is generally held, bombardment by aircraft within the theatre of operations is lawful, even though there is no intention to occupy the bombarded area, similar bombardment by long-range guns would appear to be legitimate.[3] However this may be, Article 26 of the Hague Regulations enacts that the commander of the attacking forces, except in the case of an assault, shall do all he can to notify his intention to resort to bombardment. But it must be emphasised that a strict duty of notification in all cases of bombardment is not thereby imposed, for a commander only has to *do all he can to* send notification. He cannot do it when the circumstances of the case prevent him, or when the necessities of war demand an immediate bombardment. The purpose of notification is to enable private individuals within the locality to be bombarded to seek shelter for their persons and for their valuable personal property.

Article 27 of the Hague Regulations enacts the former customary rule that all necessary steps must be taken to spare, as far as possible, all buildings devoted to religion, art, science, and charity, and

[1] See above, vol. i. § 399, and Wharton, i. § 97.

[2] See Fauchille in *R.G.*, xxiv. (1917), pp. 56-76.

[3] This expression of opinion has been put together from a rough note by the author, and he evidently intended to reconsider it.

historic monuments,[1] hospitals, and all other places where the sick and wounded are collected, provided these buildings, places, and monuments are not used at the same time for military purposes. To enable the attacking forces to spare them, they must be indicated by some signs, which must be previously notified to the attacking forces, and must be visible from the far distance from which the besieging artillery carries out the bombardment.

No bombardment takes place without the sufferers accusing the attacking forces of neglecting the rule that such places must be spared. The fact is that their destruction cannot always be avoided, although the artillery of the attacking forces may not intentionally aim at them. That the forces of civilised States intentionally destroy such buildings, I cannot believe.

In practice, whenever one belligerent accuses another of having intentionally bombarded a hospital, church, or similar building, the charge is always either denied with indignation or justified by the assertion that these sacred buildings have been used improperly by the accuser. Thus when France in 1870 complained that the Germans, during the siege of Paris, had deliberately bombarded the hospitals, the Germans asserted that it was an accident. Further, in 1870, during the siege of Strasburg, when the Germans bombarded the cathedral, they justified their action by asserting that the French had established an observation post thereon. Again, in the World War, when the Germans shelled and destroyed the cathedral of Rheims and other sacrosanct edifices, they again pleaded in justification that observation posts had been established thereon.[2]

However this may be, no legal duty exists for the

[1] See Zitelmann in *Z. V.*, x. (1917), pp. 1-19.

[2] For details regarding bombardment of places enumerated in Article 27 during the World War, see Garner, i. §§ 285-289.

attacking forces to restrict bombardment to fortifications only. On the contrary, destruction of private and public buildings through bombardment has always been, and is still, considered lawful, as it is one of the means of impressing upon the authorities the advisability of surrender. Some writers[1] assert either that bombardment of a town, in contradistinction to its fortifications, is never lawful, or, at any rate, only when bombardment of the fortifications has not induced surrender. But this opinion does not represent the actual practice of belligerents, and the Hague Regulations did not adopt it.

X

ESPIONAGE AND WAR TREASON

Grotius, iii. c. 4, § 18, No. 3—Vattel, iii. §§ 179-182—Hall, § 188—Westlake, ii. pp. 89-91—Lawrence, § 199—Phillimore, iii. § 96—Halleck, i. pp. 571-575, and in *A.J.*, v. (1911), pp. 590-603—Taylor, §§ 490, 492—Wharton, iii. § 347—Moore, vii. § 1132—Hershey, No. 383—Bluntschli, §§ 563-564, 628-640—Heffter, § 125—Lueder in *Holtzendorff*, iv. pp. 461-467—Ullmann, § 176—Bonfils, Nos. 1100-1104—Despagnet, Nos. 536-542—Pradier-Fodéré, vi. Nos. 2762-2768—Rivier, ii. pp. 282-284—Nys, iii. pp. 209-218—Calvo, iv. §§ 2111-2122—Fiore, iii. Nos. 1341, 1374-1376, and *Code*, Nos. 1492-1497—Martens, ii. § 116—Longuet, §§ 63-75—Mérignhac, iii[a]. pp. 285-299—Pillet, pp. 97-100—Zorn, pp. 174-195—Holland, *War*, Nos. 84-87—Bordwell, pp. 291-292—Meurer, §§ 35-38—Spaight, pp. 202-215, 333-335—Ariga, §§ 98-100—Takahashi, pp. 185-194—*Kriegsbrauch*, pp. 30-31—*Land Warfare*, §§ 155-173—Friedemann, *Die Rechtslage der Kriegskundschafter und Kriegsspione* (1892)—Detourbet, *L'Espionnage et la Trahison* (1898)—Violle, *L'Espionnage militaire en Temps de Guerre* (1904)—Adler, *Die Spionage* (1906)—Routier, *L'Espionnage et la Trahison en Temps de Paix et en Temps de Guerre* (1915)—Bentwich in the *Journal of the Society of Comparative Legislation*, New Ser. x. (1910), pp. 243-249—M'Kinney in the *Illinois Law Review*, xii. (1918), pp. 591-628.

Twofold Character of Espionage and War Treason.

§ 159. War cannot be waged without all kinds of information about the forces and the intentions of the enemy, and about the character of the country

[1] See, for instance, Pillet, pp. 104-107; Bluntschli, § 554*a*; Mérignhac, iii[a]. pp. 280-284. Vattel (iii. § 169) does not deny the right to bombard the town, although he does not recommend it.

within the zone of military operations. To obtain the necessary information, it has always been considered lawful to employ spies, and also to make use of the treason of enemy soldiers or private enemy subjects, whether they were bribed,[1] or offered the information voluntarily and gratuitously. Article 24 of the Hague Regulations enacted the old customary rule that the employment of methods necessary to obtain information about the enemy and the country is considered allowable. The fact, however, that these methods are lawful on the part of the belligerent who employs them does not prevent the punishment of such individuals as are engaged in procuring information. Although a belligerent acts lawfully in employing spies and traitors, the other belligerent, who punishes them, likewise acts lawfully. Indeed, espionage and war treason bear a twofold character. For persons committing acts of espionage or war treason are—as will be shown below[2]—considered war criminals and may be punished, but the employment of spies and traitors is considered lawful on the part of the belligerents.

Espionage in contradistinction to Scouting and Despatch-bearing.

§ 160. Espionage must not be confounded, firstly, with scouting, or secondly, with despatch-bearing. According to Article 29 of the Hague Regulations, espionage is the act of a soldier or other individual who clandestinely, or under false pretences, seeks to obtain information concerning one belligerent in the zone of belligerent operations with the intention of communicating it to the other belligerent.[3] Therefore, soldiers not in disguise, who penetrate into the zone of operations of the enemy, are not spies. They are scouts who enjoy all the privileges of members of armed

[1] Some writers maintain, however, that it is not lawful to bribe enemy soldiers into espionage; see below, § 162.

[2] § 255.

[3] Assisting or favouring espionage, or knowingly concealing a spy are, according to a customary rule of International Law, acts punishable as though they were themselves acts of espionage; see *Land Warfare*, § 172.

forces, and they must, if captured, be treated as prisoners of war. Likewise, soldiers or civilians charged with the delivery of despatches for their own army or for that of the enemy, and carrying out their mission openly, are not spies. And it matters not whether despatch-bearers make use of balloons, aircraft, or other means of communication. Thus, a soldier or civilian trying to carry despatches from a force besieged in a fortress to other forces of the same belligerent, whether making use of a balloon, or an air-vessel, or riding or walking at night, may not be treated as a spy. On the other hand, spying can well be carried out by despatch-bearers, or by persons in a balloon or an air-vessel.[1] The mere fact that a balloon or air-vessel is visible does not protect the persons using it from being treated as spies; since spying can be carried out under false pretences quite as well as clandestinely. But special care must be taken really to prove the fact of espionage in such cases, for an individual carrying despatches is *prima facie* not a spy, and must not be treated as a spy until proved to be such.

A remarkable case of espionage is that of Major André,[2] which occurred in 1780 during the American War of Independence. The American General Arnold, who was commandant of West Point, on the North River, intended to desert the Americans and join the British forces. He opened negotiations with Sir Henry Clinton for the purpose of surrendering West Point, and Major André was commissioned by Sir Henry Clinton to make the final arrangements with Arnold. On the night of September 21, Arnold and André met outside the American and British lines, but André, after having changed his uniform for plain clothes,

[1] See below, § 356 (4), concerning wireless telegraphy.

[2] See Halleck in *A.J.*, v. (1911), p. 594.

undertook to pass the American lines on his return, furnished with a passport under the name of John Anderson by General Arnold. He was caught, convicted as a spy, and hanged. As he was not seeking information,[1] and therefore was not a spy according to Article 29 of the Hague Regulations, a conviction for espionage would not, if such a case occurred to-day, be justified. But it would be possible to convict for war treason, for André was no doubt negotiating treason. Be that as it may, George III. considered André a martyr, and honoured his memory by granting a pension to his mother and a baronetcy to his brother.[2]

§ 161. The usual punishment for spying is hanging or shooting; though less severe punishments are, of course, admissible, and are sometimes inflicted. However, according to Article 30 of the Hague Regulations a spy may not be punished without trial before a court-martial; and according to Article 31, a spy who is not captured in the act, but rejoins the army to which he belongs, if subsequently captured by the enemy, may not be punished for his previous espionage, but must be treated as a prisoner of war. But Article 31 applies only to spies who belong to the armed forces of the enemy; civilians who act as spies, and are captured later, may be punished. No regard is paid to the status, rank, position, or motive of a spy. He may be a soldier or a civilian, an officer or a private. He may be following instructions of superiors, or acting on his own initiative from patriotic motives. A case of espionage, remarkable on account of the position of the spy, is that of the American Captain Nathan Hale, which occurred in 1776. After the American forces had withdrawn from Long Island,

Punishment of Espionage.

[1] Halleck, *loc. cit.*, p. 598, asserts the contrary.

[2] See Phillimore, iii. § 106; Halleck, i. p. 573; Rivier, ii. p. 284.

Captain Hale recrossed under disguise, and obtained valuable information about the English forces that had occupied the island. But he was caught before he could rejoin his army, and he was executed as a spy.[1]

War Treason.

§ 162. War treason is a comprehensive term for a number of acts hostile to the belligerent within whose lines they are committed[2]; it must be distinguished from real treason, which can only be committed by persons owing allegiance, albeit temporary, to the injured State. War treason can be committed by a soldier or an ordinary subject of a belligerent, but it can also be committed by an inhabitant of occupied enemy territory, or even by a subject of a neutral State temporarily staying there, and it can take place after an arrangement with the favoured belligerent or without such an arrangement. In any case, a belligerent making use of war treason acts lawfully, although the Hague Regulations do not mention the matter at all.

This is generally recognised; but it is controversial[3] whether a belligerent acts lawfully who bribes a commander of an enemy fortress into surrender, incites enemy soldiers to desertion, bribes enemy officers for the purpose of getting important information, incites enemy subjects to rise against the legitimate Government, and the like. If the rules of the Law of Nations are formulated, not from doctrines of book-writers, but from what is done by belligerents in practice,[4] it must be asserted that such acts, detestable and immoral as they are, are not considered illegal according to the existing rules of the Law of Nations.

[1] The case of Major Jakoga and Captain Oki, which, though reported as a case of espionage, is really a case of war treason, will be discussed below in § 255.

[2] The subject is more fully discussed below in § 255.

[3] See Vattel, iii. § 180; Heffter, § 125; Taylor, § 490; Martens, ii. § 110 (8); Longuet, § 52; Mérignhac, iii[a]. p. 289. See also below, § 164.

[4] See *Land Warfare*, § 158; and Spaight, pp. 140-150, who distinguishes between incitement of enemy troops to treason and incitement of the enemy population to revolt; the former he permits, the latter he considers inadmissible.

XI

RUSES

Grotius, iii. c. 1, §§ 6-18—Bynkershoek, *Quaestiones Juris publici*, i. c. 1—Vattel, iii. §§ 177-178—Hall, § 187—Lawrence, § 207—Westlake, ii. pp. 79-81—Phillimore, iii. § 94—Halleck, i. pp. 566-571—Taylor, § 488—Moore, vii. § 1115—Bluntschli, §§ 565-566—Heffter, § 125—Lueder in *Holtzendorff*, iv. pp. 457-461—Ullmann, § 176—Bonfils, Nos. 1073-1076—Despagnet, Nos. 526-527—Pradier-Fodéré, vi. Nos. 2759-2761—Rivier, ii. p. 261—Nys, iii. pp. 204-209—Calvo, iv. §§ 2106-2110—Fiore, iii. Nos. 1334-1339—Longuet, §§ 53-56—Mérignhac, iii[a]. pp. 263-266—Pillet, pp. 93-97—*Kriegsbrauch*, pp. 23-24—Holland, *War*, Nos. 78-79—Bordwell, pp. 283, 286—Meurer, ii. pp. 151-152—Spaight, pp. 152-156—*Land Warfare*, §§ 139-154—Brocher in *R.I.*, v. (1873), pp. 325-329.

Character of Ruses of War.

§ 163. Ruses of war, or stratagems, are deceit employed in the interest of military operations for the purpose of misleading the enemy. Such deceit is of great importance in war, and, just as belligerents are allowed to employ all methods of obtaining information, so are they—and Article 24 of the Hague Regulations confirms this—allowed to employ all sorts of ruses for the purpose of deceiving the enemy. Very important objects can be attained through ruses of war, such as, for instance, the surrender of a force, or of a fortress, the evacuation of territory held by the enemy, the withdrawal from a siege, the abandonment of an intended attack, and the like. But ruses of war are also employed, and are very often the decisive factor, during battles.

Different Kinds of Stratagems.

§ 164. Of ruses there are so many kinds that it is impossible to enumerate[1] and classify them. But some instances may be given. It is hardly necessary to mention the laying of ambushes and traps, the masking of military operations (such as marches or the erection of batteries and the like), the feigning of

[1] See *Land Warfare*, § 144, where a great number of legitimate ruses are enumerated.

attacks or flights or withdrawals, the carrying out of a surprise, and other stratagems employed every day in war. But it is important to know that, when useful, feigned signals and bugle-calls may be ordered, the watchword of the enemy may be used, deceitful intelligence may be disseminated,[1] the signals and the bugle-calls of the enemy may be mimicked [2] to mislead his forces. Even such detestable acts [3] as bribery of enemy commanders and officials in high position, and secret seduction of enemy soldiers to desertion, and of enemy subjects to insurrection, are frequently committed, although many writers protest. As regards the use of the national flag, the military ensigns, and the uniforms of the enemy, theory and practice are unanimous in prohibiting such use during actual attack and defence, since the principle is considered inviolable that during actual fighting belligerent forces ought to be certain who is friend and who is foe. But many [4] publicists maintain that, until the actual fighting begins, belligerent forces may, by way of stratagem, make use of these things. Article 23(*f*) of the Hague Regulations does not prohibit their use without qualification, but only their *improper* use, thus leaving the question open,[5] what uses are proper and what are not. Those who have hitherto taught the admissibility of the use of these symbols outside actual fighting can correctly maintain that this article does not prohibit it.[6]

[1] See the examples quoted by Pradier-Fodéré, vi. No. 2761.

[2] See Pradier-Fodéré, vi. No. 2760.

[3] The point has been discussed above in § 162.

[4] See, for instance, Hall, § 187; Bluntschli, § 565; Taylor, § 488; Calvo, iv. No. 2106; Pillet, p. 95; Longuet, § 54. But the number of publicists who consider it illegal to make use of the enemy flag, ensigns, and uniforms, even before an actual attack, was before the World War becoming larger; see, for instance, Lueder in *Holtzendorff*, iv. p. 458; Mérignhac, iii[a]. p. 264; Pradier-Fodéré, vi. No. 2760; Bonfils, No. 1074; *Kriegsbrauch*, p. 24; Spaight, pp. 104-110. As regards the use of the enemy flag by men-of-war, see below, § 211.

[5] See *Land Warfare*, § 152.

[6] When members of armed forces wear the uniforms of prisoners or of

§ 165. Stratagems must be carefully distinguished from perfidy, since the former are allowed, whereas the latter is prohibited. Halleck [1] correctly formulates the distinction, by laying down the principle that, whenever a belligerent has expressly or tacitly engaged, and is therefore bound by a moral obligation, to speak the truth to an enemy, it is perfidy to betray his confidence, because it constitutes a breach of good faith.[2] Thus a flag of truce, or the cross of the Geneva Convention, must never be used for a stratagem; capitulations must be carried out to the letter; the feigning of surrender to lure the enemy into a trap, the assassination of enemy commanders, soldiers or heads of States, are treacherous acts. On the other hand, stratagem may be met by stratagem, and a belligerent cannot complain of the enemy who so deceives him. If, for instance, a spy of the enemy is bribed to give deceitful intelligence to his employer, or if an officer, who is approached by the enemy and offered a bribe, accepts it feigningly but deceives the briber and leads him to disaster, no perfidy is committed.

Stratagems in contradistinction to Perfidy.

the enemy dead, not for deceit but through shortage of clothing—and they always will if necessary—such distinct alterations in the uniform ought to be made as will make it apparent to which side the soldiers concerned belong (see *Land Warfare*, § 154). Moreover, if soldiers are, through lack of clothing, obliged to wear civilian greatcoats, hats, and the like, care must be taken that they wear a fixed distinctive emblem which marks them as soldiers, since otherwise they lose the privileges of members of armed forces. (See Article 1 of the Hague Regulations.) During the Russo-Japanese War each belligerent repeatedly accused the other of using Chinese clothing for members of their armed forces; their soldiers apparently were obliged through lack of proper clothing temporarily to use Chinese garments. See, however, Takahashi, pp. 174-178.

[1] i. p. 566.

[2] See *Land Warfare*, §§ 139-142, 146-150.

XII

OCCUPATION OF ENEMY TERRITORY

Grotius, iii. c. 6, § 4—Vattel, iii. §§ 197-200—Hall, §§ 153-161—Westlake, ii. pp. 93-116—Lawrence, §§ 176-179—Maine, pp. 176-183—Halleck, ii. pp. 432-466—Taylor, §§ 568-579—Hershey, Nos. 387-400—Wharton, iii. §§ 354-355—Moore, vii. §§ 1143-1155—Bluntschli, §§ 539-551—Heffter, §§ 131-132—Lueder in *Holtzendorff*, iv. pp. 510-524—Klüber, §§ 255-256—G. F. Martens, ii. § 280—Ullmann, §§ 183-184—Bonfils, Nos. 1156-1175—Despagnet, Nos. 567-578—Pradier-Fodéré, vii. Nos. 2939-2988, 3019-3028—Nys, iii. pp. 222-251 and 463-472—Rivier, ii. pp. 299-306—Calvo, iv. §§ 2166-2198—Fiore, iii. Nos. 1454-1481, and *Code*, Nos. 1540-1568—Martens, ii. §§ 117-120—Longuet, §§ 115-133—Mérignhac, iiie. pp. 387-415—Pillet, pp. 237-259—Zorn, pp. 213-243—Garner, ii. §§ 365-430—*Kriegsbrauch*, pp. 45-50—Holland, *War*, Nos. 102-106—Bordwell, pp. 312-330—Meurer, ii. §§ 45-55—Spaight, pp. 320-380—*Land Warfare*, §§ 340-404—Waxel, *L'Armée d'Invasion et la Population* (1874)—Litta, *L'Occupazione militare* (1881)—Löning, *Die Verwaltung des General-Gouvernements im Elsass* (1874), and in *R.I.*, iv. (1872), p. 622, v. (1873), p. 69—Bernier, *De l'Occupation militaire en Temps de Guerre* (1884)—Corsi, *l'Occupazione militare in Tempo di Guerra e le Relazioni internazionali che ne derivano* (2nd ed. 1886)—Bray, *De l'Occupation militaire en Temps de Guerre, etc.* (1891)—Magoon, *Law of Civil Government under Military Occupation* (2nd ed. 1900)—Lorriot, *De la Nature de l'Occupation de Guerre* (1903)—Deherpe, *Essai sur le Développement de l'Occupation en Droit international* (1903)—Sichel, *Die kriegerische Besetzung feindlichen Staatsgebietes* (1905)—Nowacki, *Die Eisenbahnen im Kriege* (1906), pp. 78-90—Conner, *The Development of Belligerent Occupation* (1912)—Meurer, *Die volkerrechtliche Stellung der vom Feind besetzten Gebiete* (1915)—Ferrand, *Des Réquisitions en matière de Droit international public* (1917)—Nys, *L'Occupation de Guerre* (1919)—Rolin-Jaequemyns in *R.I.*, ii. (1870), p. 666, and iii. (1871), p. 311—Stier-Somlo in *Z.V.*, viii. (1914), pp. 581-608—Cybichowski in *Z.I.*, xxvi. (1916), pp. 427-478—Oppenheim in the *Law Quarterly Review*, xxxiii. (1917), pp. 266-286 and 363-370—Visscher, *ibid.*, xxxiv. (1918), pp. 72-81—Bentwich in the *British Year-book of International Law*, i. (1920-1921), pp. 139-148.

Occupation as an Aim of Warfare.

§ 166. If a belligerent succeeds in occupying the whole, or even a part, of enemy territory, he has realised a very important aim of warfare. He can now not only use the resources of the enemy country for military purposes, but can also keep it for the time being as a pledge of his military success, and thereby impress upon the enemy the necessity of submitting to terms of peace. In regard to occupation, International Law respecting warfare has progressed more than in any other department. In former times, enemy territory occupied by a belligerent was in every point considered his State property, so that he could do what he liked with it and its inhabitants. He could devastate the country with fire and sword, appropriate all public and private property therein, and kill the inhabitants, or take them away into captivity, or make them take an oath of allegiance. He could, even before the war was decided, and his occupation was definitive, dispose of the territory by ceding it to a third State; an instance of this happened during the Northern War (1700-1718), when in 1715 Denmark sold the occupied Swedish territories of Bremen and Verden to Hanover. That an occupant could force the inhabitants of the occupied territory to serve in his own army, and to fight against their legitimate sovereign, was indubitable. Thus, during the Seven Years' War, Frederick II. of Prussia repeatedly made forcible levies of thousands of recruits in Saxony, which he had occupied.

But during the second half of the eighteenth century, things gradually began to undergo a change. That the distinction between mere temporary military occupation of territory, and real acquisition of territory through conquest and subjugation, became more and more apparent, is shown by the fact that Vattel[1] drew attention to it. However, it was not till long after the Napoleonic wars that, during the nineteenth century, the consequences of this distinction were carried to their full extent by the theory and practice of International Law. So late as 1808, after the Russian troops had militarily occupied Finland, which was at that time a part of Sweden, Alexander I. of Russia made the inhabitants take an oath of allegiance,[2] although it was only by Article 4 of the Peace Treaty of Frederiks-

[1] iii. § 197.

[2] See Martens, *N.R.*, i. p. 9.

hamm[1] of September 17, 1809, that Sweden ceded Finland to Russia; and so late as 1814, in the case of *The Foltina*,[2] Sir William Scott still asserted the validity of the principle of the common law 'that a conquered country forms immediately part of the King's Dominions.'[3]

The first writer who drew all the consequences of the distinction between mere military occupation and real acquisition of territory was Heffter in his treatise *Das Europäische Völkerrecht der Gegenwart*,[4] which appeared in 1844; but it took the whole of the nineteenth century to develop the rules regarding occupation which are now universally recognised, and in many respects have been enacted by Articles 42-56 of the Hague Regulations.

In so far as these rules touch upon the treatment of the persons and property of the inhabitants of occupied territory, and property situated thereon, they have already been considered.[5] What concerns us here are the rights and duties of the occupying belligerent in relation to his political administration of the territory, and to his political authority over its inhabitants.[6] The principle underlying these modern rules is that, although the occupant does in no wise acquire sovereignty over such territory through the mere fact of having occupied it, he actually exercises for the time being a military authority over it. As he thereby prevents the legitimate

[1] See Martens, *N.R.*, i. p. 19.

[2] 1 Dod. 450.

[3] Alluding to the fact that the island of Guadeloupe, taken from the French in 1810, was, before conclusion of peace, ceded by Great Britain to Sweden by Article 5 of the Treaty of Stockholm of March 3, 1813. But it would seem that Sweden never took possession of it. At any rate, by the Treaty of London of August 13, 1814, she consented to its restitution to France, Great Britain paying her twenty-four million francs as compensation.

[4] § 131.

[5] See above, §§ 107-154.

[6] The Hague Regulations (Articles 42-56). All French writers, and many others, treat under the heading 'occupation' not only these questions, but also other matters, such as appropriation of public and private property, requisitions and contributions, destruction of public and private property, violence against enemy subjects and enemy officials. They have, however, nothing to do with occupation, and are better discussed in connection with the means of land warfare.

sovereign from exercising his authority, and claims obedience for himself from the inhabitants, he has to administer the country, not only in the interest of his own military advantage, but also, at any rate so far as possible, for the public benefit of the inhabitants. Thus the present International Law not only gives certain rights to an occupant, but also imposes certain duties upon him.

§ 167. Since an occupant, although his power is merely military, has certain rights and duties, the first question is, when, and under what circumstances, a territory must be considered occupied. **Occupation, when effected.**

Now it is certain that mere invasion is not occupation. Invasion is the marching or riding of troops—or the flying of a military air-vessel—into enemy country. Occupation is invasion *plus* taking possession of enemy country for the purpose of holding it, at any rate temporarily. The difference between mere invasion and occupation becomes apparent by the fact that an occupant sets up some kind of administration, whereas the mere invader does not. A small belligerent force can raid enemy territory without establishing any administration, quickly rush on to some place in the interior for the purpose of reconnoitring, destroying a bridge or depot of munitions and provisions, and the like, and quickly withdraw after having realised its purpose.[1] Although it may correctly be asserted that, so long and in so far as such raiding force is in possession of a locality, and sets up a temporary administration therein, it occupies this locality, yet it certainly does not occupy the whole territory, and even the occupation of this locality ceases the moment the force withdraws.

However this may be, as a rule occupation will be coincident with invasion. The troops march into a

[1] See *Land Warfare*, § 343.

district, and the moment they get into a village or town —unless they are actually fighting their way—they take possession of the municipal offices, the post office, the police stations, and the like, and assert their authority there. From the military point of view, such villages and towns are now 'occupied.' Article 42 of the Hague Regulations enacts that territory is considered occupied when it is actually placed under the authority of the hostile army, and that such occupation applies only to the territory where that authority is established, and in a position to assert itself. This definition is not at all precise, but it is as precise as a legal definition of a fact such as occupation can be. If, as some publicists[1] maintain, only territory of which every part was held by a sufficient number of soldiers to enforce immediately and on the spot the authority of an occupant, were to be regarded as occupied, effective occupation of a large territory would be impossible, since not only in every town, village, and railway station, but also in every isolated habitation and hut the presence of a sufficient number of soldiers would be necessary. In reason no other conditions ought to be laid down as necessary to constitute effective occupation in war than those under which in time of peace a sovereign is able to assert his authority over a territory. What these conditions are is a question of fact, to be answered according to the merits of the special case. When the legitimate sovereign is prevented from exercising his powers, and the occupant, being able to assert his authority, actually establishes an administration over a territory, it matters not with what means, and in what ways, his authority is exercised. For instance, when in the centre of a territory a large force is established, from which flying columns are

[1] See, for instance, Hall, § 161. This was also the standpoint of the delegates of the smaller States at the Brussels Conference of 1874.

constantly sent round the territory, it is indeed effectively occupied, provided that there are no enemy forces present, and these columns can really keep it under control.[1] Again, when an army is marching on through enemy territory, taking possession of the lines of communication and the open towns, surrounding the fortresses with besieging forces, and disarming the inhabitants in open places of habitation, the whole territory left behind the army is effectively occupied, provided that some kind of administration is established, and that, as soon as it becomes necessary to assert the authority of the occupant, a sufficient force can within reasonable time be sent to the locality affected. The conditions vary with those of the country concerned. When a vast country is thinly populated, a smaller force is necessary to occupy it, and a smaller number of centres need be garrisoned than in the case of a thickly populated country. Thus, the occupation of the former Orange Free State and the former South African Republic became effective in 1901 some time after their annexation by Great Britain and the degeneration of ordinary war into guerilla war, although only about 250,000 British soldiers had to keep up the occupation of a territory of about 500,000 square miles. The facts that all the towns and all the lines of communication were in the hands, and under the administration, of the British army, that the inhabitants of smaller places were taken away into concentration camps, that the enemy forces were either in captivity or dispersed into comparatively small guerilla bands, and finally, that wherever such bands tried to make an attack, a sufficient British force could within reason-

[1] This is not so-called *constructive* occupation, but is really *effective* occupation. An occupation is constructive only if an invader declares districts as occupied over which he does not actually exercise control—for instance, when he actually occupies only the capital of a large province, yet proclaims that he has thereby occupied the whole of the province, although he does not take any steps to exercise control over it.

able time make its appearance, were quite sufficient to assert British authority[1] over that vast territory, although it was more than a year before peace was finally established.[2]

Occupation, when ended.

§ 168. Occupation comes to an end when an occupant withdraws from a territory, or is driven out of it. Thus, occupation remains only over a limited area of a territory if the forces in occupation are drawn into a fortress on that territory, and are there besieged by the re-advancing enemy, or if the occupant concentrates his forces in a certain place on the territory, withdrawing before the re-advancing enemy. But occupation does not cease because the occupant, after having disarmed the inhabitants, and having made arrangements for the administration of the country, is marching on to overtake the retreating enemy, leaving only comparatively few soldiers behind.

Rights and Duties in general of the Occupant.

§ 169. As the occupant actually exercises authority, and as the legitimate Government is prevented from exercising its authority,[3] the occupant acquires a temporary right of administration over the territory and its inhabitants; and all steps he takes in the exercise

[1] It may well be doubted whether, when these territories were annexed (see above, i. § 239), their occupation could be called effective. The British Government ought not, therefore, to have proclaimed their annexation at such early dates. But there ought to be no doubt that the occupation became effective some time afterwards, in 1901. See, however, Sir Thomas Barclay in the *Law Quarterly Review*, xxi. (1905), p. 307, who asserts the contrary; see also, below, §§ 264, 265. The *Times History of the War in South Africa* (v. p. 251) estimates the number of Boer fighters in May 1901 to have been about 13,000. These armed men were dispersed into a very large number of guerilla bands, and they were in a great many cases men who seemingly had submitted to the British authorities, but afterwards had taken up arms. The annexation by Italy, during the Turco-Italian War, of Tripoli and Cyrenaica in November 1911, was likewise premature. See above, i. § 239, and Rapisardi-Mirabelli in *R.I.*, 2nd Ser. xv. (1913), pp. 527-544. But see also Tambaro in the *Jahrbuch des Volkerrechts*, i. (1913), pp. 583-629, who asserts the contrary.

[2] The rules regarding effective occupation must be formulated on the basis of actual practice quite as much as other rules of International Law. Those rules are not authoritative which are laid down by theorists, but only those which are abstracted from the actual practice of warfare, and are unopposed by the Powers.

[3] As regards the rights of the

of this right must be recognised by the legitimate Government after occupation has ceased. But as the right of an occupant in occupied territory is merely a right of administration, he may neither annex it, while the war continues, nor set it up as an independent State, nor divide it (as Germany during the World War divided Belgium [1]) into two administrative districts for political purposes. Moreover, the administration of the occupant is in no wise to be compared with ordinary administration, for it is distinctly and precisely military administration. In carrying it out the occupant is totally independent of the constitution and the laws of the territory, since occupation is an aim of warfare, and the maintenance and safety of his forces, and the purpose of war, stand in the foreground of his interest, and must be promoted under all circumstances and conditions. But, although as regards the safety of his army and the purpose of war the occupant is vested with an almost absolute power, as he is not the sovereign of the territory, he has no right to make changes in the laws,[2] or in the administration, other than those which are temporarily [3] necessitated by his interest in the maintenance and safety of his army and the realisation of the purpose of war. On the contrary, he has the duty of administering the country according to the existing laws and the existing rules of administration; he must ensure public order and safety, must respect family honour and rights, individual lives, private property, religious convictions and liberty. Fundamentally important is Article 43 of the Hague

occupant of such neutral territory as has become the theatre of war, see above, § 71.

[1] Garner, ii. § 372.

[2] See below, § 172.

[3] There is no doubt therefore that the conversion by the Germans in occupation of Belgium during the World War of the University of Ghent into a Flemish institution was unlawful. See details in Garner, ii. §§ 368-370. Unlawful also was the interference by the Russians, while in occupation of Lemberg, with the schools and the language used for instruction. See Cybichowski in *Z.I.*, xxvi. (1916), at pp. 453-457.

Regulations: 'The authority of the legitimate Power having actually passed into the hands of the occupant, the latter shall take all steps in his power to re-establish and ensure, as far as possible, public order and safety, while respecting, unless absolutely prevented, the laws in force in the country.'

Rights of the Occupant regarding the Inhabitants.

§ 170. An occupant having military authority over the territory, the inhabitants are under his Martial Law, and have to render obedience to his commands.[1] Their duty to obey does not, of course, arise from their own Municipal Law, nor from International Law, but from the Martial Law of the occupant to which they are subjected. However, the power of the occupant over the inhabitants is not unrestricted, for Articles 23, 44, and 45 of the Hague Regulations[2] expressly enact that he is prohibited from compelling the inhabitants to take part in military operations against the legitimate Government, or to give information concerning the army of the other belligerent or his means of defence. Nor may he compel them to take an oath of allegiance. Since the authority of the occupant is not sovereignty, the inhabitants owe no temporary allegiance to him. On the other hand, he may compel them to take an oath—sometimes called an 'oath of neutrality'—to abstain from taking up a hostile attitude against him and willingly to submit to his legitimate commands; and he may punish them severely for breaking this oath. He may make requisitions and demand contributions[3] from them. He may compel them to render services as drivers or farriers, and may compulsorily employ them to bury the dead, collect and

[1] As to the restrictions upon personal liberty and patriotic demonstrations imposed on occupied Belgium during the World War, see Garner, ii. § 366-367.

[2] Although the Hague Regulations cannot literally be applied in occupied enemy colonies populated by natives and having only a few white settlers, the latter must not be deported, unless it is a military necessity to do so.

[3] See above, §§ 147, 148.

remove the wounded, and bring up stores, supplies, baggage, and the like,[1] provided—see Article 52 of the Hague Regulations—the services required do not oblige them to take part in military operations against their own country. He may compel them to render services for the repair of roads, bridges, buildings or other works damaged or destroyed by military operations, or necessary either for the administration of the country or for the needs of the army of occupation, always provided that the services do not involve taking part in military operations.

Yet the meaning of 'taking part in military operations' is somewhat controversial. Many writers maintain, and *Land Warfare*[2] likewise asserts, that the words extend to the construction of bridges, fortifications, and the like, even behind the front. But the practice[3] of belligerents has always distinguished between military *operations* and military *preparations*, and has not condemned as inadmissible the compulsion of inhabitants to render assistance in the construction of military roads, fortifications, and the like behind the front, or in any other works in preparation for military operations. No doubt attempts have been made to obtain the prohibition of the requisitioning of even such services as only involve taking part in military *preparations*. Thus the Russian draft put before the Conference of Brussels in 1874 proposed[4] to stipulate that the population of an occupied province might not be forced to take part in the military operations against their own Government, *or in such acts as are contributory to the realisation of the*

[1] Formerly he could likewise compel them to render services as guides, but this was prohibited by the wording which Article 44 received from the Second Hague Conference. But Germany, Austria-Hungary, Japan, Montenegro, and Russia signed with a reservation against Article 44, so that in the World War the old rule was valid that inhabitants may be compelled to serve as guides.

[2] § 391.

[3] See above, §§ 116 n., 126 n.

[4] Article 48.

aims of war detrimental to their own country; but the conference struck out the words in italics. It is true that the Oxford *Manuel des Lois de la Guerre sur Terre* of the Institute of International Law did lay down[1] the rule that an occupant must not compel inhabitants, either to take part in the military operations, *or to assist him in his works of attack or defence*; but the Hague Conferences did not adopt this rule, and Article 52 of the Hague Regulations prohibits the requisitioning of such services only as imply an obligation to take part in military operations. It is apparent that all attempts to extend the prohibition to services which imply an obligation to take part in military *preparations* and the like have hitherto failed.

During the World War, not only the Germans in Belgium and France,[2] but also the Russians in Galicia,[3] compelled the inhabitants to construct fortifications and trenches in the rear, although a generous interpretation of Article 52 ought to have prevented them from doing so. It is to be hoped that a future conference will so amend the Hague Regulations as to make the matter clear.

However this may be, there is no right to deport inhabitants to the country of the occupant, for the purpose of compelling them to work there. When during the World War the Germans deported to Germany several thousands of Belgian[4] and French men and women, and compelled them to work there, the whole civilised world stigmatised this cruel practice as an outrage.

The occupant may collect the ordinary taxes, dues, and tolls imposed for the benefit of the State by the legitimate Government. But in such case he is, accord-

[1] Article 48 (2).

[2] See details in Garner, ii. § 400.

[3] See Cybichowski in *Z.I.*, xxvi. (1916), p. 467.

[4] See Heuvel in *R.G.*, xxiv. (1917), pp. 261-300; Passelecq, *Les Déportations belges à la Lumière des Documents allemands* (1917); Basdevant, *Les Déportations du Nord de la France et de la Belgique en vue du Travail forcé et le Droit international* (1917); Garner, ii. §§ 413-430.

ing to Article 48 of the Hague Regulations, obliged to make the collection, as far as possible, in accordance with the rules in existence and the assessment in force, and he is bound to defray the expenses of the administration of the occupied territory on the same scale as that by which the legitimate Government was bound.

Whoever does not comply with his commands, or commits a prohibited act, may be punished by him; but Article 50 of the Hague Regulations expressly enacts the rule that *no general penalty, pecuniary or otherwise, may be inflicted on the population on account of the acts of individuals for which it cannot be regarded as collectively responsible.*[1] It must, however, be specially observed that this rule unfortunately does not at all prevent[2] reprisals by an occupant in case acts of illegitimate warfare are committed by enemy individuals not belonging to the armed forces, although in practice innocent individuals are thereby punished for illegal acts for which they are neither legally nor morally responsible. For instance, a village is burned by way of reprisal for a treacherous attack committed there on enemy soldiers by some unknown individuals.[3] Nor does Article 50 prevent an occupant from taking hostages[4] to safeguard lines of communication threatened by guerillas not belonging to the armed forces, or for other purposes,[5] provided that he does not kill them,

[1] The Germans during their occupation of Belgium and Northern France in the World War regularly inflicted general penalties. See details in Garner, ii. §§ 403-412, where the interpretation of Article 50 is also discussed.

[2] See Holland, *War*, No. 110, and *Land Warfare*, §§ 385-386. See also Zorn, pp. 239-243, where an important interpretation of Article 50 is discussed; and Garner in *A.J.*, xi. (1917), pp. 511-537.

[3] See below, §§ 248, 250, where objections against the existing law are formulated. This was the justification alleged by Germany for the burning of Louvain. Garner, i. §§ 282-284.

[4] But this is a moot point; see below, § 259.

[5] Belligerents sometimes take hostages for the purpose of securing compliance with demands for contributions, requisitions, and the like. As long as such hostages obtain the same treatment as prisoners of war, the practice does not seem to be illegal, although the Hague Regulations do not mention it, and many publicists condemn it; see above, § 116 n., and below, § 259 n.

although they must suffer for acts or omissions of others, for which they are neither legally nor morally responsible.

In the treatment of the inhabitants of enemy territory, the occupant need not make any difference between subjects of the enemy and subjects of neutral States;[1] and resident subjects of neutral States have no claim, any more than have subjects of the enemy, against him for compensation for losses sustained in consequence of legitimate acts[2] of war on his part.[3]

Position of Government Officials and Municipal Functionaries during Occupation.

§ 171. As, through occupation, authority over the territory actually passes into the hands of the occupant, he may, for the time of his occupation, depose all Government officials and municipal functionaries that have not withdrawn with the retreating enemy. On the other hand, he must not compel them by force to

[1] See above, § 88, and Frankenbach, *Die Rechtsstellung von neutralen Staatsangehörigen in kriegfuhrenden Staaten* (1910), pp. 46-50; Pitt Cobbett, *Cases and Opinions on International Law* (3rd ed. 1913), ii. pp. 256-270; Hirsch, *Die rechtliche Stellung der Angehörigen neutraler Staaten* (1914), pp. 80-84; Borchard, §§ 101, 103.

[2] *Hardman's case* (see *A.J.*, vii. (1913), p. 879) is a good example. William Hardman was a British subject resident in Siboney, a town in Cuba, when in 1898, during the Spanish-American War, it was occupied by armed forces of the United States. As there was an outbreak of sickness among the American troops, and fear of yellow fever, the American military authorities found it necessary, in the interest of the health of the troops, to destroy by fire a number of houses, together with all the furniture and personal belongings of the inhabitants. Hardman was one of these unfortunate inhabitants, and, after the end of the war, the British Government claimed on his behalf the sum of £93 as the value of his destroyed personal property. Both the British and American Governments agreed that a subject of a neutral Power resident in an enemy country during military occupation cannot legally claim compensation for losses sustained by an act of war on the part of the occupant; but the British Government maintained that the burning of the houses in Siboney was not an act of war, but simply a measure for better securing the health of the American troops. The case was one of those decided in 1913 by the British and American Claims Commission. The arbitrators gave their award against the British Government, because they considered the act to be an act of war, but recommended the American Government to indemnify Hardman for the loss suffered, as an act of grace.

[3] But a belligerent may, of course, grant compensation nevertheless. Thus when in 1914, during the World War, after the occupation of Liége, the Germans executed a number of civilians, and among them five Spaniards, by way of reprisal for alleged attacks by the civilian population upon German soldiers, they granted monetary compensation to the families of the unfortunate Spaniards, although they asserted that their execution was justified as reprisals.

carry on their functions during occupation, if they refuse to do so, except where military necessity for the carrying on of a certain function arises. If they are willing to serve under him, he may make them take an oath of obedience, but not of allegiance, and he may not compel them to carry on their functions in his name, though he may prevent them from doing so in the name of the legitimate Government.[1] Since, according to Article 43 of the Hague Regulations, he has to secure public order and safety, he must temporarily appoint other functionaries in case those of the legitimate Government refuse to serve under him, or are deposed by him for the time of the occupation.

Position of Courts of Justice during Occupation.

§ 172. The particular position which courts of justice have nowadays in civilised countries, makes it necessary to discuss their position during occupation.[2] As has already been explained,[3] the British and American interpretation of Article 23(*h*) of the Hague Regulations is that it prohibits an occupant of enemy territory from declaring extinguished, suspended, or unenforceable in a court of law the rights and the rights of action of the inhabitants; and Article 43 provides that the occupant must respect, unless absolutely prevented, the laws in force in the country. But an occupant may, where necessary, set up military courts instead of the ordinary courts; and in case, and in so far as, he admits the administration of justice by the ordinary courts, he may nevertheless, so far as it is necessary for military purposes, or for the maintenance of public order and safety, temporarily alter the

[1] Many publicists assert that in case an occupant leaves officials of the legitimate Government in office, he 'must' pay them their ordinary salaries. But I cannot see that there is a customary or conventional rule in existence concerning this point. But it is in an occupant's own interest to pay such salaries, and he will as a rule do this. Only in the case of Article 48 of the Hague Regulations is he compelled to do it.

[2] See Petit, *L'Administration de la Justice en Territoire occupé* (1900).

[3] See above, § 100*a*.

laws, especially the Criminal Law, on the basis of which justice is administered, as well as the laws regarding procedure.[1]

There is no doubt that an occupant may suspend the judges[2] as well as other officials. However, if he does suspend them, he must temporarily appoint others in their place. If they are willing to serve under him, he must respect their independence according to the laws of the country. He has, however, no right to constrain the courts to pronounce their verdicts in his name, although he need not allow them to pronounce verdicts in the name of the legitimate Government. A case that happened during the Franco-German War may serve as an illustration. In September 1870, after the fall of the Emperor Napoleon and the proclamation of the French Republic, the Court of Appeal at Nancy pronounced its verdicts 'in the name of the French Government and People.' Since Germany had not yet recognised the French Republic, the Germans ordered the court to use the formula 'In the name of the High German Powers occupying Alsace and Lorraine,' but gave it to understand that, if it objected to this formula, they were disposed to admit another, and were even ready to admit the formula 'In the name of the Emperor of the French,' as the Emperor had not abdicated. The court, however, refused to pronounce its verdict otherwise than 'in the name of the French Government and People,' and, consequently, suspended its sittings. There can be no doubt that the Germans had no right to order the formula 'In the name of the High German Powers, etc.,' to be used, but they were certainly not obliged to admit the formula preferred

[1] As to the practice followed by the Germans in occupied Belgium during the World War, see Garner, ii. §§ 365-367, 373-376.

[2] As to the removal of Jewish judges by the Russians during their occupation of Lemberg in the World War, see Cybichowski in *Z.I.*, xxvi. (1916), at p. 452.

by the court; and the fact that they were disposed to admit another formula ought to have made the court accept a compromise. Bluntschli[1] correctly maintains that the most natural solution of the difficulty would have been to use the neutral formula 'In the name of the Law.'

On the other hand, during the occupation of Belgium in the World War, Germany did not interfere with the practice of the Belgian courts of pronouncing and executing their verdicts in the name of the King of the Belgians.[2] But matters changed when in 1918 the Belgian courts suspended their sittings in consequence of the deportation of some of the judges, and German courts were set up in their place.[3]

[1] § 547.

[2] See *Deutsche Juristen-Zeitung* (1915), p. 805.

[3] See Garner, ii. §§ 377-378.

CHAPTER IV

WARFARE ON SEA

I

ON SEA WARFARE IN GENERAL

Hall, § 147—Lawrence, §§ 193-194—Westlake, ii. pp. 136-154—Maine, pp. 117-122—Manning, pp. 183-184—Phillimore, iii. § 347—Twiss, ii. § 73—Halleck, ii. pp. 80-82—Taylor, § 547—Wharton, iii. §§ 342-345—Wheaton, § 355—Bluntschli, §§ 665-667—Heffter, § 139—Geffcken in *Holtzendorff*, iv. pp. 547-548, 571-581—Ullmann, §§ 187-188—Bonfils, Nos. 1268, 1294-1338—Despagnet, Nos. 647-649—Pradier-Fodéré, viii. Nos. 3066-3090, 3107-3108—Nys, iii. pp. 391-432—Rivier, ii. pp. 329-335—Calvo, iv. §§ 2123, 2379-2410—Fiore, iii. Nos. 1399-1413—Pillet, pp. 118-120—Perels, § 36—Testa, pp. 147-157—Boeck, Nos. 3-153—Lawrence, *International Problems and Hague Conferences* (1908), pp. 178-206—Westlake, *Papers*, pp. 250-258—Reddie, *Researches*, *passim*—Ortolan, ii. pp. 35-50—Hautefeuille, i. pp. 161-167—Schramm, §§ 1, 8—Wehberg, §§ 1, 2—Scholz, *Die seekriegsrechtliche Bedeutung von Flottenstützpunkten* (1918), *passim*—Gessner, Westlake, Lorimer, Rolin-Jaequemyns, Laveleye, Albéric Rolin, and Pierantoni in *R.I.*, vii. (1875), pp. 236-272, 558-656—Twiss in *R.I.*, xvi. (1884), pp. 113-137—Quigley in *A.J.*, xi. (1917), pp. 22-45—Bower in *A.J.*, xiii. (1919), pp. 60-78—See also the authors quoted below, § 178.

Aims and Means of Sea Warfare.

§ 173. The purpose of war is the same in the case of warfare on land or on sea—namely, the overpowering of the enemy. But sea warfare serves this purpose by attempting the accomplishment of aims different from those of land warfare. Whereas the aims of land warfare are defeat of the enemy army and occupation of the enemy territory, the aims[1] of sea warfare are: defeat of the enemy navy; annihilation of the enemy merchant fleet; destruction of enemy coast fortifi-

[1] Aims of sea warfare must not be confounded with ends of war; see above, § 66.

cations, and of maritime as well as military establishments on the enemy coast; cutting off intercourse with the enemy coast; prevention of carriage of contraband and of rendering unneutral service to the enemy; all kinds of support to military operations on land, such as protection of a landing of troops on the enemy coast; and lastly, defence of the home coast and protection to the home merchant fleet.[1] The means by which belligerents in sea warfare endeavour to realise these aims are: attack on, and seizure of, enemy vessels, violence against enemy individuals, appropriation and destruction of enemy vessels and sea-borne enemy goods, requisitions and contributions, bombardment of the enemy coast, cutting of submarine cables, blockade, espionage, treason, ruses, and capture of neutral vessels carrying contraband or rendering unneutral service.

Lawful and Unlawful Practices of Sea Warfare.

§ 174. As in land warfare, so in sea warfare not every practice capable of injuring the enemy in offence and defence is lawful. Although no regulations regarding the laws of war on sea have as yet been enacted by a general law-making treaty corresponding to the Hague Regulations, there are treaties concerning special points —such as submarine mines, bombardment by naval forces—and customary rules of International Law which regulate the matter. Be that as it may, the rules concerning means of sea warfare, though in many points identical with the rules in force regarding warfare on land, differ from them in many respects, and therefore must be discussed separately in the following sections. Blockade and the capture of vessels carrying contraband and rendering unneutral service to the enemy, although they are means of warfare against an enemy, are of such importance as regards neutral trade that they will be discussed under 'neutrality.'[2]

[1] See the aims of sea warfare enumerated in Article 1 of the U.S. Naval War Code.

[2] §§ 368-413*a*.

Objects of the Means of Sea Warfare.

§ 175. Whereas the objects against which means of land warfare may be directed are innumerable, the number of the objects against which means of sea warfare are directed is limited to six. The chief object is enemy vessels, whether public or private; the next, enemy individuals, with distinction between those taking part in fighting and others; the third, sea-borne enemy goods; the fourth, the enemy coast; the fifth and sixth, neutral vessels attempting to break blockade, carrying contraband, or rendering unneutral service to the enemy.

Development of International Law regarding Private Property on Sea.

§ 176. It is evident that in times when a belligerent could destroy all public and private enemy property he was able to seize, no special rule existed regarding private enemy ships and private enemy property carried on the sea. But the practice of sea warfare frequently went beyond the limits of even so wide a right, treating neutral goods on enemy ships as enemy goods, and neutral ships carrying enemy goods as enemy ships. It was not until the time of the *Consolato del Mare*, in the fourteenth century, that a set of clear and definite rules with regard to private enemy vessels and private enemy property on sea in contradistinction to neutral ships and neutral goods was adopted. According to this famous collection of maritime usages observed by the communities of the Mediterranean, there is no doubt that a belligerent may seize and appropriate all private enemy ships and goods. But a distinction is made if either ship or goods are neutral. Although an enemy ship may always be appropriated, neutral goods thereon have to be restored to the neutral owners. On the other hand, enemy goods on neutral ships may be appropriated, but the neutral ships carrying such goods must be restored to their owners. However, these rules of the *Consolato del Mare* were not at all generally recognised, although they were adopted by several treaties between single

States during the fourteenth and fifteenth centuries. Neither the communities belonging to the Hanseatic League, nor the Netherlands and Spain during the War of Independence, nor England and Spain during their wars in the sixteenth century, adopted these rules; and France expressly enacted by Ordinances of 1543 (Article 42) and 1584 (Article 69) that neutral goods on enemy ships as well as neutral ships carrying enemy goods should be appropriated.[1] Although in 1650 France adopted the rules of the *Consolato del Mare*, Louis XIV. dropped them again by the Ordinance of 1681, and re-enacted that neutral goods on enemy ships, and neutral ships carrying enemy goods, should be appropriated. Spain enacted the same rules in 1718. The Netherlands, in contradistinction to the *Consolato del Mare*, endeavoured by a number of treaties to foster the principle that the flag covers the goods, so that enemy goods on neutral vessels were exempt from, whereas neutral goods on enemy vessels were subject to, appropriation. On the other hand, throughout the eighteenth century, and during the nineteenth century down to the beginning of the Crimean War in 1854, England adhered to the rules of the *Consolato del Mare*. Thus, no generally accepted rules of International Law regarding private property on sea were in existence.[2] Matters were made worse by privateering, which was generally recognised as lawful, and by the fact that belligerents frequently declared a coast blockaded without having a sufficient number of men-of-war on the spot to make the blockade effective. It was not until the Declaration of Paris in 1856 that general rules of International Law regarding private property on sea came into existence.

[1] *Robe d'ennemy confisque celle d'amy. Confiscantur ex navibus res, ex rebus naves.*

[2] Boeck, Nos. 3-103, and Geffcken in *Holtzendorff*, iv. pp. 571-578, give excellent summaries of the facts.

Declaration of Paris.

§ 177. Things began to undergo a change with the outbreak of the Crimean War in 1854; all the belligerents proclaimed that they would not issue letters of marque; Great Britain declared that she would not seize enemy goods on neutral vessels; and France declared that she would not appropriate neutral goods on enemy vessels. Although this alteration of attitude on the part of the belligerents was originally intended for the Crimean War only and exceptionally, it led after the conclusion of peace in 1856 to the famous and epoch-making Declaration of Paris,[1] which enacted the four rules—(1) that privateering is abolished, (2) that the neutral [2] flag covers enemy goods [3] with the exception of contraband of war, (3) that neutral goods, contraband of war excepted, are not liable to capture under the enemy flag, (4) that blockades, in order to be binding, must be effective, *i.e.* maintained by a force sufficient really to prevent access to the coast of the enemy. Since, with the exception of the United

[1] See Martens, *N.R.G.*, xv. p. 767, and above, vol. i. § 559. See also Piggott, *The Declaration of Paris* (1919), who is an opponent of the declaration.

[2] Only the *neutral* flag covers enemy goods, not the flag of a belligerent, who may, therefore, seize enemy goods carried by his own merchantmen (*The Roumanian*, (1915) 1 B. and C. P. C. 536. See above, § 102, and below, § 196 n.). The neutral flag protects enemy goods only so long as they are under it; they lose protection so soon as they are transhipped into lighters (*The Dandolo*, (1916) 2 B. and C. P. C. 339). On the other hand, when enemy goods shipped in enemy vessels before the outbreak of war are transhipped *in transitu* into neutral vessels, the neutral flag does not protect them (*The Jeanne*, (1916) 2 B. and C. P. C. 227; *The Bawean*, (1917) 3 B. and C. P. C. 116; *The Vesta*, [1920] P. 385). Although the Declaration of Paris is a declaration in favour of neutral commerce, not only the neutral concerned, but also the enemy can claim restitution of non-contraband goods seized in spite of being carried by a neutral vessel (*The Dirigo*, (1919) 3 B. and C. P. C. 439).

[3] It has been asserted—see, for instance, Rivier, ii. p. 429, and Schramm, p. 93—that the neutral flag covers only private, not public, enemy property, and therefore that such goods on neutral vessels as belong to the State of the enemy may be seized and appropriated. The Italian Prize Court in 1912, during the Turco-Italian War, in *The Sheffield*, *The Newa*, and *The Menzale*, gave its decision in favour of this opinion (see Coquet in *R.G.*, xxi. (1914), pp. 281-290). However, the Declaration of Paris speaks of *marchandise neutre* without any qualification, only excepting contraband goods, and it ought not therefore to be maintained that public enemy property does not enjoy the protection of the neutral flag. See below, § 319 n.

States of America and a few other States, all members of the Family of Nations are now parties to the Declaration of Paris, it may well be maintained that the rules quoted are general International Law, the more so as the non-signatory Powers have hitherto in practice always acted in accordance with those rules.[1]

However, through the application of the doctrine of continuous voyages by the United States during the Civil War in the form of the doctrine of continuous transports,[2] through the application of that doctrine even to conditional contraband during the World War, by a number of presumptions of hostile destination, by the imposition of a duty upon a neutral consignor of proving the innocent destination of the cargo, and by an enormous extension of the list of contraband,[3] the rule of the Declaration of Paris that a neutral flag covers enemy goods with the exception of contraband of war, has to a great extent been frustrated.[4]

The Principle of Appropriation of Private Enemy Vessels and Enemy Goods thereon.

§ 178. The Declaration of Paris did not touch the old rule that private enemy vessels and private enemy goods thereon, or on ships of the capturing belligerent, may be seized and appropriated, and this rule is, therefore, as valid as ever, although there is much agitation for its abolition. In 1785, Prussia and the United States of America had already stipulated by Article 23 of their Treaty of Friendship [5] that in case of war between them merchantmen should not be seized and appropriated. Again, in 1871, the United States and Italy, by Article 12 of their Treaty of Commerce,[6] stipulated that in case of war between them merchantmen, with the exception of those carrying contraband

[1] That there is an agitation for the abolition of the Declaration of Paris has been mentioned above, § 83 n.

[2] See below, § 401.

[3] See below, §§ 393, 394, 403*a*.

[4] See Quigley, *The Immunity of Private Property from Capture at Sea* (1918), and in *A.J.*, xi. (1917), pp. 22-31.

[5] See Martens, *R.*, iv. p. 37.

[6] See Martens, *N.R.G.*, 2nd Ser. i. p. 57.

of war or attempting to break a blockade, should not be seized and appropriated. In 1823, the United States had already made a proposal to Great Britain, France, and Russia [1] for a treaty abrogating the rule that enemy merchantmen and enemy goods thereon may be appropriated; but Russia alone accepted the proposal on the condition that all other naval Powers consented. Again, in 1856,[2] on the occasion of the Declaration of Paris, the United States endeavoured to obtain the victory of the principle that enemy merchantmen should not be appropriated, making it a condition of her accession to the Declaration of Paris that this principle should be recognised. But again the attempt failed, owing to the opposition of Great Britain.

In 1865 Italy, by Article 211 of her Marine Code, enacted that, in case of war with any other State, enemy merchantmen (not carrying contraband of war or breaking a blockade) should not be seized and appropriated, provided reciprocity was granted. At the outbreak of war in 1866, Prussia and Austria expressly declared that they would not seize and appropriate each other's merchantmen. At the outbreak of the Franco-German War in 1870, Germany declared French merchantmen exempt from capture, but changed her attitude when France did not act upon the same lines. The United States of America made unsuccessful attempts [3] to secure immunity from capture for enemy merchantmen and goods at sea at the First and Second Hague Conferences.

It cannot be denied that the constant agitation, since the middle of the eighteenth century, for the abolition of the rule that private enemy vessels and

[1] See Wharton, iii. § 342, pp. 260-261, and Moore, vii. § 1198, p. 465.

[2] See Wharton, iii. § 342, pp. 270-287, and Moore, vii. § 1198, p. 466.

[3] See Holls, *The Peace Conference at the Hague*, pp. 306-321, and Scott, *Conferences*, pp. 699-707.

sea-borne goods may be captured, might, during the second half of the nineteenth century, have met with success but for the decided opposition of Great Britain. Public opinion[1] in Great Britain was not, and is not, prepared to consent to the abolition of this rule; and there is no doubt that its abolition would involve a certain amount of danger to a country like Great Britain, whose position and power depend chiefly upon her navy. The possibility of annihilating an enemy's commerce by annihilating his merchant fleet is a powerful weapon in the hands of a great naval Power. Moreover, if enemy merchantmen are not captured, they can be fitted out as cruisers, or at least be used for the transport of troops, munitions, and provisions. Before the World War several maritime States made arrangements with their steamship companies to secure the building of their transatlantic liners according to plans which made them easily convertible into men-of-war, and these vessels were of great service to the belligerents in that war.

The argument that it is unjust that private enemy citizens should suffer through having their property seized has no weight in face of the probability that fear of the annihilation of its merchant fleet in case of war may well deter a State intending to go to war from doing so. It is a matter for politicians, not for jurists, to decide whether it is necessary for Great Britain to oppose the abolition of the rule that sea-borne private enemy property may be confiscated.

However this may be, from the end of the nineteenth century to the outbreak of the World War, it was not the attitude of Great Britain alone which stood in the way of the abolition of the rule. After the growth of navies among Continental Powers, these

[1] The author would doubtless have rewritten the remainder of this section in the light of experience gained during the World War.

Powers learned to appreciate the value of the rule in war, and the outcry against the capture of merchantmen became less loud. It may perhaps be said that, even if Great Britain had in or about 1912 proposed the abolition of the rule, it is probable that a greater number of the maritime States would have refused to accede. For at the Second Hague Conference, France, Russia, Japan, Spain, Portugal, Mexico, Colombia, and Panama, besides Great Britain, voted against its abolition; and there was noticeable before the World War a slow, but constant, increase in the number of Continental publicists[1] who opposed the abolition of the practice of capturing enemy merchantmen, to which so much objection was once taken.

§ 179. Be that as it may, the time did not then seem

[1] See, for instance, Perels, § 36, pp. 195-198; Röpcke, *Das Seebeuterecht* (1904), pp. 36-47; Dupuis, Nos. 29-32; Pillet, p. 119; Giordana, *La Proprietà privata nelle Guerre marittime, etc.* (1907); Niemeyer, *Prinzipien des Seekriegsrechts* (1909); Boidin, pp. 144-167; Hirschmann, *Das internationale Prisenrecht* (1912), § 2. On the other hand, the Institute of International Law has several times voted in favour of the abolition of the rule; see *Tableau général de l'Institut de Droit International* (1893), pp. 190-193, and *Annuaire*, xxv. (1912), p. 600. The literature concerning the confiscation of private enemy property at sea is abundant. See, besides those already quoted at the commencement of § 173, Upton, *The Law of Nations affecting Commerce during War* (1863); Cauchy, *Du Respect de la Propriété privée dans la Guerre maritime* (1866); Vidari, *Del Rispetto della Proprietà privata fra gli Stati in Guerra* (1867); Gessner, *Zur Reform des Kriegsseerechts* (1875); Klobukowski, *Die Seebeute oder das feindliche Privateigenthum zur See* (1877); Bluntschli, *Das Beuterecht im Kriege und das Seebeuterecht insbesondere* (1878); Boeck, *De la Propriété privée ennemie sous Pavillon ennemi* (1882); Dupuis, *La Guerre maritime et les Doctrines anglaises* (1899); Leroy, *La Guerre maritime* (1900); Röpcke, *Das Seebeuterecht* (1904); Hirst, *Commerce and Property in Naval Warfare: A Letter of the Lord Chancellor* (1906); Hammann, *Der Streit um das Seebeuterecht* (1907); Wehberg, pp. 207-256, and *Das Beuterecht im Land und Seekrieg* (1909); Cohen, *The Immunity of Enemy's Property from Capture at Sea* (1909); Macdonell, *Some plain Reasons for Immunity from Capture of Private Property at Sea* (1910); Huttenheim, *Die Handelsschiffe der Kriegführenden* (1912); Loreburn, *Capture at Sea* (1913); Schramm, § 8; Slade in the *Naval Annual* (1914), pp. 88-98; Westlake, *Papers*, pp. 613-619; Quigley in *A.J.*, xi. (1917), pp. 32-45; Stier-Somlo, *Die Freiheit der Meere und das Volkerrecht* (1917); Hays in *A.J.*, xii. (1918), pp. 283-290; Meurer, *Das Programm der Meeresfreiheit* (1918); Davison, *The Freedom of the Seas* (1918). See also the literature quoted by Bonfils, No. 1281, Pradier-Fodéré, viii. Nos. 3070-3090, and Boeck, Nos. 382-572, where the arguments of the authors against, and in favour of, the present practice are discussed.

very far distant when the Powers would perforce come to an agreement on this, as on other points of sea warfare, in a code of regulations regarding sea warfare analogous to the Hague Regulations regarding warfare on land. A beginning was made by the United States of America by her Naval War Code [1] published in 1900, although she withdrew it in 1904. Later, the Second Hague Conference produced a number of conventions dealing with some parts of sea warfare, namely: (1) the VIth, relative to the Status of Enemy Merchant-ships at the Outbreak of Hostilities; (2) the VIIth, relative to the Conversion of Merchant-ships into War-ships; (3) the VIIIth, relative to the Laying of Automatic Submarine Contact Mines; (4) the IXth, respecting Bombardments by Naval Forces; (5) the XIth, relative to certain Restrictions on the Exercise of the Right of Capture in Maritime War.[2] Codification of Law of Sea Warfare.

Since then, however, the World War has been fought, and it has become impossible to forecast the future of the movement for the immunity of private enemy property from capture at sea, or of the laws of sea warfare in general.

II

ATTACK AND SEIZURE OF ENEMY VESSELS

Hall, §§ 138, 148—Lawrence, § 182—Westlake, ii. pp. 154-162, 312-316—Phillimore, iii. § 347—Twiss, ii. § 73—Halleck, ii. pp. 105-108—Taylor, §§ 545-546—Moore, vii. §§ 1175, 1183, etc.—Walker, § 50, p. 147—Wharton, iii. § 345—Hershey, Nos. 404, 405, 423-426—Bluntschli, §§ 664-670—Heffter, §§ 137-139—Ullmann, § 188—Bonfils, Nos. 1269-1273[3], 1350-1354, 1398-1400—Despagnet, Nos. 654-659—Rivier, ii. § 66—Nys, iii. pp. 432-449—Pradier-Fodéré, viii. Nos. 3155-3165, 3176-3178—

[1] See above, vol. i. § 32, and Stockton in the *Proceedings of the American Society of International Law*, vi. (1913), pp. 115-123. As to the Naval Codes of some other Powers, see Garner, i. §§ 7-9.

[2] The Institute of International Law, at its meeting at Oxford in 1913, adopted a draft code of maritime warfare (*Manuel des Lois de la Guerre maritime*). The author does not here mention the Declaration of London because it was primarily concerned with neutrality.

Calvo, iv. §§ 2368-2378—Fiore, iii. Nos. 1414-1424, and *Code*, Nos. 1665-1671—Pillet, pp. 121-128—Perels, § 35—Testa, pp. 155-157—Lawrence, *War*, pp. 48-55, 93-111—Ortolan, ii. pp. 31-34—Boeck, Nos. 190-208—Dupuis, Nos. 150-158, and *Guerre*, Nos. 74-112—U.S. Naval War Code, Articles 13-16—Bernsten, §§ 7-8—Schramm, § 8—Wehberg, pp. 174-207—Garner, i. §§ 214-215, 220-222, ii. §§ 532-537.

Importance of Attack and Seizure of Enemy Vessels.

§ 180. Whereas in land warfare all sorts of violence against enemy individuals are the chief means, in sea warfare attack and seizure of enemy vessels are the most important means. For together with enemy vessels, a belligerent takes possession of the enemy individuals and enemy goods thereon, so that he can appropriate vessels and goods, as well as detain those enemy individuals who are liable to be interned as prisoners of war. For this reason, and compared with attack and seizure of enemy vessels, violence against enemy persons, and the other means of sea warfare, play only a secondary part, although they are certainly not unimportant. For a weak naval Power can even restrict the operations of its fleet to mere coast defence, and thus totally refrain from directly attacking and seizing enemy vessels.

Attack, when legitimate.

§ 181. All enemy men-of-war and other public vessels, which are met by a belligerent's men-of-war on the high seas, or within the territorial waters[1] of either

[1] Whether enemy merchantmen may be captured in rivers is a controverted question. See Wehberg, pp. 60-61, and Biensfeldt in *Z. V.*, x. (1917), pp. 375-381, and the several authors there quoted. There ought to be no doubt that they may be captured in parts of rivers which are navigable from the sea by sea-going vessels, and that sea-going vessels may also be captured in parts of rivers not navigable from the sea, if they have been brought there for the purpose of saving them from capture. The Institute of International Law (see Article 1 of its *Manuel de la Guerre maritime* (1913)) had answered the question in the negative; but during the World War the various Prize Courts have answered it in the affirmative. In a judgment of the Italian Prize Court (see *The Cervignano* and *The Friuli*), condemning in 1917 two dismantled Austrian vessels moored in a river port, it is mentioned that the German Prize Courts had condemned some Belgian ships moored in the German Rhine port of Duisburg, and the Russian vessel *Primula*, captured in the river Trave which leads from Lübeck to Frauenmünde.

Different is the question of the capture of enemy vessels on inland lakes not connected with, and navigable from, the sea. In *Re Craft captured on Victoria Nyanza*, (1918) 3 B. and C. P. C. 295, it was belligerent,[1] may at once be attacked, and the attacked vessel may, of course, defend [2] herself by a counter-attack. Enemy merchantmen [3] may be attacked only if they refuse to submit to visit after having been duly signalled to do so.[4] No duty exists for an enemy merchantman to submit to visit; on the contrary, she may refuse, and defend herself against an attack. But only a man-of-war is competent to attack either men-of-war or merchantmen, in a war between parties to the Declaration of Paris, by which privateering is prohibited. Any merchantman of a belligerent attacking a public or private vessel of the enemy would be considered a pirate and treated as such, and the members of the crew would be liable to be treated as war criminals [5] to the same extent as private individuals committing hostilities in land warfare. However, if attacked by an enemy vessel, a merchantman is competent to deliver a counter-attack, and need not discontinue her attack because the vessel which opened hostilities takes to flight, but may pursue and seize her.

Moreover, if merchantmen must expect to be attacked without warning by a lawless enemy, they need not wait for attack before they themselves resort to hos-

held that the right of capture can be exercised on such large inland lakes as belong in part to the territory of each belligerent, both having armed vessels thereon.

[1] But not, of course, in territorial waters of neutral States; see *The De Fortuyn*, (1760) Burrell 175; *The Bangor*, (1916) 2 B. and C. P. C. 206; *The Düsseldorf*, (1919) 3 B. and C. P. C. 466, [1920] A. C. 1034; *The Valeria*, [1920] P. 81; *The Pellworm*, [1920] P. 347. But see *The Tinos*, above, § 71 n., and *The Ekaterinoslav* and *The Mukden*, below, § 320 n.

[2] See above, § 85. That a merchant vessel could defend herself against an attack of an enemy man-of-war had formerly never been doubted. But see Schramm, p. 308, who asserts that self-defence is not admissible.

[3] The term 'enemy merchantman' is here to be taken in its wider sense, in which it is identical with 'private vessels.' There ought, therefore, to be no doubt that yachts may be captured as well as other private vessels, although Wehberg, p. 177, denies this. See the German case of *The Primavera* (1916), cited above, § 102*a* n.

[4] This rule is, of course, valid also with regard to attacks by submarines. On the practice of German and Austrian submarines during the World War, see below, § 194*a*.

[5] See above, § 85, and below, § 254.

tilities. Thus, when in 1915, during the World War, Germany resorted to her nefarious submarine practice, and merchantmen were torpedoed without warning, or if they were warned, their crews were endangered in their lives by being put in lifeboats on the high seas, it was perfectly legitimate for merchantmen of the Allies to attempt to ram German submarines, even if signalled to stop and submit to visitation. The conviction and execution by the Germans in July 1916 of Captain Fryatt,[1] the commander of the *Brussels*, for having attempted in March 1915 to ram the German submarine U 33, was nothing else than a judicial murder.

An attack upon an enemy vessel on the sea by forces on the shore, for instance, by coast batteries, is only permissible if the vessel is an enemy man-of-war. Enemy merchantmen may not be attacked in this way; for they may only be attacked by men-of-war after having been signalled in vain to submit to visit.

Attack, how effected.

§ 182. One mode of attack which was in use in the time of sailing ships, namely, boarding and fighting the crew, which can be described as analogous to assault in land warfare, is no longer common; but if an instance occurs, it is perfectly lawful. Attack is nowadays generally effected by cannonade, torpedoes,[2] and, if opportunity arises, by ramming; and except in so far as the Hague Declaration which prohibits such attacks by aircraft is binding,[3] nothing forbids an attack on enemy vessels by launching projectiles and explosives from air-vessels. In case the attacked vessel not only takes to flight, but defends herself by a counter-attack, all modes of attack are lawful against her, just as she

[1] See Scott in *A.J.*, x. (1916), pp. 865-877. The attempt of Jerusalem in *Z.V.*, xi. (1918), pp. 563-585, to justify the conviction and execution of Captain Fryatt is futile.

[2] Article 1 of Hague Convention viii. prohibits the use of torpedoes which do not become harmless if they miss their mark.

[3] See above, § 114, and below, § 214*a*.

herself is justified in applying all modes of attack by way of defence.[1]

Sub-marine Contact Mines.

§ 182*a*. A mode of attack which requires special attention[2] is by means of floating mechanical, in contradistinction to so-called electro-contact, mines. The latter need not specially be discussed, because they are connected with a battery on land, can naturally only be laid within territorial waters, and present no danger to neutral shipping except on the spot where they are laid. But floating mechanical mines can be dropped as well in the open sea as in territorial waters; they can, moreover, drift away to any distance from the spot where they were dropped, and thus become a great danger to navigation in general. Mechanical mines were extensively used by both parties in the Russo-Japanese War, during the blockade of Port Arthur in 1904, and the question of their admissibility was raised in the press of all neutral countries, the danger to neutral shipping being obvious. The Second Hague Conference took the matter up, and, in spite of the opposing views of the Powers, produced Convention VIII. relative to the Laying of Automatic Submarine Contact Mines. This convention comprises thirteen articles and was signed, with or without reservation, by the majority of the Powers represented at the conference. Twenty States ratified it, but some made reservations.[3] This convention prohibited belligerents[4] from laying *unanchored* automatic contact mines, unless they were so constructed as to become harmless one hour

[1] But air-vessels must not attack merchantmen without summoning them to surrender, and if they sink the vessel, they must save the crew. See below, § 194.

[2] See Lawrence, *War*, pp. 93-111; Wetzstein, *Die Seeminenfrage im Völkerrecht* (1909); Rocholl, *Die Frage der Minen im Seekrieg* (1910); Barclay, *Problems*, pp. 59 and 158; Lémonon, pp. 472-502; Higgins, pp. 328-345; Boidin, pp. 216-235; Dupuis, *Guerre*, Nos. 331-358; Scott, *Conferences*, pp. 576-587; Martitz in the *Report of the 23rd Conference* (1906) *of the International Law Association*, pp. 47-74; Stockton in *A.J.*, ii. (1908), pp. 276-284; Wehberg, § 5.

[3] See above, vol. i. § 568*a*.

[4] As regards neutrals, see below, § 363*a*.

at most after those who laid them had lost control over them, and from laying *anchored* automatic contact mines which did not become harmless as soon as they had broken loose from their moorings. It also prohibited them from laying automatic contact mines off the coasts and ports of the enemy, with the sole object of intercepting commercial navigation.[1]

When anchored automatic contact mines were employed, every possible precaution was to be taken for the security of peaceful navigation. The belligerents were to provide, as far as possible, for these mines becoming harmless after a limited time, and, where they ceased to be under observation, to notify the danger zones as soon as military exigencies permitted by notice to mariners, which was also to be communicated to the Governments through the diplomatic channel.

At the close of the war each Power was to remove the mines laid by it.

There was no doubt, even when the convention was drawn up, that its stipulations were totally inadequate to secure the safety of neutral shipping, and it was for this reason that the British plenipotentiaries signed it with a reservation that the mere fact that it did not prohibit a particular act or proceeding must not be held to debar Great Britain from contesting its legitimacy. The Institute of International Law studied the matter at its meetings at Paris in 1910 and at Madrid in 1911, and produced a 'Réglementation[2] internationale de l'Usage des Mines sous-marines et Torpilles,' and at Oxford in 1914 it adopted five articles dealing with the problem in its *Manuel de Guerre maritime.*

[1] France and Germany signed with reservations against this provision.

[2] See *Annuaire*, xxiv. (1911), p. 301.

The World War proved the Hague Convention to be even more unsatisfactory than had been foreseen. On the first day of the war a German vessel was sunk while laying mines in the North Sea, and on August 23, 1914, the British Admiralty announced that 'the Germans are continuing their practice of scattering mines indiscriminately upon the ordinary trade routes. These mines do not become harmless after a certain number of hours; they are not laid in connection with any definite military scheme . . . but appear to be scattered on the chance of touching individual British war or merchant vessels.' Great Britain did not pursue this policy, but on October 2, 1914, announced a system of mine-fields in certain notified areas. As the war proceeded, Germany planted mines on other trade routes. Great Britain established other notified mine-fields, and Holland protested against both policies.[1]

§ 183. As soon as an attacked or counter-attacked vessel hauls down her flag and, therefore, signals that she is ready to surrender, she must be given quarter and seized without further firing. To continue an attack although she is ready to surrender, and to sink her and her crew, would constitute a violation of customary International Law, and would only, as an exception, be admissible in case of imperative necessity or of reprisals. **Duty of giving Quarter.**

§ 184. Seizure is effected by securing possession of the vessel through the captor sending an officer and some of his own crew on board. But if, for any reason, this is impracticable, the captor orders the captured vessel to lower her flag and to steer according to his orders. Seizure of the vessel includes seizure of all the goods thereon, although neutral merchandise will be restored by the Prize Court to its owner, as will **Seizure.**

[1] See details in Garner, i. §§ 214-215, 220-222.

usually also personal effects [1] of the captain, crew, and enemy passengers.

There is no doubt that enemy merchantmen lying in an enemy port may there be seized, although the port itself is not occupied.[2] But if a town is occupied after capitulation, and merchantmen owned by enemy subjects resident in that town are found in its port, they cannot be seized according to British practice,[3] although they may by American [4] practice.

Effect of Seizure.

§ 185. The effect of seizure differs in the case of private enemy vessels and public enemy vessels.

Seizure of *private* enemy vessels may be described as parallel to occupation of enemy territory in land warfare. Since the vessel, and the individuals and goods thereon, are actually placed under the captor's authority, her officers and crew, and any private individuals on board, are for the time being submitted to the discipline of the captor, just as private individuals on occupied enemy territory are submitted to the authority of the occupant.[5] Seizure of private enemy vessels does not, however, vest the property finally in the hands of the belligerent [6] whose forces effected the capture. The prize has to be brought before a Prize Court, which, by confirming the capture through adjudication of the prize, makes the appropriation by the capturing belligerent final.[7]

[1] See Westlake, pp. 144-155, especially with regard to the so-called 'adventures' (*pacotilles*), small parcels of merchandise which a captain is allowed to carry on his own account.

[2] *The Fortuna*, (1814) 1 Dod. 450; *The Polka*, (1854) Spinks 57.

[3] *The Ships taken at Genoa*, (1803) 4 C. Rob. 388.

[4] *Herrera* v. *United States* and *Diaz* v. *United States*, (1912) 222 U.S. 558, 574. See Kingsbury in *A.J.*, vi. (1912), pp. 650-658, and below, § 227 n.

[5] Concerning the ultimate fate of the crew, see above § 85.

[6] It is asserted that a captured enemy merchantman may at once be converted by the captor into a man-of-war, but the cases of *The Ceylon*, (1811) and *The Georgiana*, (1814) 1 Dod. 105 and 397, which are quoted in favour of such a practice, are not decisive. See Higgins, *War and the Private Citizen* (1912), pp. 138-142.

[7] See below, § 192; and Smith, *The Destruction of Merchant Ships*

On the other hand, the effect of seizure of *public* enemy vessels is their immediate and final appropriation. They may be either taken into a port, or at once destroyed. All individuals on board become prisoners of war, although, if perchance there should be on board a private enemy individual of no importance or value to the enemy, he would probably not be kept for long in captivity, but liberated in due time.

As regards goods on captured public enemy vessels, there is no doubt that the effect of seizure is the immediate appropriation of such goods on the vessels concerned as are enemy property, and these goods may therefore be destroyed at once, if desirable. Should, however, neutral goods be on board a captured enemy public vessel, it is a moot point whether or no they share the fate of the captured ship. According to British practice they do, but according to American practice they do not.[1]

Immunity of Vessels charged with Religious, Scientific, or Philanthropic Mission.

§ 186. Enemy vessels engaged in scientific discovery and exploration were, according to a general international usage in existence before the Second Hague Conference of 1907, granted immunity from attack and seizure in so far, and so long, as they themselves abstained from hostilities. The usage grew up in the eighteenth century. In 1766, the French explorer Bougainville, who started from St. Malo with the vessels *La Boudeuse* and *L'Étoile* on a voyage round the world, was furnished by the British Government with safe-conducts. In 1776, Captain Cook's vessels *Resolution* and *Discovery*, sailing from Plymouth for the purpose of exploring the Pacific Ocean, were declared exempt from attack and seizure on the part of French cruisers by the French Government. Again, the French

under International Law (1917), pp. 21-27.

[1] See, on the one hand, *The Fanny*, (1814) 1 Dod. 443, and, on the other, *The Nereide*, (1815) 9 Cranch 388. See also below, § 424 n.

Count Lapérouse, who started on a voyage of exploration in 1785 with the vessels *Astrolabe* and *Boussole*, was secured immunity from attack and seizure. During the nineteenth century this usage became quite general, and had almost ripened into a custom; examples are the Austrian cruiser *Novara* (1859) and the Swedish cruiser *Vega* (1878). No immunity, however, was granted to vessels charged with religious or philanthropic missions. A remarkable case occurred during the Franco-German War. In June 1871, the *Palme*, a vessel belonging to the Missionary Society of Basle, was captured by a French man-of-war, and condemned by the Prize Court of Bordeaux. The owners appealed, and the French Conseil d'État set the vessel free, not because the capture was not justified, but because equity demanded that the fact that Swiss subjects owning sea-going vessels were obliged to sail them under the flag of another State, should be taken into consideration.[1]

The Second Hague Conference embodied the previous usage concerning immunity of vessels of discovery and exploration in a written rule, and by Article 4 of Convention XI. extended it to vessels with a religious, scientific, or philanthropic mission.

The question, what is a 'philanthropic mission,' arose during the World War, when a German vessel, the *Paklat*,[2] requisitioned by the German authorities at Tsing-tau at the outbreak of war with Japan to carry women and children to Tientsin, was captured on her way there by a cruiser, and condemned by the Hong-

[1] See Rivier, ii. pp. 343-344; Dupuis, No. 158; Boeck, No. 199; and above, vol. i. § 258.

[2] (1915) 1 B. and C. P. C. 515. See also Garner, i. § 319, who discusses the case of *The Amiral Ganteaume*, a French steamer sunk by a German submarine while carrying Belgian refugees to England soon after the outbreak of the World War. The position of the many ships chartered by the Belgian Relief Commission to carry supplies for the inhabitants of the occupied territory in Belgium which were sunk by German submarines is also discussed by Garner, i. § 328-330.

Kong Prize Court as not being engaged on a philanthropic mission.

The immunity is the same, whether the vessel concerned is a private or a public vessel.[1]

Immunity of Fishing Boats and Small Boats employed in Local Trade.

§ 187. Coast fishing-boats, in contradistinction to boats engaged in deep-sea fisheries, were, according to a general, but not universal, custom in existence during the nineteenth century, granted immunity from attack and seizure, so long, and in so far, as they were unarmed, and were innocently employed in catching and bringing in fish.[2] As early as the sixteenth century, treaties were concluded between single States stipulating such immunity for their fishing boats in the time of war. But throughout the seventeenth and eighteenth centuries there were instances of a contrary practice, and Lord Stowell refused[3] to recognise any such exemption in strict law, although he recognised a rule of comity to that extent. Great Britain had always taken the standpoint that any immunity granted by her to fishing boats was a relaxation[4] of strict right in the interest of humanity, but revocable at any moment, and that her cruisers were justified in seizing enemy fishing boats unless prevented by special instructions from the Admiralty.[5] But at the Second Hague Conference she altered her attitude, and agreed to the immunity, not only of fishing vessels, but also of small boats employed in local trade. Article 3 of Convention XI. enacted that *vessels employed exclusively in coast fisheries, and small boats employed in local*

[1] See U.S. Naval War Code, Article 13. The matter is discussed at some length by Kleen, ii. § 210, pp. 503-505. Concerning the case of the English explorer Flinders, who sailed with the *Investigator* from England, but exchanged her for the *Cumberland*, which was seized in 1803 by the French at Port Louis, in Mauritius, as she was not the vessel to which a safe-conduct was given, see Lawrence, § 182.

[2] *The Paquette Habana*, (1899) 175 U.S. 677. See U.S. Naval War Code, Article 14; Japanese Prize Law, Article 35 (1).

[3] *The Young Jacob and Johanna*, (1798) 1 C. Rob. 20.

[4] See Hall, § 148.

[5] See Holland, *Prize Law*, § 36.

trade,[1] are, together with appliances, rigging, tackle, and cargo, exempt from capture.

None the less, the immunity of coast fishing boats from capture was valueless during the World War,[2] because Germany sank British fishing boats, and all the belligerents captured and interned members of the crews of military age.

It must be specially observed that boats engaged in deep-sea fisheries [3] and large boats engaged in local trade [1] do not enjoy the privilege of immunity from capture. Moreover, coast fishing vessels, and small boats employed in local trade, lose it by taking part in hostilities, and Article 3 of Convention XI. expressly stipulates that belligerents must not take advantage of the harmless character of boats engaged in coast fisheries and in local trade, in order to use them for military purposes while preserving their peaceful appearance.

Immunity of Merchantmen at the Outbreak of War on their Voyage to and from a Belligerent's Port.

§ 188. Several times, at the outbreak of war, during the nineteenth century, belligerents decreed that an enemy merchantman on its voyage to one of their ports at the outbreak of war, should not be seized at sea during its voyage to and from that port. Thus, at the outbreak of the Crimean War, Great Britain and France decreed such immunity for Russian vessels, Germany did the same with regard to French vessels in 1870,[4] Russia with regard to Turkish vessels in 1877, the United States with regard to Spanish vessels in 1898, and Russia and Japan with regard to each other's

[1] On the meaning of the term 'small boats employed in local trade,' see *H.M. Procurator in Egypt* v. *Deutsches Kohlen Depot Gesellschaft*, 2 B. and C. P. C. 439; 3 B. and C. P. C. 264. See also *The Maria*, (1915) 1 B. and C. P. C. 259. It is a question of fact in each case.

[2] See Garner, i. § 232.

[3] *The Berlin*, (1914) 1 B. and C. P. C. 29. However, the term 'coast fisheries,' which is not defined in the Hague Convention, certainly must not be construed to mean only fisheries within the maritime belt, for fishermen engaged in so-called coast fisheries frequently fish outside territorial waters. The size and character of the boat must determine whether it is engaged in coast or deep-sea fisheries.

[4] See, however, above, § 178.

vessels in 1904. But there was no rule of International Law which compelled a belligerent to grant such days of grace, and it appeared possible when the last edition of this book was published, that they would not be granted in future wars, for the reasons which have already been stated in considering the provisions of Hague Convention VI. How far that surmise was correct, so far as the World War was concerned, has already been pointed out.[1]

§ 189. Instances have occurred when enemy vessels which were forced by stress of weather to seek refuge in a belligerent's harbour were granted exemption from seizure.[2] Thus, when in 1746, during war with Spain, the *Elisabeth*, a British man-of-war, was forced to take refuge in the port of Havana, she was not seized, but was offered facilities for repairing the damage, and furnished with a safe-conduct as far as the Bermudas. Thus, further, when in 1799, during war with France, the *Diana*, a Prussian merchantman, was forced to take refuge in the port of Dunkirk and there seized, she was restored by the French Prize Court. But these, and other cases, have not created any rule of International Law whereby immunity from attack and seizure is granted to vessels in distress, and no such rule is likely to grow up, especially in the case of men-of-war and merchantmen easily convertible into cruisers. Vessels in Distress.

§ 190. According to the Hague Convention which adapted the principles of the Geneva Convention to warfare on sea, hospital ships are inviolable, and therefore may be neither attacked nor seized.[3] Concerning the immunity of cartel ships, see below.[4] Immunity of Hospital and Cartel Ships.

§ 191. No general rule of International Law exists granting enemy mail-boats immunity from attack and

[1] See above, § 102a.

[2] See Ortolan, ii. pp. 286-291; Kleen, ii. § 210, pp. 492-494.

[3] See below, §§ 204-209.

[4] § 225.

Immunity of Mail-Boats and of Mail-Bags.

seizure, and they were not granted any during the World War; but the several States have frequently stipulated such immunity in the case of war by special treaties.[1] Thus, for instance, Great Britain and France by Article 9 of the Postal Convention of August 30, 1890, and Great Britain and Holland by Article 7 of the Postal Convention of October 14, 1843, stipulated that all mail-boats navigating between the countries of the parties should continue to do so in time of war without impediment or molestation, until special notice was given by either party that the service was to be discontinued.

Whereas there is no general rule granting immunity from capture to enemy mail-boats, enemy *mail-bags* were, according to Article 1 of Hague Convention XI.,[2] to enjoy immunity, for it is there enacted that the postal correspondence of neutrals or belligerents, whether official or private in character, which may be found on board a neutral[3] or enemy ship at sea, is inviolable, and that, in case the ship is detained, the correspondence is to be forwarded by the captor with the least possible delay. There is only one exception to this rule; correspondence destined to, or proceeding from, a blockaded port does not enjoy immunity.

During the World War, the Central Powers used the mails to disseminate propaganda literature, to forward contraband, to send securities abroad to sustain their credit, to transmit information, and to organise incendiarism and *sabotage* in factories in neutral countries.[4] These devices assumed such proportions that the Allies proceeded to open and examine mail-bags destined for certain countries and found on neutral steamers

[1] See Kleen, ii. § 210, pp. 505-507.

[2] See Hershey in *A.J.*, x. (1916), pp. 580-584, who correctly states that this convention was not binding during the World War, because not all the belligerents were parties to it.

[3] See below, §§ 319, 411.

[4] See details in Garner, ii. §§ 532-534.

entering British territorial waters or ports. This action provoked protests from neutral States;[1] but the immunity from capture at sea granted to mail-bags does not include immunity from being censored when found on vessels which enter the territorial waters and harbours of a belligerent.[2]

It must also be specially observed that postal correspondence,[3] and not parcels sent by parcel post,[4] are immune from capture according to the Hague Convention.

III

APPROPRIATION AND DESTRUCTION OF ENEMY MERCHANTMEN

Hall, §§ 149-152, 171, 269—Lawrence, §§ 183-191—Westlake, ii. pp. 309-312—Phillimore, iii. §§ 345-381—Twiss, ii. §§ 72-97—Halleck, ii. pp. 362-431, 510-526—Taylor, §§ 552-567—Wharton, iii. § 345—Wheaton, §§ 355-394—Hershey, Nos. 428-432—Moore, vii. §§ 1206-1214—Bluntschli, §§ 672-673—Heffter, §§ 137-138—Geffcken in *Holtzendorff*, iv. pp. 588-596—Ullmann, § 189—Bonfils, Nos. 1396-1440[8]—Despagnet, Nos. 670-682—Pradier-Fodéré, viii. Nos. 3179-3207—Rivier, ii. § 66—Nys, iii. pp. 695-710—Calvo, iv. §§ 2294-2366, v. §§ 3004-3034—Fiore, iii. Nos. 1426-1443, and *Code*, Nos. 1715-1728—Martens, ii. §§ 125-126—Pillet, pp. 342-353—Perels, §§ 36, 55-58—Testa, pp. 147-160—Valin, *Traité des Prises*, 2 vols. (1758-60), and *Commentaire sur l'Ordonnance de 1681*, 2 vols. (1766)—Pistoye et Duverdy, *Traité des Prises maritimes*, 2 vols. (1854-1859)—Upton, *The Law of Nations affecting Commerce during War* (1863)—Boeck, Nos. 156-209, 329-380—Dupuis, Nos. 96-149, 282-301—Bernsten, § 8—Roscoe, *The Growth of English Law* (1911), pp. 92-140—Schramm, §§ 2, 13-15—Marsden, *Early Prize Jurisdiction and Prize Law in England* in the *English Historical Review*, xxiv. (1909), p. 675; xxv. (1910), p. 243; xxvi. (1911), p. 34. See also the literature quoted by Bonfils at the commencement of No. 1396.

---

[1] For the diplomatic controversies between Great Britain and the United States of America regarding interference with mails, see *Parl. Papers*, Cd. 8173, 8223, 8261, 8294, 8438, or *A.J.*, x. (1916), Special Supplement, pp. 404-426; for those with Sweden, see *Parl. Papers*, Cd. 8322; for those with Holland, see *R.G.*, xxiv. (1917), Documents, p. 79. See also Hall, pp. 743-746.

[2] See Cd. 8438, p. 4.

[3] If letters contain, not only correspondence, but also goods, or if goods are sent by letter post, such goods, if contraband, may be confiscated. As to securities, see *The Frederick VIII.*, (1916) 2 B. and C. P. C. 395; *The Noordam*, (1919) 3 B. and C. P. C. 488 and (on appeal) in [1920] A. C. 904; and Cd. 8261, p. 4.

[4] As regards parcel post, see *The Simla*, (1915) 1 B. and C. P. C. 281, and also Cd. 8173.

Prize Courts.

§ 192. It has already been stated above[1] that the capture of a private enemy vessel has to be confirmed by a Prize Court, and that it is only through its adjudication that the vessel becomes finally appropriated. The origin[2] of Prize Courts is to be traced back to the end of the Middle Ages. During the Middle Ages, after the Roman Empire had broken up, a state of lawlessness established itself on the high seas. Piratical vessels of the Danes covered the North Sea and the Baltic, and navigation of the Mediterranean Sea was threatened by Greek and Saracen pirates. Merchantmen, therefore, associated themselves for mutual protection, and sailed as a merchant fleet under a specially elected chief, the so-called Admiral. They also occasionally sent out a fleet of armed vessels for the purpose of sweeping pirates from certain parts of the high seas. Piratical vessels and goods which were captured were divided among the captors according to a decision of their Admiral. During the thirteenth century the maritime States of Europe themselves endeavoured to keep order on the open sea. By and by, armed vessels were obliged to be furnished with letters patent, or letters of marque, from the sovereign of a maritime State, and their captures submitted to the official control of such State as had furnished them with their letters. A board, called the Admiralty, was instituted by maritime States, and officers of that Board of Admiralty exercised control over the armed vessels and their captures, inquiring in each case[3] into the legitimation

[1] § 185.

[2] I follow the excellent summary of the facts given by Twiss, ii. §§ 74-75, but see also Marsden, *Documents relating to Law and Custom of the Sea* (i. 1915, ii. 1916), and the same author in the *English Historical Review*, xxiv. (1909), p. 675, xxv. (1910), p. 243, xxvi. (1911), p. 34, and in the *Journal of the Society of Comparative Legislation*, New Ser. xv. (1915), pp. 90-94. See also Senior in the *Law Quarterly Review*, xxxv. (1919), pp. 73-83.

[3] The first case that is mentioned as having led to judicial proceedings before the Admiral in England dates from 1357; see Marsden in the *English Historical Review*, xxiv. (1909), p. 680.

of the captor, and the nationality of the captured vessel and her goods; and after modern International Law had grown up, it was a recognised customary rule that in time of war the Admiralty of maritime belligerents should be obliged to institute a court[1] or courts, whenever a prize was captured by public vessels or privateers, in order to decide whether the capture was lawful or not. These courts were called Prize Courts. This institution has come down to our times, and nowadays all maritime States either constitute permanent Prize Courts, or appoint them specially in each case of an outbreak of war. The whole institution is essentially one in the interest of neutrals, since belligerents want to be guarded by a decision of a court against claims by neutral States regarding alleged unjustified capture of neutral vessels and goods.[2] The capture of any private vessel, whether *prima facie* belonging to an enemy or a neutral, must, therefore, be submitted to a Prize Court. Prize Courts are not international courts, but national courts instituted by Municipal Law, and the law they administer is Municipal Law,[3] based on custom, statutes, or special regulations of their State. Every State is, however, bound by International Law to enact only such statutes and regulations[4] for its Prize Courts as

[1] In England an Order in Council, dated July 20, 1589, first provided that all captures should be submitted to the High Court of Admiralty; see Marsden, *ibid.*, p. 690.

[2] The fact that in Great Britain the Prize Courts are competent to condemn British vessels found guilty of trading with the enemy has nothing to do with International Law, but is entirely a matter of Municipal Law, just as is the question—see above, § 101—whether trading with the enemy is permitted or prohibited. But, according to British practice, British Prize Courts are likewise competent to condemn merchantmen of an ally which have been found guilty of trading with the enemy. This practice is based on the fact that—see above, § 101—British Prize Courts consider it to be a rule of International Law that trading with the enemy is *ipso facto* by the outbreak of war prohibited. See *The Panariellos*, (1915) 1 B. and C. P. C. 195; 2 B. and C. P. C. 47.

[3] See below, § 434.

[4] The constitution and procedure of Prize Courts in Great Britain are governed by the Naval Prize Act, 1864 (27 & 28 Vict. c. 25), the Prize Courts Act, 1894 (57 & 58 Vict. c. 39), the Prize Courts (Procedure) Act, 1914 (4 & 5 Geo. v. c. 13), the Prize Courts Act, 1915 (5 & 6 Geo. v. c. 57), the Naval Prize (Procedure) Act, 1916 (6 Geo. v. c. 2), the

are in conformity with International Law.[1] A State may, therefore, instead of making special regulations, directly order its Prize Courts to apply the rules of International Law, and it is understood that, when no statutes are enacted or regulations are given, Prize Courts have to apply International Law. Prize Courts may be instituted by belligerents in any part of their territory, or the territories of allies, but not on neutral territory. It would nowadays constitute a breach of neutrality on the part of a neutral State to allow the institution on its territory of a Prize Court.[2]

Whereas the ordinary Prize Courts are national courts, Convention XII. of the Second Hague Conference provided for the establishment of an International[3] Prize Court at the Hague, which, in certain matters, was to serve as a court of appeal in prize cases; but this convention was never ratified, and during the World War there was no International Prize Court.

Conduct of Prize to Port of Prize Court.

§ 193. As soon as a vessel is seized, she must be conducted to a port where a Prize Court is sitting. As a rule, the officer and the crew sent on board the prize by the captor will navigate her to the port. This officer may ask the master and crew of the vessel to assist him, but, if they refuse, cannot compel them. The captor need not accompany the prize to the port, except where an officer and crew cannot be sent on board, and the captured vessel is ordered to lower her

Naval Prize Act, 1918 (8 & 9 Geo. v. c. 30), and the Prize Court Rules, 1914. The Institute of International Law has in various meetings occupied itself with capture, and embodied rules relating to it in Articles 100-115 of its *Manuel des Lois de la Guerre maritime* adopted at its meeting at Oxford in 1913 (see *Annuaire*, xxvi. pp. 667-671).

[1] The position of a Prize Court in relation to Municipal and International Law was fully considered by the Privy Council during the World War in *The Zamora*, (1916) 2 B. and C. P. C. 1, which is the leading case, so far as British Prize Courts are concerned. See also Picciotto, *The Relation of International Law to the Law of England and The United States* (1915).

[2] See below, § 327, and Article 1 of Convention XIII. of the Second Hague Conference.

[3] See above, vol. i. § 476*a*, and below, §§ 442-447.

flag, and to steer according to orders. The captor must in that case conduct the prize to the port. To which port a prize is to be taken is not for International Law to determine; it only provides that the prize must be taken straight to a port where a Prize Court sits, and only in case of distress or necessity is delay allowed. A prize may, in case of distress, or in case she is in such bad condition as prevents her from being taken to such a port, if the neutral State concerned gives permission,[1] be taken to a near neutral port, and in that event the capturing man-of-war as well as the prize enjoy there the privilege of exterritoriality. But as soon as circumstances allow, the prize must be conducted from the neutral port to a port where a Prize Court sits, and only if the condition of the prize makes this absolutely impossible, may the Prize Court give its verdict in its absence after hearing proper evidence.

The whole crew and cargo ought, as a rule, to remain on board the prize until they reach the port of adjudication. But if any cargo is in a condition which prevents it from being sent there, it may, according to the needs of the case, either be destroyed or sold in the nearest port, and, if sold, an account of the proceeds has to be sent to the Prize Court. This applies also to neutral goods, although they have, according to the Declaration of Paris, to be restored to their neutral owners.

Destruction of Prize.

§ 194. Since through adjudication by the Prize Courts the ownership of captured private enemy vessels becomes finally transferred to the belligerent whose forces made the capture, it is evident that after transfer the captured vessel as well as her cargo may be destroyed. On the other hand, it is likewise evident that, since a judgment of a Prize Court is necessary before the appro-

[1] See below, § 328, and Articles 21-23 of Convention XIII. of the Second Hague Conference.

priation of the prize becomes final, a captured merchantman must not, as a rule, be destroyed [1] on capture instead of being conducted to the port of adjudication. There are, however, exceptions to the rule, but no unanimity exists in theory or practice as regards those exceptions. Whereas some [2] consider the destruction of a prize allowable only in case of imperative necessity, others [3] allow it in nearly every case of convenience. Thus, the Government of the United States of America, on the outbreak of war with England in 1812, instructed the commanders of American vessels to destroy at once all captures, the very valuable excepted, because a single cruiser, however successful, could man a few prizes only, but by destroying each capture would be able to continue capturing, and thereby constantly diminish the enemy merchant fleet.[4] During the Civil War in America, the cruisers of the Southern Confederated States destroyed all enemy prizes, because there was no port open for them to bring prizes to. During the Russo-Japanese War, Russian cruisers destroyed twenty-one captured Japanese merchantmen.[5] According to British practice,[6] the captor is allowed to destroy the prize in only two cases—namely, first, when the prize is in such a condition as prevents her from being sent to any port of adjudication; and, secondly, when the capturing vessel is unable to spare a prize crew to navigate the prize into such a port. The *Manuel des Lois de la Guerre maritime* of the Institute of International Law has suggested for the consideration of the States in Article 104 a rule prohibit-

[1] See Smith, *The Destruction of Merchant Ships under International Law* (1917), pp. 27-54.

[2] See, for instance, Bluntschli, § 672.

[3] See, for instance, Martens, ii. § 126, who moreover makes no difference between the prize being an enemy or a neutral ship.

[4] U.S. Naval War Code (Article 14) allowed destruction 'in case of military or other necessity.'

[5] See Takahashi, pp. 284-310.

[6] *The Acteon*, (1815) 2 Dod. 48; *The Felicity*, (1819) 2 Dod. 381; *The Leucade*, (1855) Spinks 217. See also Holland, *Prize Law*, §§ 303-304.

ing destruction of a captured enemy merchantman except 'in face of exceptional necessity, *i.e.* when necessary to secure the safety of the vessel making the capture or the success of the operations of war in which it is at the time engaged.'[1] Be that as it may,[2] in every case of destruction of a prize the captor must remove crew, ship papers, and, if possible, the cargo, beforehand, and must afterwards send crew, papers, and cargo to a port of adjudication for the purpose of satisfying the Prize Court that both the capture and the destruction were lawful.

If destruction of a captured enemy merchantman can, as an exception, be lawful, the question as to compensation for the neutral owners of goods on board requires attention.[3] It seems to be obvious that, if the destruction of the vessel herself was lawful, and if it was not possible to remove her cargo, no compensation need be paid.[4] An illustrative case happened during the Franco-German War. On October 21, 1870, the French cruiser *Desaix* seized two German merchantmen, the *Ludwig* and the *Vorwärts*, but burned them because she could not spare a prize crew to navigate the prizes into a French port. The neutral owners of part of the cargo claimed compensation, but the French Conseil d'État refused to grant indemnities on the ground that the action of the captor was lawful.[5] A similar decision was given by the Hamburg Prize Court in 1915 during the World War. The *Glitra* was an English merchantman captured by a German submarine, and then sunk, because she

[1] See *Annuaire*, xxvi. p. 669.

[2] The whole matter is thoroughly discussed by Boeck, Nos. 268-285; Dupuis, Nos. 262-268; and Calvo, v. §§ 3028-3034. As regards destruction of a neutral prize, see below, § 431.

[3] See Wright in *A.J.*, xi. (1917), pp. 358-379.

[4] Wehberg, p. 295, and Smith, *op. cit.*, pp. 54-58, object to this statement; but Noldecke in *Z.V.*, ix. (1916), pp. 447-458, approves of it.

[5] See Boeck, No. 146; Barboux, pp. 53, 155; Calvo, v. § 3033; Dupuis, No. 262; Hall, § 269; Westlake, ii. p. 309. See also Article 3 of unratified Hague Convention XII.

could not be brought into a German port. The Norwegian owners of the cargo claimed compensation, but the Prize Court refused to grant it, on the ground that the sinking was lawful.[1]

Destruction of Prizes by Submarines.

§ 194*a*. The question of the destruction of prizes has become of particular importance through the use of submarines.[2] That submarines can legitimately exercise the right of visit and search over enemy merchantmen, and capture them, there is not the slightest doubt. But a submarine can never spare a prize crew to navigate a prize into any port of adjudication, nor is there any room in a submarine to take on board the crew of the prize. For this reason the opinion is widely held that a submarine may never destroy a captured merchantman. But the practice of the Central Powers during the World War was very different. German submarines, even before the general order to torpedo without warning all enemy merchantmen within the war area proclaimed by Germany around the British Isles,[3] destroyed several of their English prizes, after having given ten minutes to the crews to lower their boats and leave the ship. Although in these cases no lives were lost, because the crews were either picked up by passing vessels or otherwise reached the shore, they were exposed to considerable danger. After February 1915, German submarines frequently torpedoed both enemy and neutral merchantmen, and great loss of life was caused thereby. The most appalling case was that of the *Lusitania*, a transatlantic liner, which was torpedoed on May 7, 1915, near the coast of Ireland, and over 1100 non-combatant men, women, and children

[1] See *Deutsche Juristen Zeitung* (1915), p. 456. See also the Hamburg case of *The Indian Prince*, *A.J.*, x. (1916), pp. 930-935.

[2] On this question see Garner, i. §§ 228-243; *A.J.*, ix. (1915), pp. 666-680; Minor in the *Proceedings of the American Society of International Law*, x (1916), pp. 51-60; Hyde, *ibid.*, xi. (1917), pp. 26-35; Perrinjaoquet in *R.G.*, xxiv. (1917), pp. 117-203.

[3] See above, i. § 50*a*.

perished. Unfortunately, however, this was but one of many.[1]

§ 195. Although prizes have, as a rule, to be brought before a Prize Court, International Law nevertheless does not forbid the ransoming of the captured vessel, either directly after the capture, or after she has been conducted to port, but before adjudication. However, the practice of accepting and paying ransom, which grew up in the sixteenth[2] century, is in many countries now prohibited by Municipal Law. Thus, for instance, Great Britain by § 45 of the Naval Prize Act, 1864, prohibits ransoming except when specially provided for by Order in Council. Where ransom is accepted, a contract of ransom is made between the captor and the master of the captured vessel; t e latter gives a so-called ransom bill to the former, in which he promises the amount of the ransom. He is given a copy of the ransom bill for the purpose of a safe-conduct to protect his vessel from again being captured, provided that he keeps his course to the port agreed upon in the ransom bill. To secure the payment of ransom, an officer of the captured vessel can be detained as hostage; otherwise the whole of the crew is to be liberated with the vessel, ransom being an equivalent for both the restoration of the prize and the release of her crew from captivity. So long as the ransom bill is not paid, the hostage can be kept in captivity. But it is exclusively a matter for the Municipal Law of the State concerned to determine whether or no the captor can sue upon the ransom bill, if the ransom is not voluntarily paid.[3] Should the capturing vessel, Ransom of Prize.

[1] The author had intended to discuss and condemn the German practice; but his manuscript does not indicate the precise form which his arguments would have taken.

[2] See Senior in the *Law Quarterly Review*, xxxiv. p. 50.

[3] See for British practice, prior to the Naval Prize Act, 1864, *Cornu* v. *Blackburne*, (1781) 2 Douglas 640; *Anthon* v. *Fisher*, (1782) 2 Douglas 649 n.; *The Hoop*, 1 C. Rob. 201; Hall, § 151; and for American practice, *Goodrich and De Forest* v. *Gordon*, (1818) 15 Johnson 6.

with the hostage or the ransom bill on board, be herself captured, the hostage is liberated, and the ransom bill loses its effect, and need not be paid.[1]

Loss of Prize, especially Recapture.

§ 196. A prize is lost—(1) when the captor intentionally abandons her, (2) when she escapes through being rescued [2] by her own crew, or (3) when she is recaptured. The property in a prize which, according to International Law, the belligerent whose forces made the capture acquires, provided that a Prize Court confirms the capture, is lost when the prize is lost; and it seems to be obvious, and everywhere recognised by Municipal Law, that as soon as a captured enemy merchantman succeeds in escaping, the title of the former owners revives *ipso facto*. But the case is different when an abandoned prize, whose crew have been taken on board the capturing vessel, is afterwards met and taken possession of by a neutral vessel, or by a vessel of her home State. It is certainly not for International Law to determine whether, or not, the original ownership revives through abandonment; this is a matter for Municipal Law.

The case of recapture is likewise different from escape. Here too Municipal Law has to determine whether, or not, the former ownership revives, since International Law only lays down the rule that by recapture the property in the vessel reverts to the belligerent whose forces made the recapture. Municipal Law of the individual States has settled the matter in different ways. Thus for Great Britain § 40 of the Naval Prize Act, 1864, enacts that the recaptured vessel, except when she has been used by the captor as a ship of war, shall be restored to her former owner on his paying one-eighth to one-fourth of her value, as the Prize

[1] The matter of ransom is discussed with great lucidity by Senior in the *Law Quarterly Review*, xxxiv. pp. 49-62; see also Twiss, ii. §§ 180-183; Boeck, Nos. 257-267; Dupuis, Nos. 269-277.

[2] See Gregory in *A.J.*, xi. (1917), pp. 315-326.

Court may award, as prize salvage, whether the recapture is made before or after the enemy Prize Court had confirmed the capture. Other States restore a recaptured vessel only when the recapture is made within twenty-four hours [1] after capture, or before the captured vessel is conducted into an enemy port, or before she is condemned by an enemy Prize Court.

§ 197. Through being captured, and afterwards condemned by a Prize Court, a captured enemy vessel and captured enemy goods [2] become, as already explained, the property of the belligerent whose forces made the capture. But according to the Declaration of Paris, neutral goods, contraband excepted, found on enemy ships may not be condemned. Nevertheless, all goods found on enemy vessels are presumed [3] to be enemy unless claimed as neutral by neutral owners; moreover, only neutral *merchandise* is exempt from confiscation, and not neutral goods other than merchandise.[4] Further, neutral mortgagees [5] or pledgees [6] of enemy vessels, or enemy cargoes, have no claim to be indemnified out of the proceeds of their sale. Fate of Prize.

What becomes of the prize after condemnation is not for International Law, but for Municipal Law, to determine. A belligerent can hand the prize over to the captors, or keep her for himself, or sell her and divide the whole or part of the proceeds among the captors, or among members of the naval forces generally. For Great Britain the Naval Prize Act, 1918,[7] established a naval prize fund into which the proceeds of sale of

[1] For instance, France; see Dupuis, Nos. 278-279.

[2] It does not, of course, matter whether the goods concerned were captured on enemy ships or on merchantmen sailing under the flag of the capturing belligerent. See above, §§ 102, 177 n.

[3] See above, § 90.

[4] *The Schlesien*, (1914) 1 B. and C. P. C. 13.

[5] *The Marie Glæser*, (1914) 1 B. and C. P. C. 38; [1914] P. 218, and the German case of *The Fenix*, *Z. V.*, ix. (1915), p. 103, and *A.J.*, x. (1916), p. 909.

[6] *The Odessa*, (1914) 1 B. and C. P. C. 163, 554.

[7] 8 & 9 Geo. v. c. 30.

certain prizes and prize cargoes were paid, and out of which prize money was distributed among members of the naval and marine forces. If a neutral subject buys a captured ship after her condemnation, she may certainly not be attacked and captured by the belligerent to a subject of which she formerly belonged; but if she is bought by an enemy subject, and afterwards captured, she might be restored[1] to her former owner.

Vessels belonging to Subjects of Neutral States, but sailing under Enemy Flag.

§ 198. As merchantmen owned by subjects of neutral States but sailing under an enemy flag are vested with enemy character,[2] they may be captured and condemned. This bears hardly upon vessels belonging to subjects of non-littoral States which have no maritime flag; they are forced to navigate under the flag of another State,[3] and are, therefore, in case of war exposed to capture.

Vessels sailing under Neutral Flag, but possessing Enemy Character.

§ 199. Moreover, a vessel flying a neutral flag may be captured and condemned if, for the reasons mentioned above in §§ 89, 91, she possesses enemy character.

Goods sold to Neutrals *in transitu.*

§ 200. As regards goods consigned to enemy subjects, but sold *in transitu* to subjects of neutral States, no unanimous practice is in existence, and the attitude of the different States has been considered above in § 92.

IV

VIOLENCE AGAINST ENEMY PERSONS

See the literature quoted above at the commencement of § 107. See also Bonfils, Nos. 1273-1273[3], and Schramm, § 16.

Violence against Combatants.

§ 201. As regards killing and wounding combatants in sea warfare, and the means used for the purpose, customary rules of International Law are in existence, according to which only those combatants may be killed or wounded who are able and willing to fight,

[1] See above, § 196.
[2] See above, § 89.
[3] See above, vol. i. § 261.

or who resist capture. Men disabled by sickness or wounds, or such men as lay down arms and surrender, or do not resist capture, must be given quarter, except in a case of imperative necessity or of reprisals. Poison, and such arms, projectiles, and materials as cause unnecessary injury, are prohibited, as is also killing and wounding in a treacherous way.[1] The Declaration of St. Petersburg[2] and the Hague Declaration prohibiting the use of expanding (dum-dum)[3] bullets, apply to sea warfare as well as to land warfare, as also do the Hague Declarations concerning projectiles and explosives launched from balloons, and projectiles diffusing asphyxiating or deleterious gases.[4]

All combatants, and also all officers and members of the crews of captured merchantmen, could formerly[5] be made prisoners of war. According to Articles 5 to 7 of Convention XI. of the Second Hague Conference,[6] such members of the crews of captured merchantmen as were subjects of neutral States might never be made prisoners of war; but those of the captain, officers, and members of the crews who were enemy subjects, and, further, the captain and officers, even though subjects of neutral States, might be made prisoners of war in case they refused to be released on parole. During the World War this convention was not binding, because not all the belligerents were parties to it, and enemy subjects who were members of the crews of merchantmen were made prisoners of war. As soon as such prisoners are landed, they fall under Articles 4-20 of the Hague Regulations;

[1] See the corresponding rules for warfare on land, which are discussed above in §§ 108-110. See also U.S. Naval War Code, Article 3.

[2] See above, § 111.

[3] See above, § 112.

[4] See above, §§ 113, 114.

[5] This was almost generally recognised, but was refused recognition by Count Bismarck during the Franco-German War (see below, § 249) and by some German publicists, as, for instance, Lueder in *Holtzendorff*, IV. p. 479, n. 6.

[6] See above, § 85.

but as long as they are on board, the old customary rule of International Law, that prisoners must be treated humanely,[1] and not like convicts, must be complied with. Moreover, the Hague Convention for the Adaptation of the Principles of the Geneva Convention to Maritime Warfare enacts some particular rules concerning the shipwrecked, the wounded, and the sick who, through falling into the hands of the enemy, become prisoners of war.[2]

Violence against non-Combatant Members of Naval Forces.

§ 202. Just as military forces consist of combatants and non-combatants, so do the naval forces of belligerents. Non-combatants, as, for instance, stokers, surgeons, chaplains, members of the hospital staff, and the like, who do not take part in the fighting, may not be attacked directly and killed or wounded.[3] But they are exposed to all injuries indirectly resulting from attacks on, or by, their vessels; and they may certainly be made prisoners of war, unless they are members of the religious, medical, and hospital staff, who are inviolable according to Article 10 of Hague Convention x.[4]

Violence against Enemy Individuals not belonging to the Naval Forces.

§ 203. Likewise enemy individuals who are not members of the naval forces at all, but are found on board an attacked or seized enemy vessel, if, and so far as, they do not take part in the fighting, may not directly be attacked and killed or wounded, although they are exposed to all injury indirectly resulting from an attack on, or by, their vessel. If they are mere private individuals, they may as an exception only, and under the same circumstances as private individuals on occupied territory, be made prisoners of war.[5] But they are nevertheless, for the time they are on board

[1] See Holland, *Prize Law*, § 249, and U.S. Naval War Code, Articles 10, 11.

[2] See below, § 205.

[3] See U.S. Naval War Code, Article 3.

[4] See below, § 209.

[5] See Schramm, § 16; see also U.S. Naval War Code, Article 11, and above, § 116.

the captured vessel, under the discipline of the captor. All restrictive measures against them which are necessary are therefore lawful, as are also punishments, in case they do not comply with lawful orders of the commanding officer. If they are enemy officials in important positions,[1] they may be made prisoners of war.

V

TREATMENT OF WOUNDED AND SHIPWRECKED

Perels, § 37—Pillet, pp. 188-191—Westlake, ii. pp. 185-189—Moore, vii. § 1178—Hershey, Nos. 408-422—Bernsten, § 12—Bonfils, Nos. 1280-1280[9]—Pradier-Fodéré, viii. No. 3209—U.S. Naval War Code, Articles 21-29—Ferguson, *The Red Cross Alliance at Sea* (1871)—Houette, *De l'Extension des Principes de la Convention de Genève aux Victimes des Guerres maritimes* (1892)—Cauwès, *L'Extension des Principes de la Convention de Genève aux Guerres maritimes* (1899)—Holls, *The Peace Conference at the Hague* (1900), pp. 120-134—Boidin, pp. 248-262—Dupuis, *Guerre*, Nos. 82-105—Meurer, ii. §§ 74-87—Higgins, pp. 382-394—Lémonon, pp. 526-554—Nippold, ii. § 33—Scott, *Conferences*, pp. 599-614—Takahashi, pp. 375-385—Wehberg, § 10—Garner, i. §§ 319-327—Fauchille in *R.G.*, vi. (1899), pp. 291-302—Bajer in *R.G.*, viii. (1901), pp. 225-230—Renault in *A.J.*, ii. (1908), pp. 295-306—Higgins, *War and the Private Citizen* (1912), pp. 73-87, and in the *Law Quarterly Review*, xxvi. (1910), pp. 408-414. See also the literature quoted above at the commencement of § 118.

Adaptation of Geneva Convention to Sea Warfare.

§ 204. Soon after the ratification of the Geneva Convention, the necessity of adapting its principles to naval warfare was generally recognised, and among the non-ratified additional articles of 1868 were nine which aimed at this.[2] But it was not until the Hague Conference in 1899 that this was accomplished by a convention[3] which comprised fourteen articles. This convention was replaced at the Second Hague Conference by Convention x. for the Adaptation of the Principles of the Geneva Convention to Maritime Warfare, which comprises twenty-eight articles. It was

[1] See above, § 117.

[2] See above, § 118, and vol. i. § 560.

[3] Martens, *N.R.G.*, 2nd Ser. xxvi. p. 979.

signed, although with some reservations, by all the Powers represented at the conference, except Nicaragua which acceded later, and it has been ratified, with or without reservations, by most of the signatory Powers. It provides rules concerning the wounded, sick, shipwrecked, and dead; hospital ships; sick-bays on men-of-war; the distinctive colour and emblem of hospital ships; neutral vessels taking on board belligerent wounded, sick, or shipwrecked; the religious, medical, and hospital staff of captured ships; the carrying out of the convention, and the prevention of abuses and infractions.

The Wounded, Sick, and Ship-wrecked.

§ 205. Soldiers, sailors, and other persons officially attached to fleets or armies, whatever their nationality, who are taken on board when sick or wounded, must be respected and tended by the captors (Article 11). All enemy shipwrecked, sick, or wounded persons who fall into the power of a belligerent are prisoners of war. It is left to the captor to determine whether they are to be kept on board, or sent to a port of his own, or a neutral port, or even a hostile port. If sent to a hostile port, they may not again serve in the war (Article 14). If landed at a neutral port with the consent of the local authorities, they must be guarded by the neutral State so as to prevent them from again taking part in the war[1] (Article 15). After each engagement, both belligerents must, so far as military interests permit, take measures to search for the shipwrecked, wounded, and sick, and protect them against pillage and maltreatment (Article 16). They must send to the enemy authorities a list of names of enemy sick and wounded picked up by them, and information regarding internments, transfers, admissions to hospital, and deaths amongst the sick and wounded in their hands. They must also forward all objects of personal use, valuables,

[1] See below, § 348a.

letters, etc., that are found in captured ships for transmission to the persons concerned (Article 17).

Treatment of the Dead. § 205*a*. After each engagement both belligerents must, so far as military interests permit, take measures to protect the dead against pillage and maltreatment, and they must see that their burial, whether by land or sea, or cremation, is preceded by a careful examination in order to determine that life is really extinct (Article 16). They must send to the enemy authorities the military identification marks or tokens found on the dead; they must also forward all the objects of personal use, valuables, letters, etc., which have been left by the wounded and sick who die in hospital, for transmission to the persons concerned (Article 17).

Hospital Ships. § 206. Three different kinds of hospital ships must be distinguished—namely, military hospital ships; hospital ships equipped by private individuals or relief societies of the belligerents; and hospital ships equipped by private neutral individuals and neutral relief societies.

(1) Military hospital ships (Article 1) are ships constructed or assigned by States specially and solely to assist the wounded, sick, and shipwrecked. Their names must be communicated to the belligerents at the commencement of, or during, hostilities, and in any case before they are employed. They must be respected by the belligerents, they may not be captured while hostilities last, and they are not on the same footing as men-of-war during their stay in a neutral port.

(2) Hospital ships equipped wholly, or in part, at the cost of private individuals, or officially recognised relief societies of the *belligerents*, must also be respected (Article 2), and are exempt from capture, provided their home State has given them an official commission, and a special certificate, and has notified their names to

the other belligerent at the commencement of, or during, hostilities, and in any case before they are employed.

(3) Hospital ships, equipped wholly, or in part, at the cost of private individuals, or officially recognised relief societies of *neutral* States (Article 3), must likewise be respected, and are exempt from capture, provided that they are placed under the control of one of the belligerents, with the previous consent of their own Government and with the authorisation of the belligerent himself, and that their names have been similarly notified.

According to Article 4 all hospital ships must afford relief and assistance to the wounded, sick, and shipwrecked of either belligerent. The respective Governments are prohibited from using them for any military purpose. Their commanders must not in any way hamper the movements of the combatants, and during and after an engagement they act at their own risk and peril. Both belligerents have a right to control and visit all hospital ships, to refuse their assistance, to order them off, to make them take a certain course, to put a commissioner on board, and to detain them temporarily, if important circumstances require this.

The protection to which hospital ships are entitled ceases if they are used to commit acts harmful to the enemy (Article 8). But it is not lost merely because the staff are armed for the purpose of maintaining order and defending the wounded and sick, or because wireless telegraphic apparatus is on board. However, any man-of-war of either belligerent may, according to Article 12 (against which Great Britain made an interpretative reservation), demand the surrender of wounded, sick, or shipwrecked who are on board hospital ships of any kind.

It is to be regretted that, in practice, cases of the abuse of hospital ships for military purposes have occurred. Thus, in 1905, during the Russo-Japanese War, the *Orel*[1] (also called the *Aryel*), a Russian hospital ship, was captured and condemned by the Japanese Prize Courts for having performed, while serving as a hospital ship, certain services to the Russian fleet, which amounted to use for military purposes. Again, in 1915, during the World War, the *Ophelia*,[2] a German hospital ship, was captured and condemned by the British Prize Court, because, while adapted as a hospital ship, she was also fitted up as a signalling ship for military purposes.

Worse than the misuse of hospital ships for military purposes was the deliberate policy proclaimed by Germany[3] during the World War of sinking at sight without visit or search all hospital ships found in certain waters. In January 1917, after charging Great Britain and France with using hospital ships for the transport of troops and munitions and otherwise violating Hague Convention x. (charges which were promptly repudiated), the German Government declared that they would 'no longer suffer any enemy hospital ship in the English Channel or parts of the North Sea.'[4] In March of the same year, after making further charges, they declared that enemy hospital ships met in a prescribed area of the Mediterranean would be 'regarded by the German naval forces as belligerent' and would be 'attacked forthwith.'[5] Even before these pronouncements hospital ships had been attacked by German submarines; thereafter they were freely sunk

[1] See Takahashi, pp. 620-625; Hurst, ii. p. 354; and Higgins, *op. cit.*, p. 74, and in the *Law Quarterly Review*, xxvi. (1910), p. 408.

[2] 1 B. and C. P. C. 210; 2 B. and C. P. C. 150.

[3] See Des Gouttes in *R.G.*, xxiv. (1917), pp. 469-486.

[4] *Parl. Papers*, Misc., No. 16 (1917), Cd. 8692, p. 4. It appears that on only one occasion did the Germans exercise the right to stop and visit a hospital ship conferred by Article 4 of Hague Convention x., and then found nothing to support any charge. Had there been any truth in the allegations made by them against the Allied Governments, they could have proved them beyond question by availing themselves of this article.

[5] *Ibid.*, p. 6.

without warning, visit or search, and sometimes with great loss of life. Among the many victims of this policy were the *Asturias*, the *Gloucester Castle*, the *Donegal*, the *Lanfranc*, the *Dover Castle*, the *Rewa*, the *Glenart Castle*, and the *Llandovery Castle*.[1]

Hospital Ships in Neutral Ports.

§ 206*a*. For the purpose of defining the status of hospital ships when entering neutral ports, an international conference met at the Hague in 1904.[2] A convention (to which Great Britain was not a party) was signed on December 21, 1904, and provided that hospital ships complying with the Hague Convention should be exempt from State dues and taxes, but should nevertheless be subject to search and other formalities demanded by the laws in force in the port concerned.

Sick-Bays.

§ 206*b*. According to Article 7 of Hague Convention x., in case of a fight on board a man-of-war, the sick-bays must, as far as possible, be respected and spared. These sick-bays, and the material belonging to them, remain subject to the laws of war; they may not, however, be used for any purpose other than that for which they were originally intended so long as they are required for the wounded and sick. But should the military situation require it, a commander into whose power they have fallen may nevertheless apply them to other purposes, provided that he has previously arranged proper accommodation for the wounded and sick on board. The protection to which sick-bays are entitled ceases if they are used to commit acts harmful to the enemy (Article 8). But it is not lost because the staff is armed in order to defend the wounded and sick.

§ 207. All military hospital ships must be painted white outside with a horizontal band of green about

[1] Details in Garner, i. §§ 320-326, who mentions the various unsuccessful attempts to stop the German practice.

[2] See above, vol. i. § 592.

one metre and a half in breadth. Other hospital ships must also be painted white outside, but with a horizontal band of red. The boats and small craft of hospital ships used for hospital work must likewise be painted white. Besides being painted a distinguishing colour, all hospital ships (Article 5) must hoist, together with their national flag, the white flag with a red cross stipulated by the Geneva Convention.[1] If they belong to a neutral State, they must also fly at the mainmast the national flag of the belligerent under whose control they are placed. The distinguishing marks of hospital ships may at no time be used for any other purpose. All hospital ships which wish to ensure by night the freedom from interference to which they are entitled, must, subject to the assent of the belligerent they are accompanying, take the necessary measures to render their special painting sufficiently plain.

Distinctive Colour and Emblem of Hospital Ships.

Neutral Vessels assisting the Wounded, Sick, or Shipwrecked.

§ 208. A distinction must be made between neutral men-of-war and private vessels assisting the sick, wounded, and shipwrecked.

(1) If men-of-war take on board wounded, sick, or shipwrecked persons, precaution must be taken, so far as possible, that they do not again take part in the operations of war (Article 13). They must not, however, be handed over to the adversary, but must be detained till the end of the war.[2]

(2) Neutral merchantmen,[3] yachts, or boats which have of their own accord rescued sick, wounded, or shipwrecked men, or who have taken such men on board at the appeal of the belligerent, must, according to Article 9, enjoy special protection and certain im-

[1] There is no objection to the use by non-Christian States, who object to the cross on religious grounds, of another emblem. Thus Turkey reserved the right to use a red crescent, and Persia to use a red sun.

[2] See below, § 348.

[3] See below, § 348a.

munities. In no case may they be captured merely because they have such persons on board. But, subject to any undertaking that may have been given to them, they remain liable to capture for any violation of neutrality they may have committed. Moreover, according to Article 12,[1] any man-of-war of either belligerent may demand from them the surrender of the wounded, sick, or shipwrecked on board.

The Religious, Medical, and Hospital Staff.

§ 209. Convention x. provides that the religious, medical, and hospital staff of any captured vessel are inviolable, and may not be made prisoners of war, but must continue to discharge their duties while necessary. If they do this, the belligerent into whose hands they have fallen has to give them the same allowances and the same pay as are granted to persons holding the same rank in his own navy. They may leave the ship, when the commander-in-chief considers it possible, and on leaving they are allowed to take with them all surgical articles and instruments which are their private property (Article 10).

Application of Convention x., and Prevention of Abuses.

§ 209*a*. The provisions of Convention x. are only binding so long as the war is a war between contracting Powers only (Article 18). In the case of operations of war between land and sea forces of belligerents, its provisions only apply to forces on board ship (Article 22). The contracting Powers undertook, in case their criminal laws were inadequate, to enact, or submit to their legislatures, measures necessary for checking individual acts of pillage or maltreatment of the wounded and sick in the fleet, and for punishing improper use of the distinguishing marks of hospital ships (Article 21).

[1] Against which Great Britain made an interpretative reservation.

VI

ESPIONAGE, TREASON, RUSES

See, besides the literature quoted above at the commencement of §§ 159 and 163, Pradier-Fodéré, viii. No. 3157, and Bentwich in the *Journal of the Society of Comparative Legislation*, New Ser. x. (1910), pp. 243-249.

Espionage and Treason. § 210. Espionage[1] and war treason do not play as large a part in sea warfare as in land warfare;[2] but they may be employed. Since the Hague Regulations deal only with land warfare, there is no legal necessity of trying a spy in sea warfare by court-martial according to Article 30, although this is advisable.

Ruses. § 211. Ruses are customarily allowed in sea warfare within the same limits as in land warfare, perfidy being excluded. As regards the use of a false flag, it is by most publicists considered perfectly lawful for a man-of-war to use a neutral or enemy flag (1) when chasing an enemy vessel, (2) when trying to escape, and (3) for the purpose of drawing an enemy vessel into action.[3] On the other hand, it is universally agreed that, immediately before an attack, a vessel must fly her national flag. Halleck[4] relates the following two instances:—In 1783 the *Sybille*, a French frigate of thirty-eight guns, enticed the British man-of-war *Hussar* by dis-

[1] As regards the case of *The Haimun*, see below, § 356.

[2] See above, §§ 159-162.

[3] The use of a false flag on the part of a belligerent man-of-war is analogous to the use of the enemy flag and the like in land warfare; see above, § 164. British practice—see Holland, *Prize Law*, § 200—permits the use of false colours. U.S. Naval War Code, Article 7, forbade it altogether, but as late as 1898, during the war with Spain, two American men-of-war used the Spanish flag (see Perels, p. 183). During the war between Turkey and Russia, in 1877, Russian men-of-war in the Black Sea used the Italian flag (see Martens, ii. § 133, p. 566). The use of a neutral or enemy flag is considered to be lawful, among others, by Ortolan, ii. p. 29; Fiore, iii. No. 1340; Perels, § 35, p. 183; Pillet, p. 116; Bonfils, No. 1274; Calvo, iv. 2106; Hall, § 187. See also Pillet in *R.G.*, v. (1898), pp. 444-451. But see the arguments against the use of a false flag in Pradier-Fodéré, vi. No. 2760, and Wehberg, pp. 261-262. The right of a belligerent merchantman to use a false flag was discussed by the British and United States Government during the World War. See *Parl. Papers*, Misc., No. 6 (1915), Cd. 7816.

[4] vol. i. p. 568.

playing the British flag, and intimating herself to be a distressed prize of a British captor. When the *Hussar* approached to succour her, she at once attacked without showing the French flag, but was overpowered and captured. The commander of the *Hussar* then publicly broke the sword of the commander of the *Sybille*, whom he justly accused of perfidy, although the French commander was acquitted when subsequently brought to trial by the French Government. In 1813 two merchants of New York carried out a plan for destroying the British man-of-war *Ramillies* in the following way. A schooner, with some casks of flour on deck, was laden with several casks of gunpowder having trains leading from a species of gunlock, which, by the action of clock-work, was to go off at a given time after it had been set, and came up to the *Ramillies* in order to be captured. The *Ramillies* then sent a boat with thirteen men and a lieutenant to cut her off. Subsequently the crew of the schooner abandoned her, and she blew up with the lieutenant and his men on board.

Vattel[1] relates the following case of perfidy:—In 1755, during war between Great Britain and France, a British man-of-war appeared off Calais, made signals of distress, and then seized a French sloop and some sailors who came to bring her help. Vattel was himself not certain whether this case was fact or fiction. But there is no doubt that, if true, it is an example of perfidy, which is not allowed.

On the other hand, the following is a perfectly legitimate ruse which occurred during the World War. At the end of October 1914, the German cruiser *Emden*, hiding her identity by rigging up a dummy fourth funnel and flying the Japanese flag, passed the guardship of the harbour of Penang in the Malay States, made no reply to its signals, came down at full speed

[1] vol. iii. § 178.

on the Russian cruiser *Zhemshug*, and then, after lowering the Japanese flag and hoisting the German flag, opened fire and torpedoed her.

VII

REQUISITIONS, CONTRIBUTIONS, BOMBARDMENT

Hall, § 140*—Lawrence, § 204—Westlake, ii. pp. 182-184—Moore, vii. §§ 1166-1174—Hershey, No. 427—Taylor, § 499—Bonfils, Nos. 1277-1277[1] —Despagnet, Nos. 618-618 *bis*—Fiore, *Code*, Nos. 1655-1664—Pradier-Fodéré, viii. Nos. 3153-3154—Nys, iii. pp. 392-396—Pillet, p. 117—Perels, § 35, p. 181—Holland, *Studies*, pp. 96-111—Dupuis, Nos. 67-73, and *Guerre*, Nos. 42-47—Barclay, *Problems*, p. 51—Higgins, pp. 352-357—Lémonon, pp. 503-525—Bernsten, § 7, iii.—Boidin, pp. 201-215 —Nippold, ii. § 28—Scott, *Conferences*, pp. 587-598, and in *A.J.*, ii. (1908), pp. 285-294—Wehberg, pp. 93-97—Garner, i. §§ 273-278.

Requisitions and Contributions upon Coast Towns.

§ 212. No case has to my knowledge occurred in Europe[1] of requisitions or contributions imposed by naval forces upon enemy coast towns. The question of their legality was raised long ago by an article on naval warfare of the future, published in 1882 by the French Admiral Aube in the *Revue des Deux Mondes*.[2] Aube pointed out that one of the tasks of a fleet would be to attack and destroy by bombardment fortified and unfortified military and commercial enemy coast towns, or at least to compel them mercilessly to submit to requisitions and contributions. During the British naval manœuvres of 1888 and 1889 imaginary contributions were imposed upon several coast towns, and this prompted Hall[3] to consider carefully under what conditions requisitions and contributions would be lawful in sea warfare. Starting from the principles regarding requisitions and contributions in land warfare, he concluded that they might also be levied in sea warfare, provided a force was landed which actually took possession of

[1] Holland, *Studies*, p. 101, mentions a case which occurred in South America in 1871.

[2] vol. l. p. 331.

[3] § 140*.

a coast town and established itself there, although only temporarily, until the imposed requisitions and contributions had been complied with; but that no requisitions or contributions could be demanded by a single message sent on shore under threatened penalty of bombardment in case of refusal. There is no doubt that Hall's arguments are, logically, correct; but it was not at all certain how the naval Powers regarded them until the Second Hague Conference met. That conference produced a convention (IX.),[1] two articles of which—3 and 4—deal with requisitions and contributions.

According to Article 3 undefended ports, towns, villages, dwellings, or other buildings may be bombarded by a naval force, if the local authorities, on a formal summons being made to them, decline to comply with requisitions for provisions or supplies *necessary* for the *immediate* use of the naval force concerned. These requisitions must be proportional to the resources of the place; they can only be demanded by the commander of the naval force concerned; they must be paid for in cash, and, if this is not possible for want of sufficient ready money, their receipt must be acknowledged.

As regards contributions, Convention IX. does not directly forbid a demand for them, but Article 4 expressly forbids bombardment of undefended places by a naval force on account of non-payment of money contributions; in practice, therefore, the demand for contributions will not occur in naval warfare.

Bombardment of the Enemy Coast.

§ 213. There is no doubt whatever that enemy coast towns which are defended may be bombarded by naval forces, acting either independently, or in co-operation with a besieging army. But before the Second Hague Conference of 1907 the question was not settled as to

[1] See above, vol. i. § 568*a*.

whether or not *open and undefended* coast places might be bombarded by naval forces. The Institute of International Law in 1895, at its meeting at Cambridge, appointed a committee to investigate the matter.[1] On the basis of the report of this committee the Institute adopted for consideration by the States a body of rules declaring that the law of bombardment was the same in both land warfare and sea warfare.

The First Hague Conference did not settle the matter, but suggested that it should be considered at a subsequent conference. The Second Hague Conference, by Convention IX., provided detailed rules concerning all the points in question:—

(1) The bombardment of undefended ports, towns, villages, dwellings, or other buildings by naval forces is under all circumstances and conditions prohibited (Article 1). To define the term 'undefended,' Article 1 expressly enacted that 'a place cannot be bombarded solely because automatic submarine contact mines are anchored off the harbour,' but Great Britain, France, Germany, and Japan entered a reservation against this, since they correctly considered such a place to be 'defended.'

(2) Although undefended places themselves are exempt, nevertheless military works, military or naval establishments, depots of arms or war material, workshops or plant which could be utilised for the needs of the hostile fleet or army, and men-of-war in the harbour of undefended places, may be bombarded; and no responsibility is incurred for any unavoidable damage caused thereby to the undefended place or its inhabitants. As a rule, however, the commander must, before re-

[1] Interesting extracts from its report (see *Annuaire*, xv. (1896), pp. 148-150, 313), drafted by Professor Holland with the approval of the Dutch General Den Beer Portugael, and presented in 1896 at the meeting of the Institute at Venice, were printed in the last edition of this treatise. But the World War has robbed them of much of their importance.

sorting to bombardment of these works, ships, and the like, give warning to the local authorities so that they may themselves destroy them. Only if, for military reasons, immediate action is necessary, and no delay can be allowed to the enemy, may bombardment be resorted to without previous warning, the commander being compelled to take all due measures in order that the undefended place itself may suffer as little harm as possible (Article 2).

(3) In case undefended places do not comply with legitimate requisitions,[1] they may be bombarded.

(4) In case of bombardments, all necessary steps must be taken to spare buildings devoted to public worship, art, science, or charitable purposes; historical monuments; hospitals, and places where the sick or wounded are collected, provided they are not at the time used for military purposes. To enable the attacking force to carry out this article, the privileged buildings, monuments, and places must be indicated by visible signs, consisting of large stiff rectangular panels, divided diagonally into two coloured triangular portions, the upper portion black, the lower portion white (Article 5). Unless military exigencies render it impossible, the commander of an attacking naval force must, before commencing the bombardment, do all in his power to warn the authorities (Article 6).

(5) The giving over to pillage of a town or place, even when taken by assault, is forbidden (Article 7).

The first case in which these rules were tested in practice occurred during the Turco-Italian War. On February 25, 1912, Admiral Faravelli, the commander of an Italian squadron, surprised, at dawn, the Turkish gunboat *Awni-Illa*, and a torpedo boat, in the port of Beirut, and called upon them to surrender, giving them until nine o'clock to do so. The demand was com-

[1] See above, § 212.

municated to the governor and the consular authorities. At nine o'clock the Turkish vessels were again, by signal, summoned to surrender, and as no reply was received, they were fired at and destroyed, though at first they vigorously answered the fire of the Italians. Shells missing the vessels and bursting on the quay killed and wounded a number of individuals and damaged several buildings. The Turkish Government protested against this procedure as a violation of Convention IX., but, if the report of Admiral Faravelli was accurate, the protest was unfounded.

During the World War the Hague Convention was not, or may not, have been in strict law binding, since not all the belligerents were parties to it. However this may be, the German bombardments of Scarborough, Hartlepool, Whitby, Whitehaven, and other English coast towns ignored the spirit of the convention, for these raids had no military purpose whatever, unless it is a legitimate military purpose to attempt to frighten and terrorise the civil population of the enemy.

VIII

INTERFERENCE WITH SUBMARINE TELEGRAPH CABLES

Moore, vii. § 1176—Hershey, No. 397—Westlake, ii. pp. 116-119—Liszt, § 41, iii.—Bonfils, No. 1278—Pradier-Fodéré, vi. No. 2772—Nys, iii. pp. 314-327—Fiore, iii. No. 1387, and *Code*, Nos. 1672-1677—Perels, § 35, p. 185—Perdrix, *Les Câbles sousmarins et leur Protection internationale* (1902)—Kraemer, *Die unterseeischen Telegraphenkabel in Kriegszeiten* (1903)—Scholz, *Krieg und Seekabel* (1904)—Jouhannaud, *Les Câbles sousmarins* (1904)—Zuculin, *I Cavi sottomarini e il Telegrafo senza Fili nel Diritto di Guerra* (1907)—Wehberg, pp. 134-138—Holland in *Journal de Droit international* (Clunet), xxv. (1898), pp. 648-652, and *War*, No. 114—Goffin in the *Law Quarterly Review*, xv. (1899), pp. 145-154—Bar in the *Archiv fur Oeffentliches Recht*, xv. (1900), pp. 414-421—Rey in *R.G.*, viii. (1901), pp. 681-762—Dupuis in *R.G.*, x. (1903), pp. 532-547—Nordon in the *Law Magazine and Review*, xxxii. (1907), pp. 166-184—Cybichowski in *Z.I.*, xvii. (1907), pp. 160-201—Garner, ii. § 560—See also the literature quoted above, vol. i., at the commencement of § 286.

Uncertainty of Rules concerning Interference with Submarine Telegraph Cables.

§ 214. As the International Convention for the Protection of Submarine Telegraph Cables of 1884 [1] expressly stipulates by Article 15 that freedom of action is reserved to belligerents, the question is not settled how far belligerents are entitled to interfere with submarine telegraph cables. The Second Hague Conference inserted in Article 54 of the Hague Regulations a provision that submarine cables connecting occupied enemy territory with a neutral territory should not be seized or destroyed, and that, if a case of absolute necessity compelled the occupants to seize or destroy such a cable, it must be restored after the conclusion of peace and compensation paid. But there are no rules for other possible cases of seizure and destruction.[2]

During the World War, the belligerents cut, and in many cases diverted and used, cables communicating with enemy territory, and at the Peace Conference at Paris questions arose as to the legality of these actions, and also as to whether cables belonging to an enemy company or an enemy State were subject to the right of capture of enemy property at sea.[3] By the Treaty of Peace with Germany, Germany renounced on behalf of herself and her subjects all rights in any of the cables there mentioned, though the value of those that were privately owned was to be credited to the reparation account.[4] But neither this provision, nor the provisions of other treaties of peace, can be regarded as enunciating any rule of law on a subject quite unsettled.[5]

[1] See above, vol. i. §§ 286, 287.

[2] The Institute of International Law adopted five rules at its meeting at Brussels in 1902 (see *Annuaire*, xix. (1902), p. 331); but they were superseded by Article 54 of the *Manuel des Lois de la Guerre maritime*, adopted by the Institute at its meeting at Oxford in 1913. (See *Annuaire*, xxvi. (1913), p. 657.)

[3] Latifi, *Effects of War on Property* (1909), p. 114, says that they are not, and so does Scholz, *op. cit.*, but I have no doubt that they are.

[4] Article 244, and Annex vii. thereto.

[5] It is impossible for a treatise to discuss the details of this absolutely unsettled branch of the law. Readers who take a particular interest in it may be referred to the excellent monograph of Scholz, *Krieg und Seekabel* (1904).

CHAPTER IVA

AIR WARFARE

Bonfils, §§ 1440[4-21]—Despagnet, No. 721 *bis*—Mérignhac, iii[a]. pp. 299-345—Meyer, *Die Luftschiffahrt in kriegsrechtlicher Beleuchtung* (1909)—Philit, *La Guerre aérienne* (1910)—Stael-Holstein, *La Réglementation de la Guerre des Airs* (1911)—Bellenger, *La Guerre aérienne et le Droit international* (1912)—Spaight, *Aircraft in War* (1914)—Garner, i. §§ 291-312—Nys, Fauchille and Bar in *Annuaire*, xix. (1902), pp. 58-114, xxiv. (1911), pp. 23-133—Fauchille in *R.G.*, viii. (1901), pp. 414-485, xxiv. (1917), pp. 56-74—Ellis in *A.J.*, viii. (1914), pp. 256-277—Picciotto in the *Journal of Comparative Legislation*, New Ser. xv. pt. ii. (1915), pp. 150-155—Winfield in the *Law Magazine and Review*, xl. (1914-1915), pp. 257-271, and the literature quoted above, vol. i. p. 352.

Rules before the World War.

§ 214*a*. When the First Hague Conference met in 1899, the destructive possibilities of aircraft were beginning to arouse speculation everywhere. Some small use of balloons had, indeed, been made in previous wars; but navigable air-vessels, capable of extensive use as engines of war, then for the first time seemed to be within the reach of practical science. In this atmosphere, the conference adopted an easy but inconclusive solution of the difficulties by forbidding the launching of projectiles or explosives from balloons or air-vessels for a term of five years.[1] Between the First and the Second Hague Conferences there was marked progress in aerial invention, which led to a change of attitude on the part of many important States, and though the conference of 1907 renewed the prohibition against launching explosives or projectiles from aircraft up to the close of the Third Hague Conference, many of the stronger military Powers

[1] See above, § 114.

refused to sign the declaration by which the prohibition was prolonged. However, to Article 25 of the Hague Regulations, which prohibits attack or bombardment of towns, habitations or buildings which are not defended,[1] were added the words 'by any means whatever,' and these words were designed to cover bombardment by aircraft. The legal position of aircraft in war was again considered by the Institute of International Law, at its meeting at Madrid in 1911, and the principle was adopted[2] that aerial warfare must not comprise greater danger to the person and the property of the peaceful population than land or sea warfare. But the deliberations of the Institute could not, of course, create International Law; and the Hague declaration and Article 25 of the Hague Regulations were almost[3] the only rules relating to aircraft in war existing at the outbreak of the World War. Of these, the declaration was certainly not binding, for, among other belligerents, neither France nor Germany had signed it,[4] and even the binding force of Article 25 was controversial.[5] Assuming that Article 25 was binding, there was at any rate no rule to determine what constitutes a 'defended' place within its meaning. In truth, only during this war were the larger possibilities and lines of development of air warfare for the first time discovered, and the Law of Nations, as it stood at its outbreak, was inadequate to cope with the new problems raised by practical experience.

§ 214*b*. For aircraft were used freely by all the belli-

[1] See above, § 156.

[2] See *Annuaire*, xxiv. (1911), p. 346.

[3] See, however, Article 29 of the Hague Regulations (above, § 160), which deals with the carrying of despatches by balloons, and Article 53 (above, § 137), which deals with the seizure by an occupying belligerent of 'les moyens affectés . . . dans les airs à la transmission des nouvelles, au transport des personnes ou des choses.'

[4] See above, § 114.

[5] See Garner, i. § 297.

gerents in the World War, and for many different kinds of work. They were the eyes of armies in the field, and of the fleets at sea. They searched out the dispositions of enemy formations, and the location of his defences and reserves; they watched his fleets, and followed the course of his submarines. They also played their part in naval and military operations, dropping bombs on ships during actions at sea, and on munition dumps, billets, supply columns, reserve troops, and a hundred other objects during actions on land. However, these were not the activities which provoked indignation and controversy; but the raids upon cities far from the theatre of war, made first by Germany and her allies and eventually undertaken by her adversaries reluctantly and by way of reprisals. Some of these raids aimed at the destruction of objects of military value; others were merely to strike terror among the civilian population by waging war upon them.[1] The objection to raids on objects of military importance far from the battlefield is that aircraft are by no means certain of their aim, and their bombs are just as likely to fall among a dense civilian population from whom all fit men of military age have already been taken for the armies. It seems clear that the damage to objects of military value done by such raids during the World War was unimportant, while the damage to civilian life and property was great. The legal objection to raids upon civilians is that they violate the rule that private enemy individuals, in so far as they do not take part in the fighting, may not be directly attacked and killed or wounded.[2]

Practice during the World War.

§ 214*c*. The present rules of International Law are inadequate for the regulation of air warfare.[3] Not

The Present Position.

[1] Details in Garner, i. §§ 292-296.

[2] See above, § 116.

[3] The International Air Convention does not affect the freedom of action of the parties in war, whether as belligerents or as neutrals. See above, vol. i. § 197*c*.

only are the limits within which aircraft ought to be allowed to raid outside the theatre of naval and military operations undetermined; there are a number of other unsettled questions, such as those connected with bombardment *within* the theatre of naval and military operations,[1] attacks on merchantmen at sea,[2] destruction of prizes,[3] dropping proclamations,[4] and the duties of neutrals towards crews and material rescued from aircraft wrecked at sea and brought within their jurisdiction,[5] in regard to which points of doubt occur.

However this may be, there can be no doubt that the general principles laid down in the Declaration of St. Petersburg of 1868, in the two declarations adopted by the First Hague Conference concerning expanding bullets and projectiles diffusing asphyxiating or deleterious gases, in the Hague Regulations concerning land warfare, and the like, must find application as regards violence directed from aircraft.

[1] See above, § 155.

[2] See above, § 182.

[3] See above, § 194.

[4] See below, § 255, and Garner, i. § 312.

[5] See below, § 341*a*, and Garner, i. § 302.

CHAPTER V

NON-HOSTILE RELATIONS OF BELLIGERENTS

I

ON NON-HOSTILE RELATIONS IN GENERAL BETWEEN BELLIGERENTS

Grotius, iii. c. 19—Pufendorf, viii. c. 7, §§ 1-2—Bynkershoek, *Quaestiones Juris publici*, i. c. 1—Vattel, iii. §§ 174-175—Hall, § 189—Lawrence, § 210—Phillimore, iii. § 97—Halleck, ii. pp. 345-349—Taylor, § 508—Wheaton, § 399—Bluntschli, § 679—Heffter, § 141—Lueder in *Holtzendorff*, iv. pp. 525-527—Ullmann, § 185—Bonfils, Nos. 1237-1238—Despagnet, No. 555—Pradier-Fodéré, vii. Nos. 2882-2887—Rivier, ii. p. 360—Nys, iii. p. 473—Calvo, iv. §§ 2411-2412—Fiore, iii. No. 1482, and *Code*, Nos. 1744-1746—Martens, ii. § 127—Longuet, §§ 134-135—Mérignhac, iii^{a}. pp. 358-360—Pillet, pp. 355-356—*Kriegsbrauch*, p. 38—*Land Warfare*, §§ 221-223—Emanuel, *Les Conventions militaires dans la Guerre continentale* (1904).

Fides etiam hosti servanda.

§ 215. Although the outbreak of war between States as a rule brings non-hostile intercourse to an end, necessity of circumstances, convenience, humanity, and other factors call, or may call, some kinds of non-hostile relations of belligerents into existence. And it is a universally recognised principle of International Law that, where such relations arise, belligerents must carry them out in good faith. *Fides etiam hosti servanda* is a rule which was adhered to in antiquity, when no International Law in the modern sense of the term existed. But it had then a religious and moral sanction only. Since in modern times war is not a condition of anarchy and lawlessness between belligerents, but a contention in many respects regulated, restricted, and modified by law, it is obvious that, where non-hostile relations between belligerents occur, they are protected by law. *Fides etiam hosti servanda* is, therefore, a principle which nowadays enjoys a legal as well as a religious and moral sanction.

Different Kinds of non-Hostile Relations.

§ 216. As through the outbreak of war all diplomatic[1] intercourse and other non-hostile relations come to an end, it is obvious that non-hostile relations between belligerents must originate, either from special rules of International Law, or from special agreements between the belligerents.

No special rules of International Law demanding non-hostile relations between belligerents existed in former times; but of late a few rules of this kind have arisen. Thus, for instance, release on parole[2] of prisoners of war creates an obligation on the part of the enemy not to re-admit them into the forces while the war lasts. To give another example, by Article 4 of the Geneva Convention of 1906, and Article 14 of the Hague Regulations —see also Article 17 of Hague Convention x.—it is the duty of either belligerent to return to the enemy, through his prisoners of war bureau, all objects of personal use, letters, jewellery, and the like found on the battlefield or left by those who died in hospital.[3] Non-hostile relations of this kind, however, need not be considered in this chapter, since they have already been discussed.

Non-hostile relations may also originate from special agreements between belligerents (so-called *commercia belli*), concluded either in time of peace for the purpose of creating certain non-hostile relations in case war breaks out, or during a war. Such non-hostile relations are created through passports, safe-conducts, safe-

[1] There is no doubt that all *direct* diplomatic intercourse comes to an end; but indirect diplomatic intercourse may nevertheless go on through the legations of neutral Powers. By this means a great number of arrangements were made during the World War between the Allies and the Central Powers.

[2] See above, § 129.

[3] See above, § 144.

guards, flags of truce, cartels, surrender, capitulations, and armistices, and also by peace negotiations.[1] Each kind must be discussed separately.

Licences to Trade.

§ 217. Several writers [2] speak of the creation of non-hostile relations between belligerents by limited or general licences to trade granted by a belligerent to enemy subjects. It has been explained above,[3] that it is for Municipal Law to determine whether or not through the outbreak of war all trade and the like is prohibited between the subjects of belligerents. If the Municipal Law of one or both belligerents does contain such a prohibition, it is of course within his or their discretion to grant exceptional licences to trade to their own or the other belligerent's subjects, and such licences naturally include certain privileges. Thus, for instance, if a belligerent allows enemy subjects to trade with his own subjects, enemy merchantmen engaged in such trade are exempt from capture and appropriation by him. Yet it is not International Law which creates this exemption, but the licence, granted by the belligerent and revocable at any moment; and no non-hostile international relations between the belligerents themselves originate from such licences. The matter would be different if, either before or in the course of a war, the belligerents agreed to allow certain trade between their subjects during war; but non-hostile relations originating from such an agreement would not be relations arising from a licence to trade, but from a cartel.[4]

[1] See below, § 267.

[2] See, for instance, Hall, § 196; Halleck, ii. pp. 371-388; Lawrence, § 214; Manning, p. 168; Taylor, § 512; Wheaton, §§ 409-410; Fiore, iii. No. 1500; Pradier-Fodéré, vii. No. 2937.

[3] § 101.

[4] See below, § 224.

II

PASSPORTS, SAFE-CONDUCTS, SAFEGUARDS

Grotius, iii. c. 21, §§ 14-22—Vattel, iii. §§ 265-277—Hall, §§ 191, 195—Lawrence, § 213—Phillimore, iii. §§ 98-102—Hershey, p. 400, n. 68—Halleck, ii. pp. 358-361—Taylor, § 511—Wheaton, § 408—Moore, vii. §§ 1158-1159—Bluntschli, §§ 675-678—Heffter, § 142—Lueder in *Holtzendorff*, iv. pp. 525-529—Ullmann, § 185—Bonfils, Nos. 1246-1247—Despagnet, Nos. 558-561—Pradier-Fodéré, vii. Nos. 2854, 2932-2938—Nys, iii. pp. 477-478—Calvo, iv. §§ 2413-2418—Fiore, iii. No. 1499, and *Code*, Nos. 1765-1772—Longuet, §§ 142-144—Mérignhac, iii[a]. pp. 384-386—Pillet, pp. 359-360—*Kriegsbrauch*, p. 41—Holland, *War*, No. 101—*Land Warfare*, §§ 326-337.

Passports and Safe-conducts.

§ 218. One belligerent on occasions arranges that passports and safe-conducts shall be given to certain subjects of another.

A passport is a written permission given by a belligerent to enemy subjects, or others, allowing them to travel within his territory, or enemy territory occupied by him.

A safe-conduct is a written permission given by a belligerent to enemy subjects, or others, allowing them to proceed to a particular place for a defined object; for instance, to a besieged town for conducting certain negotiations, or to enable them return home across the sea.[1] Safe-conducts may also be given for goods, to allow them to be carried without molestation to a certain place. But a safe-conduct given to an individual does not, unless it is expressly stated, cover goods which he may carry with him. Thus when in 1915, during the World War, Captain von Papen, military attaché to the German Embassy at Washington, secured a safe-conduct from Great Britain to return home, his luggage was searched at Falmouth, and important papers, throwing

[1] Thus during the World War in 1915, Dr. Dumba, the retiring Austrian ambassador, and in 1917 Count Bernsdorff, the retiring German ambassador, to the United States, received safe-conducts for returning home on neutral vessels calling at British ports.

light upon his conspiracies in the United States, were seized.

Passports and safe-conducts make the grantee inviolable so long, and in so far, as he complies with the conditions specially imposed upon him, or made necessary by the circumstances of the special case. They are not transferable, and may be granted for a limited or an unlimited period ; in the former case their validity ceases with the expiration of the period. They may be withdrawn, not only when the grantee abuses the protection, but also for military expediency. Moreover, they are only a matter of International Law when the granting of them has been arranged between the belligerents or their responsible commanders, or between belligerents and neutral Powers. If they are granted without such an arrangement, unilaterally on the part of one of the belligerents, they fall outside the scope of International Law.[1]

§ 219. One belligerent sometimes arranges to grant protection against his forces to certain subjects or property of another belligerent in the form of safeguards, of which there are two kinds. One consists of a written order, given to an enemy subject or left with enemy property, addressed to the commander of armed forces of the grantor, and charging him with the protection of the individual or the property. Thereby he or it become inviolable. The other kind of safeguard is given by detailing one or more soldiers to accompany enemy subjects, or to guard the spot where certain enemy property is, for the purpose of protection. Soldiers on this duty are inviolable on the part of the other belligerent ; they must neither be attacked nor made prisoners, and they must, on falling into the hands of the enemy, be fed, well kept, and eventually safely Safeguards.

[1] This distinction would seem to be necessary, although it is not generally made.

sent back to their corps. Safeguards, like passports and safe-conducts, are only a matter of International Law when the granting of them has been arranged by the belligerents, or when they fall under Articles 8 and 9 of the Geneva Convention of 1906,[1] and not otherwise.

III

FLAGS OF TRUCE

Grotius, iii. c. 24, § 5—Hall, § 190—Lawrence, § 211—Westlake, ii. p. 91—Hershey, No. 384—Moore, vii. § 1157—Phillimore, iii. § 115—Halleck, ii. p. 369—Taylor, § 510—Bluntschli, §§ 681-684—Heffter, § 141—Lueder in *Holtzendorff*, iv. pp. 421-423—Ullmann, § 180—Bonfils, Nos. 1239-1245—Despagnet, Nos. 556-557—Pradier-Fodéré, vii. Nos. 2927-2931—Rivier, ii. pp. 279-280—Nys, iii. pp. 474-476—Calvo, iv. §§ 2430-2432—Fiore, iii. No. 1378, and *Code*, Nos. 1500-1505—Martens, ii. § 127—Longuet, §§ 136-138—Mérignhac, iii[a]. pp. 361-366—Pillet, pp. 356-358—Zorn, pp. 195-199—Meurer, ii. §§ 39-40—Bordwell, pp. 293, 294—Spaight, pp. 216-231—*Kriegsbrauch*, pp. 26-29—Holland, *War*, Nos. 88-91—*Land Warfare*, §§ 224-255.

Meaning of Flags of Truce.

§ 220. Certain circumstances and conditions make it necessary or convenient for the armed forces of belligerents to enter into negotiations for various purposes. Since time immemorial, a white flag has been used as a symbol by an armed force wishing to negotiate with the enemy, and always, and everywhere, it has been considered a duty of the enemy to respect this symbol. In land warfare the flag of truce is used in the following manner.[2] An individual—soldier or civilian—charged with the task of negotiating with the enemy, approaches the latter, either carrying the flag himself, or accompanied by a flag-bearer, and, often, also by a drummer, a bugler, or a trumpeter, and an interpreter. In sea warfare the individual charged with the task of negotiating approaches the enemy in a boat flying the white flag. The Hague Regulations, by Articles 32 to 34,

[1] See above, § 121.

[2] See Hague Regulations, Article 32.

enacted most of the customary rules of International Law regarding flags of truce without adding any new rule. These rules are the same for land warfare as for sea warfare, although their validity for land warfare is now grounded on the Hague Regulations, whereas their validity for sea warfare is still based on custom only.

Treatment of Unadmitted Flag-bearers.

§ 221. As a commander of an armed force is not, according to Article 33 of the Hague Regulations, compelled to receive a bearer of a flag of truce, a flag-bearer who makes his appearance may at once be signalled to withdraw. Yet even then he is inviolable from the time he displays the flag to the end of the time necessary for withdrawal. During this time he may neither be intentionally attacked nor made prisoner. However, an armed force in battle is not obliged to stop its military operations on account of the approach of an enemy flag-bearer who has been signalled to withdraw. Although he may not be fired upon intentionally, should he be wounded or killed accidentally, during the battle, no responsibility or moral blame would rest upon the belligerent concerned. In former times the commander of an armed force could inform the enemy that, within a certain defined or indefinite period, he would under no circumstances or conditions receive a flag-bearer; and if, in spite of such notice, a flag-bearer approached, he did not enjoy any privilege, and could be attacked and made prisoner like any other member of the enemy forces. But this rule is now obsolete, and its place is taken by the rule that a commander must never, except in a case of reprisals, declare beforehand, even only for a specified period, that he will not receive a bearer of a flag of truce.[1]

[1] This becomes quite apparent from the discussions at the First Hague Conference; see Martens, *N.R.G.*, 2nd Ser. xxvi. p. 465; *Land Warfare*, § 234; Spaight, pp. 221-223.

Treatment of Admitted Flag-bearers.

§ 222. Bearers of flags of truce and their parties, when admitted by the other side, must be granted the privilege of inviolability. They may neither be attacked nor taken prisoners, and they must be allowed to return safely in due time to their own lines. But they need not be allowed to acquire information about the receiving forces, and may, therefore, be blindfolded by them, or be conducted by roundabout ways, or be prevented from entering into communication with individuals other than those who confer officially with them, and they may even temporarily be prevented from returning, until a certain military operation of which they have obtained information is carried out. Article 33 of the Hague Regulations specifically enacts that a commander to whom a flag of truce is sent 'may take all steps necessary to prevent the envoy taking advantage of his mission to obtain information.' Bearers of flags of truce are not, however, prevented from reporting information they have gained by observation while passing through the enemy lines and in communicating with enemy individuals. But they are not allowed to sketch maps of defences and positions, to gather information secretly and surreptitiously, to provoke or to commit treacherous acts, and the like. If they do, they may be court-martialled. Articles 33 and 34 of the Hague Regulations expressly enact that a flag-bearer may be temporarily detained in case he abuses his mission for the purpose of obtaining information, and that he loses all privileges of inviolability 'if it is proved beyond doubt that he has taken advantage of his privileged position to provoke or commit an act of treachery.' Bearers of white flags and their party must carry [1] some authorisation with them, to show that they are charged with the

[1] Article 32 of the Hague Regulations confirms this customary rule by speaking of an individual who is 'authorised' by one of the belligerents to enter into communication with the other.

task of entering into negotiations (Article 32); otherwise they may be detained as prisoners, since it is his mission, and not the white flag itself, which protects the flag-bearer. This mission protects every one who is charged with it, whatever his rank and whether a civilian or a soldier; but it does not protect a deserter. A deserter may be detained, court-martialled, and punished, notice being given to the army sending him of the reason of his punishment.[1]

§ 223. Different from abuse of his mission by an authorised flag-bearer is abuse of the flag of truce itself, which may take one of two different forms :— **Abuse of Flag of Truce.**

(1) The force which sends an authorised flag-bearer to the enemy has to take up a corresponding attitude, the ranks which the flag-bearer leaves being obliged to halt and to cease fire. It constitutes an abuse of the flag of truce if it intentionally fails to do so. The case is even worse when a flag-bearer is intentionally sent on a feigned mission in order that military operations may be carried out under cover of the protection due from the enemy to the flag-bearer and his party.

A case of this kind is related in Halleck.[2] 'On July 12, 1882, while the British fleet was lying off Alexandria, in support of the authority of the Khedive of Egypt, and the rebels under Arabi Pasha were being driven to great straits, a rebel boat, carrying a white flag of truce, was observed approaching H.M.S. *Invincible* from the harbour, whereupon H.M. ships *Temeraire* and *Inflexible*, which had just commenced firing, were ordered to suspend fire. So soon as the firing ceased, the boat, instead of going to the *Invincible*, returned to the harbour. A flag of truce was simultaneously hoisted by the rebels

[1] See Hall, § 190.

[2] ii. p. 315. Spaight, p. 229, denies that this was a case of abuse of the white flag.

on the Ras-el-Tin fort. These deceits gave the rebels time to leave the works and to retire through the town, abandoning the forts, and withdrawing the whole of their garrison under the flag of truce.'

(2) A white flag is liable to be used to make the enemy believe that a flag of truce is about to be sent, although it is not sent, so that operations may be carried out under the protection granted by the enemy to this pretended flag of truce.

Both forms of abuse are gross perfidy, and may be met with reprisals, or with punishment of the offenders in case they fall into the hands of the enemy.

IV

CARTELS

Grotius, iii. c. 21, §§ 23-30—Vattel, iii. §§ 278-286—Hall, § 193—Lawrence, § 212—Westlake, ii. p. 162—Phillimore, iii. §§ 111-112—Halleck, ii. pp. 361-363—Taylor, § 509—Bluntschli, §§ 679-680—Heffter, § 142—Lueder in *Holtzendorff*, iv. pp. 525-529—Ullmann, § 185—Bonfils, Nos. 827 and 1280—Despagnet, No. 658—Pradier-Fodéré, vii. Nos. 2832-2837, 2888—Rivier, ii. p. 360—Nys, iii. pp. 484-487—Calvo, iv. §§ 2419-2421—Longuet, §§ 140, 141—Pillet, pp. 358, 359—*Kriegsbrauch*, p. 38—Holland, *War*, No. 100, and *Prize Law*, §§ 32-35—*Land Warfare*, §§ 338-339.

Definition and Purpose of Cartels.

§ 224. Cartels are conventions between belligerents concluded for the purpose of permitting certain kinds of non-hostile intercourse between them which would otherwise be prevented by war. Cartels may be concluded during peace in anticipation of war, or during a war, and they may provide for numerous purposes. Thus, communication by post, telegraph, telephone, and railway, which would otherwise not take place, can be arranged by cartels, as can also the exchange of prisoners, or certain treatment for the wounded, and the like. Thus, further, intercourse between their subjects through trade [1] can, either with or without limits, be agreed upon by belligerents. All rights and duties originating from cartels must be complied with in the same manner and good faith as rights and duties arising from other treaties.

§ 225. Cartel ships [2] are vessels of belligerents which are commissioned for the carriage by sea of exchanged prisoners from the enemy country to their own country, or for the carriage of official communications to and from the enemy. Custom has sanctioned the following rules regarding cartel ships for the purpose of securing protection for them and also securing their exclusive employment as a means for the exchange of prisoners: Cartel ships must not do any trade, or carry any cargo or despatches; [3] they are, in particular, not allowed to carry ammunition or instruments of war, except one gun for firing signals. They have to be furnished with a proper document declaring that they are commissioned as cartel ships. They are under the protection of both belligerents, and may neither be seized nor appropriated. They enjoy this protection, not only when actually carrying exchanged prisoners or official communications, but also on their way home after such carriage and on their way to fetch prisoners or official communications.[4] They lose it at once, and may consequently be seized and be appropriated, in case they do not comply, either with the general rules regarding cartel ships, or with the special conditions imposed upon them. Cartel Ships.

[1] See above, § 217. But arrangements for granting passports, safe-conducts, and safeguards—see above, §§ 218 and 219—are not a matter of cartels.

[2] See above, § 190.

[3] *The La Rosina*, (1800) 2 C. Rob. 372; *The Venus*, (1803) 4 C. Rob. 355.

[4] *The Daifje*, (1800) 3 C. Rob. 139; *The La Gloire*, (1804) 5 C. Rob. 192.

V

CAPITULATIONS AND SIMPLE SURRENDER

Grotius, iii. c. 22, § 9—Vattel, iii. §§ 261-264—Hall, § 194—Lawrence, § 215—Westlake, ii. p. 91—Phillimore, iii. §§ 122-126—Halleck, ii. pp. 354-357—Taylor, §§ 514-516—Wheaton, § 405—Moore, vii. § 1160—Bluntschli, §§ 697-699—Heffter, § 142—Lueder in *Holtzendorff*, iv. p. 527—Ullmann, § 185—Bonfils, Nos. 1259-1267—Despagnet, No. 562—Pradier-Fodéré, vii. Nos. 2917-2926—Rivier, ii. pp. 361-362—Nys, iii. pp. 487-491—Calvo, iv. §§ 2450-2452—Fiore, iii. Nos. 1495-1497, and *Code*, Nos. 1756-1763—Martens, ii. § 127—Longuet, §§ 151-154—Mérignhac, iii[a]. pp. 366-373—Pillet, pp. 360-364—Bordwell, p. 294—Meurer, ii. §§ 41-42—Spaight, pp. 249-259—*Kriegsbrauch*, pp. 38-41—Holland, *War*, No. 92—*Land Warfare*, §§ 301-325.

Character and Purpose of Capitulations, in contradistinction to Simple Surrender.

§ 226. Capitulations are conventions between armed forces of belligerents stipulating the terms of surrender of fortresses and other defended places, or of men-of-war, or of troops. It is, therefore, necessary to distinguish between a *simple* and a *stipulated* surrender. If one or more soldiers lay down their arms and surrender, or if a fortress or a man-of-war surrenders without making any terms whatever, there is no capitulation, for a capitulation is a convention stipulating special terms of surrender.

Nevertheless, simple surrender, though not a capitulation, is a convention, for it is an agreement for the cessation of hostilities whereby the vanquished party agrees that his forces shall be taken into captivity, and in the case of the surrender of a certain place, that he will give up possession without resistance, and in return the victor agrees to give quarter.

Capitulations are military conventions only and exclusively; they must not, therefore, contain arrangements other than those of a local and military character concerning the surrendering forces, places, or ships. If they do contain such arrangements, the latter are not valid, unless they are ratified by the political authorities of both belligerents.[1] The surrender of a certain place or force may, of course, be arranged by some convention containing other than military stipulations, but then such surrender would not originate from a capitulation. Just as the character of capitulations is merely military, so is their purpose—the abandonment of a hopeless struggle and of resistance which would only involve useless loss of life on the part of a hopelessly beset force. Therefore, whatever may be the indirect consequences of a capitulation, its direct consequences have nothing to do with the war at large, but are local only, and concern the surrendering force exclusively.

Contents of Capitulations.

§ 227. Unless otherwise expressly provided, a capitulation is concluded under the obvious condition that the surrendering forces become prisoners of war, and that all war material and other public property in their possession, or within the surrendering place or ship, are surrendered in the condition in which they were at the time when the capitulation was signed. Nothing prevents forces fearing surrender from destroying their provisions, munitions, arms and other instruments of war which, when falling into the hands of the enemy, would be useful to him. Again, nothing prevents a commander, even after negotiations regarding surrender have begun, from destroying such articles. But when once a capitulation has been signed,[2] such destruction

[1] See Phillimore, iii. § 123, who discusses the promise of Lord William Bentinck to Genoa, in 1814, regarding its independence, which was disowned by the British Government. Phillimore himself disapproves of the attitude of Great Britain, and so do some foreign publicists, as, for instance, Despagnet (No. 562); but the rule that capitulations are military conventions, and that, therefore, such stipulations are not valid as are not of a local military character, is indubitable.

[2] When, during the Russo-Japanese War, in January 1905, General Stoessel, the commander of Port Arthur, had fortifications blown up and vessels sunk, during negotiations for surrender, but before the capitulation was signed, the press undeservedly accused him of perfidy. U.S. Naval War Code, Article 52, enacted the right principle: '*after agreeing upon or signing* a capitulation, the capitulator must neither injure nor destroy the vessels, property, or stores in his possession that he is to deliver up, unless the right to do so is expressly reserved to him in the agreement or capitulation.'

is no longer lawful, and, if carried out, constitutes perfidy, which may be punished by the other party as a war crime.

But special conditions may be agreed upon between the forces concerned, and they must then be faithfully adhered to by both parties. The only rule which Article 35 of the Hague Regulations enacts regarding capitulations is that they must be in accordance with the demands of military honour, and, when once settled, must be scrupulously observed. Among possible conditions may be one that the convention shall be valid only if within a certain period relief troops are not approaching, or one that the surrendering forces shall not in every respect be treated like ordinary prisoners of war. Thus it may be stipulated that the officers, or even the soldiers, shall be released on parole, and that officers remaining prisoners shall retain their swords. Whether or not a belligerent will grant, or even offer, such specially favourable conditions depends upon the importance of the force, place, or ship to be surrendered, and upon the bravery of the surrendering force. There are even instances[1] of capitulations which stipulated that the surrendering forces should leave the place with full honours, carrying their arms and baggage away, and joining their own army, unmolested by the enemy through whose lines they had to march.[2]

Form of Capitulations, and of Simple Surrender.

§ 228. No rule of International Law exists regarding the forms of capitulations, which may, therefore, be concluded either orally or in writing. But they are usually

[1] During the Franco-German War the Germans granted these most favourable conditions to the French forces that surrendered Belfort on February 15, 1871.

[2] The question whether enemy merchantmen belonging to enemy subjects residing in a capitulating town and found in the harbours there after capitulation can be seized and confiscated was decided in the negative by Sir W. Scott in *The Ships taken at Genoa*, (1803) 4 C. Rob. 388; but it would seem that in *Herrera* v. *United States*, and *Diaz* v. *United States*, (1912) 222 U.S. 558, 574, the Supreme Court of the United States has taken a different view. See Kingsbury in *A.J.*, vi. (1912), pp. 650-658, and above, § 184.

concluded in writing. Negotiations for capitulation, from whichever side they emanate, are usually sent under a flag of truce. On the other hand, a force which is ready to surrender without special conditions of surrender, *i.e.* without a capitulation, can indicate their intention by hoisting a white flag as a signal that they abandon all resistance. The question whether the enemy must at once cease firing and accept the surrender, is to be answered in the affirmative, provided that he is certain that the white flag was hoisted by order, or with the authority, of the commander of the force. As, however, such hoisting may well have taken place without the authority of the commander and may, therefore, be disowned by him, no duty exists for the enemy to cease his attack until he is convinced that the white flag really indicates the intention of the commander to surrender.

Competence to conclude Capitulations.

§ 229. The competence to conclude capitulations is vested in the commanders of the forces opposing each other. Capitulations entered into by unauthorised subordinate officers may, therefore, be disowned by the commander without breach of faith. As regards the special conditions of capitulations, it must be particularly noted that the competence of a commander to grant them is limited [1] to those the fulfilment of which depends entirely upon the forces under his command. If he grants conditions against his instructions, or conditions the fulfilment of which depends upon forces other than his own, and upon superior officers, his superior officer may disown them. The capitulation in El Arish [2] on January 24, 1800, arranged between the French General Kléber and the Turkish Grand Vizier, and approved by the British Admiral, Sir Sidney Smith, illustrates this. As General Kléber, who was command-

[1] See U.S. Naval War Code, Article 51.
[2] Martens, *R.*, vii. p. 1.

ing the French army in Egypt, thought that he could not remain in Egypt, he proposed surrender under the condition that his army should be safely transported to France, carrying away their arms and baggage. The Grand Vizier accepted these conditions. The British Admiral, Sir Sidney Smith, who approved of them, was the local commander on the coast of Egypt, but was an officer inferior to Lord Keith, the commander of the British Mediterranean fleet. Lord Keith had, on January 8, 1800, received secret orders, dated December 15, 1799, from the British Government instructing him not to agree to any capitulation which stipulated the free return of Kléber's army to France. Sir Sidney Smith did not, however, receive instructions based on these orders until February 22, 1800, and, therefore, when he approved of the capitulation of El Arish in January, was not aware that he acted against orders of the British Government.[1] Lord Keith, after having received the above orders on January 8, 1800, wrote at once to General Kléber, pointing out that he was not allowed to grant the return of the French army to France.[2] On the other hand, the British Government, after having been informed that Sir Sidney Smith had approved of the return of the French army, sent, on March 28, 1800, fresh orders [3] to Lord Keith, received by him at the end of April, advising him, although Sir Sidney Smith had exceeded his competence, to allow the capitulation to be carried out, and the French army to be safely transported to France. Meanwhile, however, circumstances had entirely changed. When General Kléber had on March 17, 1800, received Lord Keith's letter of January 8, he addressed a proclamation [4] to his troops embodying Lord Keith's letter, and asking them to prepare themselves for battle. He began

[1] Martens, *R.*, vii. pp. 8, 9.
[2] Martens, *R.*, vii. p. 10.
[3] Martens, *R.*, vii. p. 11.
[4] Martens, *R.*, vii. p. 15.

hostilities again on March 20, but was assassinated on June 14, and General Menou took over the command. It was Menou who received, on June 20, 1800, information of the changed attitude of the British Government regarding the capitulation of El Arish. Hostilities having been renewed as far back as March, General Menou refused [1] to consent to the carrying out of the capitulation, and continued hostilities.

It is obvious that Sir Sidney Smith, in approving the capitulation, accepted a condition which did not depend entirely upon himself and the forces under him, but upon Lord Keith and his fleet. Lord Keith as well as the British Government could have lawfully disowned it. That the British Government did not do so, but was ready to ratify Sir Sidney Smith's approval, was because it did not want to disavow the promises of Sir Sidney Smith, who was not at the time aware of the orders of his Government to Lord Keith. On the other hand, the French generals were not wrong in resuming hostilities after having received Lord Keith's first information, as thereby the capitulation fell to the ground.

Violation of Capitulations, and of Simple Surrender.

§ 230. That capitulations must be scrupulously adhered to is an old customary rule, since enacted by Article 35 of the Hague Regulations. Any act contrary to a capitulation would constitute an international delinquency if ordered by a belligerent Government, and a war crime if committed without such order. Such violation may be met with reprisals or punishment of the offenders as war criminals.

When there is no capitulation, but a simple surrender, it is a duty of the surrendering force to stop firing as soon as the white flag has been hoisted, and the enemy is approaching to take possession. Those members of the surrendering force who continue to fire lose their

[1] Martens, *R.*, vii. p. 16.

claim to receive quarter,[1] and may therefore be killed on the spot. Or, if taken prisoners, they may be punished as war criminals.

VI

ARMISTICES

Grotius, iii. c. 21, §§ 1-13, c. 22, § 8—Pufendorf, viii. c. 7, §§ 3-12—Vattel, iii. §§ 233-260—Hall, § 192—Lawrence, § 216—Westlake, p. 92—Phillimore, iii. §§ 116-121—Halleck, ii. pp. 346-354—Hershey, No. 386—Moore, vii. § 1162—Taylor, §§ 513 and 516—Wheaton, §§ 400-404—Bluntschli, §§ 688-696—Heffter, § 142—Lueder in *Holtzendorff*, iv. pp. 531-544—Ullmann, § 186—Bonfils, Nos. 1248-1258—Despagnet, Nos. 563-566—Pradier-Fodéré, vii. Nos. 2889-2916—Rivier, ii. pp. 362-368—Nys, iii. pp. 491-494—Calvo, iv. §§ 2433-2449—Fiore, iii. Nos. 1484-1494, and *Code*, Nos. 1773-1786—Martens, ii. § 127—Longuet, §§ 145-149—Mérignhac, iii[a]. pp. 373-384—Pillet, pp. 364-370—Zorn, pp. 201-206—Bordwell, pp. 294-296—Meurer, ii. §§ 43-44—Spaight, pp. 232-248—*Kriegsbrauch*, pp. 41-44—Holland, *War*, Nos. 93-99—*Land Warfare*, §§ 256-300.

Character and Kinds of Armistices.

§ 231. Armistices or truces, in the wider sense of the term, are all agreements between belligerent forces for a temporary cessation of hostilities. They are in no wise to be compared with peace, and ought not to be called temporary peace, because the condition of war remains between the belligerents themselves, and between the belligerents and neutrals, on all points beyond the mere cessation of hostilities. In spite of such cessation the right of visit and search over neutral merchantmen therefore remains intact, as does likewise the right to capture neutral vessels attempting to break a blockade, and the right to seize contraband of war. Although all armistices are essentially alike in so far as they consist of cessations of hostilities, three different kinds must be distinguished—namely, (1) suspensions of arms, (2) general armistices, and (3) partial armistices.[2]

[1] See above, § 109.

[2] Although, as will be seen from the following sections, this distinction is absolutely necessary, it is not made by several publicists. Holland, *War*, No. 93, even says: 'There is no difference of meaning, according to British usage at least, between a

The Hague Regulations deal with armistices in Articles 36 to 41 but very incompletely, so that the gaps must be filled from old customary rules.

Suspensions of Arms.

§ 232. Suspensions of arms, in contradistinction to armistices in the narrower sense of the term, are cessations of hostilities agreed upon between military or naval forces, large or small, for a very short time, and regarding momentary and local military purposes only. Such purposes may be—collection of the wounded; burial of the dead; negotiations regarding the surrender or evacuation of a defended place, or for an armistice in the narrower sense of the term; or to enable a commander to ask for and receive instructions from a superior authority,[1] and the like. Suspensions of arms have nothing to do with political purposes, or with the war generally, since they are of momentary and local importance only. They concern exclusively those forces, and that spot, which are the object of the suspension of arms. The Hague Regulations do not specially mention suspensions of arms, since Article 37 speaks of local armistices only, apparently including suspensions of arms among local armistices.

General Armistices.

§ 233. A general armistice is a cessation of hostilities which, in contradistinction to suspensions of arms with their momentary and local military purposes, is agreed upon between belligerents for the whole of their forces, and the whole region of war.[2] General

"truce," an "armistice," and a "suspension of arms."' *Land Warfare*, § 256—see in particular note (*a*)—accepts the distinction as indispensable.

[1] An instructive example of a suspension of arms for such purposes is furnished by the convention between the German forces besieging Belfort and the French forces holding this fortress during the Franco-German War, signed on February 13, 1871; see Martens, *N.R.G.*, xix. p. 646.

[2] However, for particular reasons, small parts of the belligerent forces and small parts of the theatre of war may be specially excluded without detracting from the general character of the armistice, provided that the bulk of the forces, and the greater part of the region of war, are included. Thus, Article 1 of the general armistice at the end of the Franco-German War of January 28, 1871, specially excluded all military operations in the Départements du Doubs, du Jura, de la Côte d'Or, and likewise the siege of Belfort.

armistices [1] are always conventions of vital political importance affecting the whole of the war. They are as a rule, although not necessarily, concluded for a political purpose. It may be that negotiations of peace have ripened so far that the end of the war is in sight, and that, therefore, military operations appear superfluous; or that the forces of either belligerent are exhausted and need rest; or that the belligerents have to face domestic difficulties, the settlement of which is more pressing than the continuation of the war; or for any other political purpose.[2] Thus Article 2 of the general armistice at the end of the Franco-German War dated January 28, 1871,[3] expressly declared the purpose of the armistice to be to enable the French Government to convoke a Parliamentary Assembly which might determine whether the war was to be continued, or what conditions of peace should be accepted. On the other hand, each of the Central Powers asked for, and were granted, an armistice in the World War because they could no longer continue the struggle, and desired peace.

Under pressure of military disaster, Bulgaria sought a general armistice [4] which was granted on September 29, 1918. Early in October, Austria-Hungary made overtures [5] to the United States for an armistice which was eventually concluded on November 3, 1918, between representatives of the Austro-Hungarian Supreme Command

[1] In the practice of belligerents the terms 'suspension of arms' and 'general armistice' are sometimes not sufficiently distinguished, but are interchangeable. Thus, for instance, the armistice between France and Germany mentioned in n. 2 on p. 321 is entitled 'Convention entre l'Allemagne et la France pour la Suspension des Hostilités . . .,' whereas the different articles of the convention always speak correctly of an armistice, and an annex to the convention signed on January 29 is entitled 'Annexe à la Convention d'Armistice' (Martens, *N.R.G.*, xix. p. 634).

[2] Sometimes, where several States are together waging war against a common foe, some of them conclude a general armistice, and others decline. Thus in 1912, during the Balkan War, Bulgaria, Serbia, and Montenegro entered into an armistice with Turkey, but Greece refused to join.

[3] Martens, *N.R.G.*, xix. p. 626.

[4] *A J.*, xiii. (1919), Supplement, p. 402.

[5] *Ibid.*, p. 77.

and representatives of the Italian Supreme Command acting on behalf of the Allied and Associated Powers.[1] A general armistice with Turkey had already been signed on October 30, 1918. On October 3-6, 1918, the German Government had requested the President of the United States to take steps for the restoration of peace, 'and in order to avoid further bloodshed,' it had requested him 'to bring about the immediate conclusion of a general armistice on land, on water, and in the air.'[2] After correspondence and assurances, the President informed Germany on October 23, 1918,[3] that he was taking up with the Associated Powers the question of an armistice, and on November 5,[4] he notified her that 'Marshal Foch has been authorised by the Government of the United States and the Allied Governments to receive properly accredited representatives of the German Government, and to communicate to them terms of an armistice.' A meeting took place, and a general armistice was concluded between Marshal Foch, commander-in-chief of the Allied armies, acting on behalf of the Allied and Associated Powers, in conjunction with Admiral Wemyss of the one part, and the German delegation of the other part, on November 11, 1918.[5]

§ 234. Partial armistices are agreements for cessation of hostilities which are not concluded by belligerents for their whole forces and the whole region of war, yet do not, like suspensions of arms, merely serve momentary and local military purposes. Partial armistices are concluded by belligerents for a considerable part of their forces and front; they are always of political importance affecting the war in general; and they are very often, although they need not be, agreed upon for political purposes. Article 37 of the Hague Regula- Partial Armistices.

[1] *A.J.*, xiii. (1919), Supplement, p. 80.

[2] *Ibid.*, p. 85.

[3] *Ibid.*, p. 92.

[4] *Ibid.*, p. 95.

[5] *Ibid.*, p. 97. *Parl. Papers*, Misc., No. 25 (1918), Cd. 9212.

tions apparently includes partial armistices together with suspensions of arms under the term 'local' armistices. A partial armistice may be concluded for the military or the naval forces only; for cessation of hostilities in the colonies only; and the like. But it is always a condition that a considerable part of the forces and of the region of war must be included, and that the purpose is not only a momentary one.

Competence to conclude Armistices.

§ 235. As regards the competence to conclude armistices, a distinction is necessary between suspensions of arms and general and partial armistices.

(1) Since the character and purpose of a suspension of arms are military, local, and momentary only, every commander is supposed to be competent to make such an agreement, and no ratification by superior officers or other authorities is required. Even commanders of the smallest opposing detachments may arrange a suspension of arms.

(2) On the other hand, since general armistices are of vital political importance, only the belligerent Governments themselves or their commanders-in-chief are competent to conclude them, and ratification,[1] whether specially stipulated or not, is necessary. Should a commander-in-chief conclude a general armistice which would not find ratification, hostilities may at once be recommenced without breach of faith, it being a matter of common knowledge that a commander-in-chief is not authorised to agree upon exclusion of ratification, unless he received special powers thereto.

(3) Partial armistices may be concluded by the commanders-in-chief of the respective forces, and ratification is not necessary, unless specially stipulated;

[1] The general armistices which brought about a cessation of hostilities in the World War in 1918 were in no case submitted for ratification, and the author would probably have wished to revise this paragraph.

the commanders being responsible to their own Governments in case they agree upon a partial armistice without being specially authorised thereto.

§ 236. No legal rule exists regarding the form of armistices, which may therefore be concluded either orally or in writing. However, the importance of general and partial armistices makes it advisable to conclude them by signing written documents containing all items which have been agreed upon. No instance is known of a general or partial armistice in modern times concluded otherwise than in writing. But suspensions of arms are often only orally concluded. Form of Armistices.

§ 237. That hostilities must cease is the obvious content of all kinds of armistices. Usually, although not at all necessarily, the parties embody special conditions in the armistice agreement. If, and so far as, this has not been done, the legal consequences of an armistice are in some respects much controverted. Everybody agrees that belligerents during an armistice may, outside the line where the forces face each other, do everything and anything they like regarding defence and preparation of offence; for instance, they may manufacture and import munitions and guns, drill recruits, build fortresses, concentrate or withdraw troops. But no unanimity exists regarding such acts as must be left undone, or may be done, within the very line where the belligerent forces face each other. The majority of writers, led by Vattel,[1] maintain that, in the absence of special stipulations, it is an implied condition of an armistice that within that line no alteration of the *status quo* shall take place which the other party, were it not for the armistice, could by application of force, for instance by a cannonade or by some other means, prevent. These writers consider it a breach of faith for a belligerent to make such alterations under Contents of Armistices.

[1] iii. §§ 246-248.

the protection of the armistice. On the other hand, a small minority of writers, but led by Grotius [1] and Pufendorf,[2] assert that cessation of hostilities and of further advance are the only implied terms of an armistice; all other acts, such as strengthening positions by concentration of more troops on the spot, erecting and strengthening defences, repairing breaches in besieged fortresses, withdrawing troops, and the like, being allowed. As the Hague Regulations do not mention the matter, the controversy still remains unsettled. I believe the opinion of the minority to be correct, since an armistice does not mean anything else than a cessation of actual hostilities, and it is for the parties themselves to stipulate such special conditions as they think necessary or convenient. It seems to be the intention of the Hague Regulations that they should do this. This applies particularly to the other controversial questions as to revictualling besieged places and as to intercourse, commercial and otherwise, with the inhabitants of the region where actual fighting was going on before the armistice. As regards revictualling, it has been correctly maintained that, if it were not allowed, the position of the besieged forces would thereby be weakened by the action of the armistice. But I cannot see why this should be an argument to hold revictualling permissible. The principle *vigilantibus jura sunt scripta* applies to armistices as well as to all other legal transactions. It is for the parties to advise such arrangements as really suit their needs and wants. Thus, during the Franco-German War, an armistice for twenty-five days, proposed in November 1870, fell to the ground on the Germans refusing to permit the revictualling of Paris.[3] As to intercourse, Article 39 of the Hague

[1] iii. c. 21, § 7.

[2] viii. 7, § 10.

[3] See Pradier-Fodéré, vii. No. 2908, where the question of revictualling during an armistice is discussed at some length, and the opinions of many publicists from Grotius to our own day are quoted.

Regulations provides that: 'It is for the contracting parties to settle in the terms of the armistice what communications may be held within the theatre of war with the population and with each other.'

For the purpose of preventing the outbreak of hostilities during an armistice, it is usual to agree upon so-called lines of demarcation[1]—that is, a small neutral zone between the forces facing each other which must not be entered by members of either force. But there are no lines of demarcation in default of special agreement.

§ 238. In case the contrary is not stipulated, an armistice commences the very moment the agreement upon it is complete. But often the parties expressly stipulate the time from which it shall begin. If the very hour is stipulated, there is no cause for controversy. But sometimes the parties only provide that the armistice shall last from one stated day to another, *e.g.* from June 15 to July 15. In such a case the actual commencement is controversial. Most publicists maintain that the armistice begins at 12 o'clock of the night between the 14th and the 15th of June, but Grotius maintains that it begins at 12 o'clock of the night between the 15th and the 16th of June.[2] Therefore, to avoid difficulties, armistice agreements ought always to be more precise. Commencement of Armistices.

When the forces included in an armistice are dispersed over a very large area, the parties have very often stipulated different dates of commencement for the different parts of the front, because it has not been possible to announce the armistice at once to all the forces affected. Thus, for instance, Article 1 of the general armistice at the end of the Franco-German War[3] stipulated that it should take effect at once for the forces in and around Paris, but that with regard to the

[1] See Pradier-Fodéré, vii. No. 2901.

[2] Grotius, iii. c. 21, § 4. See Pradier-Fodéré, vii. No. 2897. The controversy occurs again with regard to the end of an armistice; see below, § 240.

[3] Martens, *N.R.G.*, xix. p. 626.

other forces its commencement should be delayed three days. Article 38 of the Hague Regulations enacts that an armistice must be notified officially and in good time to the competent authorities and the troops, and that hostilities are suspended immediately after notification or at a fixed time, as the case may be.[1]

It sometimes happens that hostilities are carried on after the commencement of an armistice by forces which did not know of its commencement. In such cases the *status quo* at the date of the commencement of armistice has to be re-established so far as possible, prisoners made and enemy vessels seized being liberated, capitulations annulled, places occupied, evacuated, and the like; but the parties may, of course, stipulate the contrary.

Violation of Armistices.

§ 239. Any violation [2] of armistices is prohibited, and, if ordered by the Governments concerned, constitutes an international delinquency. In case an armistice is violated by members of the forces on their own account, the individuals concerned may be punished by the other party in case they fall into his hands. But apart from this no unanimity exists among the writers on International Law as to the rights of the injured party in case of violation by the other party; many [3] assert that the injured may at once, without giving notice, reopen hostilities; others [4] maintain that he may not, but has only a right to denounce the armistice. The Hague Regulations endeavoured to settle the controversy, Article 40 enacting that any serious violation of an armistice by one of the parties gives the other the right to denounce it, and even, in case of urgency, to

[1] The general armistice with Germany in the World War in 1918 was signed at 6 A.M. and was to take effect at 11 A.M.

[2] Such as the scuttling of German vessels at Scapa Flow on June 21, 1919, by order of Admiral von Reuter.

[3] See, for instance, Grotius, iii. c. 21, § 11; Pufendorf, viii. c. 7, § 12; Vattel, iii. § 242; Phillimore, ii. § 121; Bluntschli, § 695; Fiore, iii. No. 1494.

[4] See, for instance, Calvo, iv. § 2436; Despagnet, No. 566; Pradier-Fodéré, vii. No. 2913.

recommence hostilities at once. Three rules may be formulated from this—(1) violations which are not serious do not even give a right to denounce an armistice; (2) serious violations do empower the other party to denounce the armistice, but not, as a rule, to recommence hostilities at once without notice; (3) only in case of urgency is a party justified in recommencing hostilities without notice. But since the terms 'serious violation' and 'urgency' lack precise definition, the course to be taken is in practice left to the discretion of the injured party.

Violation of an armistice by private individuals, acting on their own initiative, is to be distinguished from violation by members of the armed forces. For a violation by unauthorised private persons, the injured party has, according to Article 41 of the Hague Regulations, only the right of demanding punishment of the offenders, and, if necessary, compensation for losses sustained.

End of Armistices.

§ 240. In case an armistice has been concluded for an indefinite period, the parties having made no stipulations regarding notice to recommence hostilities, notice may be given at any time, and hostilities recommenced at once after notification. In most cases, however, armistices are agreed upon for a definite period, and then they expire at the end of it without special notice, unless notification has been expressly stipulated. If, in case of an armistice for a definite period, the exact hour of the termination has not been agreed upon, but only the date, the armistice terminates at twelve o'clock midnight. In case an armistice has been arranged to last from one certain day to another, *e.g.* from June 15 to July 15, it is controversial[1] whether July 15 is excluded or included. An armistice may, lastly, be concluded under a resolutive condition, in which case the occurrence of the condition brings the armistice to an end.

[1] See above, § 238.

CHAPTER VI

MEANS OF SECURING LEGITIMATE WARFARE

I

ON MEANS IN GENERAL OF SECURING LEGITIMATE WARFARE

Bonfils, Nos. 1014-1017—Spaight, p. 461—*Land Warfare*, §§ 435-438—Garner, ii. §§ 578-595.

Legitimate and Illegitimate Warfare.

§ 241. Since war is not a condition of anarchy and lawlessness, International Law requires that belligerents shall comply with its rules in carrying on their military and naval operations. So long, and in so far, as belligerents do this, their warfare is legitimate; if they do not, their warfare is illegitimate. Now, illegitimate acts and omissions can be committed by belligerent Governments themselves, by commanders or members of the forces, and by individuals who do not belong to the forces. Experience teaches that, on the whole, illegitimate acts and omissions on the part of individual soldiers are unavoidable during war, since the passions which are aroused by, and during, war will always carry away some. But belligerents bear a vicarious responsibility for internationally illegal acts of their soldiers, which turns into original responsibility if they refuse to repair the wrong done by punishing the offenders and, if necessary, compensating the sufferers.[1] Cases in which belligerent Governments

[1] See above, vol. i. §§ 149-150.

themselves commit illegitimate acts, and also cases in which they refuse to punish their soldiers for illegitimate acts, constitute international delinquencies.[1] Now, if in time of peace an international delinquency is committed, the injured State can, if the worst comes to the worst, make war against the offender to compel adequate reparation.[2] But if an international delinquency is committed during warfare itself, no means whatever exist at present for compelling reparation.

How Legitimate Warfare is to a certain extent secured.

§ 242. Now legitimate warfare is, at any rate to a certain extent, secured through several means recognised by International Law. These means fall into three classes. The first class comprises measures of self-help:—reprisals; punishment of war crimes committed by enemy soldiers and other enemy subjects; the taking of hostages. The second class comprises:—complaints lodged with the enemy; complaints lodged with neutral States; good offices, mediation, and intervention on the part of neutral States. The third class comprises rights to compensation. Thus, according to Article 3 of Hague Convention IV., belligerents are responsible for all acts committed by members of their forces, and are liable to make compensation, if the case demands it, for any violation of the Hague Regulations. These means secure to a certain extent legitimate warfare, because it is to the interest of both belligerents to prevent the enemy from getting a justifiable opportunity of making use of them. In spite of this, many illegitimate acts of individual enemy soldiers will always occur; but they will in many cases meet with punishment by one belligerent or the other. Hostile acts of private enemy individuals not belonging to the armed forces, belligerents have a right[3] to punish severely as acts of illegitimate warfare.

[1] See above, vol. i. § 151.
[2] See above, vol. i. § 156.
[3] See below, § 254.

However, although to a certain extent legitimate warfare is in fact secured by these means, the two Balkan Wars of 1912 and 1913, and especially the World War, in which most appalling atrocities, and many violations of fundamental principles of the law of war, were committed, have clearly demonstrated that new means must be found to compel belligerents to conduct war within the limits of the laws of war.[1]

II

COMPLAINTS, GOOD OFFICES AND MEDIATION, INTERVENTION

Land Warfare, §§ 439.440.

Complaints lodged with the Enemy.

§ 243. Commanders of forces engaged in hostilities frequently lodge complaints with each other regarding single acts of illegitimate warfare committed by members of their forces, such as abuses of the flag of truce, violations of the flag of truce, or of the Geneva Convention, and the like. The complaint is sent to the enemy under the protection of a flag of truce, and the interest which every commander takes in the legitimate behaviour of his troops should always make him attend to complaints and punish the offenders, provided that the complaints are found to be justified. Very often, however, it is impossible to verify the charges, and then charge and denial face each other without there being any way of solving the difficulty. It also often happens during war that the belligerent Governments lodge with each other mutual complaints of illegitimate acts and omissions. Since diplomatic intercourse is broken off during war, such complaints are sent to the enemy, either under

[1] The only available means—intervention by the League of Nations—is discussed below in § 246.

the protection of a flag of truce, or through a neutral[1] State which lends its good offices. But here too indignant charges and emphatic denials frequently face each other without there being a way of solving the conflict.

§ 244. If certain grave illegitimate acts or omissions of warfare occur, belligerents frequently lodge complaints with neutral States, either asking their good offices, mediation, or intervention to make the enemy comply with the laws of war, or simply drawing their attention to the facts. Thus, at the beginning of the Franco-German War, France lodged a complaint with Great Britain, and asked her intervention on account of the intended creation of a volunteer fleet by Germany, which France considered to be a violation of the Declaration of Paris.[2] Conversely, in January 1871, Germany, in a circular addressed to her diplomatic envoys abroad, to be communicated to the neutral Governments, complained of twenty-one cases in which the French forces had, deliberately and intentionally it was alleged, fired on bearers of a flag of truce. Again, in November 1911, and in February 1912, during the Turco-Italian War, Turkey lodged complaints with the Powers on account of the execution of Arabs in Tripoli as war criminals, and on account of the bombardment of Turkish war-vessels in the harbour of Beirut.[3]

Complaints lodged with Neutrals.

During the World War all the belligerents lodged innumerable complaints with the neutral Powers, accusing one another of countless violations of the laws of war and neutrality.

§ 245. Complaints lodged with neutral States may instigate one or more of them to lend their good offices

[1] Thus, in October 1904, during the Russo-Japanese War, Japan sent a complaint concerning the alleged use of Chinese clothing by Russian troops to the Russian Government, through the Government of the United States of America; see Takahashi, pp. 174-178, and above, § 164. See also above, § 216 n.

[2] See above, § 84.

[3] See above, § 213.

Good Offices and Mediation.

or mediation to the belligerents for the purpose of settling the conflict arising from charges and denials of illegitimate acts or omissions of warfare; and resort to reprisals may thus be prevented. Good offices and mediation so offered do not differ from those which settle a difference between States in time of peace;[1] they are friendly acts in contradistinction to intervention, which is dictatorial interference for the purpose of making the belligerents comply with the laws of war.

Intervention on the part of Neutrals.

§ 246. There can be no doubt that neutral States (whether a complaint has been lodged with them or not) may, either singly, or jointly and collectively, exercise intervention whenever illegitimate acts or omissions of warfare are committed (1) by belligerent Governments, or (2) by members of belligerent forces, if the Governments concerned do not punish the offenders. It has already been stated[2] that other States have a right to intervene, in case a State violates, in time of peace or war, those principles of the Law of Nations which are universally recognised. There is not the slightest doubt that such principles of International Law are endangered in case a belligerent Government commits acts of illegitimate warfare or does not punish the offenders in case such acts are committed by members of its armed forces. But apart from this, the Hague Regulations make illegitimate acts of warfare on land now appear as by right the affair of all signatory States to the convention, and therefore, in case of war between signatory States, the neutral signatory States certainly have a right of intervention if acts of warfare are committed which are illegitimate according to the Hague Regulations. If any such intervention occurred, it would have nothing to do with the war in general, and would not make the intervening State a party to the war, but would concern only the international delinquency committed

[1] Discussed above, §§ 7-11.

[2] Above, vol. i. § 135 (4)

by the one belligerent through acts of illegitimate warfare.

But although neutral States have without doubt a *right* to intervene, they have at present no duty to do so, with the consequence that a great many violations of the laws are committed. The two Balkan Wars of 1912 and 1913, and still more the World War, in which most appalling atrocities and many violations of fundamental principles of the law of war were committed, have shown that belligerents are frequently ready to brush aside all rules of warfare for the sake of some military purpose. It would seem that the only way in which, in the future, such violations can be prevented, is by making it a duty of the League of Nations to exercise intervention in case a belligerent violates fundamental principles of law concerning the conduct of war.[1]

III

REPRISALS

Vattel, iii. § 142—Hall, § 135—Westlake, ii. pp. 123-126, and *Papers*, pp. 259-264—Taylor, §§ 487, 507—Wharton, iii. § 348*b*—Hershey, No. 337—Moore, vii. § 1114—Bluntschli, §§ 567, 580, 654, 685—Lueder in *Holtzendorff*, iv. p. 392—Pradier-Fodéré, viii. Nos. 3214-3221—Bonfils, Nos. 1018-1026—Despagnet, No. 543—Rivier, ii. pp. 298-299—Calvo, iv. §§ 2041-2043—Martens, ii. § 121—Mérignhac, iii[a]. pp. 349-358—Holland, *War*, Nos. 119-120—Bordwell, p. 305—Spaight, pp. 462-465—*Land Warfare*, §§ 452-460—Lammasch, *Das Volkerrecht nach dem Kriege* (1917), pp. 17-20—Le Fur, *Des Représailles en Temps de Guerre* (1919)—Halleck in *A.J.*, vi. (1912), pp. 107-118—Wilkinson in the *Law Magazine and Review*, xl. (1914-15), pp. 289-298—Woolsey in the *Proceedings of the American Society of International Law*, ix. (1915), pp. 62-67—Renault in the *Journal de Droit international* (Clunet), xlii. (1915), pp. 313-344—Mérignhac in *R.G.*, xxiv. (1917), pp. 9-26.

§ 247. Whereas reprisals in time of peace are to be distinguished from retorsion, and are injurious acts committed for the purpose of compelling a State to

[1] See above, vol. i. § 167*a* (5).

Reprisals between Belligerents in contradistinction to Reprisals in Time of Peace.

consent to a satisfactory settlement of a difference created through an international delinquency,[1] reprisals between belligerents are retaliation by means of illegitimate acts of warfare,[2] whether constituting international delinquencies or not, for the purpose of making the enemy comply in future with the rules of legitimate warfare.[3] Reprisals between belligerents [4] are terrible means,[5] because they are in many cases directed against innocent enemy individuals, who must suffer for real or alleged offences for which they are not responsible. Reprisals cannot be dispensed with, because without them illegitimate acts of warfare would be innumerable. As matters stand, every belligerent, and every member of his forces, knows for certain that reprisals are to be

[1] See above, §§ 33, 42.

[2] The author had noted that the confiscation on August 25, 1916, of the Palais de Venice in Rome, the seat of the Austrian Legation at the Holy See, and the property of Austria-Hungary, as a measure of reprisals against the bombardment of Venice by Austrian aircraft (see above, vol. i. p. 566 n. and Scelle in *R.G.*, xxiv. (1917), pp. 244-255), would not seem to be in accordance with the definition of reprisals given in the text, which presupposes the resort to such acts as are themselves violations of the laws of war. He had intended to reconsider his definition on this ground.

[3] The author had intended to draw a distinction, based upon the experience of the World War, between reprisals really intended to make the enemy comply with the rules of legitimate warfare and 'reprisals' (if they can be called by this name at all) which were nothing else than 'tit for tat.' He would have quoted, as an illustration of the former kind, the segregation of the crews of German submarines (see below, § 249 (4)), and, as an illustration of the latter kind, the action of the Allies in following the German example in the use of poison gas and liquid fire (see above, §§ 110, 113), in bombing 'open' towns (see below, n. 5), etc.

[4] The question how far reprisals are justified which, although directed against the enemy, hit neutrals, is discussed below, §§ 319, 360.

[5] There was never a war in which the belligerents resorted so often to reprisals as during the World War. To mention only a few instances, the German army in Belgium committed appalling atrocities in the name of reprisals. The French bombarded from the air the undefended German towns of Stuttgart, Karlsruhe, and Trèves by way of reprisals because the Germans had so bombarded English and French undefended places. Because Great Britain refused to carry out all the rules of the unratified Declaration of London, Germany declared all the waters around the British Isles a war area, and ordered her submarines to torpedo all British merchantmen without warning; in this way the *Lusitania* was sunk, and over 1100 innocent civilians drowned. To meet these reprisals, Great Britain resorted to counter-reprisals, and prohibited all imports to, and exports from, Germany. Because Great Britain segregated the captured crews of German submarines from other prisoners, Germany put an equal number of captive English officers into solitary confinement.

expected in case they violate the rules of legitimate warfare. But while reprisals are frequently an adequate means for making the enemy comply with these rules, they frequently miss their purpose, and call forth counter-reprisals on the part of the enemy.

Reprisals admissible for every Illegitimate Act of Warfare.

§ 248. Whereas reprisals in time of peace are admissible for international delinquencies only, reprisals between belligerents are admissible [1] for any and every act of illegitimate warfare,[2] whether it constitutes an international delinquency or not. Thus, the Germans during the Franco-German War frequently, by way of reprisal, bombarded and fired undefended open villages where their soldiers had been treacherously killed by enemy individuals in ambush who did not belong to the armed forces. Again, Lord Roberts, during the South African War, ordered,[3] by way of reprisal, the destruction of houses and farms in the vicinity of a place where damage was done to the lines of communication. Or, again, the appalling atrocities committed in 1914 during the World War by the German soldiery in Belgium, Germany,[4] in so far as she did not deny them altogether, declared to have been necessary as measures of reprisal. That this practice is objectionable, and ought therefore to be prohibited, is pointed out below in § 250.

Danger of Arbitrariness in Reprisals.

§ 249. The right to exercise reprisals carries with it great danger of arbitrariness, for often the alleged facts

[1] It is for the injured belligerent to consider whether he will at once resort to reprisals, or, before doing so, will lodge complaints with the enemy or with neutral States. In practice, however, a belligerent will rarely resort at once to reprisals, if the violation of the rules of legitimate warfare is not very grave, and the safety of his troops does not require prompt and drastic measures.

[2] That prisoners of war may be made the objects of reprisals for acts of illegitimate warfare committed by the enemy, there is hardly any doubt; see Beinhauer, *Die Kriegsgefangenschaft* (1908), p. 74; Spaight, pp. 89, 465.

[3] See Section 4 of the Proclamation of June 19, 1900 (Martens, *N.R.G.*, 2nd Ser. xxxii. p. 147), and Beak, *The Aftermath of War* (1906), p. 11.

[4] See the White Book published in 1915 by the German Foreign Office, *Die Volkerrechtswidrige Führung des Belgischen Volkskrieges*, and the Belgian Grey Book, *Réponse au Livre blanc Allemand du 10 Mai 1915*, (1916).

which make belligerents resort to them are not sufficiently verified; sometimes the rules of war which they consider the enemy to have violated are not generally recognised; often the act of reprisal performed is excessive compared with the precedent act of illegitimate warfare.[1] Some cases may illustrate this danger.

(1) In 1782 Joshua Huddy, a captain in the army of the American insurgents, was taken prisoner by loyalists and handed over to a Captain Lippencott for the ostensible purpose of being exchanged, but was arbitrarily hanged. The commander of the British troops had Lippencott arrested, and ordered him to be tried for murder. Lippencott was, however, acquitted by the court-martial, as there was evidence to show that his command to execute Huddy was in accordance with orders of a Board which he was bound to obey. Thereupon some British officers who were prisoners of war in the hands of the Americans were directed to cast lots to determine who should be executed by way of reprisal for the execution of Huddy. The lot fell on Captain Asgill, a young officer only nineteen years old, and he would have been executed but for the supplication of the Queen of France, who saved his life.[2]

(2) 'The British Government, having sent to England, early in 1813, to be tried for treason, twenty-three Irishmen, naturalised in the United States, who had been captured on vessels of the United States, Congress authorised the President to retaliate. Under this act, General Dearborn placed in close confinement twenty-three prisoners taken at Fort George. General Prevost, under express directions of Lord Bathurst, thereupon ordered the close imprisonment of double the number of commissioned or uncommissioned United States' officers. This was followed by a threat of "unmitigated severity

[1] See Le Fur, *op. cit. passim.*

[2] See the case reported in Martens, *Causes célèbres*, iii. pp. 311-321. See also Phillimore, iii. § 105.

against the American citizens and villages" in case the system of retaliation was pursued. Mr. Madison having retorted by putting in confinement a similar number of British officers taken by the United States, General Prevost immediately retorted by subjecting to the same discipline all his prisoners whatsoever. . . . A better temper, however, soon came over the British Government, by whom this system had been instituted. A party of United States' officers, who were prisoners of war in England, were released on parole, with instructions to state to the President that the twenty-three prisoners who had been charged with treason in England had not been tried, but remained on the usual basis of prisoners of war. This led to the dismissal on parole of all the officers of both sides.'[1]

(3) During the Franco-German War the French had captured forty German merchantmen, and made their captains and crews prisoners of war. Count Bismarck, who considered it against International Law to detain these men as prisoners, demanded their liberation, and when the French refused this, ordered forty French private individuals of local importance to be arrested by way of reprisal and sent as prisoners of war to Bremen, where they were kept until the end of the war. Count Bismarck was decidedly wrong,[2] since France had, as the law then stood, in no way committed an illegal act by detaining the German crews as prisoners of war.[3]

(4) During the World War, when in 1915 the German Government ordered her submarines to torpedo British merchantmen at sight without warning, the British Admiralty declared that they would not in future regard the captured crews of German submarines as

[1] See Wharton, iii. § 348*b*.

[2] That Bismarck's standpoint was wrong has been pointed out above in § 201. Some German writers, however, take his part; see, for instance, Lueder in *Holtzendorff*, iv. p. 479, n. 6. As regards the present law on the subject, see above, §§ 85, 201.

[3] The case is one of reprisals, and has nothing to do with the taking of hostages; see below, § 258.

'honourable' prisoners of war, but would keep them separate from other German prisoners. Accordingly, thirty-nine captured officers and men were segregated by way of reprisal in naval detention barracks. Germany promptly resorted to counter-reprisals, and placed the same number of British officers in solitary confinement. Great Britain soon afterwards abandoned the policy of differential treatment.[1]

(5) In September 1914, during the World War, the German armies in Belgium burned the university of Louvain, including its world-famed library, and other buildings in other towns by way of reprisals, alleging that Belgian civilians had fired upon the German troops. The Belgian Government denied these charges and maintained that German soldiers in Louvain had shot one another; the civilised world was horrified at these reprisals.[2]

Proposed Restriction of Reprisals.

§ 250. The Hague Regulations did not mention reprisals at all, because the Brussels Conference of 1874, which accepted the unratified Brussels Declaration, had struck out several sections of the Russian draft code regarding reprisals. These original sections[3] (69-71) stipulated—(1) that reprisals should be admitted only in extreme cases of absolutely certain violations of the rules of legitimate warfare; (2) that the acts performed by way of reprisal should not be excessive, but in proportion to the violation; (3) that reprisals should be ordered by commanders-in-chief only.

In face of the arbitrariness with which, according to the present state of International Law, resort can be had to reprisals, it cannot be denied that an agreement upon some precise rules regarding them is an imperative

[1] Details from Garner, ii. § 356.

[2] Details from Garner, i. §§ 282-284. See also the Belgian and German official publications mentioned above, § 248 n.

[3] See Martens, *N.R.G.*, 2nd Ser. iv. pp. 14, 139, 207. See also Articles 85 and 86 of the Manual of the Laws of War, adopted by the Institute of International Law (*Annuaire*, v. p. 174).

necessity. The events of the World War illustrate the present condition of affairs. The appalling atrocities committed by the German army in Belgium and France, if avowed at all, were always declared by the German Government to be justified as measures of reprisal. There is no doubt that Article 50 of the Hague Regulations, enacting that *no general penalty, pecuniary or otherwise, may be inflicted on the population on account of the acts of individuals for which it cannot be regarded as collectively responsible,* does not prevent the burning, by way of reprisals, of villages, or even towns, for a treacherous attack committed there on enemy soldiers by unknown individuals, and this being so, a brutal belligerent has his opportunity. It should, therefore, expressly be enacted that reprisals, like ordinary penalties, may not be inflicted on the whole population for acts of individuals for which it cannot be regarded as collectively responsible.

IV

PUNISHMENT OF WAR CRIMES

Hall, § 135—Bluntschli, §§ 627-643*a*—Spaight, p. 462—Holland, *War*, Nos. 117-118—Hershey, p. 411, n. 4—Ariga, §§ 96-99—Takahashi, pp. 166-184—*Land Warfare*, §§ 441-451—Renault, *De l'Application du Droit pénal aux Faits de Guerre* (1915)—Dumas, *Les Sanctions pénales des Crimes Allemands* (1916)—Garner, ii. §§ 581-588—Landa in *R.I.*, x. (1878), pp. 182-184—Woolsey in the *Proceedings of the American Society of International Law*, ix. (1915), pp. 67-69—Pic in *R.G.*, xxiii. (1916), pp. 243-268—Oppenheim in the *Law Quarterly Review*, xxxiii. (1917), pp. 266-286—Mérignhac in *R.G.*, xxiv. (1917), pp. 28-56.

§ 251. In contradistinction to hostile acts of soldiers by which the latter do not lose their privilege of being treated as members of armed forces who have done no wrong, war crimes are such hostile or other acts of soldiers or other individuals as may be punished by

Conception of War Crimes.

the enemy on capture of the offenders.[1] It must, however, be emphasised that the term 'war crime' is used, not in the moral sense of the term 'crime,' but only in a technical legal sense, on account of the fact that perpetrators of these acts may be punished by the enemy. For, although among the acts called war crimes are many which are crimes in the moral sense of the term (such, for instance, as the abuse of a flag of truce or assassination of enemy soldiers), there are others which may be highly praiseworthy and patriotic (such as taking part in a levy *en masse* on territory occupied by the enemy). But because every belligerent may, and actually must, in the interest of his own safety, punish these acts, they are termed war crimes, whatever may be the motive, the purpose, and the moral character of the act.[2]

Different Kinds of War Crimes.

§ 252. In spite of the uniform designation of these acts as war crimes, four different kinds of war crimes must be distinguished on account of the essentially different character of the acts: namely (1) violations of recognised rules regarding warfare committed by members of the armed forces, (2) all hostilities in arms committed by individuals who are not members of the enemy armed forces, (3) espionage and war treason, (4) all marauding acts.

Violations of Rules regarding Warfare.

§ 253. Violations of rules regarding warfare are war crimes only when committed without an order of the belligerent Government concerned. If members of the armed forces commit violations *by order* of their Government, they are not war criminals, and may not be punished[3] by the enemy; the latter may, however,

[1] This definition makes it clear that a belligerent may punish captured enemy soldiers who before capture committed violations of the rules of warfare which constituted—see below, § 253—war crimes. Strupp in *Z I.*, xxv. (1915), p. 359, answers the question in the negative. See above, vol. i. § 445.

[2] See above, § 57. Particular objection is taken to the term 'war treason' as used below, § 255; but this term is generally recognised. See Spaight, pp. 334-335.

[3] The contrary is sometimes asserted; see, for instance, Bellot in the *Grotius Society*, ii. (1917), pp. 31-56, and Mérignhac in *R.G.*, xxii.

resort to reprisals. In case members of forces commit violations ordered by their commanders, the members may not be punished, for the commanders are alone responsible, and the latter may, therefore, be punished as war criminals on their capture by the enemy.[1]

The following are the more important violations that may occur :—

(1) Making use of poisoned, or otherwise forbidden, arms and ammunition.

(2) Killing or wounding soldiers disabled by sickness or wounds, or who have laid down arms and surrendered.

(3) Assassination, and hiring of assassins.

(4) Treacherous request for quarter, or treacherous feigning of sickness and wounds.

(5) Ill-treatment of prisoners of war, or of the wounded and sick. Appropriation of such of their money and valuables as are not public property.

(6) Killing or attacking harmless private enemy individuals. Unjustified appropriation and destruction of their private property, and especially pillaging. Compelling the population of occupied territory to furnish information about the army of the other belligerent, or about his means of defence.

(7) Disgraceful treatment of dead bodies on battlefields. Appropriation of such money and other valuables found upon dead bodies as are not public property, nor arms, ammunition, and the like.

(1917), pp. 51-53. But Dumas, *Les Sanctions pénales des Crimes Allemands* (1916), pp. 29-34, and Renault in the *Journal de Droit international* (Clunet), xlii. (1915), pp. 341-342, agree with me. The law cannot require an individual to be punished for an act which he was compelled by law to commit. See also § 366 of the American *Rules of Land Warfare* of 1914, and Garner, ii. § 588.

[1] The author did not live to discuss the legal responsibility of the former German Emperor in relation to the World War, or Article 227 of the Treaty of Peace with Germany, which arraigned him, not as being responsible for the war crimes committed by order by members of the German forces, but 'for a supreme offence against international morality and the sanctity of treaties.' However, the Dutch Government refused to compel him to leave Holland, and the trial has not been proceeded with. See Garner, ii. §§ 589-591.

(8) Appropriation and destruction of property belonging to museums, hospitals, churches, schools, and the like.

(9) Assault, siege, and bombardment of undefended open towns and other habitations. Unjustified bombardment of undefended places by naval forces.

(10) Unnecessary bombardment of historical monuments, and of such hospitals and buildings devoted to religion, art, science, and charity, as are indicated by particular signs notified to the besiegers bombarding a defended town.

(11) Violations of the Geneva Convention.

(12) Attack on, or sinking of, enemy vessels which have hauled down their flags as a sign of surrender. Attack on enemy merchantmen without previous request to submit to visit.

(13) Attack or seizure of hospital ships, and all other violations of the Hague Convention for the Adaptation to Maritime Warfare of the Principles of the Geneva Convention.

(14) Unjustified destruction of enemy prizes.[1]

(15) Use of enemy uniforms and the like during battle; use of the enemy flag during attack by a belligerent vessel.

(16) Violation of enemy individuals furnished with passports or safe-conducts; violation of safeguards.

(17) Violation of bearers of flags of truce.

(18) Abuse of the protection granted to flags of truce.

(19) Violation of cartels, capitulations, and armistices.

(20) Breach of parole.[2]

[1] Unjustified destruction of neutral prizes—see below, § 431—is not a war crime, but is nevertheless an international delinquency, if ordered by the belligerent government.

[2] By Article 228 of the Treaty of Peace with Germany 'the German Government recognises the right of the Allied and Associated Powers to bring before military tribunals persons accused of having committed acts in violation of the laws and customs of war. Such persons shall, if found guilty, be sentenced to punishments laid down by law.' See also Treaty of Peace with Austria, Article 173; with Bulgaria, Article 118; with Hungary, Article

§ 254. Since International Law is a law between States only and exclusively, no rules of International Law can exist to prohibit private individuals from taking up arms, and committing hostilities against the enemy. But private individuals committing such acts do not enjoy the privileges of members of armed forces, and the enemy has, according to a customary rule of International Law, the right to consider, and punish, such individuals as war criminals. Hostilities in arms committed by private individuals are not war crimes because they really are violations of recognised rules regarding warfare, but because the enemy has the right to consider and punish them as acts of illegitimate warfare. The conflict between praiseworthy patriotism on the part of such individuals and the safety of the enemy troops does not allow of any solution. It would be unreasonable for International Law to impose upon a belligerent a duty to forbid the taking up of arms by his private subjects, because such action may occasionally be of the greatest value to him, especially for the purpose of freeing a country from the enemy who has militarily occupied it. Nevertheless the safety of his troops compels the enemy to consider and punish such hostilities as acts of illegitimate warfare, and International Law gives him a right to do so.

Hostilities in Arms by Private Individuals.

It is usual to make a distinction between hostilities in arms by private individuals against an invading or retiring enemy and hostilities in arms committed by

157; with Turkey, Article 226. Before these treaties were drawn up the Peace Conference at Paris appointed a commission, consisting of representatives of ten Allied and Associated Powers, to consider the responsibility of the authors of the war, the facts as to breaches of the laws and customs of war by the Central Powers, the degree of responsibility for them attaching to particular individuals, and the constitution and procedure of a tribunal to try them. The commission presented a majority and two minority reports, and these important documents have been published by the Carnegie Endowment for International Peace (Division of International Law, Pamphlet No. 32).

the inhabitants against an enemy occupying a conquered territory. In the latter case one speaks of war rebellion, whether inhabitants take up arms singly or rise in a so-called levy *en masse*. Articles 1 and 2 of the Hague Regulations make the greatest possible concessions regarding hostilities committed by irregulars.[1] Beyond the limits of these concessions belligerents will never be able to go without the greatest danger to their troops.

It must be particularly noted that a merchantman of a belligerent, which attacks enemy vessels without previously having been attacked by them, may be considered and treated as a pirate,[2] and that the captain, officers, and members of the crew may, therefore, be punished as war criminals to the same extent as private individuals who commit hostilities in land warfare.[3]

Espionage and War Treason.

§ 255. Espionage and war treason, as has been explained above,[4] bear a twofold character. International Law gives a right to belligerents to use them. On the other hand, it gives a right to belligerents to consider them, when committed by enemy soldiers or enemy private individuals within their lines,[5] as acts of illegitimate warfare, and consequently punishable as war crimes.

Espionage has already been treated above.[6] War treason consists of all such acts (except hostilities in arms on the part of the civilian population, and espionage) committed within the lines of a belligerent as are harmful to him and are intended to favour the enemy. War treason may be committed,

[1] See above, §§ 80-81.

[2] See above, §§ 85, 181.

[3] As regards the execution of Captain Fryatt, see above, § 181.

[4] § 159.

[5] Espionage outside their lines—a notable feature of the World War—is punishable according to the Municipal Law of the State in which it takes place.

[6] §§ 159-161.

not only in occupied enemy country, or in the zone of military operations, but anywhere within the lines of a belligerent.[1]

The following are the chief cases of war treason that may occur :—

(1) Information of any kind given to the enemy.

(2) Voluntary supply of money, provisions, ammunition, horses, clothing, and the like, to the enemy.

(3) Any voluntary assistance to military operations of the enemy, be it by serving as guide in the country by opening the door of a defended habitation, by repairing a destroyed bridge, or otherwise.

(4) Attempting to induce soldiers to desert, to surrender, to serve as spies, and the like; negotiating desertion, surrender, and espionage offered by soldiers.

(5) Attempting to bribe soldiers or officials in the interest of the enemy, and negotiating such bribe.

(6) Liberation of enemy prisoners of war.[2]

(7) Conspiracy against the armed forces, or against individual officers and members of them.

(8) Wrecking of military trains, destruction of the lines of communication or of telegraphs or telephones in the interest of the enemy, and destruction of any war material for the same purpose.

(9) Circulation of enemy proclamations dangerous to the interests of the belligerent concerned.[3]

[1] See Oppenheim in the *Law Quarterly Review*, xxxiii. (1917), p. 266, and see above, § 251 n., with regard to the objection raised against this term.

[2] During the World War Germany executed Miss Cavell, who was nursing in Brussels, on a charge of having assisted Allied soldiers to escape. Even if, at the secret trial, the charge was proved, so that the sentence might perhaps have been justified according to the letter of the law, the execution was an outrage, especially as the victim was a woman who had with equal devotion nursed German as well as French and English wounded. See Garner, ii. §§ 382-386.

[3] As to the treatment, during the World War, of airmen who dropped proclamations within the enemy lines, see Garner, i. § 312.

(10) Intentional false guidance of troops by a hired guide, or by one who offered his services voluntarily.

(11) Rendering courier, or similar, services to the enemy.

Enemy soldiers—in contradistinction to private enemy individuals—may only be punished for war treason when they have committed the act of treason during their stay within a belligerent's lines under disguise. If, for instance, two soldiers in uniform are sent to the rear of the enemy to destroy a bridge, they may not, when caught, be punished for war treason, because their act was one of legitimate warfare. But if they exchange their uniforms for plain clothes, and thereby appear to be members of the peaceful private population, they may be punished for war treason. A remarkable case of this kind occurred in 1904, during the Russo-Japanese War. Two Japanese disguised in Chinese clothes were caught in an attempt to destroy, with the aid of dynamite, a railway bridge in Manchuria, in the rear of the Russian forces. Brought before a court-martial, they confessed themselves to be Shozo Jakoga, forty-three years of age, a major on the Japanese General Staff, and Teisuki Oki, thirty-one years of age, a captain on the Japanese General Staff. They were convicted, and condemned to be hanged, but the mode of punishment was changed, and they were shot. All the newspapers which mentioned this case reported it as a case of espionage; but it was in fact one of war treason. Although the two officers were in disguise, their conviction for espionage was impossible according to Article 29 of the Hague Regulations, provided, of course, they were court-martialled for no other act than the attempt to destroy a bridge.

There are many acts of the inhabitants of occupied enemy country which a belligerent may forbid and punish, in the interests of order and the safety of his army, although they do not fall under the category of war treason, and are not therefore punishable as war crimes. To this class belong all acts which violate the orders legitimately given by an occupant of enemy territory.[1]

§ 256. Marauders are individuals roving, either singly or collectively in bands, over battlefields, or following advancing or retreating forces, in quest of booty. They have nothing to do with warfare in the strict sense of the term; but they are an unavoidable accessory to warfare, and frequently consist of soldiers who have left their corps. Their acts are considered to be acts of illegitimate warfare, and they are punished in the interest of the safety of either belligerent. **Marauding.**

§ 257. All war crimes may be punished[2] with death, but belligerents may, of course, inflict a more lenient punishment, or commute a sentence of death into a more lenient penalty. If this be done and imprisonment take the place of capital punishment, the question arises whether persons so imprisoned must be released at the end of the war, although their term of imprisonment has not yet expired. Some publicists[3] answer this question in the affirmative, maintaining that it could never be lawful to inflict a penalty extending beyond the duration of the war. But I believe that the question has to be answered in the negative. If a belligerent has a right to pronounce a sentence of capital punishment, it is obvious that he may select a more lenient penalty and carry it out even beyond the duration of the war. It would in no wise be in the interest of humanity to deny this right, for otherwise belligerents would have always to pronounce and carry **Mode of Punishment of War Crimes.**

[1] See *Land Warfare*, § 446.

[2] The proposal of Woolsey (see the *Proceedings of the American Society of International Law*, ix. (1916), pp. 67-69), that an International Court of neutrals should try, and pronounce judgment in, all cases of war crimes is well meant; but the question is whether it is capable of being realised.

[3] See, for instance, Hall, § 135, p. 437.

V

TAKING OF HOSTAGES

Grotius, iii. c. 4, § 14 and c. 11, § 18—Hall, §§ 135, 156—Taylor, § 525—Bluntschli, § 600—Lueder in *Holtzendorff*, iv. pp. 475-477—Klüber, §§ 156, 247—G. F. Martens, ii. § 277—Ullmann, § 183—Bonfils, Nos. 1145 and 1151—Pradier-Fodéré, vii. Nos. 2843-2848—Rivier, ii. p. 302—Calvo, iv. §§ 2158-2160—Fiore, iii. Nos. 1363-1364—Martens, ii. § 119—Longuet, § 84—Bordwell, p. 305—Spaight, pp. 465-470—Breton, *Les Non-belligérants: leurs Devoirs, leurs Droits, et la Question des Otages* (1904)—Garner, i. §§ 195-201—*Kriegsbrauch*, pp. 49, 50—*Land Warfare*, §§ 461-464.

Former Practice of taking Hostages.

§ 258. The practice of taking hostages, as a means of securing legitimate warfare, prevailed in former times much more than nowadays. It was frequently resorted to in cases in which belligerent forces depended more or less upon each other's good faith, as, for instance, in the case of capitulations and armistices. To make sure that no perfidy was intended, officers or prominent private individuals were taken as hostages, and could be held responsible with their lives for any perfidy committed by the enemy. This practice has totally disappeared, and is hardly likely to be revived. But it must not be confounded with the still existing practice of seizing enemy individuals for the purpose of making them the object of reprisals. Thus, when in 1870, during the Franco-German War, Count Bismarck ordered forty French notables to be seized, and to be taken away into captivity, by way of retaliation upon the French for refusing to liberate the crews of forty captured merchantmen, these forty French notables were not taken as hostages, but were made the object of reprisals.[1]

[1] The case has been discussed above in § 249. All the French writers who comment upon it make the mistake of referring to it as an instance of the taking of hostages.

§ 259. A new practice of taking hostages was resorted to by the Germans in 1870 during the Franco-German War for the purpose of securing the safety of forces against possible hostile acts by private inhabitants of occupied enemy territory. Well-known men were seized and detained, in the expectation that the population would refrain from hostile acts out of regard for the fate of the hostages. Thus, when unknown people frequently wrecked the trains transporting troops, the Germans seized prominent enemy citizens, and put them on the engines, a device which always proved effective, and soon put a stop to further train-wrecking. The same practice was resorted to, although for a short time only, by Lord Roberts [1] in 1900 during the South African War. It has been condemned by the majority of publicists. But, with all due deference to the authority of so many prominent men who oppose the practice, I cannot agree with their opinion. Matters would be different if hostages were seized, and exposed to dangers, for the purpose of preventing legitimate hostilities on the part of members of the armed forces of the enemy.[2] But no one can deny that train-wrecking on occupied enemy territory by private enemy individuals is an act which a belligerent is justified in considering and punishing as war treason.[3] It is for the purpose of guarding against an act of illegitimate warfare that these hostages are put on the engines. The danger to which they are exposed comes from their fellow-citizens, who are informed that hostages are on

Modern Practice of taking Hostages.

[1] See Section 3 of the Proclamation of Lord Roberts, dated Pretoria, June 19, 1900, but this section was repealed by the Proclamation of July 29, 1900. See Martens, *N.R.G.*, 2nd Ser. xxxii. pp. 147, 149.

[2] *Land Warfare*, § 463, does not consider the practice commendable, because innocent citizens are thereby exposed to legitimate acts of train-wrecking on the part of raiding parties of armed forces of the enemy. Spaight, pp. 466-470, admits the practice in principle, but considers it to have been unjustified during the Franco-German as well as during the South-African War, because there was no certainty that the train-wrecking had not been committed by raiding parties of the armed forces of the enemy.

[3] See above, § 255 (8).

the engines, and ought therefore to refrain from wrecking the trains. It cannot, and will not, be denied that the measure is a harsh one, and that it makes individuals liable to suffer for acts for which they are not responsible. But the safety of the troops and lines of communication of the occupying belligerent is at stake, and I doubt, therefore, whether even the most humane commanders will be able to dispense with this measure, since it alone has proved effective. It must further be taken into consideration that the amount of cruelty connected with it is no greater than in reprisals, where also innocent individuals must suffer for illegitimate acts for which they are not responsible. Moreover, is it not more reasonable to prevent train-wrecking by putting hostages on the engines than to resort to reprisals when it has been done? For there is no doubt that a belligerent is justified in resorting to reprisals[1] in each case of train-wrecking by private enemy individuals,[2] and no objection is ever raised against his doing so, although it is possible that the train-wrecking was a legitimate act committed by a raiding party of the armed forces of the enemy.

During the World War Germany adopted a terrible practice of taking hostages in the territories occupied by her armies, and shooting them when she believed that civilians had fired upon German troops. Garner, after considering the evidence in detail, summarises it in the following words: ‘It is clear that the German practice of taking hostages was very general. There is indeed reason to believe that it was resorted to in most of the towns and villages in Belgium and France which fell under their occupation. For the most part, the pur-

[1] See above, § 248.

[2] Belligerents sometimes take hostages to secure compliance with requisitions, contributions, ransom bills, and the like, but such cases have nothing to do with illegitimate warfare; see above, § 116, p. 175, n. 2, and § 170, p. 241, n. 5. The Hague Regulations do not mention the taking of hostages for any purpose.

pose . . . was to ensure the good behaviour of the inhabitants and strict obedience to the German authority. . . . The hostages were sometimes stationed on bridges to ensure the latter against destruction; sometimes they were assembled on the public square; frequently they were marched in front of the German columns to protect the latter against attack, and the like. Considerable numbers were shot.'[1]

VI

COMPENSATION

Bonfils, No. 1026[1]—Despagnet, No. 510 *bis*—Lémonon, pp. 344-346—Higgins, pp. 260-261—Scott, *Conferences*, p. 528—Nippold, ii. § 24—Boidin, pp. 83-84—Spaight, p. 462—Holland, *War*, No. 19—*Land Warfare*, § 436—Hofer, *Der Schadenersatz im Landkriegsrecht* (1913)—Schoen, *Die völkerrechtliche Haftung der Staaten aus unerlaubten Handlungen* (1917), pp. 92-94 and 122-143—Garner, ii. § 580—Fauchille in *R.G.*, xxiii. (1916), pp. 280-297—Pic, *ibid.*, pp. 243-268—Mérignhac in *R.G.*, xxiv. (1917), p. 8.

259*a*. There is no doubt that, if a belligerent can be made to pay compensation for all damage done by him in violating the laws of war, this will be an indirect means of securing legitimate warfare. In former times no rule existed which stipulated such compensation, although, of course, violation of the laws of war was always an international delinquency. On the contrary, it was an established customary rule[2] that claims for reparation for damages caused by violations of the rules of legitimate warfare could not be raised after the conclusion of peace, unless the contrary was expressly stipulated.[3] It was not until the Second Hague Conference that matters underwent a change. In revising

How the Principle of Compensation for Violations of the Laws of War arose.

[1] i. § 198.
[2] See below, § 274.
[3] Express provision for the payment of reparation for damages of this kind was made by the Treaty of Peace with Germany after the World War. See Articles 231 and 232, and the annex to Article 244.

the Convention concerning the Laws and Customs of War on Land, besides other alterations, it adopted a new article (3) which enacts that a belligerent who violates the provisions of the Hague Regulations, shall, if the case demand, be liable to make compensation, and that he shall be responsible for all acts committed by persons forming part of his armed forces.

Germany, on whose initiative this principle was adopted, proposed two articles concerning the matter, the one dealing with the payment of compensation for violations of the Hague Regulations with regard to subjects of neutral States,[1] and the other for violations of these Regulations with regard to enemy subjects. The conference, however, preferred to make no distinction between the different cases of violation, but to adopt the general principle.

Compensation for Violations of the Hague Regulations.

§ 259*b*. It is apparent that Article 3 of Convention IV. enacts two different rules: (1) that a belligerent who violates the Hague Regulations shall, if the case demand, pay compensation; (2) that a belligerent is responsible for all acts committed by any persons forming part of his armed forces.

To take this second rule first, the responsibility of a State for internationally illegal acts on the part of members of its armed forces is, provided the acts have not been committed by its command or authorisation, only a vicarious responsibility, but nevertheless it must, as was pointed out above,[2] pay damages for these acts when required. For this reason, Article 3 did not create a new rule in so far as it enacted that belligerents must pay for damage caused by members of their forces.

On the other hand, the rule that compensation must be paid by belligerents for damage done through violations of the Hague Regulations, was a new rule, at any rate in so far as it is laid down in a general way.

[1] See below, § 357.

[2] vol. i. § 163.

If interpreted according to the letter, Article 3 of Convention IV. provides for payment of compensation for violations of the Hague Regulations only, and not for violations of other rules of International Law concerning land warfare or even concerning sea warfare. I have, however, no doubt that the Powers would recognise that the principle of Article 3 must find application to any rule of the laws of war, by the violation of which subjects of the enemy, or of neutral States, suffer damage. For instance, if the commander of a naval force, in contravention of Hague Convention IX., were to bombard an undefended place, compensation could be claimed for such subjects of the enemy and of neutral States as suffered damage through the bombardment.

However, Article 3, although it establishes the obligation to pay compensation, does not stipulate anything concerning the time, or the way, in which claims for compensation are to be settled. This is clearly a case for arbitration, and it is to be hoped that an international conference will make arbitration obligatory for claims for compensation arising from violations, on the part of a belligerent, of the Hague Regulations as well as of other laws of war.

CHAPTER VII

END OF WAR, AND POSTLIMINIUM

I

ON TERMINATION OF WAR IN GENERAL

Hall, § 197—Lawrence, 217—Phillimore, iii. § 510—Taylor, § 580—Moore, vii. § 1163—Heffter, § 176—Kirchenheim in *Holtzendorff*, iv. pp. 791-792—Ullmann, § 198—Bonfils, No. 1692—Mérignhac, iiie. pp. 121-133—Despagnet, No. 605—Calvo, v. § 3115—Fiore, iii. No. 1693—Martens, ii. § 128—Longuet, § 155—Charleville, *La Validité juridique des Actes de l'Occupant en Pays occupé* (1902)—Focherini, *Il Postliminio nel moderno Diritto internazionale* (1908)—Phillipson, *Termination of War* (1916).

War a Temporary Condition.

§ 260. The normal condition between two States being peace, war can never be more than a temporary condition; whatever may have been the cause, or causes, of a war, it cannot possibly last for ever. For either the purpose of war will be realised, and one belligerent will be overpowered by the other, or both will sooner or later be so exhausted by their exertions that they will desist from the struggle.

Three Modes of Termination of War.

§ 261. A war may be terminated in three different ways. (1) Belligerents may abstain from further acts of war, and glide into peaceful relations without expressly making peace through a special treaty; (2) they may formally establish the condition of peace through a special treaty of peace; (3) a belligerent may end the war through subjugation of his adversary.[1]

[1] That a civil war may come to an end through simple cessation of hostilities, or through a treaty of peace, need hardly be mentioned. But it is of importance to state that there is a difference between civil war and other war in a case of subjugation. For to terminate a civil war, conquest *and* annexation, which together constitute subjugation, are unnecessary (see below, § 264); conquest alone is sufficient.

II

SIMPLE CESSATION OF HOSTILITIES

Hall, § 203—Phillimore, iii. § 511—Taylor, § 584—Bluntschli, § 700—Heffter, § 177—Kirchenheim in *Holtzendorff*, iv. p. 793—Ullmann, § 198—Bonfils, No. 1693—Despagnet, No. 605—Nys, iii. p. 738—Rivier, ii. pp. 435-436—Calvo, v. § 3116—Fiore, iii. No. 1693—Martens, ii. § 128—Longuet, § 155—Mérignhac, iii[a]. p. 121—Pillet, p. 370—Phillipson, *Termination of War* (1916), pp. 3-8.

Exceptional Occurrence of Simple Cessation of Hostilities.

§ 262. The regular modes of termination of war are treaties of peace or subjugation; but cases have occurred in which simple cessation of all acts of war on the part of both belligerents has actually and informally brought the war to an end. Thus ended in 1716 the war between Sweden and Poland, in 1720 the war between Spain and France, in 1801 the war between Russia and Persia, in 1867 the war between France and Mexico, and in the same year the war between Spain and Chili. Thus ended also the World War as between Germany and China, since China did not sign the Treaty of Peace with Germany. So also the World War as between the United States and Germany will have ended, unless a separate treaty of peace is negotiated between these two powers.[1]

Although termination of war through simple cessation of hostilities is for many reasons inconvenient, and is, therefore, as a rule avoided, it may nevertheless in the future, as in the past, occasionally occur.

Effect of Termination of War through Simple Cessation of Hostilities.

§ 263. Since, in the case of termination of war through simple cessation of hostilities, no treaty of peace embodies the conditions of peace between the former belligerents, the question arises whether the *status* which existed between the parties before the outbreak of war,

[1] Whereas the war between Prussia and several German States in 1866 came to an end through subjugation of some States and treaties of peace with others, Prussia never concluded a treaty of peace with the Principality of Lichtenstein, which was also a party to the war.

the *status quo ante bellum*, should be revived, or the *status* which exists between the parties at the time when they simply ceased hostilities, the *status quo post bellum* (the *uti possidetis*), can be upheld. The majority of publicists[1] correctly maintain that the *status* which exists at the time of cessation of hostilities becomes silently recognised through such cessation, and is, therefore, the basis of the future relations of the parties. This question is of the greatest importance regarding enemy territory militarily occupied by a belligerent at the time hostilities cease. According to the correct opinion, it can be annexed by the occupier, the adversary, through the cessation of hostilities, having dropped all rights he possessed over it. On the other hand, termination of war through cessation of hostilities does not dispose of claims of the parties which have not been settled by the actual position of affairs at the termination of hostilities, and it remains for the parties to settle them by special agreement, or to let them stand over.

III

SUBJUGATION

Vattel, iii. §§ 199-203—Hall, §§ 204-205—Lawrence, § 77—Phillimore, iii. § 512—Halleck, i. pp. 501-534—Taylor, §§ 220, 585-588—Moore, i. § 87—Walker, § 11—Wheaton, § 165—Bluntschli, §§ 287-289, 701-702—Heffter, § 178—Kirchenheim in *Holtzendorff*, iv. p. 792—Liszt, § 10—Ullmann, §§ 92, 97, 197—Bonfils, Nos. 535 and 1694—Despagnet, Nos. 387-390, 605—Rivier, ii. pp. 436-441—Nys, iii. p. 738—Calvo, v. §§ 3117-3118—Fiore, ii. No. 863, iii. No. 1693, and *Code*, Nos. 1083-1086—Martens, i. § 91, ii. § 128—Longuet, § 155—Pillet, p. 371—Holtzendorff, *Eroberungen und Eroberungsrecht* (1872)—Heimburger, *Der Erwerb der Gebietshoheit* (1888), pp. 121-132—Westlake in the *Law Quarterly Review*, xvii. (1901), p. 392, now reprinted in Westlake, *Papers*, pp. 475-489—Phillipson, *Termination of War* (1916), pp. 8-51.

§ 264. Subjugation must not be confounded with conquest, although there can be no subjugation without

[1] See, however, Phillimore, iii. § 511, who maintains that the *status quo ante bellum* has to be revived.

conquest. Conquest is taking possession of enemy territory by military force, and is completed as soon as the territory is effectively[1] occupied. Now it is obvious that conquest of *a part* of enemy territory has nothing to do with subjugation, because the enemy may well reconquer it. Even the conquest of *the whole* enemy territory need not necessarily involve subjugation; for in a war between more than two belligerents, the troops of one of them may evacuate their own country and join the allied army, so that the armed contention is continued, although the territory of one of the allies is completely conquered. Again, a belligerent, although he has annihilated the forces and conquered the whole of the territory of his adversary, and thereby brought the armed contention to an end,[2] may nevertheless not choose to exterminate the enemy State by annexing the conquered territory, but may conclude a treaty of peace with the expelled or imprisoned head of the defeated State, re-establish its Government, and hand back to it the whole or a part of the conquered territory. Subjugation takes place only when a belligerent, after having annihilated the forces and conquered the territory of his adversary, destroys his existence by annexing the conquered territory. Subjugation may, therefore, correctly be defined as *extermination in war of one belligerent by another through annexation*[3] *of the former's territory after conquest, the enemy forces having been annihilated.*[4]

Subjugation in contradistinction to Conquest.

§ 265. Although complete conquest, together with

[1] The conditions of effective occupation have been discussed above in § 167. Regarding subjugation as a mode of acquisition of territory, see above, vol. i. §§ 236-241.

[2] The continuation of guerilla war after the termination of a real war is discussed above in § 60.

[3] That conquest alone is sufficient for the termination of civil wars has been pointed out above, § 261.

[4] Premature annexation can become valid through the occupation becoming soon afterwards effective. Thus, although the annexation of the South African Republic, on September 1, 1900, was premature, it became valid through the occupation becoming effective in 1901. See above, § 167 n.

Subjugation a Formal End of War.

annihilation of the enemy forces, brings the armed contention, and thereby the war, actually to an end, the formal end of the war is thereby not yet realised, as everything depends upon the resolution of the victor regarding the fate of the vanquished State. If he be willing to re-establish the captive or expelled head of the vanquished State, it is a treaty of peace concluded with the latter which terminates the war. But if he desires to acquire the whole of the conquered territory for himself, he annexes it, and thereby formally ends the war through subjugation. That the expelled head of the vanquished State protests and keeps up his claims, matters as little as do protests of neutral States. These protests may be of political importance for the future ; legally they are of no importance at all.

History presents numerous instances of subjugation. Although no longer so frequent as in former times, subjugation is not at all of rare occurrence. Thus, modern Italy came into existence through the subjugation by Sardinia in 1859 of the Two Sicilies, the Grand Dukedom of Tuscany, the Dukedoms of Parma and Modena, and in 1870 the Papal States. Thus, further, Prussia subjugated in 1866 the Kingdom of Hanover, the Dukedom of Nassau, the Electorate of Hesse-Cassel, and the Free Town of Frankfort-on-the-Main ; and Great Britain annexed in 1900 the Orange Free State and the South African Republic.[1]

[1] Since Great Britain annexed these territories in 1900, the agreement of 1902, regarding 'Terms of Surrender of the Boer Forces in the Field'—see *Parl. Papers*, South Africa (1902), Cd. 1096—was not a treaty of peace, and the South African War came formally to an end through subjugation, although—see above, § 167 n.—the proclamation of the annexation was somewhat premature. The agreement embodying the terms of surrender of the routed remnants of the Boer forces had, therefore, no internationally legal basis (see also below, § 274, p. 369 n.). The case would be different if the British Government had really—as Sir Thomas Barclay asserted in the *Law Quarterly Review*, xxi. (1905), pp. 303, 307—recognised the existence of the Government of the South African Republic down to May 31, 1902.

IV

TREATY OF PEACE

Grotius, iii. c. 20—Vattel, iv. §§ 9-18—Phillimore, iii. §§ 513-517—Halleck, i. pp. 306-324—Taylor, §§ 590-592—Moore, vii. § 1163—Wheaton, §§ 538-543—Bluntschli, §§ 703-707—Heffter, § 179—Kirchenheim in *Holtzendorff*, iv. pp. 794-804—Ullmann, § 198—Bonfils, Nos. 1696-1697, 1703-1705—Despagnet, Nos. 606-611—Rivier, ii. pp. 443-453—Nys, iii. pp. 737-753—Calvo, v. §§ 3119-3136—Fiore, iii. Nos. 1694-1700, and *Code*, Nos. 1954-1964—Martens, ii. § 128—Longuet, §§ 156-164—Mérignhac, iiie. pp. 121-123—Pillet, pp. 372-375—Phillipson, *Termination of War* (1916), pp. 75-204.

Treaty of Peace the most frequent End of War.

§ 266. Although occasionally war ends through simple cessation of hostilities, and although subjugation is not at all rare or irregular, the most frequent end of war is a treaty of peace. Many publicists correctly call a treaty of peace the normal mode of terminating war. Simple cessation of hostilities is certainly an irregular mode, while subjugation is in most cases, either not within the scope of the intention of the victor, or not realisable; and it is quite reasonable that a treaty of peace should be the normal end of war. States which are driven from disagreement to war will, sooner or later, when the fortune of war has given its decision, be convinced that the armed contention ought to be terminated. Thus a mutual understanding and agreement upon certain terms is the normal mode of ending the contention; and it is a treaty of peace which embodies such understanding.

Peace Negotiations.

§ 267. However, as the outbreak of war interrupts all regular non-hostile intercourse between belligerents, negotiations for peace are often difficult of initiation. Each party, although willing to negotiate, may have strong reasons for not opening negotiations. Good offices and mediation on the part of neutrals, therefore, are often of great importance, as thereby negotiations are called into existence which otherwise might have been long delayed. But neither formal nor informal peace negotiations *ipso facto* bring hostilities to a standstill, although a partial or general armistice may be concluded for the purpose of such negotiations. The fact that peace negotiations are going on directly between belligerents does not create any non-hostile relations between them apart from those negotiations themselves. Such negotiations can take place by the exchange of letters between the belligerent Governments, or through special negotiators, who may meet on neutral territory, or on the territory of one of the belligerents. In case they meet on belligerent territory, the enemy negotiators are inviolable, and must be treated on the same footing as bearers of flags of truce, if not as diplomatic envoys. For it can happen that a belligerent receives an enemy diplomatic envoy for the purpose of peace negotiations.[1] Be that as it may, negotiations,

[1] The World War (except as between Germany and China, and as between the United States and those of the Central Powers with which she was at war—see above, § 262) ended as follows:—On October 3-6, 1918, the German Government forwarded to the President of the United States of America through the Swiss diplomatic channel a Note requesting him to take steps for a general armistice (see above, § 233) and for the restoration of peace, suggesting as a basis for peace negotiations the programme laid down by him in his Message to Congress of January 8, 1918 (which contained 'the fourteen points'), and in his subsequent pronouncements, particularly in his Address of September 27, 1918 (see *A.J.*, xiii. (1919), Supplement, p. 85). After an exchange of Notes the President informed Germany on November 5, 1918 (*ibid.*, p. 93) that he had been in communication with the Governments associated with the United States in the war, and that, subject to two qualifications as to reparation and the so-called 'freedom of the seas,' they were prepared to conclude peace on the suggested basis. A general armistice was signed on November 11 (see above, § 233), and a peace conference, at which all the victorious and none of the vanquished Powers were represented, assembled at Paris in January 1919 (see above, vol. i. § 50*b*). The draft treaty was handed to the German delegation, which had been summoned to Paris to receive it, in May 1919. Germany stated her objections in writing, and the treaty, after some modification, was signed on June 28, 1919. There was no pre-armistice agreement as to the basis of peace negotiations between the Allied and Associated Powers and any of Germany's allies. Armistices were granted to them (see above, § 233), and eventually draft treaties were presented to each of them for their comment in writing and subsequent signature (see above, vol. i. § 50*b*, to which it is now possible to add that the Treaty of Peace with Austria came into force on July 16, 1920, and that with Bulgaria on August 9, 1920. The Treaty of Peace with Hungary was signed at Trianon on June 4, 1920; the Treaty of Peace with Turkey was signed at Sèvres on August 10, 1920; but these two treaties have not yet (February 1921) come into force.)

wherever taking place and by whomsoever conducted, may always be broken off before an agreement is arrived at.

§ 268. Although ready to terminate the war through a treaty of peace, belligerents are frequently not able to settle all the terms at once. In such cases hostilities are usually brought to an end through so-called preliminaries of peace, the definitive treaty to take the place of the preliminaries being concluded later on. Such preliminaries are a treaty in themselves, embodying an agreement between the parties regarding such terms of peace as are essential. Preliminaries are as binding as any other treaty, and therefore need ratification. Very often, but not necessarily, the definitive treaty of peace is concluded at a place other than that at which the preliminaries were settled. Thus, the war between Austria, France, and Sardinia was ended by the Preliminaries of Villafranca of July 11, 1859, yet the definitive treaty of peace was concluded at Zurich on November 10, 1859. The war between Austria and Prussia was ended by the Preliminaries of Nickolsburg of July 26, 1866, yet the definitive treaty of peace was concluded at Prague on August 23. In the Franco-German War the Preliminaries of Versailles of February 26, 1871, were the precursor of the definitive treaty of peace concluded at Frankfort on May 10, 1871.[1] Preliminaries of Peace.

The purpose for which preliminaries of peace are agreed upon makes it obvious that such essential terms as are stipulated by them are the basis of the definitive treaty of peace. It may happen, however, that neutral States protest for the purpose of preventing

[1] No preliminaries of peace were agreed upon at the end of the Russo-Japanese War. After negotiations at Portsmouth (New Hampshire) had led to a final understanding on August 29, 1905, the treaty of peace was signed on September 5, and ratified on October 1. Nor at the end of the World War (see above, § 267 n. and vol. i. § 50b).

this. Thus, when the war between Russia and Turkey had been ended through the Preliminaries of San Stefano of March 3, 1878, Great Britain protested, a congress met at Berlin, and Russia had to be content with less favourable terms of peace than those stipulated at San Stefano.

Form and Parts of Peace Treaties.

§ 269. International Law does not contain any rules regarding the form of peace treaties; they may, therefore, be concluded verbally or in writing. But their importance makes the parties always conclude them in writing, and there is no instance of a treaty of peace verbally concluded.

According to the different points stipulated, it is usual to distinguish different parts within a peace treaty. Besides the preamble, there are general, special, and separate articles. General articles are those which stipulate the points which are to be agreed upon in every treaty of peace, such as the date of termination of hostilities, the release of prisoners of war, and the like. Special articles are those which stipulate the special terms of the particular agreement of peace. Separate articles are those which stipulate points with regard to the execution of the general and special articles, or which contain reservations and other special remarks by the parties.[1] Sometimes *additional* articles occur. They are stipulations agreed upon in a special treaty and intended to supplement the treaty of peace.[2]

§ 270. As the treaty-making power is, according to the Law of Nations, in the hands of the head[3] of the

[1] The Treaty of Peace with Germany (see above, vol. i. § 568*e*), upon which all the treaties of peace after the World War were modelled, first names the parties, then in a preamble recites the origin of the war and the armistice, then names the plenipotentiaries, and then fixes the date of the end of war and resumption of diplomatic relations. Next follows, in fifteen chapters, the substantive part of the treaty. At the end come general articles providing for ratification and coming into force, followed by the signatures and date and place of execution.

[2] For instance, a supplementary protocol to the Treaty of Peace with Germany was signed on the same day as the treaty itself.

[3] See above, vol. i. § 495.

State, it is he who is competent to conclude peace. But just as constitutional restrictions imposed upon heads of States regarding their general power of concluding treaties [1] are of importance for International Law, so are constitutional restrictions imposed upon heads of States regarding their competence to make peace. Therefore, treaties of peace concluded by heads of States which violate constitutional restrictions are not binding upon the States concerned, because the heads have exceeded their powers. The constitutions of the several States settle the matter differently, and it is not at all necessary that the power of declaring war and that of making peace should be vested by them in the same hands. In Great Britain the power of the Crown to declare war and to make peace is indeed unrestricted. But the constitutions of other States provide otherwise.[2] Competence to conclude Peace.

The controverted question as to whether a head of a State who is a prisoner of war is competent to make peace ought to be answered in the negative. The reason is that the head of a constitutional State, although he does not by becoming a prisoner of war lose his position, nevertheless thereby loses the power of exercising the rights connected therewith.[3]

§ 271. Unless the treaty provides otherwise,[4] peace commences with the signing of the peace treaty. Should it not be ratified, hostilities may be recommenced, and the unratified peace treaty is considered as an armistice. Sometimes, however, the peace treaty fixes a future date for the commencement of peace, stipulating that hostilities must cease on a certain future day.[5] This Date of Peace.

[1] See above, vol. i. § 497.

[2] See examples in Rivier, ii. p. 445.

[3] See Vattel, iv. § 13.

[4] The Treaties of Peace after the World War provided that peace should commence when they came into force, *i.e.* when a procès-verbal had been drawn up recording the deposit of ratifications by the vanquished Power and certain other Powers. See above, vol. i. § 568*e*.

[5] This was unnecessary in the treaties after the World War because general armistices had long ago been concluded.

is the case when war is waged in several, or widely separated, parts of the world, so that it is impossible at once to inform the opposing forces of the conclusion of peace.[1] Different dates may even be stipulated for the termination of hostilities in different parts of the world.

The question has arisen whether, in a case where a peace treaty provides a future date for the termination of hostilities in distant parts, if the forces in those parts hear of the conclusion of peace before that date, they must abstain at once from further hostilities. Most publicists correctly answer this question in the affirmative. But the French Prize Courts in 1801 condemned as good prize the English vessel *Swineherd* which was captured by the French privateer *Bellona* in the Indian Seas within the period of five months fixed by the Peace of Amiens for the termination of hostilities in those seas.[2]

V

EFFECTS OF TREATY OF PEACE

Grotius, iii. c. 20—Vattel, iv. §§ 19-23—Hall, §§ 198-202—Lawrence, § 218—Phillimore, iii. §§ 518-528—Halleck, i. pp. 328-348—Taylor, §§ 581-583—Wheaton, §§ 544-547—Bluntschli, §§ 708-723—Heffter, §§ 180-183, 184a—Kirchenheim in *Holtzendorff*, iv. pp. 804-817—Ullmann, § 199—Bonfils, Nos. 1698-1702—Despagnet, No. 607—Rivier, ii. pp. 454-461—Nys, iii. pp. 747-757—Calvo, v. §§ 3137-3163—Fiore, iii. Nos. 1701-1703, and *Code*, Nos. 1965-1985—Martens, ii. § 128—Longuet, §§ 156-164—Mérignhac, iii[a]. pp. 124-132—Pillet, pp. 375-377—Phillipson, *Termination of War* (1916), pp. 214-277.

§ 272. The chief and general effect of a peace treaty is the restoration of a condition of peace between the

[1] The ending of the Russo-Japanese War was quite peculiar. Although the treaty of peace was signed on September 5, 1905, the agreement concerning an armistice pending ratification of the peace treaty was not signed until September 14, and hostilities went on till September 16.

[2] Details in Hall, § 199; see also Phillimore, iii. § 521.

former belligerents. As soon as the treaty is ratified or otherwise comes into force, all rights and duties which exist in time of peace between the members of the family of nations are *ipso facto*, and at once, revived between the former belligerents.

Restoration of Condition of Peace.

On the one hand, all acts legitimate in warfare cease to be legitimate. Neither contributions nor requisitions, nor attacks on members of the armed forces or on fortresses, nor capture of ships, nor occupation of territory, are any longer lawful. If forces, ignorant of the conclusion of peace, commit such hostile acts, the condition of things at the time peace was concluded must as far as possible be restored.[1] Thus, ships captured must be set free, territory occupied must be evacuated, members of armed forces taken prisoners must be liberated, contributions imposed and paid must be repaid.

On the other hand, all peaceful intercourse between the former belligerents, and between their subjects, is resumed as before the war. Thus diplomatic intercourse is restored, and consular officers recommence their duties.[2]

The condition of peace created by a peace treaty is legally final, in so far as the order of things set up and stipulated by the treaty of peace is the settled basis of future relations between the parties, however contentious the matters concerned may have been before the outbreak of war. In concluding peace, the parties expressly or implicitly declare that they have come to an understanding regarding such settled matters. They may indeed make war against each other in future on other grounds, but they are legally bound not to go to war over matters settled by a previous treaty of

[1] *The Mentor*, (1799) 1 C. Rob. 179. Matters are, of course, different in case a future date—see above, § 271—is stipulated for the termination of hostilities.

[2] As to pre-war contracts, see above, § 101.

peace. That the practice of States does not always conform with this rule is a well-known fact which, although it discredits the rule, cannot shake its theoretical validity.

Principle of *Uti Possidetis.* § 273. Unless the parties stipulate otherwise, the effect of a treaty of peace is that conditions remain as at the conclusion of peace. Thus, all moveable State property, such as munitions, provisions, arms, money, horses, means of transport, and the like, seized by an invading belligerent, remain his property, as likewise do the fruits of immoveable property seized by him. Thus further, if nothing is stipulated regarding conquered territory, it remains in the hands of the possessor, who may annex it. But it is nowadays usual, although not at all legally necessary, for a conqueror desirous of retaining conquered territory to secure its cession in the treaty of peace.[1]

Amnesty. § 274. Since a treaty of peace is considered a final settlement of the war, one of the effects of every peace treaty is the so-called amnesty—that is, an immunity for all wrongful acts done by the belligerents themselves, the members of their forces, and their subjects during the war, and due to political motives.[2] It is usual, but not at all necessary, to insert an amnesty

[1] A case of concealed cession occurred with regard to Tripoli and Cyrenaica at the end of the Turco-Italian War in 1912. Inasmuch as Turkey did not want to cede these territories *expressis verbis*, and Italy insisted on acquiring them, the parties agreed in a protocol of October 15, 1912, that before the conclusion of peace which took place at Lausanne on October 18, 1912—see Martens, *N.R.G.*, 3rd Ser. vii. p. 7—Turkey should within three days grant complete autonomy to these territories, and thereby renounce sovereignty over them. This having been done, and peace concluded, Italy notified their annexation to the Powers. See Diena in *Z.I.*, xxiii. (1913), who, however, does not consider this to be a case of concealed cession, but of dereliction by Turkey and occupation of no man's land by Italy.

[2] This immunity is only effective in regard to the other party to the war. For instance, while it prevents an occupant of enemy territory from punishing war criminals after the conclusion of peace, it does not prevent a belligerent from punishing members of his own forces, or any of his own subjects, who during war committed violations of the laws of war, *e.g.* killed wounded enemy soldiers and the like.

clause in a treaty of peace. Therefore, unless the contrary is expressly stipulated in the treaty,[1] so-called war crimes [2] which were not punished before the conclusion of peace may no longer be punished after its conclusion. Individuals who have committed such war crimes, and have been arrested for them, must be liberated.[3] International delinquencies committed intentionally by belligerents through violation of the rules of legitimate warfare are considered to have been condoned. Formerly, even claims for reparation for damages caused by such acts could not be set up after the conclusion of peace, unless the contrary was expressly stipulated; but Article 3 of Hague Convention IV. has changed this.[4] On the other hand, the amnesty has nothing to do with ordinary crimes, or with debts incurred during war. A prisoner of war who commits murder during captivity may be tried and punished after the conclusion of peace, just as a prisoner who runs into debt during captivity may be sued after the conclusion of peace, or an action be brought on a ransom bill.

But here again the amnesty grants immunity only for wrongful acts done by the subjects of one belligerent against the other. Wrongful acts committed by the subjects of a belligerent against their own Government are not covered by it. Therefore a belligerent may after the conclusion of peace punish treason, desertion,

[1] The contrary was expressly stipulated in the Treaties of Peace after the World War. See above, § 253.

[2] See above, §§ 251-257. Clause 4 of the 'Terms of Surrender of the Boer Forces in the Field'—see *Parl. Papers*, South Africa (1902), Cd. 1096—expressly excluded from the amnesty 'certain acts, contrary to usages of war, which have been notified by the Commander-in-Chief to the Boer Generals, and which shall be tried by court-martial immediately after the close of hostilities.' But—see above, § 265, p. 360, n. 1—the agreement embodying these terms of surrender was not a treaty of peace, the Boer War having been terminated through subjugation.

[3] This applies only to those who have not yet been convicted. Those undergoing a term of imprisonment need not be liberated at the conclusion of peace; see above, § 257.

[4] See above, § 259*a*.

and the like committed during the war by his own subjects, unless the contrary has been expressly stipulated in the treaty of peace.[1]

Release of Prisoners of War.

§ 275. A very important effect of a treaty of peace is to end the captivity of prisoners of war.[2] This, however, does not mean that with the conclusion of peace all prisoners of war must at once be released. It only means—to use the words of Article 20 of the Hague Regulations—that 'after the conclusion of peace, the repatriation of prisoners of war shall take place as speedily as possible,' or to employ the phraseology of the Treaty of Peace with Germany, that their repatriation 'shall take place as soon as possible after the coming into force of the . . . treaty, and shall be carried out with the greatest rapidity.'[3] The instant release of prisoners at the very place where they were detained, would be inconvenient, not only for the State which kept them in captivity, but also for themselves, as in most cases they would not possess means to pay for their journey home. Therefore, although with the conclusion of peace they cease to be captives in the technical sense of the term, prisoners of war remain, as a body, under military discipline until they are brought to the frontier, and handed over to their Government. That prisoners of war may be detained after the conclusion of peace until they have paid debts incurred during captivity seems to be an almost generally[4] recognised rule, and the Treaties of Peace after the World War provided that prisoners 'awaiting disposal or undergoing sentence for offences other than those against discipline' might be detained.[5] But it is con-

[1] Thus Russia stipulated by Article 17 of the Preliminaries of San Stefano, in 1878—see Martens, *N.R.G.*, 2nd Ser. iii. p. 252—that Turkey must accord an amnesty to such of her own subjects as had compromised themselves during the war.

[2] See above, § 132.

[3] Article 214.

[4] See, however, Pradier-Fodéré, vii. No. 2839, who objects to it.

[5] See, for example, Treaty of Peace with Germany, Article 219.

troversial whether prisoners of war may be detained who are undergoing a term of imprisonment for offences against discipline. After the Franco-German War in 1871 Germany detained such prisoners,[1] whereas Japan after the Russo-Japanese War in 1905 released them. After the World War the Allied and Associated Powers released such German prisoners unless the offence had been committed after a certain date.[2]

§ 276. The question how far a peace treaty revives treaties concluded between the parties before the outbreak of war is much controverted. The answer depends upon the other question, how far the outbreak of war cancels existing treaties between belligerents.[3] There can be no doubt that treaties which have been cancelled by the outbreak of war do not revive. On the other hand, there can likewise be no doubt that treaties which have only been suspended by the outbreak of war do revive. But no certainty or unanimity exists regarding treaties which do not belong to the above two classes, and no rule of International Law exists concerning them. It is for the parties to make special stipulations in the peace treaty. Revival of Treaties.

VI

PERFORMANCE OF TREATY OF PEACE

Grotius, iii. c. 20—Vattel, iv. §§ 24-34—Phillimore, iii. § 597—Halleck, i. pp. 339-342—Taylor, §§ 593-594—Wheaton, §§ 548-550—Bluntschli, §§ 724-726—Heffter, § 184—Kirchenheim in *Holtzendorff*, iv. pp. 817-822 —Ullmann, § 199—Bonfils, Nos. 1706-1709—Despagnet, Nos. 612 and 613—Rivier, ii. pp. 459-461—Nys, iii. p. 753—Calvo, v. §§ 3164-3168—Fiore, iii. Nos. 1704-1705—Martens, ii. § 128—Longuet, §§ 156-164—Mérignhac, iii[a]. pp. 132-133—Phillipson, *Termination of War* (1916), pp. 205-213.

[1] See Pradier-Fodéré, vii. No. 2840; Bienhauer, *Die Kriegsgefangenschaft* (1908), p. 79; Payrat, *Le Prisonnier de Guerre* (1910), pp. 364-370.

[2] See, for example, Treaty of Peace with Germany, Article 218.

[3] See above, § 99, and the very detailed discussion of the question in Phillimore, iii. §§ 529-538.

Treaty of Peace, how to be carried out.

§ 277. The general rule that treaties must be performed in good faith applies to peace treaties as well as to others. The great importance, however, of a treaty of peace, and its special circumstances and conditions, make it necessary to draw attention to some points connected with its performance. Occupied territory may have to be evacuated, a war indemnity may have to be paid in cash, boundary lines of ceded territory may have to be drawn, and many other tasks performed. These tasks often necessitate the conclusion of numerous treaties for the execution of the peace treaty in detail, and the appointment of commissioners. Difficulties may arise in regard to the interpretation[1] of certain stipulations, which will be settled by arbitration or otherwise if the parties cannot agree. Arrangements may have to be made for the case in which a part, or the whole, of the territory occupied during the war is to remain for some period under military occupation as a means of securing the performance of the peace treaty.[2] One can form an idea of the numerous points of importance to be dealt with during the performance of a treaty of peace if one takes into consideration that, after the Franco-German War was terminated in 1871 by the Peace of Frankfort, more than a hundred conventions were successively concluded for the purpose of carrying out this treaty of peace, or if one studies the texts of the treaties of the peace after the World War, and considers the questions arising under them from day to day.[3]

Breach of Treaty of Peace.

§ 278. Just as is the performance, so is the breach of peace treaties of great importance. A peace treaty can be violated in its entirety, or in one of its stipulations only. Violation by one of the parties does not

[1] See above, vol. i. §§ 553-554.
[2] See above, vol. i. § 527.
[3] See above, vol. i. §§ 568*d*-568*g*.

ipso facto cancel the treaty; but the other party may cancel it on this ground. Just as with violation of treaties in general, so with violations of treaties of peace, some publicists maintain that a distinction must be drawn between essential and non-essential stipulations, and that only violation of essential stipulations creates a right for the other party to cancel the treaty of peace. It has been shown above,[1] that the majority of publicists rightly oppose the distinction.

But a distinction must be made between a violation during the period in which the conditions of the peace treaty have to be fulfilled, and a violation afterwards. In the first case, the other party may at once recommence hostilities, the war being considered not to have terminated through the violated peace treaty. The second case, which might happen soon or not until several years after the period for the fulfilment of the peace conditions, is in no way different from violation of any treaty in general. If a party cancels a peace treaty, and wages war against the State which violated it, this war is a new war, and in no way a continuation of the previous war, which was terminated by the violated treaty of peace. Just as in case of violation of a treaty in general, so in case of violation of a peace treaty, the injured party who wants to cancel it on that ground must do this within reasonable time after the violation has taken place; otherwise the treaty, or at least the non-violated parts of it, remain valid. A mere protest neither constitutes a cancellation nor reserves the right of cancellation.[1]

[1] See above, vol. i. § 547.

VII

POSTLIMINIUM

Grotius, iii. c. 9—Bynkershoek, *Quaestiones Juris publici*, i. c. 15 and 16—Vattel, iii. §§ 204-222—Hall, § 162-166—Manning, pp. 190-195—Phillimore, iii. §§ 539-590—Halleck, ii. pp. 535-564—Taylor, § 595—Wheaton, § 398—Bluntschli, §§ 727-741—Heffter, §§ 188-192—Kirchenheim in *Holtzendorff*, iv. pp. 822-836—Bonfils, No. 1710—Despagnet, No. 614—Nys, iii. pp. 757-758—Rivier, ii. pp. 314-316—Calvo, v. §§ 3169-3226—Fiore, iii. Nos. 1706-1712—Martens, ii. § 128—Pillet, p. 377.

Conception of Postliminium.

§ 279. The term 'postliminium' is originally one of Roman Law derived from *post* and *limen* (*i.e.* boundary). According to Roman Law, the relations of Rome with a foreign State depended upon whether or not a treaty of friendship[1] existed. If such a treaty was not in existence, Romans entering the foreign State concerned could be enslaved, and Roman goods taken there could be appropriated. Now, *jus postliminii* denoted the rule (1) that a Roman so enslaved, should he ever return into the territory of the Roman Empire, became *ipso facto* a Roman citizen again, with all the rights he possessed previous to his capture, (2) that Roman property, appropriated after entry into the territory of a foreign State, at once upon being taken back into the territory of the Roman Empire *ipso facto* reverted to its former Roman owner. Modern International and Municipal Law have adopted the term to indicate the fact that territory, individuals, and property, after having come in time of war under the authority of the enemy, return, either during the war or at its end, under the sway of their original sovereign. This can occur in different ways. Occupied territory can voluntarily be evacuated by the enemy, and then at once be reoccupied by the owner; or it can be reconquered by the legitimate sovereign; or

[1] See above, vol. i. § 40.

it can be reconquered by a third party, and restored to its legitimate owner. Conquered territory can also be freed through a successful levy *en masse*. Property seized by the enemy can be retaken, but it can also be abandoned by the enemy, and subsequently revert to the belligerent from whom it was taken. Further, conquered territory can, in consequence of a treaty of peace, be restored to its legitimate sovereign. In all such cases, the question has to be answered what legal effects the postliminium has in regard to the territory, the individuals thereon, or the property concerned.

Postliminium according to International Law, in contradistinction to Postliminium according to Municipal Law.

§ 280. Most writers confound the effects of postliminium according to Municipal Law with those according to International Law. For instance: whether a private ship which is recaptured reverts *ipso facto* to its former owner;[1] whether the former laws of a reconquered State revive *ipso facto* by the reconquest; whether sentences passed on criminals during occupation by the enemy should be annulled; these, and many similar questions treated in books on International Law, have nothing at all to do with International Law, but have to be determined exclusively by the Municipal Law of the respective States. International Law can deal only with such effects of postliminium as are international. These may be grouped under the following heads: revival of the former condition of things, validity of legitimate acts, invalidity of illegitimate acts.

Revival of the Former Condition of Things.

§ 281. Although a territory, and the individuals thereon, come through military occupation in war under the actual authority of the enemy, neither it nor they, according to the rules of International Law of our times, fall under the sovereignty of the invader. They remain, if not acquired by the conqueror through subjugation, under the sovereignty of the other belli-

[1] See above, § 196.

gerent, although the latter is in fact prevented from exercising his supremacy over them. Now, the moment the invader voluntarily evacuates such territory, or is driven away by a levy *en masse*, or by troops of the other belligerent, or of his ally, the former condition of things *ipso facto* revives. The territory and individuals concerned are at once, so far as International Law is concerned, considered to be again under the sway of their legitimate sovereign. For all events of international importance taking place on such territory the legitimate sovereign is again responsible towards third States, whereas during the time of occupation the occupant was responsible.

However, a case in which an occupant of territory is driven out of it by the forces of a third State not allied with the legitimate sovereign of such territory is not one of postliminium, and, consequently, the former state of things does not revive, unless the new occupant hands the territory over to the legitimate sovereign. If this is not done, the military occupation of the new occupant takes the place of that of the previous occupant.

Validity of Legitimate Acts.

§ 282. Postliminium has no effect upon such acts of a former military occupant connected with the occupied territory, and the individuals and property thereon, as he was, according to International Law, competent to perform; these acts are legitimate acts. Indeed, the State into whose possession such territory has reverted must recognise these legitimate acts, and the former occupant has by International Law a right to demand this. Therefore, if the occupant has collected the ordinary taxes, has sold the ordinary fruits of immoveable property, has disposed of such moveable state property as he was competent to appropriate, or has performed other acts in conformity with the laws of war, this may not be ignored by the legitimate sovereign after he has again taken possession of the territory.

However, this only extends to acts which have occurred during the occupation. A case which illustrates this happened after the Franco-German War. In October 1870, during occupation by German troops of the *Départements de la Meuse* and *de la Meurthe*, a Berlin firm entered into a contract with the German Government to fell 15,000 oak trees in the State forests of these *départements*, paying in advance £2250. The Berlin firm sold its contractual rights to others, who after having felled 9000 trees sold, in March 1871, their right to fell the remaining 6000 trees to yet another party. The last-named party felled some of them during the German occupation; but when the French Government again took possession of the territory, the contractors were without compensation prevented from further felling trees.[1] The question whether the Germans had a right to enter into the contract at all is doubtful. But even if they had, it covered the felling of trees during their occupation only, and not afterwards.

Invalidity of Illegitimate Acts.

§ 283. If the occupant has performed acts which, according to International Law, he was not competent to perform, postliminium makes the invalidity of these illegitimate acts apparent. Therefore, if the occupant has sold immoveable State property, such property may afterwards be claimed from the purchaser, whoever he is, without compensation. If he has given office to individuals, they may afterwards be dismissed. If he has appropriated and sold such private or public property as may not legitimately be appropriated by a military occupant, it may afterwards be claimed from the purchaser without payment of compensation.

[1] The protocol of signature added to the Additional Convention to the Peace Treaty of Frankfort, signed on December 11, 1871—see Martens, *N.R.G.*, xx. p. 868—comprised a declaration that the French Government did not recognise any liability to pay compensation.

No Postliminium after Interregnum.

§ 284. Cases of postliminium occur only when a conquered territory reverts, either during or at the end of the war, into the possession of the legitimate sovereign. No case of postliminium arises when a territory, ceded to the enemy by the treaty of peace, or conquered and annexed without cession at the end of a war terminated through simple cessation of hostilities,[1] later on reverts to its former owner State; or when the whole of the territory of a State which was conquered and subjugated regains its liberty, and becomes again the territory of an independent State. In these cases the territory has actually been under the sovereignty of the conqueror; the period between the conquest and the revival of the previous condition of things was not one of mere military occupation during war, but one of an interregnum during time of peace, and therefore the revival of the former condition of things is not a case of postliminium. An illustration of this is furnished by the case of the domains of the Electorate of Hesse-Cassel.[2] This hitherto independent State was subjugated in 1806 by Napoleon, and became in 1807 part of the Kingdom of Westphalia constituted by Napoleon for his brother Jerome. Jerome governed it up to the end of 1813, when, with the downfall of Napoleon, the Kingdom of Westphalia fell to pieces, and the former Elector of Hesse-Cassel was reinstated. During his reign Jerome had sold many of the domains of Hesse-Cassel. The Elector, on his return, did not recognise these contracts, but deprived the owners of their property without compensation, maintaining that a case of postliminium had arisen, and that Jerome had no right to sell the domains. The courts of the electorate pronounced against the Elector, denying that a case of postliminium had arisen, since Jerome, although

[1] See above, § 263.
[2] See Phillimore, iii. §§ 568-574, and the literature there quoted.

a usurper, had been King of Westphalia during an interregnum, and the sale of the domains was therefore no wrongful act. But the Elector, who was absolute in the electorate, did not comply with the verdict of his own courts, and the Vienna Congress, which was approached by the unfortunate proprietors of the domains, refused to intervene, although Prussia strongly took their part. It is generally recognised by all writers on International Law that this case was not one of postliminium, and the attitude of the Elector cannot therefore be defended by appeal to International Law.

PART III

NEUTRALITY

CHAPTER I

ON NEUTRALITY IN GENERAL

I

DEVELOPMENT OF THE INSTITUTION OF NEUTRALITY

Hall, §§ 208-214—Lawrence, § 223—Westlake, ii. pp. 198-206—Phillimore, iii. §§ 161-226—Twiss, ii. §§ 208-212—Hershey, No. 446—Taylor, §§ 596-613—Walker, *History*, pp. 195-202, and *Science*, pp. 374-387—Geffcken in *Holtzendorff*, iv. pp. 614-634—Ullmann, § 190—Bonfils, Nos. 1494-1521—Despagnet, No. 687—Rivier, ii. pp. 370-375—Nys, iii. pp. 535-546—Calvo, iv. §§ 2494-2591—Fiore, iii. Nos. 1503-1535—Martens, ii. § 130—Dupuis, Nos. 302-307—Mérignhac, iii[a]. p. 495—Boeck, Nos. 8-153—Kleen, i. pp. 1-70—Cauchy, *Le Droit maritime international* (1862), ii. pp. 232-439—Gessner, pp. 1-69—Bergbohm, *Die bewaffnete Neutralität 1780-1783* (1884)—Fauchille, *La Diplomatie française et la Ligue des Neutres 1780* (1893)—Schweizer, *Geschichte der schweizerischen Neutralität* (1895), i. pp. 10-72—Boye, *De Vaebnede Neutralitetsforbund* (1912)—Wehberg, § 2—Pyke, *The Law of Contraband* (1915), pp. 20-88—Piggott and Ormond, *Documentary History of the Armed Neutralities* (1919)—Roxburgh in the *Journal of Comparative Legislation*, 3rd Ser. i. p. 17.

Neutrality not practised in Ancient Times.

§ 285. Since in antiquity there was no notion of an International Law,[1] it is not to be expected that neutrality as a legal institution should have existed among the nations of old. Neutrality did not exist even in practice, for belligerents never recognised an attitude of impartiality on the part of other States. If war broke out between two nations, third parties had to choose between the belligerents, and become allies or enemies of one or other. This does not mean that third parties had actually to take part in the fighting. Nothing of the kind was the case. But they had, if necessary,

[1] See above, vol. i. § 37.

to render assistance; for example, to allow the passage of belligerent forces through their country, to supply provisions and the like to the party they favoured, and to deny all such assistance to the enemy. Several instances are known of efforts [1] on the part of third parties to take up an attitude of impartiality; but belligerents never recognised such impartiality.

Neutrality during the Middle Ages.

§ 286. During the Middle Ages matters only changed to the extent that, in the latter part of this period, belligerents did not exactly force third parties to a choice; legal duties and rights connected with neutrality did not exist. A State could maintain that it was no party to a war, although it furnished one of the belligerents with money, troops, and other kinds of assistance. To prevent such assistance, which was in no way considered illegal, treaties were frequently concluded, during the latter part of the Middle Ages, specially stipulating that neither party was to assist the enemies of the other in any way during time of war, or allow his subjects to do so.[2] Through the influence of such treaties, the difference between real and feigned impartiality of third States during war became recognised; and neutrality, as an institution of International Law, gradually developed during the sixteenth century.[3]

It was of great importance that the Swiss Confederation from the end of the sixteenth century adopted

[1] See Geffcken in *Holtzendorff*, iv. pp. 614-615.

[2] The collection of rules and customs of maritime law which goes under the name of the *Consolato del Mare* made its appearance about the middle of the fourteenth century. One of its rules, *i.e.* that in time of war enemy goods on neutral vessels might be confiscated, but that, on the other hand, neutral goods on enemy vessels must be restored, became of great importance, since Great Britain acted accordingly from the beginning of the eighteenth century until the outbreak of the Crimean War in 1854. See above, § 176.

[3] See 'Neutrality and Neutralisation in the Sixteenth Century—Liége,' by W. S. M. Knight (*Journ. Comp. Leg.*, 3rd Ser. ii. p. 98), and 'Neutrality of the Channel Islands during the Fifteenth, Sixteenth, and Seventeenth Centuries,' by E. T. Nicolle (*Journ. Comp. Leg.*, 3rd Ser. ii. p. 238).

the new and changed policy of always remaining neutral during wars between other States. Although this former neutrality of the Swiss can in no way be compared with modern neutrality, since Swiss mercenaries for centuries afterwards fought in all European wars, the Swiss Government itself succeeded in each instance in taking up, and preserving, an attitude of impartiality, which complied with the rules of neutrality then current.

Neutrality during the Seventeenth Century.

§ 287. At the time of Grotius, neutrality was recognised as an institution of International Law, although it was only in its infancy and needed a long time to reach its present range. Grotius did not know, or at any rate did not use, the term neutrality.[1] He treats neutrality in the very short seventeenth chapter of the Third Book on the Law of War and Peace, under the title *De his, qui in Bello medii sunt*, and only establishes two doubtful rules.[2] The first is that neutrals shall do nothing which may strengthen a belligerent whose cause is unjust, or hinder the movements of a belligerent whose cause is just. The second rule is that in a war in which it is doubtful whose cause is just, neutrals shall treat both belligerents alike, in permitting the passage of troops, in supplying provisions for the troops, and in not rendering assistance to persons besieged.

The treatment of neutrality by Grotius shows, on the one hand, that, apart from the recognition of the fact that third parties *could* remain neutral, not many rules regarding the duties of neutrals existed, and, on the other hand, that the granting of passage to troops of belligerents, and the supply of provisions to them, were not considered illegal. Indeed, the practice of the seventeenth century shows in numerous instances

[1] That the term was known at the time of Grotius may be inferred from the fact that Neumayr de Ramsla in 1620 published his work *Von der Neutralität und Assistenz in Kriegszeiten*; see Nys in *R.I.*, xvii. (1885), p. 78.

[2] § 3.

that neutrality was not really an attitude of impartiality, and that belligerents did not respect the territories of neutral States. Thus, although Charles I. remained neutral, the Marquis of Hamilton and six thousand British soldiers were fighting in 1631 under Gustavus Adolphus. 'In 1627 the English captured a French ship in Dutch waters; in 1631 the Spaniards attacked the Dutch in a Danish port; in 1639 the Dutch were in turn the aggressors, and attacked the Spanish Fleet in English waters; again, in 1666, they captured English vessels in the Elbe . . .; in 1665 an English fleet endeavoured to seize the Dutch East India Squadron in the harbour of Bergen, but were beaten off with the help of the forts; finally, in 1693, the French attempted to cut some Dutch ships out of Lisbon, and on being prevented by the guns of the place from carrying them off, burnt them in the river.'[1]

Progress of Neutrality during the Eighteenth Century.

§ 288. It was not until the eighteenth century that theory and practice agreed that it was the duty of neutrals to remain impartial, and of belligerents to respect the territories of neutrals. Bynkershoek and Vattel formulated adequate conceptions of neutrality. Bynkershoek[2] does not use the term 'neutrality,' but calls neutrals *non hostes*, and he describes them as those who are of neither party—*qui neutrarum partium sunt*—in a war, and who do not, in accordance with a treaty, give assistance to either party. Vattel,[3] on the other hand, uses the term 'neutrality,' and gives the following definition: 'Neutral nations, during a war, are those who take no one's part, remaining friends common to both parties, and not favouring the armies of one of them to the prejudice of the other.' But although Vattel's book appeared in 1758, twenty-

[1] See Hall, § 209.
[2] *Quaestiones Juris publici*, i. c. 9.
[3] iii. § 103.

one years after that of Bynkershoek, his doctrines are in some ways less advanced than those of Bynkershoek. Bynkershoek, in contradistinction to Grotius, maintained that neutrals had nothing to do with the question as to which party to a war had a just cause; that neutrals, being friends to both parties, have not to sit as judges between them, and, consequently, must not give or deny to one party or the other more or less in accordance with their conviction as to the justice or injustice of the cause of each. Vattel, however, taught [1] that a neutral, although he may generally allow the passage of troops of the belligerents through his territory, may refuse it to a belligerent making war for an unjust cause.

Although the theory and practice of the eighteenth century agreed that it was the duty of neutrals to remain impartial, the impartiality demanded was not at all strict. For throughout the greater part of the century, a State was considered not to violate neutrality by furnishing one of the belligerents with such limited assistance as it had previously promised by treaty.[2] In this way troops could be supplied by a neutral to a belligerent, and passage through neutral territory could be granted to his forces. Secondly, either belligerent might use the resources of neutrals. It was not considered a breach of neutrality for a State to allow one or both belligerents to levy troops on its territory, or to grant letters of marque to its merchantmen. It is true that during the second half of the eighteenth century, theory and practice became aware that neutrality was not consistent with these, and other, indulgences. But this only led to a distinction between neutrality in the strict sense of the term and imperfect neutrality. However, as regards the duty of belli-

[1] iii. § 135.

[2] See Nys in *R.I.*, 2nd Ser. xv. (1913), pp. 173-181, and the examples in Hall, § 211.

gerents to respect neutral territory, progress was made during this century. Whenever neutral territory was violated, reparation was asked for and made. Nevertheless it was considered lawful for a victor to pursue a vanquished army into neutral territory, and for a fleet to pursue[1] a defeated enemy fleet into neutral territorial waters.

First Armed Neutrality.

§ 289. Whereas, on the whole, the duty of neutrals to remain impartial, and the duty of belligerents to respect neutral territory, became generally recognised during the eighteenth century, the members of the Family of Nations did not come to an agreement during this period regarding the treatment of neutral vessels trading with belligerents. It is true that the right of visit and search for contraband of war, and the right to seize contraband, were generally recognised, but in other respects no general theory and practice were agreed upon. France and Spain upheld the rule that neutral goods on enemy ships and also neutral ships carrying enemy goods could be seized by belligerents. England, on the other hand, while conceding from time to time the rule 'free ship, free goods,' by particular treaties with certain States, throughout the eighteenth century generally followed the rule of the *Consolato del Mare*, according to which enemy goods on neutral vessels might be confiscated, whereas neutral goods on enemy vessels had to be restored.

England also upheld the principle that the commerce of neutrals should in time of war be restricted to the same limits as in time of peace, since most States in time of peace reserved *cabotage* and trade with their colonies for vessels of their own merchant marine. It was in 1756 that this principle first came into question. In that year, during war with England, France found that the naval superiority of England prevented her

[1] See below, §§ 320, 347 (4).

from carrying on her colonial trade by her own merchant marine, and therefore threw it open to vessels of the Netherlands, which had remained neutral. England then ordered her fleet to seize all such vessels with their cargoes, on the ground that they had become incorporated with the French merchant marine, and had thereby acquired enemy character. Ever since that time the above principle has been commonly called the 'rule[1] of 1756,' although it is now proved[2] that, as early as 1745, the English Prize Courts considered it a settled rule of law that a neutral vessel had no right in time of war to carry on such trade of a belligerent as was closed to it in time of peace.

In the practice of declaring enemy coasts to be blockaded, and condemning captured neutral vessels for breach of blockade, although the blockades were by no means always effective, England followed other Powers.

As privateering was legitimate and in general use, neutral commerce was considerably disturbed during every war between naval States. Now in 1780, during war between Great Britain, her American colonies, France, and Spain, Russia sent a circular[3] to England, France, and Spain, in which she proclaimed the following five principles: (1) that neutral vessels should be allowed to navigate from port to port of belligerents,

[1] *The Immanuel*, (1799) 2 C. Rob. 186. A clear statement of the rule and the facts is given by Reddie, *Researches*, i. pp. 307-313. See also the literature quoted below, § 400 n.; Phillimore, iii. §§ 212-222; Hall, § 234; Manning, pp. 260-267; Westlake, ii. p. 294; Moore, vii. § 1180; Boeck, No. 52; Dupuis, Nos. 131-133. Note that the original meaning of the rule of 1756 is different from the meaning it received by its extension in 1793. From that year onwards, England not only considered those neutral vessels which embarked upon the French coasting and colonial trade thrown open to them during the war with England as having acquired enemy character, but also those which carried neutral goods from neutral ports to ports of a French colony. This extension of the rule was clearly unjustified, and it is not possible to believe that it will ever be revived.

[2] See Marsden, *Law and Custom of the Sea*, ii. (1916), p. 436, who mentions the case of *The Ceres*.

[3] Martens, *R.*, iii. p. 158. See Reddie, *Researches*, i. pp. 321-357.

and along their coasts; (2) that enemy goods on neutral vessels, contraband excepted, should not be seized by belligerents; (3) that, with regard to contraband, Articles 10 and 11 of the Treaty of 1766 between Russia and Great Britain should be applied in all cases; (4) that a port should only be considered blockaded if the blockading belligerent had stationed vessels there, so as to create an obvious danger for neutral vessels entering the port; (5) that these principles should be applied in the proceedings and judgments on the legality of prizes. In July 1780 Russia [1] entered into a treaty with Denmark, and in August 1780 with Sweden, for the purpose of enforcing those principles by equipping a number of men-of-war. Thus the 'Armed Neutrality' made its appearance. In 1781 the Netherlands, Prussia, and Austria, in 1782 Portugal, and in 1783 the Two Sicilies joined the league. France, Spain, and the United States [2] of America accepted its principles without formally joining. The war between England, the United States, France, and Spain was terminated in 1783, and the war between England and the Netherlands in 1784; but in the treaties of peace the principles of the 'Armed Neutrality' were not mentioned. This league had no direct practical consequences, since England retained her former standpoint. Moreover, some of the States that had joined it acted contrary to some of its principles when they themselves went to war—Sweden, for example, during her war with Russia in 1788-1790, and France and Russia in 1793—and some of them concluded treaties in which were stipulations at variance with those principles. Nevertheless, the First Armed Neutrality has proved of great importance, because its principles furnished the basis of the Declaration of Paris of 1856.

[1] Martens, *R.*, iii. pp. 189, 198.
[2] See Albrecht in *Z.V.*, vi. (1912), pp. 436-449.

The French Revolution and the Second Armed Neutrality.

§ 290. The wars of the French Revolution and the Napoleonic Wars showed that the time was not yet ripe for the progress[1] aimed at by the First Armed Neutrality. Russia, the very same Power which had initiated the Armed Neutrality in 1780 under the Empress Catharine II. (1762-1796), joined Great Britain in 1793 in order to interdict all neutral navigation into ports of France, with the intention of subduing France by famine. Russia and England justified their attitude by the exceptional character of their war against France, which had proved to be the enemy of the security of all other nations. The French Convention answered with an order to the French fleet to capture all neutral ships carrying provisions to enemy ports, or carrying enemy goods.

But although Russia had herself acted in defiance of the principles of the First Armed Neutrality, she called a Second Armed Neutrality into existence in 1800, during the reign of the Emperor Paul. The Second Armed Neutrality was caused by the refusal of England to concede immunity from visit and search to neutral merchantmen under convoy.[2] Sweden was the first to claim in 1653, during war between Holland and Great Britain, that the belligerents should not visit and search Swedish merchantmen under convoy of Swedish men-of-war, provided that a declaration was made by the men-of-war that the merchantmen had no contraband on board. Other States later raised the same claim, and many treaties were concluded which stipulated the immunity from visit and search of neutral merchantmen under convoy. But Great Britain refused to recognise the principle, and when, in July 1800, a British squadron captured a Danish man-of-war and her convoy of several merchantmen for having resisted

[1] See Reddie, *Researches*, i. pp. 418-468, ii. pp. 1-232.

[2] See below, § 417.

visit and search, Russia invited Sweden, Denmark, and Prussia to renew the 'Armed Neutrality,' and to add to its principles the further principle, that belligerents should not have a right of visit and search in case the commanding officer of the man-of-war, under whose convoy neutral merchantmen were sailing, should declare that the convoyed vessels did not carry contraband of war. In December 1800 Russia concluded treaties with Sweden, Denmark, and Prussia consecutively, by which the 'Second Armed Neutrality' became a fact.[1] But it lasted only a year on account of the assassination of the Emperor Paul of Russia on March 23, and the defeat of the Danish fleet by Nelson on April 2, 1801, in the battle of Copenhagen. Nevertheless, the Second Armed Neutrality likewise proved of importance, for it led to a compromise in the 'Maritime Convention' concluded between England and Russia under the Emperor Alexander I, on June 17, 1801, at St. Petersburg,[2] to which Denmark and Sweden acceded on October 23, 1801. By Article 3 of this treaty, England recognised, as far as Russia was concerned, the rules that neutral vessels might navigate from port to port, and on the coasts, of belligerents, and that blockades must be effective. But in the same article England forced Russia to recognise the rule that enemy goods on neutral vessels might be seized, and did not recognise the immunity of neutral vessels under convoy from visit and search, although, by Article 4, she conceded that the right should in that case be exercised only by men-of-war, and not by privateers.

[1] Martens, *R.*, vii. pp. 127-202. See also Martens, *Causes célèbres*, iv. pp. 219-302.

[2] Martens, *R.*, vii. p. 260, and Krauel in *Festschrift der Berliner Juristenfakultät für Heinrich Brunner* (1914), pp. 69-107. Krauel (*op. cit.*, p. 97) denies that the stipulations of the 'Maritime Convention' contained a compromise, because they did not concern all maritime Powers; but surely they did constitute a compromise between England on the one hand, and, on the other, Russia, Denmark, and Sweden.

But this compromise did not last long. When, in November 1807, war broke out between Russia and England, Russia, in her declaration of war,[1] annulled the Maritime Convention of 1801, proclaimed anew the principles of the First Armed Neutrality, and asserted that she would never again drop them. Great Britain, in her counter-declaration,[2] proclaimed her return to those principles against which the First and the Second Armed Neutralities were directed, and she was able to point out that no Power had applied these principles more severely than had Russia under the Empress Catharine II. after she had initiated the First Armed Neutrality.

Thus all progress made by the Maritime Convention of 1801 fell to the ground. Times were not favourable to any progress. After Napoleon's Berlin Decrees in 1806, ordering the boycott of all English goods, England declared all French ports, and all the ports of the allies of France, blockaded, and ordered her fleet to capture all ships destined to them. Russia, after having solemnly asserted in her declaration of war against England in 1807 that she would never again drop the principles of the First Armed Neutrality, by Article 2 of an ukase [3] published on August 1, 1809, violated one of the most important of these principles, by ordering neutral vessels carrying enemy (English) goods to be stopped, and the enemy goods seized, together with the vessels themselves if more than half their cargoes consisted of enemy goods.

Neutrality during the Nineteenth Century.

§ 291. The development of the rules of neutrality during the nineteenth century was due to four factors.

(1) The most prominent and influential factor was the attitude of the United States of America towards

[1] Martens, *R.*, viii. p. 706.
[2] Martens, *R.*, viii. p. 710.
[3] Martens, *N.R.*, i. p. 484.

neutrality from 1793 to 1818. When England in 1793 joined the war which had broken out in 1792 between the so-called First Coalition and France, Genêt, the French diplomatic envoy accredited to the United States, granted letters of marque to American merchantmen manned by American citizens in American ports. These privateers were destined to cruise against English vessels, and French Prize Courts were set up by the French minister in connection with French consulates in American ports. On the complaint of Great Britain, the Government of the United States ordered these privateers to be disarmed and the French Prize Courts to be closed down.[1] As the trial of Gideon Henfield,[2] who was acquitted, proved that the Municipal Law of the United States did not prohibit the enlistment of American citizens in the service of a foreign belligerent, Congress in 1794 passed an Act temporarily forbidding American citizens from accepting letters of marque from a foreign belligerent or enlisting in the army or navy of a foreign State, and forbidding the fitting out and arming of vessels intended as privateers for foreign belligerents. Other Acts were passed from time to time. Finally, on April 20, 1818, Congress passed a Foreign Enlistment Act, which contained provisions intended to be permanent, and was the basis of the British Foreign Enlistment Act of 1819. Thus the United States initiated the present practice, according to which it is the duty of neutrals to prevent the fitting out and arming on their territory of cruisers for belligerents, to prevent enlistment on their territory for belligerents, and the like.

(2) Of great importance became the permanent neutralisation of Switzerland and Belgium. These States naturally adopted, and retained, throughout every war during that century an exemplary attitude

[1] See Wharton, iii. §§ 395-396. [2] See Taylor, § 609.

of impartiality towards the belligerents; and each time war broke out in their vicinity, they took effectual military measures to prevent belligerents from using their neutral territory and resources.

(3) The third factor was the Declaration of Paris of 1856, which incorporated into International Law the rule 'free ship, free goods,' the rule that neutral goods on enemy ships cannot be appropriated, and the rule that blockades must be effective.

(4) The fourth factor was the general development of the military and naval resources of all members of the Family of Nations. As during the second half of the nineteenth century, all the larger States were obliged to keep their armies and navies in constant readiness for war, it followed that, whenever war broke out, each belligerent was anxious not to injure neutral States lest they should take the part of the enemy. On the other hand, neutral States were always anxious to fulfil the duties of neutrality for fear of being drawn into the war. Thus the general rule, that the development of International Law has been fostered by the interests of the members of the Family of Nations, applies also to neutrality. Unless it had been to the interest of belligerents to remain during war on good terms with neutrals, and to the interest of neutrals not to be drawn into war, the institution of neutrality would never have developed so favourably as it actually did during the nineteenth century.

Neutrality in the Twentieth Century.

§ 292. This development continued up to the outbreak of the World War in 1914. The South African and Russo-Japanese Wars produced several incidents which gave occasion for the Second Hague Conference of 1907 to bring neutrality within the range of its deliberations, and to agree upon Convention v. respecting the Rights and Duties of Neutral Powers and Persons in War on Land,[1] and Convention XIII. respecting the Rights and Duties of Neutral Powers in Naval War.[2] Moreover, some of the other conventions agreed upon at this conference, although they do not directly concern neutral Powers, are indirectly of great importance to them. Thus Convention VII. relative to the Conversion of Merchant-ships into War-ships indirectly concerns neutral trade as well as the Convention VIII. relative to the Laying of Automatic Submarine Contact Mines, and Convention XI. relative to certain Restrictions on the Exercise of the Right of Capture. By Convention XII. the conference agreed upon the establishment of an International Prize Court to serve as a Court of Appeal from decisions of the Prize Courts of either belligerent which concerned the interests of neutral Powers or their subjects. But this convention secured no ratifications, and in order to find a basis of generally accepted prize law on which the proposed court might found its judgments, a Naval Conference of London met in 1908, and in 1909 produced the Declaration of London concerning the laws of naval war, which represented a code comprising rules respecting blockade, contraband, unneutral service, destruction of neutral prizes, transfer to neutral flag, enemy character, convoy, resistance to search and compensation.

During the Turco-Italian War, the first naval war

[1] All the States represented at the conference signed this convention except China and Nicaragua, which acceded later, and at least twenty-three States have ratified it. But Great Britain entered a reservation against Articles 16-18 (see above, § 88), and Argentina against Article 18, and Great Britain has not ratified. See above, vol. i. § 568*a*; and Lémonon, pp. 407-425; Higgins, pp. 290-294; Boidin, pp. 121-134; Nippold, § 25; Scott, *Conferences*, pp. 541-555; Bustamante in *A.J.*, ii. (1908), pp. 95-120.

[2] This convention was signed by all the Powers represented at the conference, except the United States of America, China, Cuba, Nicaragua, and Spain; but the United States, China, and Nicaragua acceded later. At least twenty Powers have ratified, but there are a number of reservations. See above, vol. i. § 568*a*; and Lémonon, pp. 555-603; Higgins, pp. 457-483; Bernsten, § 13; Boidin, pp. 237-247; Dupuis, *Guerre*, Nos. 277-330; Nippold, § 34; Scott, *Conferences*, pp. 620-648; Hyde in *A.J.*, ii. (1908), pp. 507-527.

fought after the declaration had been drawn up, both belligerents complied with it, although it had not been ratified by any Power, and Turkey was not even a signatory. When the World War came, the declaration was still unratified; but the United States of America at once invited both groups of belligerents to adopt it, although it had not become legally binding. Germany and Austria-Hungary agreed on condition that their enemies did the same; but Great Britain, France, and Russia were only prepared to adopt the declaration with certain modifications.[1] This they in fact did during the first part of the war. Great Britain, for example, by an Order in Council of August 20, 1914,[2] put the declaration into force, rejecting, however, its lists of contraband, and modifying its rules as to false papers,[3] destination of contraband,[4] and knowledge of the existence of a blockade.[5] This order also directed the courts to regard the General Report of the Drafting Committee as an authoritative statement of the meaning and intention of the declaration.[6] For the order of August 20, 1914, a new order was substituted on October 29, 1914.[7] By this new order the declaration remained in force, but with additional modifications as to the carriage of contraband [8] and without any direction as to the General Report. A further order of October 20, 1915,[9] withdrew Article 57, which provided that the neutral or enemy character of a vessel was to be determined by the flag which she was entitled to fly; [10] and an order of March 30, 1916,[11]

[1] Above, vol. i. § 50*a*; *A.J.*, ix. (1915), Special Supplement, pp. 1-8.

[2] The Declaration of London Order in Council (No. 1), 1914; *London Gazette*, August 21, 1914.

[3] See below, § 404.

[4] See below, § 403*a*.

[5] See below, § 384.

[6] See above, vol. i. § 554 (8).

[7] The Declaration of London Order in Council (No. 2), 1914; *London Gazette*, October 30, 1914.

[8] See below, § 403*a*.

[9] The Declaration of London Order in Council, 1915; *London Gazette*, October 26, 1915.

[10] See above, § 89.

[11] The Declaration of London Order in Council, 1916; *London Gazette*, March 31, 1916.

withdrew Article 19, relating to capture for breach of blockade,[1] and made further modifications in the rules as to contraband.

This was the last of the Declaration of London Orders in Council. For by a joint memorandum of July 7, 1916,[2] Great Britain and France notified the neutral Powers that, whereas at the beginning of the war the Allied Governments had adopted the declaration because it seemed to present in its main lines a statement of the rights and duties of belligerents based on the experience of previous naval wars, as the World War had developed it became clear that its rules, while not in all respects improving the safeguards afforded to neutrals, did not provide belligerents with the most effective means of exercising their admitted rights. These rules, they argued, could not stand the strain imposed by the test of rapidly changing conditions and tendencies which could not have been foreseen, and they had therefore come to the conclusion that they must confine themselves simply to applying the historic and admitted rules of the Law of Nations. In pursuance of this policy Great Britain, by the Maritime Rights Order in Council of July 7, 1916,[3] withdrew all the Declaration of London Orders in Council, declared that she would exercise her belligerent rights at sea in strict accordance with the Law of Nations, and laid down four special rules with regard to contraband[4] and continuous voyage.[5]

From July 7, 1916, therefore, the Declaration of London was no longer applied, even in part, and it still remains unratified.[6] Uncertainties in maritime

[1] See below, § 385*a*.

[2] *Parl. Papers*, Misc., No. 22 (1916), Cd. 8293; and above, vol. i. § 50*a*.

[3] *Ibid.* and *London Gazette*, July 11, 1916.

[4] See below, §§ 391-406*a*.

[5] See below, §§ 385*a*, 403*a*.

[6] For the arguments for and against ratification as they appeared before the World War, see Smith, *International Law*, 4th ed. (1911), pp. 353-371, and the literature cited above, vol. i. § 568*b* n.

law, which the declaration was intended to abolish, were before the war regarded as among the chief obstacles to the proposed International Prize Court, and as many uncertainties still exist to-day. There is, therefore, no hope of seeing that court established, unless another attempt to codify prize law proved to be more successful than the attempt made at the Naval Conference of London.

Apart from the fate of the Declaration of London, the World War wrought many changes in current conceptions of neutrality. All the Great Powers and very many others took part in the fighting, and among their war-tried peoples the view was widely held that a neutral 'shirks his share of the burden of humanity.' Such an attitude was natural enough in the circumstances, but may well disappear in years to come. More enduring perhaps will be the lesson then learned that in a protracted modern war the position of neutrals becomes hardly more tolerable than that of belligerents, while the increased value of neutral support, and the great efforts which the belligerents will make to obtain it, may make a policy of neutrality more difficult to follow. Moreover, it is now understood that to make neutrality easy is not necessarily to lessen the danger of war, because a State may be encouraged to begin hostilities by a conviction that its neighbours will stand aside.

Reflections such as these may have inspired Article 16 of the Covenant of the League of Nations, which would abolish neutrality in all wars in which the League takes part. Accordingly, the institution of neutrality has entered upon a new phase, and might in future find a place only in wars waged apart from the League. Whether such wars will be many or few cannot yet be foretold.

II

CHARACTERISTICS OF NEUTRALITY

Grotius, iii. c. 17, § 3—Bynkershoek, *Quaestiones Juris publici*, i. c. 9—Vattel, iii. §§ 103-104—Hall, §§ 19-20—Lawrence, § 222—Westlake, ii. pp. 190-198—Phillimore, iii. §§ 136-137—Hershey, No. 447—Halleck, ii. p. 161—Taylor, § 614—Moore, vii. §§ 1287-1291—Walker, § 54—Wheaton, § 412—Bluntschli, §§ 742-744—Heffter, § 144—Geffcken in *Holtzendorff*, iv. pp. 605-606—Gareis, § 87—Liszt, § 42—Ullmann, § 190—Bonfils, Nos. 1441 and 1443—Despagnet, No. 686—Rivier, ii. pp. 368-370—Pradier-Fodéré, viii. Nos. 3222-3224, 3232-3233—Nys, iii. pp. 547-559—Calvo, iv. §§ 2491-2493—Fiore, iii. Nos. 1536-1541, and *Code*, Nos. 1791-1798—Martens, ii. § 129—Dupuis, Nos. 316—Mérignhac, iii[a]. pp. 496-509—Pillet, pp. 273-275—Heilborn, *System*, pp. 336-351—Perels § 38—Testa, pp. 167-172—Kleen, i. §§ 1-4—Hautefeuille, i. pp. 195-200—Gessner, pp. 22-23—Schopfer, *Le Principe juridique de la Neutralité et son Évolution dans l'Histoire de la Guerre* (1894)—Lifschütz in *Z.I.*, xxvii. (1918), pp. 40-124.

Conception of Neutrality.

§ 293. Such States as do not take part in a war between other States are neutrals.[1] The term 'neutrality' is derived from the Latin *neuter*. Neutrality may be defined as *the attitude of impartiality adopted by third States towards belligerents and recognised by belligerents, such attitude creating rights and duties between the impartial States and the belligerents.* Whether or not a third State will adopt an attitude of impartiality at the outbreak of war is not a matter for International Law but for International Politics. Therefore, unless a previous treaty stipulates it expressly, no duty exists for a State, according to International Law, to remain neutral when war breaks out. Every sovereign State, as an independent member of the Family of Nations, is master of its own resolutions, and the question of remaining neutral or not at the outbreak of war is, in absence of a treaty stipulating otherwise, one of policy and not of law. However, all States which do not

[1] Grotius (iii. c. 17) calls them *medii in bello*; Bynkershoek (i. c. 9) *non hostes qui neutrarum partium sunt.*

expressly declare the contrary by word or action, are supposed to be neutral, and the rights and duties arising from neutrality come into existence, and remain in existence, through the mere fact of a State taking up an attitude of impartiality, and not being drawn into the war by the belligerents. A special assertion of intention to remain neutral is not therefore legally necessary on the part of neutral States, although they often expressly and formally proclaim [1] their neutrality.

Neutrality an Attitude of Impartiality.

§ 294. Since neutrality is an attitude of impartiality, it excludes such assistance and succour to one of the belligerents as is detrimental to the other, and, further, such injuries to the one as benefit the other. But it requires, on the other hand, active measures from neutral States. For neutrals must prevent belligerents from making use of their neutral territories, and of their resources, for military and naval purposes during the war. This applies not only to actual fighting on neutral territories, but also to the transport of troops, war materials, and provisions for the troops, the fitting out of men-of-war and privateers, the activity of Prize Courts, and the like. Further, neutrals must prevent each belligerent from interfering with their legitimate intercourse with the other belligerent through commerce and the like, because a belligerent cannot be expected passively to suffer vital damage resulting to him from the violation by his enemy of a rule which, while it operates directly in favour of neutrals, indirectly operates in his favour as well.

But it is important to remember that the necessary attitude of impartiality is not incompatible with sympathy with one belligerent, and antipathy against the other, so long as these feelings do not find expression in actions violating impartiality. Thus, not only public opinion and the press of a neutral State, but also its

[1] See below, § 309.

Government,[1] may show their sympathy to one party or another without thereby violating neutrality. Moreover, acts of humanity on the part of neutrals and their subjects, such as the sending to military hospitals of doctors, medicine, provisions, dressing material, and the like, and the sending of clothes and money to prisoners of war, can never be construed as acts of partiality, even if these comforts are provided for the wounded and the prisoners of one belligerent only.

Again, the necessary attitude of impartiality due to the fact that neutrals have nothing to do with quarrels between the belligerents, does not compel them to remain inactive when a belligerent in carrying on hostilities violates the rules of International Law. On the contrary, as has been pointed out above,[2] neutrals have then a *right* to intervene, although—as the law stands at present—they have no duty to do so.

Neutrality an Attitude creating Rights and Duties.

§ 295. Since neutrality is an attitude during a state of war only, it calls into existence special rights and duties which do not generally obtain. They come into existence through the outbreak of war having been notified, or having otherwise [3] unmistakably become known to third States who take up an attitude of impartiality, and are not dragged into the war by the belligerents; they expire *ipso facto* with the termination of the war, or with the outbreak of war between neutrals and a belligerent.

Rights and duties deriving from neutrality do not exist before the outbreak of war, although it may be expected every moment. Even a so-called neutralised State, like Switzerland, has during time of peace no duties connected with neutrality, although as a neutralised State

[1] See, however, Geffcken in *Holtzendorff*, iv. p. 656, and Frankenbach, *Die Rechtsstellung von neutralen Staatsangehorigen in kriegführenden Staaten* (1910), p. 53, who assert the contrary.

[2] vol. i. § 135 (4); vol. ii. § 246.

[3] See Article 2 of Hague Convention III.

it has even then certain duties. These duties are not duties connected with neutrality, but duties imposed upon the neutralised State as a condition of its neutralisation. They include restrictions for the purpose of safeguarding the neutralised State from being drawn into war.[1]

Neutrality an Attitude of States.

§ 296. As International Law is a law between States only and exclusively, neutrality is an attitude of impartiality on the part of *States*, and not on the part of individuals.[2] Individuals derive neither rights nor duties, according to International Law, from the neutrality of those States whose subjects they are. Neutral States are indeed obliged by International Law to prevent their subjects from committing certain acts, but the duty of these subjects to comply with such injunctions of their sovereigns is a duty imposed upon them by Municipal Law, not by International Law. Belligerents, on the other hand, are indeed permitted by International Law to punish subjects of neutrals for breach of blockade, for carriage of contraband, and for rendering unneutral service to the enemy; but the duty of subjects of neutrals to comply with these injunctions of belligerents is a duty imposed upon them by these very injunctions of the belligerents, and not by International Law. Although as a rule a State has no jurisdiction over foreign subjects on the open sea,[3] International Law gives each belligerent an exceptional right to punish foreign subjects by confiscation of cargo, and in certain circumstances of the vessel itself, in case their vessels break blockade, carry contraband, or render unneutral service to the enemy; but punish-

[1] See above, vol. i. § 96.

[2] It is inaccurate to speak (as is commonly done in certain cases) of individuals as being neutral. For instance, Article 16 of Hague Convention v. designates the nationals of a State which is not taking part in a war as 'neutrals.' Again, belligerents occupying enemy territory frequently compel enemy individuals who are not members of the armed forces of the enemy to take a so-called 'oath of neutrality.'

[3] See above, vol. i. § 146.

ment[1] is threatened and executed by the belligerents, not by International Law. Therefore, if neutral merchantmen commit such acts, they neither violate neutrality nor do they act against International Law; they simply violate injunctions of the belligerents concerned. If they choose to run the risk of punishment in the form of losing their property, this is their own concern, and their neutral home State need not prevent them from doing so. But to the right of belligerents to punish subjects of neutrals for the acts specified corresponds the duty of neutral States to acquiesce in the exercise of this right by either belligerent.

Apart from carriage of contraband, breach of blockade, and unneutral service to the enemy, which a belligerent may punish by capturing and confiscating the vessels or goods concerned, subjects of neutrals are perfectly free in their movements, and neutral States have in particular no duty to prevent their subjects from selling arms, munitions, and provisions to a belligerent, from enlisting in his forces, and the like.

No Cessation of Intercourse during Neutrality between Neutrals and Belligerents.

§ 297. Neutrality as an attitude of impartiality involves the duty of abstaining from assisting either belligerent whether actively or passively; but it does not involve a duty to break off all intercourse with the belligerents. Apart from certain restrictions necessitated by impartiality, all intercourse between belligerents and neutrals takes place as before, a condition of peace prevailing between them in spite of the war between the belligerents. This applies particularly to the working of treaties, to diplomatic intercourse, and to trade. But indirectly, of course, the condition of

[1] Schramm, pp. 39-41, argues against the general opinion that confiscation of vessel and cargo for breach of blockade, carriage of contraband, and the like, bears the character of punishment. He overlooks the fact that such confiscation is not a punishment threatened by International Law, but only by the belligerents, who by International Law are permitted to inflict it.

war between belligerents may have a disturbing influence upon intercourse between belligerents and neutrals. Thus the treaty rights of a neutral State may be interfered with through occupation of enemy territory by a belligerent; its subjects living on enemy territory bear in a sense enemy character; its subjects trading with the belligerents are hampered by the right of visit and search, and the right of the belligerents to capture blockade-runners and contraband of war.

§ 298. Since neutrality is an attitude during war, the question arises as to the necessary attitude of foreign States towards civil war. As civil war becomes real war through recognition[1] of the insurgents as a belligerent Power, a distinction must be made between cases where recognition has taken place and those where it has not. There is no doubt that a foreign State commits an international delinquency by assisting insurgents in spite of being at peace with the legitimate Government. But matters are different after recognition. The insurgents are then a belligerent Power, and the civil war is then real war. Foreign States can either become a party to the war or remain neutral, and in the latter case all the duties and rights of neutrality devolve upon them. Since, however, recognition may be granted by foreign States independently of the attitude of the legitimate Government, and since recognition granted by the legitimate Government is not binding upon foreign Governments, it may happen that insurgents are granted recognition by the legitimate Government while foreign States refuse it, and *vice versa*.[2] In the first case, the rights and duties of neutrality devolve upon foreign States as far as the legitimate Government is concerned. Its men-of-war may visit and search their merchantmen for contraband;

Neutrality an Attitude during War (Neutrality in Civil War).

[1] See above, §§ 59 and 76, and Rougier, *Les Guerres civiles et le Droit des Gens* (1903), pp. 414-447.

[2] See above, § 59.

a blockade declared by it is binding upon them, and the like. But no rights and duties of neutrality devolve upon foreign States as regards the insurgents. A blockade declared by them is not binding, and their men-of-war may not visit and search merchantmen for contraband. On the other hand, if insurgents are recognised by a foreign State but not by the legitimate Government, that foreign State has all the rights and duties of neutrality so far as the insurgents are concerned, but not so far as the legitimate Government is concerned.[1] In practice, however, recognition of insurgents by foreign States will, if really justified, always cause the legitimate Government to grant recognition also.

Neutrality to be recognised by the Belligerents.

§ 299. Although third States have no duty to remain neutral when war breaks out,[2] and may take up the cause of one of the belligerents, they have a right[3] to demand that neither belligerent should force them into war. A belligerent who, at the outbreak of war, refuses to recognise a third State as a neutral, does not indeed violate neutrality, because neutrality does not come into existence in fact and in law until both belligerents have acquiesced in the attitude of impartiality taken up by third States. For neutrality to come into being it is not sufficient that a third State should take up an attitude of impartiality; it is also necessary that both belligerents should recognise this attitude by acquiescing in it, and not forcing the would-be neutral

[1] See the nine rules regarding the position of foreign States in case of an insurrection, adopted by the Institute of International Law at its meeting at Neuchâtel in 1900 (*Annuaire*, xviii. p. 227). The question whether, if foreign States refuse recognition to insurgents, although the legitimate Government has granted it, the legitimate Government has a right of visit and search for contraband, is controversial; see *Annuaire*, xviii. pp. 213-216.

[2] See above, § 293.

[3] The doctrine propounded by me in the previous editions of this work, and also by other writers, that third States have no right to demand to be neutral, cannot be upheld in face of the modern development of the institution of neutrality.

to take part in the war.[1] But the Law of Nations in its present development objects to a would-be neutral State being forced into war, and a belligerent who refuses to recognise it as neutral violates International Law, although not neutrality.

But though the acquiescence of belligerents in the attitude of impartiality taken up by third States is necessary to bring neutrality into existence, this does not mean, as has been maintained,[2] that neutrality is based on a contract concluded either *expressis verbis*, or by unmistakable actions, between both belligerents and third States, with the consequence that a third State might at the outbreak of war take up the position of being neither neutral nor a party to the war, and thereby reserve for itself freedom of action for the future. Since the normal relation between the members of the Family of Nations is peace, when war breaks out between some of the members, the others become neutrals *ipso facto* by taking up an attitude of impartiality and by not being treated by the belligerents as parties to the war. It is not a contract that calls neutrality into existence; it is rather the legal consequence of a certain attitude on the part of third States on the one hand, and the belligerents on the other, taken up at the outbreak of war.

Once third States have taken up an attitude of impartiality and the belligerents have recognised it, neutrality exists in fact and in law, and belligerents as well as neutrals violate neutrality if they commit any act incompatible with it.[3] Belligerents, therefore, violate it if at any time afterwards they declare war upon a neutral State just because it does not serve their

[1] History records several cases in which States which intended to be neutral were compelled by one or both belligerents to throw in their lot with one or the other.

[2] See Heilborn, *System*, pp. 347, 350.

[3] See above, § 293, and below, § 312.

purpose any longer to acquiesce in its neutrality. Likewise, a neutral violates neutrality if at any time afterwards he declares war upon a belligerent just because it does not suit his purpose any longer to remain neutral. Yet, although in such cases a declaration of war is *ipso facto* a violation of neutrality, neutrality is nevertheless thereby brought to an end, and thenceforth the former neutral is a belligerent with all the rights granted to him and all the duties imposed upon him by International Law.[1]

III

DIFFERENT KINDS OF NEUTRALITY

Vattel, iii. §§ 101, 105, 107, 110—Westlake, ii. pp. 206-207—Phillimore, iii. §§ 138-139—Halleck, ii. p. 142—Taylor, § 618—Wheaton, §§ 413-425—Bluntschli, §§ 745-748—Geffcken in *Holtzendorff*, iv. pp. 634-636—Ullmann, § 190—Despagnet, Nos. 685, 686—Pradier-Fodéré, viii. Nos. 3225-3231—Rivier, ii. pp. 376-379—Calvo, iv. §§ 2592-2642—Fiore, iii. Nos. 1542-1545—Mérignhac, iii[a]. 509-512—Pillet, pp. 277-284—Kleen, i. §§ 6-22.

Perpetual Neutrality.

§ 300. The very first distinction to be made between different kinds of neutrality is that between perpetual neutrality and other neutrality. Perpetual or permanent neutrality is the neutrality of States which are neutralised by special treaties of the members of the Family of Nations, as at the present time is Switzerland. Apart from the duties arising from their neutralisation which are to be performed in time of peace as well as in war, the duties and rights of neutrality are the same for them as for other States. This applies not only to the obligation not to assist either belligerent, but also to the obligation to prevent both from using the neutral territory for their military purposes. Thus, Switzerland in 1870 and 1871, during the Franco-

[1] The assertion that a declaration of war which is *ipso facto* a violation of International Law is not operative, has been refuted above, § 61.

German War, properly prevented the transport of troops, recruits, and war material of either belligerent over her territory, disarmed the French army which had saved itself by crossing the Swiss frontier, and detained its members until the conclusion of peace.[1]

General and Partial Neutrality.

§ 301. The next distinction is between general and partial neutrality which derives from the fact that a part of the territory of a State may be neutralised,[2] as are, for instance, the Ionian Islands of Corfu and Paxo, which are part of the territory of Greece. Such a State has a duty always to remain partially neutral—namely, as far as its neutralised part is concerned. General neutrality, on the other hand, is the neutrality of States no part of whose territory is neutralised by treaty.

Voluntary and Conventional Neutrality.

§ 302. A third distinction is that between voluntary and conventional neutrality. Voluntary (or simple or natural) is the neutrality of a State which is not bound by a general or special treaty to remain neutral in a certain war. Neutrality is in most cases voluntary. On the other hand, the neutrality of a State by treaty bound to remain neutral in a war is conventional. Of course, the neutrality of neutralised States is in every case conventional; States which are not neutralised can also be obliged by treaty to remain neutral in a particular war, just as they can by treaty of alliance be obliged not to remain neutral, but to take the part of one of the belligerents.

Armed Neutrality.

§ 303. One speaks of an armed neutrality when a neutral State takes military measures for the purpose of defending its neutrality against possible or probable attempts by either belligerent to make use of the neutral territory. Thus, the neutrality of Switzerland during the Franco-German War was an armed neutrality. The

[1] See below, § 339.

[2] See above, § 72. As to the occupation of Corfu by the Allies during the World War, see Garner, ii. § 464.

term 'armed neutrality' is also used, and in a different sense, when neutral States take military measures for the purpose of defending the real or pretended rights of neutrals against threatened infringements by either belligerent. The First and Second Armed Neutralities[1] of 1780 and 1800 were armed neutralities in the latter sense of the term.

Benevolent Neutrality.

§ 304. Treaties stipulating neutrality often provide for a 'benevolent' neutrality in a certain war. The term is likewise frequently used during diplomatic negotiations. However, there is now no distinction between benevolent neutrality and neutrality pure and simple.[2] The idea dates from earlier times, when the obligations imposed by neutrality were not so stringent, and neutral States could favour one of the belligerents in many ways without thereby violating their neutral attitude. If a State remained neutral in the lax sense in which neutrality was then understood, but otherwise favoured a belligerent, its neutrality was called benevolent.

Perfect and Qualified Neutrality.

§ 305. A distinction of great practical importance in former times was that between perfect, or absolute, and qualified, or imperfect, neutrality. The neutrality of a State was qualified if it remained neutral on the whole, but actively or passively, directly or indirectly, gave some kind of assistance to one of the belligerents in consequence of an obligation entered into by a treaty previous to the war, and not for that particular war exclusively. On the other hand, neutrality was termed perfect if a neutral State neither actively nor passively, neither directly nor indirectly, favoured either belligerent. There is no doubt that, in the eighteenth century, when it was recognised that a State could be considered neutral, although it was by a previous treaty

[1] See above, §§ 289, 290.

[2] As to the neutrality of Greece during part of the World War, see below, p. 435.

bound to render more or less limited assistance to one of the belligerents, this distinction between neutrality perfect and qualified was justified.[1] But, during the second half of the nineteenth century, it became controversial whether so-called qualified neutrality was neutrality at all, or whether a State, which, in fulfilment of a treaty obligation, rendered some assistance to one of the belligerents, violated its neutrality. The majority of modern writers[2] maintained, correctly I think, that a State was either neutral or not, and that it violated its neutrality if it rendered any assistance whatever to a belligerent from any motive whatever. In this case, a State which had entered into such obligations as those just mentioned would in time of war frequently have conflicting duties; in fulfilling its treaty obligations, it would frequently be obliged to violate its duty of neutrality, and *vice versa*. Several writers,[3] on the other hand, maintained that such a fulfilment of treaty obligations would not constitute a violation of neutrality. All doubt in the matter ought now to have been removed, since Article 2 of Hague Convention v. categorically enacts that 'belligerents are forbidden to move across the territory of a neutral Power troops or convoys either of munitions of war or of supplies.' The principle at the back of this enactment no doubt is that a qualified neutrality has no longer any *raison d'être*, and that neutrality must in every case be perfect.[4]

[1] See Nys in *R.I.*, 2nd Ser. xv. (1913), pp. 173-181.

[2] See, for instance, Ullmann, § 190; Despagnet, No. 686; Rivier, ii. p. 378; Calvo, iv. § 2594; Taylor, § 618; Fiore, iii. No. 1541; Kleen, i. § 21; Hall, § 215 (see also Hall, § 219, concerning passage of troops). Phillimore, iii. § 138, goes with the majority of publicists, but in § 139 he thinks that it would be too rigid to consider acts of 'minor' partiality which are the result of conventions previous to the war as violations of neutrality.

[3] See, for instance, Heffter, § 144; Manning, p. 225; Wheaton, §§ 425-427; Bluntschli, § 746; Halleck, ii. p. 142.

[4] See above, § 77, where it has been pointed out that a neutral who takes up an attitude of qualified neutrality may nowadays be considered as an accessory belligerent party to the war.

Some Historical Examples of Qualified Neutrality.

§ 306. For the purpose of illustration, the following instances of qualified neutrality may be mentioned :—

(1) By a Treaty of Amity and Commerce concluded in 1778 between the United States of America and France, the United States granted to French privateers and their prizes the right of admission to American ports during war, and undertook not to admit the privateers of the enemies of France. When in 1793, during war between England and France, England complained of the admission of French privateers to American ports, the United States met the complaint by advancing their treaty obligations.[1]

(2) Denmark had by several treaties, especially by a treaty of 1781, undertaken to furnish Russia with a certain number of men-of-war and troops. In 1788, during war between Russia and Sweden, Denmark fulfilled her obligations towards Russia, and nevertheless declared herself neutral; although Sweden protested against the possibility of such qualified neutrality, she acquiesced, and did not consider herself at war with Denmark.[2]

(3) In 1848, during war between Germany and Denmark, Great Britain, fulfilling a treaty obligation towards Denmark, prohibited the exportation of arms to Germany, but permitted exportation to Denmark.[3]

(4) In 1900, during the South African War, Portugal, to comply with a treaty obligation[4] towards Great Britain regarding the passage of British troops through Portuguese territory in South Africa, allowed the passage of an English force which had landed at Beira[5] and was destined for Rhodesia.

(5) In 1915, during the World War, British and

[1] See Wheaton, § 425, and Phillimore, iii. § 139.

[2] See Phillimore, iii. § 140.

[3] See Geffcken in *Holtzendorff*, iv. p. 610, and Rivier, n. p. 379.

[4] Article 11 of the treaty between Great Britain and Portugal concerning the delimitation of spheres of influence in Africa. Martens, *N.R.G.*, 2nd Ser. xviii. p. 185.

[5] See below, § 323; Baty, *International Law in South Africa* (1900), p. 75; and *The Times History of the War in South Africa*, iv. p. 366.

French troops were landed at Salonika, which was part of the territory of Greece, then neutral, in order to aid Serbia, which was also an ally of Greece. Greece protested, but did not oppose the landing.[1]

IV

COMMENCEMENT AND END OF NEUTRALITY

Hall, § 207—Westlake, ii. pp. 208-210—Phillimore, i. §§ 392-392[a], iii. §§ 146-149—Taylor, §§ 610-611—Wheaton, §§ 437-439, and Dana's note 215—Heffter, § 145—Bonfils, Nos. 1445-1446—Despagnet, No. 689—Pradier-Fodéré, viii. Nos. 3234-3237—Rivier, ii. pp. 379-381—Martens, ii. § 138—Kleen, i. §§ 5, 36-42.

Neutrality commences with Knowledge of the War.

§ 307. Since neutrality is an attitude of impartiality deliberately taken up by a State and acquiesced in by the belligerents, it cannot begin before the outbreak of war becomes known. It is only then that third States can make up their minds whether or not they intend to remain neutral. As soon as they determine to adopt an attitude of impartiality, and the belligerents acquiesce in their choice, the duties deriving from neutrality are incumbent upon them. It has long been the usual practice of belligerents to notify the outbreak of war to third States so as to enable them to make their decision, but formerly this was not in strict law necessary. Knowledge of the outbreak of war, however obtained, gave a third State an opportunity of coming to a decision, and, if it remained neutral, its neutrality dated from the time when it first knew of the outbreak of war. But it is apparent that an immediate notification of war by belligerents is of great importance, as excluding all doubt and controversy regarding knowledge of the outbreak of war. For it must always be remembered that a neutral State may in no way be made responsible for acts of its own or of its subjects which have been performed before it knew of the war, although the

[1] Garner, ii. § 466.

outbreak of war might have been expected. For this reason Article 2 of Hague Convention III. enacted that belligerents must without delay send a notification of the outbreak of war [1] to neutral Powers, and that the condition of war should not take effect in regard to neutral Powers until after receipt of a notification, unless it was established beyond doubt that they were in fact aware of its outbreak.[2]

Commencement of Neutrality in Civil War.

§ 308. As civil war becomes real war through recognition of the insurgents as a belligerent Power, neutrality during a civil war begins for every foreign State from the moment recognition is granted.[3]

Establishment of Neutrality by Declarations.

§ 309. Neutrality being an attitude of States creating rights and duties, active measures on the part of a neutral state are required for the purpose of preventing its officials and subjects from committing acts incompatible with its duty of impartiality. Now, the manifesto by which a neutral State orders its organs and subjects to comply with the attitude of impartiality adopted by itself is called a 'declaration of neutrality' in the special sense of the term. Such a declaration must not, however, be confounded with manifestoes by the belligerents proclaiming to neutrals the rights and duties devolving upon them through neutrality, or with the assertions made by neutrals to belligerents or *urbi et orbi* that they will remain neutral, although these manifestoes and assertions are often also called declarations of neutrality.[4]

Municipal Neutrality Laws.

§ 310. International Law leaves it to the discretion of each State to take the measures necessary to ensure neutrality. Since in constitutional States the powers

[1] It may even be made by telegraph.

[2] See above, §§ 94, 95.

[3] That recognition may be granted or refused by foreign States independently of the attitude of the legitimate Government has been stated above, § 298, where an explanation is also given of the consequences of recognition granted, either by foreign States alone, or by the legitimate Government alone.

[4] See above, § 293.

of Governments are frequently so limited by Municipal Law that they may not take adequate measures without the consent of their parliaments, and since, so far as International Law is concerned, it is no excuse for a Government to plead that its Municipal Law prevents it from taking adequate measures, several States have once for all enacted so-called Neutrality Laws, which prescribe the attitude to be taken up by their officials and subjects in case they remain neutral in a war. These Neutrality Laws are latent in time of peace; but their provisions become operative *ipso facto* by the respective States making a declaration of neutrality to their officials and subjects.

British Foreign Enlistment Act.

§ 311. The United States of America enacted[1] a Neutrality Law on April 20, 1818; Great Britain followed her example in 1819 by passing a Foreign Enlistment Act,[2] which was in force till 1870. As this Act did not give adequate powers to the Government, Parliament passed on August 9, 1870, a new Foreign Enlistment Act,[3] which is still in force. This Act, in the event of British neutrality, prohibits: (1) the enlistment by a British subject in the military or naval service of either belligerent, and similar acts (§§ 4-7); (2) the building, equipping,[4]

[1] Printed in Phillimore, i. pp. 667-672. On the resolution of Congress of March 4, 1915, see *A.J.*, ix. (1915), pp. 490-493. See also the Act 'to punish Acts of Interference with the Foreign Relations, the Neutrality, and the Foreign Commerce of the United States, etc.,' passed on June 15, 1917 (*A.J.*, xi. (1917), Supplement, pp. 178-198).

[2] 59 Geo. iii. c. 69.

[3] 33 & 34 Vict. c. 90. See Sibley in the *Law Magazine and Review*, xxix. (1904), pp. 454-467, and xxx. (1905), pp. 37-53.

[4] According to § 30, the interpretation clause of the Act, 'equipping' includes 'the furnishing a ship with any tackle, apparel, furniture, provisions, arms, munitions, or stores, or any other thing which is used in or about a ship for the purpose of fitting or adapting her for the sea or for naval service.' It is, therefore, not lawful for British ships, in case Great Britain is neutral, to supply a belligerent fleet direct with coal. Thus during the Russo-Japanese War, while German steamers laden with coal followed the Russian fleet on her journey to the Far East, British shipowners were prevented from doing the same by the Foreign Enlistment Act. It was under this Act that in 1904 the British Government ordered the detention of the German steamer *Captain W. Menzel*, which had

and despatching[1] of vessels for employment in the military or naval service of either belligerent (§§ 8-9); (3) the increase by any individual living on British territory of the armament of a man-of-war of either belligerent being at the time in a British port (§ 10); (4) the preparing or fitting out of a naval or military expedition against a friendly State (§ 11).

The British Foreign Enlistment Act goes beyond the requirements of International Law, in so far as it tries to prohibit and penalises a number of acts which, according to the present rules of International Law, a neutral State is not required to prohibit and penalise. Thus, for instance, a neutral State need not prohibit its private subjects from enlisting in the service of a belligerent; from supplying coal, provisions, arms, and ammunition direct to a belligerent fleet, provided that the fleet is not within, or just outside, the territorial waters of that neutral; or from selling ships to a belligerent, although it is known that they will be converted into cruisers, or used as transport ships. For Article 7 of Convention v. and Article 7 of Convention XIII. categorically enact that 'a neutral Power is not bound to prevent the export or transit, on behalf of either belligerent, of arms, munitions of war, or, in general, of anything which could be of use to an army or fleet.'

taken on board Welsh coal at Cardiff for the purpose of carrying it to the Russian fleet *en route* to the Far East. See below, § 350.

[1] An interesting case occurred during the Russo-Japanese War. Messrs. Yarrow and Co., the shipbuilders, possessed a partly completed vessel, the *Caroline*, capable of being finally fitted up either as a yacht or as a torpedo boat. In September 1904 a Mr. Sinnet and the Hon. James Burke Roche called at their shipbuilding yard, bought the *Caroline*, and ordered her to be fitted up as a high-speed yacht. The required additions were finished on October 3. On October 6 the vessel left Messrs. Yarrow's yard and was navigated by a Captain Ryder, *via* Hamburg, to the Russian port of Libau, there to be altered into a torpedo boat. That § 8 of the Foreign Enlistment Act applied to this case there is no doubt. But there is also no doubt that it was this Act, and not the rules of International Law, which required the prosecution of Messrs. Sinnet and Roche by the British Government. For, in International Law, the case was merely one of contraband. See below, §§ 321, 334, 397.

§ 312. Neutrality ends with the war, or through a hitherto neutral State beginning war against one of the belligerents, or through one of the belligerents commencing war against a hitherto neutral State. But two classes of cases must be distinguished. **End of Neutrality.**

There is, in the first place, the class of cases in which war breaks out between one of the belligerents and a hitherto neutral State, either (*a*) on account of a dispute not connected with the cause of the war then in progress, or (*b*) because the belligerent has violated fundamental rules of warfare, or (*c*) because either the belligerent or the neutral has committed a violation of neutrality so grave that the injured party considers it necessary to answer it by a declaration of war. In such and similar cases a declaration of war does not *ipso facto* constitute a violation of neutrality.

There is, secondly, the class of cases in which war breaks out between one of the belligerents and a hitherto neutral State simply because it does not suit the belligerent any longer to recognise its impartial attitude, or because it does not suit the neutral to remain neutral any longer. For instance, a belligerent may desire to march troops through a neutral country, and the neutral will not permit this; or a neutral may desire to abandon neutrality although it can find no cause for war in the events which have occurred since it decided to remain neutral. In such cases a declaration of war *ipso facto* constitutes a violation of neutrality because, neutrality having previously come into existence in fact and in law, a neutral ought not to abandon it except for a reason not connected with the cause of the war in progress, nor ought a belligerent to draw the neutral into the war.[1]

[1] See above, § 299. The doctrine propounded by me in the previous editions of this work that a belligerent has no duty to allow a hitherto neutral State to remain neutral, and that a neutral State has no duty to remain neutral, cannot be upheld in face of the modern development of the in-

However this may be, duties of neutrality exist only so long as a State remains neutral. They come to an end *ipso facto* by a neutral State throwing up its neutrality, or by a belligerent beginning war against a hitherto neutral State. Yet the ending of neutrality must not be confounded with mere violation of neutrality. A mere violation does not *ipso facto* bring neutrality to an end.[1]

stitution of neutrality. Once a State has made up its mind to remain neutral and the belligerents have recognised such neutrality, neither party can, without violating neutrality, declare war in case it does not suit its purpose any longer to observe the duties deriving from neutrality.

[1] See below, § 358.

CHAPTER II

RELATIONS BETWEEN BELLIGERENTS AND NEUTRALS

I

RIGHTS AND DUTIES DERIVING FROM NEUTRALITY

Vattel, iii. § 104—Hall, § 214—Phillimore, iii. §§ 136-138—Twiss, ii. § 216—Heffter, § 146—Geffcken in *Holtzendorff*, iv. pp. 656-657—Gareis, § 88—Liszt, § 42—Ullmann, § 191—Bonfils, Nos. 1441-1444—Despagnet, Nos. 684 and 690—Rivier, ii. pp. 381-385—Nys, iii. pp. 560-625—Calvo, iv. §§ 2491-2493—Fiore, iii. Nos. 1501, 1536-1540, and *Code*, Nos. 1799-1801, 1807—Martens, ii. § 131—Kleen, i. §§ 45-46—Mérignhac, iii[a]. pp. 512-516—Pillet, pp. 273-275.

Conduct in general of Neutrals and Belligerents.

§ 313. Neutrality can be carried out only if neutrals as well as belligerents follow a certain line of conduct in their relations with one another. It is for this reason that from neutrality derive rights and duties, for belligerents as well as for neutrals, and that, consequently, neutrality can be violated by both belligerents and neutrals. These rights and duties are correlative :—the duties of neutrals to the rights of the belligerents, and the duties of the belligerents to the rights of the neutrals.

What Rights and Duties of Neutrals and of Belligerents there are.

§ 314. There are two rights and two duties deriving from neutrality for neutrals, and likewise two for belligerents.

Duties of neutrals are, in the first place, to act toward belligerents in accordance with their attitude of impartiality ; and, secondly, to acquiesce in the exercise by either belligerent of the right to punish neutral merchantmen for breach of blockade, carriage of contraband, and rendering unneutral service to the enemy, and, accordingly, to visit, search, and eventually capture them.

The duties of belligerents are, in the first place, to act towards neutrals in accordance with their attitude of impartiality; and, secondly, not to suppress their intercourse, and in particular their commerce, with the enemy.[1]

Either belligerent has a right to demand impartiality from neutrals; on the other hand, neutrals have a right to demand such behaviour from either belligerent as is in accordance with their attitude of impartiality. Neutrals have a right to demand that their intercourse, and in particular their commerce, with the enemy shall not be suppressed; on the other hand, either belligerent has a right to punish subjects of neutrals for breach of blockade, carriage of contraband, and unneutral service, and, accordingly, to visit, search, and capture neutral merchantmen.

Rights and Duties of Neutrals contested.

§ 315. Some writers[2] maintain that no rights derive from neutrality for neutrals, and, consequently, no duties for belligerents, because everything which must be left undone by a belligerent regarding his relations with a neutral must likewise be left undone in time of peace. But this opinion has no foundation. It is true indeed that the majority of the acts which belligerents must leave undone in consequence of their duty to respect neutrality must likewise be left undone in time of peace in consequence of the territorial supremacy of every State. But there are several acts which do not belong to this class—for instance, the non-

[1] All writers on International Law resolve the duty of impartiality incumbent upon neutrals and the duty of belligerents to act toward neutrals in accordance with their impartiality into many distinct duties. In this way quite a large catalogue of duties and corresponding rights is produced, and the whole matter is unnecessarily complicated.

[2] Heffter, § 149; Gareis, § 88; Heilborn, *System*, p. 341.

appropriation of enemy goods on neutral vessels. And those acts which do belong to this class also fall at the same time under another category. Thus, a violation of neutral territory by a belligerent for military and naval purposes of the war is indeed an act prohibited in time of peace, because every State has to respect the territorial supremacy of other States; but it is at the same time a violation of neutrality, and therefore totally different from other violations of foreign territorial supremacy. This becomes quite apparent when the true inwardness of such acts is regarded. For while every State has a right to demand reparation for an ordinary violation of its territorial supremacy, it need not take any notice of it, and it has no duty to demand reparation. But in case a violation of its territorial supremacy constitutes at the same time a violation of its neutrality, the neutral State not only has a right to demand reparation, but has a duty [1] to do so. For, if it did not, it would violate its duty of impartiality by favouring one belligerent to the detriment of the other.[2]

On the other hand, it has been asserted [3] that, apart from conventional neutrality, from which treaty obligations arise, it is incorrect to speak of duties deriving from neutrality, since at any moment during the war neutrals can throw up neutrality and become parties to the war. This assertion is based on the erroneous doctrine [4] that a neutral does not violate neutrality by abandoning his impartial attitude for no other reason than that it no longer serves his purpose to remain neutral. But even if that doctrine were correct, it

[1] See, for instance, Article 3 of Hague Convention XIII. which enacts: 'When a ship has been captured in the territorial waters of a neutral Power, such Power must, if the prize is still within its jurisdiction, employ the means at its disposal to release the prize with its officers and crew, and to intern the prize crew. If the prize is not within the jurisdiction of the neutral Power, the captor Government, on the demand of that Power, must liberate the prize with its officers and crew.'

[2] See below, § 360.

[3] See Gareis, § 88.

[4] See above, §§ 299, 312.

would not follow from it that, so long as a State remained neutral, no duties derived from neutrality.

For to say that duties derive from neutrality only means that, so long as neutrals intend neutrality, and so long as belligerents intend to recognise that neutrality, duties derive from neutrality for both belligerents and neutrals.

Contents of Duty of Impartiality.

§ 316. It has already been stated above,[1] that impartiality *excludes* such assistance and succour to one of the belligerents as is detrimental to the other, and, further, such injuries to one of the belligerents as benefit the other, and that it *includes* active measures on the part of a neutral for the purpose of preventing belligerents from making use of neutral territories and neutral resources for their military and naval purposes, and of preventing either of them from interfering with his legitimate intercourse with the other. But all this does not exhaust the contents of the duty of impartiality.

For, according to the present strict conception of neutrality, the duty of impartiality *excludes* in addition all facilities whatever for military and naval operations of the belligerents, even if granted to both belligerents alike. In former times assistance was not considered a violation of neutrality, provided it was given to both belligerents in the same way, and States were considered neutral although they allowed an equal number of their troops to fight on the side of each belligerent. To-day this could no longer happen. From Hague Conventions V. and XIII., which deal with neutrality in land and sea warfare respectively, it becomes quite apparent that any facility whatever directly concerning military or naval operations, even if it consists only in granting passage over neutral territory to belligerent forces, is illegal, although granted to both belligerents alike. *The*

[1] § 294.

duty of impartiality to-day comprises abstention from any active or passive co-operation with belligerents.

Secondly, the duty of impartiality *includes* in addition the equal treatment of both belligerents regarding such facilities as do not directly concern military or naval operations, and which may, therefore, be granted or refused to belligerents according to the discretion of a neutral. If a neutral grants such facilities to one belligerent, he must grant them to the other in the same degree. If he refuses them to the one, he must likewise refuse them to the other.[1] Thus, since it does not, according to the International Law of the present day, constitute a violation of neutrality for a neutral to allow his subjects to supply either belligerent with arms and ammunition in the ordinary way of trade, it would constitute a violation of neutrality to prohibit the export of arms destined for one of the belligerents only. Thus, further, if a neutral allows men-of-war of one of the belligerents to bring their prizes into neutral ports, he must grant the same facility to the other belligerent.

Duty of Impartiality continuously growing more intense before the World War.

§ 317. Although neutrality has already for centuries been recognised as an attitude of impartiality, it has taken two hundred years for the duty of impartiality to attain its present range and intensity. This continuous development had by no means ceased, but was slowly and gradually going on when the World War broke out. During that war the detailed rules concerning the relations between neutrals and belligerents which result from the duty of a neutral State to be impartial were put to proof, and it will be necessary to discuss them at greater length.[2]

[1] See Articles 7, 8, 9, 11, 13, 14 of Hague Convention v., and Articles 7, 9, 11, 17, 19, 21, 23 of Hague Convention xiii.

[2] See below: Neutrals and Military Operations (§§ 320-328a); Neutrals and Military Preparations (§§ 329-335); Neutral Asylum to Land Forces, War Material and Airmen (§§ 336-341a); Neutral Asylum to Naval Forces (§§ 342-348a); Supplies and Loans to Belligerents (§§ 349-352); Services to Belligerents (§§ 353-356).

Contents of Duty of Belligerents to treat Neutrals in accordance with their Impartiality.

§ 318. On the other hand, the contents of the duty of belligerents to treat neutrals in accordance with their impartiality are so manifest that elaborate treatment is unnecessary. This duty *excludes*, in the first place, any violation of neutral territory for military or naval purposes of the war,[1] and any interference with the legitimate intercourse of neutrals with the enemy; and, secondly, the appropriation of neutral goods, contraband excepted, on enemy vessels.[2] On the other hand, it *includes*, in the first place, due treatment of neutral diplomatic envoys accredited to the enemy and found on occupied enemy territory; and, secondly, due treatment of neutral subjects and neutral property on enemy territory. A belligerent who conquers enemy territory must at least grant to neutral envoys accredited to the enemy the right to quit the occupied territory unmolested.[3] He must likewise abstain from treating neutral subjects and property established on enemy territory more harshly than the laws of war allow; for, although neutral subjects and property, by being established on enemy territory, have acquired enemy character, nevertheless they have not lost the protection of their neutral home State.[4] He must, lastly, pay full damages in case he exercises his right of angary[5] against neutral property in course of transit through enemy territory.

§ 319. The duty of each belligerent not to suppress intercourse between neutrals and the enemy requires no detailed discussion either. It is a duty which is in accordance with the development of the institution of

[1] See Articles 1-4 of Hague Convention v., and Articles 1-5 of Hague Convention xiii.

[2] This is stipulated by the Declaration of Paris of 1856.

[3] The position of foreign envoys found by a belligerent on occupied enemy territory is not settled as regards details. But there is no doubt that a certain consideration is due to them, and that they must at least be granted the right to depart. See above, vol. i. § 399.

[4] See above, § 88.

[5] See below, §§ 364-367.

Contents of Duty not to suppress Intercourse between Neutrals and the Enemy.

neutrality. It is of special importance with regard to commerce of subjects of neutrals with belligerents, since formerly attempts were frequently made to intercept all neutral trade with the enemy although no effective blockade had been established. A consequence of the now recognised freedom of neutral commerce with either belligerent is, in the first place, the rule enacted by the Declaration of Paris of 1856, that enemy goods, with the exception of contraband, on neutral vessels on the open sea or in enemy territorial waters may not be appropriated by a belligerent,[1] and, secondly, the rule, enacted by Article 1 of Hague Convention XI., that the postal correspondence of neutrals or belligerents, except correspondence destined for, or proceeding from, a blockaded port, which may be found on a neutral or enemy vessel at sea, is inviolable.[2] But the recognised freedom of neutral commerce necessitates, on the other hand, certain measures on the part of belligerents. It would be unreasonable to impose on a belligerent a duty not to prevent the subjects of neutrals from breaking a blockade, from carrying contraband, and, lastly, from rendering unneutral service to the enemy. International Law gives, therefore, a right to either belligerent to prevent neutral merchantmen, so far as is in his power, from doing such things, and, accordingly, to visit, search, capture, and confiscate them.[3]

But the duty of a belligerent not to suppress intercourse, and especially legitimate commerce, between neutrals and the enemy has an exception in the case

[1] That not only goods owned by enemy individuals, but also goods owned by the enemy State, ought to be exempt from appropriation when on neutral vessels, has already been pointed out, although the practice of Italy is to the contrary; see above, § 177 n.

[2] See above, § 191, and below, § 411.

[3] That a subject of a neutral State who tries to break a blockade, or carries contraband to the enemy, or renders the enemy unneutral service, violates injunctions of the belligerents, but not International Law, has been shown above in § 296; see also below, §§ 383, 398.

of reprisals. It has been pointed out above[1] that neutrals must prevent each belligerent from interfering with their legitimate intercourse with the other belligerent, because a belligerent cannot be expected passively to suffer vital damage to himself in consequence of the violation by his enemy of a rule which, although it operates directly in favour of neutrals, indirectly operates in his favour also. If, therefore, the enemy resorts to measures which suppress, or aim at suppressing, his intercourse with neutrals, and they do not prevent these measures from being carried out, he is justified in resorting to reprisals, and in turn preventing intercourse between his enemy and neutrals, provided that these reprisals do not extend further than to prevent imports to, and exports from, the enemy country.

Thus when in February 1915, during the World War, Germany, as a measure of reprisals against the Allies, mainly because they would not carry out the rules of the unratified Declaration of London,[2] decreed all the waters surrounding the British Isles to be a war zone, in which every enemy merchant vessel would be destroyed by submarines without it being always possible to save crew and passengers, and neutral ships might be exposed to danger, Great Britain by Order in Council of March 11, 1915,[3] and France by decree of March 13, 1915,[4] retaliated by ordering their fleets to prohibit all exports from, and imports to, Germany, and by an Order in Council of January 10, 1917, the order of March 11, 1915, was extended to all enemy countries.[5] The United States of America protested[6] against these British and French reprisals, asserting that the measures resorted to were a violation of neutral

[1] § 294; see also §§ 316, 318.
[2] See above, § 292.
[3] *London Gazette*, March 15, 1915.
[4] Dalloz, *Jurisprudence Générale* (1915), pp. 78-79.
[5] *London Gazette*, January 12, 1917.
[6] *Parl. Papers*, Misc., No. 14 (1916), Cd. 8233.

rights. Now this was certainly the case; but neutrals could not complain, because they did not prevent Germany from carrying out her nefarious submarine practice, which attempted to cut off entirely all communication with Great Britain. Just as neutrals who do not, or are not able to, prevent a belligerent from marching troops through their neutral territories cannot complain if the other belligerent likewise invades these territories and attacks the enemy there, so neutrals cannot complain if a belligerent prevents commercial intercourse between another belligerent and neutrals because they did not prevent that other belligerent from resorting to measures designed to stop intercourse between the first belligerent and neutrals. The rule that belligerents must not interfere with the legitimate commerce of neutrals is based on a compromise—just as is the rule that belligerents must not violate neutral territory; and it presupposes that both belligerents will carry it out, and that neutrals will prevent both of them from violating it. If, on the contrary, neutrals acquiesce in the violation of this rule by one belligerent to the vital disadvantage of the other belligerent, the latter cannot be expected to suffer this without redress, and must be excused if, in retaliating upon the enemy, he also violates the rule.[1]

On February 1, 1917, Germany embarked upon a further extended submarine practice, and thereby provoked a new reprisals Order in Council of February 16,

[1] See below, § 360, n. 2. Whether a belligerent is justified in resorting to reprisals which injure neutrals as well as the enemy is a very controversial question. See Phillimore in the *Grotius Society*, ii. p. 175; Pyke, *The Law of Contraband of War* (1915), p. 4; *A.J.*, ix. (1915), pp. 673, 680. The British Prize Courts have recognised the Order in Council of March 11, 1915, as being in accordance with International Law. See *The Stigstad*, (1916) 2 B. and C. P. C. 179, affirmed by the Privy Council, 3 B. and C. P. C. 347; *The United States*, (1916) 2 B. and C. P. C. 390; *The Frederick VIII.*, (1916) 2 B. and C. P. C. 395; and in particular *The Leonora*, (1918) 3 B. and C. P. C. 181, 385.

1917,[1] which decreed that any vessel carrying goods with an enemy destination, or of enemy origin, should be liable to capture and condemnation in respect of the carriage of such goods unless she called before capture at a British or Allied port for the examination of her cargo, and that goods found on examination to be goods of enemy origin or enemy destination should be liable to condemnation. This Order in Council was in my opinion *ultra vires*, because it threatened punishment and assumed jurisdiction over neutral ships for acts which, according to International Law, are perfectly legitimate. That a belligerent may in certain cases as a matter of reprisals attempt to prevent all exports from, and imports to, the enemy country, I consider to be in accordance with International Law; but he transgresses the permissible limits of action if he condemns and confiscates neutral ships and their cargoes for carrying enemy goods from or to the enemy country.[2]

II

NEUTRALS AND MILITARY OPERATIONS

Vattel, iii. §§ 105, 118-135—Hall, §§ 215, 219, 220, 226—Westlake, ii. pp. 227-232—Lawrence, §§ 229, 234-240—Manning, pp. 225-227, 245-250—Twiss, ii. §§ 217, 218, 228—Taylor, §§ 618, 620, 632, 635—Walker, §§ 55, 57, 59-61—Wharton, iii. §§ 397-400—Moore, vii. §§ 1293-1303—Wheaton, §§ 426-429—Bluntschli, §§ 758, 759, 763, 765, 769-773—Heffter, §§ 146-150—Geffcken in *Holtzendorff*, iv. pp. 657-676—Ullmann, § 191—Bonfils, Nos. 1449-1457, 1460, 1469, 1470—Despagnet, Nos. 690-692—Rivier, ii. pp. 395-408—Calvo, iv §§ 2644-2664, 2683—Fiore, iii. Nos. 1546-1550, 1574-1575, 1582-1584—Martens, ii. §§ 131-134—Kleen, i. §§ 70-75, 116-122—Mérignhac, iii[a]. pp. 516-547—Pillet, pp. 284-289—Perels, § 39—Testa, pp. 173-180—Heilborn, *Rechte*, pp. 4-

[1] *London Gazette*, February 23, 1917.

[2] See, however, the judgment in *The Leonora*, (1918) 3 B. and C. P. C. 181, which declared the Order in Council of February 16, 1917, to be in accordance with International Law. It was affirmed by the Privy Council (*ibid.*, 385).

12—Dupuis, Nos. 308-310, 315-317, and *Guerre*, Nos. 277-294—*Land Warfare*, §§ 465-471—Einicke, *Rechte und Pflichten der neutralen Mächte im Seekrieg* (1912), pp. 22-70—Wehberg, § 11.

§ 320. The duty of impartiality incumbent upon a neutral must obviously prevent him from committing hostilities against either belligerent. This would need no mention, except to distinguish between hostilities on the one hand, and, on the other, military or naval acts of force by a neutral for the purpose of repulsing violations of his neutrality committed by either belligerent. Hostilities by a neutral are acts of force performed for the purpose of attacking a belligerent. They are acts of war, and they create a condition of war between such neutral and the belligerent concerned. If, however, a neutral does not attack a belligerent, but only repulses him by force when he violates, or attempts to violate, the neutrality of the neutral, this does not constitute hostilities. Thus, if men-of-war of a belligerent attack an enemy vessel in a neutral port and are repulsed by neutral men-of-war, or if belligerent forces try to make their way through neutral territory and are forcibly prevented by neutral troops, no hostilities have been committed by the neutral, who has done nothing else than fulfil his duty of impartiality. Article 10 of Convention v. enacts categorically that 'the fact of a neutral Power repelling, even by force, attacks on its neutrality, cannot be considered as a hostile act.' And stress must be laid on the fact that it is no longer legitimate for a belligerent to pursue [1] military or naval forces who take refuge on neutral territory; should a belligerent nevertheless do this, he must, if possible, be repulsed by the neutral.

Hostilities by and against Neutrals.

It is, on the other hand, likewise obvious that hostilities against a neutral on the part of either belligerent are acts of war, and not mere violations of

[1] See above, § 288, and below, § 347 (4).

neutrality. Thus the German attack on Belgium in 1914, to enable German troops to march through Belgian territory and attack France, created war[1] between Germany and Belgium. If, however, forces of one belligerent attack forces of the other belligerent, which have taken refuge on neutral territory, or which are there for other purposes, such attacks do not constitute hostilities against the neutral, but are mere violations of neutrality; and they must be repulsed or reparation must be made for them, as the case may be.

Quite a peculiar condition arose at the outbreak of, and during, the Russo-Japanese War. The ends for which Japan went to war were the expulsion of the Russian forces from the Chinese Province of Manchuria and the liberation of Korea, which was at the time an independent State, from the influence of Russia. Manchuria and Korea became therefore part of the region of war, although both were neutral territories, and neither China nor Korea became parties to the war. The hostilities which occurred on these neutral territories were in no wise directed against the neutrals concerned. This anomalous situation arose out of the inability of both China and Korea to free themselves from Russian occupation and influence, Japan considering her action, which must be classified as an intervention, to be justified on account of her vital interests. The Powers recognised this situation by influencing China not to take part in the war, and by influencing the belligerents not to extend military operations beyond the borders of Manchuria. Manchuria and Korea having become part of the region of war,[2] the hostilities committed there by the belligerents against one another cannot be classified as violations of neutrality. The cases of *The Variag* and *The Korietz*,

[1] See above, § 71.
[2] See above, § 71; Lawrence, *War*, pp. 268-294; Ariga, §§ 16-22.

and the case of *The Reshitelni*, may illustrate the peculiar condition of affairs :—

(1) On February 8, 1904, a Japanese squadron under Admiral Uriu entered the Korean harbour of Chemulpo and disembarked Japanese troops. The next morning Admiral Uriu requested the commanders of two Russian ships in that harbour, the *Variag* and the *Korietz*, to leave the harbour and engage him in battle outside, threatening to attack them inside the harbour in case they refused. But they did not refuse, and the battle took place outside the harbour, but within Korean territorial waters.[1] The complaint made by Russia that in this case the Japanese violated Korean neutrality, would seem to be unjustified, since Korea fell within the region of war.[2]

(2) The Russian destroyer *Reshitelni*, one of the vessels that escaped from Port Arthur on August 10, 1904, took refuge in the Chinese harbour of Chifu. On August 12, two Japanese destroyers entered the harbour, captured her, and towed her away.[3] There ought to be no doubt that this was a violation of neutrality,[4] since Chifu does not belong to the part of China which fell within the region of war.

Anomalous also was the situation during the World War, when, while Greece was still neutral,[5] the Allies occupied Salonika and also Corfu and certain other Greek islands. The forces which had landed at Salonika were attacked by Bulgaria and the other Central Powers.[6]

[1] See Lawrence, *War*, pp. 279-289, and Takahashi, pp. 462-466.

[2] It was for this reason that the Japanese Prize Courts in 1904, during the Russo-Japanese War, condemned the Russian vessels *Ekaterinoslav* (Hurst and Bray, ii. p. 1) and *Mukden* (*ibid.*, ii. p. 12), although they were captured, not on the open sea, but in the territorial waters of Korea. See *The Tinos*, above, § 71 n.

[3] See Lawrence, *War*, pp. 291-294, and Takahashi, pp. 437-444.

[4] See below, §§ 360 and 361, where the cases of *The Dresden* and *The General Armstrong* are discussed.

[5] See above, § 306.

[6] See below, § 323, and Garner, ii. §§ 464-473.

Furnishing Troops and Men-of-War to Belligerents.

§ 321. If a State remains neutral, it violates its impartiality by furnishing a belligerent with troops or men-of-war; and it matters not whether it renders such assistance to one of the belligerents, or to both alike. Whereas Convention v. does not mention the furnishing of troops, Article 6 of Convention XIII. enacts that 'the supply, in any manner, directly or indirectly, by a neutral Power to a belligerent Power, of warships, ammunition, or war material of any kind whatever, is forbidden.'

However, it is controversial whether a neutral State, which in time of peace had concluded a treaty with one of the belligerents to furnish him in case of war with a limited number of troops, would violate its neutrality by fulfilling its treaty obligation. Several writers [1] have answered the question in the negative, and there is no doubt that during the eighteenth century such cases happened. But no case happened during the nineteenth century, and there ought to be no doubt that nowadays the answer must be in the affirmative, since a qualified neutrality [2] is no longer admissible.

As regards furnishing men-of-war to belligerents, the question arose during the Russo-Japanese War whether a neutral violates his duty of impartiality by not preventing his national steamship companies from selling to a belligerent such of their liners as are destined in case of war to be incorporated as cruisers in the national navy. The question was discussed on account of the sale to Russia of the *Augusta Victoria* and the *Kaiserin Maria Theresia* by the North German Lloyd, and the *Fürst Bismarck* and the *Columbia* by the Hamburg-American Line; for these vessels were at once enrolled in the Russian Navy as second-class

[1] See, for instance, Bluntschli, § 759, and Heffter, § 144. See above, § 306 (2), where the case is quoted of Denmark furnishing troops to Russia in 1788 during a Russo-Swedish war.

[2] See above, § 305.

cruisers, re-named *Kuban, Ural, Don,* and *Terek.* Had these vessels by an arrangement with the German Government really been auxiliary cruisers to the German Navy, and had the German Government given its consent to the transaction, a violation of neutrality would have been committed by Germany. But the German Press maintained that they had not been auxiliary cruisers, and Japan did not lodge a protest with Germany on account of the sale. If these liners were not auxiliary cruisers to the German Navy, their sale to Russia was a legitimate sale of articles of contraband.[1]

Subjects of Neutrals fighting among Belligerent Forces.

§ 322. Although several States, as, for instance, Great Britain[2] and the United States of America, by their Municipal Law prohibit their subjects from enlisting in the military or naval service of belligerents, the duty of impartiality incumbent upon neutrals does not at present include any necessity for such prohibition, provided that the individuals concerned cross the frontier singly[3] and not in a body. But a neutral must recall his military and naval officers who may have been serving in the army or navy of either belligerent before the outbreak of war; and must retain military and naval officers who want to resign their commissions for the obvious purpose of enlisting in the service of either belligerent. Therefore, when in 1877, during war between Turkey and Serbia, Russian officers left the Russian Army and entered the Serbian Army as volunteers with permission of the Russian Government, there was a violation of the duty of impartiality on the part of neutral Russia.

On the other hand, there is no violation of neutrality in a neutral allowing surgeons and other non-combatant members of his army vested with a character

[1] See below, § 397.

[2] See § 4 of the Foreign Enlistment Act, 1870.

[3] See Article 6 of Convention v.

of inviolability according to the Geneva Convention to enlist, or to remain, in the service of either belligerent.

Passage of Troops and War Material through Neutral Territory.

§ 323. In contradistinction to the practice of the eighteenth century,[1] it is now generally recognised that a violation of the duty of impartiality is involved when a neutral allows a belligerent the passage of troops or the transport of war material or supplies over his territory.[2] And it matters not whether a neutral gives such permission to one of the belligerents only, or to both alike.

(a) *The Passage of Troops*

The practice of the eighteenth century was unavoidable at that time, since many German States consisted of parts distant one from another, so that their troops had to pass through other sovereigns' territories for the purpose of reaching outlying parts. At the beginning of the nineteenth century, the passing of belligerent troops through neutral territory still occurred. Prussia, although she at first repeatedly refused, at last in 1805 entered into a secret convention with Russia granting Russian troops passage through Silesia during war with France. On the other hand, even before Russia had made use of this permission, Napoleon ordered Bernadotte to march French troops through the then Prussian territory of Anspach without even asking the consent of Prussia. In spite of the protest of the Swiss Government, Austrian troops passed through the Swiss territory in 1813, and when in 1815 war broke out again through the escape of Napoleon from the island of Elba and his return to France, Switzerland granted to the allied troops passage through her territory.[3] But since that time it has become universally recognised that all passage of belligerent troops through neutral territory must be prohibited, and the Powers declared *expressis verbis* in the

[1] See Vattel, iii. §§ 119-132.

[2] See Dumas in *R.G.*, xvi. (1909), pp. 289-316.

[3] See Wheaton, §§ 418-420.

Act of November 20, 1815, which neutralised Switzerland, and was signed at Paris,[1] that 'no inference unfavourable to the neutrality and inviolability of Switzerland can and must be drawn from the facts which have caused the passage of the allied troops through a part of the territory of the Swiss Confederation.' The few instances[2] in which during the nineteenth century States pretended to remain neutral, but nevertheless allowed the troops of one of the belligerents passage through their territory, led to war between the neutral and the other belligerent.

As has been already stated,[3] in October 1915 during the World War, while Greece was still neutral, the Allies, on the invitation of M. Venizelos, then prime minister of Greece, disembarked troops at Salonika for the purpose of bringing aid to Serbia. The Greek Government protested *pro forma*, but did not put any obstacle in the way of their landing. This led to an attack on Salonika by the Central Powers, but war between the Central Powers and Greece did not ensue until much later.[4]

However, just as in the case of furnishing troops, it is a moot point whether passage of troops can be granted without violating the duty of impartiality incumbent upon a neutral, in case a neutral is required to grant it in consequence of an existing State servitude, or of a treaty previous to the war. There ought to be no doubt that, since nowadays qualified neutrality is no longer admissible, the question must be answered in the negative.[5]

(b) *The Transport of War Material and Supplies*

With regard to the transport of war material and supplies, Article 2 of Hague Convention v. categorically

[1] See Martens, *N.R.*, ii. p. 741.

[2] See Heilborn, *Rechte*, pp. 8-9.

[3] Above, §§ 306, 320.

[4] Above, § 320, and Garner, ii. §§ 464-473.

[5] See above, §§ 305-306, and vol. i. § 207. Clauss, *Die Lehre von den Staatsdienstbarkeiten* (1894), pp. 212-217, must likewise be referred to. See also Dumas in *R.G.*, xvi. (1909), pp. 289-316.

enacts that 'belligerents are forbidden to move across the territory of a neutral Power troops or convoys either of munitions of war or of supplies.' But different from this case is the case in which munitions and the like are sent by private individuals to a belligerent across neutral territory. As to this, Article 7 of that convention lays down the rule that 'a neutral Power is not bound to prevent the export or transit, for one or the other of the belligerents, of arms, munitions of war, or, in general, of anything which can be of use to an army or fleet.'

The distinction between these two articles was incidentally considered[1] during the controversy that arose in the World War between Great Britain and Holland concerning the transit of metals from Belgium (then under German military occupation) to Germany, and of sand and gravel from Germany to occupied Belgium through Dutch territory. Great Britain argued that Holland, by permitting such traffic (whatever the purpose for which the materials were used), was giving direct assistance to Germany, and so committing a violation of neutrality. Holland, on the other hand, argued that she was only bound to prevent the transit of these materials when they were connected with military operations, and that the consignments which had passed through were not so connected.

Passage of Wounded through Neutral Territory.

§ 324. The passage of wounded soldiers is different from that of troops. If a neutral allows the passage of wounded soldiers, he certainly does not render direct assistance to the belligerent concerned. But it may well be that he gives indirect assistance because a belligerent, being relieved from transporting his wounded, can now use the lines of communication for the transport of troops, war material, and provisions. Thus when in 1870, after the battles

[1] *Parl. Papers*, Misc., No. 17 (1917), Cd. 8693, and Garner, ii. § 570.

of Sedan and Metz, Germany applied to Belgium and Luxemburg to allow her wounded to be sent through their territories, France protested on the ground that the relief thereby given to the German lines of communication would be an assistance to the military operations of the German Army. Belgium, on the advice of Great Britain, did not grant the request, but Luxemburg did.[1]

According to Article 14 of Convention v. a neutral Power *may* grant the passage of the wounded or sick at the request of a belligerent. If he does, the trains bringing them must carry neither combatants nor war material, and those of the wounded and sick who belong to the army of the other belligerent must remain on the neutral territory, must there be guarded by the neutral Government, and, after having recovered, must be prevented from returning to their home State and rejoining their corps.[2] By Article 14 it is left to the discretion of a neutral whether or not he will allow the passage of wounded and sick; he must, therefore, investigate every case, and come to a conclusion according to its merits. During the World War, the United States, while neutral, did not allow certain wounded or disabled Canadian soldiers to pass through American territory on their way home after discharge.[3]

Passage of Men-of-War.

§ 325. In contradistinction to passage of troops through his territory, the duty of impartiality incumbent upon a neutral does not require him to forbid the passage of belligerent men-of-war[4] through the maritime belt forming part of his territorial waters. Article 10 of Convention XIII. categorically enacts that 'the neutrality of a Power is not violated (*n'est pas*

[1] See Hall, § 219, and Geffcken in *Holtzendorff*, iv. p. 664.

[2] According to Article 15 of Convention v., the 'Geneva Convention applies to the sick and wounded interned in neutral territory.'

[3] See Garner, ii. § 570.

[4] See Trainé, *Das Gastrecht im Seekrieg* (1912), §§ 8-12.

compromise) by the mere passage of belligerent men-of-war and their prizes.' Since[1] every littoral State may, even in time of peace, prohibit the passage of foreign men-of-war through its maritime belt unless it forms a part of the highways for international traffic, it may certainly prohibit the passage of belligerent men-of-war in time of war. Thus, at the outbreak of the World War in 1914, Holland declared that belligerent war-vessels would not be allowed passage through her maritime belt in Europe, and later she seized German and British submarines which, though not in distress, had entered Dutch territorial waters, and interned their crews. Again, in 1916, Norway declared that thenceforth belligerent submarines would not be allowed to pass through her territorial waters.[2] However, no duty exists for a neutral to prohibit such passage in time of war. Nor need he exclude belligerent men-of-war from his ports, although he may do this likewise. The reason is that such passage and such admission to ports involves very little assistance indeed, and is justified by the character of the sea as an international high-road. But it is obvious that belligerent men-of-war must not commit any hostilities against enemy vessels during their passage, and must not use the neutral maritime belt and neutral ports as a basis for their operations against the enemy.[3]

Occupation of Neutral Territory by Belligerents.

§ 326. In contradistinction to the practice of the eighteenth century,[4] the duty of impartiality must nowadays prevent a neutral from permitting belligerents to occupy a neutral fortress, or any other part of neutral territory. Even if a treaty previously entered into stipulates such occupation, it cannot be granted without violation of neutrality.[5] On the con-

[1] See above, vol. i. § 188.
[2] See Garner, ii. § 562.
[3] See below, § 333.
[4] See Kleen, i. § 116.
[5] See Klüber, § 281, who asserts the contrary.

trary, the neutral must even use force to prevent belligerents from occupying any part of his neutral territory.[1] The question whether such occupation on the part of a belligerent would be excusable in case of extreme necessity in self-defence on account of the neutral's inability to prevent the other belligerent from making use of the neutral territory as a base for his military operations must, I think, be answered in the affirmative, since an extreme case of necessity in the interest of self-defence must be considered as an excuse.[2] But necessity of this kind and degree exists only when the use of the territory by the enemy is imminent; it is not sufficient that a belligerent should merely fear that his enemy might perhaps attempt so to use it.

Prize Courts on Neutral Territory.

§ 327. It has long been universally recognised that the duty of impartiality must prevent a neutral from permitting a belligerent to set up Prize Courts on neutral territory. The intention of a belligerent in so doing can only be to facilitate the plundering by his men-of-war of the commerce of the enemy; a neutral tolerating such Prize Courts would, therefore, indirectly assist the belligerent in his naval operations. During the eighteenth century, however, it was not considered illegitimate for neutrals to allow the setting up of Prize Courts on their territory. The 'Règlement du Roi de France concernant les Prises qui seront conduites dans les Ports étrangers, et les Formalités que doivent remplir les Consuls de S.M. qui y sont établis' of 1779, furnishes a striking proof of it. But after the United States of

[1] As to the occupation of parts of Greek territory during the World War, see above, § 320.

[2] See Vattel, iii. § 122; Bluntschli, § 782; Calvo, iv. § 2642. Kleen, i. § 116, seems not to recognise an extreme necessity of the kind mentioned above as an excuse.—There is a difference between this case and the case which arose at the outbreak of the Russo-Japanese War, when both belligerents invaded Korea, for, as was explained above in § 320, Korea and Manchuria fell within the region of war.

America in 1793 closed down the French Prize Courts set up by the French envoy Genêt on her territory,[1] it became recognised that such Prize Courts are inconsistent with the duty of impartiality incumbent upon a neutral, and Article 4 of Convention XIII. so enacts.

Belligerent's Prizes in Neutral Ports.

§ 328. It would, no doubt, be an indirect assistance to the naval operations of a belligerent if a neutral allowed him to organise on neutral territory the safe-keeping or sale of prizes.

But the case of a temporary stay of a belligerent man-of-war with her prize in a neutral port is different. Neutral Powers may—although most maritime States no longer do—allow prizes to be brought temporarily into their ports.[2] Articles 21 and 22 of Convention XIII. lay down the following rules: A prize may only be brought into a neutral port on account of unseaworthiness, stress of weather, or want of fuel or provisions; it must leave as soon as the circumstances which justified its entry are at an end, and if it does not, the neutral Power must order it to leave at once, and must, in case of disobedience, employ the means at its disposal to release the prize with its officers and crew, and to intern the prize crew; a prize brought into a neutral port for reasons other than unseaworthiness, stress of weather, or want of fuel or provisions,—for instance, to avoid recapture—must forthwith be released by the neutral Power. Article 22 does not mention that in such a case the prize crew must be interned, but there is no doubt that they must be.[3]

The question requires attention whether a prize, whose unseaworthiness is so great that it cannot be repaired, may be allowed to remain in the neutral port, and be there sold [4] after the competent Prize Court has

[1] See above, § 291 (1).

[2] See Trainé, *Das Gastrecht im Seekrieg* (1912), § 20; Scott in *A.J.*, x. (1916), pp. 104-112.

[3] The United States interned the prize crew in the case of *The Appam*. See below, § 328*a*.

[4] See Kleen, i. § 115.

condemned it. Since Article 21 enacts that an admitted prize must leave the neutral port as soon as the circumstances which justified its entry are at an end, there is no doubt that it may remain if it cannot be repaired so as to be made seaworthy. There ought, consequently, to be no objection to its sale in the neutral port, provided it has previously been condemned by the proper Prize Court.

While Article 21 cannot meet with any objection, Article 23 of Convention XIII. is of a very doubtful character. It enacts that a neutral Power may allow prizes to enter its ports, whether under convoy or not, when they are brought there to be sequestrated pending the decision of a Prize Court; and the restrictions imposed by Article 21 do not apply to prizes brought into a neutral port under Article 23. It would in practice enable a belligerent to safeguard all his prizes against recapture, and a neutral Power which allowed belligerent prizes access to its ports under it would indirectly render assistance to the naval operations of the belligerent concerned. For this reason, Great Britain, Japan and Siam, and also the United States of America when she acceded to the convention in December 1909, entered a reservation against Article 23. Be that as it may, those Powers which have accepted Article 23 will not, I believe, object to the sale in the neutral port of such sequestrated prizes, provided they have previously been condemned by the proper Prize Court.

The case of *The Appam*.

§ 328*a*. On several occasions during the World War German cruisers brought their prizes into neutral ports. Thus in March 1915 the German cruiser *Prinz Eitel Friedrich* conducted a French prize into a Chilian port, and at other times German war-vessels took the captured steamers *Valentine*, *Helicon*, and *Sacramento* into the Chilian harbour of Juan Fernandez. These acts were the subject of various protests.[1] But the case which attracted most attention was that of *The Appam*. This British liner was captured by a German war-vessel off the coast of Africa, and was navigated across the Atlantic by a prize crew, unaccompanied by the captor, to the then neutral American port of Newport News. The American Government thereupon liberated the ship's crew and passengers, and interned the prize crew, and the owners of the vessel instituted proceedings in the American courts for her release. The court of first instance held that Articles 21 and 22 of Hague Convention XIII.[2] were declaratory of existing rules of International Law, under which neutral ports might not become places of asylum or permanent rendezvous for belligerent prizes; that the *Appam* had been brought to the United States for reasons other than unseaworthiness, stress of weather, or want of fuel or provisions, and must be set free. The Supreme Court affirmed this decision.[3]

III

NEUTRALS AND MILITARY PREPARATIONS

Hall, §§ 217-218, 221-225—Lawrence, §§ 234-240—Westlake, ii. pp. 210-227—Manning, pp. 227-244—Phillimore, iii. §§ 142-151*b*—Twiss, ii. §§ 223-225—Halleck, ii. pp. 165-185—Taylor, §§ 616, 619, 626-628—Walker, §§ 62-66—Wharton, iii. §§ 392, 395-396—Wheaton, §§ 436-439—Moore, vii. §§ 1293-1305—Heffter, §§ 148-150—Geffcken in *Holtzendorff*, iv. pp. 658-660, 676-684—Ullmann, § 191—Bonfils, Nos. 1458-1459, 1464-1466—Despagnet, Nos. 692-693—Rivier, ii. pp. 395-408—Calvo, iv. §§ 2619-2627—Fiore, iii. Nos. 1551-1570—Kleen, i. §§ 76-89, 114—Mérignhac, iii[a]. pp. 522-547—Pillet, pp. 288-290—Dupuis, Nos. 322-331, and *Guerre*, Nos. 290-294—*Land Warfare*, §§ 472-476—Einicke, *Rechte und Pflichten der neutralen Mächte im Seekrieg* (1912), pp. 71-153—Wehberg, § 11.

---

[1] See Garner, ii. § 566.

[2] See above, § 328.

[3] (1917) 243 U.S. 124; Garner, ii. § 567. See also Scott in *A.J.*, x. (1916), pp. 809-831; Coudert in *A.J.*, xi. (1917), pp. 270-314; and the documents in *A.J.*, x. (1916), Special Supplement, pp. 387-403, and xi. (1917), pp. 443-453.

Depots and Factories on Neutral Territory.

§ 329. Although, according to the present intense conception of the duty of impartiality, neutrals need not [1] prohibit their subjects from supplying belligerents with arms and the like in the ordinary way of trade, a neutral must [2] prohibit belligerents from erecting, and maintaining on his territory, depots and factories of arms, ammunition, and military provisions. However, belligerents can easily evade this rule by not keeping depots and factories, but contracting with subjects of the neutral concerned in the ordinary way of trade for any amount of arms, ammunition, and provisions.[3]

Levy of Troops, and the like.

§ 330. In former centuries neutrals were not required to prevent belligerents from levying troops on their neutral territories; indeed, a neutral often himself levied troops on his territory for belligerents without thereby violating his duty of impartiality as understood in those times. In this way the Swiss Confederation frequently used to furnish belligerents, and often both parties, with thousands of recruits, although she herself always remained neutral. But at the end of the eighteenth century a movement was started which tended to change this practice. In 1793, President Washington of the United States of America interdicted the levy of troops for belligerents on American territory, and by and by many other States followed the example. During the nineteenth century, the majority of writers maintained that the duty of impartiality must prevent a neutral from allowing the levy of troops; and the few [4] writers who differed made it a condition that a neutral, if he allowed it at all, must allow it to both

[1] See below, § 350.

[2] See Bluntschli, § 777, and Kleen, i. § 114.

[3] The distinction made by some writers between an occasional supply by subjects of neutrals and an organised supply in large proportions, and the assertion that the latter must be prohibited by the neutral State, is not justified. See below, § 350.

[4] See, for instance, Twiss, ii. § 225, and Bluntschli, § 762.

belligerents alike. The controversy was settled by Articles 4 and 5 of Hague Convention v., which lay down the rules that corps of combatants may not be formed, nor recruiting offices opened, on the territory of a neutral Power, and that neutral Powers must not allow these acts.

The duty of impartiality must likewise prevent a neutral from allowing a belligerent man-of-war reduced in her crew to enrol sailors in his ports, with the exception of such few men as are absolutely necessary to navigate the vessel to the nearest home port.[1]

Akin to the levy of troops on neutral territory was the granting of letters of marque to vessels belonging to the merchant marine of neutrals. Since privateering has disappeared, the question whether neutrals must prohibit their subjects from accepting letters of marque from a belligerent[2] need not be discussed.

Passage of Bodies of Men intending to Enlist.

§ 331. A neutral is not obliged by his duty of impartiality to prohibit passage through his territory of men who intend to enlist, whether they pass singly or in numbers. Thus, in 1870, Switzerland did not object to Frenchmen travelling through Geneva for the purpose of reaching French corps, or to Germans travelling through Basle for the purpose of reaching German corps, under the condition, however, that these men travelled without arms and uniform. On the other hand, when France during the Franco-German War organised an office[3] in Basle for the purpose of sending bodies of Alsatian volunteers through Switzerland to the south of France, Switzerland correctly closed it down because this *official* organisation of the passage of whole bodies of volunteers through her neutral

[1] See Article 18 of Convention XIII. and below, § 333 (3), and § 346.

[2] See above, § 83. With the assertion of many writers that a subject of a neutral who accepts letters of marque from a belligerent may be treated as a pirate, I cannot agree. See above, vol. i. § 273.

[3] See Bluntschli, § 770.

territory was more or less equal to a passage of troops.

The Second Hague Conference sanctioned this distinction, for Article 6 of Convention v. enacts that 'the responsibility of a neutral Power is not involved by the mere fact that persons cross the frontier individually (*isolément*) in order to offer their services to one of the belligerents.' An *argumentum e contrario* justifies the conclusion that the responsibility of a neutral *is* involved in case it allows men to cross the frontier *in a body* in order to enlist in the forces of a belligerent.

Organisation of Hostile Expeditions.

§ 332. Since the levy and passage of troops, and the forming of corps of combatants, must be prevented by a neutral, *a fortiori* he is required to prevent the organisation of a hostile expedition from his territory against either belligerent. This takes place when a band of men combine under a commander for the purpose of starting from the neutral territory and joining the belligerent forces. The case, however, is different if a number of individuals, not organised into a body under a commander, start in company from a neutral State for the purpose of enlisting with one of the belligerents. Thus in 1870, during the Franco-German War, 1200 Frenchmen started from New York in two French steamers for the purpose of joining the French Army. Although the vessels carried also 96,000 rifles and 11,000,000 cartridges, the United States did not interfere, since the men were not organised in a body, and the arms and ammunition were carried in the way of ordinary commerce.[1]

§ 333. Although a neutral is not required by his duty of impartiality to prohibit[2] the passage of belligerent men-of-war[3] through his maritime belt, or to

[1] See Hall, § 222, and Curtis in *A.J.*, viii. (1914), pp. 1-37, 224-255.

[2] See Curtius, *Des Navires de Guerre dans les Eaux neutres* (1907).

[3] As regards submarine vessels, see below, § 344*a*.

Use of Neutral Territory as Base of Naval Operations.

prohibit the temporary stay of such vessels in his ports, it is universally recognised that he must not allow admitted vessels to make the neutral maritime belt and neutral ports the base of their naval operations against the enemy.[1] Thus Article 5 of Hague Convention XIII. enacts that 'belligerents are forbidden to use neutral ports and waters as a base of naval operations against their adversaries.' The following rules may be formulated as emanating from this principle :—

(1) A neutral must, so far as is in his power, prevent belligerent men-of-war[2] from cruising within his portion of the maritime belt for the purpose of capturing enemy vessels as soon as they leave it. However, a neutral is only required to do all that lies in his power. It is absolutely impossible to prevent such cruising under all circumstances and conditions, especially in the case of neutrals who own possessions in distant parts of the globe. How many thousands of vessels would be necessary, if Great Britain, for instance, were unconditionally obliged to prevent such cruising in every portion of the maritime belt of all her numerous possessions scattered over all parts of the globe ?

(2) A neutral must prevent a belligerent man-of-war

[1] See Trainé, *Das Gastrecht im Seekrieg* (1912).

[2] The rules here laid down with regard to men-of-war apply also to vessels assimilated to men-of-war, *i.e.* vessels used as transports or fleet auxiliaries or in any other way for the purpose of prosecuting or aiding hostilities. It is true that the relevant articles of Hague Convention XIII. speak only of 'belligerent men-of-war,' and do not mention vessels assimilated thereto. But paragraphs 3 and 4 of the preamble state 'that it is not possible at present to concert measures applicable to all circumstances which may arise in practice,' and 'that in cases not covered by the present convention account must be taken of the general principles of the Law of Nations.' Without doubt, therefore, its stipulations concerning belligerent vessels of war apply to auxiliary vessels.

During the World War the question was much discussed—see Scott in *A.J.*, x. (1916), pp. 113-116, and Garner, i. §§ 246-249—whether merchantmen of belligerents which had been armed for defence only, were to be considered as men-of-war, and were therefore to be denied the privileges usually accorded to merchantmen in neutral harbours. The German Government contended that they should; but all the neutral maritime States, with the exception of Holland, correctly said no.

from leaving a neutral port at the same time as an enemy man-of-war or an enemy merchantman, or must make other arrangements which prevent an attack so soon as both reach the open sea.[1] Thus Article 16 of Hague Convention XIII. enacts :—'When warships belonging to both belligerents are present simultaneously in a neutral port or roadstead, a period of not less than twenty-four hours must elapse between the departure of the ship belonging to one belligerent and the departure of the ship belonging to the other. The order of departure is determined by the order of arrival, unless the ship which arrived first is so circumstanced that an extension of its stay is permissible. A belligerent warship may not leave a neutral port or roadstead until twenty-four hours after the departure of a merchant-ship flying the flag of its adversary.'

(3) A neutral must prevent a belligerent man-of-war, whose crew is reduced from any cause whatever, from enrolling sailors in his neutral ports, with the exception of such few hands as are necessary to navigate the vessel safely to the nearest port of her home State.[2]

(4) A neutral must prevent belligerent men-of-war admitted to his ports or maritime belt from taking in such a quantity of provisions and coal as would enable them to continue their naval operations, for otherwise he would make it possible for them to cruise on the open sea near his maritime belt for the purpose of attacking enemy vessels.

There is, however, no unanimity among the Powers concerning the quantity of provisions and coal which belligerent men-of-war may be allowed to take in. Articles 19 and 20 of Hague Convention XIII. enact the following :—

Article 19: 'Belligerent warships may only re-

[1] See below, § 347 (1).
[2] See Article 18 of Convention XIII. and above, § 330.

victual in neutral ports or roadsteads to bring up their supplies to the peace standard. Similarly these vessels may only ship sufficient fuel to enable them to reach the nearest port in their own country.[1] They may, on the other hand, fill up their bunkers built to carry fuel, when in neutral countries which have adopted this method of determining the amount of fuel to be supplied. If, in accordance with the law of the neutral Power, the ships are not supplied with coal within twenty-four hours of their arrival, the duration of their permitted stay is extended by twenty-four hours.'

Article 20: 'Belligerent warships which have shipped fuel in a port belonging to a neutral Power may not, within the succeeding three months, replenish their supply in a port of the same Power.'

But Great Britain, which upholds the rule that belligerent warships must not take in more provisions and fuel in neutral ports than is necessary to bring them safely to the nearest port of their own country, and Japan and Siam reserved against Article 19, and Germany reserved against Article 20. Therefore the matter is not settled.

It is agreed, however, that it makes no difference whether the man-of-war intends to buy provisions and coal on land or to take them in from transport vessels which accompany or meet her in neutral waters.

(5) A neutral must prevent belligerent men-of-war admitted into his ports or maritime belt from replenishing their ammunition and armaments, and from adding to their armaments, as otherwise he would indirectly assist them in preparing for hostilities (Article 18 of

[1] As the amount of fuel necessary to enable a British or German war-vessel in a Chilian port to reach the nearest British or German port was sufficient to enable it to carry on hostilities in the Atlantic or the Pacific for a long period, Chili found great difficulty during the World War in reconciling this article with the obligation to prevent British or German war-vessels from taking in such quantities of coal as would enable them to continue their operations. See Garner, ii. § 561.

Convention XIII.). It makes no difference whether the ammunition and armaments are to come from the shore, or are to be taken in from transport vessels.

Similarly, although a neutral may allow the repair of slight damage, he must prevent belligerent men-of-war in his ports from carrying out such repairs as would add to their fighting force. He may not therefore allow extensive repairs necessary to render crippled war-vessels again fit for action. During the Russo-Japanese War this was generally recognised, and the Russian men-of-war *Askold* and *Grossovoi* in Shanghai, the *Diana* in Saigon, and the *Lena* in San Francisco had therefore to be disarmed, and they and their crews detained. Article 17 of Hague Convention XIII. formally embodied this distinction by providing that 'in neutral ports and roadsteads belligerent warships may only carry out such repairs as are absolutely necessary to render them seaworthy, and may not add in any manner whatsoever to their fighting force.' The local authorities must decide what repairs are necessary, and such repairs must be carried out with the least possible delay.

Accordingly, in February 1913, during the Balkan War, the Turkish cruiser *Hamidieh* was allowed to remain a couple of days in the harbour of Malta to repair slight damage caused by the stress of weather. On the other hand, during the World War, the German cruisers *Prinz Eitel Friedrich* and *Kronprinz Wilhelm*, and the German gunboat *Geier* and her naval tender *Locksun*, which entered neutral American ports for repairs, were allowed only a limited time within which to execute them, and as they failed to depart within the prescribed period, they were interned and dismantled until the end of the war.[1] During the World War the question also arose whether *slight* damage might be repaired, even though

[1] See Garner, ii. § 563; *A.J.*, ix. (1915), p. 486; Hall, p. 671.

it was caused, not by weather, but by hostile action in battle. As Article 17 of Convention XIII. draws no distinction between damage by weather and damage in battle, Holland decided to permit such repairs.

(6) A neutral must prevent belligerent men-of-war admitted to his ports from remaining there longer than is necessary for ordinary and legitimate purposes. It could not be said at the outbreak of the World War that the rule adopted in 1862[1] by Great Britain, and followed by some other maritime States, not to allow a longer stay than twenty-four hours, was a rule of International Law. It was left to the discretion of neutrals to adopt by their Municipal Law any rule they thought fit, so long as the admitted men-of-war did not prolong their stay for other than ordinary and legitimate purposes. Article 12 of Convention XIII. confirmed this arrangement by prescribing the twenty-four hours rule only for those neutral countries which had not special provisions to the contrary in their Municipal Laws.[2] In fact, however, during the World War, most, if not all, neutral States adopted the twenty-four hours rule.[3]

It is agreed—and Article 14 of Convention XIII. enacts it—that belligerent men-of-war, except those for the time exclusively devoted to religious, scientific, or philanthropic purposes, must not prolong their stay in neutral ports and waters beyond the time permitted, except on account of damage or stress of weather. A neutral would certainly violate his duty of impartiality if he were to allow belligerent men-of-war to winter in his ports, or to stay there for the purpose of waiting for other vessels of the fleet or transports.

[1] See Hall, § 231.

[2] Germany, Domingo, Siam, and Persia entered a reservation against Article 12.

[3] See Garner, ii. § 563, and *A.J.*, x. (1916), Supplement, pp. 121-178, where the regulations of several States governing the admission of belligerent men-of-war to their ports are collected.

The rule that a neutral must prevent belligerent men-of-war from staying too long in his ports or waters, became of considerable importance during the Russo-Japanese War, when the Russian Baltic Fleet was on its way to the Far East. Admiral Rojdestvensky is said to have stayed in the French territorial waters of Madagascar from December 1904 till March 1905, for the purpose of awaiting there a part of the Baltic Fleet that had set out at a later date. The press likewise reported a prolonged stay by parts of the Baltic Fleet during April 1905 at Kamranh Bay and Hon-kohe Bay in French Indo-China. If the reported facts were true, France would seem to have violated her duty of impartiality by not preventing such an abuse of her neutral ports.

(7) A neutral must prevent more than three men-of-war belonging to the same belligerent from being simultaneously in one of his ports or roadsteads unless his Municipal Law provides the contrary (Article 15 of Convention XIII.).

(8) Belligerent men-of-war must not shelter in a neutral port for an undue length of time in order to escape capture.[1]

(9) At the outbreak of war, a neutral must warn all belligerent men-of-war then in his ports, roadsteads, or territorial waters, to depart within twenty-four hours, or such other time as the local law prescribes (Article 13 of Convention XIII.).[2]

Building and Fitting-out of Vessels intended for Naval Operations.

§ 334. Whereas a neutral is in no [3] wise obliged by his duty of impartiality to prevent his subjects from selling armed vessels to the belligerents, such armed vessels being merely contraband of war, a neutral is bound to employ the means at his disposal to prevent his subjects from building, fitting out, or arming, to the

[1] See below, § 347 (4).

[2] Germany reserved against Article 13.

[3] See below, §§ 350, 397.

order of either belligerent, vessels intended to be used as men-of-war, and to prevent the departure from his jurisdiction of any vessel which, by order of either belligerent, has been adapted to warlike use.[1] The difference between selling armed vessels to belligerents and building them to order is usually defined in the following way :—

An armed ship, being contraband of war, is in no wise different from other kinds of contraband, provided that she is not manned in a neutral port, so that she can commit hostilities at once after having reached the open sea. A subject of a neutral who builds an armed ship, or arms a merchantman, not to the order of a belligerent, but intending to sell her to a belligerent, does not differ from a manufacturer of arms who intends to sell them to a belligerent. There is nothing to prevent a neutral from allowing his subjects to sell armed vessels, and to deliver them to belligerents, either in a neutral port or in a belligerent port. In the cases of *The La Santissima Trinidad*[2] (1822) and *The Meteor*[3] (1866), American courts have recognised this;[4] and so did the unratified Declaration of London, which in Article 22 (10) enumerated as absolute contraband 'warships, including boats, and their distinctive component parts.'

On the other hand, if a subject of a neutral builds armed ships to the order of a belligerent, he prepares the means of naval operations, since the ships, on sailing outside the neutral territorial waters and taking in a crew and ammunition, can at once commit hostilities. Thus, through the carrying out of the order of the belligerent, the neutral territory has been made the base of naval operations; and as the duty of impartiality

[1] See Article 8 of Convention XIII.
[2] 7 Wheaton, p. 340.
[3] See Balch, 201, 202; Wharton, iii. § 396, p. 561.
[4] See Phillimore, iii. § 151*b*, and Hall, § 224; but see also Wehberg, pp. 411-413, who asserts that neutrals must prevent their subjects from selling armed vessels to belligerents. Hershey, p. 467, n. 8, would seem to be of the same opinion.

includes an obligation to prevent either belligerent from making neutral territory the base of military or naval operations, a neutral violates his neutrality by not preventing his subjects from carrying out an order of a belligerent for the building and fitting out of men-of-war.

This distinction, although of course logically correct, is hair-splitting. But as, according to the present law, neutral States need not prevent their subjects from supplying[1] arms and ammunition to belligerents, it will probably continue to be drawn.

However this may be, submarines are in the same category as surface vessels, and when, in 1914 during the World War, one of the Allied Powers ordered a number of submarines to be built by a firm in the United States, the American Government was of opinion that they could not permit the carrying out of the contract.[2]

The Alabama Case and the Three Rules of Washington.

§ 335. The movement for recognition of the fact that the duty of impartiality requires a neutral to prevent his subjects from building and fitting out to order of belligerents vessels intended for naval operations began with the famous case of *The Alabama.* In 1862,[3] during the American Civil War, the attention of the British Government was drawn by the Government of the United States to the fact that a vessel for warlike purposes was built in England to order of the insurgents. This vessel, afterwards called the *Alabama,* left Liverpool in July 1862 unarmed, but was met at the Azores by three other vessels, also coming from England, which

[1] See below, § 350.

[2] See *A.J.*, ix. (1915), pp. 177-187.

[3] For details, see Mountague Bernard, *Neutrality of Great Britain during the American Civil War* (1870), pp. 338-496; Geffcken, *Die Alabama Frage* (1872); Pradier-Fodéré, *La Question de l'Alabama* (1872); Caleb Cushing, *Le Traité de Washington* (1874); Bluntschli in *R.I*, ii. (1870), pp. 452-485; Balch, *The Alabama Question* (1900) and *L'Évolution de l'Arbitrage international* (1908), pp. 43-70; Westlake in the *Cambridge Modern History,* xii. pp. 16-22.

supplied her with guns and ammunition, so that she could at once begin to prey upon the merchantmen of the United States. On the conclusion of the Civil War, the United States claimed damages from Great Britain for the losses sustained by her merchant marine through the operations of the *Alabama* and other vessels likewise built in England. Negotiations went on for several years, and finally on May 8, 1871, the parties entered into the Treaty of Washington [1] for the purpose of having their difference settled by arbitration, Great Britain, the United States, Brazil, Italy, and Switzerland each choosing one arbitrator. The treaty contained three rules, since then known as 'The Three Rules of Washington,' to be binding upon the arbitrators, namely: [2]— 'A neutral Government is bound—

'*Firstly.* To use due diligence to prevent the fitting out, arming, or equipping within its jurisdiction, of any vessel which it has reasonable ground to believe is intended to cruise or carry on war against a Power with which it is at peace, and also to use like diligence to prevent the departure from its jurisdiction of any vessel intended to cruise or carry on war as above, such vessel having been specially adapted in whole or in part, within such jurisdiction, to warlike use.

'*Secondly.* Not to permit or suffer either belligerent to make use of its ports or waters as the base of naval operations against the other, or for the purpose of the renewal or augmentation of military supplies or arms, or the recruitment of men.

'*Thirdly.* To exercise due diligence in its own ports and waters, and as to all persons within its jurisdiction, to prevent any violations of the foregoing obligations and duties.'

In consenting that these rules should be binding upon the arbitrators, Great Britain expressly declared that

[1] Martens, *N.R.G.*, xx. p. 698.

[2] See Moore, vii. § 1330.

in her view these rules were not recognised rules of International Law at the time when the case of *The Alabama* occurred, but the treaty contained a stipulation that the parties 'agree to observe these rules as between themselves in future, and to bring them to the knowledge of other maritime Powers, and to invite them to accede to them.'

The arbitrators [1] met at Geneva in 1871, held thirty-two conferences there, and gave their decision [2] on September 14, 1872, according to which England had to pay 15,500,000 dollars damages to the United States.

The arbitrators put a construction upon the term '*due diligence*' [3] and asserted other opinions in their decision which are very much contested, and to which Great Britain never consented. Though Great Britain and the United States agreed upon the three rules, they did not at all agree upon their interpretation, and could not agree upon the contents of the communication to other maritime States stipulated by the Treaty of Washington. It ought not, therefore, to be said that the Three Rules of Washington [4] have literally become universal rules of International Law. Nevertheless, they were the starting-point of the movement for the universal recognition of the fact that the duty of impartiality obliges neutrals to prevent their subjects from building and fitting out, to order of belligerents, vessels intended for warlike purposes, and to prevent the departure from their jurisdiction of any vessel, which, by order of a belligerent, has been adapted to warlike use. Article 8 of Hague Convention XIII. copies almost verbally the first of the Three Rules of Washington, but with the important difference that it re-

[1] See Moore, *Arbitrations*, i. pp. 495-682.

[2] The award is printed in full in Moore, *Arbitrations*, i. pp. 653-659, and in Phillimore, iii. § 151*a*.

[3] See below, § 363.

[4] As regards the seven rules adopted by the Institute of International Law, at its meeting at the Hague in 1875, as emanating from the Three Rules of Washington, see *Annuaire*, i. (1877), p. 139.

places the words 'to use due diligence' by 'to employ the means at its disposal.' For this reason the construction put by the Geneva arbitrators upon the term *due diligence* is *not* applicable to Article 8, the question whether a neutral employed the means at his disposal being a mere question of fact.

IV

NEUTRAL ASYLUM TO LAND FORCES, WAR MATERIAL AND AIRMEN

Vattel, iii. §§ 132-133—Hall, §§ 226, 230—Halleck, ii. p. 150—Taylor, § 621—Wharton, iii. § 394—Moore, vii. §§ 1314-1318—Bluntschli, §§ 774, 776-776*a*, 785—Heffter, § 149—Geffcken in *Holtzendorff*, iv. pp. 662-665—Ullmann, § 191—Bonfils, Nos. 1461-1462—Rivier, ii. pp. 395-398—Calvo, iv. §§ 2668-2669—Fiore, iii. Nos. 1576, 1582, 1583—Martens, ii. § 133—Mérignhac, iii[a]. pp. 577-586—Pillet, pp. 286-287—Kleen, ii. §§ 151-157—Holland, *War*, Nos. 131-133—Zorn, pp. 316-352—Heilborn, *Rechte*, pp. 12-83—Garner, i. §§ 301-307—*Land Warfare*, §§ 485-501—Rolin-Jaequemyns in *R.I.*, iii. (1871), pp. 352-366.

On Neutral Asylum in general.

§ 336. Neutral territory, being outside the region of war,[1] offers an asylum to members of belligerent forces, to the subjects of the belligerents and their property, and to war material belonging to the belligerents. Since, according to the present rules of International Law, the duty of either belligerent to treat neutrals according to their impartiality must—the case of extreme necessity in self-defence excepted—prevent them from violating the territorial supremacy of neutrals, enemy persons and goods are perfectly safe on neutral territory. It is true that neither belligerent has a right to demand from a neutral[2] such asylum for his subjects, their property, and his State property. But neither has he any right to demand that a neutral should refuse

[1] See above, §§ 70, 71.

[2] The generally recognised usage by which a neutral grants temporary hospitality in his ports to vessels of either belligerent in distress is an exception discussed below in § 344.

it to the enemy. The territorial supremacy of the neutral enables him to use his discretion in granting or refusing asylum. However, his duty of impartiality must compel him, if he grants it, to take all such measures as are necessary to prevent his territory from being used as a base of hostile operations.

Now, neutral territory may be an asylum (1) for private property, (2) for public enemy property, especially war material, cash, and provisions, (3) for private subjects of the enemy, (4) for enemy land forces, (5) for enemy airmen, and (6) for enemy naval forces. Details, however, need only be given with regard to asylum to land forces, war material[1] and airmen, and to naval forces.[2] For with regard to private property and private subjects it need only be mentioned that private war material brought into neutral territory stands on the same footing as public war material of a belligerent brought there, and, further, that private enemy subjects are safe on neutral territory even if they are claimed by a belligerent as having committed war crimes.

As regards asylum to land forces, a distinction must be made between (1) prisoners of war, (2) single fugitive soldiers, and (3) troops, or whole armies, pursued by the enemy, and thereby induced to take refuge on neutral territory.

Neutral Territory and Prisoners of War.

§ 337. Neutral territory is an asylum to prisoners of war of either belligerent; they become free[3] *ipso facto* by coming into neutral territory, whether they have escaped from a place of detention and taken refuge on neutral territory, or whether they are brought as

[1] §§ 337-341.

[2] §§ 342-348.

[3] Thus when, in November 1917, a Russian prisoner who had escaped from a German prison camp in Schleswig was shot before reaching the Danish frontier but succeeded in crossing it, and two German soldiers went over and dragged him back to German territory, Germany apologised for the violation of Danish territory, and declared that she would not have hesitated to transfer the prisoner to the Danish authorities if he had not meanwhile died. See *The Times*, February 16, 1917.

prisoners into neutral territory by enemy troops who themselves take refuge there.[1] This principle has been generally recognised for centuries. An illustration occurred in 1588, when several Turkish and Barbary captives escaped from one of the galleys of the Spanish Armada which was wrecked near Calais; although the Spanish ambassador claimed them, France considered them to be freed by coming on her territory, and sent them to Constantinople.[2] But has the neutral on whose territory a prisoner has taken refuge the duty to retain him and thereby prevent him from rejoining his own army? Formerly this question was not settled. In 1870, during the Franco-German War, Belgium believed that it had such a duty, and detained a French non-commissioned officer who had been a prisoner in Germany and had escaped into Belgian territory with the intention of rejoining the French forces at once. Doubts were expressed upon this case;[3] but all writers agreed that it was different if escaped prisoners wanted to remain on the neutral territory; as they might at any subsequent time wish to rejoin their own forces, the neutral was considered to be obliged by his duty of impartiality to take adequate measures to prevent their so doing. There was likewise no unanimity as to whether prisoners brought into neutral territory by enemy forces taking refuge there, could be detained in case they intended at once to leave the neutral territory. Some writers[4] maintained that they could not; others asserted that they might always be detained, and had to comply with such measures as the neutral considered necessary to prevent them from rejoining their forces.[5]

[1] The case of prisoners on board a belligerent man-of-war which enters a neutral port is different; see below, § 345.

[2] See Hall, § 226.

[3] See Rolin-Jaequemyns in *R.I.*, iii. (1871), p. 355; Bluntschli, § 776; Heilborn, *Rechte*, pp. 32-34.

[4] For instance, Heilborn, *Rechte*, pp. 51-52.

[5] See Sauser-Hall in *R.G.*, xix. (1912), pp. 40-57, where this case, and the cases previously mentioned, are discussed.

Article 13 of Hague Convention v. settled the controversy by enacting that a neutral who receives prisoners of war who have escaped, or who are brought there by troops of the enemy taking refuge on neutral territory, shall leave them at liberty, but that, if he allows them to remain on his territory, he *may*—he need not!—assign them a place of residence so as to prevent them from rejoining their forces. Since, therefore, everything is left to the discretion of the neutral, he has to take into account the merits and needs of every case and to take such steps as he thinks adequate; a belligerent certainly cannot, as of right, call upon the neutral to detain them.

The case of unwounded prisoners who, with the consent of the neutral, are transported through neutral territory is different. Such prisoners do not become free on entering the neutral territory; but there is no doubt that a neutral, by consenting to the transport, violates his duty of impartiality, because it is equivalent to passage of troops through neutral territory (Article 2 of Convention v.).

Different again is the case where enemy soldiers are amongst the wounded whom a belligerent is allowed by a neutral to transport through neutral territory. Such wounded prisoners become free, but they must, according to Article 14 of Convention v., be guarded by the neutral, so as to ensure that they do not again take part in military operations.[1]

Fugitive Soldiers and Deserters on Neutral Territory.

§ 338. A neutral may grant asylum to single soldiers of belligerents who take refuge on his territory, although he need not do so, but may at once send them back. If he grants such asylum, his duty of impartiality obliges him to disarm them, and to take such measures as are necessary to prevent them from rejoining their forces. But it is in practice impossible for a neutral to

[1] See also Article 15 of Convention x. and below, § 348a.

be so watchful as to detect every single fugitive who enters his territory. It will always happen that such fugitives steal into neutral territory and leave it again later on to rejoin their forces without the neutral being responsible. Moreover, before he can incur responsibility for not doing so, a neutral must actually be in a position to detain such fugitives. Thus Luxemburg, during the Franco-German War, could not prevent hundreds of French soldiers, who fled into her territory after the capitulation of Metz, from rejoining the French forces, because it was a condition [1] of her neutralisation that she should not keep an army, and therefore, in contradistinction to Switzerland, was unable to mobilise troops for the purpose of fulfilling her duty of impartiality.

Different from the case of fugitive soldiers is the case of fugitive deserters. If they desert and cross the neutral territory for the purpose of joining the enemy, their case is hardly different from the case of men who pass through neutral territory, intending to enlist in the army of a belligerent.[2] For this reason they need not be interned if they come *individually*; but they must be interned if they come *in a body*. On the other hand, if they desert without any such intention, they need not be interned, even though they come in a body.

Neutral Territory and Fugitive Troops.

§ 339. On occasions during war large bodies of troops, or even a whole army, are obliged to cross the neutral frontier for the purpose of escaping captivity. A neutral need not permit this, and may repulse them on the spot; but he may also grant asylum. It is, however, obvious that the presence of such troops on neutral territory is a danger to the other party. The duty of impartiality incumbent upon a neutral obliges him, therefore, to disarm them at once, and to guard them so as to ensure that they do not again perform military acts

[1] See above, vol. i. § 100.

[2] See above, § 331.

against the enemy during the war. In this case Hague Convention v. enacts the following rules :—

Article 11 : 'A neutral Power which receives in its territory troops belonging to the belligerent armies shall detain them, if possible, at some distance from the theatre of war. It may keep them in camps, and even confine them in fortresses or localities assigned for the purpose. It shall decide whether officers are to be left at liberty on giving their parole that they will not leave the neutral territory without authorisation.'

Article 12 : 'In the absence of a special convention, the neutral Power shall supply the interned with the food, clothing, and relief which the dictates of humanity prescribe. At the conclusion of peace, the expenses caused by internment shall be made good.'

It is usual for troops who are not actually pursued by the enemy—if pursued they have no time to do it—to enter through their commander into a convention with the representative of the neutral concerned, stipulating the conditions upon which they cross the frontier and give themselves into his custody. Such conventions are valid without ratification, provided that they contain only such stipulations as do not disagree with International Law, and concern only the requirements of the case.

Although the detained troops are not prisoners of war captured by the neutral, they are nevertheless in his custody, and therefore under his disciplinary power, just as prisoners of war are under the disciplinary power of the State which keeps them in captivity. They do not enjoy the exterritoriality[1] due to armed forces abroad, because they are disarmed. As the neutral is required to prevent them from escaping, he must apply stern measures, and he may punish severely every member of the detained force who attempts to frus-

[1] See above, vol. i. § 445.

trate such measures, or does not comply with the disciplinary rules regarding order, sanitation, and the like.

The most remarkable instance known in history is the asylum granted by Switzerland during the Franco-German War to a French army of about 82,000 men with 10,000 horses, which crossed the frontier on February 1, 1871.[1] France had, after the conclusion of the war, to pay about eleven million francs for the maintenance of this army in Switzerland during the rest of the war.

Other instances occurred during the World War, when after the fall of Antwerp in 1914 Holland interned British troops which crossed into Holland, south of the River Scheldt, to escape the German Army,[2] and when the local authorities in Spanish New Guinea interned 900 Germans and 14,000 natives who crossed the Spanish frontier from German Cameroon.[3]

Neutral Territory and non-Combatant Members of Belligerent Forces.

§ 340. The duty of impartiality incumbent upon a neutral obliges him to detain in the same way as soldiers non-combatant[4] members of belligerent forces who cross his frontier. He may not, however, detain army surgeons and other non-combatants who are privileged according to Article 9 of the Geneva Convention.[5]

Neutral Territory and War Material of Belligerents.

§ 341. It can happen during war that war material belonging to one of the belligerents is brought into neutral territory for the purpose of saving it from capture by the enemy. It may be brought by troops crossing the neutral frontier to evade captivity, or it may be purposely sent there by order of a commander. Now, a neutral is by no means obliged to admit such material, just as he is not obliged to admit soldiers of

[1] See the convention regarding this asylum between the Swiss General Herzog and the French General Clinchant in Martens, *N.R.G.*, xix. p. 639.

[2] *The Times*, October 11, 1914.

[3] *The Times*, February 7, 1916.

[4] See Heilborn, *Rechte*, pp. 43-46. Convention v. does not mention this.

[5] See above, § 121.

belligerents. But if he does, his duty of impartiality obliges him to seize and retain it till after the conclusion of peace. War material includes arms, ammunition, provisions, horses, means of military transport (such as carts and the like), and everything else that belongs to the equipment of troops. But means of military transport are war material only so far as they are the property of a belligerent. If they are hired, or requisitioned, from private individuals, they may not be detained by the neutral.

It can likewise happen during war that war material which was originally the property of one of the belligerents but later had been seized and appropriated by the enemy, is brought by the latter into neutral territory. Does such material, through coming into neutral territory, become free, and must it be restored to its original owner? Or must it be retained by the neutral, and after the war be restored to the belligerent who brought it into the neutral territory? In analogy with prisoners of war who become free through being brought into neutral territory, it is maintained [1] that such war material becomes free, and must be restored to its original owner. To this, however, I cannot agree.[2] Since war material through seizure by the enemy becomes his property, and remains his property unless the other party re-seizes and thereby re-appropriates it, there is no reason for it to revert to its original owner upon being brought into neutral territory.[3]

§ 341*a*. No customary or conventional rules as yet

[1] See Hall, § 226.

[2] See Heilborn, *Rechte*, p. 60, and *Land Warfare*, § 492. The Dutch Government at the Second Hague Conference proposed a rule according to which captured war material brought by the captor into neutral territory should be restored, after the war, to its original owner, but—see *Deuxième Conférence*, *Actes*, vol. i. p. 145—this proposal was not accepted.

[3] See Heilborn, *Rechte*, pp. 61-65, where the question is discussed as to whether a neutral may claim a lien on war material brought into his territory for expenses incurred for the maintenance of detained troops belonging to the owner of the war material.

Neutral Territory and Belligerent Airmen.

exist for the case in which a belligerent air-vessel crosses into neutral air space, be it inadvertently or intentionally, and is compelled to land. During the World War the general practice of neutrals seems to have been always to detain the air-vessel and the airmen. Moreover, when belligerent aircraft passed over neutral territory without intending to land, they were fired at for the purpose of compelling them to do so.[1] But in case they came down, not on neutral territory, but on the open sea, and their crews were there rescued by neutral merchantmen and so brought into neutral territory, they were treated as shipwrecked soldiers, and were not detained.[2]

V

NEUTRAL ASYLUM TO NAVAL FORCES AND SHIPWRECKED WAR MATERIAL

Vattel, iii. § 132—Hall, § 231—Westlake, ii. pp. 234-242—Twiss, ii. § 222—Taylor, §§ 635, 636, 640—Wharton, iii. § 394—Wheaton, § 434—Moore, vii. §§ 1314-1317—Bluntschli, §§ 775-776*b*—Heffter, § 149—Geffcken in *Holtzendorff*, iv. pp. 665-667, 674—Ullmann, § 191—Bonfils, No. 1463—Despagnet, No. 692 *ter*—Rivier, ii. p. 405—Calvo, iv. §§ 2669-2684—Fiore, iii. Nos. 1576-1581, 1584, and *Code*, Nos. 1811-1815—Martens, ii. § 133—Kleen, ii. § 155—Pillet, pp. 305-307—Perels, § 39, p. 213—Testa, pp. 173-187—Dupuis, Nos. 308-314, and *Guerre*, Nos. 304-328—Ortolan, ii. pp. 247-291—Hautefeuille, i. pp. 344-405—Takahashi, pp. 418-484—Garner, ii. §§ 561-564—Trainé, *Das Gastrecht im Seekrieg* (1912), §§ 14-20—Einicke, *Rechte und Pflichten der neutralen Machte im Seekrieg* (1912), pp. 153-325—Popy, *Les Problèmes soulevés par l'Asile maritime en Temps de Guerre* (1913), and in *R.G.*, xx. (1913), pp. 574-599—Wehberg, § 11—Bajer in *R.I.*, 2nd Ser. ii. (1900), pp. 242-247—Lapradelle in *R.G.*, xi. (1904), pp. 531-564.

Asylum to Naval Forces in contradistinction to Asylum to Land Forces.

§ 342. Whereas it is a condition of the granting of asylum by a neutral to land forces, and single members of them, that he should disarm them and detain them for the purpose of preventing them from joining in further military operations, a neutral may grant tem-

[1] See the details given by Garner, i. §§ 301-303.

[2] See below, § 348a.

porary asylum to men-of-war of[1] belligerents without being obliged to disarm and detain them.[2] This is so, whether belligerent men-of-war seek neutral asylum because they are chased into neutral waters by the enemy[3] or from other causes. The reason is that the sea is considered to be an international highway, that the ports of all nations serve more or less the interests of international traffic on the sea, and that the conditions of navigation make it necessary to extend a certain hospitality in ports to vessels of all nations. Thus the rules of International Law regarding asylum in neutral ports to men-of-war of belligerents have developed on somewhat different lines from the rules regarding asylum to land forces. But the rule, that the duty of impartiality incumbent upon a neutral must prevent him from allowing belligerents to use his territory as a base of operations of war, is nevertheless valid regarding asylum granted to their men-of-war.

Neutral Asylum to Naval Forces optional.

§ 343. Although a neutral may grant asylum to belligerent men-of-war in his ports, he has no duty to do so. He may prohibit all belligerent men-of-war from entering any of his ports, whether these vessels are pursued by the enemy, or desire to enter for other reasons. However, his duty of impartiality must prevent him from denying to one party what he grants to the other; he may not, therefore, allow men-of-war of one belligerent to enter his ports and exclude men-of-war of the other belligerent (Article 9 of Convention XIII.). Neutrals, as a rule, admit men-of-war of both parties, often, however, excluding them from certain ports. Thus, during the Crimean War, Austria prohibited all belligerent men-of-war from entering the port of Cattaro.

[1] What is here said with regard to neutral asylum to men-of-war of belligerents applies also to such of their vessels as are assimilated to men-of-war; see above, § 333.

[2] See, however, below, § 347, concerning the abuse of asylum, which must be prohibited.

[3] But this is not universally admitted; see, for instance, Kleen, ii. pp. 29-31. The point has not been settled by Convention XIII.

Thus, further, Great Britain during the American Civil War closed to all belligerent men-of-war the ports of the Bahama Islands, stress of weather excepted.

Be that as it may, since a neutral must prevent belligerents from making his territory the base of military operations, he must not, as has already been explained,[1] allow an unlimited number of men-of-war belonging to one of the belligerents to stay simultaneously in one of his ports.

Asylum to Naval Forces in Distress.

§ 344. To the rule that a neutral need not admit men-of-war of the belligerents to his ports there is no exception in strict law. However, there is an international usage that belligerent men-of-war in distress should never be prevented from making for the nearest port. In accordance with this usage, vessels in distress have always been allowed to enter even such neutral ports as are closed to belligerent men-of-war. There are even instances known of belligerent men-of-war in distress having asked for, and been granted, asylum by the enemy in an enemy port.[2]

Asylum to Submarine Vessels.

§ 344*a*. During the World War the question arose whether submarine vessels forming part of the belligerent forces should have the same status as other men-of-war, and therefore be granted temporary asylum in neutral ports. In August 1916 the Allies proposed to neutral Powers that no asylum should be granted to belligerent submarine vessels of any description. They argued[3] that in their case the application of the principles of the Law of Nations was affected by special and novel conditions: (1) submarines could navigate and remain at sea submerged, and thus escape all control and observation; (2) it was impossible to identify them and to establish their national character, whether neutral or

[1] See above, § 333 (7).
[2] See above, § 189.
[3] *Parl. Papers*, Misc., No. 33 (1916), Cd. 8349. See Reeves in *A.J.*, xi. (1917), p. 147, and Hall, § 231*a*.

belligerent, combatant or non-combatant, and to remove the capacity for harm inherent in their nature; (3) any place which provided a submarine war-vessel far from its base with opportunity for rest and replenishment of its supplies thereby furnished such an addition to its powers that the place became in fact, through the advantages it gave, a base of naval operations.

However, no agreement was reached upon this proposal, the various Powers acting differently. Thus whereas the United States of America rejected it, and admitted the German submarine war-vessel U 53 to the American harbour of Newport,[1] Norway by a decree of October 13, 1916,[2] forbade all belligerent submarine war-vessels from entering Norwegian territorial waters, except in case of *force majeure*. Sweden by a decree of July 19, 1916,[1] and Holland by its declaration of neutrality of August 4, 1914,[3] had adopted a similar policy. Spain by a decree of June 29, 1917, prohibited all belligerent submarines from entering Spanish waters and ports, from whatever cause.

Exterritoriality of Men-of-War during Asylum.

§ 345. The exterritoriality which, according to a universally recognised rule of International Law, men-of-war enjoy [4] in foreign ports, obtains even in time of war during their stay in neutral ports. Therefore, for example, prisoners of war on board do not become free by coming into the neutral port [5] so long as they are not brought on shore. On the other hand, belligerent men-of-war are expected to comply with all orders made by the neutral to prevent them from making his ports the base of their operations of war—an order, for instance, not to leave the ports at the same time as vessels of the other belligerent. And, if they do not comply voluntarily, they may be made to do so through appli-

[1] Garner, ii. § 564. As to *The Deutschland*, see Garner, ii. § 565.

[2] *Journal de Droit international* (Clunet), xliv. (1917), p. 322.

[3] *R.G.*, xxiv. (1917), Documents, pp. 110-114, 186.

[4] See above, vol. i. § 450.

[5] See above, § 337.

cation of force, for a neutral has a duty to prevent by all means at hand the abuse of the asylum granted.

Special provision is made by Article 24 of Convention XIII. for the case of a belligerent man-of-war which refuses to leave a neutral port: 'If, notwithstanding the notification of the neutral Power, a belligerent ship of war does not leave a port in which it is not entitled to remain, the neutral Power is entitled to take such measures as it considers necessary to render the ship incapable of putting to sea so long as the war lasts, and the commanding officer of the ship must facilitate the execution of such measures. When a belligerent ship is detained by a neutral Power, the officers and crew are likewise detained. The officers and crew so detained may be left in the ship or kept either on another vessel or on land, and may be subjected to such measures of restriction as it may appear necessary to impose upon them. A sufficient number of men must, however, be always left on board for looking after the vessel. The officers may be left at liberty on giving their word not to quit neutral territory without permission.'

If an officer, left at liberty on giving his word, nevertheless escapes from the neutral country, his Government is in duty bound to compel him to return, and the neutral Government can subject him to disciplinary punishment for having broken his parole.[1]

If a vessel is interned, and therefore dismantled, she loses the character of a man-of-war. She no longer enjoys the privilege[2] of exterritoriality due to men-of-war in foreign waters, and prisoners on board become free, although they must be detained by the neutral concerned.[3]

[1] See the remarkable case of the escape of members of the crews of German cruisers interned on parole in the United States, reported by Scott in *A.J.*, x. (1916), pp. 877-882, and Garner, ii. § 563.

[2] See Scott in *A.J.*, x. (1916), pp. 355-357.

[3] See below, § 348*a* (6).

§ 346. A belligerent man-of-war, to which temporary asylum is granted in a neutral port, is not only not disarmed and detained; as has already been stated, facilities may even be rendered to her as regards slight repairs,[1] the supply in limited quantities of provisions and coal,[2] and, under certain circumstances, the enrolment of a very small number of sailors.[3] **Facilities to Men-of-War during Asylum.**

§ 347. However, it would be easy for belligerent men-of-war receiving temporary asylum in neutral ports to abuse it, if neutrals were not required to prohibit such abuse. **Abuse of Asylum to be prohibited.**

(1) It can abuse asylum, in the first place, by ascertaining whether any, and if so what kind of, enemy vessels are in the same neutral port, accompanying them when they leave, and attacking them immediately they reach the open sea. To prevent such abuse, in the eighteenth century several neutral States arranged that, if belligerent men-of-war or privateers met enemy vessels in a neutral port, they were not to be allowed to leave together, but an interval of at least twenty-four hours was to elapse between the sailing of the vessels. During the nineteenth century this so-called twenty-four hours rule was enforced by the majority of States, and the Second Hague Conference, as has already been mentioned,[4] expressly enacted it.

(2) Asylum can, secondly, be abused by wintering in a port in order to wait for other vessels of the same fleet, or by similar intentional delay. There is no doubt that neutrals must prohibit this abuse by ordering such belligerent men-of-war to leave the neutral ports.[5]

(3) Asylum can, thirdly, be abused by repairing a belligerent man-of-war which has become unseaworthy. Although, as has already been explained,[6] small repairs

[1] See above, § 333 (5).
[2] See above, § 333 (4).
[3] See above, § 333 (3).
[4] See above, § 333 (2).
[5] See above, § 333 (6).
[6] See above, § 333 (5).

are allowed, a neutral would violate his duty of impartiality by allowing such repairs as would make good the unseaworthiness of a belligerent man-of-war.

(4) Asylum can, lastly, be abused by remaining in a neutral port an undue length of time in order to escape attack and capture by the other belligerent.[1] Since nowadays a right of pursuit into neutral waters, which was asserted by Bynkershoek,[2] is no longer recognised, it would be an abuse of asylum if an escaping vessel were allowed to make a prolonged stay in the neutral waters, and a neutral who allowed it would violate his duty of impartiality by assisting one of the belligerents to the disadvantage of the other.[3] Therefore, when, after the battle off Port Arthur in August 1904, the Russian battleship *Cesarewitch*, the cruiser *Novik*, and three destroyers escaped and took refuge in the then German port of Tsing-Tau, the *Novik*, which was uninjured, had to leave the port after a few hours,[4] whereas the other vessels, which were too damaged to leave the port, were disarmed and, together with their crews, detained till the conclusion of peace. Again, when, at the end of May 1905, after the battle of Tsu Shima, three damaged Russian men-of-war, the *Aurora*, *Oleg*, and *Jemchug*, escaped into the harbour of Manila, the

[1] See above, § 333 (8).

[2] *Quaestiones Juris publici*, i. c. 8. See also above, §§ 288, 320.

[3] It was only during the Russo-Japanese War in 1904 that this became generally recognised; but Article 24 of Convention XIII. places it beyond all doubt. Until that war, it was controverted whether a neutral was obliged either to dismiss or to disarm and detain men-of-war which had fled into his ports to escape attack and capture. See Hall, § 231, and Perels, § 39, p. 213, in contradistinction to Fiore, iii. No. 1579. The 'Règlement sur le Régime légal des Navires et de leurs Équipages dans les Ports étrangers,' adopted by the Institute of International Law in 1898 at its meeting at the Hague—see *Annuaire*, xvii. (1898), p. 273—answered (Article 42) the question in the affirmative.

[4] This case marks the difference between the duties of neutrals as regards asylum to land forces and asylum to naval forces. Whereas land forces crossing neutral frontiers must either be at once repulsed or else detained, men-of-war may be granted the right to stay for some limited time within neutral harbours and then leave unhindered; see above, § 342. The supply of a small quantity of coal to the *Novik* in Tsing-Tau was criticised by writers in the press, but unjustly; see above, § 333 (4).

United States of America ordered them to be disarmed and, together with their crews, to be detained during the war.

§ 348. It may happen during war that neutral men-of-war pick up, and save from drowning, soldiers and sailors belonging to belligerent men-of-war sunk by the enemy, or that they take them on board for other reasons. Neutral men-of-war being an asylum for the members of the belligerent armed forces so rescued, the question arose whether they must be given up to the enemy, or must be detained during the war, or may be brought to their home country. Two cases were on record before the Second Hague Conference which illustrate this matter. **Neutral Men-of-War as an Asylum.**

(1) At the beginning of the Chino-Japanese War, on July 25, 1894, after the Japanese cruiser *Naniwa* had sunk the British ship *Kow-shing*, which served as a transport carrying Chinese troops,[1] forty-five Chinese soldiers, who clung to the mast of the sinking ship, were rescued by the French gunboat *Lion*, and brought to the Korean harbour of Chemulpo. Hundreds of others saved themselves on some islands near the spot where the incident occurred, and 120 of these were taken on board the German man-of-war *Iltis* and brought back to the Chinese port of Tientsin.[2]

(2) At the beginning of the Russo-Japanese War, on February 9, 1904, after the Russian cruisers *Variag* and *Korietz* had accepted the challenge [3] of a Japanese fleet, fought a battle outside Chemulpo, and returned, crowded with wounded, to the harbour, the British cruiser *Talbot*, the French *Pascal*, and the Italian *Elba* received large numbers of the crews of the disabled Russian cruisers. The Japanese demanded that these neutral men-of-war

[1] See above, § 89 n.

[2] See Takahashi, *Cases on International Law during the Chino-Japanese War* (1899), pp. 36, 51.

[3] See above, § 320 (1).

should give up the rescued men as prisoners of war, but the neutral commanders demurred, and it was arranged that the rescued men should be handed over to the Russians under the condition that they should not take part in hostilities during the war.[1]

Article 13 of Convention x. of the Second Hague Conference settled the question raised by these cases as follows: 'If wounded, sick, or shipwrecked are taken on board a neutral man-of-war, precaution must be taken, so far as possible, that they do not again take part in the operations of the war.'

Two new classes of cases, however, which occurred during the World War, raised difficulties as to the proper interpretation of this article. (1) It speaks only of neutral *men-of-war* and says nothing concerning the case in which other neutral *public vessels*—such as lightships, revenue cutters, and the like — rescue wounded, sick, or shipwrecked soldiers or sailors. There ought to be no doubt that this article must be applied by analogy, although during the World War it was reported that Holland did not detain, but released, a number of German airmen who had been rescued by a Dutch public lightship.

(2) In the case of *The Runhild*, the question arose whether Article 13 applied if a neutral warship rescued wounded, sick, or shipwrecked soldiers or sailors, not on the open sea, but within the maritime belt of the neutral concerned. The *Runhild* was a Swedish vessel, captured in November 1916 by a German submarine. While being navigated by a prize crew towards a German port, she struck a mine and sank. All on board entered the lifeboats and rowed towards the Swedish coast; after having reached the Swedish maritime belt, they were taken on board by a Swedish torpedo boat and subsequently landed in Sweden. The prize crew were

[1] See Lawrence, *War*, pp. 63-75, and Takahashi, pp. 462-466.

at first interned by Sweden according to Article 13; but, on protest from Germany, they were released in July 1917, the Swedish Government asserting—incorrectly, I believe—that this article only applies when the rescue is effected on the open sea.

§ 348*a*. Just as in war on land members of the belligerent forces may find themselves on neutral territory, so in war on sea shipwrecked or wounded or sick belligerent soldiers and sailors may be brought into neutral territory, or reach it by their own efforts. The more important cases that may occur are the following:— **Neutral Territory and Shipwrecked Soldiers and Sailors.**

(1) A belligerent man-of-war may capture shipwrecked, wounded, or sick enemy soldiers or sailors, and, instead of sending them to one of her own ports, send them to a neutral port. The neutral concerned *need not* receive them; but he *may* grant them asylum. If he does, according to Article 15 of Convention x., he is obliged—unless there is an arrangement to the contrary between him and both belligerents—to guard them so as to prevent them from again taking part in the war;[1] and the expenses of tending and interning them have to be paid by the belligerent to whom they belong.

(2) Neutral merchantmen[2] may have rescued wounded, sick, or shipwrecked soldiers or sailors of their own accord, or may have taken them on board by request from a belligerent man-of-war. According to Article 12 of Convention x., the surrender of these men may at any time be demanded by any belligerent man-of-war. But if such a demand be not made, and the men are brought into a neutral port, it is an indirect inference from Article 13 (which stipulates the detention of men received by neutral *men-of-war*) that men brought in by a neutral *merchantman* need not be detained.

(3) Shipwrecked soldiers or sailors may, by their own

[1] See above, § 205.

[2] See above, § 208 (2).

efforts, succeed in reaching a neutral coast, be it by swimming, or by clinging to rafts, or in one of their own lifeboats. Neither Convention x. nor Convention xiii. provides for this case. However, the fact that shipwrecked soldiers and sailors rescued by a neutral merchantman and landed in a neutral harbour need not be detained, warrants the opinion that they need not be detained in case they succeed in reaching a neutral coast by their own efforts. For why should they be treated worse than those rescued and landed by neutral merchantmen?

The practice during the World War was not uniform. Thus Norway detained survivors from the sunk British vessels *India* and *Lord Alverstone* who succeeded in reaching the Norwegian coast; and Spain detained the surviving combatants from the British transport *Woodfield* who reached the Moroccan coast in their own lifeboat. On the other hand, Spain did not detain the German prize crew who gained the Spanish coast in a lifeboat belonging to their prize the *Thyra*; and Greece, while still neutral, did not detain the survivors of the *Ramazan*, a sunk British troopship.

(4) It may happen that belligerent vessels are unlawfully attacked and sunk by the other belligerent while in neutral territorial waters, and soldiers or sailors from these vessels may reach the neutral shore. Conventions x. and xiii. do not provide for this case either. Since, even if the vessel had been lawfully attacked and sunk on the open sea, these men need not be detained if they are brought to a neutral port by a neutral merchantman, or reach it by their own efforts, they surely need not be detained if their vessel was unlawfully attacked and sunk in neutral waters. Indeed, in this case, even if they are rescued by a neutral man-of-war and landed on the neutral shore, they need not be detained. The reason for this is, that the attacked

vessel, and the men on board, being legitimately in neutral territory when the vessel was unlawfully sunk, the survivors were not saved from *lawful* capture by the rescuing man-of-war. Their capture by the enemy would have been as unlawful as was the sinking of their vessel; and Article 13[1] of Convention x. does therefore not apply.

However, during the World War Denmark ruled differently. In August 1915 a British submarine ran aground in Danish territorial waters, and was notified that she must be refloated within twenty-four hours to avoid sequestration. However, before the lapse of this period she was attacked and sunk by a German destroyer. Survivors were rescued by a Danish man-of-war and landed in Denmark; and the Danish Government held that they must be detained. Again, in September 1917, a British man-of-war pursuing a German armed trawler fired on her after she had already entered Danish neutral waters, and sank her; when the survivors reached the Danish coast, the Danish Government again ruled that they must be detained and interned.[2]

(5) Armed guards placed by a belligerent on a neutral merchantman may reach a neutral port. During the World War the Allies quite generally resorted to the practice of sending neutral merchantmen stopped by their cruisers to a belligerent port for the purpose of search.[3] These vessels were not captured, but were simply ordered to navigate to a certain belligerent port; and frequently an armed guard was placed on board so as to ensure obedience. Now if one of these vessels on her way to the belligerent port of search

[1] See above, § 348.

[2] The case of *The Dresden*—see below, § 361—in which the survivors were detained by Chili, is different, because orders had been given for her to be disarmed, and her men interned, before the attack by the British occurred.

[3] See below, § 421*a*.

was compelled by distress to call at a neutral port, there would certainly be no duty upon the neutral to detain the crew, because the case is analogous to that of a prize in distress brought into a neutral port.[1] But suppose the crew of the vessel, once in a neutral port, refuse to leave, or that the vessel reaches a port of her own flag State where, of course, she would be released by the local authorities: must the neutral then detain the armed guard, or may he permit them to leave? Again, if the crew overpower the armed guard, and take refuge in a neutral port, must the neutral detain the guard?

Since in all these, and similar, cases the guard is, as it were, stranded on neutral territory, there is, in my opinion, no duty upon the neutral to detain and intern them. An illustrative case is that of *The Andrew Welch*. In 1915, during the World War, while the United States was still neutral, the *Andrew Welch*, an American vessel, was stopped on the open sea by a British cruiser and was directed to proceed to Lerwick, an armed guard of six men having been put on board. Owing to stress of weather she was compelled to enter the port of Christiansand; once there, the crew refused to proceed to Lerwick. The Norwegian Government did not detain the armed guard, but allowed them to return to England.

(6) Prisoners of war held on a belligerent vessel may reach neutral shores. Two classes of cases must here be distinguished:—

(i) It may happen that the vessel is attacked by the enemy and sunk or wrecked, and that surviving prisoners either reach a neutral coast by their own efforts or are rescued and brought there by a neutral merchantman. Or again, prisoners on a belligerent vessel may jump overboard while the vessel is at sea and reach a neutral

[1] See above, § 328, and Article 21 of Convention XIII.

coast. The case of these men is analogous to that of prisoners on land who escape into neighbouring neutral territory. For this reason the neutral must not detain them, but must allow them to leave the country; only if the neutral permits them to remain in the country may he intern them.[1]

(ii) On the other hand, it may happen that prisoners of war are held on board a belligerent vessel which is in a neutral port for legitimate purposes, but having failed to leave it in due time, is detained with its officers and crew. What is the fate of the prisoners on board? That they now become free, there is no doubt; but the question is whether the neutral may allow them to leave the country, or is in duty bound to detain and intern them. It is asserted that they need not be detained, because the case is analogous to the case of prisoners brought into neutral territory by enemy troops which take refuge there. Yet this analogy does not exist, because belligerent troops in land warfare entering neutral territory, if not repulsed on the spot, must at once be disarmed and interned, whereas men-of-war may, for certain purposes and to a certain extent, be allowed to enter neutral harbours and receive hospitality there without being disarmed and detained. It is only when they do not leave in due time that they must be detained. For this reason, in the case now under discussion, the neutral is confronted by the fact that there are on his territory a number of combatants of both belligerents, *i.e.* the officers and crew of the vessel, and the former prisoners. As both parties arrived legitimately in the neutral harbour, if the neutral afterwards detains the officers and crew, he must in justice likewise detain the former prisoners of war.[2]

§ 348*b*. During war shipwrecked war material—or

[1] See above, § 337, and Article 13 of Convention v.

[2] See above, § 345.

Neutral Territory and Shipwrecked War Material.

even an abandoned shipwrecked man-of-war—belonging to a belligerent may be brought to neutral territory. Several cases must be distinguished :—

(1) In case such shipwrecked war material is brought into neutral territory by the forces of the belligerent owner for the purpose of avoiding capture by the enemy, there is no doubt that the neutral State must sequestrate it, and must not restore it to the belligerent owner till after the war.

(2) The same is valid in case shipwrecked war material is washed up on a neutral shore, or is salved at sea by a neutral man-of-war.

(3) Different, however, is the case, which is not settled, of shipwrecked war material being picked up on the open sea by neutral *merchantmen* and carried to a neutral harbour. Several such cases occurred during the World War.[1] Thus in December 1914 the *Orn*, a Norwegian merchant vessel, salved part of the naval gear of the British cruisers *Cressy*, *Hogue*, and *Aboukir*, which had been sunk by submarine, and brought it to the Hook of Holland. In the same month the same vessel brought to the Hook of Holland a British officer and mechanic in a seaplane which had been forced to descend in the North Sea. In January 1916 a boat from the Noord-Hinder lightship approached an abandoned British seaplane, removed a Lewis machine gun and other articles, and took them to the lightship, whence they were sent to the mainland ; the seaplane, stripped of its machine gun, was ultimately recovered at sea by the British authorities. In April 1916 ship's gear and a quantity of stores of various kinds belonging to the British destroyer *Medusa*, which had been abandoned by her crew in the North Sea, were salved by Dutch fishermen, and brought to Holland. In the same month Lieutenant Beare's seaplane was obliged

[1] See *Parl. Papers*, Misc., No. 4 (1918), Cd. 8985.

to descend in the North Sea, and he was rescued together with his machine by a Dutch fishing boat which took them to a Dutch port. In September 1917 a British seaplane manned by Lieutenant Hopcroft and Petty-Officer Garner, which had been forced to descend in the North Sea, was rescued by a Dutch fishing boat, and taken to a Dutch port. In all these cases the rescued officers were released, but the shipwrecked material was retained by Holland. The British Government demanded the release of the material also, correctly contending that there was no rule of International Law which forced a neutral Government to retain it, and that the case of shipwrecked material brought by neutral merchantmen into a neutral port was essentially similar to that of rescued belligerent soldiers and sailors similarly brought into a neutral port. The Dutch Government, however, refused to agree, asserting that the duties of neutrality did not allow them to release the war material, although a special rule allowed them to release the officers.

Whatever the merits of the case may be, the arguments by which the Dutch Government defended their attitude were singularly inapplicable. They quoted Article 6 of Convention XIII. of the Second Hague Conference which forbids 'the supply, in any manner, directly or indirectly, by a neutral Power to a belligerent Power, of warships, ammunition, or war material of any kind,' but this article has nothing whatever to do with the case. They contended that the release of belligerent soldiers and sailors rescued by neutral merchantmen was an exception to a general principle sanctioned by a special rule. Yet no such special rule exists, the release of belligerent soldiers and sailors rescued by neutral merchantmen being simply, as has already been shown,[1] an inference from Article 13 of Convention X.

[1] See above, § 348*a* (2).

VI

SUPPLIES AND LOANS TO BELLIGERENTS

Vattel, iii. § 110—Hall, §§ 216-217—Westlake, ii. pp. 251-253—Lawrence, § 235—Phillimore, iii. § 151—Twiss, ii. §§ 227, 228—Halleck, ii. p. 186—Taylor, §§ 622-625—Walker, § 67—Wharton, iii. §§ 390-391—Moore, vii. §§ 1307-1312—Bluntschli, §§ 765-768—Heffter, § 148—Geffcken in *Holtzendorff*, iv. pp. 686-700—Ullmann, §§ 191-192—Bonfils, Nos. 1471-1474—Despagnet, Nos. 693-694—Rivier, ii. pp. 385-411—Calvo, iv. §§ 2624-2630—Fiore, iii. Nos. 1559-1563—Martens, ii. § 134—Kleen, i. §§ 66-69, 96-97—Mérignhac, iii[a]. pp. 547-575—Pillet, pp. 289-293—Dupuis, Nos. 317-319—*Land Warfare*, §§ 477-480—Einicke, *Rechte und Pflichten der neutralen Mächte im Seekrieg* (1912), pp. 71-117—Pyke, *The Law of Contraband of War* (1915), pp. 55-88—Gregory, *The Manufacture and Sale of Munitions of War* (1916)—Westlake, *Papers*, pp. 362-392—Nys in *R.I.*, 2nd Ser. xv. (1913), pp. 181-196—Butte in the *Proceedings of the American Society of International Law*, ix. (1916), pp. 112-134—Morey and Gregory in *A.J.*, x. (1916), pp. 467-491, 543-555—Garner, ii. §§ 546-559, and in the *Proceedings of the American Society of International Law*, x. (1916), pp. 18-32, and in *A.J.*, x. (1916), pp. 749-797.

Supply on the part of Neutrals.

§ 349. The duty of impartiality must prevent a neutral from supplying belligerents with arms, ammunition, vessels, and military provisions,[1] whether for money or gratuitously. A neutral who sold arms and ammunition to a belligerent at a profit, and one who supplied them as a gift, would each violate their duty of impartiality. So far as direct transactions regarding such supply between belligerents and neutrals are concerned, the rule is settled. The case is different, however, where a neutral does not directly and knowingly deal with a belligerent, but is, or ought to be, aware that he is indirectly supplying a belligerent. Different neutral States have taken up different attitudes regarding cases of this kind. Thus in 1825, during the War of Independence which the Spanish South American Colonies waged against their mother country, the Swedish Government sold three old men-of-war, the

[1] See Article 6 of Convention XIII.

Försigtigheten, *Euridice*, and *Camille*, to two merchants, who on their part sold them to English merchants representing the Government of the Mexican insurgents. When Spain complained, Sweden rescinded the contract.[1] Further, the British Government in 1863, during the American Civil War, after selling an old gunboat, the *Victor*, to a private purchaser and subsequently finding that the agents of the Confederate States had obtained possession of her, gave an order that during the war no more Government ships should be sold.[2] On the other hand, the Government of the United States of America, in pursuance of an Act passed in 1868 for the sale of arms which the end of the Civil War had rendered superfluous, sold in 1871, notwithstanding the Franco-German War, thousands of arms and other war material, which were shipped to France.[3] The attitude then adopted by the United States is now generally condemned, and Article 6 of Convention XIII. may be quoted against a repetition of such a practice on the part of a neutral State. This article prohibits the supply in any manner, directly or *indirectly*, by a neutral State to a belligerent, of warships, ammunition, or war material of any kind whatever.

Supply on the part of Subjects of Neutrals.

§ 350. In contradistinction to supply to belligerents by neutral States, the supply of such articles by subjects of neutrals is lawful, and neutral States are not, therefore, obliged by their duty of impartiality to prevent it. Article 7 of Convention V. and Article 7 of Convention XIII. concur in enacting the old customary rule that 'A neutral Power is not bound to prevent the export or transit, for one or other of the belligerents, of arms, munitions of war, or, in general, of anything which can be of use to an army or fleet.' Moreover,

[1] See Martens, *Causes célèbres*, v. pp. 229-254.

[2] See Lawrence, 3rd ed. p. 520.

[3] See Wharton, iii. § 391, and Moore, vii. § 1309.

Article 18 [1] of Convention v. recognises that the furnishing of supplies to one belligerent by subjects of neutrals who do not live on the territory of the other belligerent, or on territory occupied by him, does not invest them with enemy character. When, in August 1870, during the Franco-German War, Germany lodged complaints with the British Government for not prohibiting its subjects from supplying arms and ammunition to the French Government, Great Britain correctly replied that she was not by International Law under any obligation to prevent her subjects from doing so.

Again, during the World War, the Government of the United States took up the same attitude, when Germany and Austria-Hungary complained because American manufacturers and traders supplied the Allies with arms and ammunition.[2]

Of course, a neutral State which is anxious to avoid all controversy and friction can, by his Municipal Law, order his subjects to abstain from furnishing such supplies, as, for instance, did Switzerland and Belgium during the Franco-German War. But such an attitude is dictated by political prudence, and not by any obligation imposed by International Law.

The endeavour to make a distinction between furnishing supplies in single cases, or on a small scale, and furnishing supplies on a large scale, and to regard only the former as lawful,[3] has found recognition neither in theory nor in practice. As International Law stands, belligerents may make use of visit, search, and seizure to protect themselves against the conveyance of contraband to the enemy by sea by subjects of neutrals. But so far as their home State is concerned, such neutral

[1] That Great Britain entered a reservation against Article 18 was pointed out above, in § 88, n. 2, where the meaning of the reservation was explained.

[2] See *A.J.*, ix. (1915), pp. 687-694, 927-934, and the excellent article of Garner in *A.J.*, x. (1916), pp. 749-797; see also Garner, ii. §§ 546-558.

[3] See Bluntschli, § 766.

subjects, at the risk of having their property seized during transit, may supply either belligerent with any amount of arms, ammunition, coal, provisions, and even with armed ships,[1] provided always that they deal with the belligerents in the ordinary way of commerce.

The case is different when there is no ordinary commerce with a belligerent Government, and when subjects of neutrals directly supply a belligerent army or navy, or parts of them. If, for instance, a belligerent fleet is cruising outside the maritime belt of a neutral, that neutral must prevent vessels belonging to his subjects from bringing coal, arms, ammunition, and provisions to that fleet; for otherwise he would be allowing the belligerent to use neutral resources for naval operations.[2] But he need not prevent vessels belonging to his subjects from bringing coal, arms, ammunition, and provisions to belligerent ports, although the supply is destined for the navy and the army of the belligerent. Nor need he prevent belligerent merchantmen from coming into his ports and transporting arms and the like, bought from his subjects, to the ports of their home State. Nor need he prevent vessels belonging to his subjects from following a belligerent fleet, and supplying it *en route*[3] with coal, ammunition, provisions, and the like, provided that this does not take place in the neutral maritime belt.

There is no doubt then that, as the law stands at present, neutrals need not prevent their subjects from supplying belligerents with arms and ammunition. Yet there is also no doubt that such supplies are apt to prolong a war which otherwise would come to an end

[1] See above, § 334, and below, § 397.

[2] See above, § 333 (4); and the Note addressed by Austria-Hungary to the United States on June 29, 1915, during the World War, and the American reply of August 12, 1915, cited by Garner, ii. § 549 n.

[3] See above, § 311, n. 4.

at an earlier date. But it will be a long time, if it ever happens, before it is made the duty of neutrals to prevent such supplies as far as is in their power, and to punish such of their subjects as furnish them. The profit derived from such supplies being enormous, the members of the Family of Nations are not inclined to cripple the trade of their subjects by preventing them. Further, belligerents want to have the opportunity of replenishing their arms and ammunition if they run short during war. Moreover, an alteration of the present law would be to the disadvantage of an innocent belligerent, who had not expected an attack, and was therefore not prepared for war, while his adversary, who planned the attack, would have made ample preparation. However this may be, the question is one of the standard of public morality.[1] If this standard rises, and it becomes the conviction of the world at large that the supply of arms and ammunition by subjects of neutrals is apt to lengthen wars, a rule will appear under which neutrals have to prevent it.

Loans and Subsidies on the part of Neutrals.

§ 351. His duty of impartiality must prevent a neutral State from granting a loan to either belligerent. Vattel's [2] distinction between interest-bearing loans and loans carrying no interest, and his assertion that loans on the part of neutrals are lawful if they bear interest and are made with the pure intention of making money, have not found favour with other writers. Nor do I know any instance of an interest-bearing loan having been made by a neutral State during the nineteenth century.

What is valid regarding a loan is all the more valid regarding subsidies in money granted to a belligerent

[1] See above, vol. i. § 51 (7); see also Westlake, *Papers*, pp. 362-392, and Gregory, *The Manufacture and Sale of Munitions of War* (1916), where the present rule of law is very ably defended. For the contrary view, see Butte in the *Proceedings of the American Society of International Law*, v. (1916), pp. 112-134.

[2] iii. § 110.

by a neutral State. Through the granting of subsidies a neutral State becomes as much the ally of the belligerent as it would by furnishing him with troops.[1]

Loans and Subsidies on the part of Subjects of Neutrals.

§ 352. It was formerly a moot point in the theory of International Law whether a neutral is obliged by his duty of impartiality to prevent his *subjects* from granting subsidies and loans to belligerents to enable them to continue the war. Several writers[2] maintained either that a neutral was obliged to prevent such subsidies and loans altogether, or at least that he must prohibit a public subscription for them on neutral territory. On the other hand, a number of writers asserted that, since money is just as much an article of commerce as goods, a neutral was in no wise obliged to prevent on his territory a public subscription by his subjects to loans for the belligerents. In contradistinction to the theory of International Law, the practice of the States has established beyond doubt that neutrals need not prevent subscriptions on their territory to loans for belligerents. Thus in 1854, during the Crimean War, France protested in vain against a Russian loan being raised in Amsterdam, Berlin, and Hamburg. In 1870, during the Franco-German War, a French loan was raised in London. In 1877, during the Russo-Turkish War, no neutral prevented his subjects from subscribing to the Russian loan. In 1904, during the Russo-Japanese War, Japanese loans were raised in London and Berlin, and Russian loans in Paris and Berlin.

On the other hand, during the World War, President

[1] See above, §§ 305, 306, 321.

[2] See Phillimore, iii. § 151; Bluntschli, § 768; Heffter, § 148; Kleen, i. § 68. The case of *De Wutz* v. *Hendricks*, (1824) 9 Moo. 586, quoted by Phillimore in support of his assertion that neutrals must prevent their subjects from subscribing to a loan for belligerents, is not decisive, for Lord Chief Justice Best only decided 'that it was contrary to the Law of Nations for persons residing in this country to enter into any agreements to raise money by way of a loan for the purpose of *supporting subjects of a foreign State in arms against a Government in alliance with our own.*'

Wilson of the United States of America, by his advice to the American bankers,[1] at first prevented, though he did not prohibit, the raising of loans by any of the belligerents. But an Anglo-French loan was raised in the United States without objection in September 1915, for the purpose of stabilising the rate of exchange by enabling Great Britain and France to pay for their American purchases in American money, and other similar loans were raised there later.[2]

Matters differ somewhat in regard to subsidies to belligerents by subjects of neutrals. A neutral is not indeed obliged to prevent individual subjects from granting subsidies to belligerents, just as he is not obliged to prevent them from enlisting with them. But if he were to allow on his territory a public appeal for subscriptions to such subsidies, he would certainly violate his duty of impartiality; for whereas loans are a matter of commerce, subsidies are not. However, public appeals for subscriptions of money for charitable purposes, *e.g.* for the wounded, prisoners, and the like, need not be prevented, even if they are only made in favour of one of the belligerents.

This distinction, then, between loans and subsidies, public subscriptions for loans being permitted, but those for subsidies being prohibited, is certainly correct as the law stands at present. But there is no doubt that the fact of belligerents having the opportunity of getting loans from subjects of neutrals is apt to lengthen wars. The Russo-Japanese War, for instance, would have come to an end much sooner if either belligerent could have been prevented from borrowing money from subjects of neutrals. Therefore, what has been said with regard

[1] Garner, ii. § 569.

[2] The Second Hague Conference, by enacting in Article 7 of Convention v. that a neutral 'is not bound to prevent the export . . . of anything which can be of use to an army or fleet,' has indirectly recognised that he need not prevent the subscription on his territory to loans for belligerents.

to the supply of arms and ammunition applies likewise to loans: if the standard of public morality rises, and it becomes the conviction of the world at large that loans by subjects of neutrals are apt to lengthen wars, a rule will grow up under which neutral Governments will have to prevent such loans.

VII

SERVICES TO BELLIGERENTS

Westlake, ii. pp. 253-254—Despagnet, No. 696 *bis*—Bonfils, No. 1475[1]—Ullmann, § 192—Rivier, ii. pp. 388-391—Nys, iii. pp. 671-678—Calvo, iv. §§ 2640-2641—Martens, ii. § 134—Perels, § 43—Kleen, i. §§ 103-108—Lawrence, *War*, pp. 83-92, 218-220—Scholz, *Drahtlose Telegraphie und Neutralität* (1905), *passim*, and *Krieg und Seekabel* (1904), pp. 122-133—*Land Warfare*, §§ 481-484—Wehberg, § 11—Kebedgy in *R.I.*, 2nd Ser. vi. (1904), pp. 445-451—Garner, ii. § 560.

§ 353. Since pilots are in the service of littoral States, the question whether neutrals may permit them to render services to belligerent men-of-war and transport vessels is of importance. Article 11[1] of Hague Convention XIII. enacts that 'a neutral Power may allow belligerent warships to employ its licensed pilots.' Since, therefore, everything is left to the discretion of neutrals, they will have to take the merits and needs of every case into account. There would certainly be no objection to a neutral allowing belligerent vessels to which asylum is legitimately granted to be piloted into his ports, and also belligerent war-vessels to be piloted through his maritime belt, if their passage is not prohibited. But a belligerent might justly object to the men-of-war of his adversary being piloted on the open sea by pilots of a neutral Power, except in a case of distress. Pilotage.

It is worth mentioning that Great Britain, during

[1] Germany entered a reservation against Article 11.

the Franco-German War in 1870, prohibited her pilots from conducting German and French men-of-war which were outside the maritime belt, except when in distress, and that Denmark, Norway, and Sweden, which compel belligerent warships to use local pilots when entering or leaving a harbour, and the like, prohibit their pilots from conducting belligerent warships outside these areas, except when in distress.[1]

Transport on the part of Neutrals.

§ 354. It is generally recognised that the duty of impartiality incumbent upon a neutral obliges him to prevent his men-of-war and other public vessels from rendering transport services to either belligerent. Therefore, such vessels must neither carry soldiers nor sailors belonging to belligerent forces, nor their prisoners of war, nor ammunition, nor military or naval provisions, nor despatches. The question how far such vessels are prevented from carrying enemy subjects other than members of the forces depends upon the question whether, by carrying those individuals, they render services to one of the belligerents which are detrimental to the other. Thus, when in 1901, during the South African War, the Dutch Government intended to send a man-of-war, the *Gelderland*, to President Kruger to convey him to Europe, they made sure in advance that Great Britain did not object.

The question has been raised[2] whether a neutral whose rolling stock runs on the railway lines of a belligerent, may continue to leave it there although it is being used for the transport of troops, war material, and the like. The answer, I believe, ought to be in the negative; for there is no doubt that, if the rolling stock remains on the railway lines of a belligerent, the neutral concerned is indirectly rendering transport services to the belligerent. It is for this reason that Article 19 of

[1] See Wehberg, p. 419.
[2] See Nowacki, *Die Eisenbahnen im Kriege* (1906), p. 126.

Convention v. enacts that railway material coming from the territory of neutrals shall not be requisitioned or used by a belligerent, except in the case of, and to the extent required by, absolute necessity.[1]

Transport on the part of Neutral Merchantmen and by Private Neutral Rolling Stock.

§ 355. Just as a neutral is not obliged to prevent his merchantmen from carrying contraband, so he is not obliged to prevent them from rendering services to belligerents by carrying, in the way of trade, enemy troops, and the like, and enemy despatches. Neutral merchantmen rendering such services to belligerents do so at their own risk; for these are unneutral services, for which the merchantmen may be punished[2] by the belligerents, although the neutral State under whose flag they sail bears no responsibility for them whatever.

The same is valid with regard to rolling stock belonging to private railway companies of a neutral State. That such rolling stock may not be used by a belligerent without the consent of the companies owning it, for the transport of troops, war material, and the like, except in the case of, and to the extent required by, absolute necessity, follows from Article 19 of Convention v. If, however, a private railway company does give its consent, and if its rolling stock is used for warlike purposes, it acquires enemy character, Article 19 of Convention v. does not apply, and the other belligerent may seize and appropriate it as though it were the property of the enemy State.[3]

Information regarding Military and Naval Operations.

§ 356. Information regarding military and naval operations may be given and obtained in so many various ways that several cases must be distinguished:—

(1) It is obvious that the duty of impartiality incumbent upon a neutral obliges him to prevent his men-of-war from giving any information to one belligerent concerning the naval operations of the other belligerent.

[1] See below, § 365.

[2] See below, §§ 407-413.

[3] See Nowacki, *Die Eisenbahnen im Kriege* (1906), p. 128.

But a neutral bears no responsibility whatever for private vessels sailing under his flag which give such information. Such vessels run the risk, however, of being punished for rendering unneutral service.[1]

(2) It is likewise obvious that his duty of impartiality must prevent a neutral from giving information to a belligerent concerning the war through his diplomatic envoys, couriers, and the like.[2] But the question has been raised whether a neutral is obliged to prevent couriers [3] from carrying despatches for a belligerent over his neutral territory. I believe the answer must be in the negative, at least so far as those couriers are concerned who are in the service of diplomatic envoys, and those agents who carry despatches from a State to its head or to diplomatic envoys abroad. Since they enjoy [4] inviolability for their persons and official papers, a neutral cannot interfere so as to find out whether they are carrying information to the disadvantage of the enemy.

(3) According to Article 8 of Convention v., 'a neutral Power is not bound to forbid or restrict the employment, on behalf of belligerents, of telegraph or telephone cables, or of wireless telegraphy apparatus, whether belonging to it, or to companies, or to private individuals.' Since, therefore, everything is left to the discretion of the neutral concerned, he will have to take the merits and needs of every case into consideration, and act accordingly. But so much is certain, that a belligerent has no right to insist that neutrals should forbid or restrict such employment of their telegraph wires, etc., on the part of his adversary. On the other hand, their duty of impartiality must compel

[1] See below, §§ 409, 410, and Articles 45 and 46 of the unratified Declaration of London.

[2] During the World War the Swedish minister to Argentina, Baron Lowen, transmitted cipher messages on behalf of the German envoy, Count Luxburg, thereby violating Swedish neutrality (see *A.J.*, xii. (1918), pp. 135-140).

[3] See Calvo, iv. § 2640.

[4] See above, vol. i. §§ 405, 457.

neutrals to prevent the despatch from their territory of wireless messages sent to enable belligerent cruisers outside the neutral territorial waters to watch for, and capture, vessels which have been within those waters so soon as they depart, or any other wireless messages through the sending of which their neutral territory becomes a base of naval or military operations for one of the belligerents.[1]

During the World War, in order to discharge the duties so laid upon them, all the maritime neutral States of importance prevented belligerent merchantmen in their ports from using their wireless installations. Thus Sweden, which shortly after the outbreak of the war had passed a law prohibiting vessels in Swedish ports from using their wireless apparatus, in February 1916, in consequence of violations of that law by the German vessel *Mecklenburg*, sealed the wireless apparatus on that and other German vessels in Swedish ports. Again, during the course of the war, the United States of America took control of the private wireless telegraphy stations which had been erected in the United States before the war, and prevented all stations from transmitting cipher messages.[2]

A different situation arises when a belligerent intends to arrange the transmission of messages through a submarine cable laid for that very purpose over neutral territory, or through telegraph and telephone wires erected for that purpose on neutral territory. This would seem to be an abuse of neutral territory, and the neutral must prevent it. Accordingly, when in 1870, during the Franco-German War, France intended to lay a telegraph cable from Dunkirk to the north of

[1] See Garner, ii. § 560, who mentions the complaints of the British and French Governments during the World War, that wireless stations in various Latin-American States were sending messages to German war-ships in the South Atlantic and Pacific Oceans.

[2] See Garner, ii. § 560.

France—the cable to go across the Channel to England and from there back to France—Great Britain refused her consent on account of her neutrality. Again in 1898, during war between Spain and the United States of America, when the latter intended to land at Hong-Kong a cable proposed to be laid from Manila, Great Britain refused her consent.[1]

The case is likewise different when a belligerent intends to erect in a neutral country, or in a neutral port or neutral waters, a wireless telegraphy station, or any apparatus intended as a means of communication with belligerent forces on land or sea, or to make use of any installation of this kind established by him before the outbreak of war for purely military purposes, and not previously opened for the services of the public generally. According to Articles 3 and 5 of Convention v. and Article 5 of Convention xiii., a neutral is bound to prohibit this. When in 1904, in the Russo-Japanese War during the siege of Port Arthur, the Russians installed an apparatus for wireless telegraphy in Chifu, and communicated thereby with the besieged, this constituted a violation of neutrality.

(4) It is obvious that his duty of impartiality must prevent a neutral from allowing belligerents to establish intelligence bureaux on his territory. On the other hand, a neutral is not obliged to prevent his subjects from giving information to belligerents, be it by letter, telegram, telephone, or wireless telegraphy. In particular, a neutral is not obliged to prevent his subjects from giving information to belligerents by wireless telegraphy apparatus installed on a neutral merchantman. Such individuals run, however, the risk of being punished as spies, if they act clandestinely or under false pretences,[2] and the vessel is liable to be captured and confiscated for rendering unneutral service.

[1] See Lawrence, *War*, p. 219.

[2] See above, § 159.

On the other hand, newspaper correspondents making use of a wireless installation on a neutral merchantman for the purpose of sending news to their papers,[1] may not be treated as spies — although during the Russo-Japanese War Russia threatened to treat them as such—and the merchantman may not be confiscated, although belligerents need not allow the presence of such vessels at the seat of war. Thus, during the Russo-Japanese War, the *Haimun*, a vessel fitted with a wireless telegraphy apparatus for the service of *The Times*, was ordered away by the Japanese, although during the first five weeks of the war they had made no objection. But, of course, an individual can at the same time be a correspondent for a neutral newspaper and a spy, and he may then be punished for espionage.

VIII

VIOLATION OF NEUTRALITY

Hall, §§ 227-229—Lawrence, §§ 233, 238, 239—Phillimore, iii. §§ 151*a*-151*b* —Taylor, §§ 630, 642—Wharton, iii. §§ 402, 402*a*—Wheaton, §§ 429-433—Moore, vii. §§ 1319-1328, 1334-1335—Bluntschli, §§ 778-782—Heffter, § 146—Geffcken in *Holtzendorff*, iv. pp. 667-676, 700-709—Ullmann, § 191—Bonfils, No. 1476—Despagnet, No. 697—Pradier-Fodéré, viii. No. 3235—Rivier, ii. pp. 394-395—Calvo, iv. §§ 2654-2666 —Fiore, iii Nos. 1567-1570—Martens, ii. § 138—Kleen, i. § 25—Dupuis, Nos. 332-337—Einicke, *Rechte und Pflichten der neutralen Machte im Seekrieg* (1912), pp. 326-364—Schramm, pp. 79-82—Garner, ii. § 562—Harris in the *Proceedings of the American Society of International Law*, ix. (1915), pp. 31-39.

Violation of Neutrality in the Narrower and in the Wider Sense of the Term.

§ 357. Many writers who speak of violation of neutrality only treat under this head violations of the duty of impartiality incumbent upon neutrals. Indeed such violations only are meant, if one speaks of violation of

[1] See Lawrence, *War*, pp. 85-92. On the position of newspaper correspondents in naval warfare, as it was before the World War, see Higgins, *War and the Private Citizen* (1912), pp. 91-112, and in *Z.V.*, vi. (1912), pp. 19-28, and the literature and cases there cited.

neutrality in the narrower sense of the term. However, it is necessary for obvious reasons to discuss, not only violations of the duty of impartiality of neutrals, but violations of all duties deriving from neutrality, whether they are incumbent upon neutrals or upon belligerents. In the wider sense of the term, violation of neutrality comprises, therefore, every performance or omission of an act contrary to the duty of a neutral towards either belligerent as well as contrary to the duty of either belligerent towards a neutral. *Everywhere in this treatise the term is used in its wider sense.*

Violations of neutrality on the part of belligerents must not be confounded with violations of the laws of war, by which subjects of neutral States suffer damage. If, for instance, an occupant levies excessive contributions from subjects of neutral States domiciled in enemy country in contravention of Article 49 of the Hague Regulations, this is a violation of the laws of war, for which, according to Article 3 of Convention IV., he must pay compensation; but it is not a violation of neutrality.

Violation in contradistinction to End of Neutrality.

§ 358. Mere violation of neutrality must not be confounded with the ending of neutrality,[1] for neither a violation on the part of a neutral[2] nor a mere violation on the part of a belligerent *ipso facto* brings neutrality to an end. If correctly viewed, the condition of neutrality continues to exist between a neutral and a belligerent in spite of a violation of neutrality. A violation of neutrality is nothing more than a breach of a duty deriving from the condition of neutrality. This applies not only to violations of neutrality by negligence, but also to intentional violations. Even in an extreme case,

[1] See above, § 312.

[2] But this is almost everywhere asserted, as the distinction between the violation of the duty of impartiality incumbent upon neutrals and the ending of neutrality is usually not made.

in which the violation of neutrality is so great that the offended party considers war the only adequate measure in answer to it, it is not the violation which brings neutrality to an end, but the determination of the offended party. For there is no violation of neutrality so great as to oblige the offended party to declare war in answer to it, such party always having the choice whether he will keep up the condition of neutrality or not.

But this applies only to mere violations of neutrality, and not to a declaration of war or hostilities. Hostilities are acts of war, and bring neutrality to an end;[1] and a declaration of war brings neutrality to an end even before the outbreak of hostilities.

Consequences of Violations of Neutrality.

§ 359. Violations of neutrality, whether committed by a neutral against a belligerent or by a belligerent against a neutral, are international delinquencies.[2] They may at once be repulsed, and the offended party may require the offender to make reparation, and, if this is refused, may take such measures as he thinks adequate to exact the necessary reparation.[3] If the violation is only slight and unimportant, the offended State will often merely complain. If, on the other hand, the violation is very substantial and grave, the offended State will perhaps at once declare that it considers itself at war with the offender. In such a case, it is not the violation of neutrality which brings neutrality to an end, but the declaration of the offended State that it considers the violation to be of so grave a character as to oblige it to regard itself at war with the offender.

That a violation of neutrality, like any other international delinquency, can only be committed by malice or culpable negligence,[4] and that it can be committed

[1] They have been characterised in contradistinction to mere violations above in § 320.

[2] See above, vol. i. § 151.

[3] See above, vol. i. § 156.

[4] See above, vol. i. § 154.

through a State refusing to comply with the consequences of its 'vicarious' responsibility for acts of its agents or subjects,[1] is a matter of course. Thus, if a belligerent fleet attacks enemy vessels in neutral territorial waters without an order from its Government, the latter bears 'vicarious' responsibility for this violation of neutral territory by its fleet. If the Government concerned refuses to disown the act of its fleet, and to make the necessary reparation, this 'vicarious' responsibility turns into 'original' responsibility, for a case of violation of neutrality and an international delinquency has then arisen. The same is valid if an agent of a neutral State, without an order of his Government, commits such an act as would constitute a violation of neutrality in case it were ordered by the Government; for instance, if the head of a province of a neutral State, without authorisation from his Government, allows forces of a belligerent to march through the neutral province.

Neutrals not to acquiesce in Violations of Neutrality committed by a Belligerent.

§ 360. It is entirely within the discretion of a belligerent whether he will acquiesce in a violation of neutrality committed by a neutral in favour of the other belligerent. On the other hand, a neutral may not exercise the same discretion regarding a violation of neutrality committed by one belligerent and detrimental to the other. His duty of impartiality rather obliges him, in the first instance, to prevent with the means at his disposal the belligerent concerned from committing such a violation; *e.g.* to repulse an attack by men-of-war of a belligerent on enemy vessels in neutral ports. Thus Article 3 of Hague Convention XIII. enacts: 'When a ship has been captured in the territorial waters of a neutral Power, such Power must, if the prize is still within its jurisdiction, employ the means at its disposal to release the prize with its officers

[1] See above, vol. i. § 150.

and crew, and to intern the prize crew.' But in case he could not prevent and repulse a violation of his neutrality, his same duty of impartiality obliges him to exact due reparation from the offender;[1] for otherwise he would favour the one party to the detriment of the other. If a neutral neglects this obligation, he himself thereby commits a violation of neutrality, for which he may be made responsible by a belligerent who has suffered through the violation of neutrality committed by the other belligerent and acquiesced in by him.[2] For instance, if belligerent men-of-war seize enemy vessels in the ports of a neutral, and if that neutral, who could not or did not prevent this, exacts no reparation from the belligerent concerned, the other party may make the neutral responsible for the losses sustained.

Cases of *The General Armstrong* and *The Dresden*.

§ 361. Some writers[3] maintain that a neutral is freed from responsibility for a violation of neutrality committed by a belligerent in attacking enemy forces in neutral territory, if the forces attacked, instead of trusting for protection or redress to the neutral, defend themselves against the attack. This rule is adopted from the arbitral award in the case of *The General Armstrong*. In 1814, during war between Great Britain

[1] See Articles 25 and 26 of Convention XIII. This duty is nowadays universally recognised; but before the nineteenth century it did not exist, although the rule that belligerents must not commit hostilities on neutral territory, and in particular in neutral ports and waters, was well recognised. That, in spite of its recognition, this rule was in the eighteenth century frequently infringed by commanders of belligerent fleets, may be illustrated by many cases. Thus, for instance, in 1793, the French frigate *Modeste* was captured in the harbour of Genoa by two British men-of-war (see Hall, § 220); and in 1801, during war against Sweden, a British frigate captured the *Freden* and three other Swedish vessels in the Norwegian harbour of Oster-Risoer (see Ortolan, ii. pp. 411-418).

[2] It has been pointed out above, § 319, that in case one belligerent resorts to measures which aim at suppressing intercourse between another belligerent and neutrals and the neutrals do not prevent the carrying out of such measures, the injured belligerent is justified in resorting to reprisals and in himself preventing intercourse between neutrals and the first-mentioned belligerent.

[3] See, for instance, Hall, § 228, and Geffcken in *Holtzendorff*, IV. p. 701.

and the United States of America, the American privateer *General Armstrong*, lying in the harbour of Fayal, an island belonging to the Portuguese Azores, defended herself against an attack by an English squadron, but was nevertheless captured. The United States claimed damages from Portugal because the privateer was captured in a neutral Portuguese port. Negotiations went on for many years, and the parties finally agreed in 1851 upon arbitration by Louis Napoleon, then President of the French Republic. In 1852 Napoleon gave his award in favour of Portugal, maintaining that, although the attack on the privateer in neutral waters comprised a violation of neutrality, Portugal could not be made responsible, because the vessel chose to defend herself, instead of demanding protection from the Portuguese authorities.[1] It is, however, not at all certain that the rule laid down in this award will find general recognition in theory and practice.[2]

However that may be, cases similar to that of *The General Armstrong* occurred during the World War. Thus in March 1915 the German cruiser *Dresden* sought refuge within the territorial waters of Chili near the island of Juan Fernandez, and asked to be allowed to remain there for eight days in order to effect repairs. The request was refused, and the *Dresden* was ordered to depart within twenty-four hours. However, she did not depart, and received notification that she was to be interned. Meanwhile two British cruisers, *Kent* and *Glasgow*, came up and opened fire. The *Dresden* hoisted a flag of truce, and despatched one of her officers to inform the *Glasgow* that she was in neutral territorial waters. In reply, the British squadron called

[1] See Moore, *Arbitrations*, ii. pp. 1071-1132; Calvo, IV. § 2662; and Dana's note 208 in Wheaton, § 429.

[2] The case of *The Reshitelni*, which occurred in 1904, during the Russo-Japanese War, and is somewhat similar to that of *The General Armstrong*, is discussed above in § 320 (2). That no violation of neutrality took place in the case of *The Variag* and *The Korietz*, is shown above in § 320 (1).

upon her to surrender under a threat of destruction, whereupon she blew herself up and sank.[1] Again, Hall mentions a case in which a British submarine which had run aground in Danish territorial waters was there fired upon by a German destroyer.[2]

Mode of exacting Reparation from Belligerents for Violations of Neutrality.

§ 362. It is obvious that the duty of a neutral not to acquiesce in violations of neutrality committed by one belligerent to the detriment of the other obliges him to repair, so far as he can, the result of such wrongful acts. Thus, he must liberate[3] a prize taken in his neutral waters, or prisoners made on his territory, and the like. In so far, however, as he cannot, or cannot sufficiently, undo the wrong done, he must exact reparation from the offender. Now, no general rule can be laid down regarding the mode of exacting such reparation, since everything depends upon the merits of the individual case. However, as regards the capture of enemy vessels in neutral waters, a practice has grown up which must be considered binding, according to which the neutral must claim the prize, and eventually damages, from the belligerent concerned, and must restore her to the other party. Thus in 1800, during war between Great Britain and the Netherlands, Prussia claimed in the British Prize Court the *Twee Gebroeders*,[4] a Dutch vessel captured by the British cruiser *L'Espiègle* in the neutral maritime belt of Prussia. Sir William Scott ordered the restoration of the vessel, but refused costs and damages, because the captor had not violated Prussian neutrality intentionally but only by mistake and misapprehension. Thus again, in 1805, during war between Great Britain and Spain, the United States

[1] Details from Garner, ii. § 562. See also Alvarez, *La grande Guerre*, etc. (1915), p. 227, and documents in *A.J.*, x. (1916), Supplement, pp. 72-76.

[2] 7th ed. p. 663.

[3] See Article 3 of Convention XIII.

[4] 3 C. Rob. 162. This case is all the more important as the capture was really made outside the neutral maritime belt by boats sent from *L'Espiègle*. *L'Espiègle* was, however, herself within the neutral maritime belt.

claimed in the British Prize Court the *Anna*,[1] a Spanish vessel captured by the English privateer *Minerva* within her neutral maritime belt. Thus, further, in 1864, during the American Civil War, when the Confederate cruiser *Florida* was captured by the Federal cruiser *Wachusett* in the neutral Brazilian port of Bahia, Brazil claimed the prize. As the prize had sunk while at anchor in Hampton Roads, she could not be restored; but the United States expiated[2] the violation of neutrality committed by her cruiser by court-martialling the commander, by dismissing her consul at Bahia for having advised the capture, and, finally, by sending a man-of-war to the spot where the violation of neutrality had taken place for the special purpose of delivering a solemn salute to the Brazilian flag.

Many similar cases occurred during the World War. Thus, in July 1916, the British steamer *Adams* was captured by a German torpedo boat in Swedish territorial waters, and taken to the German port of Swinemunde; Sweden claimed the prize, and Germany apologised, and brought the vessel back to the spot where she had been captured, and set her free.[3] Again, when the German vessels *Pellworm*[4] and others were captured by British cruisers in July 1917, in Dutch territorial waters, the Dutch Government claimed them in the British Prize Court; similarly, Norway claimed the release of the *Dusseldorf*[5] and the *Valeria*,[6] German vessels which had been captured by British forces in Norwegian territorial waters.

It is, however, only the neutral State whose neutrality has been violated, and not the owner of the vessel, who can, at any rate according to British practice,

[1] 5 C. Rob. 373. See above, vol. i. § 234.

[2] See Moore, vii. § 1334.

[3] *The Westminster Gazette*, July 21, 1916.

[4] [1920] P. 347.

[5] (1919) 3 B. and C. P. C. 466, and *The Times*, July 29, 1920.

[6] [1920] P. 81; 37 T. L. R. 337.

successfully prosecute a claim for the release of the vessel before the Prize Court.[1]

§ 363. Apart from intentional violations of neutrality, a neutral can be made responsible only for such acts favouring or damaging a belligerent as he could by due diligence have prevented, and which by culpable negligence he failed to prevent. It is by no means obligatory for a neutral to prevent such acts under all circumstances and conditions. This is in fact impossible, and it becomes more obviously so, the larger a neutral State and the longer its boundary lines. So long as a neutral exercises due diligence for the purpose of preventing such acts, he is not responsible in case they are nevertheless performed. However, the meaning of the term *due diligence* has become controversial on account of the definition proffered by the United States of America in interpreting the Three Rules of Washington, and adopted by the Geneva Court of Arbitration.[2] According to that interpretation the *due diligence* of a neutral *must be in proportion to the risks to which either belligerent may be exposed from failure to fulfil the obligations of neutrality on his part.* Had this interpretation been generally accepted, the most oppressive obligations would have become incumbent upon neutrals. But no such general acceptance has taken place. The fact is that *due diligence* in International Law can have no other meaning than it has in Municipal Law. It means *such diligence as can reasonably be expected when all the circumstances and conditions of the case are taken into consideration.*

Negligence on the part of Neutrals.

Be that as it may, the Second Hague Conference took a step which excluded for the future the continuation of the controversy regarding the interpretation of *due*

[1] See *The Bangor*, (1916) 2 B. and C. P. C. 206, and the American cases of *The Anne*, (1818) 3 Wheaton 435; *The Lilla*, (1862) 2 Sprague 177; *The Sir William Peel*, (1866) 5 Wall. 517; *The Adela*, (1867) 6 Wall. 266.

[2] See above, § 335.

diligence, for Articles 8 and 25 of Convention XIII., instead of stipulating *due diligence* on the part of neutrals, stipulated *the employment of the means at their disposal.*

Laying of Submarine Contact Mines by Neutrals.

§ 363*a*. In order to defend themselves against possible violations of their neutral territory, neutrals may lay automatic contact mines off their coasts. If they do this, they must, according to Article 4 of Convention VIII., observe the same rules and take the same precautions as are imposed upon belligerents.[1] Moreover, they must, according to paragraph 2 of Article 4 of Convention VIII., give notice in advance to mariners of the place where automatic contact mines have been laid, and this notice must be communicated at once to the Governments through diplomatic channels.

Convention VIII. is quite as unsatisfactory in its rules concerning mines laid by neutrals as in its rules concerning mines laid by belligerents, and the danger to neutral shipping created by mines laid by neutrals is very great. However, when Article 4 speaks of the laying of contact mines by neutral Powers *off their coasts*, without limiting such operations to within the three-mile-wide maritime belt, it does not intend to give neutrals a right to lay them outside the belt.[2] For it is expressly stated :[3] 'Mais il paraîtrait entendu que l'absence de toute disposition fixant les limites dans lesquelles les neutres peuvent placer des mines ne devra pas être interprétée comme établissant, pour les neutres, le droit de placer des mines en pleine mer.'

A neutral, in laying mines within his territorial waters, must have regard to the duty of impartiality incumbent upon him, and must consider whether his mine-field favours one belligerent at the expense of

[1] See above, § 182*a*.

[2] As was erroneously stated in the second edition of this work.

[3] See *Deuxième Conférence*, Actes, iii. p. 456. See also Article 6 of the 'Règlementation internationale de l'Usage des Mines sous-marines et des Torpilles' of the Institute of International Law (*Annuaire*, xxiv. (1911), p. 302).

another. On July 14, 1916, during the World War, Sweden declared that the Kogrund Channel, leading to the Baltic Sea, was to be closed by mines, and that only Swedish shipping might pass through it. The channel was within Swedish territorial waters. The effect of this action was to force Allied ships entering or leaving the Baltic to pass through the outer channels, which were closely patrolled by German warships. Thus while German ships had access to both the east and west coasts of Sweden, Russia was confined to the east coast and the other Allied Powers to the west, Sweden having completed the German barrier between them. The Allied Powers protested.

IX

RIGHT OF ANGARY

Grotius, iii. c. 17, § 1 (see also ii. c. 2, §§ 6-9)—Vattel, ii. § 121—Hall, § 278—Lawrence, § 233—Westlake, ii. pp. 131-134—Phillimore, iii. § 29—Halleck, i. p. 519—Taylor, § 641—Walker, § 69—Bluntschli, § 795*a*—Heffter, § 150—Bulmerincq in *Holtzendorff*, iv. pp. 98-103—Geffcken in *Holtzendorff*, iv. pp. 771-773—Ullmann, § 192—Bonfils, No. 1490—Despagnet, No. 494—Mérignhac, iii[a]. pp. 586-591—Rivier, ii. pp. 327-329—Kleen, ii. §§ 165, 230—Perels, § 40—Hautefeuille, iii. pp. 416-426—Holland, *War*, Nos. 139-140—*Land Warfare*, §§ 507-510—Albrecht, *Requisitionen von neutralem Privateigenthum, insbesondere von Schiffen* (1912), pp. 24-66—Wehberg, p. 70—Borchard, § 104—Garner, i. §§ 118-119.

The Original Right of Angary.

§ 364. Under the term *jus angariae*,[1] belligerents who had not sufficient vessels often claimed and practised in former times the right to lay an embargo on, and seize, neutral merchantmen in their harbours, and to compel them and their crews to transport troops, munitions, and provisions to certain places on payment

[1] The term *angaria*, which in mediæval Latin means *post-station*, is a derivation from the Greek term ἄγγαρος for messenger. *Jus angariae* would therefore literally mean a right of transport.

of freight in advance.[1] This practice arose in the Middle Ages,[2] and was much resorted to by Louis XIV. of France. To save the vessels of their subjects from seizure under this right of angary, States began in the seventeenth century to conclude treaties under which each renounced the right with regard to the vessels of the other. And so the right fell into disuse during the eighteenth century, and there is no case in which it is reported to have been exercised during the nineteenth century. Nevertheless, many writers [3] assert that it is not obsolete, and might be exercised even in this twentieth century. They do this because, even during the nineteenth century, some States concluded treaties [4] containing articles which provided for compensation in case this right of angary should be exercised by one of the contracting parties. On the other hand, there is evidence that the right is contested. A number of writers [5] object to it. Article 39 of the 'Règlement sur le Régime légal des Navires dans les Ports étrangers' adopted by the Institute of International Law [6] rejects it: 'Le droit d'angarie est supprimé. . . .' The King's Regulations and Admiralty Instructions of 1908 (No. 494) contain the following rules under the heading, 'Coercion of a British ship': 'If any British merchant ship, the nationality of which is unquestioned, should be coerced into the conveyance of troops or into taking part in other hostile acts, the Senior Naval Officer, should there be no diplomatic or consular authority at the place, is to remonstrate with the local authorities and take such other steps to assure her release or exemp-

[1] See above, § 40.

[2] On the origin and development of the *jus angariae*, see Albrecht, *op. cit.*, pp. 24-37.

[3] See, for instance, Phillimore, iii. § 29; Calvo, iii. § 1277; Heffter, § 150; Perels, § 40; Rivier, ii. p. 328; Despagnet, No. 494.

[4] See Albrecht, *op. cit.*, pp. 34-37.

[5] See, for instance, Bulmerincq in *Holtzendorff*, iv pp. 98-103; Lawrence, § 233; Kleen, ii. § 165.

[6] See *Annuaire*, xvii. (1898), p. 284.

tion, as the case may demand, and as may be in accordance with these Regulations.'

Considering that no case of the use of this right of angary happened in the nineteenth century, and that International Law concerning the rights and duties of neutrals became much more developed during the eighteenth and nineteenth centuries, in the two preceding editions of this work I ventured the assertion that this right of angary 'is now probably obsolete.' However, although no real case occurred during the World War—the requisitioning of Dutch ships by the Allies in March 1918 being a case of the modern right of angary as discussed below[1]—that war has shown that belligerents will not easily renounce the use of any right unless it is absolutely clear that it does not exist, or no longer exists. For this reason it cannot with certainty be said that the right is obsolete.

The requisitioning during the World War of some Swedish and Dutch steamers lying in English and French harbours, against which the Swedish and Dutch[2] Governments protested, had nothing to do with the right of angary, whatever may have been the merits of the case. The British Government did indeed requisition a number of Swedish ships—the *Sphinx*, the *Bellgrove*, the *Phyllis*, and the *Cremona*,—and of Dutch ships—the *Vembergen*, *Kelbergen*, and others,—and paid compensation for their use. But the public statement made by the British Government on October 11, 1917, did not base this requisitioning upon the right of angary.[3] 'The tonnage at the disposal of H.M. Government,' so runs the statement, 'has been increased by a decision, which has recently

[1] § 365.

[2] *Parl. Papers*, Misc., No. 5 (1918), Cd. 8986.

[3] There are, however, passages in the correspondence with the Dutch Government which do seek to justify the requisitioning by reference to the right of angary, though the term is not used.

been taken, to utilise in the Government service British-owned, or mainly British-owned, ships which are in British ports, but which have hitherto sailed under neutral flag. As the German Government has by its prize court regulations decided that, notwithstanding the neutral flag, it may treat these vessels as British, it is necessary in order to protect British capital invested in these ships that they should fly the British flag and be armed for their defence.'[1]

Be that as it may, the right of angary not only empowers a belligerent to requisition *neutral ships* for military purposes, but also to compel the *neutral crews* to render services by which they acquire enemy character.

The Modern Right of Angary.

§ 365. In contradistinction to this original right of angary, the *modern* right of angary is a right of belligerents to destroy, or use, in case of necessity, for the purpose of offence and defence, neutral property on their territory, or on enemy territory, or on the open sea. This modern right of angary does not, as did the original right, empower a belligerent to compel *neutral individuals* to render services, but only extends to neutral property. In case property of subjects of neutral States is vested with enemy character,[2] it is not neutral property in the strict sense of the term 'neutral,' and all the rules respecting appropriation, utilisation, and destruction[3] of enemy property obviously apply to it. The object of the right of angary is, therefore, *either such property of subjects of neutral States as retains its neutral character from its temporary position on belligerent territory, and which therefore is not vested with enemy character, or such neutral property on the open sea as has not acquired enemy character.* All sorts of neutral property, whether it consists of vessels

[1] *The Times*, October 12, 1917.

[2] See above, § 90.

[3] See the case of *William Hardman*, above, § 170 n.

or other[1] means of transport, or arms, ammunition, provisions, or other personal property, may be the object of the right of angary, provided it is serviceable to military ends and wants. The conditions under which the right may be exercised are the same as those under which private enemy property may be utilised or destroyed; but in every case the neutral owner must be fully indemnified.[2]

A remarkable case[3] happened in 1871 during the Franco-German War. The Germans seized some British coal-vessels lying in the river Seine at Duclair, and sank them for the purpose of preventing French gunboats from running up the river. On the intervention of the British Government, Count Bismarck refused to recognise the duty of Germany to indemnify the owners of the vessels sunk, although he agreed to do so.

However, it may safely be maintained that a duty to pay compensation for any damage done in the exercise of the right of angary must nowadays be recognised. Article 53 of the Hague Regulations stipulates the payment of indemnities for the seizure and utilisation of all appliances adapted to the transport of persons or goods which are the private property of inhabitants of occupied enemy territory, and Article 52 of the Hague Regulations stipulates payment for requisitions; since in these articles the immunity from confiscation of the private property of the inhabitants is recognised, all the more must that of private neutral

[1] Thus in 1870, during the Franco-German War, the Germans seized hundreds of Swiss and Austrian railway carriages in France and used them for military purposes.

[2] See Article 6 of U.S. Naval War Code:—'If military necessity should require it, neutral vessels found within the limits of belligerent authority may be seized and destroyed, or otherwise used for military purposes, but in such cases the owners of the neutral vessels must be fully recompensed. The amount of the indemnity should, if practicable, be agreed upon in advance with the owner or master of the vessel. Due regard must be had to treaty stipulations upon these matters.' See also Holland, *War*, No. 140.

[3] See Albrecht, *op. cit.*, pp. 45-48.

property temporarily on occupied enemy territory be recognised also.

During the World War, on March 20, 1918, the United States of America, by a proclamation [1] reciting that the law and practice of nations accorded to a belligerent Power the right in time of military exigency and for purposes essential to the prosecution of the war to take over and utilise neutral vessels lying within its jurisdiction, requisitioned seventy-seven Dutch vessels lying in American harbours,[2] and undertook to make full compensation to the owners. On the following days, Great Britain, France, and Italy followed suit. Great Britain announced the decision of the Associated Governments to requisition the Dutch ships in their ports 'in exercise of the right of angary,' in a Note of March 21, 1918,[3] which stated that they had 'felt compelled to fall back on their unquestionable right to employ any shipping found in their ports for the necessities of war,' but would compensate the owners of the vessels and arrange for the repatriation of the crews if desired. On March 30, 1918,[4] the Dutch Government protested against the interpretation given to the right of angary, 'an ancient rule unearthed for the occasion and adapted to entirely new conditions in order to excuse seizure *en masse* by a belligerent of the merchant fleet of a neutral country.' To this protest, on April 25, 1918, the British Government replied in a memorandum which discussed in detail the modern right of angary in International Law.[5]

The Dutch crews belonging to the ships requisitioned by the Associated Governments were not compelled to continue to serve, although many of them did so voluntarily.

[1] Text in *A.J.*, xii. (1918), Supplement, p. 259.

[2] See Scott in *A.J.*, xii. (1918), pp. 340-356.

[3] *Parl. Papers*, Misc., No. 11 (1918), Cd. 9025, p. 2.

[4] *Ibid.*, p. 3

[5] *Ibid.*, p. 6.

As regards Great Britain, the decisions of the Privy Council in *The Zamora* [1] and *The Canton* [2] recognised the modern right of angary on the following conditions: (1) that urgency (though not absolute necessity) demanded the requisitioning, (2) that the neutral owner was fully compensated. The court somewhat extended the right of angary, in so far as it admitted requisitioning, not only in connection with offence or defence, but also in connection with 'other matters involving national security.' These cases also established that in British Prize Law the right can be exercised against captured neutral property while it is still subject to proceedings for condemnation in prize.

Right of Angary concerning Neutral Rolling Stock.

§ 366. A special case of the right of angary found recognition by Article 19 of Convention v. of the Second Hague Conference, which enacted that railway material coming from the territory of a neutral Power, whether belonging to the neutral State or to companies or private persons, shall not be requisitioned or utilised by a belligerent, *except in the case of, and to the extent required by, absolute necessity,* that it shall as soon as possible be sent back to the country of origin, and that compensation shall be paid for its use.[3] This article also gives a right to a neutral Power, whose railway material has been requisitioned by a belligerent, to retain and make use of, to a corresponding extent, railway material coming from the territory of the belligerent concerned.

Right of Angary not deriving from Neutrality.

§ 367. Whatever the extent of the right of angary may be, it does not derive from the law of neutrality. The correlative duty of a belligerent to indemnify the neutral owner of property appropriated or destroyed in the exercise of the right of angary does indeed derive

[1] (1916) 2 B. and C. P. C. 1.

[2] (1916) 2 B. and C. P. C. 264.

[3] See Nowacki, *Die Eisenbahnen im Kriege* (1906), pp. 115-126, and Albrecht, *op. cit.*, pp. 22-24.

from the law of neutrality. But the right of angary itself is rather a right deriving from the law of war. As a rule the law of war only gives the right to a belligerent, under certain circumstances and conditions, to seize, make use of, or destroy the private property of the inhabitants of occupied enemy territory; but under other circumstances and conditions, and very exceptionally, it likewise gives a belligerent the right to seize, use, or destroy neutral property temporarily on occupied enemy territory, on his own territory, or on the open sea.

The right of angary being a right deriving from the law of war, it must not be confounded with the right, which every State no doubt possesses, of seizing in case of emergency, and subject to compensation, any foreign property on its territory. One ought not therefore to speak of a right of angary belonging to neutrals[1] as well as to belligerents, or of a right of angary in peace as well as war.

[1] As does Basdevant in *R.G.*, xxiii. (1916), pp. 268-279. See also Garner, I. § 120.

CHAPTER III

BLOCKADE

I

CONCEPTION OF BLOCKADE

Grotius, iii. c. 1, § 5—Bynkershoek, *Quaestiones Juris publici*, i. c. 11—Vattel, iii. § 117—Hall, §§ 233, 257-266—Lawrence, §§ 246-252—Westlake, ii. pp. 255-276, and *Papers*, pp. 312-361—Maine, pp. 107-109—Manning, pp. 400-412—Phillimore, iii. §§ 285-321—Twiss, ii. §§ 98-120—Halleck, ii. pp. 210-242—Taylor, §§ 674-684—Walker, §§ 76-82—Wharton, iii. §§ 359-365—Moore, vii. §§ 1266-1286—Wheaton, §§ 509-523—Hershey, Nos. 477-495—Bluntschli, §§ 827-840—Heffter, §§ 154-157—Geffcken in *Holtzendorff*, iv. pp. 738-771—Ullmann, § 182—Bonfils, Nos. 1608-1673[12]—Despagnet, Nos. 620-640—Pradier-Fodéré, vi. Nos. 2776-2779, and viii. Nos. 3109-3152—Nys, iii. pp. 165-196, 691-694—Rivier, ii. pp. 288-298—Calvo, v. §§ 2827-2908—Fiore, iii. Nos. 1606-1629—Martens, ii. § 124—Pillet, pp. 129-144—Kleen, i. §§ 124-139—Ortolan, ii. pp. 292-336—Hautefeuille, ii. pp. 189-288—Gessner, pp. 145-227—Perels, §§ 48-51—Testa, pp. 221-229—Dupuis, Nos. 159-198, and *Guerre*, Nos. 113-136—Boeck, Nos. 670-726—Holland, *Prize Law*, §§ 106-140—U.S. Naval War Code, Articles 37-45—Bernsten, § 10—Nippold, ii. § 32—Schramm, § 9—Bargrave Deane, *The Law of Blockade* (1870)—Fauchille, *Du Blocus maritime* (1882)—Carnazza-Amari, *Del Blocco maritimo* (1897)—Frémont, *De la Saisie des Navires en cas de Blocus* (1899)—Guynot-Boissière, *Du Blocus maritime* (1899)—§§ 35-44 of the 'Règlement international des Prises maritimes' (*Annuaire*, ix. (1887), p. 218), adopted by the Institute of International Law—Atherley-Jones, *Commerce in War* (1907), pp. 92-252—Soderquist, *Le Blocus maritime* (1908)—Hansemann, *Die Lehre von der einheitlichen Reise im Rechte der Blockade und Kriegskonterbande* (1910)—Güldenagel, *Verfolgung und Rechtsfolgen des Blockadebruchs* (1911)—Hirschmann, *Das internationale Prisenrecht* (1912), §§ 17-23—Wehberg, pp. 138-172—Piggott, *The Neutral Merchant* (1913)—Halsbury, *The Laws of England*, xxiii. (1912), pp. 279-281—Kennedy in the *Journal of Comparative Legislation*, New Ser. ix. (1908), pp. 239-251—Myers in *A.J.*, iv. (1910), pp. 571-595—General Report presented to the Naval Conference of London by its Drafting Committee, Articles 1-21—Holtzoff in *A.J.*, x. (1916), pp. 53-64.

§ 368. Blockade is the blocking by men-of-war[1] of the approach to the enemy coast, or a part of it, for

Definition of Blockade.

[1] When in 1861, during the American Civil War, the Federal Government blocked the harbour of Charleston by sinking ships laden

the purpose of preventing ingress and egress of vessels of all nations. Blockade must not be confounded with siege, although it may take place concurrently with siege. Whereas siege aims at the capture of the besieged place, blockade endeavours merely to intercept all intercourse, and especially commercial intercourse, by sea between the coast and the world at large. Although blockade is, as shown above,[1] a means of warfare against the enemy, it concerns neutrals as well, because the ingress and egress of neutral vessels are thereby interdicted and may be punished.[2]

Blockade in the modern sense of the term is an institution which could not develop until neutrality was in some form a recognised institution of the Law of Nations, and until the freedom of neutral commerce was in some form guaranteed. The institution of blockade dates from 1584 and 1630, when the Dutch [3] Government declared all the ports of Flanders in the power of Spain to be blockaded; but it has taken several hundred years for it to reach its present condition, since, until the beginning of the nineteenth century, belligerents frequently made use of so-called paper blockades. These are no longer valid, a blockade now being binding only if effective.

It is on account of the practical importance of blockade to the interests of neutrals that it is more conveniently treated with neutrality than with

with stone, the question arose whether a so-called stone blockade is lawful. There ought to be no doubt—see below, § 380—that such a stone blockade is not a blockade in the ordinary sense of the term, and that neutral ships may not be seized and confiscated for having attempted egress or ingress. But, on the other hand, there ought to be no doubt either that this mode of obstructing an enemy port is as lawful as any other means of sea warfare, provided the blocking of the harbour is made known, so that neutral vessels can avoid the danger of being wrecked. See Wharton, iii. § 361*a*; Fauchille, *Blocus*, pp. 143-145; Perels, § 35, p. 187.

[1] §§ 173-174.

[2] As regards the so-called 'long-distance blockade,' see below, §§ 390*a*-390*b*.

[3] See Fauchille, *Blocus*, pp. 2-6, and Westlake, *Papers*, pp. 325-337.

war. But blockade as a means of warfare must not be confounded with so-called pacific blockade, which is a means of compulsive settlement of State differences.[1]

Apart from the stipulation of the Declaration of Paris that a blockade to be binding must be effective, no conventional rules concerning blockade are in existence, nor is the practice of the States governed by common rules covering all points. Articles 1-21 of the Declaration of London did indeed offer a code of the law of blockade; but this declaration remained unratified, and although, as has already been stated,[2] at the outbreak of the World War the Allies adopted all these articles with certain modifications relating to presumed knowledge of the existence of a blockade, the British Maritime Rights Order in Council of July 7, 1916, and the corresponding French decree, abandoned the declaration altogether.

Blockade, Strategic and Commercial.

§ 369. A blockade is termed *strategic* if it forms part of other military operations directed against the coast which is blockaded, or if it be declared in order to cut off supplies from enemy forces on shore. In contradistinction to strategic blockade, one speaks of a *commercial* blockade when it is declared simply in order to cut off the coast from intercourse with the outside world, and no military operations take place on shore. That commercial blockades are, according to the present rules of International Law, as legitimate as strategic blockades, is not generally denied. But several writers [3] maintained before the World War that blockades which are purely commercial ought to be abolished as not being in accordance with the guaranteed freedom of neutral commerce during war.

[1] See above, §§ 44-49.

[2] Above, § 292.

[3] See Hall, § 233, and Westlake, *Papers*, pp. 313-361; but later Westlake (ii. p. 263) withdrew his opposition to commercial blockades.

Blockade to be Universal.

§ 370. A blockade is really in being when vessels of all nations are interdicted and prevented from ingress or egress. Blockade as a means of warfare is admissible only in the form of a *universal* blockade, that is—to borrow the language of Article 5 of the unratified Declaration of London—it 'must be applied impartially to the vessels of all nations.' If the blockading belligerent were to allow the ingress or egress of vessels of one nation, no blockade would exist.[1]

On the other hand, provided that a blockade is universal, a special licence for ingress or egress may be given to a particular vessel and for a particular purpose,[2] and men-of-war of all neutral nations may be allowed to pass to and fro unhindered.[3] Thus, when during the American Civil War the Federal Government blockaded the coast of the Confederate States, neutral men-of-war were not prevented from ingress and egress. But a belligerent has a *right* to prevent neutral men-of-war from passing through the line of blockade, and it is entirely within his discretion whether or not he will admit or exclude them; nor is he compelled to admit them all, even though he has admitted one or more of them.

Blockade, Outwards and Inwards.

§ 371. As a rule, a blockade is declared for the purpose of preventing ingress as well as egress. But sometimes only ingress, or only egress, is prevented. In such cases one speaks of 'blockade inwards' and of 'blockade outwards' respectively. Thus the blockade of the mouth of the Danube declared by the Allies in 1854, during the Crimean War, was a 'blockade inwards,' since the only purpose was to prevent supply reaching the Russian Army from the sea.[4]

[1] *The Rolla*, (1807) 6 C. Rob. 364; *The Franciska*, (1855) Spinks 287. See also below, § 382.

[2] This exception to the general rule was not mentioned by the unratified Declaration of London.

[3] Recognised by Article 6 of the unratified Declaration of London.

[4] *The Gerasimo*, (1857) 11 Moore P.C. 88.

What Places can be Blockaded.

§ 372. In former times it was sometimes asserted that only ports, or even only fortified ports,[1] could be blockaded; but the practice of the States has always shown that single ports and portions of an enemy coast, as well as the whole of the enemy coast, may be blockaded. Thus, during the American Civil War, the whole of the coast of the Confederate States to the extent of about 2500 nautical miles was blockaded. Attention must also be drawn to the fact, that such ports of a belligerent as are in the hands of the enemy may be the object of a blockade. Thus during the Franco-German War the French blockaded [2] their own ports of Rouen, Dieppe, and Fécamp, which were occupied by the Germans. Article 1 of the unratified Declaration of London indirectly sanctioned this practice by enacting that 'a blockade must not extend [3] beyond the ports and coasts belonging to or occupied by the enemy.'

Blockade of International Rivers.

§ 373. It is a moot question whether the mouth of a so-called international river [4] may be the object of a blockade, in case the riparian States are not all belligerents. Thus, when in 1854, during the Crimean War, the allied fleets of Great Britain and France blockaded the mouth of the Danube, Bavaria and Würtemberg, which remained neutral, protested. When, in 1870, the French blockaded the whole of the German coast of the North Sea, they exempted the Dollart, the mouth of the river Ems, because the Dollart separates the Dutch province of Groningen from German territory. Again, when in 1863, during the blockade of the coast of the Confederate States, the Federal cruiser *Vanderbilt* captured the British vessel *Peterhoff* [5] destined for

[1] Napoleon I. maintained in his Berlin Decrees: 'Le droit de blocus, d'après la raison et l'usage de tous les peuples policés, n'est applicable qu'aux places fortes.'

[2] See Fauchille, *Blocus*, p. 161.

[3] The so-called 'long-distance blockade' (see below, §§ 390*a*-390*b*) is of course essentially a blockade extending beyond the coast of the enemy.

[4] See above, vol. i. § 176.

[5] (1866) 5 Wall. 49. See Fauchille, *Blocus*, pp. 171-183; Phillimore, iii. § 293*a*; Hall, § 266; Rivier, ii. p. 291.

Matamoros, on the Mexican shore of the Rio Grande, the American courts released the vessel on the ground that trade with Mexico, which was neutral, could not be prohibited.

The Declaration of London, had it been ratified, would only have settled the controversy as regards one point. By enacting that 'the blockading forces must not bar access to neutral ports or coasts,' Article 18 would certainly have prohibited the blockade of the whole mouth of a boundary river between a neutral and a belligerent State, as, for instance, the River Rio Grande in case the United States of America was at war and Mexico remained neutral. But no provision was made for the case of the blockade of the mouths of rivers, such as the Danube or the Rhine, for example, which pass through several States between their sources and their mouths at the sea-coast, if one or more of the upper riparian States remain neutral.

Blockade of Straits.

§ 373*a*. Similar to, but not identical with, the question whether the mouth of an international river may be blockaded, is the question whether territorial straits may be blockaded. Three cases must be distinguished:

(1) Straits which only separate territory belonging to one and the same State, and do not connect two parts of the open sea (*e.g.* the Solent), may certainly be blockaded.

(2) When straits only separate territory belonging to one and the same State, but at the same time connect two parts of the open sea, the question whether they can be blockaded is unsettled.[1] During the Turco-Italian War in 1911 Italy did not declare a blockade of the Dardanelles, which belonged to this class of straits. The Bosphorus and Dardanelles are now to be subject to a special international régime under which they may never be blockaded;[2] but the general legal

[1] Baty in *Jahrbuch des Völkerrechts*, i. (1913), pp. 630-639.
[2] See above, vol. i. § 197.

position of straits of this kind as regards blockade still remains open.

(3) Unsettled also is the case in which straits divide two different States.

Justification of Blockade.

§ 374. The question has been raised in what way blockade, which vests in a belligerent a certain jurisdiction over neutral vessels, and has detrimental consequences for neutral trade, can be justified.[1] Several writers, following Hautefeuille,[2] maintain that the establishment of a blockade by a belligerent stationing a number of men-of-war so as to block the approach to the coast amounts to conquest of that part of the sea, and that such conquest justifies a belligerent in prohibiting ingress and egress of vessels of all nations. In contradistinction to this artificial construction of a conquest of a part of the sea, some writers [3] try to justify blockade by the necessity of war. I think, however, that no special justification of blockade is necessary at all. The fact is that the detrimental consequences of blockade to neutrals stand in the same category as the many other detrimental consequences of war to neutrals. Neither the one nor the other need be specially justified. A blockade interferes indeed with the recognised principle of the freedom of the sea, and, further, with the recognised freedom of neutral commerce. But all three have developed together, and when the freedom of the sea in time of peace and war, and, further, when the freedom of neutral commerce became generally recognised, the exceptional restrictions of blockade became at the same time recognised as legitimate.

[1] The matter is thoroughly treated by Fauchille, *Blocus*, pp. 13-36, and Güldenagel, *op. cit.*, pp. 51-86.

[2] See Hautefeuille, ii. pp. 190-191.

[3] See Gessner, p. 151; Bluntschli, § 827; Martens, ii. § 124.

II

ESTABLISHMENT OF BLOCKADE

See the literature quoted above at the commencement of § 368.

Competence to establish Blockade.

§ 375. A declaration of blockade being 'a high[1] act of sovereignty,' and having far-reaching consequences upon neutral trade, it is generally recognised not to be in the discretion of a commander of a naval force to establish a blockade without the authority of his Government. Article 9 of the unratified Declaration of London recognised this by providing that 'a declaration of blockade is made by the blockading Power or by the naval authorities acting in its name.' The authority of the Government to establish a blockade may be granted to a commander of a naval force for the express purpose of a particular blockade, the Government ordering him to blockade a certain port or coast; or the Government may expressly delegate its power of declaring a blockade to a commander, for use at his discretion. Moreover, if operations of war take place at a great distance[2] from the seat of Government, and a commander finds it necessary to establish a blockade, the blockade can become valid through the Government giving its immediate consent after being informed of the act of the commander. Further, the powers vested in the hands of the supreme commander of a fleet are supposed to include the authority to establish a blockade in case he finds it necessary, provided that his Government acquiesces as soon as it is informed of its establishment.[3]

§ 376. A blockade does not come into being *ipso facto*

[1] *The Henrick and Maria*, (1799) 1 C. Rob. 146.

[2] *The Rolla*, (1807) 6 C. Rob. 364.

[3] As regards the whole matter, see Fauchille, *Blocus*, pp. 68-73.

by the outbreak of war. Even the actual blocking of the approach to an enemy coast by belligerent men-of-war need not by itself mean that the ingress and egress of *neutral* vessels are to be prohibited, since it may be for the purpose of preventing the egress and ingress of *enemy* vessels only. Continental writers, therefore, have always considered notification to be essential for the establishment of a blockade. English, American, and Japanese writers, however, have not held notification to be essential, although they have considered knowledge on the part of a neutral vessel of an existing blockade to be necessary to justify her condemnation for breach of blockade.[1]

Declaration and Notification of Blockade.

But although Continental writers have always held notification to be essential for the establishment of blockade, they have differed with regard to the kind of notification that is necessary. Some writers [2] have maintained that three different notifications must take place—namely, (1) a local notification to the authorities of the blockaded ports or coast; (2) a diplomatic or general notification to all maritime neutral States by the blockading belligerent; and (3) a special notification to every approaching neutral vessel. Other writers [3] have considered only diplomatic and special notification essential. Others again [4] have maintained that special notification to every approaching vessel is alone required, although they have recommended diplomatic notification as a matter of courtesy.

As regards the practice of States, it has always been usual for the commander who establishes a blockade to send a notification of the blockade to the authorities of the blockaded ports or coast and to the foreign

[1] See below, § 384.

[2] See, for instance, Kleen, i. § 131.

[3] See, for instance, Bluntschli, §§ 831-832; Martens, ii. § 124, Gessner, p. 181.

[4] See, for instance, Hautefeuille, ii. pp. 224 and 226; Calvo, v. § 2846; Fauchille, *Blocus*, pp. 219-221.

consuls there. It has, further, always been usual for the blockading Government to notify the fact diplomatically to all neutral maritime States. And some States, such as France and Italy, have always ordered their blockading men-of-war to board every approaching neutral vessel, and notify her of the establishment of the blockade. But Great Britain, the United States of America, and Japan have not considered notification to be essential for the institution of a blockade. They have held that the simple fact that the approach was blocked, and egress and ingress of neutral vessels actually prevented, is sufficient to make the existence of a blockade known, but when no diplomatic notification had taken place, they did not seize a vessel for breach of blockade if her master had no actual notice of the existence of the blockade. English,[1] American,[2] and Japanese [3] practice, accordingly, have made a distinction between a so-called *de facto* blockade and a notified blockade.

If the Declaration of London had been ratified, Articles 8 to 12 would have created a common practice, for the Powers came to an agreement upon the following rules :—

(1) There was to be a *declaration* as well as a *notification* in order to make a blockade binding (Article 8).

(2) A *declaration* of blockade was to be made either by the blockading Power, or by the naval authorities acting in its name, and was to specify (*a*) the date when the blockade began ; (*b*) the geographical limits of the coastline under blockade ; and (*c*) the period within which neutral vessels might come out (Article 9). If the commencement of the blockade or its geographical limits were given inaccurately the declaration was not to be valid, and a new declara-

[1] *The Vrouw Judith*, (1799) 1 C. Rob. 150.

[2] See U.S. Naval War Code, Articles 39-40.

[3] See Japanese Prize Law, Article 30.

tion was to be necessary in order to make the blockade binding (Article 10). If no mention was made of the period within which neutral vessels might come out, they were to be allowed to pass out freely (Article 16).

(3) *Notification* of the declaration of blockade was at once to be made. Two notifications were to be necessary (Article 11): (1) by the Government of the blockading fleet to all neutral Governments, the purpose of this notification being to enable neutral Governments to inform merchantmen sailing under their flag of the establishment of a blockade; (2) by the officer commanding the blockading force to the local authorities, whose duty it was to notify the foreign consuls at the blockaded port or coastline. The purpose of this notification was to enable neutral merchantmen in the blockaded port or ports to receive knowledge of the establishment of the blockade, and to prepare to leave the port within the period specified in the declaration of blockade. If this notification had not been made, neutral vessels were to be allowed to pass freely out of the blockaded port (Article 16).

(4) The rules as to declaration and notification of blockade were to apply to cases where the limits of a blockade were extended, or where a blockade was re-established after having been raised (Article 12).

But, as has been already explained, the Declaration of London remains unratified, and though the Allied Governments adopted the greater part of it at the outbreak of the World War, later they fell back upon 'the historic and admitted rules of the Law of Nations.'[1]

Length of Time for Egress of Neutral Vessels.

§ 377. As regards *ingress*, a blockade becomes valid the moment it is established; even vessels in ballast have no right of ingress. As regards *egress*, it has always been usual for the blockading commander to grant a certain length of time within which neutral vessels might leave the blockaded ports unhindered;[2]

[1] See above, §§ 292, 368.

[2] Recognised by implication in Article 9 of the unratified Declaration of London.

but no rule exists respecting the length of such time. Fifteen days have frequently been granted,[1] but in the blockades during the World War, the periods granted were very short, namely, four days in the case of the blockade of German East Africa, two days in the cases of the blockade of the Cameroons and of the Bulgarian coast on the Ægean Sea, and three days in the case of the blockade of the coast of Asia Minor.

End of Blockade.

§ 378. Apart from the conclusion of peace, a blockade can come to an end in four different ways.

It may, in the first place, be raised, or restricted in its limits, by the blockading Power for any reason it likes. In such a case it has always been usual to notify the end of blockade to all neutral maritime States.[2]

A blockade can, secondly, come to an end through an enemy force driving off the blockading squadron or fleet. In such a case, the blockade ends *ipso facto* by the blockading squadron being driven away, whatever their intention as to returning may be. Should the squadron return and resume the blockade, it must be considered as a new blockade, and not simply the continuation of the former blockade, and the steps necessary for the establishment of a blockade must again be taken.[3]

The third ground for the ending of a blockade is its failure to be effective.[4]

The fourth ground is the capture and occupation of the blockaded port or coast by the blockading force. It was indeed held in the American Civil War in the case of *The Circassian*,[5] that this did not end the blockade;

[1] According to U.S. Naval War Code, Article 43, thirty days were to be allowed 'unless otherwise specially ordered.'

[2] Article 13 of the unratified Declaration of London stipulated that 'the voluntary raising of a blockade, as also any restrictions in its limits, must, in the same way as the declaration of a blockade, be notified to all neutral Governments by the blockading Power, and to the local authorities by the officer commanding the blockading fleet.

[3] See Article 12 of the unratified Declaration of London.

[4] See below, § 382.

[5] (1864) 2 Wall. 135.

but the Mixed Commission on British and American Claims, set up after the war, considered that judgment to be wrong, and awarded compensation to all the claimants.[1]

III

EFFECTIVENESS OF BLOCKADE

See the literature quoted above at the commencement of § 368.

§ 379. The necessity that a blockade should be made effective by the presence of a blockading squadron of sufficient strength to prevent egress and ingress of vessels became gradually recognised during the first half of the nineteenth century; it became formally enacted as a principle of the Law of Nations through the Declaration of Paris in 1856, and was recognised in Article 2 of the unratified Declaration of London. Effective blockade is the contrast to so-called fictitious or paper blockade, which was frequently practised during the seventeenth, eighteenth, and at the beginning of the nineteenth century.[2] Fictitious blockade consists in declaring and notifying that a port or a coast is blockaded without, however, posting a sufficient number of men-of-war on the spot to be really able to prevent egress and ingress of every vessel. It was one of the principles of the First and of the Second Armed Neutralities that a blockade should always be effective; but it was not till after the Napoleonic wars that this principle gradually found universal recognition. During the second half of the nineteenth century, even those States which had not acceded to the Declara-

Effective in contradistinction to Fictitious Blockade.

[1] However, in 1899 during the Spanish American War, the Supreme Court of the United States in *The Adula* (176 U.S. 361) held the case of *The Circassian* to be decisive.

[2] See Fauchille, *Blocus*, pp. 74-109.

tion of Paris did not dispute the necessity of a blockade being effective.

Condition of Effectiveness of Blockade.

§ 380. The condition of effectiveness of a blockade, as defined by the Declaration of Paris, is its maintenance *by such a force as is sufficient really to prevent access to the coast.* But no unanimity exists respecting what is required to constitute an effective blockade according to this definition. Apart from differences of opinion regarding points of minor interest, it may be stated that in the main there have been two conflicting opinions.

According to one opinion, the definition of an effective blockade pronounced by the First Armed Neutrality of 1780 is valid, and a blockade is effective only when the approach to the coast is barred by a chain of men-of-war, anchored on the spot, and so near to one another that the line cannot be passed without obvious danger to the passing vessel.[1] This corresponds to the practice followed before the World War by France.

According to another opinion, a blockade is effective when the approach is watched—to use the words of Dr. Lushington [2]—'by a force sufficient to render the egress and ingress dangerous, or, in other words, save under peculiar circumstances, as fogs, violent winds, and some necessary absences, sufficient to render the capture of vessels attempting to go in or come out most probable.' According to this opinion, there need be no chain of anchored men-of-war to expose any vessels attempting to break the blockade to a cross fire; a

[1] See Hautefeuille, ii. p. 194; Gessner, p. 169; Kleen, i. § 129; Boeck, Nos. 676-681; Dupuis, Nos. 173-174; Fauchille, *Blocus*, pp. 110-142. Phillimore, iii. § 293, takes up the same standpoint in so far as a blockade *de facto* is concerned: 'A blockade *de facto* should be effected by stationing a number of ships, and forming as it were an arch of circumvallation round the mouth of the prohibited port, where, if the arch fails in any one part, the blockade itself fails altogether.'

[2] In his judgment in *The Franciska*, (1855) Spinks 287.

real danger of capture suffices, whether the danger is caused by cruising or anchored men-of-war. This is the standpoint of the theory and practice of Great Britain and the United States, and it seems likewise to be that of Germany and several German writers.[1] The blockade during the American Civil War of the whole coast of the Confederate States to the extent of 2500 nautical miles by four hundred Federal cruisers could, of course, only be maintained by cruising vessels; and the fact that all neutral maritime States recognised it as effective shows that the opinion of dissenting writers had more theoretical than practical importance.

The Declaration of London, if it had been ratified, would have settled the controversy at least to the extent of determining that 'the question whether a blockade is effective, is a question of fact,'[2] and thereby by implication recognising the before-mentioned decision of Dr. Lushington. But, as has been explained,[3] the declaration remains unratified, and it was abandoned by Great Britain and France during the World War.

If the Anglo-American standpoint be adopted, since the question of effectiveness is one of fact, and real danger to passing vessels is the characteristic of effectiveness, it must be recognised that the distance of the blockading men-of-war from the blockaded port or coast is immaterial so long as the circumstances and conditions of the special case justify it. Thus during the Crimean War the port of Riga was blockaded by a man-of-war stationed at a distance of 120 miles from the town, in the Lyser Ort, a channel three miles wide forming the only approach to the gulf.[4] Moreover, in certain cases, and in the absence of a sufficient number of men-of-war, a blockade may be made effec-

[1] See Perels, § 49; Bluntschli, § 829; Liszt, § 41, iii.

[2] Article 3.

[3] Above, §§ 292, 368.

[4] *The Franciska*, (1855) Spinks 287. See Hall, § 260, and Holland, *Studies*, pp. 166-167.

tive through planting land batteries within range of any vessel attempting to pass,[1] provided that there be at least one man-of-war on the spot. But a stone blockade,[2] so called because vessels laden with stones are sunk in the channel to block the approach, is not an effective blockade.

Amount of Danger which creates Effectiveness.

§ 381. It is impossible to state exactly what degree of danger to a vessel attempting to pass is necessary to prove an effective blockade. It is recognised that a blockade does not cease to be effective because now and then a vessel succeeds in passing the line unhindered, provided that there was so much danger as to make her capture probable. Dr. Lushington strikingly dealt with the matter in the following words:[3] 'The maintenance of a blockade must always be a question of degree—of the degree of danger attending ships going into or leaving a port. Nothing is further from my intention, nor indeed more opposed to my notions, than any relaxation of the rule that a blockade must be sufficiently maintained; but it is perfectly obvious that no force could bar the entrance to absolute certainty; that vessels may get in and get out during the night, or fogs, or violent winds, or occasional absence; that it is most difficult to judge from numbers alone. Hence, I believe that in every case the inquiry has been, whether the force was competent and present, and, if so, the performance of the duty was presumed; and I think I may safely assert that in no case was a blockade held to be void when the blockading force was on the spot or near thereto on the ground of vessels entering into or escaping from the port, where such

[1] *The Nancy*, (1809) 1 Acton 63; *The Circassian*, (1864) 2 Wall. 135; *The Olinde Rodrigues*, (1898) 174 U.S. 510. See also Bluntschli, § 829; Perels, § 49; Geffcken in *Holtzendorff*, iv. p. 750; Walker, *Manual*, § 78.

[2] See above, 368. As to laying mines off enemy ports and coasts to interrupt commercial navigation, see above, § 182*a*.

[3] In his judgment in *The Franciska*, (1855) Spinks 287.

ingress or egress did not take place with the consent of the blockading squadron.'

§ 382. A blockade is effective so long as the danger lasts which makes probable the capture of such vessels as attempt to pass the approach. It ceases *ipso facto* by the absence of such danger, whether the blockading men-of-war are driven away, or are sent away for the fulfilment of some task which has nothing to do with the blockade, or voluntarily withdraw, or allow the passage of vessels in other cases than those which are exceptionally admissible. Thus, when in 1861, during the American Civil War, the Federal cruiser *Niagara*, which blockaded Charleston, was sent away, and her place was taken after five days by the *Minnesota*, the blockade ceased to be effective, although the Federal Government refused to recognise this.[1] Thus, further, when, during the Crimean War, Great Britain allowed Russian vessels to export goods from blockaded ports, and accordingly permitted the egress of such vessels from the blockaded port of Riga, the blockade ceased to be effective, because it tried to interfere with neutral commerce only; and the capture of the Danish vessel *Franciska*[2] for attempting to break the blockade was not upheld.

Cessation of Effectiveness.

On the other hand, practice,[3] and the majority of writers, have always recognised that a blockade does not cease to be effective in case the blockading force is driven away for a short time through stress of weather, and Article 4 of the unratified Declaration of London adopted this view by providing that 'a blockade is not regarded as raised if the blockading force is temporarily withdrawn on account of stress of weather.' English[4]

[1] See Mountague Bernard, *Neutrality of Great Britain during the American Civil War* (1870), pp. 237-239.

[2] Spinks 287. See above, § 370.

[3] *The Columbia*, (1799) 1 C. Rob. 154.

[4] See Twiss, ii. § 103, p. 201, and Phillimore, iii. § 294.

writers have also denied that a blockade ceases to be effective because a blockading man-of-war is absent for a short time for the purpose of chasing a vessel which succeeded in passing the approach unhindered,[1] but the unratified Declaration of London did not recognise this.[2]

IV

BREACH OF BLOCKADE

See the literature quoted above at the commencement of § 368.

Definition of Breach of Blockade.

§ 383. Breach or violation of blockade is the unallowed ingress or egress of a vessel in spite of the blockade. An attempted breach is, so far as a punishment is concerned,[3] treated in the same way as a consummated breach; but the practice of States has differed as to the time at which, and act by which, an attempt to break a blockade commences.

No Breach without Notice of Blockade.

§ 384. Since breach of blockade is, from the standpoint of the blockading belligerent, a criminal act, knowledge on the part of a vessel of the existence of a blockade is essential for making her egress or ingress a breach of blockade.

It is for this reason that Continental theory and practice have never considered a blockade established without local and diplomatic notification, so that every vessel might have, or might be supposed to have, notice of its existence. For the same reason some States, as France and Italy, have never considered a vessel to have committed a breach of blockade unless, before her attempted ingress, one of the blockading

[1] See Article 37 of U.S. Naval War Code.

[2] See the Report of the Drafting Committee on Article 4.

[3] It has already been pointed out (above, § 296) that a blockade-runner does not violate International Law, but rules made by the belligerent, violations of which International Law permits him to punish.

cruisers stopped her, gave her special warning, and recorded the warning in her log-book.[1]

British, American, and Japanese practice regarding the necessary knowledge of the existence of a blockade on the part of a vessel has always made a distinction between actual and constructive notice, no breach of blockade having been held to exist without either the one or the other.[2] Actual notice has been understood to mean knowledge acquired by a direct warning from one of the blockading men-of-war, or knowledge acquired from any other public or private source of information. Constructive knowledge has been understood to arise when a vessel has been presumed to know of the blockade on the ground either of notoriety or of diplomatic notification. The existence of a blockade has always been presumed to be notorious to vessels within the blockaded ports; but it has been a question of fact whether it was notorious to other vessels. Knowledge of the existence of a blockade has always been presumed if sufficient time had elapsed after the home State of the vessel had received diplomatic notification of the blockade, for it to inform all vessels sailing under its flag, whether or no they had actually received, or taken notice of, the information.[3]

The unratified Declaration of London followed, to a certain extent, British, American, and Japanese practice; it differed chiefly in that the presumption of knowledge of a blockade was never to be absolute, but might in every case be rebutted. Article 14 provided that 'the liability of a neutral vessel to capture for breach of blockade is contingent on her knowledge, actual or presumptive, of the blockade.' Knowledge of the blockade was to be presumed, *failing*

[1] See above, § 376.

[2] See Holland, *Prize Law*, §§ 107, 114-127; U.S. Naval War Code, Article 39; Japanese Prize Law, Article 26.

[3] *The Vrouw Judith*, (1799) 1 C. Rob. 150; *The Neptunus*, (1799) 2 C. Rob. 110; *The Calypso*, (1799) 2 C. Rob. 298; *The Neptunus*, (1800) 3 C. Rob. 173; *The Hoffnung*, (1805) 6 C. Rob. 112.

proof to the contrary, in case the vessel had left a neutral port subsequent to the notification of the blockade to the Power to which such port belonged, and provided that the notification was made in sufficient time (Article 15). But in case a neutral vessel *approaching* a blockaded port had neither actual nor presumptive knowledge of the blockade, she was not to be considered *in delicto*, and notification had to be made to her by recording a warning in her log-book. Further, if a neutral vessel was *coming out* of a blockaded port, she had to be allowed to pass free, in case, through the negligence of the officer commanding the blockading fleet, no declaration of blockade had been notified to the local authorities, or in case, in the declaration as notified, no period had been mentioned within which neutral vessels might come out (Article 16).

However this may be, the declaration remains unratified, and modifications were made with regard to presumed knowledge of the existence of a blockade, when its rules were put into force by the Allied Powers at the outbreak of the World War.

The Former Practice as to what constitutes an Attempt to break Blockade.

§ 385. The practice of States, as well as the opinions of writers, have differed much as to what acts of a vessel constitute an attempt to break blockade.

(1) The Second Armed Neutrality of 1800 sought to restrict an attempt to break blockade to the employment of force or ruse by a vessel on the line of blockade for the purpose of passing through. This was, on the whole, the practice of France, which moreover, as stated before, required that the vessel should before the attempt have received special warning from one of the blockading men-of-war. Many writers[1] took the same standpoint.

(2) The practice of other States, such as Japan, approved by many writers,[2] went beyond this, and

[1] See Hautefeuille, ii. p. 234; Kleen, i. § 137; Gessner, p. 202; Dupuis, No. 185; Fauchille, *Blocus*, p. 322.

[2] See Bluntschli, § 835; Perels, § 51; Geffcken in *Holtzendorff*, iv.

considered that an attempt to break blockade had been made when a vessel, with or without force or ruse, endeavoured to pass the line of blockade; when, for instance, a vessel destined for a blockaded place was found anchoring or cruising near the line of blockade.

(3) The practice of Great Britain and the United States of America went furthest, since it considered that an attempt to break blockade had been made when a vessel, not destined according to her ship-papers for a blockaded port, was found near it and steering for it; or when a vessel, destined for a port the blockade of which was diplomatically notified, started on her journey knowing that the blockade had not been raised (except when the port from which the vessel sailed was so far distant from the scene of war as to justify her master in starting for a destination known to be blockaded on the chance of finding that the blockade had been removed, and with an intention of changing her destination should that not prove to be the case).[1] This practice, further, applied the doctrine of continuous voyages[2] to blockade, for it considered that an attempt to break blockade was committed by a vessel which, although ostensibly destined for a neutral or an unblockaded port, in reality intended, after touching there, to go on to a blockaded port.[3]

(4) During the Civil War, the American Prize Courts carried the practice further by condemning vessels for breach of blockade which knowingly carried to a neutral port cargo ultimately destined for a blockaded

p. 763; Rivier, ii. p. 431. See also § 25 of the Prussian Regulations (1864) concerning Naval Prizes, and Article 29 of the Japanese Naval Prize Law.

[1] See Holland, *Prize Law*, § 133, and U.S. Naval War Code, Article 42; *The Betsey*, (1799) 1 C. Rob. 332.

[2] On this doctrine, see below, § 400 n.

[3] See Holland, *Prize Law*, § 134, and the case of *The James Cook*, (1810) Edwards 261.

port, and by condemning for breach of blockade such cargo [1] as was ultimately destined for a blockaded port, when the carrying vessel was ignorant of its ulterior destination. Thus the *Bermuda*,[2] a British vessel with a cargo part of which was, in the opinion of the American courts, ultimately destined for the blockaded ports of the Confederate States, was seized on her voyage to the neutral British port of Nassau, in the Bahama Islands, and condemned for breach of blockade by the American courts. The same happened to the British vessel *Stephen Hart*,[3] which was seized on her voyage to the neutral port of Cardenas, in Cuba. And in the famous case of *The Springbok*,[4] a British vessel also destined for Nassau, in the Bahama Islands, which was seized on her voyage to this neutral British port, the cargo alone was finally condemned for breach of blockade, since, in the opinion of the court, the vessel was not cognisant that the cargo was intended to reach a blockaded port. The same happened to the cargo of the British vessel *Peterhoff* [5] destined for the neutral port of Matamoros, in Mexico. The British Government declined to intervene in favour of the British owners of the respective vessels and cargoes.[6]

It is true that the majority of authorities [7] assert the illegality of these judgments of the American Prize Courts, but it is a fact that Great Britain at the time recognised as correct the principles which are the basis of these judgments.

§ 385*a*. The unratified Declaration of London sought to effect a settlement of this controversial matter.

[1] But not the vessel.

[2] (1865) 3 Wall. 514.

[3] (1865) 3 Wall. 559.

[4] (1866) 5 Wall. 1.

[5] (1866) 5 Wall. 28.

[6] See *Parl. Papers*, Misc., No. 1 (1900).

[7] See, for instance, Holland, *Prize Law*, p. 38, n. 2; Phillimore, iii. § 298; Twiss, *Belligerent Right on the High Seas* (1884), p. 19; Hall, § 263; Gessner, *Kriegfuhrende und neutrale Machte* (1877), pp. 95-100; Bluntschli, § 835; Perels, § 51; Fauchille, *Blocus*, pp. 333-344; Martens, ii. § 124. See also Wharton, iii. § 362, p. 401, and Moore, vii. § 1276.

What constituted an Attempt to break Blockade according to the unratified Declaration of London.

Article 17 provided that 'neutral vessels may not be captured for breach of blockade except within the area of operations of the men-of-war detailed to render the blockade effective,' and Article 19 provided that 'whatever may be the ulterior destination of a vessel or of her cargo, she may not be captured for breach of blockade, if, at the moment, she is on the way to a non-blockaded port.'

According to these provisions, a neutral vessel, to be guilty of an attempt to break blockade, must actually have entered the *area of operations* (*rayon d'action*) of the blockading fleet. This *area of operations* was to be a question of fact in each case. 'When a Government decides to undertake blockading operations against some part of the enemy coast it details a certain number of men-of-war to take part in the blockade, and entrusts the command to an officer whose duty it is to use them for the purpose of making the blockade effective. The commander of the naval force thus formed posts the vessels at his disposal according to the line of the coast and the geographical position of the blockaded places, and instructs each vessel as to the part which she has to play, and especially as to the zone which she is to watch. All the zones watched taken together and so organised as to make the blockade effective, form the area of operations of the blockading force.' [1]

But the mere fact that a neutral vessel had entered the area of operations was not to be sufficient to justify her capture; she had also to be destined for, and be on her way to, the blockaded port. If she passed through the area of operations without being destined for, and on her way to, the blockaded port, she was not attempting to break the blockade. Even should the ulterior destination of a vessel or her cargo be the blockaded port, she was not to be regarded as attempting to break the blockade, if, at the moment of visit, she was really on her way to a non-blockaded port (Article 19). However, she had to be really, and not only apparently, on her way to a non-

[1] Report of the Drafting Committee on Article 17.

blockaded port; if it could be proved that in reality her immediate destination was the blockaded port and that she only feigned to be destined for a non-blockaded port, she might be captured, for she was actually attempting to break the blockade.[1]

However that may be, these provisions excluded the application to blockade of the doctrine of continuous voyage in any form. But at the outbreak of the World War the declaration had not been ratified, and though at first the Allied Governments adopted most of its rules, including Article 19, in March 1916 [2] they abandoned that article, and declared that the principle of continuous voyage or ultimate destination should apply to blockade. Later, as has already been explained, they abandoned the declaration altogether.[3]

When Ingress is not considered Breach of Blockade.

§ 386. Although blockade inwards interdicts ingress to all vessels, if not especially licensed,[4] necessity makes exceptions to the rule.

According to the practice which before the World War had been quite general, whenever a vessel either by need of repairs,[5] stress of weather,[6] want of water [7] or provisions, or upon any other ground, was absolutely obliged to enter a blockaded port, such ingress did not constitute a breach of blockade. On the other hand, according to British practice at any rate, ingress did not cease to be breach of blockade if caused by intoxication of the master,[8] ignorance [9] of the coast, loss of compass,[10] endeavour to get a pilot,[11] and the like, or an attempt to ascertain [12] whether the blockade was raised.[13]

[1] See the Report of the Drafting Committee on Article 19.
[2] *London Gazette*, March 31, 1916.
[3] See above, §§ 292, 368.
[4] See above, § 370.
[5] *The Charlotta*, (1810) Edwards 252.
[6] *The Fortuna*, (1803) 5 C. Rob. 27.
[7] *The Hurtige Hane*, (1799) 2 C. Rob. 124.
[8] *The Shepherdess*, (1804) 5 C. Rob. 262.
[9] *The Adonis*, (1804) 5 C. Rob. 256.
[10] *The Elizabeth*, (1810) Edwards 198.
[11] *The Neutralitet*, (1805) 6 C. Rob. 30.
[12] *The Spes and Irene*, (1804) 5 C. Rob. 76.
[13] See Holland, *Prize Law*, §§ 135-136.

The unratified Declaration of London recognised that necessity makes exceptions to the rule that vessels may not enter a blockaded port. Article 7 provided that 'in circumstances of distress, acknowledged by an officer of the blockading force, a neutral vessel may enter a place under blockade, and subsequently leave it, provided that she has neither discharged nor shipped any cargo there.' However, this article did not define *circumstances of distress* and made it a condition that those circumstances must be acknowledged by an officer of the blockading force.[1] Everything was therefore, *prima facie* at any rate, left to the consideration of that officer. But once he had acknowledged that the vessel was in distress, he was in duty bound[2] to allow her to enter the blockaded port, unless he relieved the distress himself.

When Egress is not considered Breach of Blockade.

§ 387. There are a few cases of egress which, according to the practice of Great Britain and most other States before the World War, were not considered breaches of blockade outwards.[3] Thus a vessel which was in a blockaded port before the commencement of the blockade[4] was allowed to sail from it in ballast, as was also a vessel that had entered during a blockade, either in ignorance of it, or with the permission of the blockading squadron.[5] Thus, further, a vessel, the cargo of which was put on board before the commencement of the blockade, was allowed to leave the port afterwards unhindered.[6] Thus, again, a vessel obliged by absolute necessity to enter a blockaded port was afterwards allowed to leave it unhindered. And a

[1] See the case of *The Clumberhall*, a British vessel condemned by the Italian Prize Court for having entered a blockaded area during the Turco-Italian War, in 1912, under a plea of distress, without first having had the cause of distress verified by the blockading fleet. The facts were stated in the House of Commons on May 25, 1914; see *Hansard*, vol. 63, p. 108.

[2] See Report of the Drafting Committee on Article 7.

[3] See Holland, *Prize Law*, § 130; Twiss, ii. § 113; Phillimore, iii. § 313.

[4] *The Frederick Moltke*, (1798) 1 C. Rob. 86.

[5] *The Juno*, (1799) 2 C. Rob. 116.

[6] *The Vrouw Judith*, (1799) 1 C. Rob. 150.

vessel employed by the diplomatic envoy of a neutral State for the exclusive purpose of sending home from a blockaded port distressed seamen of his nationality [1] was also allowed to pass unhindered.[2]

Passage through Unblockaded Canal no Breach of Blockade.

§ 388. A breach of blockade can only be committed by passing through the blockaded approach. Therefore, if the maritime approach to a port is blockaded, but an inland canal leads from it to another unblockaded port or to a neutral port, no breach of blockade is committed by the egress or the ingress of a vessel passing such canal for the purpose of reaching the blockaded port.[3]

V

CONSEQUENCES OF BREACH OF BLOCKADE

See the literature quoted above at the commencement of § 368.

Capture of Blockade-running Vessels.

§ 389. It is universally recognised that a vessel may only be captured for a breach of blockade while *in delicto*; that means during an attempt to break the blockade, or during the breach itself. But here again practice as well as theory have differed much, since there has been no unanimity with regard to the extent of time during which an attempted breach or an actual breach could be said to be continuing.

It has already been stated [4] that it has been a moot point from what moment a breach of blockade can be said to have been attempted, and that, according to

[1] *The Rose in Bloom*, (1811) 1 Dodson 55.

[2] The unratified Declaration of London recognised by Article 7—see above, § 386—that a vessel which, on account of distress, entered a blockaded port, must be allowed to leave it afterwards, provided she had neither discharged nor shipped cargo there; and Article 16—see above, § 384—provided that a vessel coming out of a blockaded port in the circumstances there mentioned must be allowed to pass free. But beyond these the declaration did not specify any cases in which egress was not to be considered breach of blockade.

[3] *The Stert*, (1801) 4 C. Rob. 65. See Phillimore, iii. § 314.

[4] Above, § 385.

the practice of Great Britain and the United States, the fact that a vessel destined for a blockaded port was starting on her voyage constituted an attempt. It is obvious that this controversy bears upon the question from what point of time a blockade-running vessel must be considered *in delicto.*

But it has been likewise a moot point when the period of time during which a blockade-running vessel might be said to be *in delicto* came to an end. According to Continental theory and practice, the vessel has been considered to be *in delicto* only so long as she is actually on the line of blockade, or, having fled from there, so long as she is being pursued by one of the blockading cruisers. On the other hand, according to the practice of Great Britain [1] and the United States,[2] a blockade-running vessel has been held to be *in delicto* so long as she *has not completed her voyage from the blockaded port to the port of her destination and back to the port from which she started originally,* the voyage out and home being considered one voyage. But a vessel has been held to be *in delicto* only so long as the blockade continued, capture being no longer admissible in case the blockade had been raised or had otherwise come to an end.

The Declaration of London sought to settle the controversy, for, according to Article 20, a vessel was to be *in delicto* so long only [3] as she was being pursued by a man-of-war of the blockading force (and not by any other cruiser), and she might no longer be captured if the pursuit was abandoned or if the blockade was raised. Under this rule, a blockade-breaking vessel was liable to capture so long as the pursuit lasted, whether or no she was still within the area of operations; even if for a while she had

[1] *The Welvaart van Pillaw,* (1799) 2 C. Rob. 128; *The General Hamilton,* (1805) 6 C. Rob. 61.

[2] See U.S. Naval War Code, Article 44.

[3] See below, § 428*a*.

taken refuge in a neutral port, she might, on coming out, be captured, provided that the captor was one of the men-of-war of the blockading force which had pursued her and waited for her outside the port of refuge.[1] However, the declaration has not been ratified.

Penalty for Breach of Blockade.

§ 390. Capture being effected, the blockade-runner must be sent to a port, to be brought before a Prize Court. For this purpose the crew may be temporarily detained, as they will have to serve as witnesses. In former times the crew could be imprisoned, and it is said that even capital[2] punishment could have been pronounced against them. But since the eighteenth century, this practice of imprisoning the crew has been abandoned, and nowadays the crew may not even be made prisoners of war, but must be released as soon as the Prize Court has pronounced its decision.[3] The only penalty which may be pronounced is confiscation of the vessel and the cargo. But the practice[4] of the several States has differed much concerning the penalty for breach of blockade. According to British and American practice before the World War, confiscation of both vessel and cargo might take place in case the owners of the vessel were identical with those of the cargo. In case vessel and cargo had not the same owners, confiscation of both took place only when the cargo consisted of contraband of war or the owners knew of the blockade at the time the cargo was shipped for the blockaded port.[5] It mattered not whether the captured vessel which carried the cargo had herself actually passed through the blockaded line, or whether the breach of

[1] See the Report of the Drafting Committee on Article 20.

[2] See Bynkershoek, *Quaestiones Juris publici*, i. c. 11.

[3] See Calvo, v. §§ 2897-2898; U.S. Naval War Code, Article 45.

[4] See Fauchille, *Blocus*, pp. 357-394; Gessner, pp. 210-214; Perels, § 51, pp. 276-278.

[5] *The Mercurius*, (1798) 1 C. Rob. 80; *The Columbia*, (1799) 1 C. Rob. 154; *The Alexander*, (1801) 4 C. Rob. 93; *The Adonis*, (1804) 5 C. Rob. 256; *The Exchange*, (1808) Edwards 39; *The Panaghia Rhomba*, (1858) 12 Moore P.C. 168. See Phillimore, iii. §§ 318-319.

blockade was effected through the combined action of lighters and the vessel, the lighters passing the line and discharging the cargo into the vessel near the line, or *vice versa.*[1] The cargo alone was confiscated according to the judgments of the American Prize Courts during the Civil War in the case of *The Springbok* and in similar cases[2] when goods ultimately destined for a blockaded port were sent to a neutral port on a vessel whose owners were ignorant of this ulterior destination of the goods.

The Declaration of London proposed to settle the matter by a very simple rule, for according to Article 21 the penalty for blockade-breaking was to be condemnation of the vessel in all cases, and condemnation of the cargo also, unless the owner proved that at the time of the shipment of the goods the shipper *neither knew, nor could have known,* of the intention of the vessel to break the blockade. The case in which the whole, or part, of the cargo consisted of contraband, was not mentioned by Article 21, but its condemnation is a matter of course. However, the declaration has not secured ratification.

VI

THE SO-CALLED LONG-DISTANCE BLOCKADE

§ 390*a*. In the foregoing sections of this chapter the conception of blockade as understood before the World War, and the rules of International Law concerning it, have been explained and discussed. The World War did not illustrate or develop these rules, because the few blockades that were declared—blockades of the coast of German East Africa, of the Cameroons, of Bulgaria on the Ægean Sea, of Asia Minor, and a few others[3]—provoked little or no controversy, and played

Conception of the Long-Distance Blockade.

[1] *The Maria,* (1805) 6 C. Rob. 201.
[2] See above, § 385 (4).
[3] Details in Garner, ii. § 510.

no part in the major operations of the war. The Central Powers, whose surface warships were only able to leave their base for an occasional raid, were certainly in no position to maintain an effective blockade in accordance with the rules set forth in this chapter, while the Allied and Associated Powers, confronted by mines and submarines along a coast-line highly organised for defence, found it impracticable to establish a blockade of Germany of a type known in former wars. Instead, they resorted to what is called a *long-distance blockade.*[1]

It has already been said[2] that when, in February 1915, Germany declared the waters round the British Isles to be a war zone, and proclaimed that all enemy ships found in that area would be destroyed, and neutral ships might be exposed to danger, Great Britain announced that, in concert with her allies, she would endeavour to prevent, as a measure of retaliation, commodities of any kind from reaching or leaving Germany. The Order in Council of March 11, 1915, which gave effect to this decision, was expressly stated to be retaliatory, and did not speak of establishing a blockade, with the recognised rules for which it did not conform. But only a few days later, the British Foreign Secretary announced the new policy to the United States ambassador in the words: 'the British fleet has instituted a blockade, effectively controlling by cruiser "cordon" all passage to and from Germany by sea.'[3]

This long-distance blockade was promptly challenged by neutrals, and in particular by the United States of America.[4] She admitted that, as great changes had occurred in the conditions and means of naval warfare

[1] See Garner, ii. §§ 509-531, and in *A.J.*, ix. (1915), pp. 843-857; Perrinjaquet in *R.G.*, xxiv. (1915), pp. 210-255; Piggott, *The Neutral Merchant* (1915).

[2] See above, § 319.

[3] *Parl. Papers*, Misc., No. 6 (1915), Cd. 7816, p. 26.

[4] In Notes dated April 2, 1915, and November 5, 1915: *Parl. Papers*, Misc., No. 14 (1916), Cd. 8233, p. 1, No. 15 (1916), Cd. 8234, p. 2.

since the rules hitherto governing legal blockade were formulated, a 'close' blockade with its cordon of ships in the immediate offing of the blockaded ports might be no longer practicable; but she complained that the British measures did not even conform with 'the spirit and principles of the essence of the rules of war.' Her main grounds of criticism were (1) that these measures amounted to a blockade of neutral ports—'so great an area of the high seas is covered, and the cordon of ships is so distant from the territory affected, that neutral vessels must necessarily pass through the blockading force in order to reach important neutral ports which Great Britain, as a belligerent, has not the legal right to blockade';[1] (2) that, as trade between Scandinavian ports and German Baltic ports was not intercepted, these measures did not 'bear with equal severity' upon all neutrals;[2] and (3) that they were not effective, since 'German coasts are open to trade with the Scandinavian countries' and 'German naval vessels cruise both in the North Sea and the Baltic and seize and bring into German ports neutral vessels bound for Scandinavian and Danish ports.'[3] The United States argued that 'measured by the three universally conceded tests above set forth' the British long-distance blockade could not be regarded as constituting 'a blockade in law, in practice, or in effect.'[4]

To these arguments the British Government replied[5] that these measures amounted to 'no more than an adaptation of the old principles of blockade to the peculiar circumstances'[6] of the World War, and that, although they ought not to be judged with strict

[1] Note of April 2, 1915. See also Note of November 5, 1915, No. 21.

[2] Note of April 2, 1915. See also Note of November 5, 1915, No. 20.

[3] Note of November 5, 1915, No. 19.

[4] Note of November 5, 1915, No. 22.

[5] In Notes dated July 23, 1915, and April 24, 1916: *Parl. Papers*, *ibid.*

[6] Note of July 23, 1915, No. 2.

reference to the rules applicable to blockade,[1] they were in harmony with the spirit of those rules.[2] To the American complaint (1) that they constituted a blockade of neutral ports, Great Britain replied that 'if the blockade can only become effective by extending it to enemy commerce passing through neutral ports, such an extension is defensible and in accordance with principles which have met with general acceptance,'[3] that the Allied Governments made every effort to discriminate between *bona fide* neutral commerce and that intended for Germany,[4] and that they had 'tempered the severity' with which their measures might press upon neutrals by imposing penalties less drastic than those invariably inflicted for a breach of the old form of blockade.[5] To the contention (2) that it was not impartial, she replied that 'the passage of commerce to a blockaded area across a land frontier or across an inland sea has never been held to interfere with the effectiveness of the blockade . . . if the doctrine of continuous voyage may rightly be applied to goods going to Germany through Rotterdam, on what ground can it be contended that it is not equally applicable to goods with a similar destination passing through some Swedish port and across the Baltic or even through neutral waters only ? '[6]

With reference to the complaint (3) that the long-distance blockade was not effective, Great Britain expressed a doubt whether there had ever been a blockade where the ships which slipped through bore so small a proportion to those which were intercepted.[7]

§ 390*b*. There the legal controversy was broken off ; [8]

[1] Note of April 24, 1916, No. 35.
[2] Note of April 24, 1916, No. 33.
[3] Note of July 23, 1915, No. 9.
[4] Note of April 24, 1916, No. 26.
[5] Note of July 23, 1915, No. 11.
[6] Note of April 24, 1916, No. 35.
[7] Note of April 24, 1916, No. 33.

[8] A rough note in the author's manuscript shows that he intended to recognise the legality of a long-distance blockade, and to lay down certain conditions with which it ought to conform. Apparently, he would have provided for notification,

The Isolation of the Central Empires during the World War.

Great Britain and her allies had in the meantime applied themselves to the difficult task of discriminating between *bona fide* neutral commerce and that intended for Germany. They set up departments which investigated the machinery, and the subterfuges, of German overseas trade; they identified goods originating in Germany, by insisting that all exports from adjacent countries should be accompanied by certificates of origin. They induced importers in these countries to form representative associations, and entered into agreements with these associations under which goods consigned to them were generally exempted from interference, in return for a guarantee that neither the goods, nor their products, should reach the enemy in any form. Of such associations the Netherlands Overseas Trust was the first; others were formed in Sweden, Norway, Denmark, and Switzerland. They persuaded many shipping lines, with a view to avoiding the costly delay of elaborate visit and search, to undertake, if so required, to bring back to England any suspected goods which were not discharged at the port of examination, or to store them until the end of the war, or to hand them to their consignees only under stringent guarantees that neither they, nor their products, would reach the enemy. They persuaded other shipping lines only to accept goods for Northern Europe when accompanied by a certificate from the Allied authorities that they would be allowed to pass the blockade. They refused to supply bunker coal to neutral vessels unless their owners would undertake that no vessel owned, chartered, or controlled by them should trade with an enemy port, or carry goods of enemy origin or destination. Finally,

and would have insisted that it should be effective, and that vessels should not be condemned for breach of it. It would seem that he had not decided whether to adopt the British or the American view with regard to so-called blockade of neutral ports when death interrupted his work.

they sought to make agreements with representative bodies of neutral traders under which the import of any given article to a neutral country was limited to the amount of its true domestic requirements.[1]

However, the aim of the Allied Governments was not wholly realised, even by these measures, as long as the United States remained neutral. But after she had entered the war, in April 1917, she prohibited exports to the neutral countries of Northern Europe except under licences which were only given in return for satisfactory guarantees. This she was legally entitled to do, and the isolation of the Central Empires was complete.[2]

[1] These measures are all described in *Parl. Papers*, Misc., No. 2 (1916), Cd. 8145.

[2] See Garner, ii. § 530.

CHAPTER IV

CONTRABAND

I

CONCEPTION OF CONTRABAND

Grotius, iii. c. 1, § 5—Bynkershoek, *Quaestiones Juris publici*, i. cc. ix.-xii.—Vattel, iii. §§ 111-113—Hall, §§ 236-247—Lawrence, §§ 253-259—Westlake, ii. pp. 277-302, and *Papers*, pp. 362-392, 461-474, 519-522—Maine, pp. 96-122—Manning, pp. 352-399—Phillimore, iii. §§ 226-284—Twiss, ii. §§ 121-151—Halleck, ii. pp. 243-270—Taylor, §§ 653-666—Walker, §§ 73-75—Wharton, iii. §§ 368-375—Hershey, Nos. 496-512—Moore, vii. §§ 1249-1263—Wheaton, §§ 476-508—Bluntschli, §§ 801-814—Heffter, §§ 158-161—Geffcken in *Holtzendorff*, iv. pp. 713-731—Gareis, § 89—Liszt, § 42—Ullmann, §§ 193-194—Bonfils, No. 1535-1588[15]—Despagnet, Nos. 705-715 *ter*—Rivier, ii. pp. 416-423—Nys, iii. pp. 626-670—Calvo, v. §§ 2708-2795—Fiore, iii. Nos. 1591-1601, and *Code*, Nos. 1850-1858—Martens, ii. § 136—Kleen, i. §§ 90-102—Boeck, Nos. 606-659—Pillet, pp. 315-330—Gessner, pp. 70-144—Perels, §§ 44-46—Testa, pp. 201-220—Lawrence, *War*, pp. 140-174—Ortolan, ii. pp. 165-213—Hautefeuille, ii. pp. 69-173—Dupuis, Nos. 199-230, and *Guerre*, Nos. 137-171—Bernsten, § 9—Nippold, ii. § 35—Takahashi, pp. 490-525—Schramm, § 10—Holland, *Prize Law*, §§ 57-87—U.S. Naval War Code, Articles 34-36—Heineccius, *De navibus ob Vecturam vetitarum Mercium commissis Dissertatio* (1740)—Huebner, *De la Saisie des Bâtiments neutres*, 2 vols. (1759)—Valin, *Traité des Prises*, 2 vols. (1763)—Martens, *Essai sur les Armateurs, les Prises, et surtout les Reprises* (1795)—Lampredi, *Del Commercio dei Populi neutrali in Tempo di Guerra* (1801)—Tetens, *Considérations sur les Droits réciproques des Puissances belligérantes et des Puissances neutres sur Mer* (1805)—Pistoye et Duverdy, *Traité des Prises maritimes*, 2 vols. (1855)—Pratt, *The Law of Contraband of War* (1856)—Moseley, *What is Contraband and what is not?* (1861)—Upton, *The Law of Nations affecting Commerce during War* (1863)—Lehmann, *Die Zufuhr von Kriegskonterbandewaren, etc.* (1877)—Kleen, *De Contrebande de Guerre et des Transports interdits aux Neutres* (1893)—Vossen, *Die Konterbande des Krieges* (1896)—Hirsch, *Kriegskonterbande und verbotene Transporte in Kriegszeiten* (1897)—Manceaux, *De la Contrebande de Guerre* (1899)—Brochet, *De la Contrebande de Guerre* (1900)—Pincitore, *Il contrabbando di Guerra* (1902)—Remy, *Théorie de la Continuauté du Voyage en matière de Blocus et de Contrebande de Guerre* (1902)—Knight, *Des États neutres au point de vue de la Contrebande de Guerre* (1903)—Wiegner, *Die Kriegskonterbande* (1904) — Atherley-Jones, *Commerce in War* (1907), pp. 1-91 and 253-283—Hold, *Die Kriegskonterbande* (1907)—Hansemann, *Die Lehre von der einheitlichen Reise im Rechte der Blockade und Kriegskonterbande* (1910)—Hirschmann, *Das internationale Prisenrecht* (1912), §§ 24-30—Wehberg, pp. 97-123—Garner, ii. §§ 495-508*a*—Piggott, *The Neutral Merchant* (1915)—Pyke, *The Law of Contraband of War* (1915), and in the *Law Quarterly Review*, xxxii. (1916), pp. 50-69 (*The Kim* case) —Westlake in *R.I.*, ii. (1870), pp. 614-635—Kleen in *R.I.*, xxv. (1893), pp. 7, 124, 239, 389, and xxvi. (1894), pp. 214-217—Bar in *R.I.*, xxvi. (1894), pp. 401-414—Brocher de la Fléchère in *R.I.*, 2nd Ser. i. (1899), pp. 337-353—Fauchille in *R.G.*, iv. (1897), pp. 297-323—Kleen in *R.G.*, xi. (1904), pp. 353-362—Gover in the *Journal of Comparative Legislation*, New Ser. ii. (1900), pp. 118-130—Kennedy and Randall in the *Law Quarterly Review*, xxiv. (1908), pp. 59-75, 316-327, and 449-464—General Report presented to the Naval Conference of London by its Drafting Committee, Articles 22-44—Moore in *R.I.*, 2nd Ser. xiv. (1912), pp. 221-247—Phillimore in the *Journal of Comparative Legislation*, New Ser. xv. (1915), pp. 223-238—Perrinjaquet in *R.G.*, xxii. (1915), pp. 127-238.

Definition of Contraband of War.

§ 391. The term contraband is derived from the Italian 'contrabbando,' which, itself deriving from the Latin 'contra' and 'bannum' or 'bandum,' means 'in defiance of an injunction.' Contraband of war[1] is the designation of such goods as by either belligerent are forbidden to be carried to the enemy on the ground that they enable him to carry on the war with greater vigour. But this definition is only formal, as it does not state what kinds of goods belong to the class of contraband. This has been much controverted. Throughout the seventeenth, eighteenth, and nineteenth centuries, the matter stood as Grotius had explained it. Although he did not employ the term contraband, which only came into general use after his time, he treated of the matter, and distinguished[2] three different

[1] Although—see above, §§ 173-174—prevention of carriage of contraband is a means of sea warfare against the enemy, it chiefly concerns neutral commerce, and is, therefore, more conveniently treated with neutrality.—A good short survey of the origin and development of the modern law of contraband is given by Pyke, *The Law of Contraband* (1915), pp. 29-54. The same work (pp. 100-104) gives an account of the attempt to abolish contraband altogether.

[2] See Grotius, iii. c. 1, § 5: 'Sunt res quæ in bello tantum usum habent, ut arma: sunt quae in bello nullum habent usum, ut quae voluptati inserviunt: sunt quae et in bello et extra bellum usum habent, ut pecuniae,

kinds of articles. Firstly, those which, as arms for instance, can only be made use of in war, and which are, therefore, always contraband. Secondly, those, as for example articles of luxury, which can never be made use of in war and which, therefore, are never contraband. Thirdly, those which, as money, provisions, ships, and articles of naval equipment, can be made use of in war as well as in peace, and which are, on account of their ancipitous use, contraband or not according to the circumstances of the case. In spite of Bynkershoek's decided opposition[1] to this distinction, the practice of most belligerents has been in conformity with it. A great many treaties have, from the beginning of the sixteenth century, been concluded between many States for the purpose of fixing what articles belonging to the class of ancipitous use should, and what should not, be regarded between the parties as contraband; but these treaties disagree with one another. And, so far as they are not bound by a treaty, belligerents exercise their discretion in every war, according to the special circumstances and conditions, in regarding, or not regarding, certain articles of ancipitous use as contraband. The endeavour of the First and the Second Armed Neutralities of 1780 and 1800 to restrict the number and kinds of articles that could be regarded as contraband failed; and the Declaration of Paris of 1856 uses the term contraband without attempting to define it. By Articles 22-29 of the Declaration of London of 1909 the Powers seemed to have come to an agreement concerning what articles are, and what are not, contraband; but the declaration remained unratified, and the World War has shown that it is impossible once and for all to settle the ques-

commeatus, naves, et quae navibus adsunt. . . . In tertio illo genere usus ancipitis, distinguendus erit belli status. . . .'

[1] *Quaestiones Juris publici*, i. c. x.

tion what articles are to be considered as contraband. Furthermore, the interests of the States when they are belligerents are opposed to their interests when they are neutrals; and for this reason all States when belligerents take up a different attitude with regard to contraband from that which they take up when neutrals.

Absolute and Conditional Contraband, and Free Articles.

§ 392. Apart from the distinction between articles which can be made use of only in war and those of ancipitous use, two different classes of contraband must be distinguished.

There are, in the first place, articles which by their very character are destined to be used in war. In this class are to be reckoned, not only arms and ammunition, but also such articles of ancipitous use as military stores, naval stores, and the like. These are termed absolute contraband. There are, secondly, articles which, by their very character, are not necessarily destined to be used in war, but which, under certain circumstances and conditions, can be of the greatest use to a belligerent for the continuation of the war. To this class belong, for instance, provisions, coal, gold, and silver. These articles are termed conditional or relative contraband.

Although hitherto not all the States have made this distinction, which is important not only in determining whether or not a particular article is contraband, but also in determining the consequences of carrying contraband,[1] nevertheless they did make a distinction in so far as they varied the list of articles which they declared contraband in their different wars. Certain articles, as arms and ammunition, have always been on the list, whilst other articles were only considered contraband when the circumstances of a particular war made it necessary. The majority of writers have

[1] See below, § 405.

always approved of the distinction between absolute and conditional contraband, although several insisted that arms and ammunition only and exclusively could be recognised as contraband, and that conditional contraband did not exist.[1] The unratified Declaration of London adopted[2] the distinction, but added a third class.[3] To this class were assigned all articles which were either not susceptible of use in war, or the possibility of the use of which in war was so remote as practically to make them not susceptible of use in war. These articles were termed *free articles*.[4]

But although till the outbreak of the World War the distinction between absolute and conditional contraband was certainly correct in theory, and of value in practice, the war has shaken its foundation. It dates from the time when armies were small, and comprised only a very small fraction of the population of the belligerent countries. But during the World War, when, as has already been explained,[5] every fit male in each belligerent State became by choice or compulsion a member of the military forces, when the whole country with all its resources was gradually mobilised, and the means of communication were nationalised and developed to an unprecedented and unforeseen degree, many declared that the distinction between absolute and conditional contraband was out of date, because a belligerent Government could at any moment, and would if necessary, lay its hand on, and requisition, all articles in the country which were, or might be, of use for carrying on the war.

§ 393. That absolute contraband cannot, and need not, be restricted to arms and ammunition only and

[1] See, for instance, Hautefeuille, ii. p. 157, and Kleen, i. § 90.

[2] Articles 23, 24.

[3] Article 27.

[4] But there are a number of other free articles, although they do not belong to the articles characterised above; see below, § 396*a*.

[5] Above, § 57*a*.

Articles absolutely Contraband.

exclusively becomes obvious, if it be remembered that other articles, although of ancipitous use, can be as valuable and essential to a belligerent for the continuance of the war. The necessary machinery and material for the manufacture of arms and ammunition are almost as valuable as the latter themselves, and warfare on sea can as little be waged without vessels and articles of naval equipment as without arms and ammunition. But no unanimity exists with regard to such articles of ancipitous use as are to be considered as absolute contraband, and States, when they go to war, increase or restrict, according to the circumstances of the particular war, the list of articles they consider absolute contraband.

But although belligerents must be free to take into consideration the circumstances of the particular war, as long as the distinction between absolute and conditional contraband is upheld, it ought not to be left altogether to their discretion to declare any articles they like to be absolute contraband. The test to be applied is whether, under the special circumstances of a particular war, or considering the development of the means used in making war, the article concerned is by its character destined to be made use of for military, naval, or air-fleet purposes, because it is indispensable to those purposes. If not, it ought not to be declared absolute contraband. However, it may well happen that an article which is not by its very nature destined to be made use of in war, acquires this character in a particular war and under particular circumstances; and in such case it may be declared absolute contraband. Thus, for instance, foodstuffs cannot, as a rule, be declared absolute contraband; but if the enemy, for the purpose of securing sufficient for his military forces, takes possession of all the foodstuffs in the country, and puts the whole population on rations, foodstuffs acquire the character essential to articles of absolute contraband, and can therefore be declared to be such. Or, to give another example, cotton was not in former wars considered to be absolute contraband, because its use for military purposes was of minor importance; but nowadays the importance of cotton for the manufacture of high explosives has become so apparent, that during the World War the Allies had, in 1915, to declare it absolute contraband. But, as has been said, the distinction between absolute and conditional contraband threatens to disappear.

Articles 22 and 23 of the Declaration of London distinguished two classes of absolute contraband. Article 22 enumerated eleven groups of articles which might *always*, without special declaration and notice, be treated as absolute contraband. Article 23 comprised articles exclusively used for war which were not enumerated amongst the eleven groups of the first class, but might also be treated as absolute contraband *after special declaration and notification*. Such a declaration might be published during time of peace, and notification thereof had then to be addressed to all other Powers; but if the declaration was published after the outbreak of hostilities, a notification had only to be addressed to the neutral Powers. Should a Power—see Article 26—waive the right to treat as absolute contraband any article comprised in the first class, notification thereof had to be made to the other Powers.

The list of articles in the first class embodied a compromise, for it included several articles—such as saddle, draught, and pack animals suitable for use in war—which Great Britain and other Powers formerly only considered as conditional contraband.

However, the Declaration of London remained unratified, and although at the outbreak of the World War Great Britain and her allies adopted most of its rules,[1] they rejected the list of absolute contraband

[1] See above, § 292.

which it contained. During the war, they so increased the number of articles of absolute contraband by successive orders that the final British list, dated July 2, 1917, covered two pages of the *London Gazette*.[1]

Among them, for example, were: aircraft, alcohols, ammonia, animals suitable for use in war, armour plates, arms and ammunition, arsenic, asbestos, barbed wire, bones, borax, camp equipment, carbolic acid, caustic potash, celluloid, clothing and equipment (military), copper, cork, cotton and cotton goods, diamonds suitable for industrial purposes, electrical appliances adapted for use in war, explosives specially prepared for use in war and materials used in their manufacture, field forges, flax, gases for war purposes, glycerine, gold, silver, paper money and securities for money, hair, harness (military), hemp, hides, implements designed exclusively for the manufacture of war material, iron, lead, leather, lubricants, mercury, mineral oils, motor vehicles, photographic films, platinum, range-finders, rubber, searchlights, silk, soap, sodium, starch, steel containing tungsten or molybdenum, sulphuric acid, tanning substances, tar, tin, turpentine, tyres, wagons (military), warships and their component parts, waxes, woods capable of use in war, zinc. The list also contained a large number of other rare metals, chemicals, and other commodities.

Articles conditionally Contraband.

§ 394. There are many articles which are not by their character destined to be made use of in war, but which are nevertheless of great value to belligerents for the continuance of war. Such articles are conditionally contraband, which means that they are contraband when it is clearly apparent,[2] having regard to the destination of the vessel carrying them, or to their consignee, that they are intended to be used for military or naval purposes. But neither the practice of the

[1] July 3, 1917.

[2] See below, § 395.

several States nor the opinion of writers agree upon the matter, and it is in particular controversial [1] whether or no foodstuffs, horses and other beasts of burden, coal and other fuel, money and the like, and cotton, may conditionally be declared contraband.

(1) That *foodstuffs* should not under ordinary circumstances be declared contraband, there ought to be no doubt. There are even several writers [2] who emphatically deny that they could ever be conditional contraband. But the majority of writers have always admitted that foodstuffs destined for the use of the enemy army or navy might be declared contraband. This has been the practice of Great Britain,[3] the United States of America, and Japan. But in 1885, during her hostilities against China, France declared rice to be absolute contraband, on the ground of the importance of this article to the Chinese population. Again, Russia in 1904, during the Russo-Japanese War, declared rice and provisions to be absolute contraband; on the protest of Great Britain and the United States of America, however, she altered her decision, and treated these articles as conditional contraband only.[4] Article 24 of the unratified Declaration of London declared foodstuffs to be conditional contraband, and they appeared as conditional contraband in the British [5] and German [6] contraband lists during the World War.

(2) The importance of *horses and other beasts of burden* for cavalry, artillery, and military transport explains their frequently being declared as contraband by belli-

[1] See Perels, § 45, and Hall, §§ 242-246, who give bird's-eye views of the controversy.

[2] See, for instance, Bluntschli, § 807.

[3] *The Jonge Margaretha*, (1799) 1 C. Rob. 189.

[4] See the cases of *The Arabia* and *The Calchas* (Hurst, i. pp. 52, 143), in which the Russian Supreme Prize Court recognised the distinction between absolute and conditional contraband.

[5] *London Gazette*, July 3, 1917. The British list referred to in these sections is the final list issued on July 2, 1917.

[6] *London Gazette*, August 7, 1917. The German list referred to in these sections is that promulgated by ordinance on June 25, 1917. There had been many earlier lists.

gerents. No argument against their character as conditional contraband can have any basis. But they were frequently declared absolute contraband, as, for instance, by Article 36 of the United States Naval War Code of 1900. Russia, which during the Russo-Japanese War altered the standpoint at first taken up by her, and recognised the distinction between absolute and conditional contraband, nevertheless adhered to her declaration of horses and beasts of burden as absolute contraband. The unratified Declaration of London, by Article 22, also declared them to be absolute contraband, and they so figured in the British and German contraband lists during the World War.

(3) Since men-of-war are nowadays propelled by steam power, the importance of *coal*, and other fuel for waging war at sea, is obvious. For this reason Great Britain has, ever since 1854, maintained that coal, if destined for belligerent men-of-war or belligerent naval ports, is contraband. But in 1859 France and Italy did not take up the same standpoint. Russia, although in 1885 she declared that she would never consent to coal being regarded as contraband, in 1904 declared coal, naphtha, alcohol, and every other kind of fuel, to be absolute contraband. And she adhered to this standpoint, although she was made to recognise the distinction between absolute and conditional contraband. Article 24 of the unratified Declaration of London declared fuel, and therefore coal, to be conditional contraband, and during the World War Great Britain so treated all fuel, except mineral oils, which were declared absolute contraband in view of their absolute necessity for use in motors, aeroplanes, and submarines. Germany declared coal, coke, and mineral oils to be absolute contraband, and other fuel to be conditional contraband.

(4) As regards *money*, unwrought precious metals

which may be coined into money, bonds, and the like, the mere fact that a neutral is prohibited by his duty of impartiality from granting a loan to a belligerent ought to bring conviction that these articles are certainly contraband if destined for the enemy State or its forces. However, these articles are seldom brought by neutral vessels to belligerent ports, since under the modern conditions of trade belligerents can be supplied in other ways with the necessary funds. Be that as it may, in 1916, during the World War, the Allies, who at the beginning of the war had declared gold, silver, and paper money to be *conditional* contraband, proclaimed that they would thenceforth treat gold, silver, paper money, all negotiable instruments, and the like as *absolute* contraband. These articles figured as absolute contraband in the German list.

(5) As regards *raw cotton,* it is asserted[1] that in 1861, during the Civil War, the United States declared it absolute contraband under quite peculiar circumstances, since it took the place of money sent abroad for the purpose of paying for vessels, arms, and ammunition. But this assertion is erroneous.[2] Be that as it may, raw cotton could not, prior to the World War, properly be considered absolute contraband. For this reason Great Britain protested when Russia, in 1904 during the Russo-Japanese War, declared raw cotton to be absolute contraband; but although Russia at first seemed inclined to give way[3] to this protest, she finally adhered to her original attitude. Article 28 of the unratified Declaration of London put raw cotton on the free list, and during the World War

[1] See Hall, § 246; Taylor, § 662; Wharton, iii. § 373.

[2] See Moore, vii. § 1254, and Holland, *Letters to the 'Times' upon War and Neutrality* (1909), pp. 108-112.

[3] See the decision of the Supreme Prize Court in the case of *The Calchas* (May 7, 1905, see Hurst, i. p. 143); whereas in the case of *The St. Kilda* (Dec. 11, 1908, see Hurst, i. p. 202) this same court decided that raw cotton was absolute contraband.

the Allies at first did not declare it contraband. But in time its importance for the manufacture of high explosives became so apparent that they declared to be *absolute* contraband: 'raw cotton, linters, cotton waste, cotton yarns, cotton piece-goods, and other cotton products capable of being used in the manufacture of explosives.'[1] Cotton also figured as absolute contraband in the German list.

By the unratified Declaration of London two classes of conditional contraband were distinguished.

Article 24 enumerated fourteen groups of articles which might *always*, without special declaration and notice, be treated as conditional contraband. Article 25 consisted of articles which were not enumerated, either amongst the eleven groups of absolute contraband contained in Article 22, or amongst the fourteen groups of conditional contraband contained in Article 24, but were nevertheless susceptible of use in war as well as for purposes of peace; these might also be treated as conditional contraband, but *only after special declaration and notification*. With regard to this declaration and notification, the same procedure was to be followed as in the case of absolute contraband.[2]

But the list contained in the unratified Declaration of London was not adopted by Great Britain during the World War. While at first only slight alterations were made in it, it was varied by successive orders, and the final list contained in the proclamation of July 2, 1917, comprised some thirty-four kinds of articles classed as conditional contraband.[3] Among them were: bladders, boots and shoes suitable for use in war, casks, clothing suitable for use in war, docks, field-glasses, foodstuffs, forage, fuel (other than mineral oils, which were absolute contraband), glue, harness,

[1] See Garner, ii. § 498.
[2] See above, § 393.
[3] *London Gazette*, July 3, 1917.

horse-shoes, nautical instruments, certain oils and fats together with oleaginous seeds, nuts and kernels, railway, telegraph and telephone materials, vehicles available for use in war (other than motors, which were absolute contraband), vessels of all kinds (other than warships, which were absolute contraband).

Hostile Destination essential to Contraband.

§ 395. Whatever may be the nature of articles, they are never contraband unless they are destined [1] for the use of a belligerent in war. Arms and ammunition destined for a neutral are as little contraband as other goods with the same destination. Hostile destination, which is essential even for articles which are obviously used in war, is all the more important for such articles of ancipitous use as are only conditionally contraband. Thus, for instance, provisions and coal are perfectly innocent and not at all contraband if they are destined for use by a neutral. However, the destination of the articles must not be confounded with the destination of the vessel which carries them. For, on the one hand, certain articles with a hostile destination are considered contraband although the carrying vessel is destined for a neutral port, and, on the other hand, certain articles, although they are without a hostile destination, are considered contraband because the carrying vessel is to touch at an intermediate enemy port and is, therefore, destined for such port, although her ultimate destination is a neutral port.

[1] Goods are destined for the use of a belligerent in war, not only when they are shipped to an enemy consignee, but also when they are shipped, after the outbreak of war, by a neutral consignor to a neutral consignee with the intention that they should ultimately become the property of the enemy. The fact that at the time of capture the legal property in the goods had not passed from the consignor does not matter, because in such case capture is regarded as delivery and the goods are treated in a Prize Court as enemy property. See *The Louisiana*, (1918) 3 B. and C. P. C. 60, and distinguish *The Kronprinzessin Victoria*, (1918) 3 B. and C. P. C. 247. See also *The Rijn*, (1917) 2 B. and C. P. C. 507; *The Hellig Olav*, (1918) 3 B. and C. P. C. 258; *The Noordam*, (1918) 3 B. and C. P. C. 317; *The Kronprins Gustaf*, (1919) 3 B. and C. P. C. 432; *The Urna*, [1920] A.C. 899.

The unratified Declaration of London, in Articles 30 to 36, comprised very detailed rules with regard to hostile destination, distinguishing clearly between the characteristics of hostile destination in the case of absolute contraband and of conditional contraband.

(1) The destination of articles of *absolute* contraband was, according to Article 30, to be considered hostile if it were shown that they were being sent either to enemy territory, or to territory occupied by the enemy, or to the armed forces of the enemy; and, according to Article 31, hostile destination of absolute contraband was to be considered as completely proved, (i) when the goods were consigned to an enemy port or to the armed forces of the enemy, (ii) when the vessel was to call at enemy ports only, or was to touch at an enemy port, or meet the armed forces of the enemy, before reaching the neutral port to which the cargo concerned was consigned.

(2) The destination of articles of *conditional* contraband, on the other hand, was, according to Article 33, considered to be hostile if they were intended for the use of the armed forces, or of a government department, of the enemy State, unless in this latter case the circumstances showed that the articles could not in fact be used for warlike purposes.[1] Gold and silver in coin or bullion and paper money were, however, in every case to be regarded as having a hostile destination if intended for a government department of the enemy State. According to Article 34, hostile destination of conditional contraband was to be presumed, unless the contrary was proved, when the articles were consigned, (i) to enemy authorities, or to an enemy contractor established in the enemy country who as a

[1] See *The Constantinos*, (1916) 2 B. and C. P. C. 140, where the Egyptian Prize Court held that the owner of certain conditional contraband consigned to Smyrna had established that it was for private consumption.

matter of common knowledge supplied articles of this kind to the enemy, or, (ii) to a fortified place of the enemy or to another place serving as a base—whether of operations or supply—for the armed forces of the enemy.[1] On the other hand, if the articles were not so consigned and if the contrary was not proved, their destination was presumed to be non-hostile. In the case of a merchantman which could herself be conditional contraband [2] if bound to a fortified place of the enemy, or to another place serving as a base for the armed forces of the enemy, there was to be no presumption of a hostile destination, but a direct proof was to be necessary that she was destined for the use of the armed forces, or of a government department, of the enemy State.

At the outbreak of the World War, Great Britain, in concert with her Allies, by the Order in Council of August 20, 1914,[3] adopted (among other articles) Articles 30, 31, 33, and 34 of the unratified Declaration of London without modification except that to the presumptions laid down in Article 34 with regard to the destination of conditional contraband was added a new presumption. This Order in Council was replaced by a new order of October 29, 1914, which again adopted these articles of the declaration, with an additional presumption that if goods which were

[1] During the World War—see the British Note of February 19, 1915, to the United States in *A.J.*, ix. (1915), Supplement, p. 176—Germany claimed to treat practically every town or port on the English East Coast as a fortified place and base of operations. Moreover, one of her cruisers sank the neutral Dutch vessel *Maria* in September 1914, while carrying grain (conditional contraband) from California to Dublin and Belfast, on the ground that Dublin and Belfast served as bases for the armed forces of Great Britain. See Garner, ii. §§ 486, 508, and text of the decision in *Z.V.*, ix. (1916), p. 408, and in *A.J.*, x. (1916), p. 927. Again—see the German Note to the United States of April 5, 1915, in *A.J.*, ix. (1915), Special Supplement, p. 181—Germany justified the sinking of the American vessel *William P. Frye* carrying a cargo of wheat to Queenstown, Falmouth, or Plymouth on the ground that these ports were 'strongly fortified English coast places, which, moreover, serve as bases for the British naval forces.'

[2] See below, § 397.

[3] See above, § 292.

conditional contraband were consigned 'to or for an agent of the enemy State,' they had the hostile destination necessary to render them liable to capture. By an Order in Council dated March 30, 1916, it was further provided that this additional presumption should apply also to absolute contraband, and that both absolute and conditional contraband should be presumed to have the hostile destination necessary to render it liable to capture, if consigned 'to or for a person who during the present hostilities has forwarded imported contraband goods to territory belonging to or occupied by the enemy.' The burden of proving that goods which came within these provisions of this order had an innocent destination was placed upon the owner. However, by the Maritime Rights Order in Council of July 7, 1916, the Declaration of London was abandoned, and it was provided that 'the hostile destination required for the condemnation of contraband articles shall be presumed to exist, until the contrary is shown, if the goods are consigned to or for an enemy authority, or an agent of the enemy State, or to or for a person in territory belonging to or occupied by the enemy, or to or for a person who during the present hostilities has forwarded contraband goods to an enemy authority, or an agent of the enemy State, or to or for a person in territory belonging to or occupied by the enemy, or if the goods are consigned "to order," or if the ship's papers do not show who is the real consignee of the goods.'

Free Articles.

§ 396. It is obvious that such articles as are not susceptible of use in war may never be declared contraband, whether their destination be hostile or not.

The unratified Declaration of London, by Article 27, expressly recognised this, and in Article 28—in a so-called *free list*—enumerated seventeen groups of articles which might never be declared contraband in spite of their hostile destination. This free list was, however, not adopted by the Allies during the World War; several articles enumerated therein were declared contraband, and thereby the free list obviously lost all value. In the future, as in the past, it will remain for the belligerents to consider whether or no they will treat an article as free, provided that they do not violate the general principle[1] that only such articles may be declared contraband as enable the enemy to carry on the war with greater vigour.

Articles destined for the use of the Carrying Vessel, or to aid the Wounded.

396*a*. However, there are two groups of articles which will always be recognised as free.

In the first place, those articles which serve exclusively to aid the sick and wounded may never be treated as contraband even if their destination is hostile. They may, however, in case of urgent military necessity, and subject to the payment of compensation, be requisitioned, if they are destined to territory belonging to, or occupied by, the enemy, or to his armed forces. The unratified Declaration of London laid down this rule, and it was adopted during the World War.

Secondly, articles intended for the use of the vessel in which they are found, or for the use of her crew and passengers during the voyage, can never be contraband. Hostile destination being essential before any kinds of articles may be considered contraband, those articles which are carried by a vessel manifestly for her own use, or for the use of her crew and passengers, must be free.[2] Merchantmen frequently carry a gun and a certain amount of ammunition for the purpose of signalling, and, if they navigate in parts of the sea where there is danger of piracy, they frequently carry a certain amount of arms and ammunition for defence

[1] See above, § 391.

[2] Article 29 of the unratified Declaration of London comprised this rule likewise.

against an attack by pirates. It will not be difficult either for the searching belligerent man-of-war or for the Prize Court to ascertain whether or no such arms and ammunition are carried *bona fide*.

Contraband Vessels.

§ 397. A neutral vessel, whether carrying contraband or not, can herself be contraband. Such is the case when she has been built or fitted out for use in war and is on her way to the enemy. Although it is the duty of neutrals[1] to employ the means at their disposal to prevent the fitting out, arming, or the departure of any vessel within their jurisdiction which they have reason to believe is intended to cruise or to engage in hostile operations against a belligerent, their duty of impartiality does not compel them to prevent their subjects from supplying a belligerent with vessels fit for use in war except where they have been built or fitted out by his order. Subjects of neutrals may therefore—unless prevented from so doing by Municipal Law, as, for instance, are British subjects by §§ 8 and 9 of the Foreign Enlistment Act, 1870—by way of trade supply a belligerent with vessels of any kind, provided that they have not been built or fitted out by his order. According to the practice which prevailed prior to the World War, such vessels, being equivalent to arms, used to be considered as absolute contraband;[2] and they need not necessarily have been fit for use as men-of-war; it sufficed that they were fit to be used for the transport of troops and the like.

According to Articles 22, 24, and 34 of the unratified Declaration of London, a distinction was to be made between warships and other vessels. Warships, including their boats, and distinctive component parts

[1] See Article 8 of Convention XIII., and above, §§ 334, 350.

[2] *The Richmond*, (1804) 5 C. Rob. 325. See also Twiss, ii. § 148, and Holland, *Prize Law*, § 86.

which by their nature could only be used on a vessel of war, might be treated as *absolute* contraband without notice. Vessels, craft, and boats of all kinds, and, further, floating docks, parts of docks and their component parts, might only be treated as *conditional* contraband, but might be so treated without notice.

During the World War the Allies adopted these rules of the Declaration of London.[1]

II

CARRIAGE OF CONTRABAND

See the literature quoted above at the commencement of § 391.

§ 398. The guaranteed freedom of commerce making the sale of articles of all kinds to belligerents by subjects of neutrals legitimate, articles of conditional as well as absolute contraband may be supplied by sale to either belligerent by these individuals. Moreover, the carriage of such articles by neutral merchantmen on the open sea is, as far as International Law is concerned, quite as legitimate as their sale. The carrier of contraband by no means[2] violates an injunction of the Law of Nations. But belligerents have, by the Law of Nations, the right to prohibit and punish the carriage of contraband by neutral merchantmen, and the carrier of contraband violates, for this reason, an injunction of the belligerent concerned. It is not International Law, but the Municipal Law of the belligerents, which makes carriage of contraband illegitimate and penal.[3] The question why the carriage of contraband articles

Carriage of Contraband Penal by the Municipal Law of Belligerents.

[1] See above, §§ 393, 394.

[2] Most writers, especially British and American, nowadays agree with this statement, although there are still some left who assert that a carrier of contraband violates an injunction of International Law. It is to be regretted that Pyke, *The Law of Contraband* (1915), pp. 89-95, and Butte in the *Proceedings of the American Society of International Law*, IX. (1915), p. 125, renew this assertion.

[3] See above, § 296.

may be prohibited and punished by the belligerents, although it is quite legitimate so far as International Law is concerned, can only be answered by reference to the historical development of the Law of Nations. In contradistinction to former practice, which interdicted all trade between neutrals and the enemy, the principle of freedom of commerce between subjects of neutrals and either belligerent has gradually become universally recognised; but this recognition included from the beginning the right of either belligerent to punish carriage of contraband on the sea. And the reason obviously is the necessity for belligerents, in the interest of self-preservation, to prevent the import of such articles as may strengthen the enemy, and to confiscate the contraband cargo, and, in certain cases, the vessel also, as a deterrent to other vessels.

The present condition of the matter of carriage of contraband is therefore a compromise. In the interest of the generally recognised principle of freedom of commerce between belligerents and subjects of neutrals, International Law does not require neutrals to prevent their subjects from carrying contraband;[1] on the other hand, International Law empowers either belligerent to prohibit and punish carriage of contraband just as it empowers either belligerent to prohibit and punish breach of blockade.[2]

Direct Carriage of Contraband.

§ 399. The simplest case of carriage of contraband occurs where a vessel is engaged in carrying to an enemy port such goods as are contraband and have a hostile destination.[3] In such cases, it makes no difference

[1] See *Ex parte Chavasse, in re Grazebrook*, (1865) 34 L. J. N. S., Bank. 17. The same applies to blockade-running and rendering unneutral service; see *The Helen*, (1865) L.R. 1 A. and E. 1.

[2] See above, § 383.

[3] The destination of the cargo being hostile, it does not matter that the cargo is intended to be reshipped to a neutral country after having undergone a certain course of treatment. The hostile destination makes it contraband; *The Axel Johnson*, (1917) 2 B. and C. P. C. 532.

whether the fact that the vessel is destined for an enemy port becomes apparent because her papers show that she is bound to such a port, or because she is found at sea sailing on a course for an enemy port, although her papers show her to be bound to a neutral port. Further, it makes no difference, according to the hitherto prevailing practice of Great Britain and the United States of America at any rate, that she is ultimately bound for a neutral port, and that the articles concerned are, according to her papers, destined for a neutral port, if only she is to call at an intermediate enemy port, or if she is to meet enemy naval forces at sea in the course of her voyage to the neutral port of destination;[1] for otherwise the door would be open to deceit, and it would always be pretended that goods which a vessel was really carrying to the intermediate enemy places were intended for the neutral port of ultimate destination. For the same reason, a vessel carrying such articles as are contraband when they have a hostile destination is considered to be carrying contraband if her papers show that her destination is dependent upon contingencies under which she may have to call at an enemy port, unless she proves that she has abandoned the intention of calling there in any event.[2]

The unratified Declaration of London distinguished between carriage of absolute and of conditional contraband:—

As regards *absolute* contraband, a vessel was, according to Article 32, considered to be carrying contraband whether the fact that she was destined for an enemy port became evident because her papers showed that she was bound for such a port, or because she was

[1] See Holland, *Prize Law*, § 69.

[2] *The Imina*, (1800) 3 C. Rob. 167; and *The Trende Sostre*, (1800) cited in *The Lisette*, (1806) 6 C. Rob. 390, n. See also Holland, *Prize Law* § 70.

found at sea sailing for an enemy port, although her papers showed her to be bound for a neutral port. Moreover, according to Article 31, it was to make no difference that the vessel was bound for a neutral port and that the articles concerned were, according to her papers, destined for a neutral port, if only she was to touch at an intermediate enemy port, or was to meet armed forces of the enemy before reaching the neutral port to which the goods in question were consigned.

As regards *conditional* contraband, a vessel was, according to Article 35, to be considered as carrying contraband if her papers showed her to be destined for an enemy port, or, if being clearly found out of her course to a neutral port indicated by her papers, she was unable to give adequate reasons to justify such deviation.

Articles 32 and 35 both stipulated that ship-papers were to be conclusive proof as to the destination of the vessel and of the cargo, unless the vessel was clearly found out of the course indicated by them; but the Report of the Drafting Committee emphasised that this rule must not be interpreted too literally, since otherwise fraud would be made easy. Ship-papers are conclusive proof—so ran the Report—*unless facts show their evidence to be false.*

From the outbreak of the World War until July 1916, the Allies adopted Articles 32 and 35 as regards direct carriage of contraband, though they modified Article 35 in other important respects.[1] By the Maritime Rights Order in Council of July 7, 1916, they abandoned the rules of the declaration altogether.

Circuitous Carriage of Contraband.

§ 400. A more usual case of carriage of contraband occurs when a neutral vessel carrying such articles as are contraband if they have a hostile destination is, according to her papers, ostensibly bound for a neutral

[1] See below, § 403*a*.

port, but is intended, after having called there, and perhaps delivered her cargo there, to carry it on (re-shipping it if need be) from there to an enemy port. There is, of course, no doubt that such vessels are carrying contraband whilst engaged in carrying the articles concerned from the neutral to the enemy port. But, during the American Civil War, the question arose whether they may already be considered to be carrying contraband when they are on their way from the port of starting to the neutral port from which they are afterwards to carry the cargo to an enemy port, since they are really intended to carry the cargo from the port of starting to an enemy port, although not directly, but circuitously, by a roundabout way. The American Prize Courts answered the question in the affirmative by applying to the carriage of contraband the principle of *dolus non purgatur circuitu*, and the so-called doctrine of continuous voyages.[1] This attitude of the American Prize Courts has called forth protests from

[1] The so-called doctrine of continuous voyages dates from the time of the Anglo-French wars at the end of the eighteenth century, and is connected with the application of the so-called rule of 1756. (See above, § 289.) Neutral vessels engaged in French and Spanish colonial trade, which had been thrown open to them during the war, sought to evade seizure by British cruisers and condemnation by British Prize Courts according to the rule of 1756, by taking their cargo to a neutral port, landing it and paying import duties there, and then re-loading it and carrying it to the mother country of the respective colony. Thus in *The William*, (1806) 5 C. Rob. 385, it was proved that this neutral vessel took a cargo from the Spanish port of La Guira to the port of Marblehead in Massachusetts—the United States being neutral—landed the cargo, paid import duties there, then re-shipped the greater part of it, and, in addition, other goods, and sailed after a week for the Spanish port of Bilbao. In all such cases, the British Prize Courts considered the voyages from the colonial port to the neutral port and from there to the enemy port as one continuous voyage, and confirmed the seizure of the ships concerned. See Reddie, *Researches*, i. pp. 307-313; Remy, *Théorie de la Continuauté du Voyage en matière de Blocus et de Contrebande* (1902); Hansemann, *Die Lehre von der einheitlichen Reise im Rechte der Blockade und Kriegskonterbande* (1910); Fauchille in *R.G.*, iv. (1897), pp. 297-323; Arias and Baldwin in *A.J.*, ix. (1915), pp. 583-593, 793-801. The American courts have applied the doctrine of continuous voyages not only to carriage of contraband but also to blockade; see above, § 385 (4), where the cases of *The Bermuda* and *The Stephen Hart* are quoted. See also Judson in the *Proceedings of the American Society of International Law*, ix. (1915), pp. 104-111.

many authorities,[1] British as well as foreign; but Great Britain did not protest, and from the attitude of the British Government in the case of *The Bundesrath* and other vessels in 1900 during the South African War, it was possible to conclude, although only by inference, that it considered the practice of the American Prize Courts to be correct and just, and that, when a belligerent, it intended to apply the same principles.[2] And in the last edition of this treatise I stated that, provided that the intention of the vessel was really to carry the cargo circuitously, by a roundabout way, to an enemy port, and further, provided that a mere suspicion was not held to be proof of such intention, I could not see why this application of the doctrine of continuous voyages should not be considered reasonable, just, and adequate.

Indirect Carriage of Contraband (Doctrine of Continuous Transports).

§ 401. Before turning to the practice during the World War, it will be convenient to consider a similar case which occurs when neutral vessels carry to neutral ports such articles as are contraband if bound for a hostile destination, arrangements having been made (of which the vessel may or may not be aware) for the articles to be brought afterwards by land or sea into the hands of the enemy. Long before the World War the question had arisen whether such vessels while on their voyage to the neutral port might be considered to be carrying contraband of war.[3] As early

[1] See, for instance, Hall, § 247. But Phillimore, iii. § 227, p. 391, says of the judgments of the Supreme Court of the United States in the cases of *The Bermuda*, (1865) 3 Wall. 514, and *The Peterhoff*, (1866) 5 Wall. 49, that they 'contain very valuable and sound expositions of the law, professedly, and for the most part really, in harmony with the earlier decisions of English Prize Courts.' On the other hand, Phillimore, iii. § 398, p. 490, disagrees with the American courts regarding the application of the doctrine of continuous voyages to breach of blockade, and reprobates the decision in the case of *The Springbok*, (1866) 5 Wall. 1.

[2] See also Holland, *Manual of Naval Prize Law*, § 71.

[3] The question is treated with special regard to the case of *The Bundesrath*, in two able articles in the *Law Quarterly Review*, xvii. (1901). See also Baty, *International Law in South Africa* (1900), pp. 1-44.

as 1855, during the Crimean War, the French Conseil-Général des Prises, in condemning the cargo of saltpetre of the Hanoverian neutral vessel *Vrow Houwina*, answered the question in the affirmative;[1] but it was not until the American Civil War that the question was decided on principle. Since goods first brought from more distant neutral ports were shipped from the British port of Nassau, in the Bahamas, and from other neighbouring neutral ports, to the blockaded coasts of the Southern States near by, Federal cruisers seized several vessels destined for, and actually on their voyage to, Nassau and other neutral ports, because all or parts of their cargoes were ultimately destined for the enemy. The American courts considered those vessels to be carrying contraband, although they were sailing from one neutral port to another, on clear proof that the goods concerned were destined to be transported by land or sea from the neutral port of landing into the enemy territory. The leading cases are those of *The Springbok* and *The Peterhoff*,[2] for the courts found the seizure of these and other vessels justified on the ground of carriage of contraband as well as on the ground of breach of blockade. Thus another application of the doctrine of continuous voyages came into existence, since vessels, whilst sailing between two neutral ports, could only be considered to be carrying contraband when the transport, first from one neutral port to another, and afterwards from the second neutral

[1] See Calvo, v. § 2767, p. 52. The case of the Swedish neutral vessel *The Commercen*, which occurred in 1814 (1 Wheaton 382), and which is frequently quoted with that of *The Vrow Houwina*, is not a case of indirect carriage of contraband. The *Commercen* was on her way to Bilbao, in Spain, carrying a cargo of provisions for the English army in Spain, and she was captured by a privateer commissioned by the United States of America, which was then at war with England. When the case came before Mr. Justice Story in 1816, he reprobated the argument that the seizure was not justified because a vessel could not be considered to be carrying contraband when on her way to a neutral port, and he asserted that the hostile destination of goods was sufficient to justify the seizure of the vessel.

[2] Above, § 385 (4).

port to the enemy territory, was regarded as one continuous voyage. This new application of the doctrine of continuous voyages is fitly termed 'the doctrine of continuous transports.'

The Case of *The Bundesrath*.

§ 402. The application of the doctrine of continuous voyages under the new form of continuous transports was likewise condemned by many British and foreign authorities; but Great Britain did not protest in this case either—on the contrary, as was mentioned above,[1] she declined to interfere in favour of the British owners of the vessels and cargoes concerned. And that she really considered the practice of the American courts just and sound became clearly apparent from her attitude during the South African War. When, in 1900, the *Bundesrath*, *Herzog*, and *General*, German vessels sailing from German neutral ports to the Portuguese neutral port of Lorenzo Marques in Delagoa Bay, were seized by British cruisers under the suspicion of carrying contraband, Germany demanded their release, maintaining that no carriage of contraband could be said to take place by vessels sailing from one neutral port to another. But Great Britain refused to admit this principle, maintaining that articles ultimately destined for the enemy were contraband, although the vessels carrying them were bound for a neutral port.[2]

There is no doubt that the attitude then taken up by the British Government was contrary to the opinion of the prominent English [3] writers on International Law. Even the *Manual of Naval Prize Law*, edited by Professor Holland [4] in 1888, and 'issued by authority

[1] § 385 (4).

[2] See *Parl. Papers*, Africa, No. 1 (1900).

[3] See, for instance, Hall, § 247, and Twiss in the *Law Magazine and Review*, xii. (1877), pp. 130-158. See also the papers re-edited by Baty under the title *Prize Law and Continuous Voyage* (1915).

[4] In a letter to *The Times* of January 2, 1900, Professor Holland points out that circumstances had so altered since 1888 that the attitude of the British Government in

of the Lords Commissioners of the Admiralty,' reprobated the American practice, for in § 73 it laid down the following rule: '. . . If the destination of the vessel be neutral, then the destination of the goods on board should be considered neutral, notwithstanding it may appear from the papers or otherwise that the goods themselves have an ulterior hostile destination to be attained by transhipment, overland conveyance, or otherwise.' And the practice of British Prize Courts in the past would seem to have been in accordance with this rule. In 1798, during war between England and the Netherlands, the neutral ship *Imina*,[1] which had left the neutral port of Dantzig for Amsterdam carrying ship's timber, but, on hearing of the blockade of Amsterdam by the British, had changed her course for the neutral port of Emden, was seized on her voyage to Emden by a British cruiser; she was, however, released by Sir William Scott because she had no intention of breaking blockade, and because a vessel could only be considered as carrying contraband whilst on a voyage to an enemy port. 'The rule respecting contraband, as I have always understood it, is that the articles must be taken *in delicto*, in the actual prosecution of the voyage to an enemy port,' said Sir William Scott.[2]

§ 403. Although the majority of Continental writers condemned the doctrine of continuous transports,

the case of *The Bundesrath* was quite justified; see Holland, *Letters to the 'Times' upon War and Neutrality* (1909), pp. 114-119.

[1] 3 C. Rob. 167.

[2] It is frequently maintained—see Phillimore, iii. § 227, pp. 397-403—that in 1864, in the case of *Hobbs* v. *Henning*, 17 C. B. (N.S.) 791, Lord Chief Justice Erle repudiated the doctrine of continuous transports; but Westlake shows that this is not the case. See Westlake's Introduction in Takahashi, *International Law during the Chino-Japanese War* (1899), pp. xx-xxiii, and in the *Law Quarterly Review*, xv. (1899), pp. 23-30 (now reprinted in Westlake, *Papers*, pp. 461-474). See also Hart, *ibid.*, xxiii. (1907), p. 199, who discusses the case of *Seymour* v. *London and Provincial Marine Insurance Co.*, (1872) 41 L.J.C.P. 193, in which the court recognised the doctrine of continuous transports.

Continental Support to the Doctrine of Continuous Transports.

several eminent Continental authorities supported it. Thus, Gessner[1] emphatically asserted that the destination of the carrying vessel is of no importance compared with the destination of the goods. Bluntschli, although he condemned[2] the American practice regarding breach of blockade committed by a vessel sailing from one neutral port to another, expressly approved[3] the American practice regarding carriage of contraband by a vessel sailing between two neutral ports, yet carrying goods with a hostile destination. Kleen[4] condemned the rule that the neutral destination of the vessel made the goods appear likewise neutral, and defended seizure in the case of a hostile destination of the goods on a vessel sailing between two neutral ports; he expressly stated that such goods are contraband from the moment the carrying vessel leaves the port of loading. Fiore[5] reprobated the theory of continuous voyages as applied by British and American courts, but he asserted nevertheless that the hostile destination of certain goods carried by a vessel sailing to a neutral port justifies the vessel being regarded as carrying contraband, and the seizure thereof. Bonfils[6] took up the same standpoint as Bluntschli, admitting the application of the theory of continuous voyages to carriage of contraband, but reprobating its application to breach of blockade.[7] The Institute of International Law adopted the rule:[8] '*La destination pour l'ennemi est présumée lorsque le transport va à l'un de ses ports, ou à un port neutre qui, d'après des preuves évidentes et de fait incontestable, n'est qu'une étape pour l'ennemi, comme but final de la même opération commerciale.*' Thus this representative body of authorities of all nations fully

[1] p. 119.
[2] § 835.
[3] § 813.
[4] i. § 95, p. 388.
[5] iii. No. 1649.
[6] No. 1569.
[7] No. 1570.
[8] See § 1 of the 'Réglementation internationale de la Contrebande de Guerre,' *Annuaire*, xv. (1896), p. 230.

adopted the American application of the doctrine of continuous voyages to contraband, and thereby recognised the possibility of indirect as well as circuitous carriage of contraband.

Moreover, the attitude of several Continental States was in favour of the American practice. Thus, according to §§ 4 and 6 of the Prussian Regulations of 1864 regarding Naval Prizes, it was the hostile destination of the goods, or the destination of the vessel to an enemy port, which made a vessel appear as carrying contraband and which justified her seizure. In Sweden the same was valid.[1] Thus, further, an Italian Prize Court during the war with Abyssinia in 1896 justified the seizure in the Red Sea of the Dutch vessel *Doelwijk*,[2] which had sailed for the neutral French port of Djibouti, carrying a cargo of arms and ammunition destined for the Abyssinian army and to be transported to Abyssinia after having been landed at Djibouti.

The Declaration of London concerning the Doctrine of Continuous Voyages, and the Practice during the World War.

403*a*. The unratified Declaration of London offered a compromise which, if it had been accepted, would have settled the controversy respecting the application of the doctrine of continuous voyages to the carriage of contraband, whether circuitous or indirect carriage be concerned.

(1) On the one hand, Article 30 recognised with regard to *absolute* contraband the application of the doctrine of continuous voyages both to circuitous and indirect carriage of contraband, by providing that 'absolute contraband is liable to capture if it is shown to be destined to territory belonging to or occupied by the enemy, or to the armed forces of the enemy. *It is immaterial whether the carriage of the goods is direct or entails transhipment or a subsequent transport by land.*'

[1] See Kleen, i. p. 389, n. 2.

[2] See Martens, *N.R.G.*, 2nd Ser. xxviii. pp. 66, and Diena in the *Journal de Droit international Privé* (1897), pp. 268-297. See also below, § 436.

(2) On the other hand, Article 35 rejected the doctrine of continuous voyages with regard to *conditional* contraband by providing that 'conditional contraband is not liable to capture except when found on board a vessel bound for territory belonging to or occupied by the enemy, or for the armed forces of the enemy,[1] and when it is not to be discharged in an intervening neutral port.'

(3) In *cases where the enemy country had no seaboard*, Article 36—in contradistinction to the provisions of Article 35—expressly recognised the doctrine of continuous voyages for *conditional* contraband also by providing that 'notwithstanding the provisions of Article 35, conditional contraband, if shown to have the destination referred to in Article 33, is liable to capture in cases where the enemy country has no seaboard.'

However, the compromise offered by the Declaration of London was not accepted by the Allies during the World War, and the doctrine of continuous voyages was applied to the circuitous or indirect carriage of conditional [2] as well as of absolute contraband. Thus the British Order in Council of October 29, 1914, which replaced the first Declaration of London Order of August 20, 1914, provided that: 'Notwithstanding the provisions of Article 35 of the said Declaration

[1] Article 35 came into question during the Turco-Italian War. In January 1912 the *Carthage*, a French mail-steamer plying between Marseilles and Tunis, was captured for carriage of contraband by an Italian torpedo boat and taken to Cagliari, because she had an aeroplane destined for Tunis on board. As the destination of the vessel was neutral, and as, according to Article 24 of the declaration aeroplanes were conditional contraband, France protested against the capture of the vessel. Italy agreed to release her, and the question whether her capture was justified was submitted to the Permanent Court of Arbitration at the Hague, which, on May 6, 1913, gave its award in favour of France. See Martens, *N.R.G.*, 3rd Ser. viii. p. 174, and above, vol. i. § 151 n. See also Rapisardi-Mirabelli in *R.I.*, 2nd Ser. xv. (1913), pp. 128-135; Ruzé in *R.I.*, 2nd Ser. xvi. (1914), pp. 116-128; Basdevant, *La Leçon juridique des Incidents du 'Carthage,' du 'Manouba,' et du 'Tavignano'* (1914).

[2] *The Kim*, [1915] P. 215; 1 B. and C. P. C. 405.

conditional contraband shall be liable to capture on board a vessel bound *for a neutral port* if the goods are consigned "to order," or if the ship's papers do not show who is the consignee[1] of the goods, or if they show a consignee of the goods in territory belonging to or occupied by the enemy.' By an order of March 30, 1916, this provision was also made applicable to absolute contraband.

The Allies went even beyond this, for the order of October 29, 1914, laid down the following further rules:—'where it is shown . . . that the enemy Government is drawing supplies for its armed forces from or through a neutral country, [it may be directed] that in respect of ships bound for a port in that country, Article 35 of the said Declaration shall not apply . . . so long as such direction is in force, a vessel which is carrying conditional contraband to a port in that country shall not be immune from capture'; and the order of March 30, 1916, further provided that 'the destinations referred to in Article 30 (absolute contraband) and in Article 33 (conditional contraband) of the said Declaration shall . . . be presumed to exist, if the goods are consigned to or for a person, who, during the present hostilities, has forwarded imported contraband goods to territory belonging to or occupied by the enemy.'

In all the cases covered by these provisions of these Orders in Council the burden of proving that the destination of the goods was innocent was laid upon the owner.

However, by the Maritime Rights Order in Council of July 7, 1916, the Declaration of London was abandoned altogether, and it was provided in the simplest terms that 'the principle of continuous voyage or ultimate destination shall be applicable both in cases of contraband and of blockade.' This order also laid down

[1] See *The Kronprinzessin Victoria*, (1918) 3 B. and C. P. C. 247.

elaborate presumptions as to hostile destination which have already been mentioned.[1]

Certain new applications of the doctrine of continuous transports or indirect carriage of contraband were made by the British Prize Courts during the World War. Thus, in 1917, it was decided [2] that the doctrine of continuous transports was applicable even in a case where contraband goods, seized while on their way to a neutral country, had been intended, after having undergone a process of manufacture there, to be exported from the neutral to an enemy country. But the British Prize Court [3] expressed the view that it would not be in accordance with International Law 'to hold that raw materials on their way to citizens of a neutral country to be converted into a manufactured article for consumption in that country were subject to condemnation on the ground that the consequence might, or even would necessarily, be that another article of a like kind and adapted for a like use would be exported by other citizens of the neutral country to the enemy.'

III

CONSEQUENCES OF CARRIAGE OF CONTRABAND

See the literature quoted above at the commencement of § 391.

Capture for Carriage of Contraband.

§ 404. It has always been universally recognised by theory and practice that a vessel carrying contraband may be seized by the cruisers of the belligerent concerned. But seizure is allowed only so long as a vessel is *in delicto*; this commences when she leaves the port of starting, and ends when she has deposited the contraband goods, whether with the enemy or other-

[1] Above, § 395.

[2] *The Balto*, (1917) 2 B. and C. P. C. 398.

[3] *The Bonna*, (1918) 3 B. and C. P. C. 163.

wise. The rule was generally recognised, therefore, even prior to the Declaration of London, that a vessel which has deposited her contraband may not be seized on her return voyage. British and American practice had indeed admitted one exception to this rule—namely, in the case in which a vessel had carried contraband on her outward voyage with simulated and false papers.[1] But no such exception had been admitted by the practice of other countries. Thus, when in 1879, during war between Peru and Chili, the German vessel *Luxor*, after having carried a cargo of arms and ammunition from Monte Video to Valparaiso, was seized in the harbour of Callao, in Peru, and condemned by the Peruvian Prize Courts for carrying contraband, Germany interfered, and succeeded in getting the vessel released. Seizure for carriage of contraband was only admissible on the open sea and in the maritime territorial belts of the belligerents. Seizure within the maritime belt of neutrals would be a violation of neutrality.

Article 37 of the unratified Declaration of London confirmed these old customary rules by providing that a vessel carrying goods liable to capture as absolute or conditional contraband may be captured on the high seas or in the territorial waters of the belligerents throughout the whole of her voyage even if she is to touch at a port of call before reaching the hostile destination. But Article 38 rejected the British and American practice by providing that a vessel might not be captured on the ground that she had carried contraband[2] on a previous occasion if it was in point of fact at an end.

[1] *The Nancy*, (1800) 3 C. Rob. 122; *The Margaret*, (1810) 1 Acton 333. See Holland, *Prize Law*, § 80. Wheaton, i. § 506, n. *b*, condemns this practice; Hall, § 247, calls it 'undoubtedly severe'; Halleck, ii. p. 220, defends it. See also Calvo, v. §§ 2756-2758.

[2] But see below, § 428*a*.

During the World War, however, the Allies adopted Article 37, but did not adopt Article 38. Thus the British Order in Council of October 29, 1914, which replaced the order of August 20, 1914, provided that 'a neutral vessel, with papers indicating a neutral destination, which, notwithstanding the destination shown on the papers, proceeds to an enemy port,[1] shall be liable to capture and condemnation if she is encountered before the end of her next voyage'; and this rule was re-enacted in the Maritime Rights Order in Council of July 7, 1916, by which the declaration was abandoned.

Penalty for Carriage of Contraband according to the Practice hitherto prevailing.

§ 405. In former times neither in theory nor in practice were similar rules recognised with regard to the penalty for carriage of contraband. The penalty was frequently confiscation not only of the contraband cargo itself, but also of all other parts of the cargo, together with the vessel. Only France made an exception, since, according to an *ordonnance* of 1584, she did not even confiscate the contraband goods themselves, but only seized them against payment of their value; it was not until 1681 that an *ordonnance* proclaimed confiscation of contraband, and even then with exclusion of the vessel and the innocent part of the cargo.[2] During the seventeenth century, however, the distinction between contraband on the one hand, and, on the other, the innocent goods and the vessel was clearly recognised by Zouche and Bynkershoek, and confiscation of the contraband alone became more and more the rule, certain cases excepted. During the eighteenth century, the right to confiscate contra-

[1] In *The Alwina*, (1916) 2 B. and C. P. C. 186, affirmed on appeal (3 B. and C. P. C. 54), it was held that a neutral vessel which had been carrying contraband with false papers is not liable to capture if in the meantime she had abandoned the adventure, discharged the contraband cargo at a neutral port, and sold and delivered it to other buyers.

[2] See Wheaton, *Histoire des Progrès du Droit des Gens en Europe* (1841), p. 82.

band was frequently contested, and it is remarkable as regards the change of attitude of some States that by Article 13 of the Treaty of Friendship and Commerce[1] concluded in 1785 between Prussia and the United States of America all confiscation was abolished. This article provided that the belligerent should have the right to stop vessels carrying contraband, and to detain them for such length of time as might be necessary to prevent possible damage by them, but that they should be paid compensation for their detention. It further provided that the belligerent might seize all contraband against payment of its full value, and that, if the captain of a vessel stopped for carrying contraband delivered up all contraband, the vessel should at once be set free. I doubt whether any other treaty of the same kind was entered into by either Prussia or the United States;[2] and it is certain that, if any rule regarding the penalty for carriage of contraband was generally recognised at all, it was the rule that contraband goods could be confiscated. But there always remained the difficulty that what articles were contraband was controversial, and that the practice of States varied much as to whether the vessel herself and innocent cargo carried by her could be confiscated. For beyond the rule that absolute contraband could be confiscated, there was no unanimity

[1] Martens, *R.*, iv. p. 42. The stipulation was renewed by Article 13 of the Treaty of Friendship and Commerce of 1799 and by Article 12 of the Treaty of Commerce and Navigation concluded between the two States in 1828; Martens, *R.*, vi. p. 679, and *N.R.*, vii. p. 619. These treaties were the subject of diplomatic correspondence between the United States and Germany during the World War, Germany having sunk a neutral American vessel, the *William P. Frye* (see above, § 395), which was carrying contraband. See *A.J.*, ix. (1915), Special Supplement, pp. 180-193, and x. (1916), Special Supplement, pp. 345-352; *Z.I.*, xxvi. (1915), pp. 184-197.

[2] Article 12 of the Treaty of Commerce between the United States of America and Italy, signed at Florence on February 26, 1871—see Martens, *N.R.G.*, 2nd Ser. i. p. 57—stipulates immunity from seizure of such private property only as does not consist of contraband or attempt to break blockade. See above, § 178.

regarding the fate of the vessel and the innocent part of the cargo. Great Britain and the United States of America confiscated the vessel when the owner of the contraband was also the owner of the vessel; they also confiscated such part of the innocent cargo as belonged to the owner of the contraband goods;[1] they, lastly, confiscated the vessel, although her owner was not the owner of the contraband, if the vessel sailed with false or simulated papers for the purpose of carrying contraband,[2] or if the vessel was by a treaty with her flag State under an obligation not to carry the goods concerned to the enemy and the owner knew that his vessel was carrying contraband.[3] To these—as appears from *The Hakan*,[4] decided in the British Prize Courts during the World War—British practice added a third case. After considering the practice of the past, the Privy Council felt that 'in this state of the authorities they ought to hold that knowledge of the character of the goods on the part of the owner of the ship is sufficient to justify the condemnation of the ship, at any rate where the goods in question constitute a substantial part of the whole cargo.'

Some States allowed a vessel carrying contraband which was not herself liable to confiscation to proceed with her voyage on delivery of her contraband goods to the capturing cruiser;[5] but Great Britain[6] and other States insisted upon the vessel being brought before a Prize Court in every case.

As regards conditional contraband, those States

[1] *The Kronprinsessan Margareta*, (1917) 2 B. and C. P. C. 409; *The Annie Johnson*, (1917) 3 B. and C. P. C. 138; *The Posteiro*, (1917) 3 B. and C. P. C. 275; *The Parana*, (1919) 3 B. and C. P. C. 482; *The Antwerpen*, (1919) 3 B. and C. P. C. 486 n.

[2] See Holland, *Prize Law*, §§ 82-87.

[3] *The Neutralitet*, (1801) 3 C. Rob. 295; *The Ringende Jacob*, (1798) 1 C. Rob. 89; *The Sarah Christina*, (1799) 1 C. Rob. 237; *The Franklin*, (1801) 3 C. Rob. 217.

[4] (1916) 2 B. and C. P. C. 210 and, on appeal, 479, at p. 487.

[5] See Calvo, v. § 2779.

[6] See Holland, *Prize Law*, § 81.

which made any distinction at all between absolute and conditional contraband, frequently confiscated neither the conditional contraband nor the carrying vessel, but seized the former and paid for it. According to the British practice [1] which prevailed from the end of the eighteenth century, freight was paid to the vessel, and the usual compensation for the conditional contraband was the cost price plus ten per cent. profit. States acting in this way asserted a right to confiscate conditional contraband, but exercised pre-emption in mitigation of such a right. Those Continental writers who refused to recognise the existence of conditional contraband, denied in consequence that there was a right to confiscate articles which were not absolute contraband; but they maintained that every belligerent had, according to the so-called right of angary,[2] a right to stop all neutral vessels carrying provisions and other goods with a hostile destination of which he might have made use, and to seize such goods against payment of their full value.

Penalty according to the Declaration of London for Carriage of Contraband.

§ 406. The unratified Declaration of London offered by Articles 39 to 44 a settlement of the controversy respecting the penalty for carriage of contraband which represented a fair compromise. Contraband goods, whether absolute or conditional contraband, might be confiscated (Article 39). The carrying vessel might (Article 40) likewise be confiscated if the contraband, reckoned either by value, weight, volume, or freight, formed more than half the cargo.[3] If this was not

[1] See Holland, *Prize Law*, § 84. Great Britain likewise exercised pre-emption instead of confiscation with regard to such absolute contraband as was in an unmanufactured condition and was at the same time the produce of the country exporting it.

[2] See above, § 365.

[3] In *The Lorenzo*, (St. Lucia Prize Court), (1914) 1 B. and C. P. C. 226, it was correctly decided that under Article 40 of the Declaration of London the confiscation of the carrying vessel takes place whether or not her owner knew that she was carrying contraband. In *The Hakan*, (1916) 2 B. and C. P. C. 210 and, on appeal, 479, it was held (see above, § 405) that knowledge on the part of the owner of the vessel that a substantial part of the cargo is contraband is in itself sufficient to justify

the case, and the carrying vessel was therefore released, she might (Article 41) be condemned to pay the costs and expenses incurred by the captor in respect of the proceedings in the national Prize Court and the custody of the ship and cargo during the proceedings. But whatever might be the proportion between contraband and innocent goods on a vessel, innocent goods (Article 42) which belonged to the owner of the contraband and were on board the same carrying vessel might be confiscated.

If a vessel carrying contraband sailed before the outbreak of war (Article 43), or was unaware of a declaration of contraband which applied to her cargo, or had had no opportunity of discharging her cargo after receiving such knowledge,[1] the contraband might only be confiscated on payment of compensation,[2] and the vessel herself and her innocent cargo might not be confiscated, nor might the vessel be condemned to pay any costs and expenses incurred by the captor. But there was to be a presumption which was not to be rebuttable with regard to the *mens rea* of the vessel.

her condemnation. It was also held in this case in the court of first instance (at p. 226) and in *The Maracaibo*, (1916) 2 B. and C. P. C. 294, that, independently of the Declaration of London, it is now a rule of International Law that the carrying vessel may be condemned if the contraband, reckoned either by value, weight, volume, or freight, forms more than half the cargo. It was further held in *The Maracaibo*, that this rule applies even when the owner of the vessel is ignorant of the contraband character of the goods. But doubts were expressed on this point in *The Dirigo*, (1919) 3 B. and C. P. C. 439. See also *The Hillerod*, (1917) 3 B. and C. P. C. 48; *The Ran*, [1919] P. 317, 3 B. and C. P. C. 621; *The Kim*, [1920] P. 319.

[1] It seems to be obvious that Article 43 only applies to cargo which is neutral property. If enemy property, it may be condemned without compensation. See *The Sorfareren*, (1915) 1 B. and C. P. C. 580.

[2] It is obvious that the vessel must be brought into a port and before a Prize Court if the captor desires to seize the contraband against compensation. The question whether Article 44 applied to such a case, and whether therefore the neutral vessel might be allowed to continue her voyage if the master was willing to hand over the contraband to the captor, must be answered in the affirmative, provided that the contraband, reckoned either by value, weight, volume, or freight, formed less than half the cargo. For Article 44 precisely treated of a case in which the vessel herself was not liable to condemnation *on account of the proportion of the contraband on board* (see Article 40).

For according to the second paragraph of Article 43, a vessel was to be considered to have knowledge of the outbreak of war, or of a declaration of contraband, if she left an enemy port after the outbreak of hostilities, or if she left a neutral port after the notification of the outbreak of hostilities, or of the declaration of contraband to the Power to which such port belonged, provided that such notification was made in sufficient time. However, the declaration did not secure ratification.

The question of pre-emption of conditional contraband was not mentioned by the Declaration of London. There is, however, nothing to prevent the several maritime Powers from exercising pre-emption in mitigation of their right of confiscation.

Seizure of Contraband without Seizure of the Vessel.

§ 406*a*. Prior to the Declaration of London, the practice of the several States had differed[1] with regard to the question whether a vessel which was not herself liable to condemnation might be allowed to proceed on her voyage, on condition that she handed over the contraband carried by her to the captor. Great Britain and some other States answered it in the negative; but several States in the affirmative. The unratified Declaration of London, although it upheld the general rule that, whatever might be the ultimate fate of the vessel, she must be taken into a port of a Prize Court, admitted two exceptions to the rule :—

(1) According to Article 44, a vessel which had been stopped for carrying contraband and which was not herself liable to be confiscated on account of the proportion of contraband on board, might—not must—when the circumstances permitted it, be allowed to continue her voyage in case she handed over the contraband cargo to the captor. In such a case, the captor was to be at liberty to destroy the contraband handed over to him. But the matter had in any case to be

[1] See above, § 405.

brought before a Prize Court. The captor had therefore to enter the delivery of the contraband on the log-book of the vessel so stopped, and the master had to give duly certified copies of all relevant papers to the captor.

(2) According to Article 54, the captor might[1] exceptionally, in case of necessity, demand the handing over, or might proceed himself to the destruction, of any absolute or conditional contraband goods found on a vessel which was not herself liable to condemnation, if the taking of the vessel into the port of a Prize Court would involve danger to the safety of the capturing cruiser, or to the success of the operations in which she was engaged at the time. But the captor had nevertheless to bring the case before a Prize Court. He had, therefore, to enter the captured goods on the log-book of the stopped vessel, and obtain duly certified copies of all relevant papers. If the captor could not establish before the Prize Court that he was really compelled to abandon the intention of bringing in the carrying vessel, he was to be condemned (see Article 51) to pay the value of the goods to their owners whether contraband or not.

However, the declaration has not been ratified.

During the earlier part of the World War the Allies adopted the rules of the unratified declaration which have been mentioned in this and the preceding section; when, in July 1916, Great Britain and France abandoned the declaration altogether, they expressly retained Article 40.

[1] See below, § 431.

CHAPTER V

UNNEUTRAL SERVICE

I

THE DIFFERENT KINDS OF UNNEUTRAL SERVICE

Hall, §§ 248-253—Lawrence, §§ 260-262—Westlake, ii. pp. 302-306—Phillimore, iii. §§ 271-274—Halleck, ii. pp. 305-344—Taylor, §§ 667-673—Walker, § 72—Wharton, iii. § 374—Wheaton, §§ 502-504 and Dana's note 228—Moore, vii. §§ 1264-1265—Hershey, Nos. 513-515—Bluntschli, §§ 815-818—Heffter, § 161*a*—Geffcken in *Holtzendorff*, iv. pp. 731-738—Ullmann, § 192—Bonfils, Nos. 1584-1588—Despagnet, Nos. 716-716 *bis*—Rivier, ii. pp. 388-391—Nys, iii. pp. 671-678—Calvo, v. §§ 2796-2820—Fiore, iii. Nos. 1602-1605, and *Code*, Nos. 1859-1863—Martens, ii. § 136—Kleen, i. §§ 103-106—Boeck, Nos. 660-669—Pillet, pp. 330-332—Gessner, pp. 99-111—Perels, § 47—Testa, p. 212—Dupuis, Nos. 231-238, and *Guerre*, Nos. 172-188—Bernsten, § 9—Nippold, ii. § 35—Schramm, § 11—Holland, *Prize Law*, §§ 88-105—U.S. Naval War Code, Articles 16 and 20—Hautefeuille, ii. pp. 173-188—Ortolan, ii. pp. 209-213—Mountague Bernard, *Neutrality of Great Britain during the American Civil War* (1870), pp. 187-225—Marquardsen, *Der Trent-Fall* (1862), pp. 58-71—Hirsch, *Kriegskonterbande und verbotene Transporte in Kriegszeiten* (1897), pp. 42-55—Takahashi, *International Law during the Chino-Japanese War* (1899), pp. 52-72—Vetzel, *De la Contrebande par Analogie en Droit maritime internationale* (1901)—Atherley-Jones, *Commerce in War* (1907), pp. 304-315—Hirschmann, *Das internationale Prisenrecht* (1912), §§ 31-32—Pastureau, *Des Transports interdits aux Neutres* (1912)—Wehberg, pp. 123-132—Garner, ii. §§ 538-545—See also the monographs quoted above at the commencement of § 391, and the General Report presented to the International Naval Conference of London on behalf of the Drafting Committee, Articles 45-47, Cd. 4554, p. 55.

Unneutral Service in general.

§ 407. Before the Naval Conference of London held in 1908, the term *unneutral service* had been used by several writers with reference to the carriage by neutral vessels of certain persons and despatches for the enemy. The term had been introduced to distinguish such carriage of persons and despatches from the carriage of contraband, with which it was often confounded. Since contraband consists of certain goods only, and never of persons or despatches, a vessel carrying persons and despatches for the enemy does not carry contraband;[1] and there is another important difference. Carriage of contraband need not necessarily, and in most cases in practice does not, take place in the direct service of the enemy. On the other hand, carriage of persons and despatches for the enemy always does take place in the direct service of the enemy, and, consequently, represents much more intensive assistance to him, and a much more intimate connection with him than carriage of contraband. For these reasons, separate treatment for carriage of contraband and for carriage of persons and despatches was certainly considered desirable by many publicists. Those among them who did not adopt the term *unneutral service,* on account of its somewhat misleading character, preferred[2] the expression *analogous of contraband,* because in practice maritime transport for the enemy was always treated as analogous to, although not as identical with, carriage of contraband.[3]

The unratified Declaration of London sought to place the whole matter upon a new and very much enlarged basis, for Articles 45 to 47 treated, under the heading *De l'assistance hostile*—the official English translation of which was *unneutral service*—not only of carriage of persons for the enemy by a neutral vessel, but also of transmission of intelligence in his interest,

[1] This was recognised in *The Yangtsze Insurance Association* v. *Indemnity Mutual Marine Assurance Company,* [1908] 1 K.B. 910; [1908] 2 K.B. 504.

[2] It was also preferred in the first edition of this work. But after the official adoption, in the translation of the unratified Declaration of London, of the term *unneutral service,* it was useless to oppose it.

[3] Although—see above, §§ 173-174 —prevention of unneutral service to the enemy is a means of sea warfare, it chiefly concerns neutral commerce, and is therefore more conveniently treated with neutrality.

of taking a direct part in the hostilities, and of a number of other acts. The unratified declaration made a broad distinction between two kinds of unneutral service, meting out for the one treatment analogous in a general way to the treatment of contraband, and for the other treatment analogous to that of enemy merchant vessels. Carriage of individual members of the armed forces of the enemy, and a certain case of transmission of intelligence in the interest of the enemy, constituted the first kind; and four groups of acts bestowing enemy character on the vessel concerned constituted the second kind.

At the outbreak of the World War the Allies adopted the rules relating to unneutral service contained in the unratified Declaration of London, and applied them (subject to reprisals[1]) without modification until the whole declaration was abandoned in July 1916. Thereafter the customary rules prevailing before the Naval Conference of London again became applicable.[2] After that date, however, few (if any) cases of unneutral service came before Prize Courts in which general principles were laid down or applied: and as conditions have changed greatly since the old customary rules grew up, the present position of the law of unneutral service is unsatisfactory.

Carriage of Persons for the Enemy.

§ 408. Either belligerent may punish neutral vessels for carrying, in the service of the enemy, certain persons. Such persons included, according to the customary rules of International Law prevailing before the unratified Declaration of London, not only members of the armed forces of the enemy, but also individuals who, though not yet members of the armed forces, would have become so as soon as they reached their place of destination, and, thirdly, non-military individuals in the service of the enemy who were either in

[1] See below, § 413a. [2] See above, § 292.

such a prominent position that they could be made prisoners of war, or were going abroad as agents for the purpose of fostering the cause of the enemy. Thus, for instance, if the head of the enemy State, or one of his cabinet ministers, fled the country to avoid captivity, the neutral vessel that carried him could have been punished, as could also the vessel carrying an agent of the enemy sent abroad to negotiate a loan and the like. However, the mere fact that enemy persons were on board a neutral vessel did not in itself prove that they were carried by the vessel for the enemy, and in his service. This was the case only when the vessel knew of the character of the persons and nevertheless carried them, thereby acting in the service of the enemy, or when the vessel was directly hired by the enemy for the purpose of transporting the individuals concerned. Thus, for instance, if able-bodied men booked their passages on a neutral vessel to an enemy port with the secret intention of enlisting in the forces of the enemy, the vessel could not be considered as carrying persons for the enemy; but she could be so considered, if an agent of the enemy openly booked their passages. Thus, further, if the fugitive head of the enemy State booked his passage under a false name, and concealed his identity from the vessel, she could not be considered as carrying a person for the enemy; but she could be so considered, if she knew whom she was carrying, because she was then aware that she was acting in the service of the enemy. As regards a vessel directly hired by the enemy, there could be no doubt that she was acting in the service of the enemy. Thus the American vessel *Orozembo*[1] was in 1807, during war between England and the Netherlands, captured and condemned because, although chartered by a merchant in Lisbon ostensibly

[1] 6 C. Rob. 430.

to sail in ballast to Macao and to take from there a cargo to America, she received, by order of the charterer, three Dutch officers and two Dutch civil servants, and sailed, not to Macao, but to Batavia. The American vessel *Friendship*[1] was likewise in 1807, during war between England and France, captured and condemned, because she was hired by the French Government to carry ninety shipwrecked officers and sailors home to a French port.

According to British practice prevailing before the unratified Declaration of London, a neutral vessel was considered as carrying persons in the service of the enemy even if she had been forcibly constrained by the enemy to carry them, or if she was *bona fide* in ignorance of the status of her passengers. Thus, in 1802, during war between Great Britain and France, the Swedish vessel *Carolina*[2] was condemned by Sir William Scott for having carried French troops from Egypt to Italy, although the master endeavoured to prove that the vessel was forced to render the transport service; and the above-mentioned vessel *Orozembo* was condemned,[3] although her master was ignorant of the service for the enemy on which he was engaged: '. . . In cases of *bona fide* ignorance there may be no actual delinquency; but if the service is injurious, that will be sufficient to give the belligerent a right to prevent the thing from being done or at least repeated,' said Sir William Scott.[4]

[1] 6 C. Rob. 420.

[2] 4 C. Rob. 256.

[3] See Phillimore, iii. § 274, and Holland, *Prize Law*, §§ 90-91. Hall, § 249 n., reprobates the British practice. During the Russo-Japanese War only one case of condemnation of a neutral vessel for carrying persons for the enemy is recorded, that of *The Nigretia*, a vessel which endeavoured to carry into Vladivostok the escaped captain and lieutenant of the Russian destroyer *Ratstoropny*; see Takahashi, pp. 639-641, and Hurst and Bray, ii. p. 201.

[4] It should be mentioned that, according to the customary law hitherto prevailing, the case of diplomatic agents sent by the enemy to neutral States was an exception to the rule that neutral vessels may be punished for carrying agents sent by the enemy. The importance of this exception became apparent in

According to the unratified Declaration of London neutral merchantmen (apart from the case of the carriage of persons who in the course of the voyage directly assist the operations of the enemy) might only be considered to render unneutral service if they carried such enemy persons as were already actually members of the armed forces of the enemy. Article 45 made it quite apparent, through using the words '*embodied* in the armed forces,' that reservists and the like who were on their way to the enemy country for the purpose of there joining the armed forces, were not [1] among the classes of enemy persons which a neutral vessel might not carry without exposing herself to punishment for rendering unneutral service to the enemy.

the case of *The Trent* which occurred during the American Civil War. On November 8, 1861, the Federal cruiser *San Jacinto* stopped the British mail steamer *Trent* on her voyage from Havana to the British port of Nassau, in the Bahamas, forcibly took off Messrs. Mason and Slidell, together with their secretaries, political agents sent by the Confederate States to Great Britain and France, and then let the vessel continue her voyage. Great Britain demanded their immediate release, and the United States at once granted this, although the ground on which release was granted was not identical with the ground on which it was demanded. The United States maintained that the removal of these men from the vessel without bringing her before a Prize Court for trial was irregular, and therefore not justified, whereas release was demanded on the ground that a neutral vessel could not be prevented from carrying diplomatic agents sent by the enemy to neutrals. Now diplomatic agents in the proper sense of the term these gentlemen were not, because, although they were sent by the Confederate States, the latter were not recognised as such, but only as a belligerent Power. Yet they were political agents of a quasi-diplomatic character, and the standpoint of Great Britain was for this reason perhaps correct. The fact that the Governments of France, Austria, and Prussia protested through their diplomatic envoys in Washington shows at least that neutral vessels may carry unhindered on the open sea (though not through the territorial waters of the other belligerent — see above, vol. i. § 398, and the cases of *Tarnowski*, *Dumba*, and *Bernsdorff* there mentioned) diplomatic agents sent by the enemy to neutrals, however doubtful it may be whether the same is valid regarding agents with a quasi-diplomatic character. See *Parl. Papers*, (1862) North America, No. 5; Marquardsen, *Der Trent-Fall* (1862); Wharton, iii. § 374; Moore, vii. § 1265; Phillimore, ii. §§ 130-130*a*; Mountague Bernard, *Neutrality of Great Britain during the American Civil War* (1870), pp. 187-225; Harris, *The Trent Affair* (1896). But see *The Pontoporos*, (1915) 1 B. and C. P. C. 371; (1916) 2 B. and C. P. C. 87, where this and other cases were considered; compare also *The Svithiod*, [1920] A.C. 718.

[1] But see the French case of *The Frederico* (1915)—Garner, ii. § 544; text in *R.G.*, xxii. (1915), Jurisprudence, p. 17, xxiv. (1917), Jurisprudence, p. 11—in which the Prize Court of Appeal, in direct opposition to the Renault Report on the Declaration of London, decided that reservists on their way home from abroad are considered to be 'incorporated' in the army of their home State.

Four different cases of carrying members of the armed forces of the enemy were distinguished by the unratified declaration, namely (1) that of a neutral vessel exclusively engaged in the transport of enemy troops, (2) that of a vessel transporting a military detachment of the enemy, (3) that of a vessel transporting one or more persons who in the course of the voyage directly assist the operations of the enemy, (4) that of a vessel transporting, on a voyage specially undertaken, individual members of the armed forces of the enemy.

(1) According to Article 46 (4) a neutral vessel exclusively appropriated at the time to the transport of enemy troops acquired thereby enemy character. This case will be considered with others of the same kind below.[1]

(2) In case a vessel, not exclusively appropriated to that work, and not on a voyage specially undertaken for that purpose, transported, to the knowledge of either the owner or the charterer or the master, a military detachment of the enemy, she was, according to Article 45 (2), to be considered to render unneutral service for which she might be punished. Accordingly, if to the knowledge of either the owner or the charterer or the master, a neutral vessel *in the ordinary course of her voyage* carried a military detachment of the enemy, she was to be liable to be seized for unneutral service.

(3) In case a neutral vessel, to the knowledge of either the owner or the charterer or the master, carried one or more persons — whether a belligerent or neutral subject — who in the course of the voyage directly assisted the operations of the enemy in any way, for instance by signalling or sending a message by wireless telegraphy, she was, according to Article 45 (2), to be likewise liable to seizure for rendering unneutral service.

(4) In case a neutral vessel carried individual members of the armed forces of the enemy, she was, according to Article 45 (1), only to be liable to seizure if she was on a voyage specially undertaken for such transport, *e.g.* if she

[1] § 410.

had been diverted from her ordinary course and had touched at a port outside her ordinary course for the purpose of embarking, or was going to touch at a port outside her ordinary course for the purpose of disembarking, the enemy persons concerned. A liner, therefore, carrying individual members of the armed forces of the enemy in the ordinary course of her voyage might not be considered to be rendering unneutral service and might not be seized. However, according to Article 47, a neutral vessel carrying members of the armed forces of the enemy while pursuing her ordinary course, might be stopped for the purpose of taking off such enemy persons and making them prisoners of war.[1]

But the rules formulated by the Declaration of London are not binding, and the former customary rules remain applicable.

Transmission of Intelligence to the Enemy.

§ 409. Either belligerent may punish neutral merchantmen for transmission of intelligence to the enemy. According to customary rules of International Law either belligerent may punish neutral vessels for the carriage of political despatches from or to the enemy, and especially such despatches as relate to the war. But to this rule there have been two exceptions. First, as neutrals have a right to demand that their intercourse with either belligerent be not suppressed, a neutral vessel might not, according to the old cases, be punished for carrying despatches from the enemy to neutral Governments, and *vice versa*,[2] or from the enemy Government to its diplomatic agents and consuls abroad in neutral States, and *vice versa*.[3] The second exception was created by Article 1 of Hague Convention XI. relative to postal correspondence,[4] which provides that postal correspondence, whether private or official, is inviolable. However, the mere fact that a neutral vessel has political despatches to or from the enemy on board

[1] See below, § 413.

[2] *The Caroline*, (1808) 6 C. Rob. 461.

[3] *The Madison*, (1810) Edwards 224.

[4] As to which, see above, § 191.

does not by itself prove that she is carrying them *for and in the service of the enemy*. Just as in the case of certain enemy persons on board, so in the case of despatches, the vessel is only considered to be carrying them in the service of the enemy if she knows of their character and has nevertheless taken them on board, or if she is directly hired for the purpose of carrying them. Thus, the American vessel *Rapid*,[1] which was captured during the war between Great Britain and the Netherlands, on her voyage from New York to Tonningen, for having on board a despatch for a cabinet minister of the Netherlands hidden under a cover addressed to a merchant at Tonningen, was released by the Prize Court. On the other hand, the *Atalanta*,[2] which carried despatches in a tea chest hidden in the trunk of a supercargo, was condemned.[3]

According to the unratified Declaration of London, the carriage of despatches for the enemy might only be punished in case it fell under the category of transmitting intelligence to the enemy on the part of a neutral vessel. Two kinds of such transmission of intelligence had to be distinguished :—

First, according to Article 46 (4), a neutral vessel exclusively intended for the transmission of intelligence to the enemy acquired thereby enemy character ; this will be considered with other cases of the same kind below.[4]

Secondly, according to Article 45 (1), a neutral vessel might be seized for transmitting intelligence to the enemy if she was on a voyage specially undertaken for such transmission, *e.g.* if she had been diverted from her ordinary course and had touched or was going to touch at a port outside her ordinary course for the purpose of transmitting

[1] (1810) Edwards 228.

[2] (1808) 6 C. Rob. 440.

[3] British practice seems unsettled on the question whether the vessel must know of the character of the despatch which she is carrying. In spite of the case of *The Rapid*, quoted above, Holland, *Prize Law*, § 100, maintains that ignorance of the master of the vessel is no excuse, and Phillimore, iii. § 272, seems to be of the same opinion.

[4] § 410.

intelligence to the enemy. A liner, therefore, transmitting intelligence to the enemy in the ordinary course of her voyage might not be considered to be rendering unneutral service, and might not be punished. However, self-preservation would in a case of necessity have justified a belligerent in temporarily detaining such a liner for the purpose of preventing the intelligence from reaching the enemy.[1]

The conception 'transmission of intelligence' was not defined by the Declaration of London. It certainly meant, not only oral transmission of intelligence, but also the transmission of despatches containing intelligence. The transmission of any political intelligence of value to the enemy, whether relating to the war or not, ought to have been considered unneutral service, unless it was intelligence transmitted from the enemy to neutral Governments, or *vice versa*, or from the enemy Government to its diplomatic agents and consuls abroad in neutral States.

But the rules contained in the Declaration of London are not binding, and the old customary rules remain applicable.

Unneutral Service creating Enemy Character.

§ 410. In contradistinction to cases of unneutral service which are similar to carriage of contraband, the Declaration of London enumerated in Article 46 four cases of such kinds of unneutral service as vested neutral vessels with enemy character.[2]

(1) There was, first, the case of a neutral merchantman taking a direct part in the hostilities. This might occur in several ways, but such a vessel in every case was to lose her neutral character and acquire enemy character, just as does a subject of a neutral Power who enlists in the ranks of the enemy armed forces. But a distinction had to be made between taking a direct part in the hostilities, for instance rendering assistance to the enemy fleet during battle, and acts of a piratical character. If a neutral merchantman [3] without letters of marque during

[1] See below, § 413.

[2] See above, § 89 (1).

[3] See above, §§ 85, 181, 254.

war, and from hatred of one of the belligerents, were to attack and sink his merchantmen, she would have to have been considered, and could therefore have been treated as, a pirate.

(2) There was, secondly, the case of a neutral vessel which sailed under the orders, or the control, of an agent placed on board by the enemy Government.[1] The presence of such agent, and the fact that the vessel sailed under his orders or control, showed clearly that she was really for all practical purposes part and parcel of the enemy forces.

(3) There was, thirdly, the case of a neutral vessel in the exclusive employment of the enemy. This could have occurred in two different ways: either the vessel might have been rendering a specific service in the exclusive employment of the enemy, as, for instance, did those German merchantmen during the Russo-Japanese War which acted as colliers for the Russian fleet *en route* for the Far East; or the vessel might be chartered by the enemy so that she was entirely at his disposal for any purpose he might choose, whether connected with the war or not.[2]

(4) There was, fourthly and lastly, the case of a neutral merchantman exclusively appropriated at the time either to the transport of enemy troops, or to the transmission of intelligence for the enemy. This case is different from the case—provided for by Article 45 (1)—of a vessel on a voyage specially undertaken with a view to the carriage of individual members of the armed forces of the enemy. Whereas in that case a vessel merely rendered a specific

[1] See *The Thor*, (1914) 1 B. and C. P. C. 229; *The Hanametal*, (1914) 1 B. and C. P. C. 347.

[2] Three cases of interest occurred in 1905, during the Russo-Japanese War. *The Industrie* (Takahashi, p. 732; Hurst and Bray, ii. p. 323), a German vessel, and a French vessel, *The Quang-nam* (Takahashi, p. 735; Hurst and Bray, ii. p. 343), were condemned for being in the employ of Russia as reconnoitring vessels. *The Australia* (Hurst and Bray, ii. p. 373), an American vessel, was condemned for having been chartered by the Russian Government for the carriage of cargo and having a Russian official on board.—During the World War the interesting case of *The Zambesi*, (1914) 1 B. and C. P. C. 358, occurred, but she was a ship belonging to one belligerent and rendering service to another.

service, in this case the vessel is for the time being wholly and continuously devoted to the rendering of unneutral service. For the time being she is, therefore, actually part and parcel of the enemy marine. For this reason she was considered to have lost her neutral character, even if, at the moment an enemy cruiser searched her, she was engaged neither in the transport of troops nor in the transmission of intelligence. And it made no difference, whether the vessel was engaged by the enemy and paid for the transport of troops or the transmission of intelligence,[1] or whether she rendered the service [2] gratuitously.

However, the provisions of the Declaration of London have not secured ratification, and are therefore not legally binding.

II

CONSEQUENCES OF UNNEUTRAL SERVICE

See the literature quoted above at the commencement of § 407.

Capture for Unneutral Service.

§ 411. According to customary rules of International Law, adopted also in the unratified Declaration of London, a neutral vessel may be captured if visit or search establishes the fact, or arouses grave suspicion, that she is rendering unneutral service to the enemy. Such capture may take place anywhere on the open sea or in the territorial maritime belt of either belligerent.

Mail steamers are, in principle, not exempt from capture for unneutral service. Although, according to Article 1 of Convention XI., the postal correspondence of belligerents and neutrals, whether official or

[1] During the World War the Italian Prize Court condemned an Albanian vessel, *La Bella Scutarina*, for transmitting intelligence to the Austrians.

[2] As regards the meaning of the term transmission of intelligence, see above, § 409.

private in character, found on board a vessel on the sea is inviolable,[1] and a vessel may never therefore be considered to be rendering unneutral service by carrying amongst her postal correspondence despatches containing intelligence for the enemy, a mail steamer is nevertheless [2] not exempt from the laws and customs of naval war respecting neutral merchantmen. A mail-boat is, therefore, exposed as much as any other merchantman to capture for rendering unneutral service.

Capture is allowed only so long as the vessel is *in delicto, i.e.* during the time in which she is rendering unneutral service or is being pursued for having done so.

Penalty for Unneutral Service.

§ 412. According to the practice prevailing before the Naval Conference of London, a neutral vessel captured for carriage of persons or despatches in the service of the enemy could be confiscated. Moreover, according to British [3] practice, such part of the cargo as belonged to the owner of the vessel was likewise confiscated.[4] If the vessel was not found guilty of carrying persons or despatches in the service of the enemy, and was not therefore condemned, the Government of the captor could nevertheless detain the persons as prisoners of war and confiscate the despatches, if they were of such a character as would have made a vessel which was cognisant of their character liable to punishment for transporting them for the enemy.

The unratified Declaration of London recognised these three rules. Articles 45 and 46 declared any vessel rendering any kind of unneutral service to the enemy liable to confiscation, and also such part of the cargo as belonged to the owner of the confiscated vessel. And Article 47

[1] See above, §§ 191, 319.

[2] See Article 2.

[3] *The Friendship*, (1807) 6 C. Rob. 420; *The Atalanta*, (1808) 6 C. Rob. 440. See Holland, *Prize Law*, §§ 95 and 105.

[4] See, however, *The Hope*, (1808) 6 C. Rob. 463 n.

provided that, although a neutral vessel might not be liable to condemnation, the capturing State might nevertheless detain as prisoners of war any members of the armed forces of the enemy who were found on board. The case of despatches found on board was not mentioned by Article 47.

The mere fact that a neutral vessel is rendering unneutral service is not sufficient for her condemnation; in addition *mens rea* is required. Now as regards the four kinds of unneutral service which create enemy character, *mens rea* is obviously always in existence, and therefore always presumed to be present. For this reason Article 46, in contradistinction to Article 45, did not refer to the knowledge of the vessel of the outbreak of hostilities. But as regards the other cases of unneutral service, Article 45 provided that the vessel might not be confiscated if the vessel was encountered at sea while unaware of the outbreak of hostilities, or if the master, after becoming aware of the outbreak of hostilities, had had no opportunity of disembarking the passengers concerned. On the other hand, a vessel was to be deemed, according to Article 45, to be aware of the existence of a state of war if she had left an enemy port subsequent to the outbreak of hostilities, or a neutral port subsequent to the notification of the outbreak of hostilities to the Power to which such port belonged, provided that such notification was made in sufficient time.

Although the unratified Declaration of London meted out the same punishment for the several kinds of unneutral service which it enumerated, it did make a distinction with regard to the treatment in other respects of vessels captured for rendering unneutral service.

Article 45 provided for a neutral vessel captured for having rendered either of the two kinds of unneutral service mentioned in it treatment in a general way the same as that of a neutral vessel captured for the carriage of contraband. The vessel did not lose her neutral character, and had under all circumstances and conditions to be taken before a Prize Court, unless—see Article 49—to take her into a port of the capturing State would have involved danger to the safety of the capturing vessel or to the success of the military operations in which she was engaged at the time. And an appeal from the national Prize Courts was to lie to the proposed International Prize Court.

Article 46, on the other hand, provided treatment for a vessel captured for having rendered any of the four kinds of unneutral service enumerated in it which, in a general way, was the same as that of a captured enemy merchantman. Such a vessel acquired enemy character. Accordingly,[1] all enemy goods on the vessel might be seized, all goods on board were to be presumed to be enemy goods, and the owners of neutral goods on board were to have to prove their neutral character. Further, the rules of Articles 48 and 49 concerning the destruction of neutral vessels were not to apply. Again, no appeal was to lie from the national Prize Courts to the International Prize Court by the owner of the ship except concerning the one question, whether the act of which she was accused had the character of unneutral service.[2]

However, the rules of the declaration are not legally binding, and the old customary rules are still applicable.

Seizure of Enemy Persons and Despatches without Seizure of Vessel.

§ 413. According to the British[3] and American practice, as well as that of some other States, which prevailed prior to the Naval Conference of London, whenever a neutral vessel was stopped for carrying persons or despatches for the enemy, these could not be seized unless the vessel was seized at the same time. The release, in 1861, during the American Civil War, of Messrs. Mason[4] and Slidell, who had been forcibly

[1] See above, § 89.

[2] The question whether, if the vessel was destroyed by the captor, the innocent owners of the neutral goods on board might claim compensation, would have had to be decided in the same way as the question whether the owners of neutral goods on a destroyed enemy merchantman have a claim to compeusation; see above, § 194.

[3] See Holland, *Prize Law*, § 104.

[4] See above, § 408 n.

taken off the *Trent*, while the ship herself was allowed to continue her voyage, was based by the United States on the fact that the seizure of these men without the seizure of the vessel was illegal.

Since, according to the unratified Declaration of London, a neutral vessel rendering unneutral service of any kind was liable to be confiscated, it is evident that in such a case the enemy persons and despatches concerned might not be taken off the vessel unless the vessel herself was seized and brought into a port of a Prize Court. However, Article 47 provided that any member of the armed forces of the enemy found on board a neutral merchant vessel might be taken off and made a prisoner of war, although there might be no ground for the capture of the vessel. Therefore, if a vessel carried individual members of the armed forces of the enemy in the ordinary course of her voyage,[1] or if she transported a military detachment of the enemy and the like without being aware of the outbreak of hostilities, the members of the armed forces of the enemy on board might be seized, although the vessel herself might not be seized, as she was not rendering unneutral service.

The Declaration of London did not mention the case of enemy despatches embodying intelligence found on board

[1] Accordingly, in January 1912, during the Turco-Italian War, the Italian gunboat *Volturno*, after having overhauled, in the Red Sea, the British steamer *Africa* going from Hodeida to Aden, took off and made prisoners of war Colonel Riza Bey and eleven other Turkish officers. Although the Declaration of London was not ratified by Great Britain, she did not protest. The case of *The Manouba* ought likewise to be mentioned here. This French steamer, which plied between Marseilles and Tunis, was captured on January 18, 1912, by the *Agordat*, an Italian torpedo boat in the Mediterranean, brought to Cagliari, and then released after twenty-nine Turkish passengers, who were supposed to be Turkish officers on their way to the theatre of war, had been forcibly taken off and made prisoners. On the protest of France, it was agreed between the parties that the case should be settled by an arbitral award of the Permanent Court of Arbitration at the Hague, Italy asserting that she had only acted in accordance with Article 47 of the Declaration of London. The court, on May 6, 1913, gave its award in favour of France, because the commander of the *Agordat* did not demand from the *Manouba* the handing over of the Turks, but captured her. See Rapisardi-Mirabelli in *R.I.*, 2nd Ser. xv. (1913), pp. 135-138, and Ruzé in *R.I.*, 2nd Ser. xvi. (1914), pp. 128-136.

such a neutral vessel as might not herself be captured for such carriage. For instance, if a mail steamer, pursuing her ordinary course, carried a despatch of the enemy, not in her mail-bags, but separately (in which case, according to Article 45, the vessel was not liable to seizure), might despatches be seized without the seizure of the vessel? The question ought to be answered in the affirmative.

However, the rules of the Declaration of London are not legally binding.

Quite different from the case of the seizure of such enemy persons and despatches as a vessel cannot carry without exposing herself to punishment, is the case[1] where a vessel has such enemy persons and despatches on board as she is allowed to carry, but a belligerent believes it to be necessary in the interest of self-defence to seize them. Since necessity in the interest of self-preservation is, according to International Law, an excuse[2] for an illegal act, if such act is necessary in self-defence, a belligerent may seize such persons and despatches, provided that their seizure is not merely desirable, but absolutely necessary[3] in the interest of self-defence. For instance, seizure of an enemy ambassador on board a neutral vessel would be justifiable if he was on the way to submit to a neutral a draft treaty of alliance injurious to the other belligerent.

Seizure of Enemy Reservists during the World War.

§ 413*a*. Different too is the case where a vessel has enemy persons on board whom she is allowed to carry, but a belligerent orders them to be seized as a measure of reprisals. Notable cases of this kind occurred during the World War. On November 1, 1914, the British Foreign Office gave notice that 'In view of the action taken by the German forces in Belgium and France of removing as prisoners of war all persons

[1] See Hall, § 253; Rivier, ii. p. 390.

[2] See above, vol. i. § 129.

[3] See above, vol. i. § 130.

who are liable to military service, His Majesty's Government have given instructions that all enemy reservists on neutral vessels should be made prisoners of war.' The French Government published a similar notice. In consequence, all enemy subjects of military age found on board neutral vessels on the high seas were taken off by the cruisers of the Allies and made prisoners of war.[1] It is asserted that sixty-four neutral vessels were thus interfered with, and that about 3500 subjects of the Central Powers were taken off them and made prisoners of war. To mention a few examples:[2] the Italian steamer *Ancona*, sailing from New York to Italy, was held up by an English cruiser near Gibraltar, and seventy German passengers were removed and taken to Gibraltar as prisoners of war. The Dutch liner *New Amsterdam* was stopped by a French cruiser on the high seas off Brest, and 400 Germans and 250 Austrians were removed and made prisoners of war. Of the protests of the neutral Governments affected, only those of the United States of America were of any avail. When the American steamer *Windber*, two days after having left Colon, was stopped in November 1914 by the French cruiser *Condé* and August Piepenbrink, a German waiter, was taken off, brought to Kingston in Jamaica, and detained as a prisoner of war, the United States protested, and after some correspondence, the French and British Governments consented to set him free 'as a friendly act while reserving the question of principle involved.'[3] Again when, in February 1916, the American steamship *China* was stopped by the British cruiser *Laurentic* on the high seas about ten miles from the entrance to the Yang-tze-kiang and twenty-eight Germans, eight

[1] The legality of this measure of reprisals by the Allies may well be doubted. But see Wehberg, p. 315.

[2] For others, see Garner, ii. § 539.

[3] See *A.J.*, ix. (1915), Special Supplement, pp. 353-360, and above, vol. i. § 313 n.

Austrians, and two Turks were taken off, carried to Hong-Kong, and there detained as prisoners of war, the United States Government protested, and after some correspondence the prisoners were set free, although Great Britain reserved the question of principle.[1]

[1] See *A.J.*, x. (1916), Special Supplement, pp. 427-432.

CHAPTER VI

VISITATION, CAPTURE, AND TRIAL OF NEUTRAL VESSELS

I

VISITATION

Bynkershoek, *Quaestiones Juris publici*, i. c. 14—Vattel, iii. § 114—Hall, §§ 270-276—Manning, pp. 433-460—Phillimore, iii. §§ 322-344—Twiss, ii. §§ 91-97—Halleck, ii. pp. 271-304—Taylor, §§ 685-689—Wharton, iii. §§ 325, 346—Wheaton, §§ 524-537—Moore, vii. §§ 1199-1205—Hershey, Nos. 516-520—Bluntschli, §§ 819-826—Heffter, §§ 167-171—Geffcken in *Holtzendorff*, iv. pp. 773-781—Kluber, §§ 293-294—G. F. Martens, ii. §§ 317, 321—Ullmann, § 195—Bonfils, Nos. 1674-1691—Despagnet, Nos. 717-721—Rivier, ii. pp. 423-426—Nys, iii. pp. 679-690—Calvo, v. §§ 2939-2991—Fiore, iii. Nos. 1630-1641, and *Code*, Nos. 1876-1900—Martens, ii. § 137—Kleen, ii. §§ 185-199, 209—Gessner, pp. 278-332—Boeck, Nos. 767-769—Dupuis, Nos. 239-252, and *Guerre*, Nos. 189-204—Bernsten, § 11—Schramm, §§ 13-14—Nippold, ii. § 35—Perels, §§ 52-55—Testa, pp. 230-242—Ortolan, ii. pp. 214-245—Hautefeuille, iii. pp. 1-298—Holland, *Prize Law*, §§ 1-17, 155-230—U.S. Naval War Code, Articles 30-33—Schlegel, *Sur la Visite des Vaisseaux neutres sous Convoi* (1800)—Mirbach, *Die volkerrechtlichen Grundsätze des Durchsuchungsrechts zur See* (1903)—Loewenthal, *Das Untersuchungsrecht des internationalen Seerechts in Krieg und Frieden* (1905)—Atherley-Jones, *Commerce in War* (1907), pp. 299-360—Hirschmann, *Das internationale Prisenrecht* (1912), §§ 33-34—Wehberg, § 7—Garner, ii. § 500—Duboc in *R.G.*, iv. (1897), pp. 382-403—See also the monographs quoted above at the commencement of § 391, Bulmerincq's articles on *Le Droit des Prises maritimes* in *R.I.*, x.-xiii. (1878-1881), and the General Report presented to the International Naval Conference of London on behalf of the Drafting Committee, Article 63, Cd. 4554, p. 63.

Conception of Right of Visitation.

§ 414. The right of visitation[1] is the right of belligerents to visit and, if need be, search neutral merchant-

[1] This right of visitation is not an independent right, but is involved in the right of either belligerent—see above, § 314—to punish neutral vessels breaking blockade, carrying contraband, and rendering unneutral service. It is a *right*, in contradistinction to the *duty*, of every belligerent to visit an *enemy* merchantman if he desires to capture her. See Oppenheim in *Z.V.*, viii. (1914), pp. 154-169.

men for the purpose of ascertaining whether these vessels really belong to the merchant marine of neutrals, and, if this is found to be the case, whether they are attempting to break blockade, or carry contraband, or render unneutral service to the enemy. The right of visit and search was already mentioned in the *Consolato del Mare*, and although it has often [1] been contested, its *raison d'être* is so obvious that it has long been universally recognised in practice. It is indeed the only means by which belligerents are able to ascertain whether neutral merchantmen intend to bring assistance to the enemy and to render him unneutral services.[2]

Right of Visitation, by whom, when, and where exercised.

§ 415. The right of visit and search may be exercised by all warships [3] and military aircraft of belligerents.[4] But since it is a belligerent right, it may, of course, only be exercised after the outbreak, and before the end, of war. The right of visitation which men-of-war of all nations have in time of peace in a case of suspicion of piracy [5] has nothing to do with the belligerent right of visit and search. But since an armistice does not bring war to an end, and since the exercise of the right of visitation is not an act of warfare, it may be exercised during the time of a partial or general armistice.[6] The region where the right may be exercised

[1] See, for instance, Hübner, *De la Saisie des Bâtiments neutres* (1759), i. p. 227.

[2] A 'Règlement international des Prises maritimes' was adopted at Heidelberg in 1887 by the Institute of International Law, §§ 1-29 of which regulate visit and search. See *Annuaire*, ix. (1888), p. 218.

[3] A captured neutral merchantman does not become a commissioned vessel by having a prize crew on board, and has no right to visit, search, and capture other neutral merchantmen. When, therefore, in May 1917 during the World War, a captured Dutch trawler with a German prize crew on board captured the *Koningin Emma*, a Dutch steam trawler, which stranded while being taken to a German port, the Dutch Government protested. The German Government made an apology, and compensated the owners of the *Koningin Emma* for the loss of their vessel.

[4] In former times also by privateers.

[5] See above, vol. i. § 266 (2).

[6] But this is not universally recognised. Thus Hautefeuille, iii. p. 91, maintains that during a general armistice the right of visitation may not be exercised, and

is the maritime territorial belt of either belligerent, and the open sea, but not the maritime territorial belt of neutrals. Whether the part of the open sea in which a belligerent man-of-war meets with a neutral merchantman is near or far away from that part of the world where hostilities are actually taking place makes no difference, so long as there is suspicion against the vessel. The question whether the men-of-war of a belligerent may exercise the right of visitation in the maritime territorial belt of an ally is solely one between the belligerent and his ally, provided that the latter is already a belligerent.

Only Private Vessels may be visited.

§ 416. During the nineteenth century, it became universally recognised that neutral men-of-war are not objects of the right of visit and search of belligerents.[1] And the same is valid regarding public neutral vessels which sail in the service of armed forces, such as transport vessels, for instance. Doubt exists as to the position of public neutral vessels not sailing in the service of armed forces, *e.g.* mail-boats belonging to a neutral State. It is asserted [2] that, if commanded by an officer of the Navy, they must be treated in the same way as men-of-war, but that it is desirable to ask the commanders to give their word of honour assuring the absence of contraband and unneutral service.

Vessels under Convoy.

§ 417. Sweden in 1653, during war between Great Britain and the Netherlands, claimed [3] that the belligerents ought to waive their rights of visitation over Swedish merchantmen if they sailed under the convoy

§ 5 of the 'Règlement international des Prises maritimes' of the Institute of International Law took up the same attitude.

In strict law the right of visit and search may be exercised even after the conclusion of peace before the treaty of peace is ratified, though the above-mentioned § 5 of the 'Règlement' declares that it ceases 'avec les préliminaires de la paix.' See below, § 436.

[1] In former times Great Britain tried to extend visitation to neutral men-of-war. See Manning, p. 455.

[2] See, for instance, Gessner, p. 297, and Perels, § 52, iv.

[3] See Robinson, *Collectanea maritima* (1801), pp. 145-157.

of a Swedish man-of-war whose commander asserted that there was no contraband on board the convoyed vessels. The Peace of Westminster in 1654 brought this war to an end, and in 1756 the Netherlands, then neutral, claimed the right of convoy. But it was not until the last quarter of the eighteenth century that the right of convoy was more and more insisted upon by Continental neutrals. During the American War of Independence in 1780, the Netherlands again claimed it, and when they themselves waged war against Great Britain in 1781, they ordered their men-of-war and privateers to respect it. Between 1780 and 1800, treaties were concluded, in which Russia, Austria, Prussia, Denmark, Sweden, France, the United States of America, and other States recognised the right. But Great Britain always refused to do so, and, in July 1800, the action of a British squadron in capturing a Danish man-of-war and her convoy of six merchantmen for resistance to visitation called the Second Armed Neutrality into existence. Yet Great Britain still resisted. It was only to Russia[1] that by Article 4 of the 'Maritime Convention' of St. Petersburg of June 17, 1801, she conceded that vessels under convoy should not be visited by privateers, and though during the Crimean War she waived her claim on account of her naval co-operation with France (the latter recognising the right of convoy on principle), she waived it only for that particular war. Although during the nineteenth century more and more treaties stipulating the right of convoy were concluded, it was not mentioned in the Declaration of Paris of 1856, and Great Britain refused to recognise it throughout the century. However, Great

[1] But this concession extended to Denmark and Sweden, since these Powers (see above, § 290) acceded to the Maritime Convention on October 23, 1801.

Britain abandoned her opposition at the Naval Conference of London of 1908-1909, and the unratified Declaration of London proposed to settle the matter by Articles 61 and 62 in the following way :—

Neutral vessels under the convoy of a man-of-war flying the same flag were to be exempt from search, and might not be visited if the commander of the convoy, at the request of the commander of the belligerent cruiser which desired to visit them, gave, in writing, all the information as to the character of the convoyed vessels and their cargoes that could be obtained by search. Should the commander of the belligerent man-of-war have reason to suspect that the confidence of the commander of the convoy had been abused, he might not himself resort to visit and search, but had to communicate with the commander of the convoy. The latter had to investigate the matter, and record the result of his investigation in a report, a copy of which was to be given to the commander of the belligerent cruiser. If, in the opinion of the commander of the convoy, the facts stated in the report justified the capture of one or more of the convoyed vessels, he was to withdraw protection from the offending vessels, and the belligerent cruiser might then capture them.

In case a difference of opinion arose between the commander of the convoy and the commander of the belligerent cruiser—for instance, with regard to the question whether certain goods were absolute or conditional contraband or whether the port of destination of a convoyed vessel was an ordinary commercial port or a port which served as a base of supply for the armed forces of the enemy and the like—the commander of the belligerent cruiser was to have no power of overruling the decision of the commander of the convoy. He could only protest and report the case to his Government, which would have had to settle the matter by means of diplomacy.[1]

[1] Had the Declaration of London been ratified, its rules concerning convoy would also have applied to belligerent military aircraft meeting convoyed neutral merchantmen at sea.

However, the declaration has not been ratified, and it is apparent from the attitude of the British Government during the World War that it is no longer prepared to give effect to the concession made at the Naval Conference of London and recognise the right of convoy. Thus, when the Dutch Government announced in 1918 that a convoy would be despatched to the Dutch East Indies carrying Government passengers and goods, the British Government expressly refused to recognise the right of convoy, insisted upon the right to visit and search neutral merchantmen, even if convoyed, and only agreed to abstain from exercising that right on that occasion upon special conditions which the Dutch Government accepted.[1]

No Universal Rules regarding Mode of Visitation.

§ 418. There are no rules of International Law which lay down all the details of the formalities of the mode of visitation. A great many treaties regulate them as between the parties, for many of which Article 17 of the Peace Treaty of the Pyrenees of 1659 has served as a model; and all maritime nations have given instructions to their men-of-war regarding them. Thereby uniform formalities are practised with regard to many points; but regarding others the practice of the several States differs.

Stopping of Vessels for the Purpose of Visitation.

§ 419. A man-of-war which wishes to visit a neutral vessel must stop her, or make her bring to. Although the chasing of vessels may take place under false colours, the right colours must be shown when vessels are stopped.[2] The order for stopping can be given[3] by hailing or by firing one or two blank cartridges from the so-called affirming gun, and, if necessary, by firing a shot across the bows of the vessel.[4] If nevertheless the vessel does not bring to, the man-of-war is justified

[1] *Parl. Papers*, Misc., No. 13 (1918), Cd. 9028.

[2] See above, § 211.

[3] See above, vol. i. § 268.

[4] On emergency measures with regard to visitation resorted to by Great Britain during the World War, see Hall, § 273, p. 798, n. 2.

in using force to compel her to bring to. Once the vessel has been brought to, the man-of-war also brings to, keeping a reasonable distance. With regard to this distance, treaties very often stipulate either the range of a cannon shot, or half such width, or even a range beyond a cannon shot; but all this is totally impracticable.[1] The distance must vary according to the requirements of the case, and according to wind and weather.

The rules concerning the stopping of vessels for visitation apply also to visitation by belligerent aircraft. The order can in that case be given by hailing, or by some other sign.

Visit. § 420. The vessel, having been stopped or brought to, is visited[2] by one or two officers sent in a boat from the man-of-war. These officers examine the papers of the vessel to ascertain her nationality, the character of her cargo and passengers, and the ports from and to which she is sailing. Instead of visiting the merchantman and inspecting her papers on board, the practice is followed, by the men-of-war of some States, of summoning the master of the merchantman with his papers on board the former and examining the papers there.

If everything is found in order and there is no suspicion of fraud, the vessel is allowed to continue her course, a memorandum of the visit having been entered in her log-book. On the other hand, if the inspection of the papers shows that the vessel is carrying contraband or rendering unneutral service, or that she is for some other reason liable to capture, she is at once seized. But it may be that, although ostensibly everything is in order, there is nevertheless grave suspicion of fraud against the vessel. In such case she may be searched.

[1] See Ortolan, ii. p. 220, and Perels, § 53, pp. 284, 285.

[2] See above, vol. i. § 268, and Holland, *Prize Law*, §§ 195-216.

§ 421. Search at sea [1] is effected [2] by one or two officers, and, if need be, a few men, in presence of the master of the vessel. Care must be taken not to damage the vessel or the cargo, and no force whatever must be applied. No lock must be forcibly broken open by the search-party; the master is to be required to unlock it. If he fails to comply with the demand, he is not to be compelled to do so, since his refusal to assist the search in general, or search of a locked part of the vessel or of a locked box in particular, is at once sufficient cause for seizing the vessel. Search being completed, everything removed has to be replaced with care. If the search has satisfied the searching officers, and dispelled all suspicion, a memorandum is entered in the log-book of the vessel, and she is allowed to continue her voyage. On the other hand, if search has brought contraband, or any other cause for capture to light, the vessel is seized. But since search can never take place so thoroughly on the sea as in a harbour, it may be that, although search has disclosed no proof to bear out the suspicion, grave suspicion still remains. In such a case she may be seized and brought into a port for the purpose of being searched there as thoroughly as possible. But the commander of a man-of-war seizing a vessel in such a case must bear in mind that full indemnities must be paid to the vessel for loss of time and other losses sustained if finally she is found innocent, and the Prize Court declares that there was no reasonable ground of suspicion to justify the seizure of the vessel.[3] Therefore, after a search Search.

[1] As to the general practice followed by the Allies during the World War of taking vessels into port for search, see below, § 421*a*.

[2] See above, vol. i. § 269, and Holland, *Prize Law*, §§ 217-230.

[3] *The Baron Stjernblad*, (1917) 3 B. and C. P. C. 17; *The Sigurd* (No. 2), (1917) 3 B. and C. P. C. 87, where it was held that costs and damages will not be awarded when the validity of the seizure depends upon a difficult question of law; *The Bernisse*, (1919) 3 B and C. P. C. 517; and Article 64 of the unratified Declaration of London.

at sea has brought nothing to light against the vessel, seizure should take place only in case of grave suspicion.

Bringing Vessels into Port for Search.

§ 421*a*. During the World War, the United States of America complained that British cruisers, instead of searching American vessels on the high seas at the time of visit, made a practice of taking them into port for search. The British Government urged in justification of this procedure[1] that the size of the modern liner, the great amount of cargo carried by her, and the elaborate arrangements in vogue for concealing the identity of cargoes, made it impossible to carry out a thorough search on the high seas, especially as the danger of attacks from enemy submarines was so great, and 'the conditions during winter in the North Atlantic frequently render it impracticable for days together for a naval officer to board a vessel on her way to Scandinavian countries.' The British Notes added that ships had been taken into port for search as long ago as the American Civil War, and again during the Russo-Japanese War and the Second Balkan War. The diplomatic discussion was continued,[2] but the Allied Governments adhered to the practice of taking vessels into port for search.

Consequences of Resistance to Visitation.

§ 422. If a neutral merchantman resists visit or search, she is at once captured, and may be confiscated. The question whether the vessel only, or also

[1] The British Privy Council in *The Zamora*, (1916) 2 B. and C. P. C. 1, and the French Prize Court of Appeal in *The Frederico* (1915), *R.G.*, xxii. (1915), Jurisprudence, p. 17, xxiv. (1917), Jurisprudence, p. 11, considered the practice justifiable. See Hall, p. 800.

Concerning the Dutch claim for damages for two torpedoed Dutch vessels, the *Bernisse* and the *Elve*, which were torpedoed by a German submarine while being forcibly taken to the port of Kirkwall for examination, see *Parl. Papers*, Misc., No. 1 (1918), Cd. 8909, and (1919) 3 B. and C. P. C. 517.

[2] See the United States Notes of November 7, 1914, December 28, 1914, and November 6, 1915, and the British Notes of January 7, 1915, February 10, 1915, and April 24, 1916, in *Parl. Papers*, Misc., No. 6 (1915), Cd. 7816, and No. 15 (1916), Cd. 8234; see also Garner, ii. § 500.

her cargo, could be confiscated for resistance is controversial. According to British [1] and American theory and practice, the cargo as well as the vessel is liable to confiscation. But Continental [2] writers emphatically argue against this, and maintain that the vessel only is liable to confiscation.

According to Article 63 of the unratified Declaration of London, resistance to the legitimate exercise of the right of visit, search, and capture was to involve in all cases the confiscation of the vessel, which by her forcible resistance acquired enemy character.[3] For this reason such goods on board as belonged to the master or owner of the vessel might be treated as enemy goods and confiscated. Enemy goods on board might then likewise be confiscated, although when they were first shipped the vessel bore neutral character. Further, all goods on board were then presumed to be enemy goods, and the owners of neutral goods on board would have had to prove the neutral character of their goods. Lastly, no appeal was to lie from the national Prize Courts to the proposed International Prize Court by the owner of the ship except concerning the one question only, whether there was justification for capturing her on the grounds of forcible resistance.

However, the declaration is unratified, and therefore not legally binding. Visit and search do not take place after a vessel has been captured for resistance, for the mere fact that she has resisted makes her liable to confiscation, and it becomes irrelevant whether visit and search would show her to be guilty or innocent.

§ 423. According to the practice hitherto prevailing,[4] and also according to the unratified Declaration of London, a mere attempt on the part of a neutral mer- What constitutes Resistance.

[1] *The Maria*, (1799) 1 C. Rob. 340.

[2] See Gessner, pp. 318-321.

[3] See above, § 89.

[4] *The Maria*, (1799) 1 C. Rob. 340.

chantman to escape visitation does not in itself constitute resistance. But she may be chased and compelled by force to bring to, and she cannot complain if, in the endeavour forcibly to compel her to bring to, she is damaged or accidentally sunk. If, however, after the vessel has been compelled to bring to, visit and search show her to be innocent, she must be allowed to proceed on her course.

For resistance, to be penal, must be *forcible* resistance, *e.g.* if a vessel applies force in resisting any legitimate action by the belligerent cruiser which requires her to stop and to be visited and searched. It is not certain whether the actual application of force only, or also a refusal, on the part of the master, to show the ship-papers or to open locked parts of the vessel or locked boxes, and similar acts, would constitute forcible resistance.[1]

Sailing under Enemy Convoy equivalent to Resistance.

§ 424. Wheaton excepted, all writers would seem to agree that the fact of neutral merchantmen sailing under a convoy of enemy men-of-war is equivalent to forcible resistance on their part, whether they themselves intend to resist by force or not. But the Government of the United States of America in 1810 contested this principle. In that year, during war between Great Britain and Denmark, many American vessels sailing from Russia used to seek protection under the convoy of British men-of-war, whereupon Denmark declared all such American vessels to be good and lawful prizes. Several were captured without making any resistance whatever, and were condemned by Danish Prize Courts. The United States protested, and claimed indemnities from Denmark, and in 1830 a treaty between the parties was signed at Copenhagen,[2]

[1] Another unsettled question is whether the crew can be punished as war criminals for resorting to armed resistance; Schramm, *Das Prisenrecht* (1913), p. 358, holds that they may be.

[2] Martens, *N.R.*, viii. p. 350.

according to which Denmark had to pay 650,000 dollars as compensation. But Article 5 of this treaty expressly declared that 'the present convention is only applicable to the cases therein mentioned, and, having no other object, may never hereafter be invoked by one party or the other as a precedent or a rule for the future.'[1]

Article 63 of the Declaration of London did not define the term 'forcible resistance,' and would not, therefore, have settled the point, even if it had been ratified.

Resistance by Neutral Convoy.

§ 425. Since Great Britain does not recognise the right of convoy and has always insisted upon the right to visit neutral merchantmen sailing under the convoy of neutral men-of-war, the question has arisen whether such merchantmen are regarded as resisting visitation in case the convoying men-of-war only, and not the convoyed vessels themselves, offer resistance. British practice has answered the question in the affirmative. The rule was laid down in 1799[2] and in 1804[3] by Sir William Scott in the cases of Swedish vessels captured while sailing under the convoy of a Swedish man-of-war.

Had the Declaration of London been ratified, under Articles 61 and 62, which recognise the right of convoy, resistance by a neutral convoy to visitation could not,

[1] See Wheaton, §§ 530-537, and Taylor, § 693, p. 790. Wheaton was the negotiator of this treaty on the part of the United States. With the case of neutral merchantmen sailing under enemy convoy, the other case —see above, § 185—in which neutral goods are placed on board an armed enemy vessel is frequently confused. In the case of *The Fanny*, (1814) 1 Dod. 443, Sir William Scott condemned neutral Portuguese property on the ground that placing neutral property on board an armed vessel was equal to resistance against visitation. But the Supreme Court of the United States of America, in the case of *The Nereide*, (1815) 9 Cranch 388, held the contrary view. The court was composed of five judges, of whom Story was one, and the latter dissented from the majority and considered the British practice correct. See Phillimore, iii. § 341; Wheaton, § 529; Smith, *The Destruction of Merchant Ships* (1917), pp. 58-61.

[2] *The Maria*, (1799) 1 C. Rob. 340.

[3] *The Elsebe*, (1804) 5 C. Rob. 174.

under ordinary circumstances, have been considered to be resistance on the part of the convoyed neutral merchantman. If, however, the commander of a convoy, after having refused to give the written information mentioned in Article 61 or to allow the investigation mentioned in Article 62, forcibly resisted visitation of the convoyed merchantmen by a belligerent cruiser, the question whether resistance by a convoy was equivalent to resistance by a convoyed vessel would still have arisen.

Deficiency of Papers.

§ 426. The purpose of visit is to ascertain the nationality of a vessel, the character of her cargo and passengers, and the ports from and to which she is sailing, and it is obvious that this purpose cannot be realised in case the visited vessel is deficient in her papers. As stated above,[1] every merchantman ought to carry the following papers: (1) A certificate of registry or a sea-letter (passport); (2) the muster-roll; (3) the log-book; (4) the manifest of cargo; (5) bills of lading, and (6) if chartered, the charter-party. Now, if a vessel is visited, and cannot produce one or more of the papers mentioned, she is suspect. Search is, of course, admissible for the purpose of verifying the suspicion; but it may be that search, while not producing any proof of guilt, does not dispel the suspicion. In such a case she may be seized and brought to a port for thorough examination. But, except in a case where she cannot produce either a certificate of registry or a sea-letter (passport), she ought not to be confiscated merely for deficiency in papers. Yet, if the cargo is also suspect, or if there are other circumstances which increase the suspicion, confiscation would be, I believe, in the discretion of the Prize Court.[2]

§ 427. Mere deficiency of papers does not arouse the

[1] vol. i. § 262.
[2] See Hall, § 247^{a}. p. 730, n. 2; and below, § 428 n.

same suspicion which a vessel incurs if she destroys[1] or throws overboard any of her papers, defaces them or conceals them, and, in particular, if she does any of these things when the visiting vessel comes in sight. Whatever her cargo may be, a vessel may at once be seized without further search so soon as it becomes apparent that spoliation, defacement, or concealment of papers has taken place. The practice of the several States has hitherto differed with regard to other consequences of spoliation, defacement, or concealment of papers; but confiscation is certainly admissible in case other circumstances increase the suspicion.[2]

Spoliation, Defacement, and Concealment of Papers.

§ 428. Very high suspicion is aroused if a visited vessel carries double papers, or false[3] papers, and she may certainly be seized. But the practice of the several States has differed with regard to the question whether confiscation is admissible on this ground alone. Whereas the practice of some States, such as Russia and Spain, has answered the question in the affirmative, British[4] and American[5] practice has taken a more lenient view, and condemned such vessels only on a clear inference that the false or double papers were carried for the purpose of deceiving the belligerent by whom the capture was made, and not in other[6] cases.[7]

Double and False Papers.

[1] *The Hunter*, (1815) 1 Dod. 480.

[2] See *The Apollo* in Calvo, v. § 2989.

[3] *The Sarah*, (1801) 3 C. Rob. 330.

[4] *The Eliza and Katy*, (1805) 6 C. Rob. 192.

[5] *The St. Nicholas*, (1816) 1 Wheaton 417.

[6] See Halleck, ii. p. 271; Hall, § 276; Taylor, § 690.

[7] The unratified Declaration of London did not mention double or false papers, but the Report of the Drafting Committee to Article 64 contained the following observations: 'It is perhaps useful to indicate certain cases in which the capture of a vessel would be justified, whatever might be the ultimate decision of the Prize Court. Notably, there is the case where some or all of the ship's papers have been thrown overboard, suppressed or intentionally destroyed on the initiative of the master or one of the crew or passengers. There is in such case an element which will justify any suspicion and afford an excuse for capturing the vessel, subject to the master's ability to account for his action before the Prize Court. Even if the court should accept the explanation given and should not find any reason for condemnation, the

Call at an Enemy Port of a Vessel with a Neutral Destination.

§ 428*a*. High suspicion is likewise aroused in case a ship with papers indicating a neutral destination proceeds to an enemy port. The practice formerly prevailing did not indeed admit capture and condemnation in such a case provided the vessel was not otherwise suspect. However, during the World War, in October 1914, the Allies laid down the following rule: 'A neutral vessel with papers indicating a neutral destination, which, notwithstanding the destination shown on the papers, proceeds to an enemy port, shall be liable to capture and condemnation if she is encountered before the end of her next voyage.' The Maritime Rights Order in Council of July 7, 1916, contained a corresponding rule with regard to a neutral vessel carrying contraband.

II

CAPTURE

Hall, § 277—Westlake, ii. pp. 309-312—Lawrence, § 191—Phillimore, iii. §§ 361-364—Twiss, ii. §§ 166-184—Halleck, ii. pp. 389-421—Taylor, § 691—Hershey, Nos. 521-522—Moore, vii. §§ 1206-1214—Bluntschli, § 860—Heffter, §§ 171, 191, 192—Geffcken in *Holtzendorff*, iv. pp. 777-780—Rivier, ii. pp. 426-428—Nys, iii. pp. 695-710—Calvo, v. §§ 3004-3034—Fiore, iii. Nos. 1644-1657, and *Code*, Nos. 1901-1912—Martens, ii. § 126—Kleen, ii. §§ 203-218—Gessner, pp. 333-356—Boeck, Nos. 770-777—Dupuis, Nos. 253-281, and *Guerre*, Nos. 205-217—Bernsten, § 11—Schramm, §§ 14-15—Nippold, ii. § 35—Perels, § 55—Testa, pp. 243-244—Hautefeuille, iii. pp. 214-298—Holland, *Prize Law*, §§ 231-314—U.S. Naval War Code, Articles 46-50—Atherley-Jones, *Commerce in War* (1907), pp. 361-646—Hirschmann, *Das internationale Prisenrecht* (1912),

---

parties interested cannot hope to recover compensation.

'An analogous case would be that in which there were found on board two sets of papers, or false or forged papers, if this irregularity were connected with circumstances calculated to contribute to the capture of the vessel.

'It appeared sufficient that these cases in which there would be a reasonable excuse for the capture should be mentioned in the present Report, and should not be made the object of express provisions, since, otherwise, the mention of these two particular cases might have led to the supposition that they were the only cases in which a capture could be justified.'

§§ 35-37—Wehberg, §§ 7 and 8—Garner, ii. §§ 474-493—See also the monographs quoted above at the commencement of § 391, Bulmerincq's articles on *Le Droit des Prises maritimes* in *R.I.*, x.-xiii. (1878-1881), and the General Report presented to the Naval Conference of London on behalf of its Drafting Committee, Articles 48-54.

Grounds and Mode of Capture.

§ 429. From what has already been said regarding blockade, contraband, unneutral service, and visitation, it is obvious that capture may take place either because the vessel, or the cargo, or both, are liable to confiscation, or because grave suspicion demands a further inquiry which can only be carried out in a port. Both cases are alike so far as all details of capture are concerned, and in the latter case Prize Courts may pronounce capture to have been justified, although no ground for confiscating either vessel or cargo has been detected.

The mode of capture is the same as that for capture of enemy vessels.[1]

Effect of Capture of Neutral Vessels, and their Conduct to Port.

§ 430. The effect of capture of neutral vessels is in every way different from the effect of capture of enemy vessels,[2] since the purpose of capture differs in these two cases. Enemy vessels are captured for the purpose of appropriating them in the exercise of the right of belligerents to appropriate all enemy property found on the open sea, or in the maritime territorial belt of either belligerent. On the other hand, neutral merchantmen are captured for the purpose of confiscating vessel or cargo, or both, as punishment for certain special acts, the punishment to be pronounced by a Prize Court after a thorough investigation into all the circumstances of the special case. Therefore,

[1] See above, § 184. The 'Règlement international des Prises maritimes,' adopted by the Institute of International Law at its meeting at Heidelberg in 1887, regulates capture in §§ 45-62; see *Annuaire*, ix. (1888), p. 218. That capture may take place on the high seas, or in the territorial waters of belligerents, but not in neutral territorial waters, is a matter of course. If capture does take place in neutral territorial waters, it is not the owner of the vessel, but the neutral State, which can claim its release before the Prize Court. See above, § 362.

[2] See above, § 185.

although the effect of capture of a neutral vessel is that the vessel, and the persons and goods thereon, are placed under the captor's authority, her officers and crew never become prisoners of war. They are indeed to be detained as witnesses for the trial of the vessel and cargo, but nothing stands in the way of releasing such of them as are not wanted for that purpose. As regards passengers, if any, they have to be released as soon as possible, with the exception of those enemy persons who may be made prisoners of war.

Regarding the conduct of neutral vessels to a port of a Prize Court, whether captured by a belligerent cruiser or by military aircraft, the same is valid as regards conduct of captured enemy vessels[1] to such port.

Destruction of Neutral Prizes.

§ 431. That, as a rule, captured neutral vessels may not be sunk, burned, or otherwise destroyed has always been universally recognised, just as that captured enemy merchantmen may not, as a rule, be destroyed.[2] But it has long been a moot question whether captured neutral vessels as well as captured enemy vessels might be destroyed in exceptional cases instead of being brought before a Prize Court. British[3] practice did not, as regards her neutral owner, hold the captor justified in destroying a neutral vessel, however exceptional the case might have been, and however meritorious the destruction of the vessel from the point of view of the Government of the captor. For this reason, should a captor, for any motive whatever, have destroyed a neutral prize, full indemnities had to be paid to the owner, although, if brought into a port of a Prize Court, condemnation of vessel and cargo would have been pronounced beyond doubt.

[1] See above, § 193.

[2] See Smith, *The Destruction of Merchant Ships under International Law* (1917), pp. 78-101.

[3] *The Acteon*, (1815) 2 Dod. 48; *The Felicity*, (1819) 2 Dod. 381; *The Leucade*, (1855) Spinks 217. See Phillimore, iii. § 333; Twiss, ii. § 166; Hall, § 277; Holland, *Letters to the 'Times' upon War and Neutrality* (1909), pp. 140-150; Garner in *A.J.*, x. (1916), pp. 12-41.

The rule was that a neutral prize must be abandoned, if for any reason it could not be brought to a port of a Prize Court. But the practice of other States did not recognise this British rule. The question became of great importance in 1905, during the Russo-Japanese War, when Russian cruisers sank the British vessels *Hipsang*, *Knight Commander*, *Oldhamia*, *St. Kilda*, *Ikhona*, and the German vessels *Thea* and *Tetartos*, and the Danish vessel *Prinsesse Marie*.[1] Russia paid damages to the owners of the *Ikhona*, *St. Kilda*, *Thea*, *Tetartos*, and *Prinsesse Marie*, because her Prize Courts declared that their capture was not justified, but she refused to pay damages to the owners of the other vessels destroyed, because her Prize Courts considered them to have been justly captured.

The Declaration of London proposed to settle the matter by a compromise. Recognising that neutral prizes may not as a rule be destroyed, and admitting only one exception to the rule, it empowered the captor under certain circumstances and conditions to demand the handing over, or to proceed himself to the destruction, of contraband carried by a neutral prize which he was compelled to abandon.

According to Article 48, as a matter of principle, captured neutral vessels might not be destroyed, but had to be taken into a port of a Prize Court. However, Article 49 permitted, as an exception, the destruction of a captured neutral vessel which would have been liable to condemnation, if the taking of the vessel into a port of a Prize Court would have involved danger to the safety of the capturing cruiser, or to the success of the operations in which she was at the time of capture engaged.

According to these provisions, a neutral prize might no longer be destroyed because the captor could not spare a prize

[1] Reported in Hurst and Bray, i. pp. 21, 54, 357, 145, 188, 226, 96, 166, 276.

crew,[1] or because a port of a Prize Court was too far distant, or the like. The only justification for destruction was to be danger to the captor or to his operations at the time of capture. As regards the degree of danger required, Article 49 did not provide any clue. But considering that Article 51 spoke of an 'exceptional necessity,' it was to be hoped and expected that Prize Courts would give such an interpretation to Article 49 as would permit the sinking of neutral prizes in cases of absolute necessity only. Be that as it may, according to Article 49, only such neutral prizes might be sunk as would be liable to confiscation if brought before a Prize Court. Sinking of captured neutral vessels—apart from those which had acquired enemy character and might for this reason be sunk under the same conditions as enemy vessels—was, therefore, chiefly admitted under the exceptional circumstances mentioned in Article 49 in three [2] cases, namely: (1) when—see Article 40—the vessel carried contraband the value of which formed more than half the value of the cargo; (2) when a vessel had been captured for rendering those kinds of unneutral service which were enumerated by Article 45; (3) when—see Article 21—a vessel had been captured for breach of blockade. In no case in which she was not liable to confiscation might a neutral vessel under any circumstances or conditions be destroyed; she had always to be abandoned if the capturing cruiser could not take her into a port of a Prize Court.

However, the compromise proposed by the Declaration of London has not been ratified, and is not therefore legally binding.

When a captor destroys a neutral prize, he must place in safety all persons found on the captured vessel, and he must take on board all the captured ship's papers which are relevant for the purpose of deciding the validity of the capture.[3]

[1] Schramm, p. 513, asserts the contrary, and quotes Wehberg in his support.

[2] As to cases in which a neutral vessel carried defective, spoiled, defaced, double, or false papers, see above, §§ 426-428.

[3] See Article 50 of the unratified Declaration of London.

Moreover, according to Article 51 of the unratified Declaration of London, if the captor failed to establish before the Prize Court that he destroyed the prize in the face of an exceptional necessity, the owners of the vessel and cargo had to receive full compensation without any examination of, and any regard to, the question whether the capture itself was justifiable. Compensation had likewise to be paid in case the capture was held by the Prize Court to be invalid, although the act of destruction was held to be justifiable (Article 52). In any case, the owners of neutral goods [1] not liable to condemnation which had been destroyed with the vessel, might always, and under all circumstances and conditions, claim damages (Article 53).

Thus many safeguards would have been established against arbitrariness in the destruction of neutral prizes. On the other hand, it seemed to be going too far to insist on the captor letting the prize go with her contraband on board, if he was compelled to abandon her. For this reason Article 54 empowered the captor of a neutral vessel herself not liable to confiscation to demand the handing over, or to proceed himself to the destruction,[2] of any goods liable to confiscation found on board, if the taking of the vessel into a port of a Prize Court would have involved danger to the captor, or to the success of the operations in which he was at the time of capture engaged.

However, the rules of the Declaration of London remain unratified, and, during the World War, the practice of the Central Powers was very different.[3]

Destruction of Neutral Prizes during the World War.

§ 431*a*. There is no case on record in which, during the World War, the Allied and Associated Powers destroyed intentionally a single neutral ship. The

[1] It has been asserted—see Schramm, pp. 515-516—that the owners of enemy goods, contraband excepted, may also claim compensation because, according to the Declaration of Paris, the neutral flag covers enemy goods. But it is doubtful if Prize Courts would recognise any such claim.

[2] Details concerning such destruction have been given above in § 406*a* (2).

[3] All rules concerning destruction of neutral prizes by belligerent cruisers apply also to destruction by belligerent military aircraft.

Central Powers, on the other hand, are believed to have sunk no less than 1716.[1] In a few cases—such as those of the American vessels *Gulflight*, torpedoed on May 7, 1915, and *Nebraskan*, torpedoed on May 25, 1915—Germany admitted or claimed that a mistake had been made,[2] and in a few others—such as those of *The Draupner*, *Saga*, and *Asta*—the German Prize Court of Appeal, reversing the lower court, declared the destruction of the vessels to have been illegal and compensated the owners. But in most cases the destruction of neutral vessels at sight without visit and search, no provision, or no adequate provision, being made for the safety of passengers and crew, was upheld by the Central Powers, mainly on the ground (which their submarines did not stop to verify) that they were carrying contraband, and that to have brought them to a port of a Prize Court would have involved danger to the captor. Among the best known cases are those of the American neutral vessel *William P. Frye*, sunk by the German cruiser *Prinz Eitel Friedrich*,[3] and the Dutch vessels *Maria* and *Medea*,[4] the sinking of which was upheld by the German Prize Courts. But the torpedoing of neutral vessels at sight became a regular feature of German submarine warfare, and no neutral maritime State was exempt. Over 2000 sailors are said to have been drowned.[5]

Ransom and Recapture of Neutral Prizes.

§ 432. Regarding ransom of captured neutral vessels, the same is valid as regards ransom of captured enemy vessels.[6]

As regards recapture of neutral prizes,[7] the rule ought to be that *ipso facto* by recapture the vessel

[1] Garner, ii. § 491.

[2] Garner, ii. § 484.

[3] See Garner, ii. § 485.

[4] *Ibid.*, §§ 486-487.

[5] Details in Garner, ii. § 491.

[6] See above, § 195.

[7] See Hautefeuille, iii. pp. 369-407; Gessner, pp. 344-356; Kleen, ii. § 217; Geffcken in *Holtzendorff*, iv. pp. 778-780; Calvo, v. §§ 3210-3216.

becomes free without payment of any salvage. Although captured, she was still the property of her neutral owners, and if condemnation had taken place at all, it would have been a punishment, and the recapturing belligerent has no interest whatever in the punishment of a neutral vessel by the enemy.

But the matter of recapture of neutral prizes is not settled, no rule of International Law, and no uniform practice of the several States, being formulated regarding it. Very few treaties touch upon it, and the municipal regulations of the different States regarding prizes seldom mention it. According to British practice, the recaptor of a neutral prize is only entitled to salvage when the recaptured vessel would have been liable to condemnation if brought into an enemy port, or when the enemy Prize Court, if the vessel had been destroyed by the captor, would have considered her destruction justifiable.[1]

Release after Capture.

§ 433. Besides the case in which captured vessels must be abandoned, because they cannot for some reason or another be brought into a port, there are cases in which they are released without trial. The rule is that a captured neutral vessel is to be tried by a Prize Court in case the captor asserts her to be suspicious or guilty. But it may happen that all suspicion is dispelled even before the trial; and then the vessel is to be released at once.[2] Even after she has been brought into the port of a Prize Court, release may take place without trial. Thus the German vessels *Bundesrath* and *Herzog*, which were captured in 1900 during the South African War and taken to Durban, were, after search had dispelled all suspicion, released without trial.

[1] *The War Onskan*, (1799) 2 C. Rob. 299; *The Pontoporos*, (1915) 1 B. and C. P. C. 371; (1916) 2 B. and C. P. C. 87; *The Svanfos*, (1919) 3 B. and C. P. C. 470. See also Holland, *Prize Law*, § 270.

[2] See Holland, *Prize Law*, § 246.

That the released vessel may claim damages is a matter of course, and Article 64 of the Declaration of London would have so enacted, if it had been ratified.

III

TRIAL OF CAPTURED NEUTRAL VESSELS

Lawrence, §§ 188-190—Maine, p. 96—Manning, pp. 472-483—Phillimore, iii. §§ 433-508—Twiss, ii. §§ 169-170—Halleck, ii. pp. 423-462—Taylor, §§ 563-567—Wharton, iii. §§ 328-330—Hershey, Nos. 523-524—Moore, vii. §§ 1222-1248—Wheaton, §§ 389-397—Bluntschli, §§ 841-862—Heffter, §§ 172-173—Geffcken in *Holtzendorff*, iv. pp. 781-788—Ullmann, § 196—Bonfils, Nos. 1676-1691—Despagnet, Nos. 677-682 *bis*—Rivier, ii. pp. 353-356—Nys, iii. pp. 711-736—Calvo, v. §§ 3035-3087—Fiore, iii. Nos. 1681-1691, and *Code*, Nos. 1913-1952—Martens, ii. §§ 125-126—Kleen, ii. §§ 219-234—Gessner, pp. 357-426—Boeck, Nos. 740-800—Dupuis, Nos. 282-301, and *Guerre*, Nos. 218-223—Nippold, ii. § 35—Perels, §§ 56-57—Schramm, § 17—Testa, pp. 244-247—Hautefeuille, iii. pp. 299-369—Atherley-Jones, *Commerce in War* (1907), pp. 361-594—Hirschmann, *Das internationale Prisenrecht* (1912), § 38—Wehberg, § 9—Picciotto, *The Relation of International Law to the Law of England and the United States* (1915), pp. 26-47—Pyke in the *Law Quarterly Review*, xxxii. (1916), pp. 144, 167—See also the monographs quoted above at the commencement of § 391, and Bulmerincq's articles on *Le Droit des Prises maritimes* in *R.I.*, x.-xiii. (1878-1881).

Trial of Captured Vessels a Municipal Matter.

§ 434. Although belligerents have, under certain circumstances, according to International Law, the right to capture neutral vessels, and although they have the duty to bring these vessels for trial before a Prize Court, such trials are in no way an international matter. Just as Prize Courts are municipal [1] institutions, so trials of captured neutral vessels by these Prize Courts are municipal matters. The neutral

[1] See above, § 192. The matter is regulated, so far as Great Britain is concerned, by the Naval Prize Act, 1864 (27 & 28 Vict. c. 25); the Prize Courts Act, 1894 (57 & 58 Vict. c. 39); the Prize Courts (Procedure) Act, 1914 (4 & 5 Geo. v. c. 13); the Prize Court Rules, 1914; the Prize Court Act, 1915 (5 & 6 Geo. v. c. 57); the Naval Prize (Procedure) Act, 1916 (6 Geo. v. c. 2); the Naval Prize Act, 1918 (8 & 9 Geo. v. c. 30). The 'Règlement international des Prises maritimes,' adopted in 1887 at Heidelberg by the Institute of International Law, suggested in §§ 63-118 detailed rules concerning the organisation of Prize Courts and the procedure before them; see *Annuaire*, ix. (1888), p. 218.

home States of the vessels are not represented and are not, directly at any rate, concerned in the trial. Nor, as commonly maintained in England and the United States, is the law administered by Prize Courts International Law. These courts apply the law of their country, although a country may have adopted as municipal law the principles of International Law concerning prizes. Great Britain and the United States have done this. The best proof that Prize Courts administer their own municipal law is to be found in the fact that the practice of the Prize Courts of the several countries differs in many points. Thus, for instance, the question of enemy character, the question what is, and what is not, contraband, and the question when an attempt to break blockade begins, and when it ends, have been differently answered by the practice of different States. In most countries, when war breaks out, the Governments draw up a body of prize rules which the Prize Courts have to apply; and although these rules are supposed to be in conformity with International Law, the Prize Courts cannot go back upon them if in fact they do not.[1]

Many writers, however, do maintain that Prize Courts are international courts, and that the law administered by them is International Law. Lord

[1] See the judgment of the German Prize Court in *The Elida*, *Z.V.*, ix. (1915), p. 109:—'The Prize Regulations contain the principles fixed by the Emperor as holder of the supreme command within his Imperial legal competency for the exercise of the right of capture appertaining to naval warfare, and therefore form, in the first instance, an authoritative rule, not only for the war navy, but in so far as the legality of acts of naval commanders in connection with the right of capture comes in question, also for the inland authorities giving decisions in this connection, and in particular for the prize courts. International Law establishes rights and obligations only as between States as such. For judging the legality of acts in connection with prize law by the prize courts, general international principles can therefore apply only in so far as the prize regulations do not contain any provisions, and consequently refer tacitly to the principles of International Law. The question itself as to whether any provision of the prize regulations is in harmony with general international principles must therefore be eliminated from the decisions of the prize courts.'

Stowell again and again[1] emphatically asserted it, and the vast majority of English and American writers[2] followed him. Indeed, although during the World War the British Prize Court of Appeal, the Privy Council, recognised[3] that Prize Courts are municipal courts, it still asserted that they administer International Law; and in a later case the Prize Court was again called 'an international tribunal.'[4]

But it is to be expected that recognition of the difference between Municipal and International Law, as expounded above,[5] and of the fact that States only, and neither their courts nor officials nor citizens, are

[1] *The Maria*, (1799) 1 C. Rob. 340; *The Recovery*, (1807) 6 C. Rob. 341; *The Fox*, (1811) Edwards 311.

[2] See, for instance, Halleck, ii. p. 411; Manning, p. 472; Phillimore, iii. §§ 433-436; Hall, § 277. But see, on the other hand, Holland, *Studies*, p. 196; Westlake, ii. pp. 317-318; Scott, *Conferences*, p. 467; Maine, p. 96; Pyke in the *Law Quarterly Review*, xxxii. (1916), pp. 144-167.

[3] *The Zamora*, (1916) 2 B. and C. P. C. 1 at p. 12. The judgment in this case is of the greatest importance, because it lays down the principle that British Prize Courts are not bound by Orders in Council which are contrary to International Law unless they amount to a mitigation of the rights of the Crown in favour of the enemy or a neutral, or authorise reprisals justified by the circumstances of the case and not entailing upon neutrals a degree of unreasonable inconvenience. See above, § 319; *The Alwina*, (1918) 3 B. and C. P. C. 54 at p. 58; *The Proton*, (1918) 3 B. and C. P. C. 125.

On the other hand, the judgment in *The Zamora* recognised that British Prize Courts are bound by such Acts of Parliament as are contrary to International Law, thereby disproving the assertion that Prize Courts were bound to apply International Law. If they were, how could an Act of Parliament which was contrary to International Law be binding upon them? Municipal Law cannot *per se* change International Law. The fact that British Prize Courts *are* bound to apply an Act of Parliament shows clearly that the law which they apply is Municipal Law, although it is in substance International Law, which has been adopted by Municipal Law, and has not been abrogated by an Act of Parliament, or by an Order in Council in mitigation of the rights of the Crown, or by an order authorising justified reprisals.

Be that as it may, it is remarkable that the Privy Council does not consider British Prize Courts bound to apply the *whole* of International Law, but only the International Law of Prize in the narrower sense of the term. See *The Sudmark*, (1917) 2 B. and C. P. C. 473, in which the court declared that the jurisdiction of a court of prize does not embrace the whole region covered by International Law, but is confined to taking cognisance of, and adjudicating upon, certain matters (including capture at sea) which in former times were enumerated in the Royal Commissions under which the court was constituted, and are now defined both by statute and by the Royal Commission issued at the beginning of a war.

[4] *The Kronprinzessin Victoria*, (1918) 3 B. and C. P. C. 247 at p. 254.

[5] vol. i. §§ 20-25.

subjects of International Law, will lead also to the general recognition of the fact that the law applied by national Prize Courts is not, and cannot be, International Law, even when, as in Great Britain and the United States of America, the rules of International Law concerning prizes have for the most part[1] been adopted by Municipal Law.

And matters will remain as they are even should an International Prize Court be established, and an international code of prize law, similar to the unratified Declaration of London, become universally accepted. The law of such a code would certainly be International Law; yet it could only bind the States concerned. They, in their turn, would have to embody it in their Municipal Law, with the consequence that their Prize Courts would be obliged to administer such Municipal Law in prize cases as was in conformity with the international code. It would be the task of the International Prize Court[2] to control the national Prize Courts in that respect. If a State, having accepted such an international code of prize law, by a statute ordered its Prize Courts to apply a law in opposition to the international code, it would commit an international delinquency; nevertheless, its Prize Courts would be obliged to apply the law laid down by the statute.

As regards the procedure in Prize Courts, no general rules of International Law exist as yet; and so every State settles the matter according to discretion. But of course a fair hearing must be afforded to all claims. The procedure in Prize Courts cannot be compared with

[1] The fact that if a vessel is captured in neutral waters and the neutral State does not claim her in the Prize Court, she is, according to British practice, condemned, shows that Prize Courts in England do not in every point apply International Law. If they did, they would have to liberate the prize, whether the neutral State claimed it or not. See also n. 3 on p. 628.

[2] Trial before this court would, of course, be an international matter.

the procedure in civil or criminal courts, for in Prize Courts the burden of proof is in practice everywhere laid upon the owner of the captured vessel or cargo. Everywhere in the first instance, no doubt, evidence must come from the ship-papers and the depositions of the master and officers—'out of the vessel's own mouth'; but other evidence is also admitted in practice,[1] and it could not be otherwise without keeping the door wide open to deceit.

Result of Trial.

§ 435. The trial of a captured neutral ship can have one or more of five results: (1) vessel and cargo may be condemned,[2] or (2) the vessel alone may be condemned, or (3) the cargo alone may be condemned, or the vessel and cargo may be released either (4) with or (5) without costs and damages. Costs and damages must be allowed when capture was not justified. But capture may be justified, as, for instance, in the case of spoliation of papers, although the Prize Court does not condemn the vessel, and in that case costs and damages will not be awarded; further, costs and damages are never allowed if even a part of the cargo is condemned, although the vessel herself and the greater part of the cargo are released. That, in case the captor is unable to pay the costs and damages allowed to a released neutral vessel, his Government has to indemnify the vessel, there ought to be no doubt, for a State bears 'vicarious' responsibility[3] for internationally injurious acts of its naval forces.

Trial after Conclusion of Peace.

§ 436. Prior to the World War, it was a moot question whether neutral vessels captured before conclu-

[1] See Pyke in the *Law Quarterly Review*, xxxii. (1916), p. 56.

[2] It would seem to be obvious that condemnation of the vessel involves the loss of the vessel at the date of capture; see *Andersen* v. *Marten*, [1907] 2 K.B. 248, [1908] A.C. 334. See also *The Odessa*, (1915) 1 B. and C. P. C. 554 at p. 559: 'The effect of a condemnation is to divest the enemy subject of his ownership as from the date of the seizure.' Contrast the project of the Institute of International Law in *Annuaire*, ix. (1888), p. 218.

[3] See above, vol. i. § 163.

sion of peace might be tried after the conclusion of peace.[1] The author thought that the answer must be in the affirmative, even if a special clause was contained in the Treaty of Peace, which stipulated that vessels of the belligerents captured but not yet condemned should be released. A trial of neutral prizes is in any case necessary for the purpose of deciding whether capture was justified or not, and if not, whether costs and indemnities should be awarded to the owners. Thus, after the conclusion of the Abyssinian War, in December 1896, the Italian Prize Commission, in the case of *The Doelwijk*,[2] claimed the right to try the vessel in spite of the fact that peace had been concluded between the time of capture and trial, and declared the capture of the vessel and cargo to have been justified; but it pronounced that, peace having been concluded, confiscation of vessel and cargo would no longer be lawful.

Different, however, from the question whether neutral prizes might be tried after the conclusion of peace was the question whether they might be condemned and confiscated. In the above-mentioned case of *The Doelwijk* the question was answered in the negative, but the author believed that it ought to have been answered in the affirmative.[3] Confiscation of vessel and cargo having the character of a punishment, it

[1] See Perels, § 57, p. 309, Wehberg, p. 58, and Borchard, § 100, in contradistinction to Bluntschli, § 862. But there is, of course, no doubt that a belligerent can exercise an act of grace and release such prizes. Thus, in November 1905, at the end of the Russo-Japanese War, the Mikado proclaimed the unconditional release of all neutral prizes captured after the signing but before the ratification of the Peace of Portsmouth. Thereby, three German vessels, two English, and one Norwegian escaped confiscation, which in strict law—see above, § 415 n.—would have been justified.

[2] See Martens, *N.R.G.*, 2nd Ser. xxviii. pp. 66-90, and Diena in the *Journal de Droit international privé* (1897), pp. 268-297. See also above, § 403.

[3] After the conclusion of the Russo-Japanese War, in November 1905 and February 1906, the Japanese Prize Courts condemned two American vessels, *The Australia* and *The Montara*, which had been captured shortly before the conclusion of peace (Hurst and Bray, ii pp. 373, 403).

seemed to him that the punishment might be inflicted after the conclusion of peace provided the offence was consummated before peace was concluded. But nothing, of course, stood in the way of a belligerent taking a more lenient view, and ordering his Prize Courts not to pronounce confiscation of neutral vessels after the conclusion of peace.

At the end of the World War, the author's opinion was confirmed, at any rate so far as British practice is concerned, since in March 1920, after the Treaty of Peace with Germany had come into force, the *Rannveig*, a Norwegian vessel captured on March 6, 1919, for carrying a full cargo of contraband to a German base of supply during the armistice, was condemned by the British Prize Court.[1]

Protests and Claims of Neutrals after Trial.

§ 437. If a trial leads to condemnation, which is confirmed by the Court of Appeal, the matter, as between the captor and the owner of the captured vessel and cargo, is finally settled. But the right of protection,[2] which a State exercises over its subjects and their property abroad, may nevertheless give rise to diplomatic protests and claims on the part of the neutral home State of a condemned vessel or cargo, in case the verdict of the Prize Courts is considered to be not in accordance with International Law, or formally or materially unjust. It is through such protests and claims that the matter, which was hitherto a mere municipal one, becomes of *international* importance. History records many cases in which neutral States have intervened after trials of vessels which had sailed under their flags. Thus, for instance, in the famous case of the Silesian loan,[3] it was because Frederick II. of Prussia considered the procedure of British Prize Courts regarding a number of Prussian merchantmen

[1] [1920] P. 177.
[2] See above, vol. i. § 319.
[3] See above, § 37.

captured during war between Great Britain and France in 1747 and 1748 as unjust, that in 1752 he resorted to reprisal and sequestrated the payments of the interest on the Silesian loan. The matter was settled[1] in 1756, through the payment of £20,000 as indemnity by Great Britain. Again, after the American Civil War, Articles 12-17 of the Treaty of Washington[2] provided that three commissioners should be appointed for the purpose, amongst others, of deciding all claims against verdicts of the American Prize Courts. Again, when in 1879, during war between Peru and Chili, the German vessel *Luxor* was condemned by the Peruvian courts, Germany interposed and the vessel was released.[3]

[1] See Martens, *Causes célèbres*, ii. p. 167, and Satow, *The Silesian Loan and Frederick the Great* (1915).

[2] See Martens, *N.R.G.*, xx. p. 698, and Satow, *op. cit.*, p. 198.

[3] See above, § 404.

CHAPTER VII

THE PROPOSED INTERNATIONAL PRIZE COURT

I

PROPOSALS FOR INTERNATIONAL PRIZE COURTS

Westlake, ii. pp. 317-324—Geffcken in *Holtzendorff*, iv. pp. 785-788—Boeck, Nos. 743-766—Dupuis, No. 289, and *Guerre*, Nos. 224-231—Higgins, pp. 432-435—Lémonon, pp. 280-293—Nippold, i. § 15—Trendelenburg, *Lucken im Volkerrecht* (1870), pp. 49-50—Gessner, *Kriegfuhrende und neutrale Machte* (1877), pp. 52-58—Pohl, *Deutsche Prisengerichtsbarkeit* (1911), pp. 47-96—Schramm, § 18—Wehberg, § 9—Bulmerincq and Gessner in *R.I.*, xi. (1879), pp. 173-191, and xiii. (1881), pp. 260-267.

Early Projects.

§ 438. Numerous inconveniences must naturally result from the condition of International Law which has hitherto prevailed, according to which the courts of the belligerent whose forces have captured neutral vessels exercise jurisdiction without any control by neutrals.[1] Although neutrals frequently interfere after trial and succeed in obtaining recognition for their claims in spite of the judgments of Prize Courts, great dissatisfaction has long been felt, and proposals have been made for so-called mixed Prize Courts.

The first proposal of this kind was made in 1759 by Hübner,[2] who suggested a Prize Court composed of judges nominated by the belligerent and of consuls or councillors nominated by the home State of the captured neutral merchantmen. A number of other proposals[3] followed during the eighteenth century. A

[1] See above, § 437.

[2] *De la Saisie de Bâtiments neutres* (1759), vol. ii. p. 21. On Hubner, see Reddie, *Researches*, i. pp. 291-305.

[3] See Pohl, *op. cit.*, pp. 64-70.

proposal somewhat similar to that of Hübner was made by Tetens [1] in 1805, and several others were made during the nineteenth century.

In 1875 the Institute of International Law took up the matter, appointing, on the suggestion of Westlake, at its meeting at the Hague, a commission for the purpose of drafting a *Projet d'Organisation d'un Tribunal international des Prises maritimes.* In the course of time there were mainly two proposals before the Institute, Westlake's and Bulmerincq's. Westlake proposed [2] that courts of appeal should be instituted in each case of war, and that each court should consist of three judges—one to be nominated by the belligerent concerned, one by the home State of the neutral prizes concerned, and the third by a neutral Power not interested in the case. According to Westlake's proposal there would therefore have to be instituted in every war as many courts of appeal as there were neutrals concerned. Bulmerincq proposed [3] that two courts should be instituted in each war for all prize cases, the one to act as Prize Court of First Instance, the other to act as Prize Court of Appeal, and each consisting of three judges, one appointed by each belligerent, and the third by all neutral maritime Powers acting in concert. Finally, the Institute agreed, at its meeting at Heidelberg in 1887, upon a proposal,[4] under which at the beginning of a war each belligerent would institute a court of appeal consisting of five judges, the president and one of the other judges being appointed by the belligerent, and the other three being nominated by three neutral Powers, and this court would be competent for all prize cases.

[1] *Considérations sur les Droits réciproques des Puissances belligérantes et des Puissances neutres sur Mer*, etc. (1805), p. 163. On Tetens, see Reddie, *Researches*, ii. pp. 130-231.

[2] See *Annuaire*, ii. (1878), p. 114.

[3] See *R.I.*, xi. (1879), pp. 191-194.

[4] §§ 100-109 of the 'Règlement international des Prises maritimes,' *Annuaire*, ix. (1888), p. 239.

No further step was taken during the nineteenth century. But, during the South African War, the conviction became general that the exclusive jurisdiction of belligerents over captured neutral vessels was incompatible with the modern conditions of the oversea commerce of neutrals. At the Second Hague Conference of 1907, therefore, Germany and Great Britain each brought forward a project for a real International Prize Court.

German Project of 1907.

§ 439. The German project[1] was that national Prize Courts should only be competent in the first instance, and that every appeal should go to the International Prize Court, which should be competent, not only in case of capture of neutral vessels, but in every case of capture of merchantmen. At the beginning of every war an International Prize Court was to be established; in case there were more than two parties to a war, as many International Prize Courts were to be established as there were couples of States fighting against each other. Each court was to consist of five judges sitting together, three of whom were to be members of the Permanent Court of Arbitration at the Hague, and two admirals. The admirals were to belong to the navies of the belligerents, but the three members of the Permanent Court of Arbitration were to be chosen by neutral Powers, each belligerent authorising one neutral Power to select one member, and these two neutrals appointing a third neutral Power to select the third member. Each belligerent and the owners of captured vessels or cargoes were to have the right to bring an appeal before the court.

British Project of 1907.

§ 440. The British project[2] was as follows: The International Prize Court was to be competent in such cases only as directly concerned a neutral Power or

[1] *Deuxième Conférence, Actes*, II. p. 1071.
[2] *Ibid.*, p. 1076.

its subjects, and had already been decided by the highest national Prize Court of the belligerent concerned. Neutral Powers only, and not their subjects, were to have the right to enter an appeal, and to represent their subjects in a prize case. In contradistinction to the German project, the British draft proposed the establishment of a permanent International Prize Court, of which each Power whose mercantile marine at the date of the signature of the proposed convention exceeded a total of 800,000 tons, might nominate a prominent jurist as a member and another as his deputy. The President of the court was to be nominated by the signatory Powers in their alphabetical order. If a legal question was to be decided which had already been provided for in a convention between the parties in dispute, the court was to base its decision upon it. In the absence of such a convention, if all civilised nations were agreed on a point of legal interest, the court was to base its decision thereon; otherwise it was to decide according to the principles of International Law.

Convention XII. of the Second Hague Conference.

§ 441. The Second Hague Conference, after having discussed the German and British projects, produced Convention XII. relative to the Establishment of an International Prize Court which, on the whole, followed more closely the lines of the British project, but included several features of the German project, and others which originated in neither. The convention was signed by all the Powers represented at the conference, except Brazil, China, Domingo, Greece, Luxemburg, Montenegro, Nicaragua, Roumania, Russia, Serbia, and Venezuela; but ten States—namely, Chili, Cuba, Ecuador, Guatemala, Haiti, Persia, Salvador, Siam, Turkey, and Uruguay—entered a reservation against Article 15 because they did not agree with the principle of the composition of the court embodied in it. Moreover, none of the Powers had ratified the convention before the outbreak of the World War, and no International Prize Court was established during that war. Nevertheless, it is of interest to give some details of the proposals.

II

THE HAGUE PROJECT FOR AN INTERNATIONAL PRIZE COURT

Westlake, ii. pp. 317-324—Lawrence, § 192—Hershey, Nos. 525-531—Ullmann, § 196—Bonfils, Nos. 1440[1]-1440[3]—Despagnet, Nos. 683-683 *bis*—Nys, iii. pp. 714-736—Fiore, *Code*, Nos. 1915-1924—Dupuis, *Guerre*, Nos. 232-276—Bernsten, § 14—Lémonon, pp. 293-335—Higgins, pp. 435-444—Barclay, *Problems*, pp. 105-108—Scott, *Conferences*, pp. 466-511—Nippold, i. §§ 16-19—Fried, *Die zweite Haager Konferenz* (1908), pp. 121-130—Lawrence, *International Problems* (1908), pp. 132-159—Hirschmann, *Das internationale Prisenrecht* (1912), §§ 39-41—Pohl, *Deutsche Prisengerichtsbarkeit* (1911), pp. 103-211—Schramm, §§ 18-19—Wehberg, § 9—Gregory, White, and Scott in *A.J.*, ii. (1908), pp. 458-475, and 490-506, and v. (1911), pp. 302-324—Donker Curtius in *R.I.*, 2nd Ser. xi. (1909), pp. 5-36.

The Court.

§ 442. The International Prize Court which the unratified Hague Convention xii. proposed to set up was to consist of judges and deputy judges appointed by the contracting Powers from among jurists of known proficiency in maritime International Law, and of the highest moral reputation. Each Power might appoint one judge and one deputy for a period of six years. The judges—and the deputies when taking the places of judges—were, when outside their own country, to be granted diplomatic privileges and immunities in the performance of their duties; and might not, during their tenure of office, appear as agent or advocate before the court, nor act for one of the parties in any capacity whatever.

The judges so appointed were not, as a body, to decide the appeal cases brought before the court.

From among them a deciding tribunal was to be formed composed of fifteen judges, nine of whom were to constitute a quorum. A judge who was absent or prevented from sitting was to be replaced by a deputy. The judges appointed by Great Britain, Germany, the United States of America, Austria-Hungary, France, Italy, Japan, and Russia were always to sit, but the judges appointed by the remaining contracting Powers were only to sit in rotation. If a belligerent Power had, according to the rota, no judge sitting in the deciding tribunal, it was to have a right to demand that the judge appointed by it should take part in the settlement of all cases arising from the war. No judge might sit who had been a party to the judgment of the national Prize Court under appeal.

The belligerent captor, and also a neutral Power which was herself, or whose national was, a party, might appoint a naval officer of high rank to sit as *Assessor*, but he was to have no voice in the decision.

The seat of the deciding tribunal was to be at the Hague.

§ 443. The general principle underlying the proposals of Convention XII. concerning the competence of the court was that on the whole, *although not exclusively*, it was to be competent in cases where neutrals were directly or indirectly concerned. The International Prize Court was to be, as a rule, a court of appeal, and all prize cases had, in the first instance, to be decided by a national Prize Court of the captor. However, should the national courts fail to give final judgment within two years from the date of capture, the case might be carried direct to the International Prize Court. Competence.

An appeal against the judgments of national Prize Courts might be brought before the international court: (1) when the judgment concerned the property of a neutral Power or a neutral individual; (2) when the judgment concerned enemy property and related to (*a*) cargo on board a neutral vessel, (*b*) an enemy vessel captured in the territorial waters of a neutral Power, provided that it had not made the capture the subject of a diplomatic claim, and (*c*) a claim based upon the allegation that the seizure had been effected in violation, either of the provisions of a convention in force between the belligerent Powers, or of an enactment issued by the belligerent captor. In any case, the appeal might be based on the ground that the judgment was wrong either in fact or in law.

The following Powers and individuals were to be entitled [1] to appeal.

(1) Neutral Powers, if the judgment injuriously affected their property or the property of their subjects, or if the capture was alleged to have taken place in their territorial waters.

(2) Neutral individuals,[2] if the judgment injuriously affected their property. But the home State of such an individual might intervene and either forbid him to bring the appeal, or itself undertake the proceedings in his place.

(3) Subjects of the enemy, if the judgment injuriously affected their cargoes on neutral vessels, or if it injuriously affected their property in case the seizure was alleged to have been effected in violation, either of the provisions of a convention in force between the belligerent Powers, or of an enactment issued by the belligerent captor.

(4) Subjects of neutral Powers or of the enemy deriving rights from such individuals as were themselves qualified to appeal, provided they had taken part in the proceedings of the national court or courts.

[1] But note Article 51 of Convention XII.
[2] See above, vol. i. § 289.

(5) Subjects of neutral Powers or of the enemy deriving rights from a neutral Power whose property was the subject of the judgment, provided that they had taken part in the proceedings of the national court or courts.

§ 444. As regards the law to be applied by the proposed International Prize Court, Article 7 contained the following provisions and distinctions :— **What Law to be applied.**

(1) If a question of law to be decided was covered by a treaty in force between the belligerent captor and a Power which was itself, or whose subject was, a party to the proceedings, the court had to apply the provisions of that treaty.

(2) In absence of such a treaty, the court had to apply the rules of International Law.

(3) If there were no generally recognised rules of International Law which could be applied, the court had to base its decision on the general principles of justice and equity.

(4) If the ground of appeal was the violation of an enactment issued by the belligerent captor, the court had to apply such enactment.

(5) The court was to be empowered to disregard failure on the part of an appellant to comply with the procedure laid down by the Municipal Law of the belligerent captor, if it was of opinion that the consequences of such Municipal Law were unjust or inequitable.

§ 445. The proceedings before the International Prize Court were to comprise two distinct phases, namely, written pleadings and oral discussion. **Proceedings and Judgment.**

(1) The written *pleadings* were to consist of the deposit and exchange of cases, counter-cases, and, if necessary, of replies, and to these pleadings all papers and documents which the parties intended to use had to be annexed.

(2) After the close of the pleadings the court was to fix a day for a public sitting at which the *discussion* was to take place. The parties were then to state their views both as to the law and as to the facts, but the court might at any stage suspend the speeches of counsel in order that supplementary evidence might be obtained. After the discussion the judgment of the court was to be given. Questions were to be decided by a majority of the judges present; if the number of the judges was even and equally divided, the vote of the junior judge in the order of precedence was not to be counted. The judgment was to be taken down in writing, was to state the reasons upon which it was based, give the names of the judges taking part in it and of the assessors, if any, and was to be signed by the President and Registrar.

If the court pronounced the capture of a vessel or cargo to be valid, they might be disposed of in accordance with the Municipal Law of the belligerent captor. If the court pronounced the capture to be invalid, restitution of the vessel or cargo had to be ordered, and the amount of damages, if any, had to be fixed, especially in case the vessel or cargo had been sold or destroyed. If the national Prize Court had already declared the capture to be invalid, the International Prize Court might only determine on appeal the damages due to the owner of the captured vessel or cargo.

Action in Damages instead of Appeal.[1]

§ 446. According to the constitution of the United States of America, and probably that of some other States, no appeal may be brought against a judgment of their highest courts. These States could not, therefore, in any case, ratify Convention XII. or take part in the establishment of the International Prize Court without previously altering their constitution. As such

[1] See Scott in *A.J.*, v. (1911), pp. 302-324; Butte, *Amerikanische Prisengerichtsbarkeit* (1913), pp. 18-65, and in *A.J.*, VI. (1912), pp. 799-829.

alteration would be a very complicated and precarious matter, the Naval Conference of London of 1908-1909 agreed to call the attention of the Governments to the advantage of concluding an arrangement according to which the States involved in such constitutional differences would, in depositing their ratifications, have power to add a reservation to the effect that the right of recourse to the International Prize Court in connection with decisions of their national courts, should take the form of a direct action for damages, provided, however, that this reservation should not impair the rights guaranteed by Convention XII. to private individuals as well as to Governments.

To carry out this recommendation, Great Britain, Germany, the United States of America, Argentina, Austria-Hungary, Chili, Denmark, Spain, France, Japan, Norway, Holland, and Sweden signed on September 19, 1910, at the Hague an Additional Protocol [1] to the convention relative to the establishment of an International Prize Court. According to Article 1 of the protocol, States prevented by difficulties of a constitutional nature from accepting Convention XII. in its unaltered form, were to have the right, in ratifying the convention or acceding to it, to declare that in prize cases over which their national courts had jurisdiction, recourse to the International Prize Court might only be had in the form of an action in damages for the injury caused by the capture. If such a declaration were made the procedure in the International Prize Court was to be modified as provided in the protocol.

Present Position of the Hague Project.

§ 447. The very wide powers proposed to be given to the court with regard to the law to be applied by it led the Powers to convene the Naval Conference of

[1] Sharply criticised by Butte in *A.J.*, vi. (1912), pp. 799-829, and in *Amerikanische Prisengerichtsbarkeit* (1913), pp. 18-65.

London of 1908-1909 to formulate a code of prize law. But that code, embodied in the Declaration of London, was not ratified; and until some such code has been agreed upon and ratified, there is no hope of seeing an International Prize Court established. With the Declaration of London fell also Hague Convention XII. and the Additional Protocol. The World War was fought without any International Prize Court. Whether any further steps will ever be taken with regard to the Hague project time alone can show.

INDEX

A

G

H

M

Q

R

W

Z

Printed by T. and A. CONSTABLE LTD.
at the Edinburgh University Press, Scotland

This page intentionally left blank

Made in United States
Cleveland, OH
05 November 2026

47673326R10427